The Joan Palevsky Imprint in Classical Literature

In honor of beloved Virgil—

"O degli altri poeti onore e lume . . ."

—Dante, *Inferno*

The publisher gratefully acknowledges the generous contribution to this book provided by the Classical Literature Endowment Fund of the University of California Press Associates, which is supported by a major gift from Joan Palevsky.

There Is No Crime for Those Who Have Christ

TRANSFORMATION OF THE CLASSICAL HERITAGE

Peter Brown, General Editor

There Is No Crime for Those Who Have Christ

Religious Violence in the Christian Roman Empire

MICHAEL GADDIS

University of California Press

BERKELEY   LOS ANGELES   LONDON

University of California Press
Berkeley and Los Angeles, California

University of California Press, Ltd.
London, England

© 2005 by The Regents of the University of California

First Paperback Printing 2015

Library of Congress Cataloging-in-Publication Data

Gaddis, Michael, 1970–.
   There is no crime for those who have Christ : religious violence
in the Christian Roman Empire / Michael Gaddis.
     p.   cm. — (The transformation of the classical heritage ; 39)
   Includes bibliographical references and index.
   isbn 978-0-520-28624-5 (pbk.: alk. paper).
   1. Persecution.   2. Violence—Religious aspects—Christianity.
   3. Church history—4th century.   4. Church history—5th century.
   5. Martyrdom.   I. Title.   II. Series.
   br1604.23.g33   2005
   270.2—dc22   2005005288

Manufactured in the United States of America

21 20 19 18 17 16 15
10 9 8 7 6 5 4 3 2 1

For Constantina, my inspiration

Contents

Preface and Acknowledgments

This is a book about violence, its reality, its perceptions, and its consequences. It takes as its premise that violent acts cannot be understood apart from the moral and ideological context in which they take place. It seeks to approach the problem from multiple perspectives, illuminating the views and voices of both violent actors and victims, of apologists, observers, and opponents both praising and condemning the same deeds. In studying religious violence in late antiquity, it aims not simply to catalog events but also to explore the relationship between action, ideology, and mentality. In the context of the Christian Roman Empire, arguments about violence and its proper use formed the leading edge of broader controversies over the nature of legitimate power, the definition of religious community, and the proper relation between the spiritual and the secular.

This book began as a dissertation, which itself started with an attempt to make sense of the puzzling behavior of violent monks who assaulted pagan temples and seemed to welcome death in doing so. In disregard of repeated cautions about the sprawling and potentially limitless nature of a topic such as "religious violence in late antiquity," each effort to circumscribe my inquiry within practicable limits led me instead to broaden it, as I read further and further on topics ranging from martyrdom and persecution, to the Donatist controversy and other intra-Christian sectarian conflicts, to the misbehavior of powerful bishops, and finally to the political machinations and ideological clashes of church councils. I soon realized that a comprehensive survey of violence in all its varieties and manifestations was neither desirable nor feasible, and this book does not attempt any such thing. Instead, I searched for a thematic focus, a synthesis to connect disparate and seemingly unrelated forms of conflict. I found in ideologies of martyrdom and resistance a continuity between the suffering of violence and violent action, making sense of the behavior of zealots not only in their violence against non-Christians but also in sectarian conflict between Christians, and in their mixture of martyrial ideology and ascetic zeal I began to see common elements underlying a paradigm of religious extremism, a justification for zealous action enacting the anger of God against enemies of the faith.

But the extremists, whose words and deeds by their very nature tended to attract notice out of all proportion to their numbers, formed only one part of the picture. A more fully balanced perspective required me to look also at their counterparts at the centers of establishment power. Emperors, magistrates, and leading bishops, though speaking and acting in more measured and moderate tones, commanded and often employed a far greater preponderance of coercive power than the zealots, and justified their repression of dissidents through a rhetoric of hierarchical discipline and compassionate, paternalistic concern. I have, then, framed this study as a contrast between the violence of the extremists, arising from zealous anger, and that of the center, grounded in the authorities' desire to maintain order and harmony at all costs.

Although this work is firmly focused upon the Constantinian empire, the Roman world of the fourth and fifth centuries, it is my hope that the book will be of use not only to late-antique specialists but also to readers with general interests in the comparative and thematic dimensions of religious conflict and violence in more recent times. Once thought to belong safely to the realm of the premodern, religious violence has in recent years thrust itself explosively into our consciousness—a fact brought home to me most clearly, as no doubt to many others, when awakened on a terrible morning in September of 2001. This book makes no claim to offer explanations, still less solutions, for the violent convulsions of our own times. Each era must be interpreted in its own right and according to its own principles and standards. Present-day conflicts, while in many cases drawing upon religious discourses, identities, and symbols with roots in the ancient past, nevertheless employ thoroughly modern techniques of political organization and communication and technologies of repression or destruction. The issues, ideologies, and grievances fought over are unique to their own time. But behind all these particularities what we see—in the fourth century no less than the twenty-first—are human actors who must justify their actions both to themselves and to others and whose strategies of rationalization and contestation look surprisingly similar across dramatically different historical and cultural contexts. In what sometimes seemed a distraction from my central focus on late antiquity, I have read widely (if haphazardly) in subjects ranging from Reformation-era Europe to contemporary Hindu nationalism and Islamic radicalism and even to extremisms of both the right and the left within my own country's recent history. Without making any claim to expertise on these subjects, I have nevertheless gained from them many insights that have allowed me to approach familiar late Roman material from new and different directions.

Late antiquity stands out as a time of unique importance, offering us the first opportunity to explore the consequences arising from the combination of universalizing monotheistic religion with political power on a world stage. The dynamic history of contest and conflict between church and state would dominate European politics for the next fifteen centuries. But this study is not about institutions. It is, rather, about mentalities, the ideologies, moral postures, and emotional dispositions of violent actors, victims, critics, and observers. In these areas too the Christian Roman Empire laid down patterns and precedents. It saw the fruition of an ideology of martyrial resistance, and the transformation of martyrdom from commemoration of violence suffered to justification for violence inflicted—from dying for God to killing for God. Its emperors and bishops responded in turn by laying out a centrist ideology of coercive consensus that would be invoked time and again over the centuries by those in power, justifying their own lethal repression with a language of disciplined compassion by which they claimed to act for the greater good of their subjects. In the clash between these two paradigms we can begin to perceive the supreme irony that similar violent ends could be arrived at from opposite paths of rationalization and justification, as all parties convinced themselves that their actions were not only necessary but just.

This book, and the dissertation (Princeton, 1999) that preceded it, have been far too many years in the making. It would not have been possible without the assistance of people and institutions whose help I gratefully acknowledge. Institutional support for my initial dissertation research came from Princeton University's Program in the Ancient World, the Group for the Study of Late Antiquity, and the Graduate School, as well as the Harry Frank Guggenheim Foundation. I remain indebted to the staff of the Princeton History Department for invaluable logistical assistance and moral support. In 1998–99 I finished the dissertation amid the hospitality, scholarly resources, and congenial atmosphere of Dumbarton Oaks. During subsequent years and through the long process of turning dissertation into book, I have found a new home and a welcoming and stimulating environment at Syracuse University, its Maxwell School of Citizenship and Public Affairs, and its History Department, all of which have provided support for my continuing research and writing. Special thanks are due to my faculty colleagues, the staff, and students here.

The arguments in this book have been presented and discussed at a variety of public fora over the years, and have emerged greatly refined and improved by the suggestions and comments of colleagues and audiences: at Princeton, the Group for the Study of Late Antiquity and the Dissertation Writers' Group; several iterations of the annual Byzantine Studies Conference; the Shifting Frontiers Conference; the International Institute at the University of Michigan; here at Syracuse, the Maxwell School's Samuel Goekjian lecture series; the History Department's Religion and Society Workgroup, and twice before the friendly and informal company of regional colleagues meeting under the delightful acronym LARCNY (Late Antique Religion in Central New York.) Many thanks are due to all who participated in these colloquies.

Peter Brown, former advisor and continuing mentor, has been a source of inspiration and erudition both during my time at Princeton and through subsequent years. He remained patient while I floundered and procrastinated, and helped me find my way but did not dictate a destination. I would also like to thank others who have read all or parts of the manuscript and offered valuable advice and criticism: William Jordan, Susan Ashbrook Harvey, Tia Kolbaba, Brent Shaw, Judith Herrin, Michael Cook, David Potter, Claudia Rapp, Richard Lim, Pat Miller. Susan Harvey, David Frankfurter, Dan Caner, and Beatrice Caseau generously shared pre-publication drafts of their work with me. Richard Price offered valuable assistance and saved me from several errors in translating the *Acts of Chalcedon*. I have profited also from consultation and discussion with Jennifer Hevelone-Harper, Derek Krueger, Noel Lenski, Christopher MacEvitt, Jackie Maxwell, Leonora Neville, Elizabeth Oram, Caroline Schroeder, Kevin Uhalde, Cynthia Villagomez, Joel Walker, and many others. I would particularly like to thank the editors of University of California Press and especially the anonymous readers for the Press, in response to whose suggestions this work is greatly improved. Needless to say, all remaining errors or infelicities are solely mine.

A special debt of gratitude is due my parents, without whose support and patience over the years none of this would have been possible. Finally and above all I dedicate this book to Constantina Scourtis Gaddis, my beloved wife, who has brought new meaning and inspiration to my life.

Abbreviations

AB	*Analecta Bollandiana*
ACO	*Acta Conciliorum Oecumenicorum,* ed. Schwartz
ACW	Ancient Christian Writers series
AHC	*Annuarium Historiae Conciliorum*
AHR	*American Historical Review*
ANF	Ante-Nicene Fathers series
BZ	*Byzantinische Zeitschrift*
CAH	*Cambridge Ancient History*
CCSL	Corpus Christianorum Series Latina
CJ	Corpus Juris Civilis
CSCO	Corpus Scriptorum Christianorum Orientalium series
CSEL	Corpus Scriptorum Ecclesiasticorum Latinorum series
C.Th.	*Codex Theodosianus,* the Theodosian Code
DOP	*Dumbarton Oaks Papers*
Epp.	*Epistulae,* Letters
FOTC	Fathers of the Church series
GCS	Die Griechischen christlichen Schriftsteller der ersten Jahrhunderte series
GRBS	*Greek Roman and Byzantine Studies*
HE	*Ecclesiastical History*
HTR	*Harvard Theological Review*
JECS	*Journal of Early Christian Studies*
JEH	*Journal of Ecclesiastical History*

JRS	*Journal of Roman Studies*
JTS	*Journal of Theological Studies*
LCL	Loeb Classical Library series
MP	Lactantius, *On the Deaths of the Persecutors*
NPNF	Nicene and Post-Nicene Fathers series
Or.	Oration
PCBE	*Prosopographie chrétienne du bas-empire*, ed. Mandouze
PG	Patrologia Graeca series
PL	Patrologia Latina series
PLRE	*Prosopography of the Later Roman Empire*, ed. Jones, Martindale, and Morris
PO	Patrologia Orientalis series
SC	Sources Chrétiennes series
SP	*Studia Patristica*
TM	*Travaux et Mémoires*
VC	*Vigiliae Christianae*

Introduction

In the early fifth century, the Egyptian monk Shenoute issued an open letter containing a thundering denunciation of a local pagan magnate. Shenoute and his followers had taken the law into their own hands, ransacked the pagan's house, and smashed his idols.[1] In response to the magnate's accusation of *lesteia*—banditry, crime, illegal violence—against him, Shenoute proclaimed that "there is no crime for those who have Christ."[2] The statement neatly expresses a paradigm of religious extremism, a belief that righteous zeal for God transcended considerations of worldly law and order. Religious conflict, and the attitudes that drove it, form the subject of this book.

Shenoute made his declaration in a unique context, the world of the Christian Roman Empire. Constantine's embrace of Christianity began a process that would elevate what had been the persecuted religion of a minority to the status of a dominant, hegemonic religious community. The new relationship between Christian religion and state power raised complicated questions of secular power, spiritual authority, and moral legitimacy. Would society be uplifted, as some hoped, into a new and universal community of

---

1. Shenoute's letter: Leipoldt and Crum 1906, pp. 79ff. English trans. in Barns 1961. The pagan, though not named in this text, was most likely Gesius, a local magnate with whom Shenoute had come into conflict on several occasions: see Besa, *Life of Shenoute*, 88, 125–126 (probably referring to this incident); Emmel 1993, pp. 891–893; and Frankfurter 1998, pp. 77–82. Emmel 2002, pp. 106–111, has now made the intriguing suggestion, *contra* Frankfurter, that Gesius was not an open supporter of pagan worship but rather a "crypto-pagan" who concealed his continued devotions behind the façade of a politically expedient Christian conversion. I owe this reference to Caroline Schroeder.

2. *N the gar ete mn mnt-lestes shoop n nete ou-ntau Iesous hn oume. Mnt-lestes*, adapted from Greek *lesteia*, is equivalent to Latin *latrocinium*, on whose meaning of "criminal violence" or "brigandage" see below pp. 20–21.

Christian piety, or—as others feared—would religion be dragged down by the world, corrupted by its newfound power and wealth? This study will explore how Christians in the fourth and fifth centuries grappled with these problems. The temporal and chronological focus of this study is therefore the Christian Roman Empire, a unique environment shaped by the marriage of Christian ideology and Roman imperial power. One of the most important defining characteristics of the late antique period, the fourth through seventh centuries A.D., was the tendency of individuals, groups, and societies to construct their identity more and more exclusively in confessional religious terms. Late antiquity saw the formation of what could be called "imagined communities" (borrowing from Benedict Anderson's study of modern nationalism)[3] based on religion. Such identities were constructed both in terms of consensus, through appeal to a universal or "ecumenical" community of believers, and also in terms of division and confrontation—self-definition in opposition to hostile outsiders or by reference to past experiences of violent persecution.

Late antiquity can be defined as beginning with Constantine—the rise of one exclusive monotheistic religion to hegemonic status—and ending with Muhammad—the appearance of another. My study will cover approximately the first half of that period, staying largely within the boundaries of the Christian empire, up to the Council of Chalcedon in 451. In some sense any stopping point is arbitrary; as today's headlines remind us, religious violence is not simply a matter of ancient history. But I have chosen to end with Chalcedon because that occasion, illuminated by source material of unparalleled detail, offers us the opportunity to examine the convergence of several key themes of religious conflict, as different parties put forward competing paradigms of spiritual authority in a great debate over the proper role of secular power in the church, a contest about how the church was to relate to the world. I chose to investigate these larger concerns through a particular study of the role of violence in religious conflicts under the Christian empire. This is not a book about how Rome became Christian, or why Constantine converted, but rather an exploration of the consequences that followed from that event. My study is not dedicated to proving the facts of religious violence in the late antique world by cataloguing and enumerating riots, attacks on temples, and other incidents—previous scholarship has already done that. Rather, I have sought to explore what violence *meant* to those involved, both actors and victims, how it was experienced, represented, justified, or contested.

3. Anderson 1991.

DEFINING VIOLENCE

Beginning such a study requires that one define exactly what is meant by violence in a late Roman context and how that might differ from our own modern concepts. Such a question could not be answered merely by a simple philological analysis of terms such as Latin *violentia* or *latrocinium* and their equivalents in Greek, Coptic, or Syriac. The language of violence in late antiquity was far more than just words. Violence did not have a fixed and consistent meaning on which all late Romans, or even all our surviving sources, agreed. It was itself an object of struggle, a contested field upon which conflicting ideas about power, authority, and religious identity could be played out. Arguments seeking to defend or denounce particular uses of violence were also debates about the proper exercise of power, about legitimacy and authority, about right and wrong. My study accordingly devotes great attention to the representation of violence, and I argue that discourse about violence affected the ways in which violence could be used in practice.

At first glance, the need to define exactly what "violence" meant might seem pedantic. Accounts of religious conflict in late antiquity abound with murder, torture, and beating, from the sufferings of the martyrs to the vengeful punishment of unbelievers, not to mention acts of desecration against buildings or objects of worship—all of which we would have no trouble characterizing as quite straightforward manifestations of physical violence.

But of course our own understanding of violence can reach far beyond actual use of physical force. We think of armed robbery, for instance, as a violent crime even if no shots are actually fired—or, stated more generally, a display of coercive power backed up by the threat of violence will satisfy the definition even if the threat is not carried out. Entire systems of government can be characterized as violent when they are seen to rest primarily on coercive power, from Greco-Roman concepts of tyranny to modern critiques of colonial domination or totalitarian dictatorship—and the characterization "violent" describes the normal workings of such a system, not just the actual physical violence associated with initial military conquest or seizure of power. Most recently, following Foucault, we have begun to approach the history of modern educational, medical, and penal institutions by characterizing the disciplinary power they exercise over their human subjects as a form of violence, even when the mechanisms of control are far more subtle and sophisticated than simple physical force. When we speak of "violent" rhetoric or "hate speech," we signal an understanding that words alone may have a violent quality, blurring the commonsense distinction between word and deed.

The broader the definition of violence in use, the more it is subject to controversy. As a general rule, those who suffer violence—in whatever form—are more likely to characterize it as violence than those who use it. Concepts of right and wrong thus become key to defining what constitutes violence, and these concepts depend very much on where one stands. We could provisionally define violence as a use or display of power that others consider wrong or hurtful or that transgresses their ethical or moral norms. In this sense, "violence" acquires a meaning very similar to "violation," and it becomes easier to understand how it might extend beyond the merely physical. The ancient "outrage" of *hubris*, which in legal discourse covered a semantic field that could be translated as both *assault* and *insult*, thus embraced both the violent act and, by extension, the attitude that produced it—a state of mind that, in Christian discourse, would be called pride, a rebellion of human will against God that theologians understood to be the root of all sin.

The preceding cannot help but illustrate the difficulties of pinning down a firm and consistent definition. Violence touches on many different arenas of human action, perception, and experience. The present study will explore violence in dimensions both large and small, physical and figurative, at levels both individual and systemic. Throughout, it will emphasize the importance of considering emotions and attitudes, reactions as well as actions. A useful model for such a study can be found in Peter Gay's sweeping exploration of Victorian-era mentalities, which gathers together under the rubric of "aggression" themes as various as masculinity, imperialism, Darwinism, and even laughter, exploring not only behavior but also the ideologies, discourses, and understandings—what Gay calls "alibis"—that lay behind it.[4] In recent years, scholars have begun to treat emotions, previously consigned to the realm of the intangible and irrational, as a legitimate subject of inquiry. Barbara Rosenwein has argued for a new approach focusing on the study of "emotional communities."[5] The ancient historians, of course, had always considered emotions and motivations central to their understanding of a history

4. Gay 1993. See p. 6: "In carrying on their heartfelt disputes, the Victorians developed what I shall call alibis for aggression: beliefs, principles, rhetorical platitudes that legitimated verbal or physical militancy on religious, political, or, best of all, scientific grounds."

5. See now Rosenwein 2002. On p. 846: "People lived—and live—in what I propose to call 'emotional communities.' These are precisely the same as social communities—families, neighborhoods, parliaments, guilds, monasteries, parish church memberships—but the researcher looking at them seeks above all to uncover systems of feeling: what these communities (and the individuals within them) define and assess as valuable or harmful to them; the evaluations that they make about others' emotions; the nature of the affective bonds between people that they recog-

driven by the virtues and vices of human actors.[6] This moral context demanded careful discrimination between the appropriate and the inappropriate: anger, for instance, could manifest either as righteous zeal or as jealous rage, with dramatically opposite consequences.[7] The definition of violence, or rather, the competition of discourses attempting to define it in different ways, thus becomes a broader debate about the legitimate uses of power.

I have taken as the organizing principle of this study the violence that arises from the intersection of religion and power. In the context of a late Roman world that lived under the oppressive shadow of the imperial state, we can attempt—at the risk of great oversimplification—to distinguish between the violence employed by or on behalf of established authority, in both secular and ecclesiastical varieties, and violence deployed in opposition or resistance to that authority.[8] In exploring the rationalizations and justifications put forward by actors and apologists for these categories of violence, we can identify what I call "extremist" and "centrist" outlooks, used both to justify one's own violence and to condemn that of others. This simple binary formulation of course cannot do justice to a far more complicated reality in which multiple interest groups and centers of power competed for primacy. Nevertheless, the distinction between centrist and oppositionalist mentalities allows us to understand how similar violent results could, ironically, proceed from opposite moral and emotional motivations. An exploration of the mindset, values, and hatreds behind each viewpoint will be essential to this study.

I have employed as a working definition of "extremism" any ideology taken to its extreme, interpreted and enacted in an absolute sense that allowed no compromise with practical considerations or accommodation with the world.[9] Extremist discourse, in religion as in other contexts, valued above all

---

nize; and the modes of emotional expression that they expect, encourage, tolerate, and deplore." A noteworthy and pathbreaking example of this approach as applied to Roman history is Barton 1993.

6. For a thought-provoking analysis of "vices"—cruelty, hypocrisy, and betrayal, among others—in a modern context, see Shklar 1984.

7. Anger, in its various historical contexts, has received recent scholarly attention. For the classical world, see Harris 2001; for the Middle Ages, the essays collected in Rosenwein 1998.

8. This characterization draws somewhat on a distinction posed by Hannah Arendt between "the power of all against one" and "the violence of one against all," roughly synonymous, respectively, with state repression and extremist violence. Arendt 1970, pp. 42ff.

9. Although the concept and term "extremism" has not specifically been applied in late antique studies, some scholars have discussed the role of "totalizing discourses,"

zeal and authenticity in the pursuit of its cause, and strove for a total and perfect expression of its values.[10] Those who temporized, compromised, tried to balance competing priorities or to see more than one side of an issue, it condemned as "hypocrites." Judith Shklar has cautioned against the tendency—not unusual among religious militants—to identify hypocrisy as the worst of evils, because it carries with it the implicit corollary that authenticity and sincerity in devotion to the right cause could justify any atrocity: there is no crime for those who have Christ.[11] Religious extremists convinced themselves that they enacted not their own will, but God's, and that the anger driving their violence was a righteous and godly zeal. Their targets were not limited to obvious enemies of the faith such as pagans, Jews, or heretics but also extended to the hypocrisy of an establishment that claimed to be Christian and yet protected and tolerated unbelievers. Extremist violence, then, aimed at unmasking and provoking, forcing the authorities to act in such a way as to confirm the zealots' darkest suspicions.

The motives of late antique religious zealots cannot be understood apart from a worldview shaped by martyrdom and persecution. This oppositional mentality, grounded in Christianity's early experience as a marginalized and often persecuted cult, derived legitimacy, authority, and authenticity from the actual or perceived suffering of its spiritual role models. Persecution, which loomed so large in Christian historical imagination, need not always have been literal. Even under the Christian empire, some claimed to suffer it simply because they were forced to tolerate the continued existence of pagans and heretics.[12] This "repressive tolerance," as Herbert Marcuse might have characterized it, seemed to some as little more than a subtler form of persecution—for certainly it was not right, they thought, that truth be forced to live on equal terms with falsehood.[13] Christianity, in some ways, retained

---

e.g., asceticism, in Averil Cameron 1995; or religion's displacement of secularity in Markus 1990. Chapters 5 and 6 will discuss the prominent role of ascetic holy men in extremist violence.

10. Cf. P. Brown 1983 on the holy man's role as a "moral catalyst" personifying in an absolute sense the values that the larger society claimed to espouse.

11. Shklar 1984, esp. pp. 45–86.

12. A sentiment expressed, e.g., in Augustine, *City of God* 18.51.

13. In "Repressive Tolerance" (1969), Marcuse decried liberal democracy's freedoms of speech as a sham under which the bad would drown out the good without forceful intervention: "Tolerance cannot be indiscriminate and equal with respect to the contents of expression, neither in word nor in deed; it cannot protect false words and wrong deeds which demonstrate that they contradict and counteract the possibilities of liberation" (p. 88). He advocated censorship of "reactionary" speech and freedom of expression only for "progressive" causes—as defined, of course, by

the habits of thought of a persecuted minority even into the era of its dominance. Extremist attitudes could manifest in individuals who by any reasonable criteria might seem to be at the very center of power—emperors, bishops, or others in positions of established authority, whose zeal could override the inherent conservatism of their institutional offices. I emphasize the importance of tracing this absolutist mentality not just in individuals but also in the moral discourses and habits of argument that diffused in greater or lesser degree throughout the thought-world of late Roman Christianity.

But extremists and religious zealots could hardly be said to have a monopoly on either militant attitudes or violent actions. Establishment authorities, those close to the centers of state power, typically had much greater physical means and capacity to unleash violence against their enemies. Self-consciously moderate and yet zealous in defense of the status quo, normative imperial ideology justified and indeed demanded the use of violence against those thought to threaten peace and consensus. Emperors both pagan and Christian sought above all to achieve unity and concord, in religion as in secular politics, and were willing to use repressive and coercive means to this end. This strategy of "coercive harmony," to borrow a phrase from Laura Nader's work in legal anthropology, was the natural course for an imperial system that valued hierarchy, authority, stability, and unity above all.[14] The exercise of power cloaked itself in the language of paternalistic concern, pedagogical discipline, and therapeutic medicine—behind which lurked a potential for violence no less lethal for the high-minded motives of its perpetrators. The violence of the center always justified itself as being in the best interests of its victims—for their own good, whether they knew it or not.[15] The authorities knew themselves to act from the best of intentions, and op-

---

Herbert Marcuse and those who shared his politics. Marcuse's endorsement of "revolutionary" violence (p. 103) is a classic statement of ends justifying means, excusing and endorsing the "violence of the oppressed"—as if "oppressed" and "oppressor" were fixed, objective, and unchanging categories rather than situational and changeable constructs. Cf. Shklar 1984, p. 19: "One cannot afford to pretend that victimhood improves anyone in any way. If we do not remember that anyone can be a victim . . . we will unwittingly aid the torturers of tomorrow by overrating the victims of today."

14. Briefly stated in Nader 1996. The idea is developed and applied to anthropological research in Nader 1990.

15. Brad Gregory, in his study of Reformation-era violence, delivers a sensitive analysis of "the willingness to kill" on the part of sixteenth-century magistrates who believed themselves to be acting from the highest motives of Christian charity even as they ordered the torture and execution of fellow Christians: Gregory 1999, esp. chap. 3.

position, they were certain, could only derive from the worst of motives. Those who disputed the credal compromises hammered out at church councils did so, they suspected, not from sincere conviction but from a diabolical love of controversy and a prideful spirit of rebellion.[16]

Where extremists employed violence to expose and ultimately destroy known enemies, centrists used it to smooth over disputes, to bring the errant back into the fold by a combination of persuasion and disciplinary coercion. Where zealots freely admitted that they acted upon anger and hatred, establishment authorities claimed to be guided by compassion. Each side attributed the worst of intentions to the other, allowing no possibility of disagreement in good faith. Both believed, in their different ways, that ends justified means.[17] One used violence to divide, the other employed it to unite. The conflict between extreme and center was at root a clash between different conceptions of religious and political community, the one valuing purity and the other privileging unity. Was Christianity, in the age of Constantine, to remain an uncorrupted congregation of the virtuous few, or would it strive and compromise in order to embrace all in a universal community of believers?

QUESTIONING AND CONTESTING POWER

The relationship of power and legitimacy has long been an object of intense study, particularly in theories of the state and of international relations. Charles Tilly offers a fairly straightforward definition: "Legitimacy is the probability that other authorities will act to confirm the decisions of a given authority."[18] Tilly considers legitimacy a simple extension of physical power, in which others endorse or tolerate one's actions simply in order to avoid conflict. He quotes approvingly Arthur Stinchcombe's remark that for purposes of establishing legitimacy, "The person over whom power is exercised is not usually as important as other power-holders."[19] But the

16. Lim 1995 demonstrates a growing prejudice against argument and controversy, seen as threats to concord and authority, in the course of the religious controversies of the fourth century.

17. Cf. the warning of Arendt 1970, p. 4: "The very substance of violent action is ruled by the means-end category, whose chief characteristic, if applied to human affairs, has always been that the end is in danger of being overwhelmed by the means which it justifies and which are needed to reach it."

18. Tilly 1985, p. 171.

19. Stinchcombe 1968, p. 150.

classic Weberian formulation, that the state seeks to monopolize the means of violence, places much greater emphasis on the need for the state to enforce this monopoly not just with overwhelming force but also through ideological justification.[20] Legitimacy does consist of acceptance of one's actions by others, but it also requires that those others accept the definition or justification that the actor seeks to impose on the deed.

Although other powers, defined as other agents also capable of using violent force, generally do have more influence than "those over whom power is exercised," it would be shortsighted to leave the latter out of the equation entirely. James Scott has taught us not to overlook the capacity of subordinated and seemingly "powerless" groups to oppose and frustrate the demands of the ruling order through indirect criticism and subversion where more overt resistance is not feasible.[21] Force need not always be opposed by equal force: under the right circumstances, ideological critique may succeed in limiting the ways in which power can actually be used.

Legitimacy, as defined above, rests upon acceptance by others. But certain forms of authority derive their strength not from the consent of ruling powers but rather from confrontation with those powers. Christian martyrdom in the fourth century became a politicized discourse, a rhetorical stance available to those who sought to legitimize their defiance of imperial power.[22] Peter Brown has shown how late antique holy men gained a charismatic authority in the eyes of their followers through their confrontational style of *parrhesia*, "free speech"—or what James Scott would call "speaking truth to power"—in the face of established authorities.[23] True legitimacy is an authoritative claim accepted by an audience broader than the immediate circle of a holy man's devoted disciples. But a narrative assertion of successful authority could itself help to create it in fact. When hagiography depicted emperors, generals, and bishops bowing to the will of ascetic saints, it helped to define a "proper" pattern of relations between worldly powers and the holy man, and reinforced an expectation of similar deference in future.

Power invariably attempts to justify its own use. Through ideology and discourse, simple physical force may be transformed into legitimate authority. Dominant groups construct ideological systems that legitimize their exercise of power, seeking to justify it, with varying degrees of success, to themselves, to their peers, and also to their subjects. But power de-

20. See, e.g., Weber 1947, p. 154.
21. Scott 1985 and esp. 1990.
22. See chapter 2.
23. Brown 1992.

fended by discourse can be challenged by discourse. To the degree that the ruling authorities actually take seriously the ideology upon which they base their legitimacy—or at least feel the need to give the appearance of taking it seriously—they become particularly vulnerable to a critique articulated within the framework of their own value system, accusing them of failing to live up to the ideals they claim to espouse.[24] Thus a late antique Roman regime that claimed to be Christian opened itself to criticism for its "tolerance" of pagans, Jews, and heretics, and for its halfhearted punishment of the zealous Christians who attacked them.

Bruce Lincoln presents "force" and "discourse" as parallel and complementary means of exercising power. In the form of "ideological persuasion," discourse supplements violent force by extending to places where physical coercion cannot reach.[25] But a quite different role is served by discourse *about* violence. Lincoln elsewhere has much to say about the capacity of certain types of "corrosive" discourse to undermine power and authority.[26] When the use of violence itself becomes the subject of discourse, we may find that discourse about violence has the potential to constrain the ways in which violent power can actually be used. It is not enough to control the means of violence—one must also be able to control its meaning. Much of this study will examine attempts by different parties to contest the meaning of particular episodes of violence.

HISTORIOGRAPHY ON RELIGIOUS VIOLENCE

A brief discussion of existing scholarship on late antique violence is in order. Literature on various dimensions of the subject is vast, and this is by no means a comprehensive review, but rather a quick survey of works that have been especially useful as resources for my own research. More detailed bibliography on particular issues can be found in the relevant chapters.

For much of the first half of the twentieth century, scholarship on reli-

24. Cf. Scott 1990, p. 103: "Any ruling group, in the course of justifying the principles of social inequality on which it bases its claim to power, makes itself vulnerable to a particular line of criticism. Inasmuch as these principles of inequality unavoidably claim that the ruling stratum performs some valuable social function, its members open themselves to attack for the failure to perform these functions honorably or adequately. The basis of the claim to privilege and power creates, as it were, the groundwork for a blistering critique of domination on the terms evoked by the elite."

25. Lincoln 1989, p. 4.

26. "Corrosive discourse" from Lincoln 1994, esp. chap. 5.

gious violence in late antiquity suffered from a refusal to concede that it had anything to do with religion. Doctrinal controversies and religious riots, it was thought, were "really" disguised expressions of class struggle, secular politics, or ethnic nationalism.[27] Much work in recent decades has undertaken to point out obvious flaws in these older views.[28] There is no evidence that the lines of factional division corresponded neatly to class or ethnic identity. More important is the fact that no late antique sources ever phrased it in such terms. For contemporaries, religious conflicts were first and foremost about religion, and attempts to downplay this fact smack of "false consciousness," betraying an assumption that social and economic issues are somehow more "real" than religious concerns.[29]

Although more recent scholarship has decisively refuted older secularist interpretations, no new comprehensive paradigm has arisen to take its place. Rather, a certain compartmentalization has characterized more recent work on religious violence in late antiquity. Different studies have treated separately urban riots in Christian controversies,[30] Christian attacks on pagan temples,[31] and Donatist-Catholic conflict in North Africa.[32] These works, though generally solid, are narrow in their focus. They study particular conflicts between particular groups but do not take violence itself as a subject of inquiry.

A fundamental debate in the study of violence has asked whether violence is to be seen as irrational exception, the product of a breakdown in

27. Paradigmatic of this view was Woodward 1916. This tendency was particularly influential in scholarship on the Donatist controversy in North Africa: see chapter 3, p. 107. For a general history emphasizing an economic-determinist interpretation, see Ste. Croix 1981.

28. See, among others, Jones 1959, T. Gregory 1979. Although there has been almost no serious expression of these old-fashioned secularist interpretations in the last twenty years, much scholarly effort continues to be devoted to attacking them, e.g., most recently, Barnard 1995.

29. See Scott 1990, pp. 70–107, for a thoroughgoing attack on the notion of "false consciousness." The tendency to find secular or materialist interpretations behind episodes of religious conflict is sharply criticized, for the Reformation period, in Davis 1973 and more recently in B. Gregory 1999. We should always be cautious of assuming any simplistic causal link between material deprivation and violence: see Krueger and Maleckova 2002, debunking the "poverty causes violence" commonplace with regard to modern terrorism. Of course religious and nonreligious factors need not necessarily be exclusive: see Meeks 1983, pp. 2–7, arguing against "theological reductionism."

30. See, e.g., MacMullen 1990a, McLynn 1992, and especially T. Gregory 1979, who confines his investigation of religious violence to urban riots.

31. Most recently Trombley 1993–1994; cf. also Fowden 1978. Additional bibliography in chapter 5, pp. 157–158.

32. Full bibliography in chapter 3, p. 105.

normal systems of power, or whether it functions as an integral part of such systems.[33] Scholarship outside late antiquity has demonstrated that the violent actions of mobs can be analyzed and understood within the context of the moral system of those involved.[34] Natalie Davis, in her study of Protestant-Catholic clashes in sixteenth-century France, has shown that different groups had different "styles" of violence that reflected their particular ideological and religious beliefs.[35] Brad Gregory, working in the same period, has emphasized instead what Protestant and Catholic adversaries had in common, illuminating the clashing yet fundamentally similar understandings of martyrdom, persecution, and magisterial duty that shaped their respective "confessional communities" and drove them both to die for God and to kill for God.[36] Others have emphasized the role of violence in maintaining boundaries and regulating relationships between different religious or ethnic communities.[37]

My study will build upon these models and methods of inquiry. In addition to using violent acts as a window upon the worldview of the actors, I will also study *representations* of violence as a clue to how such acts were received and understood within the moral framework of late antique observers both supportive and hostile. In the late antique context, I see violence being used to construct community in two distinct ways—to divide "us from them" as the zealots would wish, or to force the "unity" beloved by emperors.

33. MacMullen 1990a argues for the "normality" of violence, employed and directed by religious authorities; McLynn 1992 sees violent outbursts as an exceptional consequence of situations in which the restraints imposed by normal structures of authority have disappeared.

34. See, e.g., Rudé 1964, Thompson 1971.

35. Davis 1973. Many of the same scriptural arguments and justifications of violence that we will see used by Christian zealots in the fourth and fifth centuries would be invoked again by both Catholic and Protestant militants during the Reformation. In late antique scholarship, one of very few works to make use of these methodologies for studying violence is Haas 1997.

36. B. Gregory 1999.

37. An excellent recent example is Nirenberg 1996, examining violent conflict between Christians, Muslims, and Jews in fourteenth-century Spain. In the period covered by Nirenberg's study, the religious communities involved in conflict had a long and well-established history and fairly stable identities and boundaries. For the modern period, Kakar 1996 offers a valuable analysis of Hindu-Muslim communal violence in India, working from a psychoanalytic as well as sociological perspective. In the fourth and fifth centuries, religious communities as self-conscious entities can be seen in the process of formation: cf. Haas 1997, charting how only over the course of the fourth century, as a consequence of conflict with Christians, did the pagans of Alexandria come to think of themselves as a single community whose identity was defined first and foremost by religion.

PROBLEMS OF METHODOLOGY AND EVIDENCE

Particularly illuminating are those situations where a single act of violence—anything from a mass riot to the violent destruction of a temple to gruesome martyrdom, right down to something as simple as a single blow of the hand—is depicted from multiple perspectives, subjected to multiple discourses that argue over its meaning, justifying or challenging the rightness of the deed and the ideological message it seeks to express. Practices that lie on the margins of acceptability, neither broadly accepted nor broadly condemned, offer especially valuable insight.

This approach involves much reliance on stories, and of course these raise evidentiary problems. They exaggerate, slant, or invent, depending upon their agenda. Polemical denunciations seek to highlight the severity of the violence done by one's enemies, and also to cast it in certain ideological molds such as "tyranny" or "persecution." Talk of violence may refer to physical force, or may simply reflect the author's outrage at a perceived violation of moral or legal norms. Hagiographic depictions of zealous holy men destroying temples and confounding enemies of the faith, meanwhile, may indulge in a certain amount of wishful thinking. Scholars of hagiography have long grappled with problems of evidence posed by their texts, many of which were written centuries later than the events they claim to describe, and contain obvious dramatic exaggeration and miraculous intervention.[38] Recognition of these evidentiary difficulties has led scholars to question whether violence really played such an important role—in religious affairs specifically, or in Roman society more broadly—as our sources might make it seem. Their questions, essentially, boil down to this: do reports of violence reflect the pervasive presence and influence of violence throughout society—"the tip of the iceberg," as Ramsay MacMullen argues—or is violence reported precisely because it is rare and exceptional, as Neil McLynn suggests?[39] At its most fundamental level, this question cannot be answered definitively.[40]

But the significance of violence in the late Roman world was more than

38. In chapter 5, pp. 153–155, I discuss at greater length the evidentiary problems raised specifically by hagiographic stories of holy men attacking pagan temples.

39. Two good summations in recent scholarship of these opposing points of view, arguing specifically on the prevalence of urban religious riots, can be found in MacMullen 1990a and McLynn 1992.

40. As Roger Bagnall argues: "One could suppose that the relative absence of mentions of this sort of violence is here, too, an indication of its prevalence and normality; but that involves a logical trap. A society where such violence was *not*

a simple function of its frequency. Narrative representations and rhetorical arguments regarding violence exercised an influence over the imagination of society that reached far beyond the immediate scope of actual incidents. Stories of violence played a key role in shaping the evolving self-consciousness of the Christian community, by articulating boundaries between those inside—zealous and pious Christians—and those outside—pagans, Jews, heretics, and those who tolerate them. Such accounts, whether the zealous and justified violence of pious holy men, or the brutal and criminal abuses of tyrants and persecutors, spoke to the expectations of their audiences. They expressed what people thought a holy man ought to do, or what a powerful and unscrupulous tyrant might do—their hopes for the way in which power ought to be used, and their fears as to how it might be abused.

Accordingly, I devote much attention to issues of definition and construction, asking not so much how violence occurred but how it was interpreted. This requires careful attention to the bias of sources. Our sources are texts, and we must be aware of the agendas and discourses informing those texts. Parties to religious conflicts obviously sought to justify their own position, while casting the actions and motives of their opponents in as negative a fashion as possible. The same act of violence could be treated either as zealous defense of the faith or as the angry raving of a tyrant, depending on the position of the observer. Recent scholarship on the history of heresy, and on early asceticism, has stressed the importance of getting past the polemical stereotypes inherent in normative tradition.[41] In studying violent conflict, likewise, we must recognize the rhetorical strategies and polemical categories deployed by all parties, both to see what sense the actors made of their own actions, and also to understand the moral context in which their actions were challenged.

CHRISTIANITY AND INTOLERANCE

Perhaps the single longest-running historiographical debate regarding religious violence in Christian history, argued from Gibbon up to the present, has been the question of Christian "intolerance." Many have found it difficult to imagine how the same religious system could encompass Jesus' exhorta-

---

prevalent could never be identified given such assumptions and methods." Bagnall 1989, p. 214.

41. On heresy: e.g., Lyman 1993, Le Boulluec 1985. Polemical stereotypes in regard to asceticism are discussed in chapter 6.

tion, "If someone strikes you, turn the other cheek," alongside pronouncements such as that of John Chrysostom, who in 387 told his Antiochene congregation in no uncertain terms how to deal with blasphemers: "Slap them in the face, strike them around the mouth, sanctify your hand by the blow!"[42] Some have viewed Christianity as a religious system inherently intolerant and prone to violent persecution of other faiths, while others argue that those who resorted to violence did not represent "authentic" Christianity and that therefore the religious claims of violent militants must have masked cynical political or personal agendas.[43] One could say that the two sides of this argument themselves echo the polemical stereotypes of late antiquity. Many pagans would have agreed with those who argued the fundamental intolerance of Christianity,[44] while particular Christian factions preferred to characterize the violent conduct of their rivals as fundamentally un-Christian.

In this study, I have assumed that most parties to religious violence, Christian or otherwise, believed their own actions to be justified by the imperatives of their religion as they understood it. This statement should not be taken as a categorical exclusion of the importance of other, more worldly, factors in religious conflict. Certainly political and personal rivalry played a role, and our examinations of polemical literature will show that combatants on all sides engaged in much distortion and misrepresentation of opponents. But their claims, hagiographic or polemic, had to be made with reference to broadly shared religious and moral values. We must attempt to understand how late antique Christians believed violence to fit within their moral system, whether upholding it or violating it. We must also avoid the essentializing temptation to search for a single and monolithic "authentic Christian tradition" on violence: there were different and hotly contested perspectives, and each side understood its own view to be authentic and firmly grounded in scripture. Biblical tradition offers ample material to support both militant violence and pacifism, and the appropriate question is not which do we consider to be more valid, but rather which traditions were in-

---

42. Jesus: Matthew 5:29, Luke 6:39. Chrysostom: *Homilies on the Statues* 1.32.
43. The history of the debate is summarized with detailed bibliography in Drake 1996; see also Drake 2000. Stroumsa 1993 has explained the "intolerance" of early Christians in terms of a competition between "eirenic" and "eristic" tendencies intrinsic to the faith. Moore 1987 finds a structural tendency to intolerance and persecution not in the Christian religion itself but rather in its developed medieval institutions. Nirenberg 1996, by contrast, argues against "a now almost orthodox view of the steady march of European intolerance across the centuries" (p. 7) and prefers to emphasize the particularities of local situations.
44. Cf. Ammianus 22.5.4: "No wild beasts are such enemies to mankind as are most of the Christians in their deadly hatred of one another." (Rolfe trans.)

voked by Christians in the fourth and fifth centuries. This study does not seek to impose a modern judgment but rather to explore what judgments were formed by people in late antiquity, and what consequences followed from the judgments and choices they made.

THE CONTEXT: VIOLENCE IN THE ROMAN WORLD

From the beginning, ancient political discourse was inseparably bound up with discourse about violence. The fear of entrusting absolute power to corruptible mortals animated statements of anti-monarchical sentiment in both Judaic and Hellenic traditions. A king, they warned, will raise your taxes, draft your sons, and debauch your daughters. Puffed up with a pride that will lead in turn to envy and rage, he will trample upon law and custom.[45] In archaic Greece, the name of *tyrannos* originally denoted strongmen who had seized power through unlawful violence.[46] In the later Roman Empire, the word would be synonymous with "usurper," now reserved for those who sought and failed to seize power by violent means.[47] But the term, then as now, carried broader connotations of cruelty and misrule, a regime that was violent not just in its origins but in its nature and conduct. The ancients believed that each type of government came in good and bad varieties, depending on the moral character of those in charge, and "tyranny" was the dark side of monarchy. Plato, in the *Republic,* identified the moral character of the tyrant as both criminal and animalistic. Wolf-like, "tyrannized" by his base urges, he acts without the restraint of reason and sheds the blood of his fellow citizens.[48] Plato's insight was that these vices could inhere not just in individuals but in the body politic, each regime furthering in its citizens a particular mix of virtues and vices that would strain the system and lead to its downfall. Classical thinkers sought to establish a sensible "middle way" between the twin extremes of anarchy and tyranny, by controlling imbalances and excesses of power—just as philosophers advocated controlling excess of emotion in the individual.[49]

45. See, e.g., the prophet Samuel's warning to the Israelites who had asked him to select for them a king (I Samuel 8), and the similar critique of monarchy placed by Herodotus in the mouth of the Persian Otanes (Herodotus 3.80).

46. On tyranny in archaic and classical Greece, see McGlew 1993.

47. On the terminology used to distinguish legitimate emperors from usurpers and tyrants, see MacMullen 1963, Paschoud and Szidat 1997.

48. Plato, *Republic* 9.9, 571a–576b.

49. On the control of anger, see now Harris 2001.

The philosophers of later centuries, living under Hellenistic and then Roman autocrats, shifted their focus from the characteristics of constitutions to the character of the individual ruler. Under the Principate, rhetors could still teach the praises of classical "tyrannicides" but had to adapt to present reality. No longer able to question monarchy as an institution, they learned to distinguish between "good" and "bad" rulers. Panegyrists lined up to flatter the reigning emperor, while retaining the ability to admonish him indirectly via condemnation of his predecessors' misdeeds.[50] Counselors calmed down enraged emperors by appealing to philosophical ideals of decorum. In the absence of any legal or constitutional restraint on imperial power, such discourse assumed paramount importance. Lacking a close analogue to modern concepts of "human rights," ethical thought focused instead on the character and motives of those exercising power.[51] Self-control, at bottom, was about controlling violence. Its failure, at the imperial level, could literally cost lives.[52]

The first Augustus, while ruling as a monarch in fact, went to great lengths to preserve the polite fiction of continued republican government. Wise emperors were careful to make a show of respecting senatorial privileges, not least because senatorial perspectives, which overwhelmingly dominate the surviving historiography of the Principate, determined whether one would go down in history as a "good" or a "bad" emperor. All emperors were autocrats in truth, but only "tyrants" like Caligula or Nero went out of their way to act the role. They earned their evil reputation in large part because their treason trials, confiscations, and purges directed the judicial violence of the state against the social and political elites who regarded themselves as above such treatment.

Late antiquity has left us a greatly expanded variety of sources and therefore of perspectives. Early Christians, who often found themselves on the receiving end of judicial violence, adapted the rhetorical image of the "tyrant" to their own purposes, hoping to establish the persecution of Christians as a defining characteristic of "bad" emperors.[53] As Harold Drake has

50. Panegyrics: see Nixon and Rodgers, eds. and trans., 1995, *Panegyrici Latini*.
51. On the question of "rights," see Bauman 2000.
52. On imperial anger and its restraint, see generally Brown 1992. Cf. Harris 2001, p. 249: "The control of inappropriate anger had become part of the ideological basis of that particularly ideological kind of rule which was that of the Roman emperors. At the same time, an emperor needed to be thought capable of anger against contumelious or corrupt subordinates."
53. See, e.g., Lactantius' *On the Deaths of the Persecutors*, in which "bad" emperors such as Nero and Domitian are blamed for persecution, while more fondly remembered rulers such as Hadrian or Marcus Aurelius are excused.

argued, one consequence of Christian ascendance under Constantine and his successors was that Christian bishops became the new arbiters of political opinion, taking over a role traditionally played by the senatorial class in legitimating an emperor's reputation.[54] The same culture that exalted and divinized authority also created the expectation that it would act justly, and challenged it when it did not. In what Jill Harries has called a "culture of criticism," governors and magistrates walked a delicate balance, vulnerable both to the complaints of local potentates and to the distant but never absent oversight of the imperial court.[55] The emperors needed to know what people were saying about their policies and about their functionaries, and so the system demanded the careful recording and reporting of information. Acclamations and slogans, whether chanted by senators in the curia, by bishops in synod, or by crowds in the hippodrome, were carefully taken down by notaries and forwarded to the appropriate authorities. The late Roman legal system placed a growing emphasis on accurate transcription and documentation, with a view toward creating a written record to which all parties could refer in order to verify that matters had indeed been judged properly.[56]

The absence of any legal or constitutional restraint on imperial power did not free its wielders from the necessity of justifying themselves in the eyes of others. Emperors worried about public opinion, or at least about that of important constituencies such as the senatorial elite, the army, or the riot-prone populations of major cities. Their greatest fear, of course, was conspiracy and rebellion, that the same army that had placed them in power might take them out. It was with this fear in mind that the first Augustus had redeployed the army to distant frontiers, to get the soldiers away from Rome and out of politics, and to bring an end to the civil wars that had torn apart the Republic. But as the succession struggles and usurpations of the next few centuries made clear, the Roman imperial system never really solved the dilemma of separating violence from politics.

Historiography on late Roman society, meanwhile, has generally recognized the pervasive role of violence in enforcing and supporting the social structure at the regional and local level. A "normal" and unremarkable degree of violence served to maintain dependent relationships between patrons and clients, masters and servants, rich and poor, rulers and sub-

54. Drake 2000, esp. chaps. 2 and 3.
55. Harries 1999a.
56. On acclamations, see Roueché 1984. On the importance of accurate transcription in a legal setting, Teitler 1985; in disputations, Lim 1995, esp. chap. 3; cf. discussion of the fifth-century church councils in chapter 8 below.

jects.[57] The legitimacy of violence, in any particular situation, depended on who did it to whom. Roman criminal law divided society into *honestiores,* the elites, for whom the endurance of physical violence was thought to be uniquely degrading, and *humiliores,* the vast majority of ordinary people, against whom such violence aroused little comment.[58] Physical violence became controversial when applied to inappropriate targets, *honestiores* or (as we shall see) Christian clergy. Like most premodern judicial systems, the Roman state relied on gruesome exemplary punishment as a substitute for effective law enforcement.[59]

The bloody spectacles of public executions, often staged alongside games and races, served both to deter and to entertain.[60] The carefully contained violence of the arena perhaps helped deflect the ever-present fear of destabilizing civil war, violence out of control. Roman audiences revelled in the spectacle of bloodshed, even as their moralists feared its corrupting effects. Their fascination with the gladiator's seeming eagerness for death provided a context within which they could make sense of the emerging Christian phenomenon of martyrdom.[61]

Just because violence pervaded Roman society should not be taken to mean that Romans were jaded by it, or failed to worry about the rights and wrongs of it. An empire based on military power feared that same power as the greatest threat to its political stability. The system depended upon and glorified hierarchical authority, while remaining intensely aware of the dangers of its abuse by the all-too-fallible men to whom that authority was entrusted—as it was with the emperor, so too it would become with the bishop. The imperial state balanced its emphasis on order, clemency, and harmony alongside a measured and necessary violence against designated "others"—barbarians, gladiators, criminals, and (in the pagan period) occasionally Christians. But the fear was always present that this carefully contained violence could turn against inappropriate targets and spin out of control, that means might overtake ends. Rome's unrivalled army could, and often did, go from defending the frontiers to overthrowing the government.

---

57. On the role of violence as a "normal" feature of the social structure, see, e.g., MacMullen 1974, esp. pp. 1–27; Bagnall 1989; and for the Republican period Lintott 1968, esp. pp. 1–34.

58. On these categories, see esp. Garnsey 1970.

59. On exemplary punishment as characteristic of premodern justice, see Foucault 1977, pp. 3–79. In the ancient world: *Du châtiment dans la cité* 1984, MacMullen 1990b. On crime and punishment in the late Roman state see Harries 1999b, esp. chaps. 6 and 7.

60. On public executions as entertainment, see Coleman 1990.

61. See Barton 1993, esp. chap. 1.

In the same way, Christian religious zealots instead of smashing pagan idols might ultimately turn against their own bishops.

The state's capacity to maintain order was simultaneously too weak—it had no effective police force, and in many areas local elites took the law into their own hands—and too strong, relying upon excessive and indiscriminate military force to repress significant outbreaks of unrest. The imperial government possessed an overwhelming potential for organized violence that in practice was extremely difficult to employ with any precision. Catastrophic incidents such as the massacre at Thessalonica in 390 help us to understand why a regime whose legal pronouncements complain helplessly of widespread disobedience could nevertheless inspire terror in its subjects. In this study, I will explore ways in which religious discourses created a variety of new constraints on the state's ability to make effective use of its violent power.

The Roman state's first obligation was to maintain stability and public order against the threats posed by alternative concentrations of power. It did so not only through overwhelming superiority of force but also through ideological claims to legitimate authority, which served to justify its own use of violence and outlaw that of rivals.[62] The discourse of legitimacy defined who might rightfully exercise power, thus distinguishing emperors from usurpers, soldiers from brigands, *patrocinium* from *latrocinium*.[63] The term *latrocinium*, commonly translated as "banditry," served in late Roman political discourse to describe forms of unlawful violence, independent of the state, and postulated a clear distinction between "legitimate" and "illegitimate" force.[64]

When we translate these discourses of legitimacy into the religious sphere, we may envision a theoretical model that presents the church hierarchy as standing in a similar relation to groups such as ascetic holy men,

62. On the state's concern for monopolizing the means of violence, see Weber, e.g., 1947, p. 154. Cf. the discussion of "legitimacy" above. B. Shaw 1984 applies some of these ideas to state and non-state violence in the Roman period.

63. The full impact of the word *latrocinium* when used as a political accusation is lost when it is translated by the modern English word "banditry," which connotes simple criminality driven by economic greed rather than by any strong political or religious motivation. More accurate would perhaps be the modern usage of "terrorism" to denote acts of violence performed by ideologically motivated non-state groups, as opposed to "war," legitimate violence carried out by recognized nation-states. However, the translation of *latrocinium* by "banditry" or "robbery" is well established in scholarship.

64. See B. Shaw 1984, p. 6: "Almost every kind of violent opposition to established authority short of war was subsumed under the catch-all rubric of *latrocinium*, with little or no conscious differentiation of the subcategories of violence beneath that umbrella term."

Circumcellions, or other charismatic zealots as does the state to the alternative, independent, or semi-independent locally based concentrations of power grouped under the arbitrary and derogatory classification of "banditry." In like manner, secular discourses of rulership, models of good emperors and tyrants, were adapted into the religious sphere to characterize the conduct of Christian bishops.[65] The language of *latrocinium*, the opposition between legitimate state power and lawless "private" violence, between justice and tyranny, served useful polemical purposes for parties involved in religious conflicts.

The comparisons are intriguing. Like the state, a church consisted of a hierarchically organized institutional structure that attempted to exercise a monopoly of power, in this case, over spiritual authority and the definition of religious truth, as well as a monopoly in a more concrete fashion, over ecclesiastical space and public worship services. Like the state, the church's claim was absolute and exclusive: there could be only one true church, and all who did not accept its authority were labelled "heretics" or "schismatics," in the same way that those who rejected the authority of the state were defined as rebels or brigands.[66] As with the state, the actual power of such an organized religious establishment fell far short of its claims. There were large areas of society in which its influence was limited and conditional on making compromises with the alternative concentrations of religious authority that formed around a variety of non-establishment charismatic figures who might be classified under the general rubric of "holy men."[67] These alternative groups sometimes worked in the interests of the church establishment, sometimes not. The history of monasticism was in large part the story of efforts by the church hierarchy to bring the movement under control, to discipline and institutionalize what had originally been a non-establishment phenomenon.[68]

While the state could exist without a church, as did the Roman Empire before Constantine, any church organization wishing to establish itself in a dominant position needed to co-opt the power of the state if its claims to exclusive legitimacy were to be realized in any meaningful way. Enforcing a monopoly of authority and uniformity of religious belief and practice necessitated coercive power. In the Roman Empire, as in most societies, the great-

---

65. See chapter 7.
66. W. Bauer 1934 is fundamental.
67. For the formulation of "institutional" vs. "charismatic" authority, see Weber 1947, 1963. Any study of late antique holy men must begin with Brown 1971. Discussion and more detailed bibliography in chapter 5, esp. pp. 152–153.
68. See chapter 6, pp. 231–235.

est concentration of such power resided in the state. In a struggle between two ecclesiastical factions to win the state's recognition as "legitimate," it was essential for each to deny the other side's claims to religious authority.

But that does not mean that the church was necessarily the weaker partner in such an alliance. Although religious organizations were far inferior to the state in physical power and potential for violence, in the ideological realm they could lay claim to sources of legitimacy, which, deriving from heaven, were superior to those of any earthly government. This was as true, if not more so, for monks and other "alternative" figures as for the established episcopal hierarchy. Without the support of true religion, as Augustine said, the state was nothing more than *latrocinium* on a large scale.[69] This statement exemplified a Christian critique of secular power, which could be invoked to justify and even sanctify resistance to the imperial will.

Some Christians extended this idea to argue that for those who did act on behalf of true religion, violence might be appropriate even if outside the scope of secular law: thus Shenoute's assertion, "There is no crime for those who have Christ." Scholarship on Roman law and society has long recognized the concept of "self-help," private violence used by individuals in the absence of effective state justice, to redress or avenge injury or insult.[70] In the Christian empire, as we shall see, "self-help" finds its religious counterpart in "holy violence," action on the basis of one's own piety to answer an offense against the faith.[71] Holy zealots disregarded the authority of the state—and sometimes that of the established ecclesiastical hierarchy—to carry out what they understood to be the will of God.

Andrew Lintott has demonstrated how patterns of private violence, originating from small-scale individual or family feuds in the face-to-face society of archaic Rome, had devastating consequences when perpetuated on the much larger scale of political rivalries among factions in the Late Republic.[72] I will show a similar process operating in late antiquity, as Christianity developed from a small fringe group into a dominant and hegemonic church, with similarly destructive results. Lintott argues that habits and paradigms of violence which had characterized disputes between private indi-

---

69. *City of God* 4.4, quoting and reinterpreting a story (from Cicero, *Republic* 3.14.24) in which a captured pirate told Alexander the Great that the only difference between the two of them was the scale on which they operated. Compare 2.21: "True justice has no existence save in that republic whose founder and ruler is Christ." (NPNF trans.)

70. On "self-help" in archaic and Republican periods, see Lintott 1968, pp. 1–34.

71. I outline the paradigm of "holy violence" in chapter 5.

72. Lintott 1968.

viduals since archaic times exploded into the public sphere during the political turmoil of the Late Republic and shaped the course of its civil wars. In like manner, I believe, secular political and social varieties of violence found their way into the religious sphere under the Christian empire.

EARLY CHRISTIANS AND VIOLENCE

For the first three centuries of their history, Christians were in little position to employ significant violence either in defense of their faith or in their own internal disputes. Nevertheless, the worldview shaped during the early centuries is essential to understanding the violent conflicts of later times. Earliest Christianity postulated a world sharply divided between truth and falsehood, beset by perceived enemies both outside and within. Elaine Pagels has shown how theologians of the first and second centuries applied the evolving concept of "Satan" to identify a cosmic evil behind worldly adversaries, "demonizing"—in a literal sense—Jews, pagans, and heretics.[73] As early as Paul, militaristic imagery pervaded Christian devotional language:

> Put on all the armor which God provides, so that you may be able to stand firm against the devices of the devil. . . . Take up God's armor, then you will be able to stand your ground. . . . Fasten on the belt of truth; for coat of mail put on integrity . . . take up the great shield of faith, with which you will be able to quench all the flaming arrows of the evil one. Take salvation for helmet; for sword, take that which the Spirit gives you—the words that come from God.[74]

The language of spiritual combat was not exclusive to martyrdom, and indeed could be found throughout Christian discourse and practice, in baptismal ritual, prayer, and ascetic discipline.[75] Although most Christians have not normally interpreted these formulations to refer to literal violence, the possibility has always existed for them to be understood in more than a figurative sense. *Askesis,* the punishing self-discipline pursued by zealous holy men, was understood as constant battle against a very real enemy, the demons, who deceived mortals into worshipping them as gods, and who per-

73. Pagels 1995.
74. Ephesians 6:10ff. (RSV trans.)
75. A point made by Harvey 1990b, discussing Diocletian-era martyrs in Syria who seem to have drawn their inspiration and sense of militancy from ascetic tradition, rather than the other way round.

sonified the dangerous temptations of flesh and world.[76] The impulse to turn one's back on a corrupt and idolatrous world did not limit itself to explicitly ascetic circles. For Tertullian, living in pagan society was a struggle against "idolatry," which for him referred not just to the worship of pagan gods but also to the everyday pleasures of secular life—games, the theater, fine clothes. "It is not enough," he added, "that we do no such things ourselves, unless we break all connection also with those who do."[77] Such an uncompromising discipline, when followed to the letter, would have forced many Christians into a deliberate segregation from Roman society, which in turn aroused suspicion and resentment on the part of their pagan neighbors—one of many factors that fanned the flames of persecution.[78]

Even in the time of pagan persecution, Christians had never conceived of martyrs simply as passive victims of violence. The martyrs themselves, as well as the larger Christian community in which their stories circulated, understood their ordeal in terms of struggle, active spiritual combat against the forces of evil. Athletic and military metaphors pervaded early Christian literature: the martyrs were champions of God, soldiers of Christ.[79] The physical suffering of the martyrs found its counterpart in a spiritual struggle in which the champions of the faith gave as good as they got, every wound received upon their bodies becoming a blow struck against the demons who drove their persecutors.[80] The early Christian martyrs transformed their endurance of such torture and mutilation into a marker of holiness, the wounds on their bodies symbolizing their spiritual victory.[81] The

76. Numerous patristic citations on this theme can be found in Malone 1950. The relationship between martyrdom and asceticism is discussed in chapter 5.

77. Tertullian, *On Spectacles* 15 (ANF trans.).

78. Chapter 1 discusses in more detail the attitudes behind the pagan authorities' persecution of Christians.

79. Cf. Origen, *On Martyrdom* 42. On the night before she was to be thrown to the beasts, the martyr Perpetua dreamed that she was transformed into a male gladiator, and that she wrestled with Satan and threw him to the ground: *Martyrdom of Perpetua* 10. For general discussions of combat motifs and militant attitudes in early Christianity, see Swift 1983; Helgeland, Daly, and Burns 1985.

80. Thus Lactantius, *Divine Institutes* 5.22: "It is not the men themselves who persecute, for they have no cause of anger against the innocent; but those contaminated and abandoned spirits by whom the truth is both known and hated, insinuate themselves into their minds, and goad them in their ignorance and fury." (ANF trans.) On the ideological significance of bodily suffering in early Christian martyrdom, see Perkins 1995, B. Shaw 1996.

81. Martyrs, it was said, typically remained calm under torture, and even taunted their persecutors, while the magistrates and torturers gradually lost their composure, screamed and gnashed their teeth like animals, and at times seemed themselves

experience of persecution was foundational for a Christian community that would build its sense of history and identity upon the shared veneration of the martyrs.[82]

The outlook displayed by early Christians, shaped partly by the intrinsic beliefs and structure of the faith and partly by experience of persecution, closely resembles what Mary Douglas has described as a "sectarian" mindset, characterized by a strong commitment to purity, a sense of separation from a corrupt world, and an aversion to compromise.[83] The militant attitudes that were broadly characteristic of Christian sects in the first and second centuries, although moderated in later times as the religion grew and spread into the mainstream of society, retained their strength among Donatists and other rigorist sects, ascetic zealots, and violent extremists. Mistrust of doctrinal diversity and the invention of the concept of "heresy" arose long before Christian bishops were actually in any position to enforce the interpretive monopoly and hierarchical supremacy they claimed, authoritarian ideology predating authoritarian practice. Guy Stroumsa has recently located the origins of Christian "intolerance" in the combination of a universalist social ideology and a strong focus on the inward conviction of individual belief.[84] Christian scripture and doctrine contained the basis both for violence and for the condemnation of violence. As long as Christians remained a small fringe group, their ideas had little consequence for the larger Roman world. But many of the same attitudes and habits of thought would persist in the dramatically different circumstances of the Constantinian empire, with sometimes catastrophic results.

---

to be in pain: "Then indeed it was that the cruelty of ungodly men, which raged incessantly like a devouring fire, wrought for thee a wondrous and ever memorable glory. Astonishment seized the spectators themselves, when they beheld the very executioners who tortured the bodies of their holy victims wearied out, and disgusted at the cruelties; the bonds loosened, the engines of torture powerless, the flames extinguished, while the sufferers preserved their constancy unshaken even for a moment." Constantine, *Oration to the Assembly of Saints* 22 (NPNF trans.). See also, e.g., *Acts of the Abitinian Martyrs* (Tilley trans. 1996).

82. See chapters 1 and 2.

83. Douglas and Wildavsky 1982, pp. 10–11. See discussion of Douglas' model in chapter 6, pp. 238–241. Compare the pagan Celsus' evaluation: "[The Christians'] union is the more wonderful, the more it can be shown to be based on no substantial reason. And yet rebellion is a substantial reason, as well as the advantages which accrue from it, and the fear of external enemies. Such are the causes which give stability to their faith." Origen, *Against Celsus* 3.14 (ANF trans.).

84. Stroumsa 1999.

THE PLAN OF THE BOOK

Chapter 1 sets the stage for the rest of the book by discussing Diocletian, the Great Persecution, Christian martyrdom, and then the religious policies of Constantine, with particular attention to his dealings with the early Donatists. I explore the motives and justifications behind pagan emperors' persecution of Christians, and argue that some of the same attitudes toward violence and coercion will persist under the Christian empire. Emperors both pagan and Christian placed a high value on unity and consensus, and were willing to use coercive means to that end. I also discuss the formation of Christian concepts of martyrdom that will cast a shadow over the religious conflicts of later generations. Chapter 2 explores certain aspects of the complicated relationship between church and state in the fourth century, focusing mainly on the doctrinal and factional conflicts commonly known as the "Arian controversy" but also discussing pagan-Christian conflict under Julian. It examines how discourses of martyrdom and persecution, recalling prior Christian experience of pagan persecution, came to be invoked as ideological weapons in conflicts within the Christian community. A claim to martyrdom served as a means of legitimating and even sanctifying resistance to imperial authority, while reference to the polemically charged language of persecution often forced the secular powers to moderate their considerable potential for violence, for fear of being labelled "persecutors."

Chapter 3 returns to North Africa, the scene of violent struggle between the schismatic Donatists and the state-sponsored Catholics. The conflict between the two churches embodies an ongoing tension between the opposite imperatives of purity and universality. A case study in the construction and contestation of identity, the chapter examines both how the Donatists sought to present themselves as the "Church of the Martyrs," facing persecution from a Constantinian regime they believed to be Christian in name only, and also how Optatus, Augustine, and other bishops of the Catholic camp attempted to undermine Donatist claims to religious legitimacy by focusing on the violent conduct of the Circumcellions, Donatism's militant wing. A study of Circumcellion attacks on Catholic clergy, in turn, illustrates how an ideology of martyrdom could be used to justify violence against those seen as complicit in persecution. Chapter 4 uses Augustine's response to the Donatist problem as a starting point for a broader discussion of what I call a "disciplinary" paradigm of violent coercion, through which establishment authorities justify applying force to the disobedient "for their own good." But the benign language of paternalistic compassion masks a reality in which disciplinary violence could spin out of control with lethal consequences.

Chapter 5 focuses on extremist violence, specifically the attacks of ascetic holy men against perceived enemies of the faith. Using mainly sources written by disciples or apologists for the zealots, I outline an ideology of "holy violence," action pleasing to God, which elevates personal holiness and godly zeal above the restraints of secular law and order. I explore three particular strands of extremist motivation: desire for martyrdom, righteous anger against God's enemies, and determination to expose the hypocrisies of a corrupt and too-tolerant establishment. Chapter 6 continues the focus on violent holy men but turns the tables, presenting their actions through the eyes of hostile sources. I examine cases in which claims of martyrdom or holy violence were contested or rejected. Discourses of *latrocinium* ("criminal violence"), usurpation, and falsehood served to challenge and undermine the zealots' claim to religious legitimacy. I also attempt to situate and explain the violent behavior of some ascetics within the broader context of the ascetic practices and monastic institutions of the time. Where chapter 5 outlines a hagiographic ideal of holy violence, chapter 6 explores the limitations of that ideal in practice.

With chapter 7 we turn to the late antique bishop, a figure of Christian leadership in whom the holiness of the world-renouncing ascetic saint and the worldly power of the secular magnate met in an uneasy coexistence. The chapter outlines the creation of two rhetorical opposites, the hagiographic ideal of the bishop-saint and the polemical nightmare of the tyrant-bishop, and explores the application of these stereotypes to actual bishops in situations of political or doctrinal conflict. Both types are defined in large part by violence, whether the loving and considered disciplinary force with which the bishop-saint chastises the collective "body" of his congregation, or the jealous and intemperate rage of a tyrant who puts his personal hatreds above the needs of the faith. These portraits together embody the hopes and fears of late antique Christians about the proper role of worldly power within the church, how it ought to be used and how it might be abused. Chapter 8 concludes my study with the Christological controversies and episcopal rivalries of the first half of the fifth century, a true "civil war" within the church that brought together all the different aspects of violence explored in previous chapters. The successive councils of Ephesus II (449) and Chalcedon (451) set forth competing paradigms of religious authority, the first placing holy zeal above legal procedure in order to condemn heretics, the second emphasizing legitimate hierarchical authority and projecting a rhetoric of stability and consensus against the twin threats of the tyrannical power of the bishop of Alexandria and the anarchic violence of zealous holy men. The two councils represent opposite visions of idealized Christian community:

the one built upon peace and consensus, in which violence could be employed to maintain unity; the other predicated upon dividing the world between the faithful and the impious, between truth and falsehood, in which violence served to mark enemies and reinforce boundaries. Finally, a brief conclusion discusses the aftermath of Chalcedon and Monophysite opposition up to the early sixth century, looks back over the previous chapters, and ties together the themes of the book.

1. "What Has the Emperor to Do with the Church?"

Persecution and Martyrdom from Diocletian to Constantine

"THE TRIUMPHS OF GOTHS AND SARMATIANS"

In late February of 303, the emperor Diocletian and his imperial colleagues issued an edict ordering churches to be destroyed, scriptures to be burned, and Christians to be dismissed from government service and stripped of civil rights. Diocletian, Galerius, and the rest of the imperial court in Nicomedia had lately celebrated the festival of the god Terminus—a fitting occasion, they thought, to undertake a campaign of repression that would put an end to the Christian religion once and for all.[1] This marked the formal opening of the Great Persecution, the last and most brutal assault on Christians by the pagan Roman state.[2]

The preceding four decades of peace, tolerance, and growth may have "softened" the church—as Eusebius charged[3]—but some Christians were not willing to see their faith "terminated" without a fight. No sooner had the edict been posted than a prominent Christian angrily ripped it down and tore it

1. Terminalia: seventh of the Kalends of March, or 23 February.
2. The main primary sources for the Great Persecution are Eusebius' *Ecclesiastical History* (hereafter *HE*), books 8–10, and his supplementary pamphlet *The Martyrs of Palestine*, with Lactantius' *On the Deaths of the Persecutors* (hereafter *MP*). For a thorough narrative history and general analysis see Frend 1965; Lane Fox 1986, pp. 572–608; and now Drake 2000. For a thoughtful treatment of Lactantius and his political and intellectual context see now Digeser 2000. On Eusebius, Barnes 1981 is indispensable.
3. "On account of the abundant freedom, we fell into laxity and sloth, and envied and reviled each other, and were almost, as it were, taking up arms against one another, rulers assailing rulers with words like spears, and people forming parties against people, and monstrous hypocrisy and dissimulation rising to the greatest height of wickedness." (*HE* 8.1, NPNF trans.) For Eusebius, the Persecution represented God's judgment on the disunity of the church.

to shreds, scornfully exclaiming, "These are the triumphs of Goths and Sarmatians!" We are told that the unnamed martyr then displayed an "admirable patience" as he was tortured and then burned alive.[4] The opening act of the Great Persecution had already provoked defiance and brought imperial authority into contempt. This would not be the only such display.[5] The universal sacrifice demanded by the authorities could not be reconciled with Christian faith. If God had not forbidden us to engage in idolatry, wrote Tertullian a century earlier, there would be no occasion for martyrdom![6] The "spiritual combat" long imagined by Christians was now a grim reality.

But the persecuting authorities were equally firm in their conviction that they, too, had no choice. Why did the odd and exclusive practices of a religious minority cause such concern to the leaders of the Roman state? Nearly a decade after the Persecution had begun, the pagan citizens of Tyre begged the emperor Maximinus Daia not to relent. Their petition did not fall on deaf ears. Maximinus' answer laid out, in stark language, exactly what was at stake:

> For who can be found so ignorant or so devoid of all understanding as not to perceive that it is due to the kindly care of the gods that the earth does not refuse the seed sown in it, nor disappoint the hope of the husbandmen with vain expectation; that impious war is not inevitably fixed on earth, and wasted bodies dragged down to death under the influence of a corrupted atmosphere; that the sea is not swollen and

---

4. The incident is described in both Eusebius *HE* 8.5 and Lactantius *MP* 13, with the exclamation recorded by the latter. Neither Eusebius nor Lactantius names the Christian, although later tradition identifies the martyr as Euethius. "Goths and Sarmatians" was presumably a slur on Galerius' trans-Danubian ancestry: Lactantius mocked the junior emperor as a "wild beast" with "a native barbarity and a savageness foreign to Roman blood." (*MP* 9, ANF trans.)

5. For similar acts of defiance, see Eusebius, *Martyrs of Palestine* 4 (a young man seized the governor's arm to prevent him from performing a sacrifice), 8 (a woman kicked over an altar and extinguished its fire), and 9 (three Christians rushed on the governor and disrupted his sacrifice). The Cappadocian Christians Ariston and Severianus had distributed a *libellus* containing insulting language toward the emperors, and when interrogated before the governor claimed also to have burned pagan temples: see Maraval 1990, *La passion de S. Athénogène*. In Spain, meanwhile, church authorities found it necessary to deny the title of "martyr" to Christians killed while smashing pagan idols: Council of Elvira, *Canon* 60. Scholars have been unable to agree on when exactly the Council of Elvira took place; see summary of arguments in Drake 2000, pp. 223–225. *Contra* Lane Fox 1986, p. 664, who would date the council to after 312, Suberbiola Martinez 1987, *Elvira*, pp. 46–47, puts *Canon* 60 in 298 and suggests that the extant text may be a compilation of canons from more than one council. On idol-smashing and provocation, see generally Kötting 1979, Thornton 1986.

6. Tertullian, *Scorpiace* 4.

raised on high by blasts of intemperate winds; that unexpected hurricanes do not burst forth and stir up the destructive tempest; moreover, that the earth, the nourisher and mother of all, is not shaken from its lowest depths with a terrible tremor, and that the mountains upon it do not sink into the opening chasms?

No one is ignorant that all these, and evils still worse than these, have oftentimes happened hitherto. And all these misfortunes have taken place on account of the destructive error of the empty vanity of these impious men.[7]

The Christians' refusal to worship the gods—"atheism," to right-thinking pagans—threatened the hard-earned peace bestowed by those gods. Emperors as far back as Octavian Augustus had held that their primary duty was to safeguard the *pax deorum*, the ancient arrangement by which the gods provided peace, security, and prosperity to the human race in return for proper worship and sacrifices.[8] If those gods did not receive what was due to them, disaster might result. It is intriguing to note the conflation of natural and man-made catastrophes in the imagination of Maximinus Daia and his contemporaries: flood, earthquake, famine, and plague loomed alongside barbarian invasion and civil war, all part of the same moral universe.[9] The gods worked their will through agents both natural and human. Above all the emperors feared internal division, and the political violence that might erupt therefrom. The decade-long Great Persecution coincided with the gradual and bloody unravelling of the precarious Tetrarchic peace.[10] In an irony that would be characteristic of both pagan authorities and also their later Christian counterparts, official attempts to impose unity often unleashed the very violence they sought to avoid.

Pagans' fear of their gods' anger expressed itself in ways surprisingly similar to Christian discussions of God's wrath. Lactantius' treatise *On the Anger of God*, penned in the aftermath of the Persecution, offered a powerful argument for the place of anger in divine justice. Without divine anger, Lactantius argued, there would be no fear among mortals. Without fear of God, there could be no religion and no morality. Just as God himself is an-

---

7. Imperial rescript quoted in Eusebius *HE* 9.7 (trans. NPNF).

8. A century after Constantine's conversion, Augustine had to devote several books of his *City of God* to refuting the notion that Rome's prosperity and security depended on the favor of the gods.

9. A commonplace expression of this attitude can be seen in the habit of referring to earthquakes simply as "the wrath of God," as, e.g., throughout Malalas' *Chronicle* ("in this year the wrath of God struck Antioch.")

10. For political background and narrative of events in the Tetrarchic period, see S. Williams 1985; Barnes 1981, pp. 3–77.

gry at those who transgress his laws, so does he command us to imitate that anger, and act upon it, in opposing and punishing evil.[11] When the divine law was transgressed by a few, risking a wrath that might fall upon everyone, then leniency toward the guilty equalled cruelty to the innocent. Even while rejecting their authority in religious matters, the Christians had always conceded to the pagan emperors a special role in enforcing God's justice.[12] Most pagans, meanwhile, saw the righteous anger of their own gods as providing moral force to worldly law for the punishment of evildoers.[13] Despite their sharp disagreements over religion, the underlying conceptions of justice and of a ruler's responsibilities did not differ greatly between pagans and Christians. Both sides projected onto their respective divinities their own anger at the other's behavior. In ordering the punishment of Christians, the pagan authorities would have understood themselves to be undertaking an unpleasant but necessary duty.[14]

Christians had long been scapegoats for popular fears of divine anger, as Tertullian had famously complained: "If the heavens give no rain, if there is an earthquake, if there is famine or pestilence, straightaway the cry is, 'Christians to the lion!'"[15] In the first two centuries after Christ, persecution of Christians had been mainly local and sporadic. In the absence of any coherent imperial policy or sense of urgency from the center, magistrates typically acted in response to popular prejudice.[16] A significant shift took place in the late third century, as first Decius and Valerian and then (after a forty-year hiatus) the Tetrarchs launched coordinated, empire-wide attempts to enforce religious unity and stamp out Christian "atheism." A number of

11. Lactantius, *On the Anger of God*. Lactantius argued against philosophers who believed that divinity and anger were incompatible. On the theme of divine anger, see Micka 1943.

12. Cf. Romans 13:1–4: "For rulers are not a terror to good conduct, but to bad. Would you have no fear of him who is in authority? Then do what is good, and you will receive his approval, for he is God's servant for your good. But if you do wrong, be afraid, for he does not bear the sword in vain; he is the servant of God to execute His wrath on the wrong-doer." (RSV trans.)

13. On pagan conceptions of divine anger, see now Harris 2001, esp. pp. 5–6, 136–138.

14. In a much later historical context, B. Gregory 1999, pp. 74–96, offers a sensitive and compelling presentation of what might be called the persecutor's point of view, explaining how both Protestant and Catholic magistrates in sixteenth-century Europe could justify to themselves the infliction of torture and death on religious dissidents.

15. Tertullian, *Apology* 40 (ANF trans.).

16. On persecution prior to Decius, see generally Ste. Croix 1963; T. Barnes 1968; Lane Fox 1986, pp. 419–450.

factors had combined to drive this shift in imperial religious policy. Earlier emperors' concern for the *pax deorum* had led them to legislate on the practices and morals of Rome's senatorial and equestrian elites. By the third century, grants of universal citizenship and the long process of Romanization had expanded the definition of "Roman" to encompass more or less everyone in the empire. Now the gods of Rome were, at least in theory, everyone's gods.[17] The military and political turmoil of the mid-third century created a new sense of urgency in which traditionalists such as Decius became convinced that only collective expressions of devotion by all Romans could assuage the gods' anger and restore Rome's fortunes. The universal sacrifice first demanded by the emperor Decius in 250 was intended as a gesture as much patriotic as pious. Christians were not initially its targets, but their refusal to take the emperor's "Pledge of Allegiance" rendered them suspect on grounds both religious and political. Subsequent persecutions took aim more directly at the Christians and their church.[18]

Diocletian and his colleagues envisioned a Roman people united in common loyalty to the traditional gods as a necessary concomitant to their hard-won restoration of security and political order. "Unity" as an ideological program was more critical than ever to a precarious imperial college system that depended on maintaining consensus and harmony among military strongmen whose ambitions and rivalries could easily unleash yet another catastrophic round of civil war.[19] The "problem" of Christians first came to imperial attention in the military, when some soldiers earned martyrdom through their refusal to sacrifice. Diocletian was subsequently shocked to discover Christians in the imperial household itself, and began to listen to pagan intellectuals who advocated a hard line against the Christians.[20] Even

---

17. *Constitutio Antoniniana* of 212, which granted citizenship to all free inhabitants of the empire, completed this process. On the significance of citizenship see Garnsey 1970. On the process of Romanization under the Principate, see now MacMullen 2000. Drake 2000, pp. 147–148, argues that the Principate's traditional emphasis on imperial deference to the senators had given way by the third century to a more explicit dependence of the emperor's legitimacy on the "favor of the gods"—and therefore the "atheism" of Christians posed a much greater political problem.

18. On the persecutions of the mid-third century, Lane Fox 1986, pp. 450–492, is useful.

19. On Diocletian and the Tetrarchic system generally, see S. Williams 1985. Good discussions of Tetrarchic religious politics can be found in Drake 2000, pp. 113–153, and Digeser 2000, pp. 25–32 and 46–56.

20. These were Hierocles Sossianus and (probably) Porphyry: see Digeser 2000, pp. 91–114; cf. Lane Fox 1986, pp. 592–595. Constantine and later Christian emperors would single out Porphyry's anti-Christian writings for special condemnation.

the oracles, apparently, endorsed persecution.[21] Each attempt to force these Christians into "loyalty" or purge them provoked unexpected resistance, and revealed to the authorities that Christian intransigence was a larger problem than they had thought, which in turn led them to broader repressive measures, until finally imperial policy—at least in some parts of the empire—aimed at the elimination of the Christian religion.[22]

The pagan belief in the *pax deorum*, like the conviction of later Christian emperors that God's favor depended on proper worship by a unified church, created the preconditions for official intolerance. The greater the emphasis on unity, the more severe the threat posed by the arrogant nonconformity of a small minority. If divine anger was taken seriously, this meant that dangerous and destructive power rested in the hands of marginalized sects. In theory, the late Roman government could no more tolerate their religious dissent than a modern government could tolerate weapons of mass destruction in the hands of terrorists.

But a high-minded concern for the general welfare did not by itself exhaust the complicated motives that drove the persecutors. Pious fear of the gods and sense of public duty blended with anger, frustration, and sometimes outright prejudice against the obstinate disobedience of the Christians. Magistrates took offense not so much at the content of Christian belief and practice as at the attitude displayed in their courtrooms by its adherents—an arrogant and reckless refusal to yield to higher authority. Where Christian martyrs were in fact driven to disobedience by sincere religious objections to the actions demanded of them, pagan authorities could see only *contumacia*, a stubborn and treasonous contempt for the emperor's lawful command.[23]

Ironically, as we shall see, the same disconnect would prevail under the Christian empire when secular authorities and establishment bishops looked at those they called "heretics" or "schismatics." They, likewise, preferred to characterize religious dissidence as a result of pride, obstinacy, or *philoneikia* ("quarrelsomeness" or "love of controversy") rather than sincere belief, emphasizing the personal vendettas or character flaws of its proponents.[24]

21. Constantine himself blamed the oracle of Apollo at Didyma for misleading Diocletian: Eusebius *VC* 2.50–54. Cf. Eusebius, *Praeparatio Evangelica* 4.2.10–11, blaming "cloaked philosophers" for misleading the emperors.

22. For the details, see Frend 1965, pp. 351–392.

23. Early in the second century, Pliny had complained to Trajan of the *pertinaciam et inflexibilem obstinationem* of the Christians (Pliny the Younger, *Letters* 10.96–97). Marcus Aurelius (*Meditations* 11.3) opined that the Christians' proverbial willingness to die reflected "mere stubbornness." See generally Wilken 1984.

24. Tertullian had set the tone earlier in his *Prescription Against Heretics*: 14, blaming heresy on "restless curiosity," 30 on the bad character of Marcion, 41–43

Where martyrs had seen the devil driving their persecutors, establishment Christians would see Satan inspiring the very disobedience they sought to suppress. For both pagans and Christians, attribution of the worst possible motives to one's opponents helped to justify violence against them.

In practice, the violence of the Persecution varied dramatically from one region to the next, depending—as did the effectiveness of any government policy—upon the willingness of the local officials directed to carry it out. Large parts of the empire escaped persecution altogether, as did the far west under Constantius Chlorus.[25] At the other extreme, some magistrates went beyond the letter of the edicts in prosecuting their hatred of Christians. Christian sources complain of sadistic officials and savage torments; these accounts, while probably exaggerated, are not inherently implausible given the Roman system's normal reliance on judicial torture. The persecution of Christians simply involved the regular workings of the Roman state's machinery of coercion, aimed at a new target. Judicial torture and spectacular public executions were the normal violence one would expect to be directed against those perceived as disobedient or dangerous. Because religious dissent—unlike more conventional crimes such as murder or assault—could be undone by a simple change of mind, the persecutors' aim was fundamentally coercive rather than punitive. Arrested Christians typically received numerous invitations to sacrifice and opportunities to reconsider—and their refusal to take advantage of this leniency made them all the more infuriating in the eyes of the authorities.[26]

What impact did these spectacular displays of official persecution and Christian martyrdom have on their intended audience? Traditional Roman criminal justice assumed that gruesome public punishment of wrongdoers would impress onlookers with the power of the state and deter future transgressions. Roman authorities clearly believed persecution would work the same way: the execution of a few Christians would emphasize society's unanimous condemnation of their behavior, and frighten the rest into com-

---

on the "inherent" disorder and loose morals of heretics. In the fourth century, Athanasius' polemics against his "Arian" adversaries would elevate rhetorical abuse to an art form: see chapter 2, pp. 70–87. Lim 1995 outlines a general hardening of official attitudes against disputation and argument during the fourth and early fifth centuries. On *philoneikia*, see Lim, pp. 142–143 and 201.

25. Constantius apparently demolished a few churches, but otherwise did not vigorously enforce the edicts: Eusebius *VC* 1.13–16.

26. See numerous examples from the acts of the martyrs, e.g., *Martyrdom of Perpetua*; *Passion of Maxima, Donatilla and Secunda* in Tilley 1996, *Donatist Martyr Stories.*

pliance. But this strategy assumed that authorities, potential wrongdoers, and the general public shared the same basic assumptions about what constituted criminal behavior. Common murderers and thieves usually did not have a community of supporters who regarded their executions as unjust and would venerate their memory and hold them up as role models.[27]

Contemporary Christian apologists, as well as later Christian tradition, believed in contrast that persecution only made the church stronger: the blood of the martyrs, they argued, was the seed of the church.[28] Not only did the example of the martyrs strengthen the faith of fellow believers, but the spectacle of brave Christians going willingly to death also inspired pagan onlookers and brought new converts.[29] Our evidence for the latter effect comes exclusively from Christian sources with an apologetic or hagiographic agenda, of course, but it is not entirely implausible when one considers Roman culture's traditional fascination with dramatic stories of self-sacrifice, both in exemplary history and also in the gladiatorial arena.[30]

In contrast to the triumphalist narrative of Christian tradition, skeptical modern historians have pointed out the small number of martyrs (probably a few thousand, in contrast to the far greater toll of early modern Europe's wars of religion, for example) and have drawn attention to the widespread apostasy, lapsing, or simple evasion with which the vast majority of Christians met the demands of persecution.[31]

The truth must lie somewhere in between. Christian numbers seem to have enjoyed dramatic growth during the four decades of peace between Valerian and Diocletian, and of course again under Christian emperors in the

27. A point made by B. Gregory 1999, pp. 18–19.

28. Tertullian, *Apology* 50 (trans. ANF): "The oftener we are mown down by you, the more in number we grow; the blood of the Christians is seed." Compare Lactantius, *Divine Institutes* 5.23.

29. Thus Clement of Alexandria: "By their witness and confession all may be benefited—those in the Church being confirmed, and those of the heathen who have devoted themselves to the search after salvation wondering and being led to the faith; and the rest seized with amazement." *Stromateis* 4.9 (trans. ANF).

30. Exempla from Rome's Republican tradition include Lucretia, Regulus, Decius Mus, Mucius Scaevola, and others—several of whom are explicitly cited by Tertullian (*Apology* 50) as analogous to Christian martyrs. On the violence of the arena and its symbolism, see Barton 1993; she develops the martyrial parallels explicitly in Barton 1994. Bowersock 1995 locates the origin of "martyrdom" in Greco-Roman civic culture, though see criticism of this view in Boyarin 1999, chap. 4.

31. Beginning with H. Dodwell's treatise, *De paucitate martyrum*, in 1684, and followed by Edward Gibbon in *Decline and Fall of the Roman Empire*, vol. 1, chap. 16: see discussion in Frend 1965, pp. ix-xiii. Frend pp. 393–394 discusses numerical estimates in more recent scholarship, and arrives at a likely death toll of three thousand to thirty-five hundred for the whole empire.

fourth century, rather than during actual episodes of persecution.[32] Certainly only a very small proportion of Christians were actually martyred: for every one who defied the authorities and suffered punishment, surely many others sacrificed or feigned to do so, and even more simply left town or found some other means of evading the edicts. Some more enthusiastic Christians not only admitted this fact but regarded it as a good thing, a "winnowing" process that would distinguish the strong from the weak: those who lapsed, they argued, had never been true Christians to begin with. Most agreed that God allowed them to suffer persecution in order to punish them for their sins and test their faith.[33] Even if it would be an exaggeration to say that more than a very few zealots actually looked forward to persecution, certainly Christians in later and more comfortable times looked back with some nostalgia on the days of Diocletian as they listened to heroic and exemplary tales of martyrdom.

Still, one could argue that Christianity itself was deeply damaged by the experience, not so much by the violence directed against it from outside, but by the rancorous divisions unleashed within the Christian church by the consequences of persecution: hostility between those who stood firm and those who lapsed, and disagreement over how leniently or harshly to deal with the latter. Controversy over appropriate responses to persecution was nearly as old as Christianity itself. Early Christians argued over the lessons to be drawn from the tales of the Apostles: if persecuted, should they "flee to the next city" (as Matthew 10:23 suggested) or would flight constitute denial of Christ (as in the *quo vadis* story in the apocryphal *Acts of Peter*)?[34] Tertullian, characteristically, took a hard line: "The refusal of martyrdom is denial."[35] His

32. It should go without saying that estimates of Christian numbers or growth over time are subject to tremendous uncertainties and cannot be based on any firm quantitative evidence. For one recent attempt nevertheless, see Stark 1996. Although many of his assumptions have been challenged (see review articles in *JECS* 6.2, Summer 1998), the numbers he generates seem as plausible as any. Hopkins 1998 offers a thoughtful discussion of the significance of Stark's demographic model. Regardless of its accuracy, it seems safe to say that over the course of the third century, Christians went from a tiny minority to a substantial minority, and that during the fourth century, they would become the majority. But Lane Fox 1986, pp. 585–595, is skeptical of claims for Christian growth prior to Constantine.

33. See esp. Tertullian, *On Flight from Persecution* 1; Eusebius *HE* 8.1. Likewise, heresies also played a role in God's plan because they forced the orthodox to sharpen their arguments and defend the true faith more effectively: Augustine, *City of God* 16.2.

34. Boyarin 1999, chap. 2, finds analogous controversies taking place in late antique rabbinic Judaism.

35. *On Flight from Persecution* 12.

contemporary, Clement of Alexandria, sought a middle ground, arguing against those who rejected all martyrdom as "suicide" but also condemning those who too eagerly rushed forward to give themselves up.[36] Bishop Cyprian of Carthage decided that the responsibilities of his office outweighed his personal desire for martyrdom, and spent the Decian persecution hiding on a country estate. Cyprian was forced to defend his own conduct, even as controversy erupted over the treatment of the many who had lapsed. But when renewed persecution broke out under Valerian a decade later, Cyprian would be ready for martyrdom.[37]

Sometimes, a bishop's absence created a vacuum into which others might step. Bishop Peter of Alexandria kept a low profile during the early stages of the Great Persecution, only to see Melitius take over and perform unauthorized ordinations. The resulting schism would divide the Egyptian church for generations.[38] Later in the fourth century, Alexandria's most famous bishop, Athanasius, faced persecution, this time at the hands of a Christian emperor. He also felt it necessary to explain his failure to attain martyrdom, making the novel argument that his flight into the desert was analogous to the monastic practice of *anachoresis*, withdrawal from the world.[39] In the early fifth century, Augustine would face a similar dilemma in advising his fellow clerics how to respond to barbarian invasion.[40]

In the hagiographies of later centuries, those who attained holiness by means other than martyrdom often felt compelled to apologize for that fact.[41] Persecution strained the principle of hierarchical authority, since the martyr's crown could fall upon laymen or even women, while priests and bishops were not always immune to lapsing. The "confessors," those who suf-

---

36. Clement of Alexandria, *Stromateis* 4.4. See discussion in Bowersock 1995, pp. 65–71; Frend 1965, pp. 260–264; Boyarin 1999, pp. 61–64.

37. Cyprian, *On the Lapsed*; Pontius, *Life of Cyprian*. See now Burns 2002.

38. On Peter and the Melitians, see Vivian 1988. Peter was eventually martyred, in 311 (Eusebius *HE* 9.6). On the subsequent history of the schism see Martin 1974.

39. Athanasius, *Apology for his Flight*. See next chapter. Athanasius was less interested in attaining martyrdom for himself than in painting the emperor as a persecutor: "The flight of those who are persecuted is a strong argument against those who persecute" (8) (NPNF trans.).

40. Augustine *Ep.* 228, written during the Vandal invasion of North Africa in 428–29. Clerics had a duty not to desert their congregations, he argued, but if the congregation had already fled, it was pointless for the cleric to sacrifice himself by remaining in harm's way. Tertullian, in contrast, had argued that it was all the more important for leaders of the church to set an example for their congregations in facing martyrdom bravely: *On Flight from Persecution* 11.

41. See examples in chapter 5, pp. 163–168 below.

fered torture but survived, could display their scars as proof of their triumph. As their name testified, they too had borne witness to the faith. Their very presence was simultaneously a rebuke to the lapsed and an inspiration to the ordinary believer. Already in the time of Cyprian, church authorities watched uneasily as their congregants ignored them and lined up to receive forgiveness from jailed confessors.[42]

By the fourth century, it seems, a consensus had emerged among leaders of the mainstream church that emphasized a cleric's duty to his congregation in preference to individual zeal: accept martyrdom when the time comes, but do not seek it out. But the more extreme position had its appeal, as evidenced by popular veneration of martyrs both during the persecutions and in subsequent generations.

We have already seen, however, that not all Christians were content to turn the other cheek. During the Great Persecution, zealous enthusiasm drove some to seek out martyrdom aggressively, confronting magistrates or even attacking temples, rather than waiting patiently for the persecutors to come to them.[43] Although we have little specific evidence for such behavior in earlier centuries, Clement of Alexandria's condemnation of martyrdom-seeking suggests that it was not unheard of even then. He argued that those who acted provocatively not only courted their own death but endangered others when they risked igniting further persecution:

> If he who kills a man of God sins against God, he also who presents himself before the judgment-seat becomes guilty of his death. And such is also the case with him who does not avoid persecution, but out of daring presents himself for capture. Such a one, as far as in him lies, becomes an accomplice in the crime of the persecutor. And if he also uses provocation, he is wholly guilty, challenging the wild beast. And similarly, if he afford any cause for conflict or punishment, or retribution or enmity, he gives occasion for persecution.[44]

Martyrs should not fight back, lest they "by retaliating make our persecutors savage against ourselves, and stir them up to blaspheme the name."[45] The fear that provocative action would only provoke more violence, that the

---

42. See, e.g., Cyprian *Epp.* 10, 15–17; Burns 2002, chap. 2. This situation could be characterized as a perfect Weberian moment of tension between hierarchical and charismatic forms of authority.

43. Examples discussed above, pp. 29–30. On the idea of martyrdom-seeking, see generally Butterweck 1995.

44. Clement, *Stromateis* 4.10. (trans. ANF).

45. *Stromateis* 4.10. (trans. ANF).

deeds of zealous individuals might bring reprisals against all, may have been the background to the Council of Elvira's declaration that those who were killed breaking idols were not to be honored as martyrs.[46]

But at least for the moment, the behavior of the lapsed presented a more immediate threat to the unity of the church than the excesses of zealots. Persecution revealed far worse forms of behavior than mere evasion. Some had actually sacrificed, while others pretended to do so or obtained certificates claiming they had done so. How quickly, if at all, should they be forgiven once the persecution ended? Controversy over the treatment of the lapsed had already triggered schism in the mid-third century, when Novatian, who had permanently barred the lapsed from communion, broke with the church establishment in Rome. The Novatianists, who called themselves *cathari*, "the pure," persisted as a rigorist sect well into the fifth century.[47] But a far more serious schism broke out in North Africa. Where lapsing among the congregants had been the divisive issue in Cyprian's time, fifty years later the focus was squarely upon the conduct of the clergy, many of whom had sacrificed to idols or had collaborated with the imperial edicts by handing over *(tradere)* their scriptures to be burned. This *traditio*, "treason," lay at the root of what would come to be called the Donatist controversy. Such a sin, thought the hard-liners, was not only unforgivable for the perpetrator, but created an ongoing stain that disqualified all subsequent clergy ordained by the *traditor*. Only a new baptism, administered by clerics who had remained pure, could cleanse the taint.[48]

The martyrs and confessors who had stood firm in the face of imprisonment, torture, and death had little use for *traditores* within the church hierarchy. Even as the martyrs of Abitina, languishing in prison in February 304, proclaimed that "whoever holds communion with *traditores* shall have no part with us in the Kingdom of Heaven," one of those alleged *traditores*, then-archdeacon Caecilian of Carthage, posted guards outside the jail to prevent the prisoners from receiving any aid or visitation from their fellow

---

46. Council of Elvira, *Canon 60*. The council nevertheless took a hard line on the lapsed: those who had sacrificed were permanently barred from communion (*Canons 1 and 2*).

47. On the Novatians, see T. Gregory 1975.

48. See, e.g., Augustine, *On Baptism, Against the Donatists*. The question of rebaptism had already come up in the mid-third century. Cyprian favored it (which put him at odds with Rome) but strongly condemned hard-liners who would separate themselves from the unified church in the name of purity: see Burns 2002, chap. 6. Thus, in the next century, both Donatists and Catholics could appeal to Cyprian's legacy.

Christians.[49] Accusations of *traditio* resurfaced when Caecilian was elected bishop in 311, and a group of rigorists led by Donatus, who claimed to represent the true "Church of the Martyrs," refused to recognize the authority of Caecilian and his colleagues. The split soon hardened into permanent schism, as each side ordained its own bishops and clergy and refused to recognize those of the other.[50] With different factions competing to be recognized as the one true church, it became increasingly important to challenge the legitimacy of "martyrdoms" claimed by rival groups regarded as heretical or schismatic. For the Donatists, their self-conception as the "Church of the Martyrs" was central to their identity and ideology—and thus the need for Catholic opponents to deny the validity of Donatist martyrdom, particularly in the case of those who died resisting "unity" on Catholic terms, became paramount.[51]

The catastrophe of persecution had a divisive impact not only on the church but also, apparently, on the empire as a whole. It further strained the already delicate relations among the Tetrarchs. Constantius chose not to enforce the persecuting edicts in his own territories, and continued to count Christian clergy among his advisors.[52] Licinius used Maximinus Daia's mistreatment of Christians as a *casus belli,* and Constantine later did the same against Licinius himself. It has been suggested that the persecutions commanded little popular support even among pagans.[53] The evidence for that—mainly from Christian sources—is mixed. Against known examples of mobs baying for Christian blood, or cities petitioning for renewal of per-

---

49. *Passion of the Martyrs of Abitina* 21: *Si quis traditoribus communicaverit, nobiscum partem in regnis caelestibus non habebit.* They made this pronouncement "by the authority of the holy spirit" *(sancti spiritus auctoritate),* implicitly rejecting the more formal clerical authority of Caecilian, tainted as it was by *traditio.* Bishop Felix of Apthungi, Caecilian's consecrator, had been accused of *traditio,* and thus Caecilian was equally culpable. Caecilian's action against the jailed martyrs also damned him in the eyes of their supporters. Caecilian may well have felt a need to distance the larger Christian community from the zealots, in order to avoid provoking more sweeping official reprisals, as Tilley 1996, *Donatist Martyr Stories,* pp. 25–26, suggests. But Tilley is simply incorrect to point to an "imperial law" prohibiting assistance to imprisoned Christians—the edict she cites (Eusebius *HE* 10.8) was issued by the eastern emperor Licinius well over a decade after the martyrdoms at Abitina, at a time when North Africa was already under the Christian-friendly regime of Constantine.

50. For a detailed narrative of events at the origin of the schism, see Frend 1985, pp. 1–24.

51. For Donatist self-identity see Tilley 1997b. See my chapter 3 for a lengthier treatment of Donatism.

52. Eusebius *VC* 1.13–17.

53. Drake 2000, pp. 150–153; Lane Fox 1986, pp. 596–601.

secution, can be set the likelihood that many other pagans, now used to knowing Christians as relatives and neighbors, no longer considered them to be as much a threat as did the regime.[54] They must have wondered at the sudden explosion of official violence against law-abiding fellow citizens who differed from themselves only in religion. Final proof that the policy of persecution was a bloody failure became apparent when one of its original architects, the emperor Galerius, abandoned it in 311.[55]

It had long been standard in the political lexicon of the later Roman Empire for emperors to refer to their defeated rivals as "tyrants," with all the negative connotations that term had come to bear.[56] Now Christians such as Eusebius and Lactantius began to adapt the political discourse of tyranny into a religious context, to describe persecuting emperors.[57] Paul had instructed Christians to obey their secular rulers, since they derived their authority from God. But persecutors, who fought against the divine law, forfeited that authority and became tyrants, illegitimate usurpers whose edicts Christians had a positive duty to defy.[58] As we shall see in later chapters, this duty of defiance—conceived in response to pagan persecution—could also be turned against Christian emperors, and ultimately against the church itself.

The emperor Constantine, having aligned himself on the side of the Christians, did not mince words: his persecuting predecessors were "champions of wickedness" and "fearful cowards" deceived by the lies of pagan oracles, who needlessly unleashed the evils of civil war upon an empire that had been at peace.[59] Their cruelty toward the Christians led directly to their own downfall.[60] Constantine went so far as to suggest that polytheism caused civil war: the fratricidal politics of the Tetrarchs simply reflected the rival-

54. Several of these anti-Christian petitions have survived, and are discussed in Barnes 1981, p. 160.

55. Edict quoted in Lactantius *MP* 34, Eusebius *HE* 8.17. Shortly thereafter, however, Maximinus Daia renewed persecution in the eastern provinces.

56. On the discourse of "tyrant-usurper," see MacMullen 1963.

57. Lactantius, *Divine Institutes* 5.6: Diocletian's "Jupiter" identification renders his rule illegitimate, since Jupiter stands for lawlessness—thus Diocletian is a tyrant. Compare, e.g., Eusebius *HE* 9.1; *VC* 1.3, 1.23.

58. Paul, in Romans 13:1–7. Compare Augustine *City of God* 19.17, promising obedience to the secular power in everything except religion. Cf. Eusebius *SC* 5.2: "Surely one abandoned to vices such as these, however he may be deemed powerful through despotic violence, has no true title to the name of Emperor." (NPNF trans.)

59. Quoted in *VC* 2.27 and 2.50 (Cameron and Hall trans.).

60. *VC* 2.27: "From such policies arise harsh wars, from such policies, destructive spoliation . . . For the extent of the disasters each one has suffered shows how

ries and disorderly immoralities of their pagan gods.[61] In later generations, this conflation of religious and political chaos would be made once again as Christians likened schism in the church to civil war.[62] But for now, at least, the world could enjoy peace, under one God—and one emperor.

In all these ways, the experience of persecution exercised a powerful impact on the consciousness of early Christians, one that would persist for centuries afterwards. The number of martyrs may have been small, in the larger scheme of things, but they would not be forgotten. We commonly think of the conversion of Constantine as marking the end of the age of the martyrs, the point at which actual persecution and martyrdom ceased and the cult of martyrs and saints got under way. The word "martyr" for us conveys images, drawn from ancient hagiography and modern Hollywood alike, of heroic and peaceful Christians willing to suffer torture and death for their beliefs. This kind of martyrdom requires a certain type of persecutor, of course: the pagan emperor, or his magistrate, who demands that the Christians burn incense, sacrifice to idols, or simply deny the name of Christ.[63] Traditional Christian martyrology emphasized the contrast between the brutal coercive violence applied by agents of the pagan state, and the steadfast endurance of the believers who were willing to die for their faith. These confrontations, in popular imagination both medieval and modern, form one of the most enduring images of the earliest history of Christianity.[64]

---

far he was swept on by folly in his idea that he could even defeat the divine Law." (Cameron and Hall trans.)

61. Constantine, *Oration to the Assembly of the Saints* 3: "For if the dominion of these things, numberless as they are, were in the hands, not of one but of many, there must be a partition and distribution of the elements, and the old fables would be true; jealousy, too, and ambition, striving for superior power, would destroy the harmonious concord of the whole, while each of the many masters would regulate in a manner different from the rest the portion subject to his control . . . Hence anger, discords, mutual censure, and finally universal confusion, would ensue, while each departed from his proper sphere of action, dissatisfied, through ambitious love of power, with his allotted portion"—ostensibly a discussion of divinity and the natural world, but also, clearly, a not-so-subtle swipe at Diocletian's constitutional arrangements. (NPNF trans.) Cf. a similar analogy between polytheism and political chaos in Eusebius *LC* 3.6 and *SC* 16.2–6.

62. See chapters 7 and 8.

63. Harries 1999a discusses the archetype of the "persecuting judge" who becomes progressively more enraged and sadistic in fourth-century and later martyrology: "unbridled rage, sadistic inventiveness, the readiness to inflict every form of torture and pain" (p. 230). Earlier texts, by contrast, portrayed reluctant magistrates driven, Pilate-like, by the fury of the pagan mob.

64. Modern scholarship on early Christian martyrdom and persecution has tended to focus primarily on this "traditional," pre-Constantinian martyrdom. It is

The value system of early Christianity held up the martyr's crown as the most glorious honor a Christian could achieve. Martyrs and "confessors" (those who endured torture but survived) were widely credited with the power to hear confessions and absolve sins, despite numerous attempts by the institutionalized church hierarchy to regulate the charismatic authority that these holy men and women had gained through their endurance of violence.[65] The martyrs were the first Christians to be venerated as saints, their physical relics treasured, their anniversaries commemorated. Ordinary Christians prayed for their intercession and credited them with miracles.[66]

By the beginning of the fourth century, veneration of the martyrs gathered momentum even as the end of the Great Persecution would seem to have curtailed the possibilities for creating new martyrs. In the new and complex circumstances created by the Constantinian alliance of church and state, many Christians looked back on the age of pagan persecution as a "heroic age," remembered for its stories of foundational violence that played an integral role in the formation and self-definition of the Christian religious community.

The word "community" can be understood on two levels, referring not just to particular local Christian congregations bound together by shared veneration of individual martyr cults, but more broadly to what could be called the "imagined community" of late Roman Christianity, to borrow a concept from Benedict Anderson's study of the origins of modern nationalism.[67] This

---

impossible to do more than scratch the surface of the immense bibliography on this subject. Fundamental are Delehaye 1907 and 1912, representing a tradition of scholarship good at sorting out the historical from the legendary, but too quick to condemn a large mass of the latter as being of little use for the historian. Although a martyr legend written at the end of the fourth century may add very little to our historical knowledge of the Great Persecution a century earlier, it may nevertheless yield valuable insight into the thought-world of late fourth-century Christianity. For a detailed narrative history of martyrdom and persecution up to Constantine, see Frend 1965. Musurillo 1972, *Acts of the Christian Martyrs*, translates a good selection of some of the most famous pre-Constantinian martyrdoms, including those of Polycarp, Perpetua, Cyprian, and many others. For stories of martyrs as retold in post-Constantinian sources, see, e.g., Prudentius, *Peristephanon* (with Roberts 1993); Gregory of Tours, *Glory of the Martyrs*. See also Bowersock 1995; Boyarin 1999; B. Shaw 1996, emphasizing the martyrs' presentation of *hypomone* or "endurance of suffering" as an active, positive virtue; G. Clark 1998.

65. See, e.g., Tertullian, *On Martyrdom* 1 and *On Modesty* 22; Cyprian, *Ep.* 26; Eusebius *HE* 5.2.

66. On martyr- and saint-cult generally: Hackel 1981, Brown 1981, Duval 1982, Saxer 1980, assorted articles in Lamberigts and Van Deun 1995. On the visual iconography of martyrdom in North Africa, see Salomonson 1979.

67. Anderson 1991.

paradigm can fruitfully be applied to religious communities as well as modern nation-states, and is particularly useful for the late antique period, an era whose defining characteristic was the tendency of individuals and groups to construct their identity more and more exclusively in confessional religious terms. Lacking the ethnic or territorial basis claimed by most modern nationalisms, religious communities must construct their identity exclusively upon a shared idea, value system, and sense of "communion"—the last factor especially and literally meaningful in the Christian church, which used the ritual of communion as the chief means for representing both inclusion in and (through excommunication) exclusion from the community.[68]

Communities shape their identity in large part through their sense of history, and when we read church histories and other Christian sources from the fourth and fifth centuries, we are struck by their emphasis on the Christian church as a community shaped by its endurance of persecution. Stories of martyrdom and persecution helped define Christian identity, by reminding believers what it was about their faith that was worth fighting for, and by distinguishing heroes from villains, martyrs from persecutors, Christians from pagans, insiders from outsiders. To this day, the calendar of the Coptic Church numbers years not from the birth of Christ, but according to the "Era of the Martyrs," beginning in 284 A.D. with the accession of Diocletian, the emperor responsible for the last and worst of the pagan persecutions.

CONSTANTINE

The end of persecution had been accompanied by an even more dramatic development: for the first time in history, an emperor had openly embraced Christianity. Clearly, a new era had begun. What else might be possible? Many Christians gave free expression to utopian hopes. Already in the third century, Origen had allowed himself to imagine a future in which all Romans would follow Christ.[69] Eusebius' optimism had already been apparent in the early editions of his *Ecclesiastical History*, completed before the Persecution, when he explained the Roman Empire as part of God's design and envisioned a church ever expanding—a happy ending, rudely postponed

---

68. Cf. Anderson 1991, p. 6: "[The nation] is imagined because the members of even the smallest nation will never know most of their fellow-members, meet them, or even hear of them, yet in the minds of each lives the image of their communion."

69. Origen, *Against Celsus* 8.70. In such a world, Origen confidently predicted, there would be no occasion for war.

by Diocletian, that could now be completed with Constantine.[70] A Christian emperor, perhaps, could lead his subjects in the right direction. Christian apologists like Lactantius, who blamed polytheism and idolatry for all the world's evils, could easily imagine that Christianity would provide the cure:

> But if God only were worshipped, there would not be dissensions and wars, since men would know that they are the sons of one God; and, therefore, among those who were connected by the sacred and inviolable bond of divine relationship, there would be no plottings, inasmuch as they would know what kind of punishments God prepared for the destroyers of souls . . . There would be no frauds or plunderings if they had learned, through the instruction of God, to be content with that which was their own, though little, so that they might prefer solid and eternal things to those which are frail and perishable. There would be no adulteries, and debaucheries, and prostitution of women, if it were known to all, that whatever is sought beyond the desire of procreation is condemned by God. Nor would necessity compel a woman to dishonor her modesty, to seek for herself a most disgraceful mode of sustenance; since the males also would restrain their lust; and the pious and religious contributions of the rich would succor the destitute. There would not, therefore, as I have said, be these evils on the earth, if there were by common consent a general observance of the law of God, if those things were done by all which our people alone perform . . .
>
> In short, there would be no need of so many and varying laws to rule men, since the law of God alone would be sufficient for perfect innocence; nor would there be any need of prisons, or the sword of rulers, or the terror of punishments, since the wholesomeness of the divine precepts infused into the breasts of men would of itself instruct them to works of justice.[71]

While idealists might hope that the enactment of God's law on earth would allow the state to wither away, Christians such as Constantine would have answered that worldly rulers and secular laws remained as necessary as ever. Scholars have questioned whether Constantine's laws on nonreligious matters show any discernible influence from Christian values, but the evidence clearly shows that Constantine did not believe that the time for "prisons, the sword, or the terror of punishments" had passed.[72] Moral ex-

---

70. On the successive editions and reworkings of the *Ecclesiastical History,* see Barnes 1981, pp. 148–163.

71. Lactantius, *Divine Institutes* 5.8 (ANF trans.).

72. MacMullen 1990b shows that a Christian empire brought no moderation in judicial violence. On the specific question of Christian influence on Constantine's legislation, see D. Hunt 1993, Grubbs 1995.

hortation had always struck a dominant tone in the language of imperial legislation, and Constantine was no exception.[73] But admonition went hand in hand with sanction and punishment. The state's coercive power—as imperfect as it might be in comparison to God's justice—needed to exist in order to enforce morality in this world.[74] Constantine told the Christian bishops that he, too, regarded himself as a "bishop" of sorts—ordained by God to look over all those outside the church.[75] The bishop combined moral and spiritual authority with canonical powers to impose repentance and forgive sins. Constantine, whose grants of judicial powers and privileges would considerably increase the bishops' effective power, may have envisioned for himself a role that similarly combined didactic and disciplinary obligations. Far from withering away, then, a Christian imperial state would need to take on more responsibilities than ever.

The traditional role of the emperor had always been, first and foremost, to dispense justice.[76] What kind of justice could be expected from the new, Christian emperor? The first and most obvious manifestation came in an end to a persecution that all Christians and apparently many pagans had regarded as cruel and pointless. Few would have quarrelled with the immediate measures taken by Constantine and Licinius to undo the damages of persecution, by freeing prisoners, restoring civil rights, and returning confiscated property.[77] But should justice extend also to vengeance against those responsible?

To Lactantius, God's justice had manifested itself in the fate of the per-

73. This rhetorical tendency was not entirely new to the Christian empire, nor specific to religious legislation: similar language can be found, e.g., in Diocletian's *Edict on Maximum Prices*.

74. Augustine, a century later, admitted this point and even accepted the inevitability of mistaken judgments and the necessity of judicial torture as a consequence of the "wretchedness" of human existence: *City of God* 19.6.

75. Eusebius *VC* 4.24. Eusebius added: "In accordance with this saying, he exercised a bishop's supervision over all his subjects, and pressed them all, as far as lay in his power, to lead the godly life." (Cameron and Hall trans.) The emperor's remark has occasioned much discussion by theorists of church-state relations: see, e.g., Dagron 1996, pp. 146–147; Rapp 1998a. For the implications of similar terminology used of Constantine's son and successor see Girardet 1977.

76. See Millar 1977 on the tremendous amount of time an emperor could expect to spend hearing appeals and petitions. See now Brown 2002, showing how late antique Christian emperors and bishops revived ancient Near Eastern and Biblical discourses of "justice" to create a new obligation of leadership that claimed to focus on defending the "powerless."

77. See, e.g., the 313 "Edict of Milan" in Lactantius *MP* 48; Constantine's letter to the proconsul Anulinus in Eusebius *HE* 10.5; cf. Eusebius *VC* 2.20 for measures taken by Constantine upon assuming control of the east in 324.

secuting emperors. His treatise *On the Deaths of the Persecutors* set out to demonstrate that every ruler from Nero to Maximinus Daia who had dared to persecute Christians had met with an unhappy end:

> They who insulted over the Divinity, lie low; they who cast down the holy temple, are fallen with more tremendous ruin; and the tormentors of just men have poured out their guilty souls amidst plagues inflicted by Heaven, and amidst deserved tortures. For God delayed to punish them, that, by great and marvellous examples, He might teach posterity that He alone is God, and that with fit vengeance He executes judgment upon the proud, the impious, and the persecutors. Of the end of those men I have thought good to publish a narrative, that all who are afar off, and all who shall arise hereafter, may learn how the Almighty manifested His power and sovereign greatness in rooting out and utterly destroying the enemies of his name.[78]

The excruciating death of Galerius, described in equally excruciating detail by both Eusebius and Lactantius, offered Christians a most impressive example of God's vengeance.[79] Maximinus Daia's slow and painful end also showed God's hand at work.[80] Lactantius, careful to contrast the Christians' willing embrace of death with the violence of their pagan persecutors, emphasized that this vengeance belonged only to God: "For we trust in the majesty of Him who has power to avenge contempt shown towards Himself, as also He has power to avenge the calamities and injuries inflicted on His servants. And therefore, when we suffer such impious things, we do not resist even in word; but we remit vengeance to God."[81]

We should keep in mind, however, Christians' common understanding that God often worked through human agents. Just as God could stir up pagan persecutors in order to punish the sins and test the strength of the faithful, so too could he turn to other men in order to punish those same persecutors: "God has raised up princes to rescind the impious and sanguinary edicts of the tyrants," as Lactantius said.[82] This was an age, after all, in which

---

78. Lactantius *MP* 1 (ANF trans.).

79. Lactantius *MP* 33; Eusebius *HE* 8.16. Horrible bowel diseases and infestations of worms seem to have been a fitting end for persecutors, such as Antiochus Epiphanes (2 Maccabees 9:5–28) and Herod (Josephus, *Antiquities* 17.6.5). Similarly disgusting deaths would befall arch-heretics: see, e.g., Socrates *HE* 1.37–38 for the death of Arius; Zacharias of Mytilene, *Chronicle* 3.1, and John Rufus, *Plerophoriae* 33, for the demise of Nestorius in Monophysite legend.

80. Eusebius *HE* 9.10; Lactantius *MP* 49. Lactantius claims his agony was brought on by a failed attempt at suicide through poison.

81. *Divine Institutes* 5.21 (ANF trans.).

82. *MP* 1.

Romans were accustomed to seeing their rulers die by violence. Constantine made no secret of his conviction that God had chosen him to carry out his will on earth.[83] This belief helped add an extra legitimacy to some of the more brutal measures that came with an emperor's job. It had always been common practice for victors in civil war to punish families, close associates, and prominent supporters of their defeated rivals, whether by execution, exile, or confiscation—such vengeance made sound political sense and was usually only objectionable insofar as it was seen to be carried out excessively or indiscriminately. Thus family and associates of Galerius and Maximinus Daia were killed by Licinius, whose supporters, in turn, would be purged by Constantine a decade later.[84] To the extent that Constantine regarded the persecutions and the civil wars as two aspects of the same catastrophe, it was not unreasonable for him also to punish particular pagan intellectuals or cults regarded as having helped instigate persecution.[85] Constantine's exhortation to the eastern provincials that "no one should use what he has received by inner conviction as a means to harm his neighbor" has been interpreted as a plea that Christians not attempt to avenge themselves on their former persecutors.[86] Constantine's own actions belied any notion of a complete renunciation of vengeance, and the emperor may simply have wished to ensure that retribution was carefully targeted and cleanly executed by his own agents.

Much ink has been expended trying to make sense of Constantine's policies toward pagans and pagan worship.[87] But equally pressing, for him, was the problem of disunity within the Christian church. Questions regarding lapsed Christians and accused *traditores*, which had continued to fester in the years since the end of persecution, demanded judicial resolution. The worsening schism in North Africa was the first issue to be brought to his attention. Constantine was now promising financial assistance and legal privileges

83. See, e.g., Constantine, *Oration to the Assembly of Saints* 26; Eusebius, *LC*.

84. Licinius' purges: Barnes 1981, p. 64, gives details. Constantine: *VC* 2.18.

85. For Constantine's anti-pagan policies, see Barnes 1992 and Barnes 1981, pp. 208–212, 245–248; cf. Lane Fox 1986, pp. 663–680, for Christian attacks on pagan oracles. Constantine particularly targeted the writings of Porphyry and others thought to have incited persecution.

86. Letter to the eastern provincials, quoted in *VC* 2.60 (Cameron and Hall trans.). See discussion in Drake 2000, pp. 286–291.

87. Barnes 1992; Drake 2000, pp. 273–308. Was his toleration merely a temporary and grudging acceptance of political necessity, or did he truly believe (as Drake claims) that common ground could be found between Christians and pagans on a basis of noncoercion and philosophical monotheism? Scholars still cannot agree, for instance, whether or not Constantine actually issued a general prohibition against pagan sacrifice, as Eusebius *VC* 2.45 claims: see Barnes 1984.

to bishops throughout the empire, but which of the two parties claiming the see of Carthage could claim to be legitimately entitled to such?[88] The North African church had been divided and radicalized by the experience of persecution. How would those who regarded themselves as the true "Church of the Martyrs"—who would come to be known more commonly as Donatists— react now that the same imperial government that had recently tortured and killed Christians was suddenly offering friendship and subsidies?[89]

At first, the rigorists seem to have regarded Constantine as the answer to their prayers, an opportunity for vindication in their struggle against the "tainted" Caecilian. They appealed to the emperor, asking that their case against the Caecilianists be judged by bishops outside of Africa who were not themselves suspect in *traditio*.[90] Although Constantine had already tilted toward the other side by naming Caecilian as the bishop who was to receive the new subsidies and privileges,[91] the emperor bent over backwards to give the Donatists a chance to make their case. The first hearing took place in late 313 before bishop Miltiades of Rome, who found in Caecilian's favor.[92] The Donatists, after accusing Miltiades himself of *traditio*, asked for another hearing, this time before bishops from Gaul.[93] Constantine granted them this, and in 314 a council assembled at Arles also rejected their case. By this time, the Donatists were starting to look like extremists: the Gallic bishops described them as "men of unbridled mind" who "neither had any rational ground of speech nor proper mode of accusation and proof" and expressed regret that the emperor did not impose a more severe judgment against them.[94] The Donatists' rigorist stance on the divisions created by persecu-

---

88. State involvement in intra-Christian disputes was not entirely unprecedented; in 268 the Christians of Antioch appealed to the emperor Aurelian to expel the condemned bishop, Paul of Samosata, when he refused to hand over the church building: Eusebius *HE* 7.30.

89. For Constantine's dealings with the Donatists, see Frend 1985, pp. 141–168; Barnes 1981, pp. 54–56. Major sources include the documents preserved in the appendices to Optatus; Optatus *Against the Donatists* bk. 1; Augustine *Epp.* 43 and 88; Augustine *Against Cresconius* bk. 3.

90. Optatus 1.22.

91. *Letters to Anulinus*, in Eusebius *HE* 10.5 and 10.7. See Frend 1985, p. 145. Bishop Ossius (or Hosius) of Cordoba, Constantine's trusted religious advisor throughout his reign, supported Caecilian from the beginning.

92. Optatus 1.23; Augustine *Ep.* 43.

93. Augustine, *Against Parmenian* 1.5.10. Because Gaul had escaped serious persecution under Constantius, the Donatists thought, its bishops would be free of the taint of *traditio*.

94. See the letter of the Arles bishops to Constantine, in Appendix 4 of Optatus. (Edwards trans.)

tion was increasingly out of touch with measures being taken by mainstream church authorities in the rest of the empire, which typically emphasized reconciliation of *lapsi* after reasonable penance.[95] Their disagreement embodied clashing visions of the church's role, with the ever-present tension between purity and unity, exclusivity and inclusivity. The Donatists, like earlier rigorists, saw themselves as a minority of the pure, taking action to separate themselves from the corrupting influences of the outside world. In the Constantinian era, however, the church establishment could envision a more expansive role for itself that emphasized the unity of all believers.

By this time Constantine had become visibly impatient at the Donatists' continuing stream of appeals: "They demand my judgment, when I myself await the judgment of Christ!"[96] He complained increasingly of their "madness," "arrogance," "rabid anger and vain recriminations," and worried that the continuing controversy would provoke God to anger: "Such disputes and altercations . . . might perhaps arouse the highest deity not only against the human race, but also against myself, to whose care he has . . . committed the regulation of all things earthly."[97] As early as 313, then, Constantine already believed that God had given him a special duty to maintain Christian unity. This belief, a Christian variation on the ancient idea of the *pax deorum*, would form the guiding principle of imperial religious policy for generations to come.

Meanwhile, an investigation ordered by Constantine not only failed to find any evidence of *traditio* by Felix of Apthungi, who had ordained Caecilian, but even suggested that his opponents had actually falsified documents against him.[98] The emperor was satisfied as to Caecilian's innocence, and became steadily more irritated by the Donatists' refusal to reconcile with him. It did not help the Donatist cause when a second investigation in 320 charged that at least one of their own bishops had himself been guilty of *traditio*.[99] It did not matter to the emperor that many North African Christians did not

---

95. See, e.g., Ancyra *Canons* 1–6, 8–9; Nicaea *Canons* 11, 12, 14. Nicaea *Canon* 8 condemned rigorists who refused to accept such reconciliations. The bishops at Arles agreed that a *traditor* would be unfit to hold ecclesiastical office, but insisted that any such accusation must be backed up with rigorous documentary proof—which, in their opinion, the Donatists had failed to provide. Moreover, they said, a *traditor*'s crime should not be held against those who were lawfully ordained by him: *Canon* 14. They also specifically rejected the Donatist practice of rebaptism: any baptism performed "in the name of the Father, Son, and Holy Ghost" was valid and should not be repeated.

96. *Letter to the Catholic Bishops*, Optatus App. 5 (Edwards trans.).

97. *Letter to Aelafius, Vicar of Africa*, Optatus App. 3.

98. *Gesta purgationis Felicis*, in Optatus App. 2.

99. *Gesta apud Zenophilum*, in Optatus App. 1.

accept these conclusions, and continued to support the Donatist party as the only true champions of the martyrs. Caecilian was accepted as the legitimate bishop of Carthage by all the churches outside of Africa, and so, to Constantine and to his successors, the Donatists and not their opponents were the clear obstacles to unity.

In light of Constantine's own priorities—political and religious unity and the avoidance of controversy—his decision made perfect sense. The newly converted emperor sought a Christianity that could include everyone, even *traditores*. Preferring universality and consensus over a narrow and rigorist purity, Constantine sided with the party of Caecilian, which thereafter claimed the name "Catholic" *(katholikos,* "universal") by virtue of its recognition by the imperial government and by most Christian churches outside Africa. It was not right, Constantine thought, that the Donatists—who had, after all, petitioned for his judgment in the first place—should refuse to accept a settlement and continue to cause turmoil in the North African church. Emperors were accustomed to being obeyed. Just as his pagan predecessors had done when faced with Christians' refusal to sacrifice, Constantine attributed Donatist resistance to the worst possible motives: intransigence, obstinacy, and a deliberate divisiveness. Their refusal to reconcile with the Caecilianists convicted them of an inability to forgive, a lack of Christian charity.[100]

The Caecilianist bishops and their successors shared Constantine's complaints and elaborated upon them in later polemic. Their recognition by overseas churches, particularly Rome, formed the basis of their claim to legitimacy. While the Donatists had chosen to separate themselves from the larger church, the Catholics remained part of a "universal" church. Over the next century, Catholic thinkers such as Optatus and Augustine would engage the Donatists on grounds both historical (calling attention to evidence that had acquitted Felix and Caecilian and implicated their Donatist rivals) and theological. It was in response to Donatist ideas of purity that the Catholics developed the doctrine that the sins or imperfections of an individual priest did not affect the validity of the sacraments he performed. Even if some clerics had been guilty of *traditio,* they did not pass on that taint to those whom they ordained. Once enough time had elapsed and the original *traditores* were no longer alive, the Catholics reasoned, the controversy would be moot

100. The same concern for unity and reconciliation would later drive Constantine's post-Nicaea tilt toward Arius and Eusebius of Nicomedia, and away from the hard-line Athanasius; see below. The theme of Donatist "uncharity" was picked up and emphasized in Catholic anti-Donatist polemic by Optatus and Augustine: see chapter 4, pp. 134–135.

and there ought to be no further barrier to reconciliation. Clearly, the Donatists felt differently—and so Catholics attributed the persistence of the schism to an unforgiving hard-heartedness, a lack of charity, on the Donatist side. Since none of us could claim to be sinless, Augustine would argue, the Donatists' insistence on their superior purity smacked of arrogant pride.[101] Catholic argument emphasized the value of unity, and held that schism was a sin even worse than *traditio*.[102] In this their views coincided with those of the Christian emperors, who always recognized the Catholics' legitimacy, even if they only occasionally (before the fifth century) flexed their muscles to enforce it.

Diocletian's vision of religious unity had led him to a coercive policy, and Constantine, at first, was tempted to follow the same path. Hearing that the Donatists were stirring up riots against Caecilian, the emperor threatened to come to Africa and settle the issue himself:

> Those same people who incite and do things of this nature, so that the supreme God is not worshipped with the requisite devotion, I shall destroy and scatter. And as it is sufficiently apparent that no-one can obtain the blessings of martyrdom in a manner that is seen to be foreign to and incompatible with religious truth, those whom I find to be opposed to right and religion itself, and apprehend in the violation of the due form of worship, these, without any doubt, I will cause to suffer the due penalties of their madness and their reckless obstinacy.[103]

Constantine's language here is significant. His mention—and dismissal—of martyrdom not only implies his awareness that lethal force might be necessary, but also suggests that he anticipated how the Donatists might respond to coercive violence. Clearly, Donatist leaders must have been rallying their followers to disobey the emperor's commands, and proclaiming their readiness for martyrdom. Constantine could not afford to let this claim stand: if the Donatists were martyrs, then that would make him a persecutor, no better than his pagan predecessors. Constantine had only recently aligned himself with the Christians, but was already well aware of the powerful possibilities of the discourse of martyrdom. His response echoed the standard reply of the church establishment to martyrial claims by heretics or schismatics: because their actions were "incompatible with religious

---

101. See, e.g., Augustine, *Sermon* 198.45, 52 (Dolbeau 198, Mainz 62). Augustine's anti-Donatist polemics are discussed further in chapters 3 and 4.

102. See, e.g., Optatus 1.13.

103. Constantine, *Letter to the Vicar Domitius Celsus*, in Optatus App. 7 (trans. Edwards).

truth," their deaths could not be considered martyrdom. One's willingness to die for a cause did not in and of itself make that cause right. The same argument would later be developed and used to great effect by Optatus and, especially, Augustine.[104] In this way Catholic polemic could attack what the Donatists regarded as one of their greatest strengths, their claim to be the true "Church of the Martyrs."

Although Constantine never followed through on his promise to settle the situation in person, he did make good his threat to impose ecclesiastical harmony by coercive means. In 317 an edict ordered that churches and properties held by Donatist congregations were to be seized and turned over to the Catholics.[105] This seems to have been the backdrop to a series of bloody incidents described in the Donatist *Sermon on the Passion of Donatus of Avioccala*.[106] An attempt by armed soldiers to expel Donatist worshippers from a basilica had led to a massacre, and the sermonist laid the blame squarely at Caecilian's feet:

> At that time you could have seen bands of soldiers serving the furies of the *traditores* . . . Although the people of God might have anticipated the coming slaughter and known about it from the arrangements being made, they did not flee out of fear of an imminent death. On the contrary, they flew undaunted to the house of prayer with a desire to suffer . . .
>
> Finally, bloodshed marked the end of this hatred. Now the soldiers endorsed the contract and the covenant of crime in no other way than by the seal of blood. Everyone kept their eyes shut tight while each age group and sex was killed, cut down in the middle of the basilica. It is this very basilica, I say, between whose walls so many bodies were cut down and buried. Here, in the inscriptions, memory preserves the name of the persecution as Caecilianist until the end of time, lest after his episcopate the parricide deceive others who were not privy to the things done in his name.[107]

104. The cause, not the suffering, made the martyr: see, e.g., Augustine's sermon on the martyrs of Maxula, *Sermon* 283 (Dolbeau 15, Mainz 5). Earlier examples of this argument: Clement, *Stromateis* 4.4; Eusebius *HE* 5.16. Compare the pagan emperor Marcus Aurelius' dismissive remark that early Christians sought death not in a good cause, but out of mere "stubbornness." *Meditations* 11.3.

105. The edict is not extant, but is referred to in Augustine *Ep.* 88 and *Against Petilian* 2.205; see Frend 1985, pp. 159–162.

106. The title is somewhat misleading, reflecting a later (unproven) tradition that the author of the sermon was Donatus of Carthage himself. The murdered bishop of Avioccala mentioned in the text is never named. The sermon can probably be dated c. 317–321: see Maier 1987–1989, *Dossier du Donatisme*, vol. 1, pp. 198–200. English translation in Tilley 1996, *Donatist Martyr Stories*.

107. *Sermon on Avioccala* 6–8 (trans. Tilley).

The horrific spectacle of armed soldiers intruding into a church and spilling blood within its sacred precincts could not have been better calculated to inflame Christian opinion.[108] Oral and epigraphic commemoration of the event ensured that future generations of Donatists would never forget, and never forgive. The story spoke to Donatists' deepest prejudices: the power of the state, violent by its very nature, could only corrupt the church. The sermonist charged that Caecilian had precipitated the massacre by asking the secular authorities for military assistance to coerce his rivals. This was a damning accusation, transforming a bishop already tainted by *traditio* and persecution into an ecclesiastical tyrant, a "false bishop" who could only sustain his rule by reliance on state violence.[109]

Incidents such as this did much to harden the Donatists in their oppositional stance and in their growing mistrust of the imperial power in which they had initially and briefly placed their trust. In the Donatist view, Constantine's embrace of Christianity in 312 had changed little in substance. Stung by the Donatists' unexpected resistance to his call for unity with *traditores,* Constantine did what his pagan predecessors had done when faced with resistance to their religious policies: he persecuted. The "Church of the Martyrs," true to its name, refused to yield. The *Sermon on Avioccala,* then, commemorated the first Donatist martyrs under the Christian empire. As far as the Donatists were concerned, the Great Persecution was still going on. Donatist martyr accounts written under the Christian empire show a remarkable—and very deliberate—likeness to those dating from the pagan persecutions.[110] The Catholics, descended from *traditores,* were little better than pagans in disguise. Donatists would regularly taunt them with slogans such as "Are you still pagans?" and "Be Christians!" and would insist on rebaptizing Catholics since in their eyes Catholic baptism had no validity.[111] The "original sin" of *traditio* was passed down from Caecilian and his consecrator Felix to all those who were ordained by them, its taint reaching even to Catholics who had not yet been born at the time of the Diocletianic persecution. The imperial authorities who attempted to coerce the true Chris-

108. The "soldiers in church" motif is discussed at length in chapter 2, pp. 79–88.

109. See chapter 2, pp. 76–77, on bishops' reliance on soldiers, and chapter 7 on the "tyrant-bishop."

110. Discussion of these texts in Tilley 1997a, pp. 53–76. The texts typically owed their survival to the fact that medieval Catholic copyists did not recognize them for what they were. See Monceaux 1912, vol.5, pp. 69–98.

111. Slogans reported by Optatus 3.11: *Adhuc paganus es aut pagana? Estote Christiani!* The *Sermon on Avioccala* referred to the Catholics as "Gentiles" (15).

tians into sacrilegious "unity" were doing no more than repeating the pagan persecutions under a new and false pretense of Christianity. Having failed in his direct assault against the faithful, the Donatists feared, the Devil had simply chosen a more subtle method of attack. "Christ," said the Devil, "is a lover of unity. Therefore let there be unity."[112]

There was a certain justification for this view. The judges, jailors, torturers, executioners, officers, soldiers, and other individuals who formed the coercive apparatus of the state and who carried out the repression of Christian dissidents under the Christian empire were not fundamentally different people from those who had persecuted Christians under the pagan empire. Many of them would still have been pagans.[113] Their own personal convictions aside, government officials were responsible for enforcing imperial religious policy—whatever it might be—and bringing coercive or punitive force to bear against those who dared to defy the will of the emperor. In North Africa, one example will suffice to illustrate this fundamental continuity in the methods of enforcement and coercion. Constantine's involvement in North African church affairs had begun with letters instructing the proconsul Anulinus to distribute wealth and privileges to the Catholic (i.e., Caecilianist) clergy. In all probability this Anulinus was a close relative, perhaps a son, of the Anulinus who had filled the same office just ten years before and who had presided over the torture and execution of numerous Christian martyrs, taking the villain's role in the *Passiones* of Crispina, Maxima, Secunda, Donatilla, Felix, and the martyrs of Abitina.[114]

The Donatists, then, could be forgiven for thinking that very little had changed since the time of Diocletian. Although they had originally appealed to the new Christian emperor in the hope that he would recognize the justice of their cause, subsequent experience had left them greatly disillusioned and mistrustful of imperial power. It was in this context that, during the reign of Constantine's son Constans, Donatus could make his famous remark, "What has the emperor to do with the church?"[115]

The Donatists' determined resistance and readiness for martyrdom

---

112. *Christus, inquit, amator unitatis est; unitas igitur fiat!* (*Sermon on Avioccala* 3).

113. Such as Nicomachus Flavianus, *vicarius* in 377: Mandouze, *PCBE*, s.v. Flavianus 1. Tengström 1964, pp. 170–183, surveys evidence for the religious sympathies of high-ranking imperial officials in North Africa in the period 373–420.

114. *Passiones* of the Martyrs of Abitina; of Maxima, Secunda and Donatilla; of Crispina: in Maier 1987–1989, *Dossier*, vol. 1, pp. 57–112. See s.v. Anulinus 1 and Anulinus 2 in Mandouze, *PCBE*; Anullinus 2 and Anullinus 3 in *PLRE*.

115. *Quid est imperatori cum ecclesia?* Optatus 3.3.

were rewarded, at least in the short term. Just as the fortitude of the early martyrs had outlasted the strength of their pagan persecutors, so too in this case the persecuting emperor eventually relented. By 321, Constantine seems to have abandoned any further attempt at coercion, and allowed the Donatists to live in peace.[116] Constantine may initially have failed to take the threats of martyrdom seriously, and perhaps thought that a quick show of force would be enough to bring the Donatists around without serious bloodshed. Faced with the prospect of conducting a full-scale persecution, and making martyrs of Christians, Constantine relented—and found himself in the equally unpleasant position of being forced to tolerate disobedience. It was a dilemma that would confront future Christian emperors again and again.

Perhaps attempting to make a virtue out of necessity, Constantine began preaching to fellow Christians the advantages of turning the other cheek. To the Catholic bishops in Africa, he advised:

Whatever [the Donatists'] insolence tries or does as a result of their customary intemperance, all this we are to tolerate with the virtue of tranquillity. Let nothing be done to reciprocate an injury, for it is a fool who would usurp the vengeance which we ought to reserve to God, particularly when our faith ought to be confident that whatever suffering result from the madness of people of this kind will have value in God's eyes by the grace of martyrdom.[117]

The Catholic bishops, increasingly threatened by popular violence, and learning that Constantine's support for them would no longer extend beyond the rhetorical, could at least console themselves that God would reward their suffering. Constantine's moderate tone appeared again after 324, when he advised eastern Christians against seeking vengeance on pagans.[118] In his *Oration to the Assembly of the Saints,* the emperor praised the virtue of patient suffering, reminding his audience—even as he himself prepared for war—that those who lived by the sword would die by it.[119] In 330, responding to a complaint by Numidian Catholics that Donatists had seized a basilica from them, Constantine counselled patience and offered to build them another one.[120] Not until 347, late in the reign

---

116. The edict to this effect does not survive, but was cited and read at the Conference of Carthage in 411: *Acts of the Conference of Carthage* 3.548–551.

117. *Letter to the Catholic Bishops in Africa,* in Optatus App. 9 (trans. Edwards).

118. Eusebius *VC* 2.60, discussed above.

119. Matthew 26:52. Constantine, *Oration* 15: "This is indeed heavenly wisdom, to choose rather to endure than to inflict injury." (NPNF trans.)

120. Optatus App. 10.

of his son Constans, would there be another serious attempt to coerce the Donatists into unity.[121]

There were more practical reasons for the emperor's newfound restraint. It was clear by now that forcing an end to the schism would require a significant commitment of military strength that was urgently needed elsewhere. By 321, Constantine was busily preparing for war with Licinius, his colleague and rival in the east, and could not afford any further distraction in North Africa. Part of Constantine's strategy was to paint his former ally as a "persecutor" in order to win the sympathies of Christians in the east, and the last thing he needed was to attract the same label upon himself.[122] After his victory in 324, Africa faded into the background as Constantine became entangled in the Arian controversy, the Council of Nicaea, and its difficult aftermath—quarrels that would try his patience and again tempt him toward coercion.

When the deepening dispute over the Trinity was first brought to his attention, Constantine was both irritable and dismissive. This was an argument about nothing, he hectored Alexander and Arius, a quarrel "extremely trivial and quite unworthy of so much controversy."[123] Alexander had asked a question that should never have been asked, and Arius had answered with "that opinion which either ought not to have been conceived in the first place, or once conceived ought to have been consigned to silence."[124] Constantine seems to have had, at this stage, very little understanding of the theological dilemma that would soon be debated at the Council of Nicaea—"this very silly question, whatever it actually is"[125]— nor would we, if we had to depend entirely on Eusebius' deliberately vague presentation.[126] Both the emperor and his biographer expressed a strong preference for seeking consensus by sidestepping divisive theological problems, a tendency that would emerge again and again as the Christian state tried to bring order to the Christian church. Richard Lim has documented for the fourth century a fundamental shift in values as secular and eccle-

---

121. See chapter 3, pp. 104–111, and chapter 4, pp. 135–136.

122. On Licinius as "persecutor": Eusebius *HE* 10.8 and *VC* 1.51–54 and 2.1–2; Barnes 1981, pp. 70–72.

123. *Letter to Alexander and Arius,* in *VC* 2.68.

124. *VC* 2.69.

125. *VC* 2.70.

126. Eusebius on Nicaea: *VC* 2.61, 3.4–14; Barnes 1981, pp. 226–227; Hanson 1988, pp. 159–166. Cf. Socrates *HE* 1.1: "[Eusebius] has but slightly treated of matters regarding Arius, being more intent on the rhetorical finish of his composition and the praises of the emperor, than on an accurate statement of facts." (NPNF trans.)

siastical leaders of a rapidly Christianizing empire became steadily more mistrustful of intellectual argument and open debate, instead emphasizing hierarchical authority and enforced unanimity.[127] A strong preference for consensus, and a distaste for "divisive" adversarial proceedings, pervaded the political and legal system of the late empire.[128] We should not be surprised, then, that Constantine sought a similar concord in church affairs. Addressing the bishops at Nicaea, the emperor rejoiced "to see you all with your souls in communion, and one common, peaceful harmony prevailing among you all." Division in the church was "graver than any war or fierce battle." A quick resolution to the controversy would not only gratify the emperor, but would please God.[129]

The Trinitarian controversy was anything but "trivial," and Constantine was losing sleep over it:

> Give me back therefore peaceful days and undisturbed nights [he
> entreated Arius and Alexander] so that I too may still have some
> pleasure left in the clear light and happiness of a quiet life. Otherwise
> I must weep and constantly break down in tears, and not even face
> the rest of my life with equanimity. If the peoples of God, my own
> fellow-servants I mean, are so divided by wicked and damaging strife
> between themselves, how can my thoughts any longer be collected?[130]

God had charged him with maintaining the peace of the church, and Constantine feared that God would hold him responsible for its breach. Diversity of worship threatened unity just as much as did differences of belief. One of Constantine's first priorities at Nicaea was to standardize the date of Easter, since it was "dreadful and unseemly" that Christians in one part of the empire might be feasting while their brethren elsewhere were still fasting.[131] Division and disorder undermined the dignity and honor of all Christians, who had a duty to present a united front to the outside world.

127. Lim 1995, pp. 24–30, on the fourth century's shift against disputation and toward consensus; pp. 182–216 discuss how the fifth-century church historians reconstructed the Council of Nicaea as an arena in which unlettered confessors confounded rhetoricians and philosophers with simple professions of faith.

128. Lamoreaux 1995 argues that litigants preferred bishops' courts as a more "non-adversarial"—and less expensive and less corrupt—alternative to the regular justice system. Cf. Nader 1996 on modern tendencies to enforce arbitration over "divisive" litigation.

129. *VC* 3.12, one of many instances in which Constantine assumed that his own priorities were also those of God.

130. *VC* 2.72 (Cameron and Hall trans.).

131. *VC* 3.18.

Otherwise, Constantine feared, the church would be made a laughingstock by the pagans, heretics, and Jews it hoped to convert.[132]

The purpose of Nicaea, for Constantine, was to end the controversy by producing a consensus statement of faith to which all could subscribe. Although many bishops had deep reservations about the new creed, which proclaimed Christ to be "of the same substance" *(homoousios)* as the Father, the vast majority signed. It mattered little if some of them understood the creed in a different fashion than others: as long as all accepted the same language and maintained communion with one another, unity would prevail.[133] Only a very few of the participants refused to sign, thus identifying themselves as enemies of peace. These "extremists" earned the emperor's anger, and a sentence of exile.[134] The resulting consensus—dependent as it was on a slightly coercive politics—seemed, to Constantine, to have been favored by divine inspiration: "That which has commended itself to the judgment of three hundred bishops cannot be other than the doctrine of God, seeing that the Holy Spirit dwelling in the minds of so many dignified persons has enlightened them!"[135]

The apparent comity proclaimed in the council's formal decrees covered up a fundamental gap between the emperor's politics of consensus and the agenda of theological zealots on both sides of the controversy, who preferred to expose division rather than paper it over, by clearly identifying and denouncing heretical error. Many bishops believed that the purpose of a council was to draw sharp lines between orthodoxy and heresy, to distinguish truth from falsehood. Inclusive language designed to sidestep controversial formulations could only make it easier for heresy to go undetected: the more specific and exclusive a credal statement, the better. Athanasius, who had attended the Council as a young deacon and who would champion the *homoousion* for the next half century, later explained that while he certainly had no quarrel with more moderate formulations such as "the Son is like the Father," these were insufficient because they did not explicitly exclude "Arian" interpretations.[136] The mere fact that the other side might also find

132. *VC* 3.21. Compare Socrates *HE* 1.6: "To so disgraceful an extent was this affair [the Arian controversy] carried, that Christianity became a subject of popular ridicule, even in the very theaters."

133. Eusebius had been one of many who signed only with reservations: see his letter back to his congregation in Caesarea, in Socrates *HE* 1.8. On the council generally, see Hanson 1988, pp. 152–178.

134. These were the Libyan bishops Secundus of Ptolemais and Theonas of Marmarica: Philostorgius *HE* 1.9.

135. Constantine, *Letter to the Alexandrian Church*, quoted in Socrates *HE* 1.9.

136. From this point of view, the very attempt to secure compromise through inclusive and noncontroversial credal language was itself inherently deceitful: cf.

it acceptable was enough to make it unacceptable. Such attitudes guaranteed that imperial attempts to reach unity through compromise would always encounter determined opposition from the extremes, even if the vast majority of bishops went along. The clash between these two attitudes in turn reflected a larger battle between two conflicting ideas of religious community. Was the congregation of the faithful to be inclusive, universal, built upon consensus—or was it to be marked off by firm boundaries from known enemies, the exclusive preserve of the pure who saw compromise as the work of the devil?

In contrast to the imperial, centrist viewpoint can be juxtaposed what we may call an "Athanasian" perspective. The combative bishop of Alexandria saw God's hand at work not only in the council's endorsement of the *homoousion* but also in the unhappy fates of its opponents. Athanasius took great care to publicize as widely as possible the unpleasant and embarrassing circumstances of Arius' death. The arch-heretic, who had tricked the emperor with a false pretense of repentance, spilled out his guts in a public latrine.[137] This story, which would be eagerly picked up by the pro-Nicene ecclesiastical historians in the next century, offered a powerful example of God's just hatred and violent justice against those who would divide the church. Lactantius had used the gruesome death of the persecutor Galerius in very much the same way. Both stories drew upon a tradition even older than Christianity. The horrific bowel diseases, disembowelments, and infestations of worms that afflicted villains such as Antiochus Epiphanes, Herod the Great, Herod Antipas, and of course Judas Iscariot, spelled out the terrible fate in store for God's worst enemies.[138] The authors of heresies, to Athanasius, belonged in the bad company of tyrants, persecutors, and traitors.

Constantine was second to none in condemning past emperors who had

---

Athanasius' highly unflattering portrait of Eusebius of Nicomedia and his "Arian" colleagues "nodding and winking" at hearing various suggested credal formulations whose meaning they could "twist" to support their own heresy: see, e.g., *De Decretis* 20. Only the *homoousion*, Athanasius argued, could completely exclude any possibility of "Arian" interpretation.

137. Athanasius, *Ep.* 54 and *Letter to the Bishops of Egypt and Libya;* commentary in Brakke 1995a, pp. 131–134. Cf. Socrates *HE* 1.38; Sozomen *HE* 2.29–30; Theodoret *HE* 1.14.

138. Antiochus: 2 Maccabees 9:5–28, including a last-minute repentance similar to that of Galerius; Herod the Great: Josephus *Antiquities* 17.6.5, quoted also in Eusebius *HE* 1.8; Herod Antipas: Josephus 19.8.2 and Eusebius *HE* 2.10; Judas' guts spilled out: Acts 1:16–19, in contrast to Matthew 27:3–5, where he hanged himself.

persecuted Christians, but in ecclesiastical matters he placed a higher premium on making peace than on settling scores—and on this point, Athanasius' intransigence would lead him into trouble. The fact that emperors cared more about unity than doctrinal consistency enables us to understand why Constantine, who had convoked the Council of Nicaea and endorsed the *homoousion* in 325, ten years later turned against Athanasius and a handful of other bishops known as diehard supporters of Nicene theology. In the decade after the council, Constantine reconciled with Arius, Eusebius of Nicomedia, and others who had been condemned at Nicaea, and attempted to bring them back into the church. The emperor, interested in restoring peace, did not particularly care whether or not Arius' repentance was sincere. But Athanasius and his companions were no more willing to accept or communicate with "Arians" than the Donatists would have been to forgive *traditores*. Suddenly the hard-line Nicenes, and not the Arians, were now the obstacles to unity and thus the objects of the emperor's wrath.[139]

But the Christian historical memory of later and firmly Nicene generations did not necessarily share Constantine's priorities. The defense of Nicene orthodoxy, in retrospect, far outweighed the simple preservation of unity. As Athanasius came to be venerated as a saint and Father of the Church, Constantine's own legacy grew more problematic. It began to seem, to posterity, that in the last decade of his life Constantine had backed away from a firm pro-Nicene stance and drifted uncomfortably close to heresy. Rufinus, perhaps wishing to clear the emperor of any such taint, garbled chronology in his *History* to suggest that the tilt toward the "Arian" party had only begun after 337, under Constantius; Socrates, with visible reluctance, corrected the error.[140]

To Christians in later generations, Constantine's last-minute baptism also raised eyebrows. By the late fourth and early fifth centuries, the prolonged catechumenate of Christians not yet willing to take advantage of their one opportunity to wash away a lifetime's sins remained common, but was coming under increasing criticism.[141] Later Christian emperors typically accepted proper baptism much earlier in their careers—and thus, at

---

139. Cf. Eusebius *VC* 1.44: "Such as he saw able to be prevailed upon by argument and adopting a calm and conciliatory attitude, he commended most warmly, showing how he favored general unanimity, but the obstinate he rejected." (Cameron and Hall trans.)

140. Rufinus *HE* 10.12–14; Socrates *HE* 2.1.

141. See, e.g., Augustine, *Ep.* 2*, to Firmus; Augustine recalls his own hesitation in *Confessions*. Compare Tertullian, *On Repentance* 6.9, an early complaint about catechumens who delay baptism indefinitely.

least in theory, placed themselves under the disciplinary authority of the church. To those who had seen Theodosius submit to the penitential discipline of bishop Ambrose, it did not seem right that Constantine could have dominated church politics and influenced doctrine for twenty-five years, while all the time only a catechumen. Christian ambiguity toward violence and secular power had always expressed itself in confusion over whether believers could legitimately involve themselves in the military or in public office.[142] Was the sword incompatible with faith? Both before and after Constantine, strict pacifist interpretations coexisted with more realistic views. Stories of "military martyrs" in the time of the Great Persecution reveal some Christians who refused all military service, believing that the divine law forbade them to take up the sword—but also, in other cases, veteran soldiers who apparently had served and fought for years without complaint, who only rebelled when ordered to perform pagan sacrifice.[143] Public magistracies had been a virtual impossibility for observant Christians insofar as they had required the officeholder's participation in pagan worship. Constantine quickly legislated the removal of that barrier.[144] But even if freed from the taint of idolatry, magistrates still carried blood on their hands in a judicial system that depended upon torture and execution.[145] While state officials may have regarded such unpleasantries as necessary sins, they were sins nonetheless. Delayed baptism, for such men, represented a compromise by which they could avoid addressing these contradictions until they were safely retired. Constantine, the first Christian emperor, faced a larger version of the same dilemma. Recognizing that his imperial duties—even if they were endorsed by God—necessarily involved him in sin, Constantine waited until he was finished before seeking forgiveness.[146]

142. For a survey of patristic attitudes, see Swift 1983. Many soldiers or magistrates identified themselves as Christians but nevertheless waited until the end of their lives (when they would be done with their "unchristian" profession) to receive baptism.

143. See Swift 1983, pp. 68–79 on traditions of military martyrs.

144. See, e.g., *C.Th.* 16.2.5 of 323; Eusebius *VC* 2.44.

145. A point made by Augustine, *City of God* 19.6. Ambrose, serving as governor of Milan, thought that ordering the torture of criminals (along with entertaining prostitutes at his residence) would dissuade those who sought to elect him bishop: Paulinus, *Life of Ambrose* 7–8; cf. McLynn 1994, pp. 44–47. On judicial torture, MacMullen 1990b.

146. Eusebius *VC* 4.61: "When he became aware that his life was ending, he perceived that this was the time to purify himself from the offences which he had at any time committed, trusting that whatever sins it had been his lot as a mortal to com-

If late antique Christians found Constantine's legacy problematic, then modern historiography has faced even more difficulty in trying to make sense of the emperor's character and intentions. The Constantine of Timothy Barnes—a zealous and committed Christian, whose determination to stamp out pagan idolatry only grudgingly yielded to political reality—would hardly recognize Harold Drake's "tolerant" Constantine, a skilled political operator who eschewed coercion, restrained extremists, and pursued a deliberately gentle and inclusive policy aimed at bringing Christians and moderate pagans together in a "religiously neutral" consensus.[147] The latter model has difficulty making sense of actions such as Constantine's closure of several pagan temples; the former must explain why such policies were not more extensive. Elizabeth Digeser has suggested a way to bridge the gap by distinguishing between "tolerance" as a principle (a largely modern concept) and "forbearance"—a situation in which the authorities indulge religious dissidents as a pragmatic and temporary measure, in the hope that they will eventually come around to the true faith.[148] Such a strategy would help make sense of the seeming contradiction between Constantine's frequently violent language against pagans and heretics and the weak evidence for sweeping policies to back up those words.

The policy of forbearance, in this interpretation, followed logically from the experience of the Great Persecution, which had demonstrated the failure of more coercive measures.[149] As far as the Donatists were concerned, however, it seems that Constantine needed to learn that lesson at least one more time; and it remains unclear exactly how harshly he acted towards pagans after 324.[150] A policy emphasizing persuasion over compulsion would cer-

---

mit, he could wash them from his soul by the power of the secret words and the saving bath." (Cameron and Hall trans.) Constantine then (*VC* 4.62) told the bishops, "I shall now set for myself rules of life which befit God"—a recognition, perhaps, that in his previous quarter century as a "Christian" emperor he had not yet done so.

147. See Barnes 1981 and 1992; assorted articles in Barnes 1994; Drake 2000; Drake 1995; Drake 1996.

148. Digeser 2000, esp. chaps. 4 and 5; cf. Drake 2000, p. 306, on the emperor's combination of "fierce language and mild action." Both Drake and Digeser are concerned primarily with Constantine's attitudes toward paganism, and have less to say on his approach to conflicts within the Christian camp.

149. Digeser 2000, pp. 91–114; Drake 2000, pp. 150–153, 207–212.

150. According to Barnes, Constantine saw the defeat of Licinius as an opportunity to settle scores religious as well as political, and took a hard line: Barnes 1981, pp. 208–212 and 245–248; Barnes 1992; Barnes 1984. Drake 2000, pp. 273–308 (followed by Digeser 2000, pp. 128–130) argues for a far more restrained imperial policy.

tainly explain the strong didactic and moralizing tone that dominates Constantine's official pronouncements. But imperial legislation on any subject typically carried such a tone, while simultaneously threatening sterner measures against those who did not take heed.[151] An emperor's job demanded both forbearance and harshness, and the skill to know which approach the situation called for. Constantine, in religious matters, generally showed indulgence toward the people, but impatience with those who would lead them astray. Most pagans could continue their traditional worship undisturbed, but Porphyry's anti-Christian writings—widely blamed for having instigated persecution—were to be burned.[152] Bishops who threatened the peace of the church, or teachers who spread heretical doctrine, earned the emperor's wrath, but ordinary believers were usually left untouched.

Constantine preached forbearance and restraint to his fellow Christians, even as his own actions often pointed in the opposite direction. Lactantius and Athanasius spoke of God's vengeance against persecutors and heretics, but Constantine was prepared to take action himself, when necessary, both to punish those who had persecuted the church and to deter those who would divide it. A politics of consensus does not necessarily imply tolerance—the greater the emphasis on unity, the greater the hostility against those who would threaten it with their dissent. "Coercive harmony," the violence of the center, would underpin the religious politics of the Christian empire. Whatever may have been Constantine's intentions, his actions laid the groundwork for later developments and sent his successors down a coercive path. Forbearance assumed that its beneficiaries, whether pagans or dissident Christians, would eventually find their way into the fold—and when this failed to happen, the emperors found it increasingly difficult to maintain their patience. Constans, in 347, would be enraged by the Donatists' "ungrateful" refusal of his generous gifts.[153] The tragedy of state violence lay in the fact that its perpetrators all too often believed themselves to be acting with the best of intentions: charity, didactic responsibility, and an authoritarian paternalism that allowed them to justify a "disciplinary" coercion they knew was in their subjects' own best interests.[154]

While Christian virtue might suggest forbearance in some circumstances, other times demanded action guided by a righteous zeal. Lactantius warned his readers not to expect restraint from God in the punishment of

151. See, e.g., Diocletian's *Edict on Maximum Prices.*
152. Socrates *HE* 1.9; cf. *C.Th.* 16.5.66.
153. See chapter 4, p. 135.
154. See further chapter 4 on this "disciplinary" paradigm of violence.

sin: toleration of evil is not a virtue.[155] In the decades after Constantine, zeal would drive many an extremist toward violence.[156] For an emperor to express righteous anger, however, flew in the face of centuries of philosophical advice. Imperial anger needed to be restrained and soothed by the careful *parrhesia* of sober counselors, because the consequences of its free exercise could be lethal.[157] In 387, amid the crisis of the Riot of the Statues, John Chrysostom offered to the current emperor an exemplary tale of Constantine's forbearance. When informed that rioters had defaced his imperial images, the emperor felt his face and commented, "I do not seem to have suffered any injury," before pardoning the offenders.[158] A good emperor, went the moral of the story, ought not to get upset at things like that. But of course Constantine did get angry on other occasions, most notably at those whose excessive zeal threatened consensus within the church. Religious leaders from Donatus to Athanasius had already experienced the emperor's anger. Constantine's successors would be no more successful than he had been at achieving harmony. For the next half century, ecclesiastical politics in the east would be inflamed by unceasing conflict among Nicenes, Homoians, Arians, and other factions. When imperial intervention met resistance, the result was persecution—and persecution, in turn, provoked martyrdom.

Late antique Christians were right to worry about the sword. The coercive power of the state threatened to corrupt the souls of those who employed it, to the extent that those already baptized might be advised to stay as far away from it as they could. Far more dangerous was the ease with which violence, once introduced into religious conflict, could spiral out of control and rebound against its users. The result, bloodshed within the walls of the church, will form the theme of the next chapter. Violence, Hannah

155. Lactantius, *On the Anger of God*, esp. 17–18. Compare Arendt 1970, p. 64, arguing for the appropriateness of rage in some situations; abstract detachment and lack of emotion are not necessarily the most "rational" responses.

156. See esp. chapter 5.

157. Late antique political and moral discourse placed a tremendous emphasis on containing the dangerous anger of rulers: see Brown 1992, esp. pp. 48–70; for classical antecedents see now Harris 2001, esp. chap. 10. For imperial anger and restraint in the context of disciplinary violence, see chapter 4, pp. 144–150 below. In later medieval societies, by contrast, calculated displays of rage by kings and aristocrats were expected or even encouraged: see several of the essays in Rosenwein 1998, esp. Althoff, "*Ira Regis*: Prolegomena to a History of Royal Anger" (pp. 59–74) and Stephen D. White, "The Politics of Anger" (pp. 127–152).

158. John Chrysostom, *Homilies on the Statues* 21.11. Cf. discussion of this anecdote in Drake 2000, pp. 473–474.

Arendt warns, always carries the danger that the means will overwhelm the ends for which they were employed.[159] Violence used for the sake of unity will likely shatter that unity. Lactantius, addressing the pagan persecutors, had made much the same point: "For if you wish to defend religion by bloodshed, and by tortures, and by guilt, it will no longer be defended, but will be polluted and profaned."[160]

159. Arendt 1970, p. 4.
160. Lactantius, *Divine Institutes* 5.20 (NPNF trans.).

2. "The God of the Martyrs Refuses You"

Religious Violence, Political Discourse, and Christian Identity in the Century after Constantine

In the year 355, the emperor Constantius applied heavy pressure to a group of pro-Nicene western bishops in order to persuade them to assent to a creed that avoided the controversial Nicene word *homoousios*, and to condemn the troublesome Athanasius of Alexandria. Constantius sought above all else to bring peace and consensus to a divided church, and was willing to use any means necessary, including violent force, to achieve that end. Pope Liberius of Rome, himself threatened by the emperor's representatives, praised the firm resistance of fellow bishops who had already been sent into exile: "Although under the guise of peace the enemy of the human race seems to have waxed more savage in his attacks upon the members of the church, your extraordinary and unique faith has shown you, priests most welcome to God, to be approved by God, and has marked you out already for future glory as martyrs."[1]

Christian bishops, refusing to obey the decrees of a Christian emperor, could find the same glory in their exile that the early martyrs had once achieved by death at the hands of pagan persecutors. Talk of "peace" in the church was only a cover for the devil's attack on the true faith.[2] But only a couple of years later, after he himself had been sent into exile, Liberius reversed himself and accepted the emperor's policy, signing the creed and condemning Athanasius. He did this, he said, for the sake of peace: "Because I

---

1. Liberius, *Letter to the bishops Eusebius, Dionysius and Lucifer,* in Hilary of Poitiers, *Against Valens and Ursacius* 2.4 (Wickham trans.).

2. Theodoret *HE* 4.22 records a supposed dialogue between Liberius and Constantius. The emperor angrily snapped, "How much of the universe are you, that you alone take part with an impious man and destroy the peace of the whole world?"

know you to be sons of peace, lovers of concord and harmony in the Catholic church, I address you, very dear lords and brothers, by this letter. I have not been forced by any necessity, as God is my witness, but I do it for the sake of the peace and concord which has prior place to martyrdom."[3]

It is quite likely that Liberius had changed his mind only under considerable coercive pressure. But his two statements can be taken to embody a conflict between two fundamentally different outlooks, a dichotomy that shaped the religious conflicts of the fourth century. Which was more important: zealous defense of orthodoxy, or compromise in the interest of consensus and unity? The Constantinian state sought peace in the church, and was willing to use its coercive powers to achieve that goal. The old pagan persecutions had sought to create a sense of unity among the diverse peoples of the Roman Empire by requiring universal religious observance. Those Christians who refused to sacrifice to the gods had been seen as enemies of peace, and had been treated accordingly by the same legal machinery that normally punished disobedience of imperial will. The Christian empire of Constantine and his successors likewise sought religious unity, replacing pagan sacrifice with Christian communion. Constantine summoned the Council of Nicaea in 325 in order to heal schisms within the church and to standardize the observance of Easter.[4] Those who resisted unity, because they did not wish to share communion with others whom they regarded as heretics, were troublemakers and were to be treated accordingly.

But the recusants, Christians who stood up to the emperor's will, did not accept the language of peace and unity. They justified their resistance through a different paradigm, invoking concepts of martyrdom inherited from the pagan persecutions of the past. Fourth-century Christians used discourses of martyrdom and persecution to problematize and challenge the state's exercise of power in religious affairs. Of particular interest here are situations in

---

3. Liberius, *Letter to the bishops Ursacius, Valens and Germinius*, in Hilary of Poitiers, *Against Valens and Ursacius* 2.9 (Wickham trans.). The surviving text of Liberius' letter is frequently interrupted by the bitter denunciations of a later copyist, inserting remarks such as "This is Arian falsehood!" and "Anathema to you, prevaricating Liberius!"

4. This initiative could be understood as an attempt to create the sense of "simultaneity" identified by Benedict Anderson as key to constructing an imagined community: Anderson 1991, pp. 22–36. Cf. p. 35: "Each communicant is well aware that the ceremony he performs is being replicated simultaneously by thousands (or millions) of others of whose existence he is confident, yet of whose identity he has not the slightest notion." Although Anderson is here referring to the quintessentially modern act of reading a newspaper, nevertheless the same sentence could plausibly be used to describe the Christian ritual of communion.

which Christians used the word "martyrdom" to refer to situations that did not neatly fit the traditional model inherited from pagan times.[5]

Christians in the fourth century used the memory of Diocletianic persecution to shape their own sense of history and community.[6] The prominence of martyrdom in the historical consciousness of post-Constantinian Christianity should not, however, lead us to assume that martyrdom and persecution in the fourth and fifth centuries were simply history, things of the past. The Christianization of the Roman state certainly did not bring an end to religious strife and violence. Christianity's new access to political and economic power meant that disputes within the Christian community could lead to as much bloodshed as had any previous conflict with pagans, with the added complication that those who carried out violent persecution might now call themselves Christians.[7]

The Christian experience of violence during the pagan persecutions shaped the ideologies and practices that drove further religious conflicts over the course of the fourth and fifth centuries, as Christianity both became the dominant religious faith and fragmented under the pressure of its own internal divisions. The formative experience of martyrdom and persecution determined the ways in which later Christians would both use and experience violence under the Christian empire. Discourses of martyrdom and persecution formed the symbolic language through which Christians represented, justified, or denounced the use of violence.

In the fourth and fifth centuries, Christian orthodoxy became an increasingly significant ideological underpinning of the Roman imperial state's claim to legitimacy. As we shall see, Christian emperors, though enjoying power that was theoretically absolute, often found their capacity to use that power restrained by ideological critiques articulated in terms of the Christian rhetoric of martyrdom and persecution. Invocation of "martyrdom" served to legitimize and even sanctify resistance to imperial power, and emperors were often forced to tolerate such defiance lest in crushing it they might acquire the unwholesome label of "persecutor."

In the post-Constantinian empire, the rhetorical construction and polem-

---

5. Writing of a slightly earlier historical context, Daniel Boyarin has recently argued for treating "martyrdom" not as an essence with a fixed definition, but "as a 'discourse,' as a practice of dying for God and of talking about it, a discourse that changes and develops over time." Boyarin 1999, p. 94.

6. See chapter 1, pp. 43–45.

7. B. Gregory 1999 gives a compelling treatment of a similar situation in Reformation-era Europe, when competing Christian communities each celebrated their own martyrs while justifying persecution of the others.

ical representation of violence played a key role in defining the "imagined community" of Nicene orthodox Christianity, marking the boundaries of that community and dividing "true" Christians from heretics, schismatics, pagans, and other supposed enemies of the faith. At the same time, the discourse of martyrdom and persecution also shaped and limited the ways in which the secular authorities were able to use their coercive power. These two factors played a key role in forming Christian conceptions of legitimate authority, both religious and political, in an age when the boundary between secular and ecclesiastical spheres was rapidly eroding.

The decades following the conversion of Constantine were a time of intense religious turmoil. Fourth-century church history appears to the modern student as a tangled mess of doctrinal controversies, schisms, councils, disputed episcopal elections, and riots.[8] These conflicts derived in large part from disputes over Trinitarian doctrine, specifically regarding how the relationship between God the Father and God the Son was to be understood. The "Homoousian" or Nicene party, named after the Council of Nicaea in 325 that ratified this doctrinal position, taught that the Son was "of the same substance" (*homoousios*) with the Father, and opposed itself to the doctrine of dissimilarity originally put forward by the presbyter Arius and thus commonly called "Arian." Because the Nicene party eventually prevailed—the imperial government finally threw its weight behind Homoousian doctrine at the Council of Constantinople in 381, and the Nicene creed remains an article of faith for most Christian denominations to this day—most of our sources tend to refer to the Nicenes as "the orthodox" and their rivals as "heretics." Needless to say, these are highly subjective categories whose precise definition depends very much upon where one stands.[9] Recent scholarship has warned us against being misled by the tendency of our overwhelmingly Nicene sources to press the tremendous complexity of fourth-century ecclesiastical history into a simple dichotomy of Nicene versus Arian or orthodoxy versus heresy.[10]

8. A brief and general narrative can be found in Frend 1984, pp. 473–538. Stevenson 1989 excerpts many of the relevant sources, including numerous creeds and definitions generated by different parties over the course of the fourth century. For a massive and thorough treatment of the doctrinal aspects of the Trinitarian controversy, see Hanson 1988. See also Simonetti 1975, Brennecke 1988. A detailed political narrative centered around the long and controversial career of Athanasius, bishop of Alexandria, can be found in T. Barnes 1993.

9. On this point Bauer 1934 is fundamental. On a key figure from the "Arian" side, see now Vaggione 2000.

10. See esp. Lyman 1993 in Barnes and Williams 1993, along with other essays in the same volume. On the polemical construction of Arius as "arch-heretic," see Wiles 1996.

Christian historical tradition placed great emphasis upon the role of persecution in shaping Christian identity. Eusebius had built his account of the first three centuries of Christian history around successive episodes of pagan persecution finally brought to an end by the conversion of Constantine. The church historians of the early fifth century picked up where he left off and looked back on the previous century as the time when Nicene orthodox Christianity took shape through decades of conflict and persecution by a variety of imperially-backed heresies misleadingly lumped together under the catchall label "Arian," creating a triumphalist narrative of struggle culminating in the victory of Nicene orthodoxy in 381.[11]

We do not fully appreciate the ideological and polemical power inherent in the Christian discourse of martyrdom and persecution until we consider the implications of using this language to characterize conflict within the Christian church. Although the application of this discourse became considerably more flexible over the course of the fourth century, still a Christian audience remained well aware of its original grounding in the time of pagan persecution, when "martyrdom" meant being killed for refusing to deny Christ. Where there is a martyr, of course, there must also be a persecutor. When, for instance, the emperor Constantius tried to force acceptance of a compromise creed that sidestepped Nicaea and avoided the controversial term *homoousios*,[12] Athanasius and other Nicene leaders could denounce this policy as "persecution" and celebrate those who suffered exile or violence for their adherence to the Nicene cause as "martyrs." Implicitly—or sometimes explicitly—Athanasius represented the theological position of his opponents, however sincerely Christian it might be when understood in its own context, as being equivalent to "denying Christ."[13] Thus he could redefine the very concept of Christian community, restricting it to only those who espoused Nicene Trinitarian doctrine and who remained in communion with himself.[14] All others were pushed outside the boundaries and classified as "persecutors" not fundamentally different from the pagans.

---

11. The label "Arianism" itself illustrates a key way in which the discourse of orthodoxy and heresy can be used to delegitimize a rival group. By naming "heretical" or schismatic groups after their supposed founders, one denies them the name "Christian," by which they would have undoubtedly preferred to call themselves.

12. See, e.g., the Second Creed of Sirmium in 357: text in Hilary of Poitiers, *De Synodis* 11; Athanasius *De Synodis* 28.

13. See, e.g., *Historia Arianorum* 79: "Nor will they [the Melitian schismatics] esteem it an evil thing to deny Christ."

14. Athanasius, one of the most effective and articulate Christian authors of the fourth century, whose works have survived in great quantity, is used here and throughout this chapter as a case study representative of polemical strategies used

Orthodoxy and heresy, of course, had always been used by Christian authorities to set boundaries, to include and exclude. Heretics, the "enemy within," were commonly seen as a far greater and more insidious danger to the faith than external enemies such as pagans or Jews, precisely because they disguised their iniquity under a "pretense" of Christianity.[15] But the conversion of Constantine brought Christian leaders new access to political and economic power, and specifically created the possibility for the coercive power of the state to play a role in intra-Christian conflicts. Where previously the discourse of martyrdom and persecution had served mainly to distinguish a supposedly unified Christian community from a hostile pagan world, now it helped to divide Christianity against itself.

Appeals to the familiar discourse of martyrdom and persecution in fourth-century religious conflicts allowed each side to focus its polemical efforts on the other's supposed reliance on state power. The exaggerated prominence of the emperor's role, as represented in contemporary sources, played a major part in forming historians' impression of the late Roman and Byzantine Empire as a system characterized by "caesaropapism," the supposed dominance of the emperor over the church.[16] In fact, it would be far more accurate to state the opposite proposition: late antiquity can be seen as a period in which the state's new devotion to Christianity allowed Christian religious authorities, whether bishops or charismatic holy men, to claim an unprecedented degree of secular political and economic power.[17] Most significantly, bishops whom the imperial court accepted as legitimate could employ the state's coercive apparatus to their own ends.

How was it to be decided, then, which bishops could legitimately exercise such authority? The religious conflicts of the fourth century were driven

---

by all parties (both Nicene and non-Nicene) in the fourth-century conflicts. On Athanasius' rhetoric, see Stead 1976.

15. See, e.g., *Historia Arianorum* 64, crediting the pagans as "not as bad" as the Arians. On polemical models of heresy see Le Boulluec 1985, Pagels 1995. The rhetoric of "false pretense," deriving ultimately from Jesus' warning against "false prophets" and "wolves in sheep's clothing" (Matthew 7:15), is in itself a fascinating subject: see T. Shaw 1995. The partisan rancor that characterized doctrinal conflict was considerably exacerbated by the common conviction that one's opponent was motivated not by unintentional error but by a conscious and deceitful intent to corrupt the faith.

16. For a historiographical critique of the concept, see Geanakoplos 1965, Sansterre 1972, Dagron 1996.

17. On bishops' new legal privileges and powers, see, e.g., Lamoreaux 1995. The new possibilities for exercise of political, economic, or charismatic power by Christian bishops and holy men are well illustrated by Brown 1992.

partly by theological controversy, partly by personal ambition and rivalry, but also by serious concerns over how to regulate an episcopal power that had expanded so dramatically into the secular sphere. Charges brought against bishops by their enemies devoted as much attention to issues of misconduct and abuse of power as to doctrinal error.[18] The episcopal factions that dominated the political landscape of the fourth-century church, usefully described as in many ways analogous to modern political parties, coalesced both around doctrinal positions and around powerful personalities such as Athanasius of Alexandria or Eusebius of Nicomedia.[19] Given that for the most part the fourth-century church lacked a strong and cohesive hierarchical structure above the level of the individual bishopric, and that Constantine's grants of privileges to the church had left bishops and clergy essentially immune from secular justice, the only way in which ecclesiastical conflicts could be resolved, or accusations against individual bishops adjudicated, was through the convocation of a council of bishops.[20] The Council of Nicaea, the first empire-wide or "ecumenical" gathering of Christian prelates, had set a pattern in 325 that would be followed by most subsequent synods for the remainder of the fourth century.

An assembly of bishops offered a weight of authority greater than that of any individual. When they spoke in unison, their consensus would be taken as evidence of divine inspiration. Christian emperors, who from Constantine onward believed it their divinely ordained duty to guarantee the unity and concord of the church, attempted to resolve problems primarily by summoning councils. In nearly all cases where the imperial government deposed or exiled a bishop or used coercive violence against a congregation, the secular authorities understood themselves to be doing nothing more than enforcing judgments made by a synod of bishops.[21]

Yet in fact councils were as likely to exacerbate conflict as they were to resolve it. The outcome of a particular synod depended very much on which bishops were able to attend and who had the power to set the agenda, and accordingly those bishops who enjoyed the support of the imperial authorities exercised a clear advantage. On the other hand, a council stacked too obviously in favor of one side could then be denounced by opponents as "illegitimate." Such proceedings tended to generate a barrage of charges and countercharges, of bias ("accusers allowed to sit as judges"), forgery of tran-

18. See chapter 7, pp. 268–281.
19. Political parties: see Löhr 1993.
20. On the workings of councils, see Amidon 1979.
21. As T. Barnes 1993, pp. 165–175, points out.

scripts or signatures, or coercion, bishops forced by threat of exile or violence to subscribe to the council's decision.[22]

A far deeper problem was that emperor and bishops disagreed at a fundamental level as to exactly what a council was supposed to accomplish. Hard-liners among the bishops saw a synod as occasion to define the faith more precisely, the better to distinguish truth from falsehood. But the emperor's instinct, when faced with doctrinal controversy, was to find consensus through compromise. Thus both Constantius (337–361) and Valens (364–378) threw their weight behind the so-called Homoian Trinitarian doctrine, which stated simply, "The Son is like the Father," and thus sought to renounce Arian formulations of the Son's dissimilarity and subordination while at the same time avoiding the controversial Nicene term, *homoousios*. The emperors supported Homoian doctrine as a sensible middle way between two extremes, an inclusive compromise formula to which, they hoped, all could agree.[23] If a handful of extremists on either side refused to go along, they could legitimately be punished as troublemakers bent on disturbing the peace of the church.[24] Throughout the fourth century, however, emperors seem to have been continually caught off guard by the intensity of resistance to their religious policies. Such opposition became particularly effective when expressed in the language of persecution and martyrdom.

PERSECUTION

The means of violence employed by the Roman state in fourth-century sectarian conflicts were similar to those that had been used during prior pagan persecutions, and they were deployed to the same end, to coerce obedience. But there was one important difference. Under the Christian empire, the imperial authorities often used their coercive power against Christian dissidents at the behest of Christian bishops. Constantinian legislation explic-

22. Certainly the most famous example of the ways in which councils could be delegitimized is the so-called *latrocinium* or "Robber Council" of 449, on which see chapter 8. Cf. also B. Shaw 1992 for a searching analysis of the Conference of Carthage (411), at which the Donatists were able to manipulate the proceedings of an event very much stacked against them, in such a way as to force their challenges to the council's legitimacy into the official documentary transcript.

23. On the Homoian "Reichskirche" of Constantius and Valens, see Brennecke 1988. Homoians, like all other non-Nicene groups, are lumped together in Nicene sources as "Arians," despite the fact that they themselves had formally condemned Arius.

24. Thus Constantine had eventually lost patience with Athanasius: see chapter 1, pp. 60–62.

itly directed local officials to enforce synodal decisions as law. If a bishop was deposed by an imperially recognized synod but refused to relinquish his seat, for example, secular power might be called in to force him out. Those who continued to challenge synodal authority by refusing to sign a creed could be punished by the secular authorities with exile.[25] When bishops recognized by the emperor had deposed Athanasius and appointed George to the episcopacy of Alexandria, the ensuing violent persecution of Athanasian supporters could be understood and justified as the discipline of a rebellious congregation. In many instances, as we shall see, individual bishops borrowed the services of soldiers and local magistrates to repress opponents.

But while bishops often took the initiative in employing the violence of the state, victims of such action chose to see it as persecution, emphasizing the emperor's role, in order to cast it as an unacceptable intrusion of worldly forces into church affairs. Bishops who employed the power of the state could be tarred by their association with persecution, an accusation with powerful resonance even after the end of pagan rule. One could delegitimize a bishop simply by calling attention to his use of secular violence. The image of the heretical bishop surrounded by imperial soldiers found strikingly effective use in polemic. When a bishop resorted to the coercive apparatus of the state, critics could represent him as being unduly dependent upon those powers, a mere servant of the emperor. Because he lacked the support of God and of the Christian people, he could only take possession of his see with the support of soldiers. In this manner Peter, Athanasius' successor as Nicene bishop of Alexandria, described the entrance of the emperor's candidate, the Homoian bishop Lucius, into the city:

> In this state of things when even I had withdrawn from the church—
> for how could I remain where troops were coming in—where a mob
> was bribed to violence—where all were striving for gain—where mobs
> of heathen were making mighty promises?—forth, forsooth, is sent
> a successor in my place. It was one named Lucius, who had bought the
> bishopric as he might some dignity of this world, eager to maintain
> the bad character and conduct of a wolf. No synod of orthodox bishops
> had chosen him; no vote of genuine clergy; no laity had demanded him;
> as the laws of the church enjoin. Lucius could not make his entrance
> into the city without parade, and so he was appropriately escorted not
> by bishops, not by presbyters, not by deacons, not by multitudes of the
> laity; no monks preceded him chanting psalms from the Scriptures; but
> there was Euzoius, once a deacon of our city of Alexandria, and long

25. Cf. T. Barnes 1993, pp. 165–175, stressing fourth-century emperors' deference to the will of bishops in synod.

since degraded along with Arius in the great and holy synod of Nicaea, and more recently raised to rule and ravage the see of Antioch, and there, too, was Magnus the treasurer, notorious for every kind of impiety, leading a vast body of troops.[26]

During the period after 325 and prior to 381, the bishops associated with the Nicene cause usually did not enjoy imperial support, and indeed suffered frequently for their resistance to imperial attempts to impose non-Nicene compromise doctrines, or for their refusal to communicate with bishops favored by the emperor. Nicene sources from this period tended to justify their defiance of the emperor by appeal to a rhetoric of separation between secular and ecclesiastical spheres: a good Christian emperor ought to "render unto Caesar the things that are Caesar's, and to God the things that are God's," and should not usurp the spiritual authority of bishops by presuming to intervene in the affairs of the church. Athanasius denounced Constantius' support for the "Arian" bishops attempting to depose him:

> For if a judgment [i.e. that Athanasius be deposed] had been passed
> by bishops what concern had the emperor with it? Or if it was only a
> threat of the emperor, what need in that case was there of the so-called
> bishops? When was such a thing heard of before from the beginning
> of the world? When did a judgment of the church receive its validity
> from the emperor, or rather when was his decree ever recognized by
> the church? . . . Now however we have witnessed a novel spectacle,
> which is an invention of the Arian heresy. Heretics have assembled
> together with the emperor Constantius, in order that he, alleging the
> authority of the bishops, may exercise his power against whomsoever
> he pleases, and while he persecutes may avoid the name of persecutor.[27]

This is not the place to explore the massive body of literature treating legal, theological, or moral concepts of church-state separation over the centuries. Within the specific historical circumstances of the fourth century, it is important to keep in mind that appeals for religious toleration, and criticism of state intervention in religious affairs, tended to come from those who found themselves on the wrong side of such intrusion.[28] An emperor's

26. *Letter of Peter of Alexandria,* in Theodoret *HE* 4.22 (trans. NPNF).
27. *Historia Arianorum* 52 (trans. NPNF).
28. Appeals to toleration and freedom of conscience can be found in several Christian sources dating from times of pagan persecution, e.g., Tertullian, *Apology;* Lactantius, *Divine Institutes* 5.19–20, with discussion in Digeser 2000, pp. 91–114; and see generally Garnsey 1984. Nicene sources make similar pleas against "Arian" imperial policy in the mid-fourth century: see, e.g., Hilary of Poitiers' *Letter to Constantius;* Lucifer of Cagliari. The attitude symbolized by the remark, "What has the emperor to do with the church?" attributed to Donatus of Carthage, emerged only

participation was generally welcomed when used in the service of ortho-doxy.[29] Up until the last quarter of the fourth century, then, we find Nicenes usually opposing an imperial role in church affairs and "Arians" often fa-voring it; after 381, the political situation reversed itself and ideological arguments changed accordingly. Still, the political context in which some of these critiques of imperial intervention took place should not blind us to the fact that they were able to appeal to very real concerns shared by many Christians about the proper relationship between the authority of the church and the power of the state. In the mid-fourth century, many could still remember the days when that same power had attempted to de-stroy the Christian religion entirely, and to force the faithful into pagan worship. In Constantinople in the 350s, bishop Macedonius reportedly wrenched open the mouths of recusants and physically compelled them to receive communion.[30] The response to such force was to argue that reli-gion coerced could never be true religion—and by extension, that the use of violent coercion inherently delegitimized the cause for which it was used.[31] "Arianism," in this view, could be proven wrong not only on the-

---

as a consequence of the imperial government's decision to force the Donatists into communion with the Catholic church. Pagans, too, began in the late fourth century to praise the virtues of religious toleration, when their own faith came under in-creasing pressure from the Christian regime: see, e.g., Libanius' complaint to Theo-dosius on behalf of the temples (discussed in chapter 6); Themistius' oration to Valens; or Symmachus' petitions regarding the Altar of Victory. Ando 1996 shows how these late fourth-century defenders of paganism borrowed language and arguments from second- and third-century Christian apologists.

29. Even the Donatists had initially placed their hope in imperial intervention, when they made their first appeal to Constantine: see chapter 1, pp. 50–52. For oth-ers in praise of state power, see, e.g., Firmicus Maternus, whose *Against the Errors of the Pagan Religion* argued in the 340s that the emperors should forcibly suppress paganism; or Augustine's elaborate justifications of the coercive measures applied by the state against his Donatist rivals in North Africa, on which see Brown 1963 and chapter 4 below. The fifth-century church historian Socrates sometimes endorsed imperial intervention by Theodosius and his successors, finding it a necessary anti-dote to the "divisive factionalism" of the bishops: see Urbainczyk 1997, pp. 139–167, and chapter 8, p. 316 below.

30. Extant sources for this complaint (Socrates *HE* 2.27 and 2.38; Sozomen *HE* 4.2–3 and 4.20–21) date only from the early fifth century, and no doubt contain some hyperbole, as the authors attempt to rework the story into a classic tale of persecution. They credit Macedonius with many other atrocities and explicitly com-pare his conduct to that of the pagan persecutors of old. But real coercion was used, probably by the same people, and in much the same way, and for more or less the same purpose (religious unity, by any means necessary) as in pagan times. Even Constantius—who shared Macedonius' theological views—finally lost patience with the trouble caused by the bishop's violent behavior and deposed him.

31. A point made by Lactantius, *Divine Institutes* 5.20.

ological grounds but simply because of its dependence on violence and on imperial power.[32]

The legacy of the Great Persecution had left Christians with a lingering distrust of the imperial state, and a fear that the church would be polluted or corrupted through excessive entanglement with secular power. Many centuries before Max Weber, Christians recognized state power to be essentially violent in nature. In the fourth century, some Christians still clung to earlier beliefs that professions that involved the use of violence—such as the military, or any secular magistracy responsible for judicial torture or capital punishment—were fundamentally incompatible with Christian communion.[33] In the context of fourth-century religious conflicts, as we shall see, any exercise of coercive state power was experienced and characterized by those on the receiving end as "violent," in the sense of a "violation" or intrusion of profane and worldly power into the sacred space of the church.

Though the violence associated with fourth-century religious conflicts came in a wide variety of forms, I will focus my analysis here on one type that appears quite frequently in sources representing different sides of the controversy, and in a surprisingly consistent manner: the picture of armed soldiers violently invading a church or disrupting religious services. This image is both literal—it describes a number of real incidents that happened on particular occasions, under fairly similar circumstances—and allegorical. It symbolizes for the Christian audience the destructive consequences of state intrusion into religious affairs, and the corrupting effect of worldly power and particularly of violent power upon the church.

A representative example may be taken from the petition made by the Christian followers of Athanasius in the Alexandrian church, decrying an attack upon their congregation in 356 when the imperial government made the latest in a long series of attempts to depose Athanasius from the Alexandrian episcopate and install a candidate more friendly to the Homoian "Arian" party favored by the emperor Constantius:

> While we were keeping vigil in the Lord's house, and engaged in our prayers, suddenly about midnight the most illustrious *dux* Syrianus attacked us and the church with many legions of soldiers armed with naked swords and javelins and other warlike instruments, and wearing helmets on their heads; and actually while we were praying, and while the lessons were being read, they broke down the doors. And when the

32. See, e.g., *Historia Arianorum* 67.
33. See further discussion of this issue in chapter 1, pp. 62–63.

doors were burst open by the violence of the multitude, he gave command, and some of them were shooting; others shouting, their weapons rattling, and their swords flashing in the light of the lamps; and
forthwith virgins were being slain, many men trampled down, and
falling over one another as the soldiers came upon them, and several
were pierced with arrows and perished. Some of the soldiers also
were betaking themselves to plunder, and were stripping the virgins,
who were more afraid of being even touched by them than they were
of death. . . . And when they saw that many had perished, they gave
orders to the soldiers to remove out of sight the bodies of the dead.
But the most holy virgins who were left behind were buried in the
tombs, having attained the glory of martyrdom in the time of the most
religious Constantius. Deacons also were beaten with stripes even in
the Lord's house, and were shut up there. Nor did matters stop even
here; for after all this had happened, whosoever pleased broke open
any door that he could, and searched, and plundered what was within.
They entered even into those places which not even all Christians are
allowed to enter.[34]

The irony would not be lost upon those who read the petition: Christian
martyrs were "attaining their glory" at the hands of a Christian emperor,
the son of Constantine, "the most religious Constantius." Some fifty years
later, John Chrysostom complained in nearly identical terms of an attack on
his followers:

A dense troop of soldiers, on the great Sabbath itself, as the day was
hastening toward eventide, having broken into the churches violently
drove out all the clergy who were with us, and surrounded the sanctuary with arms. And women from the oratories who had stripped
themselves for baptism just at that time, fled unclothed, from terror
at this grievous assault . . . indeed many received wounds before they
were expelled, and the baptismal pools were filled with blood, and the
sacred water reddened by it. Nor did the distress cease even at this
point; but the soldiers, some of whom as we understand were unbaptized, having entered the place where the sacred vessels were stored,
saw all the things which were inside it, and the most holy blood of

---

34. "Protest [*diamartyria*] of the Alexandrian church," quoted in Athanasius,
Historia Arianorum 81 (trans. NPNF). The wordplay between *diamartyria* ("protest" or "testimony") and martyrdom, *martyria*, both in its literal sense of testifying or bearing witness and its specifically Christian sense of dying for the faith, should
not be overlooked here. The petitioners reiterate the point by proclaiming their willingness to be martyred: "Now if an order has been given that we should be persecuted, we are all ready to suffer martyrdom."

Christ, as might happen in the midst of such confusion, was spilt upon the garments of the soldiers; and every kind of outrage was committed as in a barbarian siege.[35]

Though Chrysostom's troubles took place in an entirely different political context in which no doctrinal issues were at stake, years after the effective end of Nicene-Arian conflict, he was nevertheless able to draw upon the same tropes of martyrdom, persecution, and secular violation of ecclesiastical space that had featured so prominently in fourth-century controversy. Numerous other examples from the intervening decades can be cited, drawing upon a fairly consistent list of atrocities that all in one way or another are to be understood as violation.[36]

First and most obviously, the sacred space of the church was understood to be violated by the presence of non-Christians. Our sources make much of the supposed complicity of pagans, Jews, or Manichaeans in these attacks upon the orthodox. The Alexandrian incidents offer lurid descriptions of desecration: pagans performed blood sacrifice within the church, or sent transvestites and naked boys to dance obscenely atop the holy altar.[37] Those who attempted to cast the use of the state's coercive power as persecution had their task made easier by the fact that the mechanisms through which the state exercised coercion were fundamentally the same under the Constantinian empire as they had been in the days of pagan persecution. In the mid-fourth century, particularly, many of the individuals charged with carrying out repressive policies—soldiers, officers, magistrates, judges, jailors, torturers, etc.—were still pagans, a fact critics did not hesitate to seize upon:

Philagrius, who has long been a persecutor of the church and her virgins, and is now prefect of Egypt, an apostate already . . . and supported by Eusebius and his fellows, and therefore full of zeal against the church;

---

35. John Chrysostom, *Letter to Pope Innocent* 4 (trans. NPNF).
36. For attacks on churches specifically: at least three separate episodes in Alexandria, in 339 (Athanasius, *Encyclical Letter* and *Historia Arianorum* 10); 356 (Athanasius, *Apology for his Flight* 6, 24; *Historia Arianorum* 55–56, 59, 72, 81); and 373 (*Letter of Peter of Alexandria*, in Theodoret *HE* 4.22). The Donatist *Sermon on the Passion of Donatus of Avioccala* (see pp. 54–55 above) narrates a basilica massacre in a manner that conforms almost perfectly to the model laid out here. For attacks on clergy, monks, and virgins more generally: Socrates *HE* 2.27 and 2.38 on the persecutions of bishop Macedonius of Constantinople; letter of the Eastern bishops at the Council of Sardica (343) (quoted in Hilary of Poitiers, *Against Valens and Ursacius* 1.2), offering a nearly identical catalogue of atrocities, but this time casting Athanasius and other Nicene bishops as the villains.
37. See *Historia Arianorum* 55–56 and 59; *Letter of Peter of Alexandria*, in Theodoret *HE* 4.22.

this person, by means of promises . . . succeeded in gaining over the pagan mob, together with Jews and disorderly persons, and having excited their passions, sent them in a body with swords and clubs into the churches to attack the people.[38]

Even without deliberate acts of desecration, the mere presence of the uninitiated and unbaptized within the sanctuary constituted a violation of the holy mysteries, as Chrysostom complained in the passage quoted above. Attempts by representatives of secular authority to flaunt their power within the sacred space of the church were particularly offensive. Thus in 347 the imperial commissioner Macarius enraged Donatist opinion by displaying imperial images at church altars.[39] In Egypt, supporters of Athanasius raised similar objections to the manner in which the secular authorities conducted an investigation into charges that Athanasius or one of his henchmen had smashed a sacred chalice and overturned an altar belonging to the schismatic Melitian church. Because the subject of the inquiry necessarily touched upon the holy mysteries, it was entirely inappropriate for non-Christians and representatives of the secular power even to be in the room, let alone preside, while the matter was being discussed.[40]

Secular power polluted holy space above all because of its association with violence. Our sources dwell in considerable detail upon the sacrilege of blood spilled within the precincts of the church. John Chrysostom's graphic depiction of blood mixing with baptismal water served to charge his Christian adversaries with desecrating one of the church's holiest sacraments, a ritual that defined membership in the Christian community. At the same time, the juxtaposition of blood and water deliberately recalled traditional accounts of the martyrs, whose violent ends were often characterized as "baptism by blood."[41] Not even the body and blood of Christ, understood to be present in the form of the consecrated bread and wine, nor the sacred vessels that contained them, escaped violation. Accounts of violence in church naturally emphasized damage and desecration inflicted upon such

38. Athanasius, *Encyclical Letter* 3. Compare *Historia Arianorum* 59, "They had to assist them in their wickedness the *dux* Sebastianus, a Manichaean," and the *Letter of Peter,* describing yet another persecution ordered by the emperor and his Homoian advisors: "Palladius, governor of the province, by sect a pagan, and one who habitually prostrated himself before idols, had frequently entertained the thought of waging war against Christ . . . "

39. Optatus, *Against the Donatists* 3.11. This episode is discussed in chapter 3, p. 106.

40. Athanasius, *Apology against the Arians* 14. Charges of sacrilege against Athanasius are discussed further in chapter 7, pp. 278–279.

41. See, e.g., Tertullian, *On Baptism* 16; Origen *On Martyrdom* 30.

objects, even if in some cases it was nothing more than an inadvertent or accidental consequence of the authorities' attempt to gain control of the building. Any use of violent force within the church was inherently sacrilegious. The sacred space of the church sanctuary stood for the church as an imagined community, and the troubles of that community were symbolized and predicted in visions of such profanation. Athanasius, we are told, dreamed that he saw mules kicking over the altar in the church, and by this vision knew that persecution of the faithful would soon resume.[42]

The mere sight of weapons within the walls of the church made a shocking spectacle: the means of violence seemed nearly as sacrilegious as the violence itself. After the armed attack on the church of Alexandria in 356, the congregation carefully gathered up weapons discarded in the course of the fighting, and put them on public display within the church as proof of what had happened:

> For the bodies of the slain which were discovered and were exposed
> in public, and the bows and arrows and other arms found in the Lord's
> house, loudly proclaim the iniquity. . . . Evidence of the nature of this
> hostile assault is afforded by the fact that the armor and javelins and
> swords borne by those who entered were left in the Lord's house. They
> have been hung up in the church to this time, that they might not be
> able to deny it, and although they sent several times Dynamius the
> general, as well as the commander of the city guards, desiring to take
> them away, we would not allow it, until the circumstance was known
> to all.[43]

Rather than simply cleansing the church from the pollution of bloodshed, the Alexandrians opted instead to perpetuate the sacrilege, but turn its taint back against the perpetrators by displaying the instruments of desecration within the sacred space of the church. These unholy relics, so to speak, constituted a striking visual polemic whose effectiveness was confirmed by the repeated and embarrassed attempts of the authorities to suppress the display.[44]

Sacrilege could also be found in the violence inflicted upon the persons of clerics, monks, and virgins—groups who by virtue of their holiness and status within the church were legally and morally supposed to be immune from the violence of the secular world. This idea that physical violence was more

42. Sozomen *HE* 6.5.
43. "Protest *[diamartyria]* of the Alexandrian church," quoted in Athanasius, *Historia Arianorum* 81 (trans. NPNF).
44. Compare the Donatist *Sermon on Avioccala* (discussed in chapter 1), for commemoration of a similar massacre by an inscription "visible to this day."

wrong when suffered by certain classes of people than by others reflected the longstanding distinction made by the Roman penal system between *honestiores*, members of the elites whose crimes were usually to be punished by fines, confiscation of property, or exile, and *humiliores*, the lower orders, for whom the same crimes would bring flogging, branding, mutilation, or other forms of gruesome and exemplary bodily punishment.[45] Violence used against those who ought to be exempt from it was truly a violation of accepted norms, and on several occasions bishops or clergy arrived at a council publicly displaying the scars on their bodies, or the chains and manacles with which they had been unlawfully imprisoned, as a dramatic visual indictment of the wrongs done them by their opponents.[46] When taken within the conceptual framework of martyrdom and persecution, moreover, such a spectacle acquired a deeper meaning. Scars of persecution, proudly displayed, marked a Christian as one of the confessors, like those who had endured torture and survived during the Great Persecution. They were revered by other Christians with a devotion nearly equal to that given to actual martyrs, the very wounds upon their bodies testifying to their holiness.[47]

The violence directed against consecrated virgins, prominent in nearly every episode of persecution narrated by our sources, deserves special comment. In addition to the beatings and tortures inflicted upon male and female ecclesiastics alike, female virgins were regularly singled out for particularly degrading treatment, on some occasions actual rape, at other times what seems to have been an almost ritualized public "stripping."[48] While men might achieve spiritual authority in a variety of ways, the sacral status of these women within the church depended much more exclusively upon

45. See MacMullen 1990b and 1974.

46. At the Council of Sardica in 343, e.g.: Athanasius, *Apology against the Arians* 45.

47. Cf. Socrates *HE* 1.11 on Constantine's great reverence for confessors: "Paphnutius was bishop of one of the cities in the Upper Thebaid; he was a man so favored by God that extraordinary miracles were done by him. In the time of the persecution he had been deprived of one of his eyes. The emperor honored this man exceedingly, and often sent for him to the palace, and kissed the part where the eye had been torn out." (NPNF trans.)

48. Cf. the complaint of the Sardican bishops against Athanasius' ally, the pro-Nicene bishop, Marcellus of Ancyra: "Holy virgins vowed to God and Christ, their clothes dragged off, he exposed with horrifying foulness in the forum and the city center to the gathered populace." (Hilary of Poitiers, *Against Valens and Ursacius* 1.2.9.) Attacks on Donatist virgins are alleged in the *Sermon on Avioccala* (5). During the reign of Julian, pagan mobs in Gaza subjected Christian virgins to similar treatment: Theodoret *HE* 3.7. Sozomen *HE* 5.10 describes the same incident, but places it in Heliopolis/Baalbek.

their chastity and modesty as markers of holiness, and so an attack from that quarter was understood to be especially damaging. In contrast to the pious and chaste virgins of the orthodox, meanwhile, polemical literature pointed to rowdy and unchaste women associated with heretics, who commonly suborned prostitutes to make false accusations against orthodox bishops.[49]

But violation was not just limited to the body of the woman. The virgin's body was commonly taken to stand for the imagined "body" of the entire church, both being symbolically understood as the "bride of Christ." The church building also carried a certain bodily symbolism, so that violation either of the virgin or of the sanctuary constituted both assault and insult against the entire imagined community of Christians, and indeed against the very body of Christ. Athanasius, denouncing "Arian" opponents who had allegedly ordered consecrated virgins to be stripped and publicly scourged, made the symbolism abundantly clear:

> Pilate, to gratify the Jews of old, pierced one of our Savior's sides with a spear. These men have exceeded the madness of Pilate, for they have scourged not one but both his sides; for the limbs of the virgins are in an especial manner the Savior's own. All men shudder at hearing the mere recital of deeds like these. These men alone did not fear to strip and to scourge those undefiled limbs which the virgins had dedicated solely to our Savior Christ.[50]

Mary Douglas has identified and characterized the near-universal human tendency to build symbolic systems around the human body as a central metaphor for society. Women's bodies, in particular, often become the site upon which fears of sexual pollution or boundary transgression are played out. The violation of a single body can thus be elevated to the level

49. A prostitute named Athanasius as her lover, but then failed to recognize his face in court: Sozomen *HE* 2.25. But the story is probably a *topos*, since anti-Athanasian sources accuse the Nicenes of employing an identical stratagem against Eusebius of Nicomedia: Philostorgius *HE* 2.11. Brakke 1995a, pp. 57–79, points out that consecrated virgins in fact played a far more active role in fourth-century conflicts than these sources' presentation of entirely passive victims might suggest. There seems to have been a considerable number of virgins among the followers of Arius in Alexandria, and Athanasius' outraged account of the "insulting" behavior of Arian women may give us some idea of the role such women might have played on both sides: "They also gave permission to the females of their party to insult whom they chose; and although the holy and faithful women [of the Athanasian camp] withdrew on one side, and gave them the way, yet they gathered around them like Bacchanals and Furies, and esteemed it a misfortune if they found no means to injure them . . . " (*Historia Arianorum* 59). On stereotypes of "heretical women," see Burrus 1991.

50. Athanasius, *Apology before Constantius* 33.

of an offense against the whole community for which that body stands as a symbol.[51]

Long before Mary Douglas, of course, there was Athanasius. The bishop opened his *Encyclical Letter* of 339, which detailed the stripping of virgins alongside numerous other Arian atrocities resulting from an armed assault upon the church, by recounting a gruesome story from the Book of Judges.[52] When a Levite's concubine had been raped and murdered, the aggrieved man cut up her body and sent one piece to each of the twelve tribes of Israel, so that they might all be roused to outrage against the perpetrators of the deed. The Levite did this, Athanasius explained, "in order that it might be understood that an injury like this pertained not to himself only, but extended to all alike; and that, if the people sympathized with him in his sufferings, they might avenge him; or if they neglected to do so, might bear the disgrace of being considered thenceforth as themselves guilty of the wrong." In case his audience had not yet grasped the point, Athanasius went on:

> You know the history, brethren, and the particular account of the circumstances given in Scripture. I will not therefore describe them in more detail, since I write to persons acquainted with them, and as I am anxious to represent to your piety our present circumstances, which are even worse than those to which I have referred. For my object in reminding you of this history is this, that you may compare those ancient transactions with what has happened to us now, and perceiving how much these last exceed the other in cruelty, may be filled with greater indignation on account of them, than were the people of old against those offenders. For the treatment we have undergone far surpasses the bitterness of any persecution; and the calamity of the Levite was but small, when compared with the enormities which have now been committed against the church; or rather such deeds as these were never before heard of in the whole world, or the like experienced by any one.
>
> For in that case it was but a single woman who was injured, and one Levite who suffered wrong; now the whole church is injured, the priesthood insulted, and worst of all, piety is persecuted by impiety. On that occasion the tribes were astounded, each at the sight of part of the body of one woman; but now the members of the whole church are seen divided from one another, and are sent abroad to you, and some to others,

51. See generally Douglas 1966 and 1996. Nirenberg 1996, p. 150, makes profitable use of Douglas' ideas to explain the violent tension generated by fears of sexual contact and miscegenation between Christians, Muslims, and Jews in fourteenth-century Spain. Cf. Hannah Arendt's warning (Arendt 1970, p. 75) against the "deceptive plausibility" of body/society analogies.

52. Judges 19–20.

bringing word of the insults and injustice which they have suffered. Be ye therefore moved, I beseech you, considering that these wrongs are done to you no less than unto us.[53]

Athanasius' written narrative of the violent assault on the Alexandrian church, coupled with the oral testimony of those who would bear copies of his letter "to his fellow-ministers in every place," served the same polemical function as the weapons showcased by the Alexandrians in their church, or the manacles, chains, and scarred bodies displayed by those claiming to have suffered persecution. Like the cut-up body of the Levite woman, they provided tangible evidence of the wrongs inflicted upon the church. The circulation of this testimony throughout the Christian world in turn appealed to an imagined community of Christians, united both in shared experience of suffering and martyrdom—"these wrongs are done to you no less than to us"—and in outrage against those "persecutors" who by their crimes had placed themselves outside the boundaries of the community and forfeited the name of Christian.[54] These accounts of violence against the churches differed from traditional "acts of the martyrs" in that they meant not so much to praise the courage of individual martyrs, as to damn the conduct of the persecutors. In these narratives, the victims of persecution were nameless and plural, the better to stress that they represented a larger Christian community.[55] Nicene martyrs and confessors constituted a community of suffering and resistance, a counter to the coercive "unity" being forced upon them by the emperors. The violence done to their bodies was done to the entire body of Christ.

Allowing for the fact that the overwhelming majority of surviving sources represent the Nicene perspective, we can nevertheless perceive an interesting symmetry of polemic across sectarian lines. Anti-Nicene and anti-Athanasian sources, where they do survive, employ exactly the same polemical strategies and denounce the same kinds of symbolically charged violence as the Nicenes did in their turn. This suggests not only the obvious conclusion that neither side had a monopoly on atrocity, but also— more significantly—that what each side considered to be "atrocity" was essentially the same. In their complaints against the "violence" of their enemies, bishops grouped together an array of wrongs that included not only

53. Athanasius, *Encyclical Letter* 1 (trans. NPNF).
54. This appeal to an idealized "world opinion" can be seen as another manifestation of the "simultaneity" postulated by Anderson 1991, pp. 22–36, an invocation of shared experience across time and space based on shared identity.
55. Jewish depictions of Maccabean martyrdom, likewise, often emphasized the group over the individual: see Rajak 1997.

physical violence but also more abstract "violations" against the church: "It was our duty not to stay silent or to leave unpunished the falsehoods, the bonds, the murders, attacks, false letters, beatings, exposures of virgins, exiles, demolitions of churches, arsons, translations [of bishops] from small to larger churches and, above all, the teachings of the Arian heresy which attack orthodox belief."[56]

Despite their theological differences, Nicenes and Arians operated in the same moral and ethical universe, and shared similar fundamental concerns about the proper relationship between religion and secular power. By invoking the discourse of "persecution," these complaints allowed Christians to denounce all the evils that the patronage of the state had brought into the church.

MARTYRDOM

Up to this point we have seen the discourse of martyrdom invoked mainly to support protests against the violence used by one's enemies. It served the interests of our sources to dwell upon the innocence and peaceful nature of their own people, the better to highlight the iniquity of those who used force against them. But martyrdom in the fourth century could be used and understood in a variety of ways beyond simply providing an indictment of persecutors. Since earliest times, Christians had understood martyrdom not just as passive suffering but as spiritual combat, an active struggle against the demons that inspired their persecutors. Already during the pagan persecutions, some Christians had struck back by breaking idols, tearing down edicts or assaulting magistrates.[57] Even the dead martyrs of past persecutions continued to struggle on behalf of the faith, working miracles for those Christians who kept their relics and invoked their memory. These venerated martyrs came to be understood both as embodying the Christian community and as protecting it, like a powerful secular patron, against its enemies.[58]

The short and turbulent reign of Julian "the Apostate" (361–363), the

56. Letter of the western bishops at the Council of Sardica, 343: in Hilary of Poitiers, *Against Valens and Ursacius* 1.3.8 (trans. Edwards). Very similar language can be found in the *libellus precum*, a petition of 384 from the Luciferian clerics Faustinus and Marcellinus, complaining to Theodosius about their persecution at the hands of Pope Damasus: *Collectio Avellana Ep.* 2.

57. See chapter 1, pp. 29–30.

58. For the "patronage" exercised by the holy dead on behalf of the communities that venerated them, see Brown 1981.

last pagan emperor, produced a sharp revival of pagan-Christian conflict that temporarily overshadowed the ongoing controversies within the Christian church. Christian opposition to Julian expressed itself in the familiar language of martyrdom. But as we shall see, this language was invoked in new and more aggressive ways, to justify not only resistance but deliberate provocation against an "apostate" regime. Christian tradition looked back on Julian's reign as a time when both dead martyrs and living confessors had come together to fight on behalf of the faith.

Gregory of Nazianzus, author of the earliest extant Christian invective against the apostate emperor, assigned a key role throughout his polemical narrative of Julian's life and reign to the martyrs as champions of Christian faith against pagan iniquity.[59] At a time when the young Julian still hid his pagan leanings under an outward pretense of Christianity, "awaiting his opportunity, and concealing under the mask of goodness his evil disposition," it was the power of the martyrs that recognized and exposed him for what he was, bringing "testimony" *[martyria]* of his true nature.[60] According to a story widespread in Christian sources, Julian and his brother Gallus had been working together to construct a martyr's shrine at Macellum in Asia Minor.[61] While the side of the building belonging to Gallus— who was, and remained, a devout Christian—advanced rapidly, Julian's half repeatedly collapsed:

> Both the brothers were, as I have told you, laboring for the martyrs, and
> were zealously vying with one another in erecting an edifice to their

59. Gregory of Nazianzus, *Orations Against Julian* (*Orations* 4 and 5). The *Orations* were probably composed c. 365, only a couple of years after the emperor's death. For a strikingly similar and near-contemporary (c. 360) example of Christian polemical invective directed against a *Christian* emperor, see Hilary of Poitiers' *Against Constantius*, with excellent analysis by Humphries 1998.

60. Gregory had met the young Julian in 355, when both were students in Athens, and later claimed that signs of bad character had been clearly visible even then: "A sign of no good seemed to me to be his neck unsteady, his shoulders always in motion and shrugging up and down like a pair of scales, his eye rolling and glancing from side to side with a certain insane expression, his feet unsteady and stumbling, his nostrils breathing insolence and disdain . . . I saw the man *before* his actions exactly what I afterwards found him *in* his actions." *Or.* 5.23–24 (trans. King). On "physiognomy," the ancient art of judging inner character by physical appearance and body language, see Gleason 1995; T. Shaw 1995 explores the use of physiognomy in a Christian context to expose heretics or the demon-possessed.

61. In addition to Gregory, see, e.g., Sozomen *HE* 5.2, Theodoret *HE* 3.1. While Sozomen specified one "Mammas" as the particular martyr to be honored by this shrine, Gregory's purpose was better served here by referring to "the martyrs" as a universal collective not restricted to any particular name or local cult, and thus better suited to protect the interests of the entire Christian imagined community.

honor with a large and efficient body of workmen, but inasmuch as the work did not proceed from the same motive, so neither did the labor come to the same end with both. For the work of the one [Gallus] was finishing, and going on according to calculation, as though God readily accepted the offering, like Abel's sacrifice, rightly offered up and cut in pieces, for the donation was, in a way, the consecration of the first-fruits of the flock. But the offering of the other—alas for the dishonor of the impious, that already in this world bears testimony [*martyromenes*] to the next, and that proclaims beforehand great events by small signs— the God of the Martyrs refused it, as he did the sacrifice of Cain.

And [Julian] continued laboring, and the earth shook off what he had toiled at . . . and rejected the foundations of him that was unsound in the faith, as though she were crying aloud at the shaking of the world that was about to proceed from him, and doing honor to the martyrs through the dishonor she did to the most impious of men. This fact presaged the future obstinacy and madness of the man, and his insults to the martyrs, and his lawless conduct against the sacred edifices. . . . Oh brotherly love of the martyrs! They did not accept honor from him that was thereafter to do dishonor to many martyrs; they did not receive the gift of him that was hereafter to make many confessors.[62]

Gregory, writing with full retrospective knowledge of all the events of Julian's reign, skillfully manipulates the symbolism of the collapsing building to prefigure some of Julian's most notorious attacks on Christianity, from his abortive attempt to rebuild the Jewish Temple in Jerusalem—likewise frustrated by earthquake—to his battle with the Antiochene Christians over the bones of the martyr Babylas, which culminated in the fiery destruction of the great temple of Apollo at Daphne.[63] By invoking the biblical typology of Cain and Abel, Gregory draws a line around the community of the faithful, whose offerings are pleasing to God, and places Julian squarely outside its boundaries. Long before the apostate emperor dared openly to reject Christ, Gregory tells us, "The God of the Martyrs" had rejected him.

Julian himself, having been raised as a Christian, was well aware of the power inherent in Christian martyrial discourse. Although his ultimate aim was to overthrow the Christian church, he did his best to avoid direct, violent persecution in the manner of Diocletian—he did not wish to give the

---

62. Gregory, *Oration* 4.25–27 (trans. King).

63. On events in Antioch, see Ammianus 22.13. For contemporary Christian reaction, see, e.g., John Chrysostom's *Homily on St. Babylas, Against Julian.* Although Julian tried to blame the burning of the Apollo temple on Christian arsonists, Christian sources considered the fire miraculous, divine retribution for the pagan insults against the martyr Babylas. Ammianus, however, reported speculation that blamed the fire on a pagan priest who had carelessly left a lamp burning.

Christians more martyrs around whom they could rally opposition. Equally important, he did not wish to be cast in the unwholesome role of "persecutor" as constructed by well-established and highly effective Christian polemical discourse.

Instead of forcing Christians to sacrifice to idols through threats of imprisonment, torture, and execution, Julian relied on economic sanctions, job discrimination, confiscation of church property, and other more indirect measures in order to accomplish the same goal, of bringing Christians back to the worship of the gods, without provoking the same degree of resistance.[64] But Julian's sharply confrontational policies—covertly encouraging anti-Christian violence, aggressively promoting blood sacrifice, and attempting to ban Christians from teaching the classics—created a deliberately divisive climate that provoked some Christians to extreme acts of resistance.[65] Ironically, in his zeal for controversy Julian had more in common with hardline bishops such as Athanasius than he did with other fourth-century emperors, who were concerned above all to suppress quarrels in the interest of maintaining order and comity.[66] Even though he tried to avoid the overt violence of past persecutions, the open hostility apparent in his policies toward Christians expressed an outlook more extremist than centrist.

Christian sources, well aware of Julian's intentions, turned his very reluctance to persecute into a further indictment of his character, charging that he hoped to accomplish through "deceit" what he dared not do openly:

> He became aware . . . that to carry on the war openly, and to preside in person over the impious attempts, besides being both rash and stupid, was in all respects most damaging to his object, for [he knew] that we would become the more obstinate when oppressed, and would oppose to tyranny our zeal in the cause of religion [*antithesein te tyrannidi ten huper eusebeias philotimian*] . . . And this he discovered not only

64. Comprehensive accounts of Julian's policies toward the Christians can be found in Bowersock 1978, esp. pp. 79–93; Brennecke 1988, pp. 96–106. This policy of indirect coercion appears strikingly similar to measures advocated by Augustine and other Catholic bishops against the Donatists, and to the strategies and penalties employed in much of the anti-pagan and anti-heretical legislation of Theodosius I and successors: a disciplinary "correction" applied in order to bring about conversion. See chapter 4.

65. Bradbury 1995 argues that Julian's lavish public sacrifices were intended as a deliberately divisive challenge to Christians, for whom, as he well knew, such rituals would bring back memories of persecution. Rescript on Christian teachers: Julian, *Ep.* 42; cf. criticism of this policy at Ammianus 22.10.

66. Julian did, of course, attempt to construct a rather artificial "unity" among pagans, explicitly trying to imitate what he recognized as the organizational strengths of the Christian church. On Julian's "pagan church," see Nicholson 1994.

from reflection, but had it proved to him by the history of the previous persecutions, which have only made the Christians more honored.[67]

Gregory seems actually resentful of Julian's reluctance to persecute, accusing the emperor of begrudging Christians the honor of martyrdom. Christians were determined to make Julian a persecutor, and were ready to suffer to that end. In later historical memory, sectarian differences between Nicenes, Homoians, Anomoians, and others were buried for the duration of Julian's reign. Nicene tradition happily commemorated as martyrs many who in other circumstances might have been condemned as heretics.[68] Despite Julian's best efforts to avoid the label, later Christian sources elaborated him into a persecutor of Diocletianic proportions and repeated stories of "martyrs" who had defied him.

Julian, in his indirect measures against the church, underestimated the possibilities inherent in Christian models of martyrdom, the degree to which fifty years of Christian empowerment had altered the meaning of "spiritual combat." If Julian could practice a different kind of persecution, the Christians would respond with a different kind of martyrdom:

> Amachius, governor of Phrygia, ordered that the temple at Merum,
> a city of that province, should be opened, and cleared of the filth
> which had accumulated there by lapse of time, and that the statues
> it contained should be polished afresh. This, being done, grieved the
> Christians very much. Now a certain Macedonius, and Theodulus
> and Tatian, unable to endure the indignity thus put upon their religion,
> and impelled by a fervent zeal for virtue, rushed by night into the
> temple, and broke the images in pieces. . . . The governor seized them
> and ordered them to expiate the crime they had committed by sacrific-
> ing; on their refusal to do this, the judge menaced them with tortures,
> but they, despising his threats, being endowed with great courage,

67. Gregory, *Or.* 4.57. Cf. Socrates *HE* 3.12: "Observing that those who suffered martyrdom under the reign of Diocletian were greatly honored by the Christians, and knowing that many among them were eagerly desirous of becoming martyrs, he determined to wreak his vengeance upon them in some other way." (NPNF trans.)

68. Brennecke 1988, pp. 114–152, provides an exhaustive source-critical analysis of the martyr traditions associated with Julian, including all the incidents discussed here. Brennecke's analysis has revealed the interesting fact that nearly all of the Julianic martyrs, celebrated in our mainly Nicene sources, actually belonged to the Homoian "semi-Arian" party. This can be explained by the fact that the Homoians, long favored by Constantius, happened to be the dominant party in control of most of the major bishoprics in the east at the time of Julian's accession in 361, and so had the most to lose by Julian's economic and political disestablishment of the church. Later Nicene tradition was willing to forget the "Arian" background of these martyrs and see them simply as Christians who had stood up to pagan persecution.

declared their readiness to undergo any sufferings, rather than pollute themselves by sacrificing. After subjecting them to all possible tortures he at last laid them on gridirons under which a fire was placed, and thus slew them. . . . Thus these martyrs ended their life.[69]

The spiritual combat of the martyrs, the "soldiers of Christ," was no longer confined within the physical limits of the tortures inflicted upon the martyr's body, but now struck out directly against the enemies of the faith. "Unable to endure the indignity thus put upon their religion" by the simple reappearance of pagan worship, the Christians struck back. This time, in the words of Theodoret, "the partisans of piety returned insult for insult."[70] Studies of modern religious extremism have noted the importance of a sense of insult or humiliation—felt especially acutely by those who perceived themselves to have suffered a decline in status or power—in driving militants to violence.[71] Christian zealots, convinced that Julian was a persecutor no different from Diocletian, sought by provocative acts to force his hand, to strip away his pretended tolerance, and to galvanize broader Christian opposition. In later decades, as we shall see, militants would attempt similar provocations against a Christian government they saw as too tolerant of paganism.[72]

Merum was hardly an isolated incident. Among dozens of specific cases of Christians listed by our sources as "martyred" under Julian, it seems that the majority were actually killed by pagan mobs or by the secular authorities in retaliation for their provocative attacks against paganism—smashing idols, destroying temples, disrupting rituals. This fact is not only admitted but even celebrated by Christian sources, who without exception refer to

69. Socrates *HE* 3.15 (trans. NPNF). Cf. Sozomen *HE* 5.11. The claim that Amachius attempted to force them to sacrifice may well represent later elaboration designed to rework the story along the lines of classical martyrology. But the governor would have been well within his rights to punish them brutally for their violation of the temple, and it is not inherently implausible that a magistrate with militantly pagan sympathies might have gone beyond the limits of Julian's policy in demanding that they sacrifice. Brennecke 1988, pp. 146–147, thinks that Socrates probably drew upon a Homoian martyrial tradition going back at least to the late fourth century.

70. Theodoret *HE* 3.3, referring not specifically to the Merum incident but generally to Christian opposition to the reopening of temples. (NPNF trans.) Not all Christians accepted this highly aggressive understanding of martyrdom. Augustine's opposition to such provocative behavior is discussed in chapter 3, pp. 115–119; and the Council of Elvira's injunction against idol smashing in chapter 1, p. 40.

71. See Juergensmeyer 2000, esp. chap. 10. Certain contemporary Islamist militant groups are motivated by a desire to reverse the "humiliation" of western dominance and restore the lost glory of the classical Caliphate: L. Harris 2002.

72. See chapter 5, pp. 192–206.

the slain Christians as martyrs. In some cases, as at Merum, the Christian assailants seem to have planned their attack in the full expectation and hope of being killed for it, and thus attaining the crown of martyrdom. In other instances, pagan mobs took advantage of the permissive climate created by Julian's accession to settle longstanding scores with Christians who had previously been involved with the closure or destruction of temples under Constantine and Constantius. Bishop Mark of Arethusa, who in the reign of Constantius had pulled down a temple "under the authority then granted to the Christians," was now subjected to brutal beating and torture by pagans who demanded that he pay for the rebuilding of the shrine. He refused, and chose to endure continued torture, even when the pagans finally reduced their demand to a symbolic single gold piece:

> [He refused], that he might not throw away a single piece of gold upon his tormentors, in order that it might be clear that he was enduring all this on account of religion. For as long as the other party made the compensation for the temple very heavy, and demanded from him the amount in full, or else required him to rebuild the temple at his own cost, it might have been thought that the impossibility of the demand, and not his religious scruples, was the reason for his obstinacy [enstasis]. But when he got the better of them by his fortitude, and continually made them subtract something from the valuation, they at the end reduced it so far that the sum demanded was extremely small, and very easy for him to pay. And there was equal determination on both sides, [the pagans] to gain their point by receiving even a token sum, and [Mark] not to be subdued into paying anything at all, even though many others offered to pay it for him. . . . Thus he showed that he was carrying on the contest not for the sake of money, but for his religion.[73]

In the new and sharply polarized climate of pagan-Christian relations created by the accession of Julian, some Christians sought and found martyrdom by attacking the temples of the pagans, or by refusing even to apologize for having done so in the past. This aggressive paradigm of martyrdom pointed the way toward the more notorious, violent attacks on pagan temples and Jewish synagogues carried out by Christian holy men in the late fourth and early fifth centuries.[74]

The violent retaliations of the pagans, in turn, suggest that they too

---

73. Gregory, *Or.* 4.90.

74. See chapter 5. Harold Drake has argued that Julian's brief reign, which rudely interrupted the sense of security and empowerment Christians had enjoyed over the previous fifty years, created a harshly polarized religious climate that led directly to renewed Christian attacks on paganism in the subsequent decades: Drake 2000, pp. 431–436.

understood—and feared—the power inherent in Christian claims to martyrdom. Already in the last years of the Great Persecution, Eusebius tells us, the pagan authorities tried very hard to destroy all physical remains of the Christians they killed, burning the bodies and scattering the ashes upon the sea, in order to forestall the possibility that other Christians might venerate their relics.[75] Under Julian, pagans in Palestine attacked the Christian cult which had grown up around relics of John the Baptist and the prophet Elisha, digging up and burning the holy remains and seeking to desecrate them by mixing them with animal bones.[76] In some instances, at least as presented by Christian sources, pagans seem to have been as eager to play the persecutor as the Christians were to play the martyr. During the bloody riots that preceded the destruction of the Alexandrian Serapeum in 391, a gang of die-hard pagans barricaded themselves in the temple and then proceeded methodically to reenact the Great Persecution upon some Christians whom they had taken hostage: "These they forced to offer sacrifice on the altars where fire was kindled; those who refused they put to death with new and refined tortures, fastening some to gibbets and breaking the legs of others and pitching them into the caverns which a careworn antiquity had built to receive the blood of sacrifices and the other impurities of the temple."[77]

Julian, who was not at all eager to play the persecutor, tried as best he could to resist the Christians' new claims of martyrdom. Juventinus and Maximinus, two Christians among the imperial shield-bearers, publicly insulted the emperor by quoting scripture: "Thou hast given us over to an impious prince, an apostate beyond all nations."[78] Julian had them flogged to death. He then, according to Theodoret, took the unusual step of issuing a public proclamation claiming that the two had been executed not for any religious cause, but simply for their drunken insolence [*paroinia*, not *eusebeia*] toward their emperor, a capital crime in any context.[79] "Thus he de-

75. See, e.g., Eusebius *HE* 8.6.
76. Philostorgius *HE* 7.4; Rufinus *HE* 11.28. Cf. Brennecke 1988, pp. 119–120. Gregory of Nazianzus, *Or.* 5.29, offers a litany of pagan atrocities strikingly similar to the accusations we have already seen traded between Nicenes and Arians: "No more shall they plunder and profane the consecrated gifts, uniting rapine with sacrilege; no longer shall they insult the hoary hairs of priests, the gravity of deacons and the modesty of virgins . . . no more shall they set fire to the monuments of the martyrs, as if they could check the zeal of others to follow their example by the insults against them." (King trans.)
77. Rufinus *HE* 11.22 (trans. Amidon).
78. *Song of the Three*, verse 8.
79. Cf. also John Chrysostom's panegyric on Juventinus and Maximinus, which claims that the two were executed on charges of treasonable conspiracy: PG 50, pp. 571–578.

nied them the name of martyrs," says Theodoret, who nevertheless identifies the two as martyrs and goes on to describe how the people of Antioch gathered their relics and continued to venerate them even fifty years later.[80] Once again Christians had maneuvered Julian, against his better judgment, into acting like a "persecutor," a role in which Christian historical tradition was only too happy to cast him. Julian's pagan revival, for a brief moment, allowed the Christian community to forget its internal strife and fratricidal violence, and recall the heroic days of the Great Persecution through defiance of a common enemy whom all Christians could agree to hate. Their weapon against him was martyrdom, and for once it did not matter exactly what kind of Christianity those martyrs espoused.

These stories of martyrdom served both to strengthen group identity and to inflame hatred of the other. The "imagined community" of the late antique church defined itself in an oppositional sense, orthodox Christians against pagans, Jews, and heretics.[81] Such a mindset was not unique to Christians. Although pagans did not develop the concept of martyrdom in the same way, their own behavior shows that they too acted with a sense of history and grievance, avenging previous wrongs that Christians had done to them or to their gods and temples. A recent study of communal violence between Hindus and Muslims in modern India has stressed the role of shared stories, of education, in passing group hatreds from one generation to the next.[82] For late antique Christians, yearly liturgical commemoration of the martyrs, and the circulation of their stories both in oral tradition and in written hagiography, would have filled this role.[83] Despite the appearance of Christian unanimity presented by traditions of Julianic martyrs, the same

---

80. Theodoret *HE* 3.11. Chrysostom, writing toward the end of the fourth century, implies an already well-established cult tradition for the two in Antioch. Brennecke 1988, pp. 144–145, suggests that Theodoret may be drawing on a Homoian martyr tradition going back at least to the reign of Valens.

81. On "imagined communities" see Anderson 1991. Anderson's argument does not really explore the ways in which some identities are defined in opposition to an "other."

82. Kakar 1996, writing on Hindu-Muslim communal violence in modern India, pp. 31–32: "It is sobering to think of hundreds of thousands of children over many parts of the subcontinent, Hindu and Muslim, who have listened to stories from their parents and other family elders during the partition and other subsequent riots, on the fierceness of an implacable enemy. This is a primary channel through which historical enmity is transmitted from one generation to the next . . . Later, as the child grows up, the parental message may be amplified by the input of one or more teachers."

83. Nirenberg 1996, pp. 200–230, discusses for fourteenth-century Spain recurring episodes of anti-Jewish violence during Holy Week, when the annual commem-

processes of identity formation and opposition developed in response to violence between different Christian sects—although Nicene, Homoian, and other "communities," at least at the level of ordinary laity, were likely not so sharply separated in fourth-century reality as in later fifth-century historical memory. In the late fifth and early sixth centuries, opponents of Chalcedon likewise would use their own experiences of martyrdom and struggle against the ecclesiastical establishment to shape a new identity as a separate Monophysite church.[84]

For decades and even centuries after Julian's death, legends about that emperor's ferocious persecutions, and the spirited resistance of the martyrs, grew more and more elaborate.[85] By the sixth century, it was commonly thought that Julian's very death had been the work of the holy martyrs. Julian had been fatally wounded in combat during his abortive invasion of Persia in 363. The killer was never identified, and Christians increasingly believed that no human hand had done the deed.[86] The sixth-century chronicler John Malalas offers a fairly developed version of a highly popular and widespread legend:

> While [Julian] slept, he saw in the dream a full-grown man wearing a cuirass approaching him in his tent . . . the man struck him with a spear. The emperor was frightened and woke up with a cry, to find that he had been fatally wounded in the armpit. . . .
>
> That same night Basil, the most holy bishop of Caesarea in Cappadocia, saw in a dream the heavens opened and the Savior Christ seated on a throne and saying loudly, "Mercurius, go and kill the emperor Julian, who is against the Christians." Saint Mercurius, standing before the Lord, wore a gleaming iron breast-plate. Hearing the command, he disappeared, and then he reappeared, standing before the Lord, and cried out, "The emperor Julian has been fatally wounded and has died, as you commanded, Lord."[87]

Mercurius, a military martyr, was a soldier of Christ in every sense of the word.[88] Sanctified by his death for the faith in a long-ago persecution, he was summoned by Christ to return to the world of the living and strike down the new persecutor. The "God of the Martyrs" had taken his vengeance.

---

oration of Christ's suffering helped focus Christian hatred on the Jews they deemed responsible for it.

84. See conclusion.

85. See generally Braun and Richer 1978, de Gaiffier 1956.

86. For the development of the legends concerning Julian's death, see Baynes 1937.

87. Malalas, *Chronicle* 13.23–25 (trans. Jeffreys).

88. On Mercurius, and military saints generally, Delehaye 1909.

IMPERIAL RESTRAINT?

During the violent doctrinal conflicts that characterized the reigns of Constantius and Valens, the polemic of each side sought to paint the other as outside the boundary of legitimate Christianity, not deserving of the legal protections normally accorded to bishops and clergy—and thus rightfully subject to coercive punishment. Victims of such punishment in turn denounced it as persecution, and seized the title of "martyr" for themselves. Is there any indication that such invocation of martyrdom and persecution had any success in influencing opinions beyond the particular congregations or doctrinal camps that had produced them? Specifically, did the state authorities who were tarred with the label "persecutor" then moderate their policies as a result? Did they often back down from confrontations that threatened to produce "martyrs," or at the least did they make a conscious effort to avoid particular forms of violence that might recall the Great Persecution?

If we compare official persecution of Christians in the time of Diocletian to repression of Christian dissenters and schismatics under Constantine and his Christian successors, we do see a significant difference in the treatment of Christian bishops. Constantine's grants of privilege and immunity to the church seem to have had the effect of elevating bishops to the status of *honestiores*, that class of elite citizens normally exempt from the "judicial savagery" typical of late Roman law enforcement.[89] There seems to have been general consensus that it was not appropriate for bishops to suffer execution, torture, flogging, or other physical violence. Exile or imprisonment was by far the most common punishment formally applied to bishops who defied the emperor's will. When bishops did die, it was usually under murky circumstances in which murder by secular authorities could reasonably be suspected but not proven. The Nicene bishop Paul of Constantinople, who died in prison after being exiled to Cucusus in Cappadocia, was widely believed to have been strangled at the order of the prefect.[90] Donatists in North Africa claimed that their bishop Marculus, arrested during the Macarian "persecution" of 347, had been secretly removed from prison by night, taken out of town, and unceremoniously and unlawfully thrown off a cliff by impe-

89. See MacMullen 1990b.
90. Athanasius, *Historia Arianorum* 7. The problematic nature of Nicene traditions on Paul of Constantinople is thoughtfully discussed by Dagron 1974, pp. 422–435, correcting the overly uncritical and speculative reconstruction of Telfer 1950. See also T. Barnes 1993, pp. 212–217. Cucusus seems to have been a favored location for dumping unwanted bishops of Constantinople, as John Chrysostom later discovered.

rial authorities.[91] In some cases, exile or imprisonment under especially harsh conditions—or in dangerous areas—could be little different from a death sentence.[92] During the brutal reign of Lucius, Homoian bishop of Alexandria and client of Valens, there seems to have been a deliberate policy of sending Nicene bishops, clergy, and monks to exile in places such as Diocaesarea in Palestine or Heliopolis/Baalbek in Phoenicia, whose predominantly Jewish or pagan populations were particularly notorious for anti-Christian violence.[93] In such cases, we may suspect a conscious strategy on the part of state authorities who would gladly be rid of a troublesome bishop, but dared not be seen with a bishop's blood on their hands. The bishops, for their part, responded by claiming that a death in exile—or

91. See full discussion in chapter 3, pp. 109–111.

92. During his three years in Cucusus, Chrysostom was repeatedly endangered by the raids of Isaurian brigands, a common hazard in that area. In 407, he finally died after being forced to march long distances in extreme weather conditions as he was moved from one location to another—the imperial court may have become tired of waiting for the Isaurians to do the job. Egypt's Great Oasis (modern Kharga), another popular place of exile, was similarly exposed to frequent attacks by the fearsome Blemmyes. Nestorius, who spent nearly twenty years confined in the Oasis, was at one point captured by the Blemmyes, but then (no doubt to the consternation of the authorities) released unharmed: Evagrius *HE* 1.7. In 449, bishop Flavian of Constantinople died, apparently from excessively harsh treatment, while being sent into exile after his condemnation at the so-called Robber Council of Ephesus, on which see chapter 8. The exact circumstances are vague: see Chadwick 1955. Palladius, *Dialogue on the Life of John Chrysostom* 20, provides numerous examples and much detail on sentences of exile imposed on Chrysostom's followers.

93. The *Letter of Peter of Alexandria* (in Theodoret *HE* 4.22) mentions eleven bishops and desert ascetics sent to Diocaesarea, "a city of Christ-killing Jews," which had been the center of a major Jewish revolt a little more than twenty years previously (352 or 353). The Caesar Gallus repressed the uprising and burned the city, according to Socrates *HE* 2.33. On Palestine as a scene of religious tension, see Stroumsa 1999, esp. chap. 7, and articles in Kofsky and Stroumsa 1998. Peter also says that seventeen presbyters and deacons were sent to Heliopolis "where no man can stand the name of Christ"—an overwhelmingly pagan city that had seen some of the most violent anti-Christian incidents under Julian: *Chronicon Paschale*, pp. 546–547; Theodoret *HE* 3.3. Heliopolis' reputation as a stronghold of militant paganism persisted into the fifth century, when the young monk Rabbula chose it as an ideal venue to pursue his zealous quest for martyrdom: see chapter 5, pp. 162–164. This pattern of exile seems to have characterized repression carried out only in Egypt, not elsewhere in Valens' half of the empire, and thus probably reflected policies of bishop Lucius and of his allies, the treasurer Magnus and the governor Palladius, rather than of Valens himself. Although Nicene sources universally denounce Valens as a "persecutor," in fact specific and credible stories of violent persecution during his reign seem to come almost entirely from Egypt. On the religious policies of Valens generally, see Brennecke 1988, pp. 181–242, and now Lenski 2002, pp. 211–263.

even the endurance of exile—constituted a "martyrdom" even in the absence of a formal execution.[94]

The secular authorities' restraint in dealing with bishops did not generally extend to the lesser clergy or laity who followed those bishops. The congregations of deposed and exiled bishops frequently suffered far worse than their leaders. Armed soldiers violently invaded their churches, disrupted their services, and broke up their "unlawful" assemblies. Individuals were arrested, publicly stripped and flogged, or tortured in an attempt to force them into communion with the officially recognized bishop. Christian magistrates, like their pagan predecessors, believed that religious unity could be achieved through force, and a similar coercive purpose necessarily found expression in similar means of repression. In this context, the victims' invocations of persecution and claims of martyrdom would seem entirely appropriate.

One significant difference from the time of pagan persecution might seem to be the near absence of formal judicial execution as a means of repression in religious conflicts under the Christian empire. Although troublesome clerics might occasionally be condemned to death on trumped-up secular charges,[95] the Christian empire seems to have preferred not to impose the ultimate penalty explicitly upon religious disobedience. Classical martyrdoms, of course, always presented the martyr's formal public execution as the climax and fulfillment of a dramatic process that unfolded as the martyr was arrested, confronted the magistrate, and endured torture. Since the Christianization of the Roman state did nothing to reduce the employment of capital punishment for secular crimes, either in legislation or in practice, we may well conclude that the Christian government's reluctance to employ the sword in specifically religious matters resulted from a conscious desire to avoid making martyrs of fellow Christians in a manner that might provoke comparisons to the pagan persecutions.

It is equally clear, however, that there were limits to such restraint. Although there were few formal executions, there were many killings. Imperial law enforcement was a blunt weapon, difficult to wield with precision, and the state's violence frequently spun out of control. Soldiers were notorious for exceeding their orders, and punishing religious dissidents all too

94. Exile as martyrdom: Athanasius, *Apology against the Arians* 38 and 40; *Historia Arianorum* 40; Hilary of Poitiers, *Against Valens and Ursacius* 1.4 and 2.4 (*Letter of Pope Liberius*, quoted at the beginning of this chapter).

95. As were, for instance, the so-called Holy Notaries of Constantinople, two officials executed under Constantius (Sozomen *HE* 4.3) and decades later reinvented as "martyrs" to the Nicene cause: see discussion in Dagron 1974, pp. 422–435.

often became an occasion for plunder, rape, or extortion. Attempts to break up "schismatic assemblies" could precipitate mass slaughter when nervous soldiers confronted large and disorderly crowds in confined urban spaces.[96] Local officials might check with the emperor before taking action against a bishop, but against lesser clergy or ordinary laity they were more likely to act on their own initiative. When such officials or their soldiers were still pagans, as many in the fourth century still were, it is not unlikely that some might have taken advantage of imperial orders against Christian dissidents to act out their own anti-Christian inclinations.

Still, there is ample evidence that the discourse of martyrdom could under some circumstances restrain imperial authorities' capacity to use violent coercion in religious matters. Emperors did often relent when confronted with the possibility that they would be forced to make martyrs.[97] When the Nicene congregation of Edessa continued to hold assemblies in defiance of Valens' prohibition, the emperor reportedly threatened to slaughter all those who attended—and then backed down when the Edessenes pronounced themselves ready for martyrdom.[98] Constantius, trying to suppress news of a synod whose decisions ran counter to his policies, sent a military officer to deliver a savage threat to bishop Eusebius of Samosata, who was holding the official transcript of the council.[99] If Eusebius did not agree to hand over the document, his right hand was to be cut off. But the threat was meant only to terrify: the emperor had given his officer secret instructions that it was not to be carried out. When Eusebius extended his hands and invited the man to cut them both off, the emperor's bluff was called.[100] In the eyes of polemical sources, a "persecuting" emperor could be doubly damned if in the end he chose not to persecute: he was condemned for plotting such an evil deed, and then made to look weak and indecisive for not carrying it out.

Under emperors such as Theodosius I the Nicene party enjoyed full imperial support, and no longer had any fear of persecution on doctrinal

96. As happened in Constantinople in 345, when panicked soldiers slaughtered more than three thousand people who were too tightly packed to get out of their way: Socrates *HE* 2.16.

97. As Constantine had eventually done with the Donatists: chapter 1, pp. 57–58.

98. Rufinus *HE* 11.5; Socrates *HE* 4.18; cf. Lenski 2002, pp. 257–258.

99. The synod, held in Antioch in 360, proved an embarrassing spectacle: Melitius, elected to the episcopacy of Antioch by the imperially favored Homoian Arian party, abruptly and publicly repudiated their theological views.

100. Theodoret *HE* 2.28. Much of this story is probably fanciful—how, after all, would Theodoret know about the "secret orders"? But the kernel of truth lay in the fact that Constantius had been unable to coerce Eusebius into doing what he wanted—and this story, widely circulated, was what people believed had happened.

grounds. Yet the language of martyrdom and persecution, even in this un-likely climate, continued to be put to creative use. By legitimating and even sanctifying principled resistance to secular power, the discourse of martyr-dom attempted to limit the ways in which emperors could use their theo-retically absolute power. In several cases, as we shall see in later chapters, emperors were forced to back down or reverse themselves when confronted with the possibility of making martyrs. The unnamed bishop of Callinicum, who had burned a synagogue in 388, was, like Mark of Arethusa, faced with a demand that he undo what he had done. Ambrose of Milan, intervening on his behalf with the emperor Theodosius, argued that any attempt to force him to pay compensation would make him either an apostate if he obeyed or a martyr if he refused. In 434, the monk Hypatius announced his deter-mination to strike the urban prefect in the face—a deed for which he would certainly be put to death—rather than allow the prefect to celebrate the "pa-gan" Olympic games. When the prefect learned of the monk's intention, he cancelled the games rather than be forced to make a martyr of a holy man.[101]

The discourse of martyrdom could be used to justify a stance of defiance toward power, to carve out a space in which religion could be used to artic-ulate legitimate resistance to the emperor's will. As we shall see, the fourth century's new interpretations of martyrdom could lead yet further beyond simple endurance of persecution, to encompass active violence against per-secutors and enemies of the faith.

101. See full discussion of these two episodes in chapter 5, pp. 194–196 and 203–206.

3. An Eye for an Eye

Religious Violence in Donatist Africa

Isaac, a Christian of Carthage, had publicly confessed his faith and defied the authority of the persecuting magistrates. The enraged proconsul immediately had him seized and put to the torture. Scourged, beaten, his joints broken, his sides torn by iron claws, Isaac wore down the strength of the torturers with the endurance given him by Christ. His spirit rejoiced even as his body suffered. Isaac had seen all of this, we are told, in a vision that had come to him the previous night as he lay in prison:

> Now when he had been held for a little while by the quiet of sleep, it seemed to him that he had a contest with the ministers of the emperor. . . . His devotion therefore stood guard, engaged in the efforts of virtue, and more firmly beat back the ministers of wickedness [*ministros nequitiae*] with their imperial orders, even though they fought him boldly. After he had overcome them in a long conflict, [Isaac] caught sight of the emperor himself suddenly approaching. While he was being pushed by the emperor to fulfill his command, he bravely rejected the authority of the sacrilegious order and the menace of savage tortures. With frequent threats, that terrible man also promised to tear out his eye. Since they had fought such a long and ferocious battle between them, it was not enough [for Isaac] simply to be declared the victor. Throwing in a strong hand, he pushed aside the delay to his threats: violently tearing out [the emperor's] eye, he left the bereaved face with its seat of light empty.[1]

Following his victory in this struggle, Isaac received a shining crown from a "youth of splendid radiance" and then felt himself lifted up toward heaven. The vision presented little difficulty of interpretation: "For as he had seen

---

1. *Passion of Maximian and Isaac* 8; text of the *Passion* in Maier 1987–1989, *Dossier*, vol. 1, pp. 256–275 (my trans.).

himself fighting alone against the ministers of the king at night, so by day he now showed us how he had torn out the eye from the emperor, and thus blinded him and defeated him."[2] Isaac would defeat the devil and his servants, and receive the crown of martyrdom. The story, up to this point, is thoroughly typical of its genre. Magistrates and torturers rage like savage beasts, their uncontrolled fury smashing helplessly against the serene jubilation of the martyr.[3] The dream recalls that of Perpetua, one of North Africa's most famous martyrs, who saw herself as an athlete of Christ, wrestling and overpowering the devil in the form of an Ethiopian.[4] For Isaac, the adversary appears in the persona of the emperor in the face of whose sacrilegious command the martyrs chose to die rather than submit. The proconsul orders the bodies of the martyrs dumped into the sea, in a vain attempt to prevent the faithful from venerating their relics.[5]

But this is no typical martyrdom. The persecuting emperor is not Diocletian or Galerius, but Constans. The year is 347, a full generation after Constantine's conversion. The "sacrilegious command" that the emperor sought to impose on the Christians of Africa did not demand sacrifice to idols or renunciation of Christ but rather the celebration of a Christian mass in "unity" with the church that the emperor and most of the rest of the Christian world recognized as true, legitimate, universal, and "Catholic." Isaac, Maximian, and their companions, though they themselves undoubtedly never recognized any name other than "Christian," are known to us more commonly as Donatists.[6] Constantine, father of Constans, had been unable to reunite a North African church bitterly divided between two factions. The schism between Donatists and Catholics would persist for generations, long after the original *traditores* were dead and buried. This chapter explores the continuing confrontation between two opposite visions of religious com-

---

2. *Passion of Maximian and Isaac* 9.

3. The use of animal imagery to describe "savage" persecutors was common: see Roberts 1993, p. 55, with examples.

4. *Passion of Perpetua and Felicitas* 10.

5. Cf. Eusebius *HE* 8.6.

6. The name "Donatist" of course, was a label created by hostile polemicists. Orthodox heresiographers commonly stigmatized sects by naming them after their founders (e.g., for the other rigorist movements, "Novatians" after Novatus of Rome and "Melitians" after Melitius of Egypt) and thus denying them the name "Christian." The Donatists preferred to call themselves the Church of the Martyrs. See B. Shaw 1992, suggesting the term "African Christianity" as a less judgmental name for the Donatist movement. However, I have thought it easiest to continue using the terminology most familiar to modern readers, with due recognition of its polemical origins. On Donatist self-identification, see now Tilley 1997a and 1997b.

munity embodied in the two churches. The Donatists sought to separate themselves, a pure and zealous minority, from a corrupt world and especially from the corruptions of imperial power. The Catholics, true to their name, wished to unify the world and transform it in their image—and were willing to compromise with power to that end.[7]

The aftermath of Diocletian's persecution had given rise to similar schisms elsewhere, most notably the Melitians in Egypt and the Novatians in Rome and Asia Minor. But the North African schism was distinguished by its scope—for most of the fourth century the clear majority of Christians in the region were Donatists[8]—as well as its long history of violence on both sides. The time of Macarius, when Isaac had dreamed himself tearing out the eye of the emperor, also saw the appearance of militant Donatists known as "Circumcellions," who were as prepared to inflict violence as the martyrs had been to suffer it. By the first decade of the fifth century the Circumcellions were seizing Catholic clergy and blinding them by forcing a caustic mixture of lime and vinegar into their eyes—an act that, said Augustine, "not even the barbarians" could have thought up.[9] We turn now to these Donatist extremists, and their role in the religious violence that divided Roman North Africa in the fourth and early fifth centuries. A study of the Donatist-Catholic conflict will illuminate the relationship between the ideology of martyrdom that shaped the identity of the Donatist church, and the real violence carried out by its zealots.

"UNITY"

The imperial commissioners Macarius and Paul arrived in North Africa in 347, sent by the emperor Constans to distribute alms to the poor and to bring

---

7. On the history of Donatism generally, Frend 1985 is still fundamental. Useful surveys of scholarship can be found in A. Schindler, s.v. Afrika I in *Theologische Realenzyklopädie* 1 (1977), pp. 654–668; Frend 1988; Birley 1987; most comprehensively in Mazzucco 1993. Frend 1997 restates his views most recently. See also Tengström 1964, Kriegbaum 1987, and several useful essays on Donatism and North African Christianity generally in B. Shaw 1995. For the "worldview" of the Donatists see now Tilley 1997a. Monceaux 1912, esp. vols. 4 and 5, and Mandouze 1982, *PCBE*, are indispensable reference works.

8. A point reiterated most recently by Frend 1997, calling Donatism "the most important single movement in fourth-century North Africa" (p. 626). The Melitians and Novatians, by contrast, quickly became small minorities of comparatively marginal importance. See Greenslade 1953; on Novatians, T. Gregory 1975; on Melitians, see Goehring 1997.

9. Augustine *Ep.* 111.1 (409): *Quis enim barbarus excogitare potuit?*

the church back into unity.[10] A rumor quickly spread among the Donatists that as Macarius presided over mass he placed imperial images upon the altar, so that all those who approached to celebrate the eucharistic sacrifice would instead be participating in an act of idolatry very much like that which the pagan persecutors had demanded of the Christians a generation earlier.[11] As the agent of the Christian emperor Constans, Macarius may simply have followed usual custom in setting up imperial images wherever he was acting in his formal capacity as an imperial official, not realizing that in the context of a Christian mass such an act would be interpreted in a very different way. Though hardly evidence of a hidden agenda for restoring paganism, Macarius' act was certainly a public-relations blunder that showed considerable insensitivity to local religious concerns. Macarius' very presence at the occasion, and his address to the congregation in favor of unity, constituted a usurpation of the proper role of a bishop—an unacceptable intrusion of secular power into the religious sphere.[12] Donatus of Carthage, instructing his followers not to accept the alms offered by these "ministers of unity," angrily remarked, "What has the emperor to do with the church?"[13] Donatist resistance to the mission of Macarius led to confrontation, violence, and the persecution in which Isaac, among numerous others, attained martyrdom.

As Macarius and Paul approached southern Numidia, bishop Donatus of Bagai took even more drastic steps than had his namesake in Carthage. He sent heralds around the countryside to summon an army of supporters, a raging mob of *circumcelliones*—the first mention of the infamous

---

10. Their exact titles are not specified in the sources; *notarii* has been suggested: Mandouze, *PCBE*, s.vv. Macarius 1 and Paulus 2. They were presumably civilian officials, not military, since they had to ask the *comes* Silvester to protect them against the Circumcellions (Optatus 3.4). On the motives behind the mission of Macarius and Paul, see Cecconi 1990 and my discussion in chapter 4, pp. 135–136.

11. Optatus 3.12. Catholic sources had to admit that such an act would have been extremely sacrilegious, even while they vigorously denied that Macarius had ever actually done any such thing. The emperor Julian is said to have had images of the gods placed alongside the imperial images in every courtroom such that no one would be able to approach and carry out their legal business without appearing to pay homage to them: Sozomen *HE* 5.17. In that case, of course, the provocation against the Christians was entirely deliberate.

12. On the powerful polemical image of secular officials or soldiers inside the sacred space of the church, see chapter 2, pp. 79–88.

13. *Quid est imperatori cum ecclesia?* Optatus 3.3. The description of Macarius and Paul as *ministros operis sancti unitatis et famulos Dei* appears first in the address of Gratus, Catholic bishop of Carthage, to the council held immediately after the "persecution" of Macarius and the exile of Donatist leaders in 347: Munier 1974, *Concilia Africae*, p. 3.

fighters who would come to be known as Donatism's militant wing.[14] These malcontents, Optatus tells us, had a history. Only a few years previously, led by two self-styled "Captains of the Saints," they had terrorized the countryside and threatened public order before being ruthlessly suppressed by military force.[15] It is unclear whether the authorities at the time recognized them as religious extremists or simply as bandits, for whom, in any case, the treasure carried by the imperial almsgivers would have made a tempting target. Either way, Macarius was sufficiently worried to request and receive military protection from the *comes Africae*, Silvester. The Circumcellions, meanwhile, gathered around a large basilica in which they had stockpiled provisions in expectation of the impending confrontation. Scouts travelling ahead of Silvester's main army met with a very hostile reception, and were beaten and forced to flee. When the scouts returned to the army and told of their mistreatment, the soldiers became so enraged that their officers were unable to restrain them from perpetrating a massacre.[16]

This episode seems to have provided the pretext for a wholesale repression of Donatism, which even in Augustine's time was still remembered as the *Tempora Macariana*.[17] Optatus, even as he ridiculed Donatist comparisons to the pagan persecutions, nevertheless acknowledged a coercive subtext to Macarius' call to unity. While the persecutors had forced Christians

14. Scholarship on the Circumcellions has preoccupied itself with controversies about their social origins and the nature of their links to the broader Donatist movement, in an ongoing argument between those who seek social or economic explanations and those who understand the Circumcellions more correctly as an essentially religious phenomenon. See, e.g., Tengström 1964, pp. 24–78; Brown 1961 and 1963; Overbeck 1973; Rubin 1995. The name "Circumcellion" seems to have been a nickname meaning "those who go around the *cellae*," which likely refers to the martyrs' shrines around which the Donatist militants were known to gather: Frend 1969. (But the Donatists did not themselves use the word, preferring to be called *agonistici* or *milites Christi*: Augustine, *Enarr. in Psalmos* 132.6; Frend 1985, p. 174.) An interesting analogy might be found in fifth-century Constantinople, where monks who dwelled in the *martyria* on the outskirts of the city had a reputation for being undisciplined and rebellious: see Bacht 1951, Dagron 1970. Caner 2002, pp. 223–235 explicitly compares them to North African Circumcellions.

15. Optatus 3.4 describes the rebellion of Axido and Fasir and their suppression at the hands of Count Taurinus.

16. Optatus 3.4.

17. See, e.g., Optatus 3.10; Augustine *Epp.* 23, 44, 93; *Enarr. in Psalmos* 10.5; *Gesta* of the Conference of Carthage in 411, 1.187. Neither Paul nor the *comes* Silvester, it seems, attained the dubious honor of lending his name to an era of persecution. In Donatist eyes, at least, Macarius was the worst of the persecutors: *ex duabus bestiis taetrior fuit* (*Passion of Marculus* 3).

into the temples of the idols and had demanded that they renounce Christ, Macarius merely "compelled" the lazy into the basilica and encouraged them to pray to God, all together, in one church.[18] This strategy, compulsion for the sake of unity, concealed lethal violence under a benign rhetoric of disciplinary "correction."[19] Optatus, and Augustine after him, justified Macarius' heavy-handed enforcement by arguing that the Donatists had brought it upon themselves through their rash actions, while at the same time denying that the Catholic church bore any responsibility for actions carried out by the secular authorities. The Donatist bishops would later use a similar *quid ad nos?* ("what has that got to do with us?") strategy in distancing themselves from the Circumcellions and from unsavory characters such as Optatus of Thamugadi[20] while at the same time professing to be unaware of any certain wrongdoing by the latter.[21]

Even if it claimed no responsibility, the Catholic church clearly derived great advantage from the Macarian repression. The Catholic clergy were able to take over basilicas that the imperial authorities confiscated from the Donatists.[22] Donatus of Carthage and other major Donatist leaders were sent into exile, many of them not to return until the reign of Julian.[23] Their powerful rivals gone, in 348 the Catholic bishops prematurely proclaimed an end to schism.[24]

The Donatists did not go quietly. Maximian, in Carthage, tore up the imperial edict of unity, in a gesture of defiance that imitated, perhaps deliberately, the action of the unnamed Christian of Nicomedia in the opening days

---

18. Optatus 3.8: *Sub persecutore Floro* (governor of Numidia at the time of the Great Persecution) *christiani idolorum cogebantur ad templa; sub Macario pigri compellebantur ad basilicam! Sub Floro dicebatur ut negaretur Christus et idola rogarentur; contra sub Macario commonebantur omnes ut Deus unus pariter in ecclesia ab omnibus rogaretur.*

19. This "disciplinary" discourse, which by Augustine's time had come to guide both Catholic and imperial policy toward the Donatists, is explored at greater length in chapter 4.

20. A notorious Donatist bishop (388–398) under whose power "all of Africa groaned" (Augustine *Ep.* 108), not to be confused with Optatus of Milevis, the Catholic author. See Frend 1985, pp. 208–226.

21. See, e.g., *Against Parmenian* 1.11 (17), *Against Petilian* 2.32 (73) and 2.64–65 (143–146), *Ep.* 87.

22. Augustine, *Against Parmenian* 1.11 (18).

23. Frend 1985, pp. 180–188. Donatus died in exile (c. 355). The exact place of his exile is not known, but it was clearly outside Africa and presumably within Constans' half of the empire: see *PCBE* s.v. Donatus 5.

24. Thus bishop Gratus at the Council of Carthage: *Gratias Deo omnipotenti et Christo Iesu, qui dedit malis schismatibus finem.* Munier, *Concilia Africae*, p. 3.

of the Diocletianic persecution.[25] Isaac, inspired by his example, publicly denounced the imperial authorities as *traditores.*[26] Through these acts of provocation, both men obtained the martyrdom they sought. Meanwhile, Macarius took up residence at Vegesela, a rural estate near Bagai, and began to attack the Donatist episcopacy of southern Numidia. Bishop Donatus of Bagai, we are told, was thrown down a well and killed, either during the massacre at Bagai or soon afterwards.[27] The Donatist *Passion of Marculus* describes how Marculus and nine other local bishops came to Vegesela in order to negotiate. Macarius immediately had them seized, stripped, bound to posts, and beaten savagely with cudgels. Marculus was then dragged through various Numidian towns and displayed "as a spectacle of their cruelty." One night, in the hours before dawn, soldiers came to remove him from the prison at Nova Petra. One of the guards told him of having had a dream in which he saw himself untying Marculus' bonds. "Because of this," he reassured the prisoner, "hope for a pardon." Marculus, however, was not fooled: he, too, had had a vision, in which he received the crown of martyrdom. The guard's dream meant simply that Marculus would soon be released from his worldly body. Before the light of dawn could expose their crime, the soldiers took Marculus up a nearby mountain and hurled him from a cliff.[28]

What the *Passion of Marculus* presents to us, clearly, is not a formal execution but rather a discreet judicial murder. A public execution is a graphic demonstration of the power and authority of the state, a reminder of the legitimate violence in store for those who defy its laws. If it is not done before the eyes of all, it is pointless. A hidden killing, by contrast, expresses illegality through its very secrecy. By acting in secret, not only do the agents of the state forgo any claim to legitimacy, but they implicitly acknowledge a shameful quality in their action. The soldiers came for Marculus in the dead of the night. If the story of the guard's dream is more than hagiographical hyperbole, it may mean that they removed him from the prison under the pretext of releasing him. In a telling phrase, the author of the *Passion* likens the executioners to "bandits attacking before dawn" *(antelucano latrocinio).*[29] They chose their method of killing in the hope that his body would never be

---

25. *Passion of Maximian and Isaac* 5. The Nicomedia incident (Lactantius *MP* 13, Eusebius *HE* 8.5) is discussed at the beginning of chapter 1.

26. *Passion of Maximian and Isaac* 6. *Traditores, venite, salvate vestrae unitatis insaniam!*

27. Augustine, *Tractates on the Gospel of John* 11.15.

28. *Passion of Marculus* 8–12.

29. *Passion of Marculus* 11.

found amid the jagged rocks at the base of the precipice. "In the silence of the night they stealthily completed the crime" so that no one, not even those at the prison, would have known what happened—until a divine miracle revealed the location of the martyr's remains.[30]

A public execution, of course, would have been highly risky: popular sympathy in southern Numidia was very much on the side of the Donatists, and some sort of demonstration or even attack by Circumcellions might have been feared. More importantly, the imperial government did not wish to be seen with the blood of a bishop on its hands. Christian clergy, even those judged heretical or schismatic, were almost never executed under the Christian empire. Exile was normally the worst a bishop could expect, even when his more humble lay followers suffered far worse.[31] Macarius had already overstepped the norms of late Roman justice by subjecting the Donatist bishops to a brutal beating that effectively degraded them to the level of the *humiliores* for whom such corporal punishments were normally reserved. Above all, though, the authorities did not wish to give the Donatists a martyr—here, as with Maximian and Isaac in Carthage, they tried to dispose of the body in such a way as to prevent any recovery of relics—and yet a martyr is exactly what they got. On the very same day a large crowd of believers found Marculus' miraculously intact body. Both literary and archaeological evidence attests the rapid spread of the cult of Marculus throughout southern Numidia in the late fourth century.[32]

Augustine disbelieved the Donatist account of the deaths of Marculus and Donatus, claiming that the authorities could not have put them to death, because hurling people from cliffs or throwing them down wells were not recognized methods of execution under Roman law: "The Roman authorities never did employ such punishments: for had they not the power to put them to death openly?"[33] But that is precisely the point: these killings were

---

30. *Passion of Marculus* 14.

31. See chapter 2, pp. 98–100.

32. Already in 348, the Catholic bishops at Carthage condemned the veneration of *praecipitatos* claimed as martyrs, an obvious reference to Marculus: Munier, *Concilia Africae*, p. 4. See also, e.g., Augustine *Against Petilian* 2.14 (34): the Donatists called both Marculus and Donatus "prophets." At the Conference of Carthage in 411, the Donatist bishop Dativus of Nova Petra proudly proclaimed, "I have no [Catholic] rival, because there is the Lord Marculus, whose blood God will avenge on the day of judgment." *Gesta* 1.187. Archaeological evidence: Cayrel 1934; Courcelle 1936 on a basilica dedicated to *domnus Marculus* at Vegesela.

33. Augustine, *Tractates on the Gospel of John* 11.15, leaving aside, presumably, the ancient example of the Tarpeian Rock. Cf. also *Against Petilian* 2.20.46 and *Against Cresconius* 3.49.54.

not meant to be lawful executions. The Roman authorities had the power to put them to death openly, but feared the political consequences of using that power. Interestingly, Augustine appears to place the death of Donatus of Bagai in the same category as that of Marculus, treating both as dubious Donatist claims to martyrdom. Although no *Passio* of Donatus has survived to give us the Donatist version of his death, we might speculate that the authorities decided to dispose of the bishop of Bagai in the same quiet and embarrassed way that they had done with Marculus.

The case of Marculus merits the lengthy attention I have given it, because according to the Catholic sources it served as inspiration or pretext for what they describe as a wave of ritual mass suicides by Circumcellions motivated by a desire to be venerated as martyrs. The same Circumcellions, a few years later, would be implicated in dramatic acts of violence against Catholic churches and clergy. Current scholarship has not attempted to explore connections between Donatist expressions of martyrdom and the terroristic violence of the Circumcellions. But modern experience has shown us all too clearly that some who are willing to die for their faith may also be prepared to kill for it.[34] Making sense of the Circumcellions requires that we situate them within the context of the Donatist ideology of martyrdom, a zealotry that found expression both in dramatic self-sacrifice and in vengeance against persecutors and *traditores*.

MARTYRDOM OR SUICIDE?

Marculus—whether he had intended to die or not—had apparently inspired imitators. The Catholic bishops who assembled at the Council of Carthage in 348, while celebrating their restoration to power, took time to condemn the cults of certain "unauthorized" martyrs, particularly the "insane cliff-jumpers" *(insania praecipitatos)*.[35] For Optatus, writing in the 360s, spectacular suicide had come to seem almost characteristic of Circumcellions: "To this class [the Circumcellions] had belonged those who, in their false desire for martyrdom, used to bring assailants on themselves for their own destruction. From this source also came those who used to cast their vile souls headlong from the peaks of the highest mountains."[36]

34. Modern terrorist groups who use suicide bombers to advance their agenda, of course, would see no contradiction in this: see, e.g., the analysis of Hamas in Juergensmeyer 2000.

35. Munier, *Concilia Africae*, p. 4.

36. Optatus 3.4 (Edwards trans.).

Augustine expanded the characterization further: "It is their practice to commit suicide in various ways, particularly by leaping off cliffs, by drowning, or by fire, and they seduce others whom they can, men or women, to follow the same madness; and at times, in order that they themselves may be killed by others, they threaten the latter with death, unless they do what they are bidden."[37]

This issue poses many difficulties of interpretation. Clearly the Donatist emphasis on martyrdom was sufficiently strong to produce on occasion behavior that others might regard as suicidal. At the same time, however, we must be careful not to take our sources at face value.[38] They belonged to the side that benefited from military repression of the Circumcellions, but they were uncomfortable with the use of lethal force. Accordingly, it served their purposes to believe that all the responsibility for bloodshed rested with the other side: violence suffered by the Donatists was either the regrettable but necessary result of their own intransigence or, even better, actually self-inflicted. The Circumcellions "live as bandits and claim to die as martyrs."[39] This phrase sums up the Catholic strategy of discrediting the Circumcellions—and, by extension, the entire Donatist movement—by painting them on the one hand as common *latrones*, living by violence and driven by greed and lust, and on the other hand as fanatics who carry religious imperatives too far.

The case of Marculus illustrates the problem. In Augustine's time, some fifty years later, it was still a matter of dispute whether he had jumped from the cliff, or had been thrown by the imperial soldiers in whose custody he had last been seen.[40] Since the Donatists claimed that Marculus had in fact been murdered, it seems difficult to imagine how his example could have inspired others to suicide. And yet a variety of Catholic sources mention cliff-jumping as a habitual Circumcellion practice.[41] Nevertheless, even if the extent of the practice was exaggerated by our sources, there does seem to be some evidence for cases of suicide or "voluntary martyrdom," and the motives behind this curious practice deserve investigation.

---

37. Augustine, *De Haeresibus* 69 (Muller trans.).

38. Butterweck 1995, pp. 123–140, goes perhaps too far in the opposite direction, treating the stories of mass suicide as nothing more than an invention of Catholic polemic.

39. Augustine, *Against Petilian* 2.84 (184): *Cum vivatis ut latrones, mori vos iactatis ut martyres.* Cf. also *Against Cresconius* 3.42 (46).

40. Augustine, *Against Petilian* 2.20 (46). Cf. also *Against Cresconius* 3.49 (54), *Tractates on John* 11.5.

41. See, e.g., Optatus 3.4; Augustine *Against Parmenian* 3.6 (29), *Epistula ad Catholicos* 19.50, *Against Petilian* 2.92 (204); Filastrius, *Liber de Haeresibus* 62

The Circumcellions who "courted death" seem to have regarded themselves not as suicides but as following in the footsteps of the martyrs. A close look at their specific actions suggests that they had a very clear sense of the difference between suicide and martyrdom and took care not to cross over the line. The manner of Circumcellion death bears little relation to classical Roman Republican or early imperial traditions of suicide, which was normally done in private or among close friends, by a method—usually poison or slitting wrists—chosen for an easy, peaceful, and painless exit. The Circumcellion "suicides" as reported by our sources employed a variety of methods: jumping off cliffs, or into fire or water, or forcing others at swordpoint to be their executioners.[42] All these methods were highly public and spectacular, exactly as had been the martyrdoms of the pagan period. Their styles of death reflected those found in traditional accounts of martyrdom. By forcing other people, and particularly magistrates, to kill them, the Circumcellions recalled martyrs who rushed forward without being sought out, to proclaim their Christianity before the persecuting authorities and demand the appropriate punishment.[43] This had the additional effect of compelling the magistrate to enact the role of "persecutor" to which Donatist ideology had already consigned him, and forcing him to assume the guilt for the crime. Such a demonstration served to heighten the contradictions between the ideal and the reality of Christian empire, by revealing more clearly the "true" persecuting nature of the regime.[44]

The Catholics, clearly, could not allow this claim to stand. If they conceded Donatist martyrdom, they made themselves into collaborators in persecution, *traditores*. Augustine's assessment of Circumcellion motives,

---

(Maier, *Dossier*, vol. 2, p. 67); Praedestinatus 1.69 (Maier, *Dossier*, vol. 2, pp. 227–232). Cliff-jumping might also reflect stories of Christian women who jumped to their deaths to preserve their chastity or to escape persecutors: e.g., Victoria (*Martyrs of Abitina* 17), who was miraculously saved from the fall so that she could later undergo a more proper martyrdom at the hands of Anulinus. Cf. also the Antiochene martyr Pelagia and her sisters, celebrated by Ambrose, *On Virgins* 3.7.33–36 and *Ep.* 37; and John Chrysostom, *Homily on Pelagia* (PG 50 pp. 579–584). Some admittedly ambiguous material evidence may point toward veneration of Circumcellion cliff-jumpers: boulders at the foot of a cliff, marked with names, dates, and the word *reditus:* Frend 1985, pp. 175–176.

42. Augustine, *De Haeresibus* 69.

43. See, e.g., *Passiones* of the Martyrs of Abitina; of Secunda; of Maximian and Isaac.

44. Chapter 5, pp. 192–207, discusses how extremists' deeds served to enact the truth of their worldview, e.g., by provoking retaliation and therefore forcing the state to act brutally, exposing its "true" violent nature.

therefore, cannot be taken at face value. Certainly their choice of methods of death carried symbolic significance. The scriptural analogies adduced by Augustine, however, were entirely negative: the devil telling Jesus to throw himself off a wall, the demon-possessed Gadarene swine who ran off a cliff, and a similarly possessed youth who threw himself into fire and water.[45] Of the cliff-jumpers, Augustine said, "What martyrs? They are not doves, but they tried to fly, and fell onto the rock."[46] Augustine's intention was to deny the Circumcellions any claim to legitimate martyrdom: they were misguided, insane, and possibly possessed by demons, rather than inspired by the Holy Spirit. They went to their deaths driven by fanaticism rather than zeal, superstition rather than religion, Satan rather than God. But Augustine's comparisons surely tell us more about his own rhetorical strategy than about the Circumcellions' true motives, and we ought rather to try to make sense of their actions as they themselves might have understood them.

When speaking in general terms about the Circumcellions' "habit" of suicide, the Catholic sources tried to present it as utterly inexplicable by any rational motive. We must, however, set these remarks alongside our evidence for specific cases of Donatists who actually committed, attempted, or threatened suicide. In their presentation of Circumcellion martyr-suicides as a manifestation of insane fanaticism or demonic possession, the Catholic sources tried their best to obscure the fact that those involved might have had good reasons for choosing death. Some of the Donatist "suicides" may have believed that the imperial authorities were going to put them to death anyway.[47] All of the Donatist "suicides" known to us in any individual detail were people who either expected that they would be killed anyway, or saw death as the only alternative to forced apostasy.[48] Circumcellions who jumped from cliffs or threw themselves into lakes may well have had imperial soldiers pursuing them. Or, as in the case of Marculus, the military

---

45. Augustine, *Ep.*185.12 (417). The scriptural references are, respectively, Matthew 4:5–7 and Luke 4:9–13; Matthew 8:32 and Mark 5:13; Matthew 17:14–18 and Mark 9:16–26.

46. Augustine, *Tractates in John* 6.23: *Quos martyres? Non sunt columbae, ideo volare conati sunt, et de petra ceciderunt*—referring, probably, to the story of Simon Magus.

47. Here a comparison can be made to typical cases of suicide in earlier Roman times: those suicides were usually forced, in the sense that the person had been condemned to die or expected to be. Antiquity's most famous mass suicide, that of the Jews at Masada, becomes much more understandable when one considers what the Romans would have done to those Jews had they captured them alive.

48. Christian opinion generally praised those individuals who chose death in preference to apostasy or sexual violation: cf. Ambrose and Chrysostom on Pelagia,

or civil authorities may simply have found it convenient to report the killing of Circumcellions, or people they identified as such, as "suicides."

An important feature common to the various forms of Circumcellion voluntary death—assuming that they did in fact happen as the sources describe—is that they seem carefully chosen so that one could arguably deny the name of "suicide." In no case did the Circumcellion die by his own hand. Instead he threw himself, sometimes literally, into a situation where an external force, be it the rocks at the bottom of the cliff or the swords of the *apparitores*, would do the actual killing. This distinction may seem rather dubious, and indeed the Catholic sources ridiculed it. But it is clear that both Donatists and Catholics believed that martyrdom and suicide were two very different things, the one praiseworthy and the other not. The difference between the two sides lay in where they drew the line between martyrdom and suicide.[49] When Donatists such as Maximian and Isaac actively sought out and provoked the persecuting powers, rather than waiting to be caught and punished by them, they claimed as martyrdom actions that Catholics rejected as suicidal.[50] A suicide was guilty of his own death—but for the martyr, innocent by definition, the blood was on the hands of the persecutors.

In times of pagan persecution, or even in its absence, some zealous Christians had taken the battle to the demons' very homes, seeking martyrdom by smashing idols. In this respect the Circumcellions show themselves to be very much in tune with extremist tendencies found elsewhere in the fourth-century Christian world. Catholics and Donatists alike claimed to be dedicated to the destruction of idolatry, and both had their share of clashes with North African pagans. In Augustine's eyes, however, there was a right way and a wrong way to attack pagan worship. The correct method was to employ the power of the state: to seek imperial legislation, and convince the

---

cited above. Augustine, with his unequivocal condemnation of suicide under any circumstances, is the exception: see, e.g., *City of God* 1.17–20, explaining why women who killed themselves to avoid rape were wrong to do so. See Trout 1994. Augustine's uncompromising stand on this issue can be explained in large part by the ever-present need of the Catholic Church in North Africa to deny and delegitimize Donatist claims to martyrdom.

49. The difference Augustine wishes us to see, by contrast, is moral: true martyrdom is only that which is undergone for a good cause (*Against Parmenian* 3.6 (29); *Against Gaudentius*, passim). But certainly the Donatists were every bit as convinced of the rightness of their cause as Augustine was of his.

50. The Catholics, for their part, went out of their way to deny that there were any "persecuting powers" under the Constantinian empire. Augustine, *Against Petilian* 2.92 (204): "What Macarius is pursuing you?"

local authorities to enforce it, in order to stop sacrifice, remove idols, and close temples in a lawful and orderly manner. In this way, in 399, the imperial officials Gaudentius and Jovius had demolished the pagan temples of Carthage without provoking any disturbance.[51] In the same year, Augustine himself presided over the lawful destruction of idols on rural property that the formerly pagan owner had given to the church upon his conversion to Christianity.[52]

The wrong way, by contrast, was the Circumcellions' way. They simply rushed in and began smashing, and without the permission or protection of the authorities they risked being killed by angry pagans. Indeed, Augustine suggests, the Circumcellions' primary motive was in fact to secure a dramatic martyrdom, and it mattered little to them whether they actually succeeded in smashing the idols.

Here we must keep in mind Augustine's polemical strategy. He accepted that the suppression of idol worship was a praiseworthy enterprise that helped to advance the Christian faith. But he did not wish to concede any of the credit to his Donatist rivals. Accordingly he implied that they did not even seriously try to stamp out idolatry: they simply threw themselves on the swords of the pagans, leaving the idols undisturbed. Their method was not only illegitimate but also ineffective. Augustine even made the Circumcellions into unwitting facilitators of pagan ritual by asserting that the pagans "vowed" (*vovebant*) those whom they killed to their gods.[53]

In claiming that the Circumcellions were more interested in suicide than in idol-smashing, Augustine probably distorted their motives. It might perhaps be more accurate to say that they were determined to smash idols and did not fear the consequences. But having no fear of death, and actively seeking death, are two quite different things. We do not know, in fact, that every

51. Augustine, *City of God* 18.54; they were probably implementing *C.Th.* 16.10.18 (399). Compare *Sermon* 24 (401) on a curious incident in which the proconsul of Carthage "shaved the beard" of a cult statue of Hercules: *Fratres, puto ignominiosius fuisse Herculi barbam radi, quam caput praecidi.*

52. At Mappalia, near Carthage: *Sermon* 62.17–18 (399).

53. *Against Gaudentius* 1.28 (32): *Eorum enim est hominum genus ... qui solebant haec et antea facere, maxime cum idolatriae licentia usque quaque ferveret, quando isti paganorum armis festa sua frequentantium irruebant. Vovebant autem pagani iuvenes idolis suis quis quot occideret.* On remarks such as this, Lepelley 1980 builds an elaborate argument for continuity between pre-Christian Saturnian human-sacrifice cults and Circumcellion "suicide." It should be kept in mind, however, that whatever use the pagans may have made of such an incident tells us nothing about what the Christians themselves intended. Frankfurter 1990 offers an intelligent and sensitive methodology for evaluating claims of pagan-Christian continuities.

Circumcellion attack on a pagan temple ended in failure and a one-sided massacre of Christians. If the Circumcellions brought the same degree of violence to bear against the pagans as they did against the Catholics, we can suppose that they probably destroyed their fair share of idols. However, Catholic sources would be loath to give them the credit. In any case, the Circumcellions would have understood their own actions within a paradigm of martyrdom, not suicide.[54]

Christian sources throughout the Roman world boasted of incidents in which the destruction of a temple brought about a mass conversion of pagans.[55] Accordingly, a contest between Donatists and Catholics to attack paganism was understood at least potentially as a competition for converts. Such high stakes explain the urgency with which Augustine had to deny and delegitimize all Donatist anti-pagan activity. But reckless idol smashing was hardly unique to the Circumcellions. In many cases, Christians did not wait for the sanction of imperial law or the protection of magistrates and soldiers to begin breaking idols and destroying temples.[56] In the western church, at least, attitudes were lukewarm toward this method of attaining martyrdom. The Council of Elvira stated simply that those who were killed for breaking idols would not be received into the number of the martyrs.[57] Of course, if people had not been doing it the prohibition would not have been necessary. Augustine found it necessary to reprimand his fellow Catholics on this point. He reminded his listeners that this was no way to true martyrdom, and warned them not to act "like Circumcellions," a remark that suggests that the Circumcellions had no monopoly on the practice—or perhaps that the lines dividing Donatist from Catholic were not so clearly drawn down at the level of ordinary laity.[58]

54. Numerous examples of zealous Christians seeking martyrdom through attacks on pagan temples and statues can be found outside North Africa: see chapter 1, pp. 29–30 (during the Great Persecution); chapter 2, pp. 92–94 (under Julian); chapter 5, pp. 160–168 (under Christian emperors).

55. Most famously at the Serapeum in 391 (Rufinus *HE* 11.23–24; Socrates *HE* 5.16–17; Sozomen *HE* 7.15, 20; Theodoret *HE* 5.22) and the Marneion of Gaza in 402 (Mark the Deacon, *Life of Porphyry of Gaza*). At Minorca in 418, the same tactic was used against Jews: Severus of Minorca, *Letter on the Conversion of the Jews*.

56. See chapter 5, pp. 175–179.

57. Council of Elvira (c. 300) *Canon* 60. A likely motive may have been the fear that such acts of provocation by individuals might bring down pagan retaliation on the entire Christian community, which at that time was still a fairly weak minority. On Christian attitudes toward idol smashing, see Kötting 1979, Thornton 1986. For more on "provocation" in the context of pagan persecution, see chapter 1, pp. 39–40.

58. *Sermon* 62.17.

This insight may help set in context a mysterious incident that took place at Sufes in 399, known only from one tantalizingly brief letter of Augustine. Christians apparently destroyed a cult statue of Hercules, and the ensuing pagan reaction left sixty Christians dead. We are not told whether all sixty had taken part in the attack on the statue or if some of them were innocent victims of indiscriminate pagan vengeance, nor whether the idol smashers were residents of Sufes or outsiders. One thing conspicuous by its absence was a strong Christian reaction. One might expect sixty martyrs—more than were ever killed on any single occasion in North Africa during the Great Persecution—to receive lavish commemoration, mention in many sources both inside and outside Africa, and angry calls for imperial retaliation against the pagans of Sufes.[59] The event may be contrasted to another incident of anti-Christian violence at Calama in 408, when despite days of rioting and the burning of a church by a pagan mob, only one person actually died, but the pagans of the town were so terrified of the emperor's anger that they begged Augustine to plead with the authorities to save them from capital punishment.[60] At Sufes, however, not only was there no discussion of punishment but the pagans apparently had the nerve to demand compensation for their statue.[61] At Calama the pagans were clearly in the wrong, and the Christians could expect the full weight of the law to come down on their side. At Sufes, the lack of evidence for any legal retaliation or even threat thereof, after a much bloodier incident, might plausibly be explained by supposing that the Christians had less of a case. Those who were killed could reasonably be said to have brought it upon themselves by smashing the idol, an act of provocation that the Catholic establishment in North Africa considered to be beyond the pale of legitimate Christian zeal. If this supposition is correct, we may envision a group of zealous Christians, who gathered for the express purpose of destroying a pagan cult object and met with violent resistance from the pagans. It is impossible to tell whether or not these people were aligned with the Donatist cause. But it is significant that the Christians killed in Sufes had acted in a manner that Augustine

---

59. Augustine, *Ep.* 50 (399). The sixty are commemorated in the Roman martyrology on 30 August, apparently on the sole basis of Augustine's letter.

60. *Epp.* 90 and 91, 103 and 104.

61. Which would seem to be the occasion for Augustine's response in the surviving letter. Had the Sufites addressed themselves to him directly, and if so does that suggest that they held him somehow responsible for the conduct of the Christians? The reason for his involvement in the affair is not immediately obvious, since Sufes was far from his own diocese. It is not certain from the text of the letter, however, whether the pagans had actually written to Augustine or if he was simply expressing his indignation after receiving word of the incident.

elsewhere characterized as reckless, misguided, suicidal, and thoroughly characteristic of the Circumcellions. In this context, writing against pagans and not Donatists, Augustine could identify himself with the dead Christians, whichever church they may have represented, in order to condemn the pagans as murderers.[62]

In order to place some limits upon the charismatic authority that might be claimed by martyrs and confessors, ecclesiastical authorities throughout the Roman world endeavored to keep for themselves the power to decide who might and might not rightly be called a true martyr.[63] In situations where claims to martyrdom formed a politicized discourse, controlling its meaning became all the more important. Catholics challenged and contested Donatist martyrial ideology in order to delegitimize the religious zeal that drove Donatist violence—a violence directed increasingly against the Catholics themselves.

CLEANSING THE TEMPLE: DONATISTS IN POWER

In 362, the pagan emperor Julian allowed the Donatist bishops who had been exiled in 347 to return home. Julian knew exactly what would happen: "No wild beasts are as vicious to men as most Christians are to each other."[64] Optatus reports a wave of Donatist attacks on churches that broke out as soon as the bishops returned.[65] The Donatists sought to gain control of church buildings and expel Catholic clergy. Many of these churches had probably once been Donatist before being seized by the Catholics in 347–348. Control of worship space was often the primary object of struggle between rival Christian groups throughout the Roman Empire in the fourth century. Battles for basilicas could be quite bloody.[66] In an urban setting, large groups

---

62. Augustine's flexibility on this point parallels the ease with which Nicene orthodox historical tradition readily took up the veneration of many originally non-Nicene Christians martyred under Julian: see chapter 2, p. 92.

63. Cf. the intriguing story in Sulpicius Severus, *Life of Martin* 11, where Martin of Tours delegitimized an unauthorized local cult by "discovering" that the grave that locals had venerated as that of a martyr really contained an executed bandit: see Giardina 1983.

64. *Nullas infestas hominibus bestias, ut sunt sibi ferales plerique Christianorum expertus:* comment by Ammianus (22.5.4) on Julian's policy.

65. Optatus, bk. 2 passim. See also Frend 1985, pp. 187–192.

66. The example most often cited is Ammianus 27.3 on the Damasus-Ursinus dispute of 366, which left one hundred and sixty dead in the Sicinian basilica in Rome. Cf. also the clash over Constantine's body in 346, which reportedly killed three thousand in the courtyard of the Church of the Holy Apostles in Constantinople (Socrates

fighting in enclosed spaces could produce heavy casualties. Nevertheless the purpose of the fighting was to seize the building, and bloodshed was an incidental consequence. People were hurt or killed largely insofar as they resisted, or were simply unlucky enough to get in the way. This seems to have been the case in the one such incident described by Optatus in some detail, a Donatist attack upon the church in the *castellum* at Lemella in which a Catholic priest was killed defending the altar.[67]

Having secured possession of formerly Catholic worship space, the Donatists then began a series of symbolic actions that can be broadly interpreted as purifications. The need for such rituals arose from the particular nature of the Donatist-Catholic split, and the Donatist argument that sacraments performed by *traditores* were invalid. This included the sacrament of ordination, and therefore the entire Catholic hierarchy was seen as illegitimate even in Augustine's time when the original *traditores* were long dead.

So much we already knew from the Donatist polemics of Parmenian, Petilian, Cresconius, Gaudentius, and others, as preserved in the responses of Optatus and Augustine. But actions should speak at least as loudly as words, and these symbolic actions show us the polemicists' arguments being put into practice at the ground level. The Donatists regarded Catholic sacraments not only as invalid and lacking in divine grace but as actively evil and polluting. Thus the entire Catholic clergy and everything they touched were defiled and damned by the "original sin" of Felix and Caecilian. They could only be redeemed by purification. For most people, this took the form of rebaptism, which (both Optatus and Augustine charged) the Donatists often administered by force. Sometimes, also, they forcibly "scraped" the heads of Catholic clergy, and compelled consecrated virgins to exchange their veils for new, "pure" ones.[68] Simultaneously public humiliation, purification, and degradation, scraping the priests' heads may have been a symbolic removal of the oil of consecration. All of these rituals served to wipe away the taint of *traditio*.

The buildings themselves had to be purified as well. Thus the Donatists either scraped off, smashed up, or simply removed the altars, whitewashed

---

HE 2.37) and, in the fifth century, a similar incident at a schismatic Novatian church (Socrates *HE* 7.5). For a revisionist interpretation of these incidents see McLynn 1992.

67. Optatus 2.18.

68. 2.22. *Radere* probably refers to some sort of shaving, and not to a bloody scalping, since Optatus makes no mention of anyone being seriously injured thereby. Consecrated virgins: Optatus 6.4.

the walls, and either actually washed out the interior of the building or symbolically sprinkled it with salt water.[69] Chalices and other serving vessels used by Catholic priests in their perverted sacraments had to be melted down. The Donatists regarded the Catholics' consecrated host as useless and tainted, and accordingly they threw it to the dogs, which the Catholics of course considered to be terrible sacrilege.[70]

A parallel to the Donatists' extreme emphasis on purity and cleansing can be found in the universal Christian concern to avoid or wipe out the pollution associated with pagan blood sacrifice.[71] Christian attacks on pagan sites usually aimed for the destruction of statues, sacred trees, or other cult objects, and often an entire temple might be physically dismantled, stone by stone.[72] Such awareness of the pollution of pagan worship seems to have been particularly characteristic of ascetic zealots who conceived of life as an unending struggle against demons. Since it was believed that demons actually dwelled within the very statues and stones, the physical destruction of these objects could be seen as a form of exorcism. We have seen that the Donatists regarded Catholicism as little more than paganism in a clever disguise: rites designed to cleanse Catholic persons and places from the taint of *traditio* may well have had a similar exorcistic form and purpose. Optatus himself recognized this in a backhanded way when he accused the Donatists of "exorcising the Holy Ghost" by such rituals.[73]

We have seen, in sectarian struggles elsewhere in the Roman world, the ways in which displays of violent power within the walls of a church were understood as sacrilegious violations of sacred space. The first blood of the Donatist schism, a generation earlier, had been spilled inside the basilica at Avioccala.[74] To the Catholics, the violent "cleansing" now perpetrated by the Donatists fit neatly into this pattern, an armed invasion of the church.[75]

---

69. Cf. Augustine, *Ep.* 108, mentioning some extreme Donatists who believed that the ground should be washed with salt water wherever a Catholic priest had set foot.

70. Optatus (2.19) assures us that the dogs promptly went mad and attacked their masters.

71. Optatus 6.3 outlines the polluting qualities of pagan worship.

72. As Constantine did with the temple of Venus, which occupied the site of the Holy Sepulcher in Jerusalem: Eusebius, *VC* 3.25–30. For more examples see chapter 5, pp. 157–158.

73. Optatus 2.21.

74. *Sermon on the Passion of Donatus of Avioccala*, c. 317. See discussion in chapter 1, pp. 54–56.

75. Optatus' account of the sacrilegious behavior of the Donatists in Catholic churches thus parallels Athanasius' polemical description of the violence wrought by soldiers and pagans in the churches of Alexandria: see chapter 2, pp. 79–88.

But to the Donatists, Catholic clergy and sacraments were themselves a source of pollution, tainted by their complicity with persecuting secular powers. Barring actual bloodshed within the walls of a church, there is little indication that parties to sectarian conflicts outside North Africa ever felt the need to reconsecrate a church building simply because it had previously been used by a rival sect. In this the Donatists were unique. In their eyes the violence of their cleansing served to create a purified church that symbolized the purified community of the faithful.

DONATIST DISSENTERS

Following the Donatist resurgence under Julian, it seems that for the remainder of the fourth century the Catholics posed little challenge to Donatist ascendancy in large parts of North Africa.[76] Imperial coercion against the Donatists came only occasionally and had little effect. Circumcellion violence now directed itself against several schismatic movements that split away from the larger Donatist Church during this period. The Rogatists, a small cabal of Mauretanian bishops, broke away in the 360s specifically because they disapproved of the conduct of the Circumcellions.[77] Tyconius, a grammarian excommunicated by the Donatist bishops for his "heretical" opposition to rebaptism, wrote his critical remarks against the Circumcellions around 380.[78] Tyconius remarked disparagingly upon Circumcellions who sought out violent death either through misguided admiration of the martyrs or in the hope of themselves being venerated as martyrs. He did this in the context of discussing *superstitio*, which he defined as religious devotion taken to excess, beyond what is commanded.[79] In 392–394 a schism developed out of a disputed election to the bishopric of Carthage. Primian, the successful candidate, offended many by his abusive behavior and his violent treatment of opponents.[80] The followers of Maximian split

76. For the events of this period, see Frend 1985, pp. 193–226.
77. Augustine *Ep.* 93 (408), to Vincentius, Rogatist bishop of Cartenna.
78. On Tyconius see *PCBE* s.v. Tyconius; Frend 1997, esp. pp. 618–624.
79. Hahn 1900, *Tyconius-Studien*, pp. 68–69 (fragment preserved in Beatus of Liebana, *In Apocalypsin Commentaria*, 297.33ff.): *Superstitio dicta est, eo quod superflua aut super instituta religionis observatio. Et isti non vivunt aequaliter ut ceteri fratres, sed quasi amore martyrum semetipsos perimunt, ut violenter de hac vita discedentes et martyres nominentur.* Compare criticisms of "excessive" or "false" zeal discussed in chapters 6 and 7.
80. The Maximianist Council of Cebarsussa condemned him in 393 for a long list of abuses, one of the more bizarre of which was having a priest thrown down a drain: text in Maier, *Dossier*, vol. 2, pp. 73–81.

away from the larger Donatist church, and as a result they suffered savage persecution at the hands of the Circumcellions over the next decade.

Much of the existing scholarship suffers from the tendency to treat the Circumcellions as a tightly organized, cohesive, and homogeneous group in which all members must have been recruited from the same sources and driven by similar motives, an assumption that creates considerable difficulty in making sense of inconsistent and contradictory behavior reported by the sources.[81] The concern of some Circumcellions to avoid literal "bloodshed" by using only blunt weapons was not shared by others.[82] A better model may lie in Zeev Rubin's conception of a core group of religiously committed *agonistici*, surrounded by a much larger and less stable body of followers, diverse in origins and motives and uncertain in discipline and loyalty, whose numbers would rise and fall in tandem with the fortune and reputation of their charismatic leaders.[83] It is even possible that the same sort of thugs who moved on the outer fringes of the Circumcellion movement might occasionally have shown up in the service of Catholic bishops. Given the frequency of savage Donatist attacks on Catholic clergy, it is reasonable to suppose that the latter would have begun recruiting some sort of bodyguards.[84]

Such a model would begin to make sense of the inconsistent and ambiguous evidence we have regarding the degree of control that the Donatist clerical hierarchy exercised over the movement. Axido and Fasir, the "Captains of the Saints," had a complex relationship to the Donatist bishops, who eventually appealed to the imperial authorities to crush their uprising. Some people, including at least one priest, wished to venerate the fallen Circumcellions as martyrs, but the Donatist episcopal leadership forbade it.[85] That incident had no obvious connection with the Donatist-Catholic struggle except insofar as the followers of Axido and Fasir were the same sort of people whom Donatus of Bagai recruited a few years later to resist Macarius and

---

81. *C.Th.* 16.5.52 of 412 has misled some scholars into presenting the Circumcellions as a legally constituted *ordo*, just below plebeians and tradesmen and above *coloni* and slaves: see Atkinson 1992, Barnard 1995. But surely this neat and legalistic scheme of classification is more representative of the outlook of the imperial bureaucrats in Ravenna, who drafted the edict, than of any North African reality.

82. See below, pp. 126–127.

83. Rubin 1995, esp. pp. 178–179.

84. At the Conference of Carthage in 411, the Catholic bishop Trifolius of Abora in Proconsularis defiantly proclaimed that any Donatist caught in his town would be summarily stoned: *Nomen si illic auditum fuerit donatistarum, lapidatur* (*Gesta* 1.133). At Fussala, a village only recently converted from Donatism, we might perhaps see some of bishop Antoninus' partners in crime, as well as those who threatened violent opposition to him, as "ex-Circumcellions." (Augustine, *Epp.* 209 and 20*.)

85. Optatus 3.4.

provoke another massacre.[86] At least a few Donatists objected to the excesses of the Circumcellions.[87] In other situations, however, Circumcellion violence was clearly deployed in the Donatist cause. Seizures of basilicas and attacks on Catholic clergy obviously served Donatist interests and in some cases were personally directed by Donatist bishops and clergy. Moreover, the symbolic meaning of particular acts of violence on these occasions can only be understood within the context of Donatist ideology. Nevertheless, the Donatists' disclaimers of *quid ad nos?* were not always as disingenuous as Augustine would like us to believe.

There may well have been some truth in Augustine's charge that the Donatist bishops were afraid to condemn the misdeeds of the Circumcellions lest they lose what tenuous degree of influence they possessed over them, or even become a target of their attacks. Once called forth in the service of the Donatist church, such violence was difficult to control and occasionally turned inward.[88] When Tyconius wrote a history of the Donatist-Catholic schism, he gave it the telling title *De Bello Intestino*, "The Civil War."[89]

DONATISM ON THE DEFENSIVE

The Donatists had dominated much of North Africa for several decades, effectively tolerated if never formally supported by an imperial government distracted elsewhere. By the turn of the fifth century, that had started to change. The powerful Donatist bishop Optatus of Thamugadi had aligned himself with Gildo, Count of Africa, whose armed uprising against emperor Honorius was suppressed in 398. Both men were executed for treason.[90] The imperial regime might ignore the ecclesiastical equivalent of rebellion, but was not about to tolerate the real thing. Longstanding Catholic complaints now found a more receptive ear in Ravenna. For the first time since 347, the Catholic bishops were able to enlist the power of state on their side in a sustained effort to force the Donatists into "unity." Around 400, the Catholic church under the effective leadership of Aurelius of Carthage and Augustine of Hippo began a much more aggressive strategy against the Donatists.

86. Optatus 3.4.
87. See discussion of Rogatists and Tyconius, pp. 122–123 above.
88. Augustine, *Ep.* 108 to Macrobius, citing as example that bishop's own troubled relationship with the Circumcellions.
89. Gennadius, *De Viris Illustribus* 18. The work is not extant. Cf. similar language of "civil war" used of the fifth-century Christological controversies, in chapter 8, pp. 283–284.
90. For these events see Frend 1985, pp. 208–226.

Under the pretext of investigating Donatist violence against the Maximianists, the Catholics sent bishops and priests to missionize in areas that had long been left to the Donatists.[91] In the first decade of the fifth century, they finally succeeded in convincing the imperial government in Ravenna to apply its existing anti-heretical laws against the Donatists.[92] In 411 the imperial commissioner Marcellinus presided over a formal disputation between Donatist and Catholic bishops in Carthage, which resulted in the official condemnation of Donatism.[93] Learning from the experience of Macarius, the Catholics were careful to avoid violent and deadly repression that might only give the Donatists more martyrs.[94] Instead, they petitioned the secular authorities to impose economic penalties and legal disabilities. This heavy coercive pressure triggered a savage response from the Circumcellions, who now directed their violence entirely against their "persecutors" among the Catholic clergy.

It becomes immediately apparent that their tactics had taken a decidedly more violent turn since the time of Optatus, shifting toward brutal physical attacks on the persons of the Catholic clergy. This move toward more terroristic tactics, the violence of opposition, reflected the new political climate of the imperial crackdown. Seizing buildings would have done the Donatists little good, since they would not have been able to hold them. They shifted rather to hit-and-run ambushes targeting the leadership among their opponents. No longer were Catholics' injuries simply incidental to attacks on basilicas. Now the Circumcellions actively sought out Catholic clergy, pulling them from their homes or ambushing them on the road.[95] Restitutus, a former Donatist priest who had joined the Catholics, was pulled from his house, severely beaten, rolled in a muddy ditch and covered in straw, and dragged around to be displayed in a cage for several days. Maximian of Bagai, dragged away from the altar, beaten, stabbed in the groin and left for dead, lived to travel to Italy and shock the imperial court by displaying his

---

91. A policy announced at the Council of Carthage of September 13, 401: *Ut legatio ad Donatistas componendae pacis gratia dirigatur.* Munier, *Concilia Africae*, pp. 200–201.

92. The laws can be found under Title 16.5 *(de haereticis)* of the *Theodosian Code.*

93. On the Catholic effort and the imperial crackdown see generally Frend 1985, pp. 244–289. Introduction and commentary to the Conference in vol.1 of Lancel 1972–1991, *Actes de la Conférence de Carthage.* Needless to say, the outcome of the Conference had been decided by the authorities in advance. On the Donatist bishops' tactics at the Conference, see B. Shaw 1992, Tilley 1991b.

94. Chapter 4 discusses the Catholic strategy in detail.

95. Only a miracle saved Augustine from falling victim to such an ambush himself: Possidius, *Life of Augustine* 12.

scars. Possidius was ambushed and severely beaten at the behest of his Donatist rival, Crispinus of Calama.[96] The Catholics, it could be argued, were asking for it: this new wave of violence followed directly upon the Catholic bishops' decision in 401 to send missionaries into areas such as southern Numidia formerly conceded to the Donatists.

Some aspects of Circumcellion violence appear fairly straightforward and need no special explanation in terms of religious symbolism. Beating and burning of houses were common ways of using force to chase away a rival, or to intimidate the lay population and prevent them from supporting the Catholics. This sort of activity, aimed at harassing and intimidating enemies, was characteristic of power relations throughout the Roman world, particularly in the countryside where effective law enforcement was almost nonexistent.[97] Such force would normally be characterized by those on the receiving end as *latrocinium*. Rolling a victim such as Restitutus in mud and straw and displaying him in a cage served an obvious purpose of public humiliation, perhaps the North African equivalent of tarring and feathering.

Other features of Circumcellion personal violence deserve special comment. Augustine referred time and again to their "terrible clubs," which they called "Israels."[98] There are indications that some of the Circumcellions emphasized the fact that they did not "shed blood" with swords and therefore claimed that they could not be accused of "violence."[99] There are, equally, indications that this rule was not consistently followed among all those whom Augustine classed under the term "Circumcellions": "Look at your mobs, who are not armed only with clubs, after the old way of their parents, but have added axes, lances and swords."[100] Some of those who had more recently joined the Circumcellions felt no restraint on the kinds of

96. Restitutus: Augustine, *Ep.* 88. Maximian: *Ep.* 185.7.27. Possidius: *Against Cresconius* 3.43 (47)ff. See *PCBE* s.vv. Restitutus 6, Maximian 4, Possidius 1.

97. See generally MacMullen 1974, Bagnall 1989. Cf. in an ecclesiastical context Dioscorus' brutal treatment of opponents in Egypt, as described in the *libelli* brought against him at the third session of the Council of Chalcedon: see chapter 8, pp. 317–321.

98. See, e.g., *Enarr. in Psalmos* 10.5: *et terribiles fustes Israelis vocare*.

99. *Psalmus* 157–160: "Because it is written 'Sheathe your sword' [Matthew 26:52] they find no wrong in the cudgel," even if the victim later dies from the blows: *Quia scriptum est: reconde gladium, scelus non putant in fuste, non ut homo non moriatur, sed ut conquassatur valde et postea moriatur inde, iam cruciatus in languore. Sed tamen si miserentur, occidunt et uno fuste.*

100. *Against Petilian* 2.97 (222). *Respicite paululum catervas vestras, quae non antiquo more parentum suorum solis fustibus armantur, sed et secures et lanceas et gladios addiderunt.*

weapons they could use, and the violence intensified in direct response to the escalation of Catholic and imperial persecution.[101] This calls into question the degree of unity and cohesion among the Circumcellions, and the measure of control that the Donatist leadership exercised over them. It does seem, however, that in what we might call "normative" Donatist ideology there was a distinction between "bloodshed," which seems to connote use of weapons specifically designed to kill, and other forms of violence, which could be characterized as "nonlethal" and therefore less objectionable, even if in practice people were sometimes killed thereby. Their intent, usually, seems to have been not to kill, but to cause pain and injury for purposes of coercion and intimidation. But they do not seem to have been particularly concerned that some of their victims did in fact die of their injuries.[102]

There were more practical reasons for eschewing certain weapons: a sword was a sword and had no plausible use other than killing people. Anyone caught with a sword, who was not a soldier or otherwise authorized to have one, could be considered a *latro* and punished accordingly. But there were any number of commonly available tools with legitimate nonviolent uses that could nevertheless be used to smash skulls when the situation demanded, most obviously the Circumcellions' infamous "Israels," which may well have been the same sort of long sticks used to knock down the olives at harvest time.[103] The need to avoid being caught with an undeniably lethal weapon was particularly important for the Circumcellions, whose activities had no legal sanction.

As imperial persecution intensified, the Circumcellions struck back by imitating Isaac's triumph over the emperor. Around 406, they began blinding Catholic clergy by forcing a mixture of powdered lime and vinegar *(calce cum aceto)* into their eyes.[104] Because it is so unusual, and presents no ob-

---

101. In one incident, a Catholic priest had his hands and tongue cut off, presumably to stop him from blessing or preaching: Augustine *Ep.* 185.7.30. The priest's hands, of course, were the means by which the taint of *traditio* was "handed down" from one generation of clergy to the next.

102. See discussion of "disciplinary violence" in chapter 4, pp. 140–144.

103. As Tengström 1964, p. 52, suggests. But while it is entirely plausible that some of the Circumcellions may have doubled as itinerant laborers who worked the olive harvests, nevertheless it is a large and unwarranted jump from there to an assertion that the Circumcellions as a group were an organized and legally constituted association of harvest-workers.

104. First mentioned by Augustine in *Against Cresconius* 3.42 (46) and 3.48 (52); cf. also *Breviculus Collationis* 11.22; *Epp.* 88, 111, 185.7.30; Possidius *Life of Augustine* 10. In *Against Cresconius* (dated c. 406) Augustine describes the practice as a *novo et antehac inaudito sceleris genere* and specifically places its appearance after the visit of Maximian of Bagai to Ravenna and the new anti-Donatist edicts that

vious practical purpose, we may suspect that the Circumcellions chose this method of attack in order to make a point.[105] The explanation should be sought in the special prominence in Christian thought and expression given to seeing and light as metaphors for understanding and faith, and blindness and darkness for the lack thereof. This imagery finds its center in Acts 9, the story of the conversion of Saul on the road to Damascus. Saul, a persecutor of the Christians, was stricken with blindness so that he might see. Petilian, the Donatist apologist, invoked this story to support his argument that the Catholics, like Saul, were persecutors:

> Therefore, as we said, the Lord Christ cried to Paul: Saul, Saul, why do you persecute me? But Paul said, Who are you, Lord? And the answer to him: I am Christ of Nazareth, whom you are persecuting. And he, trembling and stupefied, said: Lord, what do you want me to do? And the Lord said to him: Get up and go into the city, and it will be told you what you are to do. And further on: Saul got up from the ground but although his eyes were open, he could not see anything [*apertisque oculis suis nihil videbat*]. O blindness, the punishment of madness [*o ultrix furoris caecitas*], you obscure the light from the eyes of the persecutor, to be removed only by baptism! Let us see then what happens in the city. Ananias went in, it says, to Saul, and when he laid his hands upon him, he said: Saul my brother, the Lord has sent me, Jesus who appeared to you on the road by which you were coming, so that you might see and be filled with the Holy Spirit. At once it was as if scales fell away from his eyes, and he received vision and arising, was baptized. When, therefore, Paul, freed by baptism from the crime of persecution, put on innocent eyes, why should you, persecutor and *traditor* blinded by false baptism, not wish to be baptized by those whom you persecute?[106]

Augustine also employed the language of sight and blindness, at one point in almost identical words. Advocating the use of coercion to bring people into the true church, he asked:

> For who can possibly love us more than Christ, who laid down His life for His sheep? And yet, after calling Peter and the other apostles by His

---

he obtained. Dr. Thomas Quinn, ophthalmologist, has informed me that such an injury would in most cases result in permanent blindness.

105. In Palestine in 453, a blind Samaritan recovered his sight and converted after smearing his eyes with the blood of murdered Christians: Zacharias of Mytilene, *Chronicle* 3.6. On sight and blindness in late antique Christian thought, see now Frank 2000, esp. pp. 114–118. On punitive blinding in the early middle ages, see Bührer-Thierry 1998.

106. *Against Petilian* 2.21 (47) (NPNF trans.).

words alone, when He came to summon Paul, who was before called Saul, subsequently the powerful builder of His Church, but originally its cruel persecutor, He not only constrained him with His voice, but even dashed him to the earth with His power; and that He might forcibly bring one who was raging amid the darkness of infidelity to desire the light of the heart, He first struck him with physical blindness of the eyes . . . since he had been wont to see nothing with his eyes open.[107]

Augustine frequently justified religious coercion with reference to the "good physician" who must inflict pain in order to save the patient.[108] In a sermon of 404 we find a metaphor that is not just medical but specifically ophthalmological:

> Imagine a man, blinded by a certain darkness. . . . The doctor [says to him]: "I am about to apply some stronger eye-salves, which will wash away the darkness from you, and from their harshness you will feel some pain. But it is necessary for you to bear this health-giving pain [*dolorem salubrem*] patiently, and not to push away my hands anxious and unable to bear the discomfort . . . I warn you that you will suffer something troublesome together with the increase of illumination."[109]

Such language, pervading the polemic of both sides, provides a context in which to view the Circumcellions' actions.[110] The Catholics, as persecutors (and the only attested victims of this practice were Catholic clergy), were "blind" even if their eyes were intact. The Circumcellions, with an extreme literalism, had taken a metaphor common to Christian discourse and made it a physical reality, reenacting both Isaac's triumph over the emperor and Christ's conversion of Paul.

In the end, however, the emperor won. The escalating savagery of Circumcellion violence and the suicide threats of Gaudentius and the priest Donatus signalled desperation in the face of a relentless imperial crackdown.[111] In the last years of his life, Augustine made little mention of the Donatists.

---

107. *Ep.*185.6.22 (NPNF trans.). Similar language in *Ep.* 93, to Vincentius the Rogatist (408): "Saul was compelled . . . by the great violence with which Christ coerced him, to know and embrace the truth; for you cannot but think that the light which your eyes enjoy is more precious to men than money or any other possession." (NPNF trans.)

108. See discussion of surgical metaphors in chapter 4, pp. 146–147.

109. *Sermon* 360B (Dolbeau 25, Mainz 61). Dolbeau dates the sermon to early 404. (My trans.)

110. The polemical exchange between Petilian and Augustine took place c. 401–405, immediately before the first reported incidents of blinding.

111. On the crackdown and its effects, see Frend 1985, pp. 290–299; Brown 1963; Lancel 1989. On Gaudentius, see chapter 4, pp. 139–140.

After the Vandal conquest of 429–435 we hear no further mention of the Circumcellions.[112] Brutal repression of both African churches by the Arian Vandals may finally have caused Donatists and Catholics to bury their differences.[113] It was a bitter irony for the Catholics, who themselves could now claim to be a persecuted "Church of the Martyrs."[114]

The collapse of Donatism, ultimately, can be traced to the failure of the "Church of the Martyrs" to co-opt the power of that same state that it saw as "persecutor." In theory, the late Roman state commanded far more violent power than any potential rival: even the most fanatical zealots would be no match for trained and armed soldiers. Nevertheless, as we shall see in chapter 5, in practice the state rarely made any serious attempt to repress the activities of revered holy men in the same way that it would stamp out an outbreak of "banditry" where no religious issues were involved.[115] In North Africa, by contrast, it was the relentless application of the state's coercive power that finally put an end to the power of the Donatists and their Circumcellions. This became possible only because one of the two rival church organizations in North Africa, the Catholic, finally managed to convince the imperial authorities to recognize it as the sole legitimate Christian church—making the Circumcellions the religious equivalent of bandits and creating the ideological justification for their merciless suppression. Isaac may have plucked out its eye, but the Constantinian empire endured.

112. Huneric's anti-Catholic edict of 484 (in Victor of Vita, *History of the Vandal Persecution* 3.10) mentions Circumcellions, but only because it is recycling the language of *C.Th.* 16.5.52 of 412.

113. On the supposed "Donatist revival" in the late sixth century, see the thoughtful analysis of Markus 1991.

114. On Catholic martyrdom under the Vandals see Victor of Vita.

115. On the response of the secular authorities to the violence of holy men, see chapters 5 and 6.

4.   *Temperata Severitas*

Augustine, the State, and Disciplinary Violence

You are of the opinion that no one should be compelled to follow righteousness, and yet you read that the householder said to his servants, "Whomsoever ye shall find, compel them to come in."[1] You also read how he who was at first Saul and afterwards Paul, was compelled, by the great violence with which Christ coerced him, to know and to embrace the truth. . . .

I have therefore yielded to the evidence afforded by these instances which my colleagues have laid before me. For originally my opinion was that no one should be coerced into the unity of Christ, that we must act only by words, fight only by arguments, and prevail by force of reason, lest we should have those whom we knew as avowed heretics feigning themselves to be Catholics. But this opinion of mine was overcome not by the words of those who controverted it, but by the conclusive instances to which they could point. For, in the first place, there was set over against my opinion my own town, which, although it was once wholly on the side of Donatus, was brought over to the Catholic unity by fear of the imperial edicts.[2]

This was the answer Augustine offered in 408 to the Donatist bishop Vincentius of Cartenna, who had spoken in opposition to the new imperial crackdown on religious dissent. Vincentius was the leader of the Rogatists, a small group of bishops who a few decades earlier had split from the larger Donatist church, apparently in protest against the forceful tactics of Parmenian and other Donatist leaders.[3] A minority of a minority, the Rogatists un-

---

1. *Cogite intrare:* Luke 14:23.
2. Augustine, *Letter to the Rogatist bishop Vincentius,* 408 (Augustine *Ep.* 93.2.5 and 93.5.17) (NPNF trans.).
3. On the Rogatists see Frend 1985, pp. 197–199.

surprisingly advocated toleration: "no one should be compelled to follow righteousness." Augustine was quick to accuse Vincentius of self-serving hypocrisy: "No wild beast is said to be gentle if, because of its not having teeth and claws, it wounds no one."[4] Vincentius would certainly use coercion if he had the means to do so. Surely, too, Vincentius would not disapprove of the imperial laws against pagan sacrifice.[5] Augustine went on to recount his own "conversion" on the issue of compulsion: at first, like Vincentius, he had worried that coercive measures would merely produce insincere converts, superficial Catholics who would remain Donatists at heart. But the effects of the new laws, he said, changed his mind and afforded him new arguments and justifications. Some had already believed, but had kept quiet from fear of Donatist violence. Others had clung to Donatist error simply through tradition and force of habit, and had never previously been compelled to consider the issues at stake.[6] Now that same force of habit would lead them back into the fold. Even those whose conformity was at first merely superficial would eventually, through repetition, take to heart what they professed.[7] This was a fundamentally utilitarian argument: coercion was acceptable because it *worked*. Practical experience had overcome Augustine's initial worries.

Augustine, having reached this useful conclusion, had little trouble convincing himself of its rightness. There was ample scriptural warrant. Christ had compelled Saul to the truth with violence. Sarah had justly chastised her servant Hagar. Moses had punished his disobedient people.[8] The process of correction might be painful, but indulgence was no kindness.[9] Eventually, those saved by severity might come to appreciate the fact.[10] Augustine took great satisfaction in describing how former Donatist congregations, once coerced, now freely thanked God for their deliverance from error— "which thanks they would not now be offering willingly, had they not first, even against their will, been severed from that impious association."[11] For Augustine, free will and compulsion were not necessarily incompatible.

---

4. *Ep.* 93.3.11.

5. *Ep.* 93.3.10.

6. See, e.g., *Epp.* 93.5.17; 93.2.5; 185.7.25.

7. *Ep.* 185.7.30.

8. *Epp.* 93.2.5, 185.6.22. Compare *Against Petilian* 2.21.47, discussed in the previous chapter, pp. 128–129.

9. *Ep.* 93.1.2.

10. *Ep.* 93.3.10: *Sed plane in eis qui sub nomine Christi errant seducti a perversis, ne forte oves Christi sint errantes, et ad gregem taliter revocandae sint, temperata severitas et magis mansuetudo servatur.*

11. *Ep.* 185.3.13 (NPNF trans.). Compare *Epp.* 93.5.18, 185.2.7.

Thus an overtly coercive paradigm came to define the Catholic and imperial approach to the Donatist problem. Augustine's change of heart on this issue has rightly been seen as a defining moment in church history, an endorsement of muscular state intervention in matters of faith.[12] What is important here is the reasoning behind the establishment's violence: the wielders of power, and their apologists, needed to believe in the rightness of their actions. Thus they reassured themselves that their might was applied not for selfish reasons but for the greater good of their subjects, whether or not the latter appreciated the fact. Their coercion justified itself through a disciplinary discourse: it employed calibrated violence not to destroy its targets but to chastise, reform, and even educate them.[13] This was the violence of the center, the establishment—the emperor and his functionaries, or ecclesiastical authorities who enjoyed the recognition and support of the state and had recourse to its means of enforcement.[14] Its motives, in theory, were not anger or vengeance but rather a paternalistic compassion. But as mildly as this approach may have sought to present itself, ultimately it depended upon a coercive power backed up by the very real possibility of violence.

The bloody futility of earlier imperial persecutions was not easily forgotten.[15] Christian authorities of the late fourth century came to favor a more indirect, "corrective" strategy because both historical experience and their own values made them shy away from a Diocletianic approach. They had learned well that persecution created martyrs, and they did not wish to be seen as persecutors, whether in the public eye or, indeed, in their own estimation. Most bishops, meanwhile, were deeply reluctant to entangle themselves in the exercise of secular power—or at least well aware of the need to *appear* so.[16] For Augustine, the necessity of compulsion came as an unwelcome distraction from the peace and quiet he preferred, and was only compelled upon him by the "restless" behavior of the Donatists.[17]

Violence—whether of the margins or of the center—cannot be understood without reference to the values, motives, and self-presentations of its authors. Where extremists used violence to polarize and to draw clear lines,

---

12. See especially Brown 1961, 1963, 1964; also Markus 1988, pp. 133–153.

13. Cameron 1995 identifies "ascetic discourse" as a guiding factor in the political and intellectual development of late antique society and comments on its fundamentally "disciplinary" nature.

14. Or what Hannah Arendt 1970, p. 42, calls "the violence of all against one."

15. See chapter 1.

16. See chapters 2 and 5 for emperors and magistrates, chapter 7 for bishops.

17. *Ep.* 93.1.1: *Nunc me potius quietis esse avidum et petentem ... Sed Donatistae nimium inquieti sunt, quos per ordinatas a Deo potestates cohiberi atque corrigi mihi non videtur inutile.*

the violence of the center sought to blur distinctions and suppress conflicts, and thereby bring all into unity.[18] Where zealots worried about authenticity, challenging Christians to live up to their values, and seeking to "expose" the true nature of their enemies, the establishment tolerated a certain degree of hypocrisy, declaring itself satisfied with outward conformity. Unlike later medieval inquisitions, anti-heretical initiatives of the fourth and fifth centuries had little concern for the private beliefs of ordinary people, placing priority on the regulation of public practice, expression, and discussion. Heretical beliefs, once renounced, could easily be forgiven—the crime lay rather in an obstinate and stubborn refusal to accept correction by ecclesiastical authority. The pastoral metaphor pervaded bishops' understanding of their duties toward the Christian laity. False teachers—"wolves in sheep's clothing"—threatened to lead the flock astray. With the help of the secular laws, the shepherds of the church could chase away heretical predators and return lost souls to the fold.[19] An inevitable consequence of the metaphor was the tendency of churchmen to see their charges as no more capable than sheep of understanding their own best interests. This conceit reflected the more generalized attitude of paternalistic condescension that defined relations between late Roman authorities both secular and ecclesiastical and their subordinates.[20] It allowed Augustine and like-minded colleagues to rationalize policies that forced people, willing or not, toward the good. Charity—the Christian duty to love one's neighbor—demanded no less.[21]

But charity went both ways. It implied not only a duty for those in authority to care for the rest, but also an obligation of gratitude and obedience on the part of those governed. Heretics and schismatics, for their conspicuous failure to accept this duty, could be portrayed as selfish, rebellious, and prideful. We have already seen how those who resisted the coercive harmony of religious consensus found themselves stigmatized as "lovers of contro-

18. This self-consciously centrist governing ideology found its antecedents in classical political discourse, which postulated a sensible "middle way" between anarchy and tyranny. Fourth-century Homoianism, likewise, sought to present itself as a unifying center against the twin extremes, Nicenes and hard-line Anomoians (see chapter 2, p. 75). A century later, Chalcedon would stake out a similarly centrist stance between the opposing heresies of Eutyches and Nestorius (chapter 8, pp. 312–314).

19. See, e.g., Augustine *Ep.* 93.3.10.

20. Under the rubric of "condescension," Peter Brown has recently linked late antique discourses of charity and poverty to the "face-to-face tyranny" of imperial rule: Brown 2002, esp. chap. 3.

21. For Augustine, all scriptural interpretation pointed toward the simple commandments, "Love God and love your neighbor." This is the defining theme of, e.g., *On Christian Doctrine*.

versy" and enemies of unity.[22] The Donatists, by setting themselves against the opinion of the whole world and refusing to make peace, displayed a profound lack of charity. For Augustine, obedience—"the daughter of charity"— distinguished the true church of the Catholics from the false one of the Donatists.[23] *Caritas*, as a Christian virtue, conveyed both this generalized "good attitude" and also our more familiar and specific sense of material assistance to the poor. The genius of Catholic polemic was to tie the two together: without the "charity" of submission, reconciliation, and restored communion, the Donatists forfeited any credit for their "good works," whether almsgiving, asceticism, or martyrdom.

Augustine was not the first to pursue this strategy. In a close reading of Optatus' account of the mission of Macarius, Giovanni Cecconi has shown how a discourse of charity formed the center of an ideology and self-definition with which the Catholic bishops countered the martyr-centric Donatist worldview.[24] The language of charity allowed Optatus to retell the story of the *Tempora Macariana* in a way that absolved the perpetrator and blamed the victim: Macarius and his imperial sponsor Constans acted with the best of intentions, and the Donatists were entirely at fault for the violence inflicted upon them. The emperor planned to offer substantial material charity to North African congregations as an inducement to bring them back into unity with the Catholic church. In return, he hoped, the Donatists would themselves display charity by forgiving and forgetting their grievances. The schismatics, in rejecting unity, showed their contempt for the Christian imperatives of love, forgiveness, and harmony. The Donatists' refusal of imperial largess in itself revealed their own uncharity, Optatus charged, because it denied Constans the chance to redeem his sins through almsgiving![25]

Donatus and his colleagues, of course, saw things very differently. The mission of Macarius was an egregious usurpation of their own prerogatives. Ordinarily, dispensing charity was the sole responsibility of local bishops, who in this case happened to be Donatist. Even if much of the money ultimately came from the emperor, it was the bishop who spent it, and the bishop who was accustomed to reap the benefits of patronage. For imperial officials to dispense charity directly, bypassing the bishops, seemed a deliberate insult. Their presence at the altar alongside imperial images represented a po-

22. See chapter 1, pp. 58–62.

23. See, e.g., *Sermon* 359B (Dolbeau 2, Mainz 5) *On Obedience* (Hill trans.), p. 343.

24. Cecconi 1990.

25. Optatus 3.3.

tentially sacrilegious intrusion of secular power into the sacred space of the church. Subsequent events of the *Tempora Macariana* seemed to confirm the Donatists' worst fears. When secular authority entered the church, violence and coercion—"persecution"—followed closely behind. Macarius and Paul travelled with a military escort, perhaps because they anticipated Donatist resistance, or perhaps simply to safeguard the treasure they carried. Optatus chided Donatist bishops and clergy for their "irrational" flight before the advance of Macarius, who he claimed used "no terror, no clubs, no guards, but exhortation only"—but Optatus then belied himself in remarking that of those who fled, "some died, but the stronger ones were captured and exiled."[26] As subsequent events proved, the Donatists were right to flee before Macarius. The clashing and highly partisan accounts of Catholic and Donatist sources make it difficult to say which side bore responsibility for the initial outbreak of violence. But the massacre at Bagai illustrates how easily things could get out of hand when the imperial government attempted to solve a religious problem with military force. Perhaps it was not the emperor's original intent that Donatists be compelled literally to accept charity at swordpoint, but means had overwhelmed ends. The grim absurdity of Circumcellion would-be martyrs who threatened magistrates, "Execute me, or I'll kill you," found its equally bizarre match in an imperial policy that effectively said, "Accept our charity, or die."

Acting, they felt, with the best of motives, the Catholics had nevertheless achieved the worst of outcomes. Augustine, decades later, conceded that Macarius had acted "excessively"—but quickly changed the subject, arguing that the more recent outrages of the Circumcellions negated any legitimate grievances the Donatists might have had about the events of 347.[27] Nevertheless, he was well aware that the old policy of direct violent coercion had achieved precisely the opposite of its intentions. Far from securing unity, the Macarian mission left a bitterly divisive memory half a century later. A more sophisticated approach was now called for.

Very much desiring and welcoming the assistance of the state's coercive power, Augustine nevertheless worried about its potential to spin out of control and escalate into murderous brutality. Even as he invoked the secular

---

26. *Nullus erat primitus terror; nemo viderat virgam, nemo custodiam; sola, ut supra diximus, fuerant hortamenta. Timuistis, fugistis, trepidastis . . . Fugerant igitur omnes episcopi cum clericis suis; aliqui sunt mortui, qui fortiores fuerunt capti et longe relegati sunt:* Optatus 3.1.

27. See, e.g., *Psalmus contra partem Donati* 151–154: *Modum si excessit Macharius conscriptum in christiana lege / Vel legem regis ferebat cum pugnaret pro unitate / Non dico istum nil peccasse, sed peiores vestros esse.*

law against his enemies, he bent over backwards to soften its impact and restrain its worst excesses. The appropriate answer to extremists steeped in an ideology of martyrdom, he thought, was not to play their game, but to deny them the deaths they so fearlessly sought. The pagan Julian, ironically, had attempted a similar strategy against his Christian opponents.[28] The Catholics, by Augustine's time, preferred to counter Donatist claims to martyrdom by depriving the Donatists of martyrs. Perhaps learning a lesson from the experience of Macarius, Catholic bishops were careful to avoid violent and deadly repression that might only confirm Donatist fears of persecution. Augustine on several occasions intervened with imperial authorities to ask that captured Circumcellions be spared torture or execution. Donatist violence was to be answered not with violent persecution but with a steady coercive pressure that used fines, legal disabilities, and confiscations to bring recusants into the Catholic church.[29] It was not retributive punishment but rather disciplinary correction, a paradigm that justified coercive force out of the necessity to "save" the Donatists from the consequences of their own error. Augustine at first had sympathized with the classic argument of the persecuted church that faith coerced is not true faith. But with the persecuting power of the state now firmly on his own side, he decided that such power, if used carefully and with the proper intentions, could find legitimate uses.

This timely change of heart was neither unique to Augustine, nor limited to the Donatist controversy. Christians of the Theodosian era were learning to appreciate the didactic power of coercive laws deployed against pagans and heretics, even as some prominent pagans conveniently voiced appeals to "tolerance" previously heard from the Christian apologists of earlier centuries.[30] When in 408 the pagans of Calama rioted, burned a church, and assaulted clergy, their spokesman Nectarius begged Augustine's intervention to head off imperial retribution.[31] Augustine's response laid out his scheme of disciplinary punishment. Of course, he promised, he would oppose any capital penalty or torture. But for their fears of losing wealth and property to confiscation, he had little sympathy. Confiscation would deprive them of the "means and opportunities of living a wicked life" and, if deprivation in this world brought them to reflect upon their error, would save them from far worse punishments in the next. Their failure to recognize

28. See chapter 2, pp. 90–96.
29. The strategy is outlined particularly well in Augustine's lengthy letter (*Ep.* 185 of 417) to the tribune Boniface. See also *Ep.* 133.
30. See Ando 1996.
31. See *Epp.* 90, 91, 103, and 104.

their own best interests in this policy of compassionate coercion did not in any way weaken its necessity:

> When any one uses measures involving the infliction of some pain, in order to prevent an inconsiderate person from incurring the most dreadful punishments by being accustomed to crimes which yield him no advantage, he is like one who pulls a boy's hair in order to prevent him from provoking serpents by clapping his hands at them; in both cases, while the acting of love is vexatious to its object, no member of the body is injured, whereas safety and life are endangered by that from which the person is deterred. . . . For, in most cases, we serve others best by not giving, and would injure them by giving, what they desire. Hence the proverb, "Do not put a sword in a child's hand. . . ." Wherefore it is for the most part an advantage to themselves when certain things are removed from persons in whose keeping it is hazardous to leave them, lest they abuse them.[32]

Pagans, Augustine concluded, could not be trusted with sharp objects. But to save them from the sword, it might be necessary to employ the surgeon's scalpel:

> When surgeons see that a gangrene must be cut away or cauterized, they often, out of compassion, turn a deaf ear to many cries. If we had been indulgently forgiven by our parents and teachers in our tender years on every occasion on which, being found in a fault, we begged to be let off, which of us would not have grown up intolerable? Which of us would have learned any useful thing? Such punishments are administered by wise care, not by wanton cruelty.[33]

Thus Augustine acknowledged that it might be necessary to employ a correction that would cause pain to its beneficiaries. The same lesson could be applied to the Donatists:

> It is indeed better, as no one ever could deny, that men should be led to worship God by teaching, than that they should be driven to it by fear of punishment or pain; but it does not follow that because the former course produces the better men, therefore those who do not yield to it should be neglected. For many have found advantage, as we have proved, and are daily proving by actual experiment, in being first compelled by fear or pain, so that they might afterwards be influenced by teaching. . . . While those are certainly better who are guided aright by love, those are certainly more numerous who are corrected by fear. . . . "He that spareth the rod hateth his son."[34]

32. *Ep.* 104.2.7 (NPNF trans.).
33. *Ep.* 104.2.7 (NPNF trans.).
34. Augustine *Ep.* 185.6.21 (NPNF trans.).

Augustine readily admitted that the Donatists would perceive this as "persecution." But, he argued, it mattered who did it to whom and why. The measured coercion of imperial law and Catholic policy was not to be compared with the wild and murderous violence of the Donatists:

> There is a persecution of unrighteousness, which the impious inflict upon the Church of Christ; and there is a righteous persecution, which the Church of Christ inflicts upon the impious. She therefore is blessed in suffering persecution for righteousness' sake; but they are miserable, suffering persecution for unrighteousness. Moreover, she persecutes in the spirit of love; they in the spirit of wrath; she that she might correct, they that they might overthrow.[35]

As with persecution, so also with martyrdom, it was the cause that mattered for Augustine. The Donatists could not claim to be "martyrs" simply by virtue of their suffering. Because they did not belong to the true church, their deaths carried no more nobility than those of common criminals.[36]

But Donatists were not discouraged from martyrdom by Augustine's attempts to redefine it. Some chose death in response to heavy coercive pressure intended to force them into communion with the Catholics. The priest Donatus, who had been seized near Hippo and brought forcibly into Catholic worship, first attempted to injure himself by falling off his horse, and then jumped into a well.[37] For the Donatists, to be forced into the Catholic church seemed no different from being forced to deny Christ and sacrifice to idols. In 420, the tribune Dulcitius advanced into southern Numidia to enforce the imperial edicts which commanded unity.[38] His approach inspired among the local Donatists the same mixture of panic and defiance with which they had awaited Macarius seventy-three years previously. Gaudentius, bishop of Thamugadi, took refuge in the great basilica and threatened to immolate himself along with his entire congregation.[39] A long standoff then ensued. Gaudentius composed a treatise in which he defended his action and claimed it as martyrdom, drawing heavily on Maccabees' examples of Jews who preferred death to apostasy.[40] Augustine's answer, *Against Gaudentius*, coun-

---

35. *Ep.* 185.2.11 (NPNF trans.).

36. See *Sermon* 359B (Dolbeau 2, Mainz 5) *On Obedience*, esp. 18.

37. Augustine *Ep.* 173 (416).

38. For what follows, the sources are Augustine, *Against Gaudentius* and *Ep.* 204.

39. Such mass suicides were rare but not unheard of. In sixth-century Phrygia, a group of Montanists would burn themselves alive in their church rather than submit to Justinian's anti-heretical edicts: Procopius, *Secret History* 11.23.

40. Particularly Razias, and the woman with her seven sons: 2 Maccabees 14:41–46 and 7, respectively. On Christian veneration of the Maccabees in late antiquity, see Schatkin 1974.

tered with a detailed exposition of Catholic doctrine on martyrdom and condemned the Donatist for seeking mere suicide.

Meanwhile, Dulcitius had also been in correspondence with the bishop of Hippo. As the tribune drew near to Thamugadi, he had apparently threatened the Donatists, "Know that you are to be given a well-deserved death." If—as the Donatists claimed—he meant this literally, it threatened to undermine the Catholic bishops' painstakingly calibrated strategy of disciplinary correction. Augustine sharply reminded the tribune that the edicts he was charged to enforce made no mention of capital punishment, but instead called for fines and confiscation. Of course, Augustine delicately suggested, Dulcitius must have been misunderstood: surely the tribune was only remarking upon the Donatists' well-known habit of suicide.[41] The final outcome of the standoff at Thamugadi is not known.[42] Dulcitius' zeal for enforcement certainly made peaceful resolution more difficult, although it is unclear whether Gaudentius' followers would have been any more receptive to a gentler approach. Some were ready to choose death before "unity," while others may have worried that they would be killed anyway. It is clear that the tribune had overstepped his authority, just as Macarius had done in 347. Although the edicts that directed Macarius have not survived, we may assume that they had not originally envisioned the torture and execution of bishops. The events of the *Tempora Macariana* had demonstrated how easily the application of military force could lead to a bloodbath even when such had not been intended by the authorities.

How could what claimed to be a policy of corrective discipline result in bloodshed and death? The idea of disciplinary violence, exercised for the greater good of its recipients, implied that force and coercion could be carefully measured and precisely calibrated. The reality, of course, was far messier. The attitudes and rationalizations behind disciplinary violence— and the unintended consequences resulting from its application—reveal broad commonalities across a range from the individual level of personal relationships to the grand scale of imperial politics. What forms of vio-

---

41. *Ep. 204: Sed quod ibi dixisti, "Noveritis vos debitae neci dandos", putaverunt sicut eorum rescripta indicant, hoc te fuisse comminatum quod tu illos apprehensos fueras occisurus, non intelligentes de illa nece, quam ipsi sibi volunt ingerere, te locutum.* Droge and Tabor 1992, pp. 167–183, in their extended discussion of *Contra Gaudentium*, overlook the significance of the tribune's behavior, which seems to have needlessly exacerbated the situation.

42. Frend 1985, p. 296, reports some archaeological evidence of fire at the basilica site, but it may date from a later century.

lence were considered acceptable in what circumstances, and where were the limits of appropriate discipline?

Certainly the norms of late Roman secular society allowed for many situations in which physical violence was thought to be entirely appropriate. A certain degree of (usually) nonlethal violence helped to enforce asymmetrical power relationships. Those in authority were expected to use disciplinary beating to control the behavior of those under their command. Masters could beat their slaves or servants, teachers their students, fathers their children. This "normal" violence helped to define the structure of Roman social relations. As we have noted, the main status distinction in late Roman society lay between *honestiores,* elites who were—in principle if not always in practice— immune to physical violence against their persons, and whose crimes were to be punished by action against their property; and *humiliores,* ordinary people, liable to gruesome physical punishment. The station of the victim ordinarily determined whether violence was acceptable or not: for *honestiores* to suffer physical violation in their bodies was uniquely degrading, and therefore an outrage against their dignity; but the same types of violence were normal and unremarkable when they fell upon *humiliores,* who had no dignity to begin with.[43] Still, there were certain rules and expectations governing how ordinary disciplinary violence should and should not be exercised. Although a master's right to discipline his slaves and servants by beating them was unquestioned, at the same time it was thought unseemly for a master to strike someone with his own hand. Elite opinion tended particularly to condemn the man who flew into a rage and beat servants "excessively"—not because the servants were thought to have any rights that were being violated but simply because it was in bad taste: unseemly displays of anger violated the decorum that lay at the heart of expectations of elite behavior.[44]

Augustine, writing to the *comes* Marcellinus in 412 to plead that captured Circumcellions be spared from torture or execution, argued that simple beating was as appropriate and useful in the judicial sphere as it was in households, schools, and even in the church:

43. Bagnall 1989, p. 213, quotes a statement to this effect in *P.Wisc.* 1.33: "It is most disgraceful for free persons to suffer *hubris.*" The term *hubris* is used here in the sense of physical assault, but also conveyed a sense of "outrage" at such violence being directed against an inappropriate target. Generally on violence as a structural aspect of social relations: MacMullen 1974, Garnsey 1970, articles in *Du châtiment dans la cité* 1984.

44. On beating servants in excessive or unseemly manner: Brown 1988, pp. 11–12, with several examples.

Fulfill, Christian judge, the duty of an affectionate father; let your indignation against their crimes be tempered by considerations of humanity; be not provoked by the atrocity of their sinful deeds to gratify the passion of revenge, but rather be moved by the wounds which these deeds have inflicted on their own souls to exercise a desire to heal them. Do not lose now that fatherly care *[paternam diligentiam]* which you maintained when prosecuting the examination, in doing which you extracted the confession of such horrid crimes, not by stretching them on the rack, not by furrowing their flesh with iron claws, not by scorching them with flames, but by beating them with rods *[virgarum verberibus]*—a mode of correction used by schoolmasters, and by parents themselves in chastising children, and often also by bishops in the sentences awarded by them [in the episcopal courts].[45]

Augustine allowed that a judge could legitimately feel "indignation" but felt that punishment should follow not from a desire for vengeance but solely from a paternal concern for correcting the sinner.[46] Fatherly discipline, in Augustine's thought, formed a far-reaching theme that bound together elements ranging from his own childhood experience, to ecclesiastical policy, even to his scheme of historical theodicy. The young Augustine's school lessons introduced him to beating for the sake of education and improvement.[47] In *Confessions*, this became a metaphor for God's paternal discipline. The long and tortured intellectual and emotional journey by which Augustine came to Christianity resulted, he believed, from the coercive and corrective application of God's power: "For You were always with me, mercifully punishing me, touching with a bitter taste all my illicit pleasures."[48] God's "beating" saved him from worse sins and their consequences: "In all this I experienced your chastisement. . . . I even dared to lust after a girl and to start an affair that would procure the fruit of death. So you beat me with heavy punishments, but not the fruit of my guilt."[49]

What the rod of correction had done for him, it could do for others—so Augustine advised fellow bishops to use it on schismatics, landlords to use it on their peasants, and fathers to use it on disobedient sons.[50] His language

---

45. Augustine *Ep.* 133.2 (412) (NPNF trans.). On episcopal courts: Cimma 1989; Raikas 1990; Lamoreaux 1995; Harries 1999b, pp. 191–211; and now the articles by Harries, Lenski, and Dossey in Mathisen 2001.

46. *Sermon* 159B.4 (Dolbeau 21, Mainz 54).

47. See *Confessions* 1.9.14–10.16.

48. *Confessions* 2.2.4 (Chadwick trans.). Russell 1999 links Augustine's thoughts on coercion to his doctrine of signs as outlined in bk. 13 of *Confessions*.

49. *Confessions* 3.3.5 (Chadwick trans.). Compare similar language in 5.8.15–5.9.16; 8.7.18; 8.11.25; 9.4.12; also *City of God* 22.22.

50. See, e.g., *Sermons* 5, 13; *City of God* 19.16.

could be taken literally, referring to actual beating. At other times it could work metaphorically, referring to nonphysical coercion, as with the anti-heretical laws that targeted property and civil rights. But it could also disguise far bloodier violence. Even such a catastrophe as the sack of Rome in 410, he argued, showed God's greater purpose—to punish us for our sins, and to teach us not to value temporal things.[51] Whether it was God chastising individuals and peoples, a teacher disciplining his student, a master punishing his slave, or a father his son, the same sense of "tough love" expressed itself, through disciplinary violence, toward the greater good of its targets.[52]

There were, of course, limits to the means that could be used in pursuit of this salutary goal—at least, when Augustine spoke literally of physical discipline applied to individuals. Beating with rods or sticks, which seems to have been a common method of punishment in familial or educational contexts, would have been painful as well as humiliating. But ordinarily it would not kill or gravely injure, nor leave lasting scars. Augustine praised Marcellinus for using rods to beat confessions out of suspected Circumcellions, in part because their confessions removed any need for more injurious forms of torture.[53] A clear distinction must be made between the simple beatings described above and the far more serious floggings often applied to slaves and criminals, which shed blood, left scars, and not infrequently resulted in death.[54] Thus Augustine, though outraged by the illegal depredations of slave-dealers, declined to enforce a particular edict against them because it called for offenders to be flogged with lead-tipped whips.[55] Flogging, even if intended for a disciplinary purpose, still carried danger. Shenoute's harsh regime of physical discipline—which he saw as "educational" *[paideuein]*—led to the accidental death of at least one of his monks. For Shenoute, the beating enacted God's anger against the sinner. Thus he found himself in a dilemma. If he flogged, he feared that he might kill; but if he did not flog, he feared offending God.[56]

51. See *Sermo de excidio urbis Romae; City of God,* esp. bk. 1.

52. For a thorough exploration of this image, with numerous examples, see de Bruyn 1999.

53. *Ep.* 133. On torture in the context of judicial interrogation, see Harries 1999b pp. 122–134.

54. de Bruyn 1999, pp. 286–289, discusses in detail the various terminologies used to describe beating, whipping, and flogging.

55. Lead-tipped whips: Augustine, *Ep.* 10*.4.

56. Sources: Emmel 1993, pp. 892ff. Shenoute's disciplinary practices have occasioned much discussion: cf. Leipoldt 1903, pp. 140–143; Elm 1994, pp. 305–306; and esp. Krawiec 2002, pp. 27–29, 40–42, 59–72, 101–106. Basil's canons acknowledged that fatal beating occasionally happened, and though worthy of severe penance

Where did one draw the line between deadly violence and corrective discipline? Scriptural injunctions such as Jesus' words to Peter—"sheathe your sword" because "those who live by the sword shall die by it"—left much room for ambiguity.[57] Did it forbid all violence, or did it refer specifically to "bloodshed" by the sword? As opposing parties in the Donatist controversy traded accusations back and forth, some said that it was not "violence" to beat or club—even to death—so long as blades were not used and blood was not shed. Where Augustine claimed to endorse only "corrective" infliction of pain, which was intended to bring about a change of heart without causing death or permanent physical damage, the Circumcellions seem to have taken the scriptural injunctions far more narrowly and literally and concluded that any form of violence not actually involving a sword was permitted.[58] But this particular evasion was not theirs alone, as Optatus tellingly let slip when he answered Donatist claims of martyrdom: "How can you call them martyrs when none of them were struck by the sword?"[59] The *Sermon on the Passion of Donatus of Avioccala*, remembering Constantine's repression of Donatists in 317, said explicitly what Optatus only hinted at: "As if they could say it was less of a martyrdom, because they were massacred by clubs instead of swords."[60] A few years earlier, Lactantius had condemned the hypocrisy of persecutors who tortured their victims to a point just short of death and then congratulated themselves for avoiding "bloodshed."[61]

The same paradigm of disciplinary correction that justified violence against individuals also found expression on an institutional scale, in the paternalistic language that pervaded the rhetoric of imperial law.[62] Whether

---

was not to be considered murder (though he was probably addressing secular heads of household): cf. Basil, *Canon* 8 (*Ep.* 38), *Canon* 43 (*Ep.* 99), *Canon* 54 (*Ep.* 217).

57. Matthew 26:52.

58. Invoking Isaiah 22:2: "They have not been killed by the sword, nor did they die in battle." Examples of Circumcellion violence against Catholic clergy are discussed in the previous chapter.

59. 3.8: "Show me one man who was ever struck by the sword under Macarius!" *Aut probate aliquem illo tempore gladio esse percussum!*

60. *Sermon on the Passion of Donatus of Avioccala* 6: *Quasi minus martyres dicerentur qui non gladiis, sed impia caede fustibus trucidabantur.*

61. Lactantius, *Divine Institutes* 5.11: "But that is the worst kind of persecutor whom a false appearance of clemency flatters; he is the more severe, he the more cruel torturer, who determines to put no one to death . . . that they may be able to boast that they have slain none of the innocent—for I myself have heard some boasting that their administration has been in this respect without bloodshed [*administratio sua . . . fuerit incruenta*]." (ANF trans.)

62. See Cameron 1995, p. 157.

confronting schismatics, heretics, stubborn pagans, or indeed those who defied laws on secular matters, imperial policy deployed the credible threat of official violence to compel offenders to choose the right path.[63] But at this level, particularly, the distinction between healthy, corrective violence and lethal force could easily blur. Constantine offered his Christian bishops a show of mildness, reassuring them, "If we reprove a fault, is not our object to admonish, not to destroy; our correction for safety, not cruelty?"[64] while adding ever-harsher measures to a penal code already noted for its physical savagery.[65] Bishops like Augustine enjoyed only intermittent success in persuading emperors and magistrates to restrain the worst excesses of criminal law. But the bishops themselves were often complicit in the violence that could erupt when they asked the state to use its power against their rivals. As we have seen in both the Trinitarian and Donatist conflicts, the use of soldiers to disperse rebellious assemblies or seize disputed basilicas brought a heavy toll of "collateral damage" that in the worst cases could result in massacre.[66]

Sometimes authorities could justify for themselves the means by which corrective discipline stumbled its way into lethal force. The church might find itself reluctantly compelled by the necessity of self-defense to ask for military assistance—as the Donatists themselves had done early in the 340s when terrified by the rebellions of Axido and Fasir. Because they were beyond the bishops' power to "correct"—*in ecclesia corrigi non posse*—it was the duty of Count Taurinus to impose a grim *disciplina* that left corpses piled around desecrated altars.[67] The Donatists' professed eagerness for martyrdom—"suicide" to the Catholics—was intended to serve a deterrent purpose: if you force us into martyrdom, our blood will be on your hands. It had worked, once, against Constantine.[68] Augustine, however, would not be deterred. Charity, he argued, did not allow us to let the possi-

<hr />

63. The strategy of disciplinary coercion, pursued by Constantine's fourth-century successors, could be seen as a more muscular alternative to that emperor's alleged "forbearance" in religious matters as proposed by Digeser 2000. See my comments in chapter 1, pp. 64–66.

64. Constantine, *Oration to the Assembly of Saints* 23 (NPNF trans.).

65. Constantine ordered, for example, that nursemaids who helped their wards elope were to have molten lead poured down their throats: *C.Th.* 9.24.1. On "judicial savagery" see MacMullen 1990b.

66. See chapters 2 and 3.

67. The incident is discussed in Optatus 3.4.

68. See chapter 1, pp. 53–57. Zealous and violent "holy men" would use the same strategy, often successfully, against other emperors and magistrates in other contexts: see next chapter.

bility of a few deaths prevent us from taking action to save many others. Whether these were deliberate suicides like Gaudentius, or simply those likely to be killed resisting the law, their deaths were a regrettable necessity and they had only their own stubbornness to blame.[69] Advocates of capital punishment—which Augustine opposed, because it left no opportunity for repentance—made a similar appeal to the greater good. If some offenders were beyond correction, perhaps their deaths would provide a salutary warning to deter others from imitating their crime. Upon this strategy of spectacular punishment and deterrence rested much of the force of imperial law.[70] Its grim example, Diocletian had assumed, would terrify Christians into abandoning their superstition—even though Christians themselves confidently proclaimed that their suffering and death would only inspire still more to martyrdom.[71]

Organic and medical imagery offered additional ways of rationalizing coercion. As we have seen, Augustine often favored medical metaphors to justify coercive punishment, invoking the physician or surgeon who must reluctantly inflict a painful treatment in order to save the patient's life.[72] Representations of the human body, of course, often stood symbolically for a collective body, whether the secular polity or the "body of Christ" that encompassed the members of the church.[73] Certain conclusions followed inevitably from the deployment of medical or surgical metaphors. Patients did not always recognize their own best interests, and might resist the doctor. It might be necessary to force them to endure bitter medicine or painful surgery, so that their lives might be preserved. It might be necessary to sacrifice

69. See, e.g., *Ep.* 185.3.14, 185.8.32–34.

70. On capital and other forms of punishment in late imperial law, see the detailed discussion in Harries 1999b, chap. 7.

71. See chapter 1, pp. 35–37. Gregory 1999, p. 86, brings out particularly well the persecutor's point of view, laying out the rationalizations by which Reformation-era authorities convinced themselves of the necessity of ending lives to save souls: "In the end and as a last resort, the public execution of criminals eliminated wrongdoers with an admonitory didacticism. Coddling heretics expressed a misplaced mercy that placed others at risk. Against his detractors, Calvin argued that it was 'more than cruel' to 'spare the wolves' and expose the sheep to possible soul-murder through the 'poisoning of [heretics'] false doctrines.' It was not contrary to but part of charity, Bonner asserted, for secular authorities to punish heretics . . . The spreading of heresy was religious reckless endangerment by spiritual serial killers. Indeed, heretics were worse than multiple murderers, because their victims lived on to harm others in turn."

72. See, e.g., *Ep.* 104.2.7, quoted above; *Sermons* 23B.11 (Dolbeau 6, Mainz 11) and 159B.11 (Dolbeau 21, Mainz 54): the doctor cuts out pride, the root of all other ills.

73. On the use of the body as social metaphor, see esp. Douglas 1966 and 1996.

a part in order to save the whole, just as a surgeon might amputate a diseased limb. When such thinking was applied to the larger context of the "body social," it became all too clear that the "diseased parts" themselves were people—individuals, or groups, whose actions or beliefs constituted a threat to the harmony of the whole. Society's surgeons, authorities charged with enforcing secular and ecclesiastical discipline, understood that not all could be saved. Thus the "deceptive plausibility" of body-society metaphors made it all too easy to justify persecution and violence.[74] Those who applied physical discipline to individuals found it fairly simple to distinguish corrective punishments from lethal. Those charged with inflicting corrective violence upon an entire society faced a much harder task in restraining its worst consequences.

Authorities liked to believe that they acted with the best of motives, but feared nevertheless that their minds might be swayed by baser instincts. Was discipline just, if administered in anger? The ancients had, in some tightly limited contexts, allowed legitimate uses for rage. In Plato's ideal polity, the guardians of the law were to display a *thumos gennaios,* a noble zeal, for its enforcement. Demosthenes found an appropriate venue for anger in the adversarial setting of the courtroom, where a successful prosecutor needed to arouse the jury's outrage against the crime.[75] Anger, then, might be necessary to the administration of justice. Lactantius, as we have seen, had faith in an angry God who punished evildoers with righteous zeal.[76] Augustine conceded that anger might have just cause, and that one might rightly be indignant at a sinner—but only for the purpose of that sinner's correction.[77] For late Roman emperors and governors, anger went hand in hand with clemency, outbursts of the one giving occasion for the indulgence of the other.[78]

But not all consequences of rage could be undone by a simple softening of the heart. Imperial contrition after the fact was of little consolation to several thousand Thessalonicans, massacred in 390 by an angry order the em-

---

74. Cf. Arendt 1970, p. 75: if the body social is "diseased" then drastic and even violent measures may seem to be justified in order to "cure" it.

75. On anger and its constraints in the classical world, see now Harris 2001, p. 188, on Demosthenes and 190–193 on Plato. Cf. Augustine's comment on Platonist views of anger in *City of God* 14.19.

76. Lactantius, *The Anger of God,* discussed in chapter 1, pp. 31–32.

77. *City of God* 9.5.

78. Brown 1992, p. 55: "A governor, or an emperor, could cancel out an act of official violence by treating it as a momentary, all-too-human lapse: he could reverse his decision . . . In this way, emphasis on anger formed part of the late Roman language of amnesty."

peror Theodosius had tried, too late, to countermand.[79] On this occasion, the disciplinary power of the state had spun catastrophically out of control into savagery and mass murder. What Antiochenes after the Riot of the Statues had been chided for fearing, Thessalonica suffered in fact. Soldiers exceeded their orders and killed without discrimination—but the real failure was not one of military discipline, but of imperial restraint. On the political scale as much as the personal, an emperor's state of mind determined not only whether an action was right or wrong, but whether the results would be salutary or horrific. Theodosius, whose punishment of errant subjects ought to have been driven by compassionate concern, instead allowed himself to be overcome by anger. He, in turn, needed to be disciplined—by the rhetorical restraints of courtiers' *parrhesia*, by a new law in which he bound himself to wait thirty days between issuing a death sentence and executing it, and by the repentance that bishop Ambrose publicly demanded of him.[80]

Late Roman political and moral discourse worried above all that the anger of the powerful might get out of hand, and stressed the difficulty of distinguishing between zealous anger, and its "near enemy," furious rage.[81] The expression of discipline could restrain violence, or it could encourage it. The same paradigm served both for self-discipline and for the disciplining of others. Pride, the root of all rebellion and sin, was to be cured or at least suppressed by discipline. This was the rationale, within monastic institutions, both for the chastisement of the self and also for the punishment of brothers by their superiors.[82] It also justified a bishop's authority over both clergy and laity, as well as the state's far more lethal power over its subjects. But there was an important difference: discipline of the self could take a violent form, such as extreme asceticism, but if applied properly it could hold in check the passions and rages that might drive one to violence against others. Discourses of self-restraint, when preached to emperors by philosophers, could save lives. But the same rhetoric of discipline, when applied in a transitive sense to the correction of others, implied or even demanded a coercion that, in extreme circumstances, could kill.

79. On the Thessalonica massacre, see Ambrose *Ep.* 51 and Sozomen *HE* 7.25, with discussion in Brown 1992, pp. 109–113.

80. Thirty-day reprieve: Sozomen *HE* 7.25. On imperial anger, and strategies for its control, see Brown 1992, pp. 48–70; Harris 2001, chap. 10.

81. Augustine, *City of God* 20.12: "For as in a good sense it is said, 'The zeal of Thine house hath consumed me,' so in a bad sense it is said, 'Zeal hath possessed the uninstructed people, and now fire shall consume the enemies.'" (NPNF trans.)

82. Asceticism and self-discipline in monastic contexts are discussed at greater length in chapter 6, pp. 235–242.

If humans could not be trusted to carry out discipline without excessive violence, even God's corrective coercion was not always more discriminating. God had intervened forcefully to compel Paul toward the good, and had worked with a similarly "surgical" precision upon Augustine himself.[83] But divine chastisement also manifested itself on a larger scale, employing persecutions and barbarian invasions as a scourge for humanity's sins. Pagans, of course, had in similar manner long credited various disasters both natural and man-made to the wrath of their own gods.[84]

Augustine could see God's justice at work through the agency of temporal laws, despite the manifest imperfections and excesses of those laws. He confidently assured the Donatist targets of coercion that "God himself is doing this for you, through us—whether by persuasion, or threat, or chastisement, or penalties, or troubles; whether through his own hidden admonitions and visitations, or through the laws of the temporal powers."[85] He was well aware, of course, that God's justice working through imperfect human agents and flawed worldly institutions could produce results that might seem far from perfect. Human judges, working from limited knowledge, could and did err. Magistrates had to employ judicial torture, for example, despite being well aware of the possibility that innocents might falsely confess while the guilty escaped. They did their proper duty, Augustine argued, while suggesting that their attitude be one of resignation to regrettable necessity, not anger or enthusiasm. This was, he concluded, a consequence of the "misery" of human existence, rather than of any malice on the part of the judge.[86]

Augustine, at least, was honest enough to admit to the messy uncertainties of worldly justice. Others were less willing to compromise with mundane reality. Some religious zealots formed an understanding of God's violence that privileged the avenging over the corrective. Lactantius, as we have seen, argued that because it would be wrong not to get angry at sin and injustice, God was fully capable of an anger both righteous and appropriate, a rage against evil that went hand in hand with compassion for the good.[87] Many people shared the belief that God acted through human agents, but "extremists" could be defined as those who believed that they them-

83. Paul: Acts 9. See discussion above, p. 142, and in chapter 3, p. 129.

84. See chapter 1, pp. 30–31.

85. *Ep.* 105.4.13: *Hoc vobis per nos Deus ipse facit, sive obsecrando, sive minando, sive corripiendo, sive damnis, sive laboribus, sive per suas occultas admonitiones vel visitationes, sive per potestatum temporalium leges.* Cf. Markus 1988, p. 145.

86. *City of God* 19.6; cf. Harries 1999b, pp. 132–134.

87. Lactantius, *Anger of God*; see discussion in chapter 1, pp. 31–32.

selves were those agents. The zealots who acted in the name of God managed to convince themselves that the anger that drove their actions, and the vengeance they exacted against perceived enemies of the faith, was not theirs but God's. Thus the hubris of establishment authorities who claimed to inflict violence in the best interests of their victims found its match in the equally arrogant certainty of extremists who identified their own hatreds with those of God. The next chapter will explore the ways in which holy zealots, many of them ascetics and would-be martyrs, used their own willingness to suffer death or to impose violent discipline upon themselves as a way of excusing, or even sanctifying, the violence they inflicted on others.

5. "There Is No Crime for Those Who Have Christ"

Holy Men and Holy Violence in the Late Fourth and Early Fifth Centuries

These words from the fifth-century Egyptian abbot Shenoute neatly express the relationship between violence and religious authority that forms the theme of this chapter. They articulate a claim to legitimacy, the idea that personal holiness can justify and even sanctify an action that under other circumstances would be regarded as criminal, that zeal for God outweighs respect for worldly law and order.[1] An investigation of the ways in which Christian zealots understood and justified "holy violence" is a study of extremism in religion, exploring the connection between sanctity and violence. The figures of holy men served to articulate the values of the larger community, and offered examples of zeal and virtue for the pious to imitate. The actions recorded of them by hagiographers, or attributed to them by other sources—whether factual or imaginary—offer us a window into the values and expectations of a broader Christian audience. Whereas the Circumcellions were known to us mainly through the views of their opponents, here we will study religious extremists as described in their own words, or at least in the words of their followers and apologists. This chapter takes a deliberately one-sided perspective, approaching violent zealots through sources sympathetic to them, in an attempt to make sense of the ways in which they understood and justified their actions. The following chapter takes an

---

1. Shenoute's monks had ransacked the house of a prominent pagan, in search of idols to smash, and Shenoute made the statement in response to the pagan's accusation of *lesteia* against him. Shenoute, "Letter to a Pagan Notable" (trans. Barns). "Crime" in Coptic is *mnt-lestes*, from Greek *lesteia*, equivalent to Latin *latrocinium*. *Lesteia/latrocinium*, usually translated as "banditry," served to describe any form of criminality, usually with violence or threat thereof, thus "illegal use of force" or even "terrorism" might better capture its sense. See discussion in introduction, pp. 20–21.

equally slanted but opposite approach, exploring the criticisms and counter-discourses that could be deployed against militants, and emphasizing the restraints imposed on extremism by practical reality. Some of the same individuals and events will reappear, this time as seen through the eyes of hostile sources. Taken together, the two chapters aim at a balanced understanding of the phenomenon of "holy violence" under the Christian Roman Empire. This section will focus mainly on religious conflict arising from the Christianization of the Roman world, that is to say conflicts of Christians against pagans or Jews, while later chapters will address the ways in which such "holy" violence could turn against the Christian community itself.

"Holy zeal" unleashed passions in the service of the faith, and we will explore the ways in which these impulses shaped actions. A desire for martyrdom—sometimes so intense as to border on the erotic—mingled with a righteous anger against enemies of the faith. This in turn led to what could be called an intolerance for tolerance, a zealous determination to expose the "hypocrisy" of a nominally Christian establishment that too readily accommodated itself to the world and allowed the continued existence of paganism and heresy. These themes, expressed in stories of holy men, simultaneously reflected the values of their audience and offered models for their imitation.

THE "HOLY MAN"

The paradigm of the late antique "holy man," established primarily in a series of articles by Peter Brown, emphasizes the saint's active participation in guiding the affairs of local communities, usurping more traditional structures of authority and patronage characteristic of Roman and Mediterranean societies.[2] The holy man derived his spiritual authority from his personal connection to God, a relationship evidenced by his ascetic feats and by miracles. This authority empowered him to ignore normal rules of hierarchy and deference, to speak boldly and bluntly [parrhesia] before the wealthy and powerful, magistrates, and even emperors, in defending the interests of the ordinary people who looked to him for leadership.[3] The holy man, in

2. Brown 1971, 1976, 1983, 1995b. Reaction to Brown's views: see the issue of *JECS* (6.3, September 1998) devoted to discussion of the "holy man" thesis, as well as articles in Howard-Johnston and Hayward 1999.

3. *Parrhesia* from Brown 1992—a style of power used by bishops as well as other saints. *Parrhesia*, as dramatic rhetorical confrontation with the powerful, can be understood as a manifestation of what James C. Scott calls "speaking truth to power," a rare moment in which the "hidden transcript" of subordinated groups penetrates into public discourse: Scott 1990, esp. chap. 8.

short, stood for the values of the community.[4] The ability to express religious authority through dramatic acts of violence, deeds readily admitted and even praised by hagiographers, became an integral part of the public role of the holy man during this period. The holy man, in hagiography, acted in such a manner as to embody a literal and absolute expression of the religious and moral values that all Christians claimed to hold.[5] Holy violence, along with the performance of miracles, the practice of asceticism, and especially the willingness to martyrdom, helped to define the personal holiness of these charismatic figures in the eyes of their audience.

METHODOLOGY

This chapter relies heavily on accounts of holy men's violent behavior as told by hagiographers. Historians have rightly expressed caution about the ability of many hagiographical texts to offer accurate information about real events. The problem becomes most acute with the *Life of Barsauma* and the *Panegyric to Macarius of Tkow,* because both texts are, in their current forms, demonstrably at least a hundred or more years later than the events of the early and mid-fifth century they claim to describe. The historicity of their accounts may legitimately be called into question, and for this reason these two texts in particular have been largely ignored by modern scholars.[6] The degree of obvious dramatic exaggeration in the Barsauma stories—fifteen thousand Jews oppose him at the synagogue of Rabbat-Moab, a building "as grand as Solomon's Temple"; one hundred and three thousand Jews are assembled at the Temple Mount—does little to inspire the researcher's confidence.

With the other hagiographical texts to be featured in this chapter—the *Lives* of Rabbula, Alexander, Hypatius, Martin, and Shenoute—we are on

4. Brown 1995b.
5. Brown 1983.
6. See Honigmann 1954, pp. 6–23, for dating the *Life of Barsauma*. He suggests late sixth century, but others have placed it possibly as late as the eighth century. Nau (1927a, 1927b), however, treats the stories of violence against Jews as more or less historical; Holum 1982, pp. 186–187, likewise accepts as fact the monks' attack on the Jews in Jerusalem and Barsauma's confrontation with Eudocia. For discussion of the *Panegyric to Macarius*, see Johnson's introduction in CSCO vol. 42. This text claims to be the work of the Alexandrian Patriarch Dioscorus (d. 454), a contemporary of Macarius, who would have known him, and would have been an eyewitness to his deeds at the Council of Chalcedon in 451, which occupy the bulk of the narrative. Unfortunately, various anachronisms in the text point to a date "no earlier than the second or third decade of the sixth century" (Johnson p. 10).

somewhat firmer ground. Modern scholarship accepts them for what they claim to be, accounts written within a few years of each saint's death, by disciples who had known him personally at least during the later stages of his career. Yet in these cases as well, doubts can be raised. Rabbula's expedition to Baalbek and Alexander's confrontation with the pagan mob both take place very early in the saints' careers, before Rabbula became bishop of Edessa and before Alexander began to collect monastic followers.[7] The early years of a saint's life, before he acquired widespread fame, often outside the living memory of his younger disciples, tend to be particularly prone to legendary elaboration or invention. Above all, we must keep in mind that hagiography is a genre written with a particularly strong agenda—to demonstrate that the subject is a holy man, favored by God's grace as demonstrated by miracles and by the saint's own virtues. This purpose guides the hagiographer's selection of stories and their incorporation into a larger narrative plan.

All of these considerations, taken together, allow a legitimate skepticism about the historicity of many specific events in hagiographic sources.[8] Many of the episodes of violence credited to these holy men—exaggerated, miraculous, and often suspiciously generic as some of them may seem—may represent not so much actual historical events, but rather a sort of wishful thinking on the part of the hagiographers and their Christian audiences. We must also remember that the agenda of a hagiographer may not necessarily reflect the priorities of the original saint: the contrast between Antony as portrayed by Athanasius, for example—simple, illiterate and unapologetically anti-intellectual, solidly anti-Arian, and suitably deferential to bishops—and the highly literate and philosophical tone of Antony's own surviving letters, should give due caution to those who would interpret such texts as transparent historical sources. David Brakke suggests that the *Life of Antony* is best approached as "social discourse between Athanasius and

---

7. But see now Bowersock 2001, arguing for the historical plausibility of the *Life of Rabbula*.

8. The problems faced by the late antique historian in dealing with late sources, texts drawing on oral tradition, legendary material, etc. are hardly unique. The historiography of the early Islamic period, for instance, has recently seen substantial debate on how much credence to give to authors writing in the ninth and tenth centuries about events of the seventh century, and how to evaluate the claims of those texts to be drawing upon meticulously documented oral transmission of *hadith:* see, e.g., Duri 1983 and the essays collected in Cameron and Conrad 1992. Behind "late" texts such as Barsauma and Macarius, of course, there lies an earlier oral tradition stretching back to the lifetime of the saint. On making sense of oral tradition, Price 1983 is quite useful.

his readers."[9] Scholarship on the *Apophthegmata Patrum* has emphasized the uncertainty of attributing particular sayings to individual monks; rather, the sayings are meant to represent a "consensus" ascetic viewpoint characteristic of the time in which they were written down.[10] In many cases, the viewpoints of individual holy men are unrecoverable beyond what can be found in the hagiographies—and the stories, whether oral or written, would have reached far wider circles of people than would ever have encountered the saint in person. One should always keep in mind not only the hagiographer's agenda, but also the expectations of the intended readers— but (as Philip Rousseau warns) it is not enough simply to take the hagiographic text itself as sufficient evidence for its own context and background.[11] A clearer and more well-rounded picture of the moral universe in which the holy man operated can be arrived at by identifying similar stories, arguments, discourses, and values expressed in a range of sources representing different genres and audiences. A recent study of modern religious terrorism advises a focus not so much on individual militants but on those who defend or celebrate them, the "ideas and communities of support" underlying extremist behavior.[12] In the late antique context, it is less important to tie particular violent acts to particular individuals than it is to explore the larger complex of attitudes, values, and prejudices that could give rise to such violence.

THE REALITY OF VIOLENCE

The first point that needs to be made is that violence really happened. There is considerable evidence from a much broader range of sources, with a variety of different agendas, that violent attacks on temples and synagogues, and other clashes between Christians and non-Christians, did in fact happen on numerous occasions and in nearly every corner of the Roman world, and that monks or holy men were often involved.[13] Sources include narra-

---

9. Brakke 1995a, p. 202: "My purpose is not to reconstruct 'what really happened'; [but] to understand the 'cultural world' that Athanasius and his readers shared." See pp. 201–265 more generally. On the letters see Rubenson 1995.

10. On the *Apophthegmata*, see discussion in Brakke 1995a, p. 204; also Burton-Christie 1993. Historians using Talmudic materials, meanwhile, face similar difficulties in attempting to reconstruct the biographies of individual rabbis: see Boyarin 1999, pp. 30–32.

11. Rousseau 1999, p. 47.

12. Juergensmeyer 2000, p. 7.

13. These statements hold true as well for violent conflict within the Christian community, which I discuss in other chapters.

tive histories by both Christians and pagans, imperial legislation, acts of church councils, letters, and other documents, above and beyond the hagiographies. Far from repeating the laudatory bias of the hagiographers, many of these sources—Christian as well as pagan—offer an opposing view, highly critical of the monks, speaking on behalf of those who fell victim to their "holy violence," and challenging their claims to religious authority.[14] Although many of the particular incidents alleged in the hagiographies are not independently corroborated elsewhere, they can be understood as plausible within the more general trends and patterns of violence that can be established from other sources.[15] How frequent or numerous such incidents actually were is not especially relevant: we have already seen that occasional, seemingly localized and small-scale incidents could have a dramatic impact on contemporary opinion through accounts told, retold, circulated, and commemorated. From the sufferings of the martyrs under pagan persecution, to the bloody church massacres associated with sectarian violence in the fourth century, stories of violence resonated deeply with Christian audiences. (This should not be surprising, particularly for a religion whose central narrative revolves around the crucifixion and death of a single individual who must have seemed utterly insignificant to first-century Romans.) Some events impressed contemporaries throughout the Roman world. The destruction in 391 of one of classical paganism's greatest centers, the Alexandrian Serapeum, dismayed pagans and emboldened Christians worldwide, the story feeding into a narrative of Christian triumph over idolatry.[16] The sack of Rome by Alaric in 410, even though the killing and destruction were limited by the standards of ancient warfare, shook the confidence of Christians and pagans alike throughout the empire.

The narratives of violence we find in hagiographies, histories, and other sources simultaneously reflected their historical context—if not for spe-

---

14. See next chapter.

15. Barsauma's attacks on pagans and Jews, for example, are not independently attested by any more contemporary source. However, contemporary sources do mention his presence at the Second Council of Ephesus (449) and the Council of Chalcedon (451)—in the latter instance, the minutes of the council record a variety of accusations brought against him by the bishops ("he has sent thousands of monks against us, he has devastated all of Syria, he is a murderer, a slayer of bishops") that prove, if nothing else, that in Christian circles he had a considerable reputation for violence in his own time: see chapter 8, p. 307. The incidents at Callinicum and Minorca, discussed below, demonstrate that attacks on synagogues were not unheard of, while the frequency of Jewish and Samaritan revolts in the fifth and sixth centuries suggests a fairly high degree of religious tension in Palestine.

16. See Brown 1995c. On Rufinus see Thelamon 1981.

cific incidents then at least in the general sense of confirming readers' expectations—and also helped to shape it. Stories affected attitudes, and offered models for individuals to imitate.[17] "Extremist" attitudes expressed in other sorts of texts—such as Firmicus Maternus' *Error of the Pagan Religions,* Shenoute's letter, or Ambrose's remarks on Callinicum—both testify and contribute to a climate of opinion that would support the sorts of "holy violence" described by the hagiographers.

Archaeology, meanwhile, has unearthed a massive accumulation of physical evidence for purposeful destruction of non-Christian cult objects and places of worship, and, in many cases, the construction of churches on their sites. Religious images were methodically hacked to pieces and thrown into wells, or mutilated by crosses carved into their faces—practices that can be understood in light of Christian beliefs about the demons that supposedly dwelled in such objects.[18] This evidence offers its own considerable methodological problems. Damage cannot be dated with any degree of precision, and the motive for destruction is not always clear. Was a temple demolished out of religious zeal, or simply looted for building material after it had been long abandoned?[19] Evidence of burning does not allow us to distinguish accidental fire from deliberate arson.[20] Except for a few very famous cases, such as the Alexandrian Serapeum, it is often very difficult to link this physical evidence to particular events known from written sources. But the evidence does suggest that stories of Christian zealots attacking temples are not inherently implausible. A suggestive analogy can be found in a surprisingly modern context: in December of 1992, a mob of Hindu militants stormed a centuries-old mosque at Ayodhya (which they believed occupied

17. Rajak 1997 suggests at p. 40 that the actions of some martyrs may well have been influenced by the model of existing martyrial literature; this was likely the case with some Donatists, as noted in chapter 3.

18. See now the excellent and thorough survey and discussion by Caseau 2001. Much evidence is assembled in Trombley 1993–1994. See the substantial recent bibliography on specific discoveries in MacMullen 1997, notes to chap. 2. Stancliffe 1983 gathers much evidence for destruction of pagan shrines, and their replacement by churches, in Gaul; see also Sauer 1996, dealing mainly with Mithraea, of particular value because it covers a geographical area very poorly represented by written sources; Hanson 1985; Spieser 1976. Major Pharaonic temple complexes of Egypt were inhabited by Coptic monks, who carved crosses and defaced images of the gods: see Winlock and Crum 1926. Synagogues converted into churches: Brenk 1991.

19. Sauer 1996 argues nonetheless that deliberate, religiously motivated desecration can be established in a great number of cases. See now Sauer 2003.

20. This could be a problem even for contemporaries. When the great temple of Apollo in Antioch burned down during the reign of Julian, different sources blamed it on heavenly fire sent by God, arson by Christians, or a lamp accidentally left burning by a careless pagan priest: Ammianus 22.13.

the site of an ancient temple of Ram) and literally tore it apart stone by stone. With no tools more elaborate than sledgehammers and crowbars, the zealots reduced a fairly substantial building down to the bare dirt in less than twenty-four hours.[21] Those familiar with late antique religious violence will recognize many parallels, from the leadership role played by ascetic "holy men," to the belated and ineffective response of the secular authorities, to the impassioned declarations of some participants that they were ready for "martyrdom."[22]

While each class of evidence has its own methodological problems, and many individual cases may be open to doubt, nevertheless when it is all taken together it presents a very compelling argument that the types of violence described in the hagiographies did in fact take place throughout the Christian Roman Empire. The written sources, in particular, prove that stories of violence made a considerable impression upon contemporaries, both Christian and non-Christian, regardless of the actual frequency of such events.

INTERPRETATION

Having established the reality of violence from a variety of other sources, we may turn to the hagiographies for an explanation of the motives and justifications of those who engaged in it, the ways in which their actions made sense to them, to their followers, and to the audiences of the hagiographers. The historical accuracy of a particular narrative is less important, for this purpose, than the values and the worldview it expresses. "Wishful thinking," meaning a tendency to depict things not so much as they are, but rather as they ought to be, is an important consideration for the historian in understanding this thought-world.

We have already seen the tremendous interest throughout the Christian world in accounts of the martyrs. Liturgical commemoration, recitation, and homiletic discussion ensured that stories of the martyrs came to the attention even of those who could not read. In the fourth century, sto-

21. Compare Libanius (*Or.* 30.8) on late fourth-century Syrian monks: "These people . . . hasten to attack the temples with sticks and stones and bars of iron, and in some cases, disdaining these, with hands and feet."

22. For extensive contemporary news coverage of the Ayodhya incident, complete with breathtaking hour-by-hour photos of the demolition in progress, see issues of *India Today* for December 1992 and January 1993; good analysis in Friedland and Hecht 1998. Compare similar scenes in, e.g., Mark the Deacon, *Life of Porphyry of Gaza*; Theodoret *HE* 5.21 on Marcellus of Apamea.

ries of holy men and women became similarly popular as pilgrims travelled to Egypt, Syria, and Palestine and reported back to audiences eager to hear the deeds and sayings of the "desert fathers."[23] Many tales may have circulated widely in oral form before being captured in writing. Some hagiographies were clearly a product of a specific monastic environment, written down some time after the holy man's death and based on oral tradition preserved by disciples. While texts such as the *Life of Barsauma* may have been little read beyond the walls of the saint's eponymous monastery, others circulated far more broadly, for example Athanasius' *Life of Antony*, originally written as a letter to "brethren" outside Egypt, and rapidly translated into Latin. The *Life of Rabbula* and the *Panegyric to Macarius of Tkow* would have been useful to anti-Chalcedonian circles beyond their immediate local context. The ecclesiastical historians took local or regional traditions and made them available to an empire-wide audience; Theodoret publicized for his Greek readers incidents from as far away as Persia and Italy.[24] It was commonly understood that one of the main purposes of hagiography was didactic. Through imitation of the pattern set by the lives of saints, Athanasius argued, Christian believers could constitute themselves into a new community that would reflect the heavenly *politeia*.[25] Recent scholarship on monasticism and its associated literature has emphasized the centrality of the master-disciple relationship, the ascetic's role as teacher and model for his followers.[26] Hagiographic accounts of prominent ascetics, likewise, used storytelling to communicate values and offer examples for imitation.[27]

Stories of holy men committing acts of holy violence tell us much about the general expectations of Christians regarding the holy man and his function as religious leader. The expression of authority through dramatic acts of violence and the understanding of such violence within a paradigm of "action pleasing to God," which can be linked in turn to late antique concepts of martyrdom, formed an integral part of the holy man's role as

23. See now Frank 2000. Harvey 1998 situates hagiography in a liturgical context.

24. Theodoret *HE* 5.38 on Abdas and other zealots in Persia; 5.26 on the monk Telemachus in Rome, both discussed below, pp. 196–200 and 204–206.

25. As discussed in Brakke 1995a, pp. 161–170.

26. See discussion in Rousseau 2000.

27. See Rapp 1998b. Krueger 1999, p. 226, defines the "presentation of instruction through third-person narration" as hagiography's "most basic feature . . . the saint speaks and enacts the teachings that the author wishes to convey." Krueger adds that hagiographers themselves hoped to imitate the virtues of the subject through the "ascetic" practice of writing.

spiritual leader—a role that often involved confrontation as well as mediation.[28] Key to the holy man's self-justification in such conflicts was the identification of his own agenda with God's will—so that what might seem to an unsympathetic observer as extralegal "self-help" became instead the performance of God's work.[29] "Self-help" had traditionally implied independence from formal law, justified by the belief that one could not depend on that law to right a wrong. In a religious context, it offered a new justification for such independence, putting one's understanding of God's law above the law of the state.

Not every late antique saint fits this pattern—there were many who led quite peaceful lives—but holy violence formed a significant part of the repertoire of behavior available to the holy man and comprehensible to his Christian audience. Stories of holy violence emphasize the role of the saint as embodiment of "community values"—the community in this sense being the larger "imagined community" of late Roman Christianity.[30] These stories, put together with tales of martyrdom and persecution, played a key role in shaping the evolving self-definition of the Christian community, by articulating boundaries between those inside (zealous Christians) and those outside (pagans, Jews, heretics, and those who tolerated them), and by presenting models of leadership and religious authority. The holy man's attacks on enemies of the faith tell us as much about power dynamics and competition for influence within the Christian camp as they do about actual relations between Christians and non-Christians.

In the hagiographies presented in this chapter, attacks on paganism served to establish the holy man's authority, emphasizing his spiritual qualifications—his zeal for God, his willingness to martyrdom—and thus laying the groundwork for his status as religious leader.

DESIRE FOR MARTYRDOM, DESIRE FOR GOD

We have seen in previous chapters that Christians understood martyrdom not in terms of passive endurance of violence but rather as active spiritual combat against the demons thought to drive their persecutors. We have also

---

28. Brown remarks briefly on the holy man's use of violence as assertion of authority (e.g., 1971, p. 124, referring specifically to rituals of exorcism) but does not pursue it at length. To my knowledge, no one has yet made a connection from this phenomenon back to concepts of martyrdom.

29. "Self-help" from Lintott 1968. See discussion in introduction, pp. 22–23.

30. "Imagined community" following, of course, the paradigm of Anderson 1991.

seen—both with Christians under Julian and with Donatists in North Africa—that an ideology of martyrdom could be used to justify a real, not merely a spiritual, combat against those perceived as "persecutors." In this chapter we will explore the ways in which concepts of martyrdom, even in the absence of persecution, served to motivate and justify "holy violence."

By the beginning of the fourth century, the cult of the martyrs was getting under way even as the end of the Great Persecution would seem to have curtailed the opportunities for attaining actual martyrdom. In order for Christians to achieve the traditional sort of martyrdom, that is, to be killed for refusing to deny Christ, there had to be persecution. But with the conversion of Constantine, the Roman imperial state, which had until very recently persecuted Christians, itself became Christian. This created an interesting question: how could Christians die for their faith in a Christian society?

For the Donatists, this was not a problem: because they had come to reject the Constantinian takeover of Christianity, considering it as nothing more than paganism in a clever disguise, they endured actual persecution and produced martyrs accordingly. Likewise for other Christian groups whom the official religious policy of the moment defined as heterodox, the old patterns of violence persisted. Power struggles between Nicenes and Arians in the fourth century, and between Monophysites and Chalcedonians in the late fifth and early sixth centuries, produced nearly as many tales of persecution, torture, resistance, and martyrdom as had the era of Diocletian.

Certain Christians' zeal for martyrdom drove them to seek it out, rather than wait for the persecuting authorities to find them. The unnamed Christian of Nicomedia, who reacted to the proclamation of the pagan persecution in 303 by publicly tearing down the emperors' anti-Christian edict and was burned alive for his defiance, found an echo, or perhaps a conscious imitator, in the Donatist Maximian, who tore down Constans' edict on ecclesiastical "unity" in Carthage in 347.[31] Some Christians seem to have responded to the pagan persecutions by striking back with violence against pagan idols and temples, thought to be the dwelling places of the demons who drove the persecutors. Two followers of the Cappadocian bishop Athe-

---

31. Nicomedia: Lactantius *MP* 13, Eusebius *HE* 8.5. The Christian shouted, "These are the triumphs of Goths and Sarmatians!" probably an ethnic slur against the "barbarian" ancestry of the junior emperor Galerius. There were other incidents during the persecutions in which Christians approached the magistrates and struck them or tried to overturn their altars: Eusebius, *Martyrs of Palestine* 4, 8, 9. See discussion in chapter 1, pp. 29–30; also Kötting 1979. Carthage: *Passion of Maximian and Isaac* 5; see discussion in chapter 3, pp. 108–109.

nogenes circulated a *libellus* containing insults against the emperors and, when interrogated by the governor, boasted that they had set fire to several temples.[32] In the early decades of the fourth century, at least, such actions would usually earn martyrdom.[33] These examples show us the focus of spiritual combat gradually moving outward from the bodies of the martyrs and toward external targets, at least at first with the idea of seeking a martyr's death through provocation of the pagans. Even as the Christianization of Roman society over the course of the fourth century lessened the risks of actual pagan retaliation, many Christians continued their attacks against idols, temples, or persons perceived as enemies of the faith, and continued to understand their own actions within a context of "martyrdom."

PURSUING MARTYRDOM

At the beginning of the fifth century, a young Syrian named Rabbula, the future bishop of Edessa, answered the call of the Gospel, followed the example of Antony, sold all his property and gave the money to the poor, and went alone into the desert.[34] For several years he lived by himself in a hole in the ground, where he prayed, recited the psalms and read scripture, and did battle with the devil, who sent snakes and scorpions to torment him and who maliciously kicked over his water jar. But these spiritual trials were not enough for Rabbula. One day he saw a band of Arab raiders passing by. "Then he rejoiced and hoped that, finally, the time of his being crowned with martyrdom was near."[35] But they only stole his clothes and food, leaving him unharmed, much to his disappointment. In the Christian empire of

32. See Maraval 1990, *La passion de S. Athénogène*, esp. pp. 51–59. Although other parts of the *Passion* are clearly of later composition, Maraval suggests that the dialogue recorded between the governor and the martyrs may preserve "un authentique procès-verbal" (p. 7).

33. As suggested by the Council of Elvira's prohibition of the practice, discussed below, p. 40. Chapter 3, pp. 115–119, deals with examples of "suicidal" attacks on pagan idols by Donatist Circumcellions in North Africa, apparently most widespread in the generation after Constantine.

34. Quotations that follow are my translations from the Syriac *Life of Rabbula*, Overbeck ed. Rabbula was bishop of Edessa 412–435, and the *Life* was composed by a disciple probably in the 440s. I will discuss Rabbula's episcopal career at greater length in chapter 7, pp. 260–268. On Rabbula see generally Blum 1969; Bowersock 2001 discusses the portion of the *Life* prior to Rabbula's ordination.

35. Overbeck 1865, p. 169. These Arabs presumably were pagans, but still one might expect that in order for it to be a proper martyrdom, they would have to try to force him to sacrifice to idols or deny Christ, and then kill him, rather than simply kill him for no particular reason.

Theodosius II, a full century after Constantine, dying for one's faith as a Christian took some effort and imagination.

Still, "the love of martyrdom burned in his heart like a glowing fire."[36] Finally Rabbula had an idea: he joined forces with Eusebius, another monk and future bishop of Tella, and the two of them headed for one of the last holdouts of paganism, the city of Heliopolis or Baalbek in Lebanon (Phoenicia Libanensis).[37] "There they went into the idol-temple, with divine zeal, to shatter the idols and to be found worthy of martyrdom. They went there not expecting to come back again alive, but in the hope of being martyred and killed, to bear witness through their deaths." Though smashing pagan idols would have been a praiseworthy deed in itself, their real intention was to provoke the pagans into killing them.[38] The pagans beat them severely, until they were taken for dead, and threw them down a great staircase.[39] But Rab-

36. Overbeck 1865, p. 169.

37. Baalbek was known as a stronghold of paganism well into the sixth century. See Ragette 1980, a general survey; detailed archaeological reports in Wiegand 1921–25.

38. Overbeck 1865, p. 170. This was precisely the sort of reckless and suicidal behavior for which Augustine condemned the Circumcellions: see chapter 3, pp. 115–117.

39. "Then they were thrown, as if they were corpses, from a great height down many stairs, on which they banged their limbs, as they followed upon each other, while each step inclined towards the next one and catapulted them to it, so that they were thoroughly smashed up when they reached the bottom." (Overbeck 1865, p. 170) In fact, the site of Baalbek does feature several great staircases, such as the one before the Propylaeum, or another at the so-called Bacchus-temple, lending a ring of truth to the episode, or at least suggesting a familiarity with the site on the part of the hagiographer. Peeters 1928, pp. 145–146, doubts the historicity of the story, on the grounds that two men by themselves could not possibly have hoped to demolish a temple—but such was not their aim. See now Bowersock 2001, pp. 268–269, arguing *contra* Peeters for the verisimilitude of this incident. The *Life of Rabbula* does, however, omit one important fact: at the time of Rabbula's visit (placed in the narrative shortly before he became bishop of Edessa in 412), the Jupiter-temple, chief among the site's temples, had already been partially demolished (by order of Theodosius I, according to Malalas 13.37) in order to make way for a Christian basilica, built directly and provocatively atop the site of the altar that had formed the focus of pagan worship there since prehistoric times. The nearby Bacchus-temple, however, continued to function at least into the sixth century (Ragette 1980, pp. 68–71) and indeed remains largely intact to this day; this would presumably have been Rabbula's target. The close proximity of temple and basilica on the same sacred ground would have made Baalbek a flashpoint of religious tension, and thus particularly attractive to Christians intent on proving their martyrial zeal. It may be significant to note that although the temple and propylaeum complex contains hundreds of niches obviously intended for the display of religious statuary, not one such statue has survived. Of course, we should not expect to find any archaeological evidence specifically reflecting Rabbula's visit—a strong and militant pagan community would surely have quickly repaired any damage that the two monks might have caused.

bula's desire for martyrdom was once again to be frustrated, because God intended him rather to have a long and fruitful career as a bishop—so the two of them survived, got up, brushed themselves off, and went home:

> They indeed dared to do this [smash the idols] but they could not be blessed with the suffering of martyrdom, for God preserved them on account of their future destiny as excellent managers of the episcopate. . . . Thus they returned, overjoyed that they were worthy of God's will, to bear the wounds of the suffering of Christ on their bodies. So indeed they endured deadly danger, as they had prayed for, but they did not die for the sake of their witness as they had hoped. Their intention was for them to become martyrs, and they had achieved this wish; only it was not completed by their death, because they were to remain kept aside so that many through them would come to share the crown of life.[40]

Whether the saint suffered martyrdom or lived on to destroy more temples, either way he bore witness to the faith. Rabbula's failed attempt at martyrdom—he was a martyr in intention, if not in fact—sufficed to demonstrate his worthiness for the later career as bishop and scourge of heretics that God had in mind for him.[41] As this example illustrates, the desire for martyrdom is in no way diminished by the absence of real persecution. Zeal for martyrdom reappears throughout Christian history in the most unlikely times and places. Francis of Assisi, in the thirteenth century, left the safety

---

40. Overbeck 1865, p. 170. Sulpicius Severus felt the need to make similar excuses for Martin of Tours' "failure" to obtain martyrdom: "For although the character of our times could not ensure him the honor of martyrdom, yet he will not remain destitute of the glory of a martyr, because both by vow and virtues he was alike able and willing to be a martyr. But if he had been permitted, in the times of Nero and of Decius, to take part in the struggle which then went on, I take to witness the God of heaven and earth that he would freely have submitted to the rack of torture, and readily surrendered himself to the flames . . . But although he did in fact suffer none of these things, yet he fully attained to the honor of martyrdom without shedding his blood. For what agonies of human sufferings did he not endure in behalf of the hope of eternal life, in hunger, in watchings, in nakedness, in fastings, in reproachings of the malignant, in persecutions of the wicked, in care for the weak, in anxiety for those in danger?" (*Ep.* 2, to Aurelius, trans. NPNF)

41. The signification is emphasized by the fact that the *Life of Rabbula* presents the Baalbek episode immediately before Rabbula's elevation to the episcopate. Susan Harvey, "Bishop Rabbula: Ascetic Tradition and Change in Fifth-Century Edessa" (unpublished paper, cited with permission) sees his attack on the Baalbek temple as prefiguring his actions as bishop to cleanse Edessa of pagans and heretics. The hagiographical traditions surrounding eastern holy men such as Rabbula, Macarius of Tkow, and Barsauma use the saints' early attacks against paganism to set the stage for their later anti-Nestorian or anti-Chalcedonian battles: see chapter 7 and conclusion.

of Christian Europe in order to preach the faith before the Sultan of Egypt, in the hope of either converting the Sultan or attaining martyrdom.[42] Teresa of Àvila, the great mystic saint of sixteenth-century Spain, a most militantly Christian kingdom, tells us in her *Autobiography* that when she was a little girl, she and her brother had been seized by a passionate desire for martyrdom, and they planned to run away to North Africa, preach the Gospel, and be beheaded by the Muslims—but their parents would not allow it.[43]

In the fourth and fifth centuries, a quest for martyrdom seems to have been a common feature in the early stages of a holy man's career. Although it is not literally true that monasticism came after martyrdom in a chronological sense, many of our hagiographic texts seem to be trying to present it that way. A frustrated attempt at martyrdom helped to establish the credentials of a monastic holy man, by linking the holiness of the ascetic with the holiness of the martyr. During the Great Persecution, Antony, whose renunciation of the world defined a paradigm of ascetic behavior that would find countless imitators, came out of the desert and entered Alexandria in the hope that he might be found worthy to join the Christians facing execution. Visiting the martyrs in prison and attending their trials, Antony did his best to make himself conspicuous so that the pagan authorities might arrest him as well. When this did not happen, he was greatly saddened:

> For, as I said before, he also prayed for martyrdom. He seemed, therefore, like one who grieved because he had not been martyred, but the Lord was protecting him to benefit us and many others, so that he might be a teacher to many. . . . When finally the persecution ended, and Peter the blessed bishop had made his witness [i.e. suffered martyrdom], Antony departed and withdrew once again to his cell, and was there daily being martyred by his conscience, and doing battle in the

---

42. According to some versions of the story, Francis challenged the learned Muslims to walk through fire and see who emerged unscathed: more on this motif of trial by fire, below. The Sultan, bemused by Francis' fearless zeal, listened politely and then sent him home with many gifts. See Kedar 1984, esp. chap. 3.

43. "I used to discuss with my brother ways and means of becoming martyrs, and we agreed to go together to the land of the Moors, begging our way for the love of God, so that we might be beheaded there. I believe that our Lord had given us courage enough even at that tender age, if only we could have seen a way. But our having parents seemed to us a great hindrance." Frustrated in her initial plan, young Teresa then pursued the venerable link between martyrdom and asceticism: "As soon as I saw that it was impossible to go anywhere where I should be put to death for God's sake, we decided to become hermits; and we used to try very hard to build hermits' cells in an orchard belonging to the house . . . " Teresa of Àvila, *Autobiography* (trans. Cohen, p. 24).

contests of the faith. He subjected himself to an even greater and more strenuous asceticism.[44]

The *Life of Antony* thus explicitly held up the ascetic life as an acceptable alternative for those unable to attain martyrdom by traditional means. Antony did not seek martyrdom in a particularly aggressive manner. He put himself in positions where he hoped to be noticed and arrested, but did not actually turn himself in or otherwise confront the authorities. He was conspicuous, but not provocative. Others, as we have seen, went further and tried harder for martyrdom. Even here, however, one is struck by the emphasis on frustrated desire—and the author's implication that the asceticism that would define Antony's career was merely a second choice.

Traditionally, Christian authors and preachers had emphasized to their congregations the need to be prepared for the possibility of martyrdom, to stand firm in their faith if and when persecution should come to them. In the later fourth century, as actual pagan persecution receded further into the background, it became a commonplace that the martyrs had not only faced death bravely but sought it eagerly.[45] Accounts of martyrdom became more and more sensational in their tone. Post-Constantinian martyr texts dwell upon torture and violent death to a shockingly graphic extent, in sharp contrast to the shorter, matter-of-fact courtroom accounts typical of earlier texts. Recent scholarship has remarked extensively on the overtly sexual and even pornographic tone found in some stories of female martyrs, such as Prudentius' accounts of Eulalia and Agnes.[46] In addition to eroticizing the violence itself, these texts also deploy the language of erotic desire to characterize their heroines' eagerness for martyrdom.[47] Stories of male martyrs—or would-be martyrs—are less obviously sexualized but often feature similar invocations of burning zeal, longing, and frustrated

44. Athanasius, *Life of Antony* 46–47 (Gregg trans.).

45. Sulpicius Severus (*Chronicle* 2.32) even made a joke of it—unfavorably comparing the zeal of early Christians seeking martyrdom to the eagerness of his own contemporaries in seeking bishoprics!

46. While Bowersock 1995, pp. 59–61, cites several examples of martyrs seeking death "zealously" and "eagerly" in pre-Constantinian martyr acts, the emphasis on erotic desire becomes much more pronounced in later texts. See, e.g., Prudentius, *Peristephanon;* Ambrose, *On Virgins.* On Prudentius generally, see Roberts 1993. The gender issues raised by these texts are extensively discussed by Burrus 1994 and 1995; Castelli 1996. A similar eroticization of martyrial violence can be seen in some of the Persian women martyrs discussed by Brock and Harvey 1998.

47. Prudentius' frankly pornographic account of Agnes welcoming the executioner's sword "like a lover" (*Peristephanon* 14.69–84) is one of the more extreme examples. See discussion in Roberts 1993, p. 101.

passion.[48] A desire for martyrdom was, fundamentally, a desire to unite one-self with God—the same impulse that underlay much mystical experience, ascetic practice, and other forms of holiness.[49] The use of nuptial or erotic language to characterize such union was quite commonplace: martyrs, like consecrated virgins, could become "brides of Christ." A martyr's violent death, then, was like a marriage, a joyous occasion, to be eagerly anticipated and celebrated.[50] The message of these texts, to a Christian audience, was that martyrdom was hardly an unpleasant "duty" to be endured—rather, they should desire it eagerly and seek it zealously. This shift in emphasis toward active pursuit of martyrdom—coming as it did at a time when real persecution was less and less likely—was what distinguished "extremist" ideologies of martyrdom from more traditional and mainstream interpretations, and it offers the key to understanding extremist violence in the fourth century and beyond.

While Christians could imagine women distinguishing themselves equally alongside men as martyrs in a traditional context of state persecution, the more provocative "holy violence" of zealous would-be martyrs seems to have been an exclusively male pursuit. Women, like men, could sometimes seek martyrdom by approaching magistrates and proclaiming their faith, rather than waiting to be arrested. But even in the context of ongoing pagan persecution, where male martyrs might actually assault magistrates and overturn altars,[51] women apparently could only fantasize about similar behavior—however bravely they might withstand the tortures inflicted upon them. Ambrose allows the virgin martyr Pelagia to imagine overthrowing an altar and smashing its idols, although even within the context of the story we are meant to understand that this did not actually happen—Pelagia merely contemplated it, before going on to die

---

48. B. Shaw 1996 argues that martyrdom's emphasis on a passive "endurance" (*hypomone*) of torture could work to "feminize" the bodily suffering even of male martyrs. Shaw, p. 296, remarks on the double meaning of *passio*—"suffering" but also "passion"—in martyrial discourse.

49. As pointed out by Boyarin 1999, pp. 93–126. Boyarin discusses Christian examples and also offers some striking parallels from late antique rabbinic tradition.

50. See, e.g., *Passion of Saints Maxima, Donatilla and Secunda* 4 (in Tilley 1996, *Donatist Martyr Stories*, p. 21); Prudentius, *Peristephanon* 14 on Agnes. Such imagery is exclusive neither to Christianity nor to the ancient world, as made clear by the chilling spectacle of videotaped statements left behind by Hamas suicide-bombers. Juergensmeyer 2000, pp. 70–71 and 198–200, describes "oddly happy" young men thanking God for the "fortunate opportunity" of martyrdom as if it were a "marriage covenant."

51. See chapter 1, pp. 29–30.

under different circumstances.[52] Women and men could equal each other in endurance and suffering, but it seems that the only violence women were allowed to inflict was upon themselves, committing suicide in order to protect their chastity.[53] It need hardly be said, of course, that we are dealing with texts written by men—although their intended audiences usually included both sexes—which accordingly reflect a male-dominated society's expectations and prejudices about the limits of permissible behavior for women. The suffering of violence, for women, could be valorized and eroticized; for men, so too could the performance of violence. Active violence, as we shall see below, depended not only upon willingness to martyrdom but also upon the enactment of anger against perceived enemies, and zeal to avenge "insults" against the honor of God—both of these being more traditionally masculine characteristics and duties.

ASCETICISM: MARTYRDOM BY OTHER MEANS?

The virgin's undefiled body symbolized the promise of resurrection, an escape from the worldly cycle of procreation and death that trapped the human race—hence, for women martyrs and ascetics, holiness demanded an extreme emphasis on maintaining chastity.[54] Male chastity came to be similarly valorized in ascetic discourse, although not to nearly the same degree—men were allowed many more different paths to holiness than women. But for both sexes, martyrdom was understood as a form of sacrifice, which demanded "victims" of special purity—if not actual virginity, then at least some form of ascetic discipline could distinguish suitable candidates.[55] The early martyrs had practiced fasting and vigils in order to prepare themselves for the ordeal of imprisonment and torture that lay ahead of them.[56] These ritual devotions also helped, however, to underline their desirability as pure offerings

52. Ambrose, *On Virgins* 3.7.33: "For who is there who wishes to die and is not able to do so, when there are so many easy ways to death? For I can now rush upon the sacrilegious altars and overthrow them, and quench with my blood the kindled fires." (NPNF trans.) According to Chrysostom (PG 50, 479ff.), she threw herself off a roof to escape her captors. See also Ambrose, *Ep.* 37.38.

53. Or so Ambrose allowed in *On Virgins* 3.7.32ff., in line with traditional Roman morality as expressed, e.g., in the story of Lucretia. But Augustine disagreed, arguing that Lucretia had not sinned by being forcibly raped, but her subsequent suicide condemned her as a murderer: *City of God* 1.16–20. Cf. Trout 1994.

54. A point made by G. Clark 1998, p. 107.

55. Compare Juergensmeyer 2000, pp. 168–171, on sacrificial undertones in the "martyrdoms" of modern militants.

56. As argued by Tilley 1991a.

before God. In ascetic discourse, as it developed in later centuries, those same disciplines and renunciations could themselves be represented as sacrificial offerings.[57] The practices and discourses associated with martyrdom and asceticism intersected in many different directions. In the absence of overt persecution, martyrial impulses could find expression by other means, the same intense zeal being diverted into ascetic or missionary directions.

It has often been said, by late antique contemporaries as well as modern scholars, that the monks were the spiritual successors to the martyrs[58]—a statement that does not take into account the ample evidence for ascetic practice among Christians of the pre-Constantinian period, not to mention the many examples of continued pursuit of violent martyrdom throughout the fourth and early fifth centuries.[59] Nevertheless, as a broad generalization, it is not without value in suggesting a relationship between martyrdom and asceticism. The early and mid-fourth century's explosion in the popularity of ascetic monasticism did coincide, at least roughly, with the end of pagan persecution. Asceticism, mortification of the flesh—whether in the form of severe fasting, sleepless vigils, wearing chains or hair shirts, or standing on a pillar for forty years—could be seen, and indeed often was seen, as a form of self-inflicted violence against the body, a substitute for the violence that the martyrs had endured. For Syrian ascetics, particularly, the wounds and deprivations inflicted on their bodies were understood as a visible sign of their inner spiritual triumphs. A Syriac hymn attributed to Ephrem instructed that ascetics were to apply to themselves the pains of the martyrs, so that their bodies in turn might become martyrs.[60] The early monks— Christians who gave up their possessions, withdrew from the secular world, and went out into the wilderness—like the martyrs, understood their endeavors in terms of spiritual combat against demons and the worldly temptations they personified.[61] Resisting temptation, doing battle with the

57. For this representation in Syriac tradition, see, e.g., Harvey 1998. Cf. Romans 12:1: "Present your bodies as a living sacrifice, holy and acceptable to God." (RSV trans.)

58. A comprehensive survey of patristic citations on this theme can be found in Malone 1950.

59. In some cases, it seems to have been the other way around: Harvey 1990b argues convincingly that accounts of early fourth-century Edessan martyrs were themselves shaped and inspired by far older motifs and discourses of Syrian asceticism.

60. On this characteristic of Syrian asceticism see, e.g., Harvey 1988b. "Ephrem" hymn cited in Vööbus 1988, vol. 3, p. 45. These hymns are more plausibly to be attributed to the fifth-century ascetic writer Isaac of Antioch: see Mathews 1990. On asceticism likened to combat: Aphrahat, *Demonstration* 7.18, urging that ascetics take the virtues of Joshua's warriors as a model.

61. Demons as personified temptations: see, e.g., *Life of Antony*. In several cases, the monk physically attacks the demon, burning its face or beheading it. See, e.g.,

demons, counted as a form of spiritual martyrdom. All of these forms of holiness, in one way or another, constituted "bearing witness" and spreading the faith.

IMITATING THE MARTYRS

In the fourth and fifth centuries, when clergy exhorted their congregations to "imitate the martyrs" they did not, ordinarily, mean to be taken literally.[62] On martyrs' feast-days, Augustine told his listeners to "take delight in imitating what we delight in celebrating."[63] But, he made clear, times had changed: "Nor should we be hoping for that kind of persecution which our ancestors endured at the hands of the earthly powers, in order to become martyrs."[64] The martyrs triumphed by resisting the temptations of idolatry, Augustine argued. Christians should not imitate their specific behavior—in the absence of true persecution, there was no good reason to "seek death" like the Donatists—but should honor their memory by resisting other forms of temptation in daily life.[65] If they fell ill, for example, they should resist the lure of "superstitious" charms, amulets, or potions, which he regarded as "idolatrous." Those who endured fever without recourse to such cures could console themselves that they, too, were "fighting in the arena"—and if they died, they would be martyrs![66] Whatever his congregants may have thought of such arguments, it is clear that the stories of the martyrs were still very much before their eyes. Their commemoration of the martyrs was sometimes too enthusiastic for Augustine, who did not conceal his disapproval of the feasting, drinking, singing, and dancing that could commonly be seen at martyrs' tombs.[67]

Sozomen *HE* 6.28. For a good general survey of Egyptian monasticism, marred however by absence of Coptic sources, see Chitty 1966.

62. On the theme of "imitation," and the various ways it could be understood in late antique martyr cult, see now Brown 2000b.

63. *Sermon* 159A (Mainz 42, Dolbeau 13), (trans. Hill, p. 135).

64. *Sermon* 306E (Mainz 50, Dolbeau 18), (trans. Hill, p. 277).

65. Unfavorable references to Donatist behavior are, unsurprisingly, commonplace in Augustine's sermons. In many cases, he used their example as an indirect way of encouraging his own listeners to do better. See, e.g., the *New Year's Sermon* 198.41 (Mainz 62), (trans. Hill, p. 215); *Sermon On Obedience* (359B, Dolbeau 2, Mainz 5).

66. *Sermon* 306E.

67. See, e.g., *Ep.* 22; *Sermon* 359B, *On Obedience*, esp. 5 (Hill trans., p. 333), confessing to his own youthful indiscretions at such festivals. Compare *Confessions* 3.3.5, and see commentary by Brown 2000a, p. 457.

The language of zeal and desire pervaded John Chrysostom's preaching on martyrs.[68] Praising the empress Eudoxia's veneration of relics, Chrysostom confessed himself swept away by the excitement of the moment: "What can I say? I'm jumping with excitement and aflame with a frenzy. . . . I'm flying and dancing and floating on air!" According to John, the empress shared the feeling: "Her desire for the martyrs, the tyranny and flame of love persuaded her to . . . display with naked enthusiasm her zeal for the holy martyrs!"[69] On another occasion, in Antioch, he praised the "magnificent spectacle, fervent love and unrestrained desire" of the crowd assembled to celebrate martyrs' festivals. Like Augustine, Chrysostom took the opportunity to rebuke his listeners for drunkenness. But when it came to honoring the martyrs, he did not urge moderation: "Take her as an advocate in your prayers, immerse yourself perpetually in the stories of his struggles. Embrace the coffin, nail yourself to the chest . . . take holy oil and anoint your whole body!"[70]

John was famous for his wildly emotional language—on occasion, it got him into trouble.[71] He was pleased to see the same enthusiasm among the people of Constantinople, when they welcomed him back from Asia Minor in 402: "What can I say about the burning desire you displayed, the mania, the frenzy, the shouting in the marketplace . . . you sanctified the air, you made the city a church."[72] His exhortations to imitate the martyrs aroused his followers to a fiery zeal that was not always metaphorical: a year later, much of the city would go up in flames as his fiercely loyal congregation rioted to protest their bishop's dismissal.[73]

68. On the context and audience for Chrysostom's sermons, see W. Mayer 1998; and the introduction to the translated sermons in Mayer and Allen 2000, *John Chrysostom*.

69. *Homily Delivered After the Remains of Martyrs*, PG 63.467–472 (trans. in Mayer and Allen 2000, pp. 86–92). The sermon was delivered in Constantinople, likely between 400 and 402.

70. *Homily on Martyrs*, PG 50.661–666 (trans. in Mayer and Allen 2000, pp. 93–97). The exact date is unknown.

71. Among the wide-ranging and often odd assortment of charges brought against Chrysostom at the Synod of the Oak in 403 were the following: "That in church he used such language as 'the table is full of furies'; that he loudly exclaimed, 'I am in love, I am mad'; that he ought to explain what 'furies' he referred to, and what he meant by 'I am in love, I am mad,' expressions unknown to the church." J. H. Freese, trans., *Epitome of the Synod of the Oak* in Photius, *Bibliotheca* 59, (London, 1920). Compare Chrysostom at PG 47.756 (trans. in Mayer and Allen 2000, p. 194): "This table is full of spiritual fire."

72. *On his Return*, text published by A. Wenger in *Revue des études byzantines* 19 (1961) 110–123 (trans. Mayer and Allen 2000, pp. 98–103).

73. See chapter 6, pp. 223–228.

While zealots who actually desired martyrdom in the literal sense were probably not that common, ordinary Christians' devotion to and "desire" for the martyrs was a powerful motivating force to which religious leaders could and did appeal. Many different forms of zealous behavior could be encouraged or justified under the rubric of imitating or honoring the martyrs. Ideologies and discourses of martyrdom, then, played a key role in developing a larger paradigm of action pleasing to God. This was made possible by a broadening in the definition of the word "martyrdom," taking it back to its original (pre-Christian) sense of "bearing witness."[74] "Witnesses" in Christianity were originally those who had seen the risen Christ and could testify about it to others. Christ told the apostles to go out and be "witnesses," to preach the faith.[75] But by the end of the first century, "martyrdom" began to refer to those who died confessing the faith, who bore witness through their blood.[76] Christians had always believed that the very spectacle of martyrs calmly and even joyously enduring torture and death was itself responsible for impressing pagan onlookers and thus bringing converts into the church. But there were many possible ways to confess the faith. In the early third century, Origen explained:

> Now every one who bears witness to the truth, whether he support it by words or deeds, may properly be called a witness [martyr]; but it has come to be the custom of the brotherhood, since they are struck with admiration of those who have contended to the death for truth and valor, to keep the name of martyr more properly for those who have borne witness to the mystery of godliness by shedding their blood for it. The Savior gives the name of martyr to every one who bears witness to the truth he declares; thus at the Ascension he says to his disciples: "You shall be my witnesses in Jerusalem and in Judaea and in Samaria and to the uttermost ends of the earth" [Acts 1:8]. . . . In the same way the martyrs bear witness, for a testimony to the unbelievers, and so do all the saints whose deeds shine before men.[77]

Although by the fourth century the word "martyr" was commonly understood in ordinary speech to refer to those who had died for proclaiming the faith, nevertheless the implicit possibility remained for a broader definition

---

74. Greek: noun *martus/marturos* as "witness," verb *martureo* "bear witness, testify." The word in its specifically Christian sense passes into Latin directly: *martyr, martyrium*.

75. See, e.g., Luke 24:48.

76. See, e.g., Revelation 2:13.

77. Origen, *Commentary on John* 2.28 (trans. ANF). Origen's expansive interpretation of the call to martyrdom poses an interesting contrast to his notoriously literal reading of Matthew 19:12.

that could encompass any action that "bore witness" to Christ by advancing the interests of the Christian faith. This reading gained new relevance after the conversion of Constantine brought the age of pagan persecution and traditional martyrdom to an end, and many Christians began to worry that it was no longer possible to imitate the virtues of the early martyrs.

In 397, three clerics sent to missionize the largely pagan valley of Anaunia (modern Val di Non) in northern Italy were burned alive by hostile locals. The three were quickly claimed as martyrs.[78] Maximus, bishop of Turin, used the incident as an occasion to remind his congregation that the possibilities for martyrdom had not been closed off by the end of the persecutions:

> For they were not condemned to death because they were Christians,
> but rather they were seized for punishment because the sacrilegious
> were being rebuked for not being Christians and devout persons. In
> a time of peace, then, when no vengeful ruler was acting oppressively,
> it was not public persecution but religious devotion that made martyrs
> of the holy men. For, desiring to provide for the salvation of the many,
> they did not fear to place their own well-being in jeopardy.[79]

Maximus has here outlined what we might call a "missionary" path to martyrdom, by which people might be killed not simply for being Christians, but for actively trying to spread the faith among a hostile audience. As the bishop's account of the incident makes clear, Anaunia was no uncharted wilderness but rather a thoroughly Romanized area already possessing a small Christian minority. The three clerics had been sent to minister to these, to build a church, and hopefully to convert the rest of the population. The clerics' intervention to prevent "apostasy"—to restrain the already-converted local Christians from taking part in a procession organized by their pagan neighbors—seems to have been the immediate provocation that drove the pagans to violence. Martyrdom could be found simply in reproaching others for their lack of faith, and Maximus made it clear

---

78. The first announcement of the incident came in two letters of Vigilius of Trent, one to Simplicianus of Milan and one to John Chrysostom in Constantinople: PL 13.549–558. Maximus, bishop of Turin, expounded upon the incident in his *Sermons* 105 and 106 (exact dates unknown), which are quoted below. The incident is also mentioned briefly by Augustine, *Ep.* 139 (412). See also Chaffin 1970, Pellegrino 1981, Lizzi 1990. Lizzi suggests (p. 172) that *C.Th.* 16.2.31 (25 April 398), prescribing harsh penalties for those who attack Catholic clergy or churches, an edict usually thought to be associated with the Donatist conflict, was originally issued in response to this incident. But Augustine and the other North African Catholic bishops did persuade the imperial court to reissue it in 409 in response to Donatist attacks. On Maximus generally: Merkt 1997.

79. *Sermon* 106 (trans. Ramsey).

to his congregation that since such "martyrdom" need not even involve risking one's life, the lesson was relevant even for the more substantially Christianized area closer to Turin, where pagan violence was not a significant danger. He warned Christian landowners of their duty to ensure the Christianization of their tenants and dependents:

> Therefore, brethren, since we have an example, let us imitate the holy men, if not by a martyr's suffering, then certainly by fulfilling the responsibilities of Christianity. And since we have heard that the *lustrum* [a festival of pagan origin] is accustomed to be celebrated by a few sacrilegious persons, by the examples of the saints let us rebuke the impious and reproach the errant, for the portion of martyrdom is to do what the martyrs did. But if we see these things and are silent, if we let them be without speaking, then we make ourselves guilty by tacit assent even if not by the commission of the crime.[80]

The duty of all Christians to spread the faith was sufficiently paramount that it might drive believers to risk their lives, as had the three clerics at Anaunia, in order to bring the gospel to the unconverted. Silence, or toleration, was not an option. Tertullian, writing in a time of actual persecution, had warned that "If you are not willing to confess, you are not willing to suffer; and to be unwilling to confess is to deny."[81] But the idea that failure to denounce idolatry actually made one complicit in that idolatry, for Maximus, was not merely confined to the case of missionaries who risked their lives in preaching to hostile pagans. The same imperative, he argued, commanded Christian elites to use all the power and influence of their position in order to compel the Christianization of those beneath them. Even this effort, which brought little or no risk to those elites, could be considered "martyrdom"—for "the whole life of a Christian is a martyrdom if he lives according to the gospel."[82]

Caesarius, bishop of Arles in Gaul at the beginning of the sixth century, again found it necessary to reassure his congregation that the absence of persecution did not make "martyrdom" impossible:

---

80. Maximus, *Sermon* 106. Similar exhortations for landlords to discipline the religious practices of their peasants can be found in *Sermons* 107 and 108. Cf. Chrysostom, *Against the Jews Oration* 1: "How much better it is to incur the hatred of your fellow servants for saving them than to provoke the Master's anger against yourselves!" (trans. Mayer and Allen 2000, p. 166)

81. Tertullian, *On Flight from Persecution* 5 (trans. ANF): *Nisi si vis confiteri, patiaris non vis; nolle autem confiteri negare est*—though, admittedly, many other contemporary Christian authorities did not share this view: see discussion in chapter 1, pp. 37–39.

82. Maximus, *Sermon* 82.

I repeat again as I have frequently admonished you, dearly beloved, that no one of you should think that martyrs cannot live in our times. "Martyr" is a Greek word, which in Latin means a witness. As we have often said, anyone who bears witness to Christ for the sake of justice is without doubt a martyr. Likewise, anyone who resists the champions of dissipation and persecutors of chastity out of love for God, will receive the crown of martyrdom. Therefore, there are martyrs even in our day. If a man reproves evildoers with justice and charity, or warns against the indiscriminate taking of oaths, perjury, calumny, and slander, he will be Christ's martyr by giving testimony to the things which please God. Moreover, one who restrains men from observing omens, wearing phylacteries, or consulting magicians and seers [practices condemned by the church as "pagan"] is known to bear testimony to Christ when he speaks against these temptations of the Devil.[83]

For Caesarius, as for Maximus, martyrdom, in the sense of bearing witness to the faith, thus extended to encompass the disciplinary correction of other people's sins. That this correction could easily take a coercive path was made clear by Caesarius in his next sermon, against Christians who continued to venerate pagan cult sites and sacred trees:

Rebuke whomever you recognize as such, admonish them quite harshly, chide them quite severely. If they are not corrected, strike them if you can; if they are not corrected thus, pull their hair. If they still continue, tie them with bonds of iron, so that a chain may hold those whom Christ's grace does not hold. Then, do not permit them to restore the shrine, but endeavor to tear to pieces and destroy them wherever they are. Cut the impious wood down to the roots, break up the altars of the Devil.[84]

For John Chrysostom, meanwhile, one way to imitate the martyrs was by rebuking "blasphemers"—with one's mouth, or with one's fists.[85] Here we have reached a definition of "martyrdom" whose meaning stretches all the way from suffering violence to inflicting it. Far from its original sense of resistance to persecuting authorities, martyrial rhetoric here is used to justify the disciplinary, corrective violence carried out by Christian authorities willing to "persecute" for the sake of spreading the gospel.[86]

Idol smashing, suicidal attacks by a handful of zealots who fully expected

---

83. Caesarius of Arles, *Sermon* 52.1 (trans. Mueller). On Caesarius' preaching against paganism, see Klingshirn 1994, esp. pp. 201–243.

84. Caesarius, *Sermon* 53.1 (trans. Mueller).

85. *Homilies on the Statues* 1.32; see discussion in chapter 7, pp. 258–259.

86. On the role of violence within a paradigm of Christian discipline, see chapter 4.

to be killed by angry pagans, represented a uniquely active and provocative quest for martyrdom, particularly characteristic of the fourth and early fifth centuries. This practice was highly controversial, for a well-established strain in patristic thought argued that it was improper to seek out and provoke persecution: Christians should rather hide or flee when possible, and then endure martyrdom bravely only when the persecuting authorities sought them out.[87] The Council of Elvira in Spain, at the beginning of the fourth century, explicitly stated that those who were killed for breaking idols were not to be honored with the title of martyr.[88] Martyrdom was a grace given by God to those found worthy, and Christians should wait until they were called to it, rather than trying to achieve it by their own efforts.[89] This argument can be seen in the context of the institutional church hierarchy's ongoing attempts to circumscribe the authority of charismatic individuals such as martyrs, confessors, and holy men, and place them more strictly under episcopal control. Augustine came down firmly against "voluntary martyrdom," in large part because martyrial zeal in North Africa seems to have been most widespread among his Donatist opponents. Temples and idols should be destroyed, he argued, but in a lawful and orderly manner, backed up by imperial edicts and supervised by imperial authorities in order to intimidate any potential resistance and therefore to prevent bloodshed and disorder.[90]

When Christians acted without such imperial support, violent retaliation by the pagans was a very real possibility. One motive behind Elvira's prohibition may have been the fear that the actions of a few zealots might bring about indiscriminate pagan vengeance against the entire Christian community, at that time still a relatively small and weak minority. The reign of Julian, as we have seen, created a new political climate suddenly, if briefly, favorable to pagan attacks on Christians. In many cases, these attacks were understood (as reported by mainly Christian sources) as retaliation for provocative and sacrilegious acts, usually involving the seizure or destruction of pagan temples or cult objects, that the Christian victims had committed earlier, during the reigns of Constantine and Constantius. Christians killed by pagans in this context seem to have been universally recognized and venerated as martyrs by the Christian community. It is far from clear,

---

87. For a survey of patristic attitudes, see Thornton, 1986, Butterweck 1995. For the post-Constantinian period see also Athanasius, *Apology for his Flight*, defending his flight in the face of the threats of the emperor Constantius.

88. Elvira, *Canon 60*.

89. A view expressed in, e.g., *Acts of Cyprian 2.1*, *Martyrdom of Polycarp 4*.

90. Full discussion in chapter 3, pp. 115–117.

of course, that most of these Christians actually "sought" martyrdom directly—at the time that they carried out their attacks on paganism, they may well have been reasonably confident that they would get away with it; the abrupt change in the political climate upon Julian's accession would have caught many of them by surprise. Others, who continued provocative attacks on paganism even under Julian's regime, more obviously had martyrdom in mind.[91]

Even in the absence of a sympathetic emperor, local pagan communities continued to strike back against those who violated their places of worship.[92] Marcellus, bishop of Apamea, had already acquired fame for his role in the destruction of that Syrian city's great temple of Zeus, for which he had secured the help of both the emperor (to restrain the pagans, by imperial edict and military supervision) and God (to overcome, by a convenient miracle, the difficult engineering problems of demolishing such a massive stone structure).[93] Now, however, attempting to repeat the deed at another temple, he was caught alone by some pagans and burned alive. Sozomen explained:

> This bishop had commanded the demolition of all the temples in the city and villages, under the supposition that it would not be easy otherwise for them to be converted from their former religion. Having heard that there was a very spacious temple at Aulon, a district of Apamea, he repaired thither with a body of soldiers and gladiators.[94] He stationed himself at a distance from the scene of conflict, beyond the reach of the arrows; for he was afflicted with the gout, and was unable to fight, to pursue, or to flee. Whilst the soldiers and gladiators were engaged in the assault against the temple, some pagans, discovering that he was alone, hastened to the place where he was separated from the combat; they arose suddenly and seized him, and burnt him alive.

In the aftermath of the incident, the issue of retribution raised an important question: by whom should "martyrs" be avenged?

> The perpetrators of this deed were not then known, but, in course of time, they were detected, and the sons of Marcellus determined upon avenging his death. The council of the province, however, prohibited

91. See chapter 2, pp. 92–94.
92. Cf. Sozomen *HE* 7.15: "The inhabitants of the last-named city [Apamea in Syria] often armed the men of Galilee and the peasants of Lebanon in defense of their temples."
93. Theodoret *HE* 5.21, placing it immediately before the destruction of the Serapeum in 391. On the destruction of the temples of Apamea see Fowden 1978; Trombley 1993, vol.1, pp. 123–146.
94. On the ability of bishops to assemble "private armies" of this sort, see Brown 1992, esp. chap. 3.

them from executing this design, and declared that it was not just that the relatives or friends of Marcellus should seek to avenge his death; when they should rather return thanks to God for having accounted him worthy to die in such a cause.[95]

Marcellus' family sought to avenge his death—presumably at first by bringing legal charges against his killers, but with the threat of retaliatory private violence not far behind. The provincial authorities, for their part, may not have wished to lend legitimacy to Marcellus' extralegal actions, and sought to prevent further bloodshed. In responding, they made use of another aspect of the discourse of martyrdom: a notion that the Christian church should not seek vengeance for its martyrs, whether by the justice of the Christian emperor or by any other agency. This was founded, ultimately, upon Stephen the Protomartyr's dying request that his killers be forgiven.[96] Vengeance would always fall upon persecutors sooner or later—as Lactantius' *On the Deaths of the Persecutors* made gruesomely clear—but it should properly be seen to come from God, in an unambiguously miraculous manner, and not from human hands. Bishop Eusebius of Samosata, fatally injured when an Arian woman dropped a stone on his head, with his last words asked his companions to forswear vengeance—an act that transformed his death into a martyrdom.[97] Public renunciation of vengeance could serve the interests of church authorities, who by interceding to save the guilty parties from capital punishment might place those parties in their debt. Augustine asked the *comes* Marcellinus not to impose the death penalty on certain Donatists who had murdered Catholic clergy, "So that the sufferings of the martyrs, which ought to shed bright glory on the church, may not be tarnished by the blood of their enemies."[98] Such a request had the added benefit of claiming the status of martyrs—an especially contested title in the North African schism—for the dead on the Catholic side. For the secular authorities, a decision to leave vengeance in God's hands allowed

95. Sozomen *HE* 7.15 (NPNF trans.).

96. Acts 7:60. This, of course, was meant in turn to echo Jesus' "Forgive them, for they know not what they do" in Luke 23:34.

97. As Theodoret *HE* 5.4, explicitly comparing him to Stephen, makes clear: "Thus he earned the martyr's crown."

98. Augustine, *Ep.* 139 (412). For this strategy, see also Augustine's intervention on behalf of the pagans of Calama, after rioting in which a church had been burned and a Christian killed: Augustine *Epp.* 90, 91, 103, 104 (408–409). See further discussion of these episodes in chapter 4, pp. 141–142. Augustine here mentions the Anaunia incident (see above, pp. 173–174), adding that in that case the imperial authorities had spared the lives of the killers, who had been caught and imprisoned, and the slain clergy were now honored as martyrs.

them to satisfy both sides—the slain were to be honored with martyrial status, while the slayers would escape punishment—and perhaps prevent further conflict, an important consideration in areas such as the Apamene, where the pagans were obviously still quite strong. Following the Alexandrian riots of 391, the emperor declared that the murdered Christians be honored as martyrs, and no legal action was to be taken against the pagans who had killed them—in this case, the intent was partly that the pagans be sufficiently grateful for being spared legal punishment not to offer serious resistance to the destruction of their temples.[99] In the case of Apamea, again, the authorities may not have wished to legitimize the extralegal violence against the temples by which Marcellus had provoked his killers.

ANGER AGAINST ENEMIES OF THE FAITH

Any discussion of retribution, of course, leads us to consider the anger and hostility that would underlie calls for revenge. The question of whether or how Christians ought legitimately to feel such emotions was far from settled. Lactantius, as we have seen, argued passionately in favor of God's anger. Insofar as God's wrath served to distinguish right from wrong and condemn transgressors, it was appropriate for pious Christians to think as God thought: "He who commands us to be angry is Himself manifestly angry."[100] But with equal conviction Lactantius asserted that vengeance properly belonged only to God.[101] Since human anger could easily be excessive or wrongly directed, its expression could lead to further injustice. Therefore, Lactantius said, God "forbids us to persevere in anger." While a quick and pure anger for the condemnation of sins would be acceptable, Christians ought not to harbor prolonged grudges or hatreds.[102] Augustine, likewise, took care to separate righteous anger from vengeful fury.[103] His admonition to "hate the sin, but love the sinner" attempted to strike a delicate balance, and hinted at just how difficult it could be to make such a distinction in practice.[104] Even the best of motives—a paternalistic urge to act upon others "for their own good"—opened the door to coercion and abuse. A missionary impulse to

99. Rufinus *HE* 11.22, Sozomen *HE* 7.15.
100. *On the Anger of God* 21.
101. *Divine Institutes* 5.21.
102. *On the Anger of God* 21. See discussion in chapter 1, pp. 31–32.
103. Augustine, *City of God* 14.15; see discussion of God's anger and human anger at, e.g., 15.25, 21.24.
104. Augustine, *City of God* 14.6.

"save" pagans and Jews, or a charitable concern to correct heretics, could operate alongside a sense of frustration at their "obstinacy" that might then overlap into resentment and hatred. Gospel commandments to love one's enemies, then, did not guarantee peace.

Christian apologists had long argued that demons were ultimately to blame for the evils of idolatry, persecution, and heresy—they tricked pagans into worshipping them as gods, and stirred up dissension and argument among Christians. This would imply, at least in theory, that pagans and heretics were not really enemies, but rather helpless victims of demonic delusion. But the ongoing struggle against the demons could all too easily slide into "demonization" of one's worldly enemies.[105]

Extremists who joined the cosmic battle against evil could act both out of vengeance—seeking retribution for past persecutions—and also out of fear. If they did not act boldly and aggressively, the demons might stir up pagans to new persecution (a particular worry after Julian's reign) or inspire new heresies to tear apart the church.[106] But fear of demonic powers in the present coexisted with an unwavering faith in the ultimate triumph of the good. The power of Christ would eventually overthrow all idolatry, and Christian idol smashers saw themselves as very much a part of that process. By attacking temples and idols sacred to the pagans, Christian zealots continued their battle against the demons whom the pagans worshipped as "gods."[107]

Violence, for the extremist, was an appropriate answer to a perceived insult or humiliation against the honor of the Christian religion. Zealous anger might be aroused by the attacks on virgins reported by Athanasius, the reopening of temples under Julian, or the prospect of Jews winning a legal judgment against Christians.[108] Extremists' exquisite sensitivity to "insult" owed much to traditional understandings of honor, shame, and masculinity, and of course was hardly unique to a Christian context.[109]

105. On this theme see generally Pagels 1995; cf. also Juergensmeyer 2000, pp. 182–185 on "Satanization" of the Other.

106. Drake 2000, pp. 431–436, emphasizes the polarizing impact of Julian's short-lived reign upon pagan-Christian relations as subsequent generations of Christians became determined to prevent another pagan revival. Cf. Juergensmeyer 2000, pp. 145–163, on the "cosmic war" mentality, and the common claim of militants that they themselves are the true "victims" and are acting defensively.

107. On Christian beliefs about demons dwelling within pagan idols and temples: Mango 1963, Saradi-Mendelovici 1990, Caseau 2001.

108. Virgins, Julian: see chapter 2, pp. 84–87 and 92–93. Jews: see discussion of Callinicum incident, pp. 194–196 below.

109. See Juergensmeyer 2000, pp. 187–215, discussing perceived threats to masculinity as a motivation for militants. On humiliation see Miller 1993. For general

The ability to perceive insult and suffer humiliation would seem to imply a sense of pride, a quality rarely praised in Christian literature, and regularly condemned, particularly in ascetic and homiletic discourse. The zealot's answer to this seeming contradiction, unsurprisingly, was that the honor he undertook to defend was not his own but that of God and the church, just as the anger with which he hated enemies of the faith was not his anger but God's. Since God was understood to work not only through the forces of nature but also through human agents, it became possible for extremists to project their own agendas and prejudices onto the divine.

A central paradox of the Christian faith was the idea of empowerment through humiliation. Christ, and the martyrs after him, allowed themselves to be degraded, abused, tortured, and killed in ways traditionally reserved for the lowest of criminals. Their very abasement and suffering became the means to victory over their persecutors. The willingness of zealous Christians to suffer violence, to expose themselves to the risk of martyrdom—even if it did not actually come to them—was central to legitimating their own actions. A claim to be acting on behalf of a transcendent and moral cause, rather than in one's own self-interest, often makes violence easier to justify in the eyes of others.[110] The contempt for death displayed by martyrs and would-be martyrs marked them as uniquely selfless and lent legitimacy to their deeds.[111] Their willingness to die gave them the right to kill.[112]

In many ways, then, the traditional "spiritual combat" of the martyr had come to be externalized. Violent acts could be undertaken to avenge a perceived insult to God or to the church, the deeds of God's servants enacting the anger of God. Christian zealots employed and understood violence within a broad paradigm of "doing God's will."

Aphrahat, an ascetic writer of early fourth-century Mesopotamia, argued

---

and comparative explorations of anger as a subject of historical study, see the essays in Rosenwein 1998, Gay 1993. See now Rosenwein's comprehensive review article, Rosenwein 2002.

110. "It is easier to be cruel, on a large scale, when you act in the name of others, or in the name of an ideal, or even for the benefit of your victim, than when you act for your own sake." Holmes 1995, p. 48.

111. Athanasius argued that freedom from "fear of death" was given to humankind by the incarnation of the Word, that this fearlessness made the martyrs' triumphs possible, and that monks could bring a similar courage to their ascetic struggles: *On the Incarnation* 28, 29; see discussion in Brakke 1995a, pp. 149–161.

112. For modern analogies of martyrial rhetoric used by terrorists, see Juergensmeyer 2000, chap. 9.

that any action pleasing to God could be understood as prayer: "A person should do the will of God, and that constitutes prayer . . . give rest to the weary, visit the sick, make provision for the poor: this is indeed prayer."[113] An equation between prayer and good deeds is not particularly unusual in Christian thought,[114] but the scriptural example Aphrahat chose to make his point is worth mention. He referred his audience to Numbers 25. When Moses was leading the Israelite community through the wilderness of Sinai, one of the Israelites had defied God's law by committing adultery with a pagan woman:

> Phinehas, son of Eleazar the priest, saw them. He picked up a spear, went into their tent, and killed both of them. The Lord spoke to Moses and said, "Phinehas son of Eleazar has turned away my wrath from Israel; for he was zealous for my zeal, so that I will not consume the people of Israel in my anger. He and his descendents shall enjoy the priesthood for all time, because he showed his zeal for God."[115]

Aphrahat commented: "Because he killed them for the sake of his God, it was reckoned as prayer for him."[116] Optatus, writing against the Donatists in North Africa, used the example of Phinehas to justify the bloody repression of the Circumcellions by the imperial commissioner Macarius in 347. For those who might be troubled by Phinehas' apparent violation of the commandment "thou shalt not kill," Optatus had this answer:

> Some evils happen for the worse, and some happen for the better. A robber [*latro*] does an evil for the worse, a judge does an evil for the better, when he avenges the sin of the robber. For this is the voice of God, "Thou shalt not kill," and this is the same God's voice, "If a man is found sleeping with a woman who has a husband, you shall kill both." One God and two contending voices. When Phinehas, son of a priest, found an adulterer with an adulteress, he raised his hand with his weapon, and stood uncertain between the two voices of God. If he struck, he would sin; if he did not strike, he would fail in duty. He chose the better sin, to strike the blow.[117]

It was demonstrated in the strongest possible terms that Phinehas had made the correct choice: God spoke, a miracle that lent legitimacy to Phine-

---

113. Aphrahat, *Demonstration* 4 "On Prayer" (trans. Brock).
114. See, e.g., Origen, *On Prayer* 12.2.
115. Numbers 25:6–13 (RSV trans.).
116. Aphrahat, *Demonstration* 4.14.
117. Optatus 3.7 (trans. Edwards). Shenoute experienced a dilemma similar to that of Phinehas: should he flog misbehaving monks, and risk fatal injury to them, or stay his hand, and risk God's anger? See chapter 4, p. 143.

has' act of violence, sanctifying the deed. It was, in the words of Optatus, a homicide pleasing to God.[118] Phinehas was commonly referred to by other patristic sources as a worthy model of "zeal for God" or as an illustration of justifiable homicide.[119] Bishop Porphyry of Gaza, famous for his role in the destruction of the temple of Zeus Marnas in 402, was hailed by his congregation as a "second Phinehas" against the idolaters.[120] The normal restraints of law and morality did not apply, Jerome argued, in punishing an offense against God: "There is no cruelty in regard for God's honor."[121] Quoting Psalm 138, Jerome argued for "hating with a perfect hatred" those who "hate God."[122] While advocates of "corrective" or "disciplinary" violence, as we have seen, might try to justify themselves with the Gospel's commands to love one's neighbors and one's enemies, extremists who emphasized anger against God's enemies found much inspiration in the Old Testament.[123]

An even more promising scriptural model could be found in the prophet Elijah, who like Phinehas carried out God's will when he ordered the massacre of four hundred and fifty "false prophets" of Ba'al.[124] Elijah challenged them to call down fire from heaven and consume their sacrificial offering, to prove which god was mightier. When he could and they could

---

118. *Et homicidium placuit Deo.* Compare the early fifth-century Pelagian treatise *On Divine Law* 5.1, whose author concedes that what is "pleasing to God" might not appear lawful to ordinary morality, and vice versa: "The divine law . . . frequently reveals a sin which does not seem to us to be a sin at all, and discovers godliness in an action in which we seek to expose an act of ungodliness. Saul and Jeoshaphat were kings of the people of Israel and, while they showed mercy to those whom God hated, incurred God's displeasure in a work of godliness. On the other hand, Phineas and the sons of Levi won the gratitude of God for human slaughter and the murder of their own relations. Do you see how greatly divine judgment differs from human sentiments . . . [so that] acts seem to be unjust which are proved to have been done justly and rightly enough in the light of knowledge of the reasons which prompted them?" (Rees trans.)

119. See, e.g., Chrysostom, *On the Priesthood* 1.7, Phinehas not a murderer; Ephrem, *Nisibene Hymns* 39.7, the lance of Phinehas guards the Tree of Life; Theodoret *Ep.* 116, the zeal of Phinehas worthy of emulation; cf. Theodoret *HR* 1.10, comparing James of Nisibis to Phinehas. In the contemporary U.S., the name "Phinehas Priests" has been used by some far-right extremists who advocate attacks on abortion clinics, Jews, homosexuals, and "race mixers": see the Anti-Defamation League report at http://www.adl.org/backgrounders/an_phineas.html.

120. Mark the Deacon, *Life of Porphyry of Gaza* 24.

121. Jerome *Ep.* 109.3 (404) to Riparius.

122. Jerome *Ep.* 109.2, quoting Psalm 138:21–22: "Do I not hate them, O Lord, that hate thee? And am I not grieved with those that rise up against thee? I hate them with perfect hatred."

123. On prophets/patriarchs as exempla see Brakke 1995a, pp. 161–170; Krueger 1997; Satran 1995.

124. 1 Kings 18:17–40.

not, he convinced the Israelites to destroy them. Elijah had always been recognized by Christians as a prototype for John the Baptist and for Jesus; in the fourth century, holy men and their hagiographers began to take him as a primary model of ascetic virtue.[125] Elijah's wild and ragged appearance, and his long sojourns in the wilderness, were particularly inspirational to the hermit-monks of the Egyptian desert and the Syrian mountains.[126] The youthful Shenoute, in a vision, received the mantle of Elijah, signifying his future as a great leader of monks.[127] When the Syrian archimandrite Barsauma was finally called home by God, after a long career battling enemies of the faith, a disciple claimed to see a column of fire carrying him to heaven, like Elijah.[128]

It should come as no surprise, then, that Elijah also represented for Christian holy men a model for holy violence, justified by zeal for God. Optatus compared the massacre of rebellious Circumcellions to the slaughter of the priests of Ba'al—in each case, an example of God's just vengeance.[129] The Alexandrian patriarch Dioscorus said to the monk Macarius, "Elijah is coming out to meet you, because you have been zealous for God as he was, when you brought down Kothos the idol."[130] Although the bulk of the *Panegyric* is dedicated to Macarius' battles against the Chalcedonians, in this passage Dioscorus is made to single out an attack on paganism as the crowning achievement of the holy man's career. Symeon the Stylite was visited by Elijah in his fiery chariot, who instructed him to be bold in his rebukes of the rich and powerful, and to care for the poor.

> For I am Elijah the prophet who in my zeal shut up the heavens and
> gave Ahab and Jezebel as food to the dogs and killed the priests of
> Ba'al. . . . For once the Lord is someone's helper, how can anyone trouble

125. See, e.g., in Athanasius, *Life of Antony* 7. On popular images of Elijah see Frankfurter 1993.

126. See, e.g., Theodoret *HR* 3.1, writing of the monk Marcianus: "How could we adequately express admiration of him? Clearly by classing him with Elijah and John and those like them, who 'went about in skins of sheep and goats, destitute, afflicted, ill-treated, of whom the world was not worthy, wandering in deserts and mountains and caves and the holes of the earth' [quoting Hebrews 11:37–38]." (Price trans.)

127. Besa, *Life of Shenoute* 8. Cf. 118, where Shenoute's disciples saw him conversing with John the Baptist, Elijah, and Elisha.

128. *Life of Barsauma*, 96th miracle.

129. Cf. Optatus 3.6: "As if no one ever deserved to die for the vindication of God!"

130. *Panegyric on Macarius* (trans. Johnson, p. 108). Macarius' anti-pagan activities are discussed below.

or hurt him? For Ahab and Jezebel could not trouble or hurt me when I decreed their death and destruction. I gave their corpses as food to animals and I killed their priests and burnt their courtiers.[131]

That the prophet chose to introduce himself by listing the most violent highlights of his career is particularly interesting in that he was not on this occasion exhorting Symeon to any specific act of violence—that ascetic's chosen lifestyle necessarily limited his potential for participating directly in such activities—but merely encouraging him to confront the rich fearlessly, suggesting that in the minds of a Christian audience the rhetorical "violence" of a holy man's *parrhesia* was not fundamentally different from real violence.

For Elijah, a miracle of fire from heaven underscored the prophet's holiness and also demonstrated God's advance approval for the killing of the pagan priests. "Fire from heaven" has been identified as a particularly characteristic theme in Syrian Christian tradition. It served as a sign sent by God to consume a worthy offering, and to distinguish truth from falsehood. Fire imagery was often used to describe the Holy Spirit, Mary's conception, and the presence of Christ within the Eucharist. Great zeal for the faith was commonly represented as "fire" within the heart.[132] It is in this context that we must understand the many stories of fire miracles by which holy men, Syrians as well as others, demonstrated their power or legitimated acts of righteous violence. The Syrian ascetic Alexander the Akoimete had first set fire to a pagan temple by his own hand, but he then followed the example of Elijah and challenged a leading pagan to see which one of them could call down fire from heaven.[133] The Egyptian monk Copres dared a Manichaean, before a crowd of spectators, to walk through fire with him. When Copres emerged unscathed, the crowd seized the Manichaean and cast him into the flames.[134] Barsauma prayed, picked up a pebble, spat on it and hurled it at a pagan temple, which immediately erupted in flames.[135] Martin, having torched a tem-

---

131. *Syriac Life of Symeon the Stylite* 42–43 (trans. Doran).

132. Brock 1993. Biblical accounts of fire consuming a sacrificial offering pleasing to God include: Leviticus 9:24, 1 Kings 18:38 (Elijah with the priests of Ba'al), 1 Chronicles 21:26, 2 Chronicles 7:1. Syrian exegetical tradition added the miracle to other biblical stories as well, claiming, e.g., that God sent fire from heaven to consume Abel's offering, but not Cain's, because Abel was pure of heart: Aphrahat, *Demonstration* 4.2. (The miracle is not found in the account of Cain and Abel in Genesis.)

133. *Life of Alexander the Akoimete* 11.

134. *Historia Monachorum* 10.32–33.

135. *Life of Barsauma*, 22nd miracle.

ple, needed a miracle to prevent the fire from spreading to nearby houses.[136] Palladius claimed to see the hand of God at work in the fires that broke out when John Chrysostom's supporters rioted to protest his exile.[137]

Miracles, then, reinforced the holy man's display of authority, and lent legitimacy to his action, divine violence backing up human.[138] The failure of the pagan gods to take vengeance for the desecration of their shrines could in itself be interpreted as a sort of "negative miracle," where the simple fact that nothing happened, proved the superior power of Christ.[139] Other miracles served to prevent retaliatory violence against the holy man.[140] The saint could call down God's wrath with a word.[141]

The preceding examples help to formulate a paradigm of holy violence for the late antique holy man, by which dramatic actions against enemies of the faith served as an expression of religious authority, legitimated by the saint's readiness to offer up his own life as a martyr. Holy men regularly flirted with martyrdom even as they did God's will and spread the gospel by destroying pagan holy places. When Martin of Tours travelled through Gaul in the late fourth century, burning temples, smashing idols, and chopping down sacred trees, he faced violent resistance from the pagans, who in one place drove him off with a beating, and in another attempted to stab him. In other instances, however, he managed to preach to the pa-

---

136. *Life of Martin of Tours* 14. When he threw his own body before the flames, a great wind arose and blew them out. Here again, the saint's willingness to risk his own life was the key to his power.

137. Palladius, *Dialogue on the Life of John Chrysostom* 10. See next chapter, pp. 227–228.

138. Other examples of miracles assisting in the destruction of pagan temples: *Life of Martin of Tours* 14, where angels with heavenly spears destroyed a shrine; Theodoret *HE* 5.21, bishop Marcellus of Apamea blessed holy water, which burst into flame as soon as it touched the temple's columns; *Life of Porphyry of Gaza*, where a child was divinely inspired to speak exact instructions for demolishing the building.

139. For instance, at the destruction of the Alexandrian Serapeum in 391: the soldier who took an axe to the cult image of Serapis was not struck dead, and the Nile did not run dry, contrary to pagan predictions (Rufinus *HE* 11.23 and 30).

140. *Martin of Tours* 15: a pagan swung a knife at the saint and was thrown down; *Life of Shenoute* 81–82: when a pagan struck Shenoute in the face, an angel appeared, dragged the man by the hair to the river and drowned him; *Shenoute* 89: when Blemmyes threatened him with spears, their arms were paralyzed.

141. Barsauma cursed various evildoers, and they died: *Life of Barsauma* miracles 37, 38, 39, 42, 67 (an entire village washed into the Euphrates), 71, 74, 76 (the empress Pulcheria, from biting her own tongue). *Shenoute* 86–87: the saint cursed some rapacious pagan landlords, and their entire island sank into the Nile. Cf. the gruesome death of the heresiarch Arius, in response to the prayers of bishop Alexander of Constantinople.

gans so quickly and effectively that they converted and then joined him in destroying their own idols.[142] Alexander the Akoimete "went out to preach the gospel, lest he be found negligent"—following the same missionary imperative outlined by Maximus of Turin. This meant, to Alexander, going into a pagan village and setting fire to the largest temple. He then proved himself an exceptionally gifted preacher, converting an angry pagan lynch mob into the beginnings of a Christian congregation. When one of the pagan community leaders asked him, "What demon has impelled you to come here and destroy the temple of the gods? What hope do you have, that you would have contempt for your life and dare such a deed?" Alexander answered, "We do not despise our lives, but rather, we desire the next life, and therefore we despise this life. We will attain the truth, and we demonstrate the truth of our speech through our actions"—a statement of purpose neatly blending the martyr's contempt of death, the ascetic's contempt for the world, and the zealot's contempt for worldly law.[143] Alexander's willingness to martyrdom became a justification of his deed. In this and many other cases, martyrdom, whether achieved in fact, or expressed instead as potential in terms of "zeal" or "worthiness," offered a visible sign of the saint's holiness. Like ascetic discipline, like the performance of miracles, it identified the holy man as chosen by God. God approved of his actions, because those actions fulfilled the will of God.

In early fifth-century Upper Egypt, the monk Macarius of Tkow received word that the idol worshippers in a nearby village had taken to sacrificing

---

142. Sulpicius Severus, *Life of Martin of Tours* 14–15.

143. *Life of Alexander the Akoimete* 11. See also Gatier 1995; and now Caner 2002, esp. chap. 4, with a new English translation of the *Life*. Other aspects of Alexander's ascetic career, which brought him into conflict with Christian authorities, will be discussed in the next chapter, pp. 243–246. The pagan interlocutor in this scene is, incidentally, none other than Rabbula, seen here as Alexander brings about his conversion to Christianity. This might lead us to suggest Chalcis/Qennesrin in Syria, Rabbula's original home, as the location of the incident—but the credibility of the story is damaged somewhat by the fact that the *Life of Rabbula* gives a completely different account of Rabbula's conversion, in which Alexander does not appear. On the other hand (as Gatier emphasizes) the precise and accurate topographical detail displayed in the *Life of Alexander*'s account of Alexander's travels in Syria suggests an eyewitness basis. A possible explanation for this discrepancy is suggested by Vööbus 1948 and by Gatier 1995, who postulate two authors, the first an early disciple present for the events in Syria, and the second a later member of the Akoimete monastery near Constantinople who translated the work into Greek and interpolated the Rabbula story from a now-lost Syriac source. Blum 1969, pp. 36–39, compares the two stories of Rabbula's conversion and declares the one in *Life of Alexander* "eine spätere legendarische Gestaltung."

Christian children on their altars.[144] Macarius and three disciples headed for the pagan village in order to overthrow the idol and temple of their god, Kothos. When warned that the pagans would resist, Macarius replied, "As the Lord lives, even if they kill me I shall not stop." When the pagan villagers saw monks approaching, men and women alike grabbed every available weapon and barricaded their doors. With the pagans seemingly terrified, Macarius and his brethren forced their way into the temple of Kothos. But it was a trap. Twenty men fell upon them, seized them, bound them up like sheep and prepared to sacrifice them on the altar, saying, "Your lifespan ends today: behold, your slaughtering-place!" It seemed as if the longstanding Christian idea of the ascetic body as sacrificial offering was about to find a gruesomely literal expression.

But Macarius, though not afraid of martyrdom, on this day was to wield violence rather than endure it. "Behold," he said, "Christ will help us." At the last minute, Besa, the disciple of the famous abbot Shenoute, stormed the temple with a large gang of monks. When they could not force open the door, they prayed, and God threw it open. The pagans were paralyzed with terror. Besa asked Macarius, "Father, do you want to set the fire, or should I?" Macarius answered, "No, rather, let us pray, and God will send down fire from heaven to destroy the temple." And so it happened. For Macarius, this act of divine violence served in turn to legitimize an act of human violence he himself was about to commit. Macarius promptly ordered the brothers to seize Homer, the high priest of the pagans. At his command, they kindled a great fire, and threw Homer into it, along with all the idols they had found in the village. Macarius illustrates neatly the connection between martyrdom and holy violence, between enduring and inflicting violence. He was both willing to die for his faith, and willing to kill for it.

Barsauma, the Syrian archimandrite, was depicted as mixing divine miracle and physical violence in a campaign of destruction, as he and his monks wandered through Palestine and Transjordan levelling synagogues and pagan temples with evenhanded thoroughness, the hagiographer pausing to point out place-names from the Book of Numbers as if Barsauma were reenacting Joshua's victories over the Canaanites.[145] During a pilgrimage to Jeru-

144. The story illustrates the degree to which popular images of "pagan" worship became more and more sensationalized as actual paganism died out. These "cartoon pagans" practice human sacrifice, use children's intestines for harp strings, etc. The *Panegyric to Macarius of Tkow* is attributed to Dioscorus, bishop of Alexandria (d. 454), but in its present form is clearly a sixth-century composition.

145. *Life of Barsauma* 26–27. Temple destroyed by fire, mentioned above, p. 185. See discussion in Nau 1927a and 1927b. Nau suggests a date in the late 420s for these incidents. Place-names: Kadesh-Barnea, river Arnon, etc. Other echoes of Joshua:

salem several years later, violence erupted when Barsauma's monks began throwing stones at Jews praying on the Temple Mount, killing many of them.[146] The bishop and the local authorities went together with the Jews to ask the help of the empress Eudocia, then resident in Bethlehem, in suppressing these "brigands in the habit of monks." The monks were quickly arrested and threatened with execution. But, at least as reported by the hagiographer, God supported his zealous servants. The monks claimed that the stones that struck the Jews had fallen from heaven, perhaps in their minds transforming their own deed into an act of God. A series of miracles then vindicated them. First, the bodies of the slain Jews were examined, and no sign of physical injury found. Then, witnesses against the monks were miraculously struck dead right in the middle of the official inquiry. Finally, a massive earthquake, an act of divine violence, terrified the governor and the empress and convinced them to release the monks.[147] So, at least, goes the story as told by Barsauma's hagiographer—but even within that text, we see indications that many contemporaries, Jewish and Christian alike, considered Barsauma and his followers to be brigands, not holy men.[148]

As implausible as some aspects of this story might be, it nevertheless reflects a historical context in which violent clashes among Christians, Jews, and pagans, fighting over sacred objects or holy places, were not unusual.[149] The temples were physical obstacles to the conversion of the pagans, and

---

Barsauma makes the sun stand still (11th miracle; cf. Joshua 10:12–13); he forbids his disciples to loot any of the treasure found in a captured synagogue, but rather orders them to burn it all; one monk conceals some treasure and is punished (21st miracle), like Achan (Joshua 7)—a story paralleled also in Mark the Deacon, *Life of Porphyry of Gaza* 65–70, suggesting perhaps that the campaigns of Joshua could be taken as a biblical type for the seizure of pagan temples. Joshua son of Nun seems to have been another popular scriptural model as a champion against the enemies of the faith. Rabbula of Edessa, in his struggles against paganism and heresy, was likened to Joshua (Overbeck ed. 1865, p. 192). Barsauma's hagiographer remarks that in Palestine "at that time" (the first half of the fifth century) "pagans, Jews and Samaritans were numerous and Christians were few" (probably not entirely accurate), presenting a picture of a Holy Land occupied by unbelievers, a veritable Canaan. Compare Gregory of Nyssa's comment on Palestine in his treatise, *On Pilgrimage:* "Nowhere in the world are people so ready to kill each other as there." On the historical context of late antique Palestine see Stroumsa 1999, chap. 7.

146. Similar incidents make the Temple Mount a flashpoint for religious tension in modern times: see Friedland and Hecht 1991.

147. *Life of Barsauma*, miracles 61–66. Earthquakes were commonly understood as signs of divine anger: cf. Malalas and other chroniclers, who referred to them simply as "the wrath of God" striking such and such a city.

148. See discussion in next chapter, pp. 246–247.

149. See generally Fowden 1978, Trombley 1993–1994, Caseau 2001. Sometimes, the pagans fought back: in addition to many incidents under Julian (see chapter 2,

they needed to be removed. The destruction of a temple frequently brought about a mass conversion of pagans, at least as reported by Christian sources.[150] Whether or not such mass conversions actually occurred, Christians' belief that they did might itself encourage some to carry out similar attacks on temples or synagogues.

In some cases, bishops, monks, and other Christians acted with the sanction and support of the imperial government.[151] When temples were closed or destroyed by imperial order, the emphasis was not so much on battling "demons" but rather on demonstrating the emptiness of pagan claims regarding their gods' power. Pagan statues and cult objects were to be brought out of their mysterious sanctuaries and exposed to public view.[152] The destruction of such objects before the eyes of a large audience—and the lack of any subsequent lightning, earthquake, or other supernatural vengeance—strengthened the Christian argument that the idols of the pagans were merely wood, stone, or metal, powerless to retaliate against their desecrators. As Augustine put it, "A hatchet can interrogate your god."[153]

In cases such as Callinicum, or the "illegal" attacks on rural shrines about which Libanius complained in his oration *For the Temples*,[154] Christian militants were clearly running ahead of imperial law, which struggled to keep

---

pp. 94–95), see, e.g., the death of Marcellus of Apamea (above); the violence in Alexandria in 391; pagan massacre of Christians at Sufes in 399 (Augustine *Ep.* 50, discussed in chapter 3, pp. 118–119); pagan rioters attack Christians at Calama in 409 and then fear imperial retribution (Augustine *Epp.* 90, 91, 103, 104).

150. Most famous examples include the Alexandrian Serapeum in 391 (Rufinus *HE* 11.23–24; Socrates *HE* 5.16–17; Sozomen *HE* 7.15–20; Theodoret *HE* 5.22) and the Marneion of Gaza in 402 (Mark the Deacon, *Life of Porphyry of Gaza*). See Haas 1997, Trombley 1993–1994, Van Dam 1985. In these cases, the destruction of the temple was accompanied by an impressive display of imperial coercive power. The Serapeum incident in particular, judging from the great impression it made on the Latin west, may have served as a model for bishop Severus' attack on the Jewish community of Minorca in 418. See Bradbury 1996, Demougeot 1982, E. D. Hunt 1982.

151. Particularly during the tenure of Maternus Cynegius, praetorian prefect of the east in 384–388. See generally Fowden 1978.

152. Thus Eusebius, *VC* 3.54–57, explaining Constantine's removal of temple treasures and statues. Bishop Theophilus' public "exposure" and ridicule of bones excavated from a pagan site angered Alexandrian pagans, provoking them to riot: Rufinus *HE* 11.22.

153. *Sermon* 23B (Dolbeau 6, Mainz 13) (Hill trans., p. 39). Compare Theophilus' encouragement of a somewhat nervous axe man, to "Give Serapis a good whack!" Theodoret *HE* 5.22.

154. This will be discussed at greater length in the next chapter, pp. 210–211.

up with their zeal.[155] Secular and religious authorities generally disapproved of such extremist behavior, as we have seen. Imperial edicts against idolatry emphasized the suppression of sacrifice and closure of temples; idols were to be removed in an orderly manner by proper authorities, not by mob action. Buildings, if possible, were to be preserved intact for other uses.[156] Augustine struggled to redirect the iconoclastic impulses of his congregants by urging them to stay away from temples and instead "smash the idols in their hearts."[157] But in many cases when this advice was ignored, the Christian state generally seems to have found it easier to let the law be violated than to punish the wrongdoers and thus risk earning those Christians the title of martyrs—and themselves that of persecutors.

In popular imagination, the relationship between martyrdom and active violence underlay the charismatic authority of the holy man and served to identify him as chosen by God. Suffering (or the willingness to suffer) violent persecution by enemies of the faith marked out a future champion who would then strike back against those same enemies. This paradigm is neatly expressed in Mark the Deacon's account of one Barochas, a Christian of Gaza, who had been beaten nearly to death and dragged through the streets by the pagans. Having been healed by the prayers of bishop Porphyry, Barochas reappeared as a "new Samson," seizing a piece of wood and smiting many pagans in "godly zeal" after they had insulted the bishop.[158] Holy violence, as an expression of the spiritual authority of the Christian holy man, involved both the willingness to expose oneself to violence and the possibility of a martyr's death, and also the willingness to carry out violent destruction, and even to kill, if such was the will of God. Zeal for God justified the deed, and as such it overrode normal considerations of secular law and order—a claim bluntly asserted in the words of Shenoute: "There is no crime for those who have Christ."

155. Imperial edicts in the late fourth century merely suppressed pagan worship and closed temples but protected the buildings, and only gradually shifted towards accepting (in many cases after the fact) their destruction. A history of Christianization written entirely from the edicts of the *Theodosian Code* would present a highly misleading picture.

156. See the edicts collected in Book 16, Title 10 of the *Theodosian Code*. Some argued for preserving pagan buildings and statuary as "artistic treasures": see Lepelley 1994.

157. Augustine, *Sermon* 62.17; see also *Sermon* 24.

158. Mark the Deacon, *Life of Porphyry of Gaza* 22–23. The incident is curiously repeated, in fundamentally similar terms, at 95–98. The name "Barochas," perhaps not coincidentally, means "blessed."

"REPRESSIVE TOLERANCE": THE VIOLENCE OF EXPOSURE

Simple hatred may have driven most extremist assaults against pagans, Jews, or heretics, but zealots and their apologists believed that behind these despised groups there lay a secondary but in some ways more insidious enemy, a corrupt establishment that hypocritically called itself "Christian" and yet allowed pagan temples to remain standing, permitted Jews to blaspheme Christ, and failed to stop heretics from spreading their poisonous doctrines.[159] Each time that zealots broke or bent the law in attacking enemies of the faith, they delivered an implicit rebuke to the imperial government for its own lack of Christian zeal. For secular authorities, religious unity and Christian orthodoxy were values that had to be weighed against considerations of expediency, political reality, and public order. But to extremists, who saw any compromise as betrayal, imperial forbearance only created an atmosphere of "repressive tolerance." It was intolerable, they felt, that truth should be forced to live on equal terms with falsehood.[160]

Reasons of state, no matter how compelling they might seem to those in power, were no excuse. When the barbarian warlord Gainas concluded a treaty with the emperor Arcadius, he asked that a single church be set aside for the use of his Arian followers—"in order to undermine the peace of the Catholic church," commented Sozomen acidly. John Chrysostom, speaking "boldly," told the emperor to keep his priorities straight: "It is better to be deprived of empire, than to become guilty of impiety, a traitor to the house of God."[161]

For Augustine, the duty of Christians to submit to the lawful authority of secular powers ended where the integrity of religious faith began.[162] He spoke not only of the pagan persecutions of the past but also of more sub-

---

159. I am indebted to Juergensmeyer 2000, esp. pp. 176–179, for this concept of a "secondary enemy" as perceived by extremists: "The secondary enemy is a less obvious threat: a moderate leader on one's own side, for example, or a governmental authority who is trying to be fair-minded" (p. 176).

160. Compare Marcuse 1969, p. 88: "Tolerance cannot be indiscriminate and equal with respect to the contents of expression, neither in word nor in deed; it cannot protect false words and wrong deeds which demonstrate that they contradict and counteract the possibilities of liberation."

161. Sozomen *HE* 8.4.

162. Thus *City of God* 19.17: "The Heavenly City . . . makes no scruple to obey the laws of the earthly city, whereby the things necessary for the maintenance of this mortal life are administered . . . [but] the Heavenly City has been compelled in this matter [of religion] to dissent, and to become obnoxious to those who think differently, and to stand the brunt of their anger and hatred and persecutions." (trans. NPNF)

tle but equally sinister "persecutions" in his own time: "Let none of you say that the Church doesn't suffer persecution nowadays, because the emperors are Catholics."[163] The very existence of heretics, and the arguments and divisions they spawned, inflicted a new form of persecution upon the church:

> The heretics themselves also, since they are thought to have the Christian name and sacraments, Scriptures, and profession, cause great grief in the hearts of the pious, both because many who wish to be Christians are compelled by their dissensions to hesitate, and many evil-speakers also find in them matter for blaspheming the Christian name, because they too are at any rate called Christians. By these and similar depraved manners and errors of men, those who will live piously in Christ suffer persecution, even when no one molests or vexes their body; for they suffer this persecution, not in their bodies, but in their hearts.[164]

Tolerating such an evil, Augustine feared, was tantamount to endorsing it.[165]

Augustine, of course, could hardly be called an extremist. He regularly condemned violent militancy and warned against the dangers of unrestrained zeal. Coercive measures against heretics or pagans should only be undertaken by lawful authority—and compassion, not anger, should guide their execution.[166] Yet even such an establishment figure as he could invoke what we might call extremist discourses, totalizing claims to religion's priority over secular law. Statements and expressions of such attitudes could be found scattered throughout scripture and Christian literature, readily available for those who might weave them together into a militant ideology or a justification for violent action. Ideas could be dangerous things.

Christians had long concerned themselves to distinguish truth from falsehood through aggressive exposure and denunciation of heresy. Violent extremists, likewise, justified their actions with a rhetoric of exposure. Their deeds unmasked the hypocrisy, corruption, and pretense of authorities who claimed to be Christian but failed to govern according to Christian values. They sought, as Hannah Arendt might have put it, "[t]o tear the mask of hypocrisy from the face of the enemy, to unmask him and the devious machinations and manipulations that permit him to rule without using violent

163. *Sermon* 359B (Dolbeau 2, Mainz 5) (Hill trans., p. 345).

164. *City of God* 18.51 (trans. NPNF).

165. Compare *Sermon* 360A (Dolbeau 24, Mainz 60) (Hill trans., p. 361): "Let none of you spring to the defense of idols. Every defender of idols is next door to being a worshipper of idols."

166. See previous chapter.

means, that is, to provoke action even at the risk of annihilation so that the truth may come out."[167]

The violence of zealous holy men served to "heighten the contradictions" in imperial policy by challenging its claims to religious authority. They knew that the Christian empire's "tolerance" was really persecution in disguise, and by their actions they hoped to expose this truth to the world. Ideally, Christian rulers and magistrates might be shamed into a change of policy. Alternatively, provoking violent official reprisals would only demonstrate the truth of the zealots' claims, by forcing the state to expose its repressive and tyrannical nature.[168] Here, as elsewhere, holy men's willingness to martyrdom justified and sanctified their deeds.

In 388, zealous Christians set fire to a synagogue in Syrian Callinicum, apparently at the instigation of the local bishop. At about the same time, some monks burned a meeting place of the Valentinian Gnostic sect, after the Valentinians had blocked the road and interrupted their procession in honor of the Maccabees.[169] The initial response of the secular authorities showed little sympathy for whatever claims of holy zeal the Christians might have put forward. Although Roman imperial legislation at this time subjected the Jews to various forms of discrimination, it nevertheless guaranteed them the right to practice their religion peacefully, and explicitly prohibited Christian attacks against them.[170] The Christians had acted violently and without the sanction of state authority, destroying property belonging to law-abiding citizens.[171] The *comes orientis* ordered, and the emperor Theodosius

---

167. Arendt 1970, pp. 65–66. Judith Shklar, meanwhile, warns that those who consider hypocrisy the worst of the vices can easily convince themselves that ends justify means if one's cause is "sincere," and are capable of intense cruelty toward anyone who fails to live up to the demands of their ideology: Shklar 1984, esp. pp. 45–86.

168. Compare Juergensmeyer 2000, p. 23, e.g., on militants deliberately seeking to provoke state repression. Stephen Spender (quoted in Arendt 1970, p. 66) remarks that "This kind of violence leads to doubletalk in which the provocateur is playing at one and the same time the role of assailant and victim."

169. The source for what follows is Ambrose, *Epp.* 40 and 41. Although most commentators have taken the burning of the synagogue and the attack on the Valentinians as a single outbreak of violence, McLynn 1994, pp. 298–309, argues that they should be considered as separate incidents. The specific location of the latter incident is not given, but McLynn suggests that the reference to the feast of the Maccabees would place it somewhat nearer to Antioch.

170. See generally edicts in *C.Th.* Title 16.8, Avi-Yonah 1976, Cohen 1976, Linder 1987, Millar 1992.

171. The emperor Arcadius, asked to order the destruction of the pagan temples of Gaza, at first refused, because the pagans were peaceful subjects and taxpayers. Mark the Deacon, *Life of Porphyry of Gaza* 41.

confirmed, that the bishop of Callinicum be compelled to pay for the re-building of the synagogue, and that the monks involved in the Valentinian incident be punished likewise. This seems to have been the usual imperial response to such situations.[172] But at this point Ambrose intervened, appealing on behalf of the bishop and monks, rebuking the emperor for valuing mere *disciplina* above the sacred cause of religion.

Extremists can answer any questioning of their tactics with a simple retort: whose side are you on?[173] Ambrose upended the normal paradigm of law and order and redefined the situation in terms of a new emphasis on religious identity that transcended all other considerations. Just as he had done with the young emperor Valentinian II in the controversy over the Altar of Victory a few years previously, Ambrose forced Theodosius to take a position on an issue he would probably much rather have left alone.[174] The bishop and the monks were Christians, and the emperor claimed to be a Christian. If Theodosius forced the bishop to pay restitution, he would in effect be siding with Jews against Christians, an act of apostasy no matter what the circumstances. In Ambrose's apocalyptic presentation of the issue, the rebuilding of a synagogue would be a humiliation to the Christian religion on a par with Julian's planned restoration of the Jerusalem temple: the Jews would celebrate this "triumph" over Christ for centuries to come.[175] Ambrose acknowledged that the bishop was "too eager" but argued that the Christians' zeal for Christ merited clemency.

> Priests are calmers of disturbances, and anxious for peace, except when even they are moved by some offense against God, or insult to the church. Let us suppose that the bishop was too eager [*ferventior*] in the matter of burning the synagogue . . . are you not afraid, o emperor,

172. The western emperor Maximus, shortly before his defeat at the hands of Theodosius in 387, had similarly ordered that a synagogue destroyed in Rome be rebuilt at Christian expense: Ambrose *Ep.* 40, suggesting to Theodosius that divine displeasure with this "un-Christian" action was a major cause of his predecessor's downfall.

173. A point made by Ellis 1998, p. 170.

174. In 384, Ambrose had issued a stinging ultimatum to Valentinian II: "The Altar of Christ rejects your gifts, because you have made an altar for idols, for the voice is yours, the hand is yours, the subscription is yours, the deed is yours. The Lord Jesus refuses and rejects your service, because you have served idols, for He said to you, 'You cannot serve two masters.' [Matthew 6:4]" Ambrose, *Ep.* 17 (trans. NPNF).

175. Several decades later, Symeon the Stylite struck a similarly uncompromising tone when he used his spiritual authority to write to the emperor Theodosius II, "burning like a blazing fire with zeal for his Lord," and condemn an imperial edict that would have allowed Jews to reclaim synagogues seized by Christians: *Syriac Life of Symeon* 122. Cf. remarks by Nau 1927a and 1927b.

that he might comply with your sentence, and fail in his faith? Are you not also afraid, lest, which will happen, he oppose your count with a refusal? He [the count] will be obliged to make him either an apostate or a martyr, either of these alien to the times, either of them equivalent to persecution.[176]

Admitting that the bishop had acted rashly, Ambrose warned that forcing the bishop to make restitution would create an intolerable situation. Either he would refuse the order, thus defying the authority of the emperor and inevitably drawing more severe punishment upon himself—which would make him a "martyr"—or he would obey and, in assisting the Jews to rebuild their synagogue, he would make himself an apostate. The bishop's willingness to suffer martyrdom—whether real, or merely inferred by Ambrose—itself served to justify the deed. Ambrose's rhetoric stretched the language, giving new meaning to old words: not only could "martyrdom" now encompass aggressive and provocative violence against non-Christians, but any apology or restitution conceded to the victims would apparently constitute "apostasy," a denial of Christ.

COURTING PERSECUTION:
CHRISTIAN EXTREMISTS AND NON-CHRISTIAN REGIMES

Such arguments worked, at least some of the time, in a Christian empire. The emperor Theodosius backed down, and refrained from punishing the zealots of Callinicum. But Christian extremism could have dramatically different consequences when expressed in the far less indulgent context of a non-Christian regime. Our next example takes us outside the Roman Empire entirely, to Persia, where in 419 or 420 a series of Christian attacks on Magian fire-temples provoked the Sasanian government to a savage persecution of Christians, which in turn led to war between the two empires in 421–422.[177] The incidents that provoked the persecution are described in Persian Christian martyr acts preserved in Syriac, and in a corresponding account

---

176. Ambrose *Ep.* 40 (trans. NPNF).
177. The link between the war of 421–422 and the persecution of Christians, which began in the final months of the reign of Yazdgard I (399–420) and continued under his successor Vahram (420–438), is convincingly argued by Peeters 1909 and Holum 1977. The persecution offered the Theodosian court, in which Pulcheria's influence was particularly dominant at that point, an opportunity to show off its zeal on behalf of the faith. After a few inconclusive battles, both sides were able to claim a nominal victory and then make peace. Theodoret's statement (*HE* 5.38) that the persecution lasted for thirty years is (as Peeters shows) an exaggeration resulting

in Theodoret.[178] The initial response of the Persian king was surprisingly lenient. Hearing that bishop Abda of Hormizd-Ardashir, or one of his priests, had destroyed a temple, he sent for him, complained "in moderate language," and ordered him to rebuild the temple—in short, exactly the way the Roman authorities had initially handled the Callinicum incident. When the ascetic Narsai was arrested for destroying a temple, the king even offered to drop the matter if Narsai would simply deny that he had done the deed.[179] Abda refused to rebuild the temple, and Narsai refused to renounce his action. For their stubbornness, both were executed. At this point the king exhausted his patience and launched a general persecution against the church. The cases illustrate the dramatically different consequences of violent Christian zeal under a non-Christian government: if these zealots had indeed been seeking martyrdom, they were so successful in their quest that they attained the martyr's crown not only for themselves but for hundreds of other Persian Christians as well.

Theodoret's judgment on Abda is well worth our attention, particularly when taken in the context of the ongoing debates about martyrdom and temple destruction then current in the Christian Roman Empire.[180] The fol-

---

from his confusing the events of 419–420 with a separate outbreak of persecution that took place under Yazdgard II in the 440s. On Persian persecutions, and generally on the status of Christians under Sasanian rule, see Labourt 1904; Christensen 1944; Asmussen 1983; Brock 1982; Brock and Harvey 1998, translating several acts of Persian female martyrs; Walker 1998.

178. Syriac *Martyrdom of Abda* in Bedjan IV, pp. 250–253, German trans. in Hoffman 1880, pp. 34–35; and Braun 1915, pp. 142–149. *Martyrdom of Narsai the Ascetic* in Bedjan IV, pp. 170–180, trans. in Hoffman 1880, pp. 36–38; and Braun 1915, pp. 142–149. Theodoret *HE* 5.38 reports the story of bishop Abdas (Abda) with some differences: where the Syriac text attributes the destruction of the fire-temple to the priest Hassu, and has Abda assume responsibility for it only afterwards, Theodoret mentions only bishop Abdas. On these incidents see Van Rompay 1995. Van Rompay, emphasizing the role of other long-term factors in bringing about the persecution (particularly Christian conversions among the Iranian Zoroastrian nobility), is unduly skeptical about the significance of these incidents. While I certainly would not deny the importance of other factors, Christian destructions of fire-temples would have offered exactly the sort of dramatic provocation necessary to galvanize elements in Persian society already hostile to Christianity, and to force a change in policy on the part of a king who had previously shown great tolerance to the church.

179. Compare Mark of Arethusa, threatened by pagans under Julian, who refused to pay even a trivial, symbolic penalty of a single coin for his previous demolition of a temple. (Gregory of Nazianzus, *Oration* 4.90, discussed in chapter 2, p. 94.)

180. Although scholars of Persian Christianity (cited above) have devoted considerable attention to the stories of Abda, Narsai, and the other martyrs, none has yet considered these incidents in a comparative context alongside the many similar

lowing should be read in juxtaposition with Ambrose's remarks on Callinicum, above:

> Now I am of the opinion that to destroy the fire-temple was wrong
> and inexpedient, for not even the divine Apostle [Paul], when he came
> to Athens and saw the city wholly given to idolatry, destroyed any one
> of the altars which the Athenians honored, but convicted them of their
> ignorance through his arguments, and made manifest the truth.[181] But
> the refusal to rebuild the fallen temple, and the determination to choose
> death rather than do so, I greatly praise and honor, and count to be a
> deed worthy of a martyr's crown; for building a shrine in honor of the
> fire seems to me to be equivalent to worshipping it.[182]

While Ambrose and Theodoret expressed their disapproval of the bishop's
recklessness in each case, they both believed it would be a far greater evil
to attempt to reverse the deed and rebuild the temple or synagogue—such
a great evil, in fact, that it would be better if the bishop chose to die. That
death, they argued, would count as a martyrdom—even though there was no
persecution. In the Persian case, persecution was the result of Abda's death,
not the cause of it. In the Roman case, the emperor Theodosius was sufficiently convinced, or intimidated, by Ambrose's intervention that he refrained from imposing any penalty on the Christians of Callinicum.[183] Martyrdom, as understood by these authors, would seem to describe and validate
a Christian's refusal to obey the orders of secular authorities when those

---

episodes of violent Christian zeal in the Roman Empire during the late fourth and
early fifth centuries; nor have studies of the latter taken the Persian evidence into
account. But the imperial frontiers of late antiquity were considerably more per-
meable than the disciplinary boundaries of modern scholarship. The story's presence in Theodoret, not to mention the war of 421–422, are ample evidence that Christians in the eastern Roman Empire (particularly in Syriac-speaking circles) were well
aware of events concerning the church in Persia, and vice versa. Indeed, it seems clear
that zealots such as Abda and Narsai, as well as the Persian Christians who honored
their memory, were drawing upon concepts of martyrdom, patterns of behavior, and
models of zealous action current in contemporary Roman Christianity. Since they
could hardly have failed to realize that a non-Christian government would treat them
far less leniently, we must assume that martyrdom was their explicit goal. They may
have looked in particular to stories of Christians who provoked martyrdom under
Julian.

181. The Council of Elvira, *Canon* 60, had used the same argument in its prohibition of idol smashing, namely, "none of the Apostles ever did it."

182. Theodoret *HE* 5.38.

183. Even as he backed down, Theodosius protested weakly that "the monks do
commit many crimes" [*monachi multa scelera faciunt*]: Ambrose, *Ep.* 41. See discussion in the next chapter, pp. 208–210.

orders were perceived as conflicting with higher religious law.[184] But what religious imperative was at stake here? In neither case was it demanded of the bishop that he sacrifice to idols or renounce the Christian religion, and yet both Ambrose and Theodoret warned against the risk of apostasy. They argued that the very act of rebuilding, or paying for the rebuilding of, a destroyed temple or synagogue would in itself constitute apostasy, a participation in Jewish or pagan worship and therefore a rejection of Christ.[185] Rebuilding a temple or synagogue would undo the progress of Christianization, which in the minds of fourth- and fifth-century Christians was so intimately connected with the destruction of such buildings. Where Rabbula had seen idol smashing primarily as a means to martyrdom, the destruction of temples and idols was also an end in itself, or rather a means to spread the faith, an integral part of Christian missionization.

The close relation between temple destruction and missionization is illustrated in the Persian case by Theodoret's juxtaposing another martyrdom story next to that of Abda. Benjamin, a deacon, was imprisoned for preaching to the Magians. The Persian authorities offered to release him in return for a promise not to preach, which he refused to give. Released anyway, possibly at the request of Roman envoys present for peace negotiations in 422,[186] he resumed his missionary efforts. When he was accused of treason, he replied that treason against a king was preferable to treason against God.[187] As presented by Theodoret, the stories of Abda and Benjamin parallel each other precisely. Both committed provocative acts in violation of Sasanian law, both with the intention of winning converts to the faith. In both cases, the Persian king offered them a chance to escape punishment if they would only cease and make amends for their offending behavior. Both refused and suffered martyrdom, feeling that failure to spread the faith—

184. In chapter 2, I discuss at greater length how in the context of fourth-century religious conflicts, Christians used martyrdom as an ideology of principled resistance to worldly power—the "sanctification of resistance."

185. Here it may be worth mentioning the similar concern of late antique Judaism to avoid any economic entanglement with pagan worship. Lest any zealous Jews be tempted to a literal application of the many scriptural commandments for the destruction of idols, rabbinic authorities warned: if anyone destroys an idol, the pagans might force him to replace it with an even more expensive one! See Lieberman 1946–47, pp. 365–366. During the Diaspora revolts of 115–117, Jewish militants in Egypt and Cyrene had made a particular point of desecrating or destroying the temples and statues of their pagan neighbors: cf. Haas 1997, p. 101.

186. As Peeters 1909 suggests.

187. Theodoret *HE* 5.38.

whether by destroying temples, or simply by preaching—would in itself constitute apostasy. Although the Persian martyrs, suffering under a non-Christian regime, are usually seen as representing the traditional model of martyrdom that had largely ceased in the Roman Empire after Constantine, these particular cases should be understood more plausibly according to the paradigm of "missionary" martyrdom outlined by Maximus of Turin. The Persian kings, unlike Diocletian, never forced Christians to sacrifice or to deny Christ. The martyrs' defiance, accordingly, reflected their determination not merely to maintain the faith but to spread it.

Although somewhat beyond the chronological focus of this study, a highly illustrative parallel can be found in ninth-century Muslim Spain. A group of Christians in Cordoba publicly and repeatedly insulted the Prophet Muhammad, knowing full well that the Muslims would treat this as a capital offense. After the Christians had turned down numerous chances to recant or apologize, the Islamic authorities reluctantly granted them the martyrdom they had so zealously sought. In scenes deliberately reminiscent of classical martyrology, Muslim jurists are shown to be every bit as befuddled by the martyrs' apparent death wish as had been the Roman magistrates of earlier centuries.[188]

As little as Christian extremists could tolerate the compromises of an insufficiently zealous Christian state, still less could they stand for the grudging and discriminatory "tolerance" conceded to Christians by a non-Christian regime such as Sasanian Iran or its Islamic successors. After the fourth century, the Sasanian state rarely persecuted Christians without significant provocation, while Islamic regimes of later centuries institutionalized both tolerance and subordination by classifying Christians and Jews alike as "Peoples of the Book." Most ordinary Christians could live and worship fairly freely under these governments, as long as they accepted a distinctly inferior status as second-class citizens. In both cases, the ruling religion took firm measures to shield itself from competition. Sasanians forbade Chris-

188. On the martyrs of Cordoba, see Wolf 1988, Coope 1995, and now Christys 2002. Christys, taking a very skeptical approach to the sources, argues that the "martyrdoms" were isolated incidents whose significance for Andalusian Christian-Muslim relations has been greatly overrated in modern historiography. It should be emphasized that some—though not all—of the Cordoba martyrs had been placed in an impossible position, as children of mixed marriages between Christians and Muslims. Islamic law demanded that such children be raised as Muslims, and so their decision to live as Christians automatically branded them as "apostates" subject to the death penalty. But even in these cases, the martyrs chose to come forward and announce themselves, instead of continuing to practice their religion in secret. A martyr's death, apparently, was preferable to a life of pretense and concealment.

tians to seek converts among the Zoroastrian aristocracy. Muslims considered both Christian proselytism and apostasy from Islam offenses punishable by death. Under the Caliphate the Christians, as *dhimmi,* were assessed special taxes, barred from riding horses or bearing arms, and forbidden to display crosses or otherwise decorate the exterior of their churches.[189] While the vast majority of Christians resigned themselves to their condition and went on with their lives, some zealots experienced the situation as both an intolerable humiliation and also an unacceptable barrier to what they understood as their missionary duty to proselytize and spread the faith. The absence of formal persecution, in their eyes, simply added insult to injury by obscuring the truth of the situation and by denying Christians the opportunity to restore their honor and prove their faith through martyrdom.[190]

These stories, from as far apart as fifth-century Persia and ninth-century Spain, show considerable similarity. Both Persian kings and Muslim *qadis* appear surprisingly lenient in their initial encounter with the martyrs, offering them multiple chances to apologize or recant—and all the more opportunity for the Christians to show their defiance. The sources do not feel any need to exaggerate the initial conditions against which the "martyrs" reacted: Christians were not forced to sacrifice or deny Christ, nor do the texts attempt to claim that they were. What was intolerable to the zealots was precisely the repressive and humiliating regime of "tolerance" under which they were forced to exist, and the limits that regime imposed on their ability to spread the faith.

Persian Christians who attacked fire temples, or the Cordoban zealots who lined up to insult the Prophet and face the executioner's sword, could not have failed to understand the swift and brutal response their actions would provoke under a non-Christian government, and we may only conclude that such provocation was exactly what they had in mind: to force the regime to abandon its "pretense" of tolerance, to expose its "true" nature as a brutal persecutor—and to compel their coreligionists, most of whom had reconciled themselves to the status quo, to make a choice. In this sense the zealots' provocations were directed as much against moderates and compromisers among their fellow Christians as against the non-Christian rulers.[191] As Ter-

---

189. On the institution of "Dhimmitude" and the fate of religious minorities under Muslim rule, see Ye'or 1996 and 2002.

190. Compare Gregory of Nazianzus, who actually resented the fact that Julian did not "persecute" more openly: chapter 2, pp. 91–92.

191. Compare Juergensmeyer 2000, p. 176, on targeting the moderates and "compromisers" on one's own side. In Cordoba, the "martyrs" may have been provoked in part by the spectacle of many of their Christian brethren converting to Islam.

tullian had said during a much earlier time of persecution, "To be unwilling to confess Christ is to deny Christ."[192]

The moderates, for their part, wanted nothing to do with such extremism. They were well aware of the precarious quality of the tolerance under which they lived and worshipped, and feared the consequences of needlessly angering their non-Christian rulers or neighbors. Five centuries after the bishops at Elvira had decreed that those who were killed smashing idols were not to be honored as martyrs, Christians in Muslim Spain showed a similar care to distance themselves from the actions of extremists. Prominent clergy and laity of Cordoba, several of whom held prestigious positions at the Caliph's court, did everything in their power to persuade the would-be martyrs—many of whom came, interestingly enough, from the more isolated and uncompromising environment of the extra-urban monasteries—to see reason. Afterwards, local church authorities discouraged any commemoration of the "martyrs" or veneration of their relics. The lack of any miracle stories associated with these martyrs, finally, constituted a telling vote of no confidence on the part of Cordoban Christians.[193]

NO JUSTICE WITHOUT TRUE RELIGION

In the eyes of true believers, a non-Christian—or insufficiently Christian—government could claim no authority in matters of religion.[194] Without the justice that could only come from religion, Augustine argued, earthly government was nothing more than *latrocinium*, organized crime on a larger scale.[195] The late Roman Empire, unlike its non-Christian neighbors or successors, was acutely sensitive to such criticism. Its rulers liked to think of themselves as good Christians, and bent over backwards to avoid situations that might force them to make martyrs out of holy men and thus earn them the unwelcome title of "persecutors." But political reality, and the need to maintain concord in a vast and diverse empire, demanded forbearance and

192. Tertullian, *On Flight from Persecution* 5. See discussion in chapter 1, pp. 37–38.

193. As soon as the relics were brought to Christian Francia and a more receptive audience, however, miracles began to be recorded immediately! See Coope 1995, p. 54.

194. A significant subset of Christian opinion, therefore, could never have accepted the political philosophy that, according to Harold Drake, underlay Constantine's policies—the creation of a "religiously neutral public space." (Drake 2000, p. xv)

195. *City of God* 4.4.

at least limited tolerance of non-Christians. To the zealots, such compromises called into question the sincerity of the regime's devotion to the faith. They deliberately sought out opportunities to expose these contradictions through violent provocation, hoping either to shame the government into more pious policies, or to earn themselves the crown of martyrdom.

In 434 or 435, Hypatius, leader of a monastery at Rufinianae, across the straits from Constantinople, got word that the urban prefect Leontius planned to reestablish the Olympic games in the theater of the nearby city of Chalcedon.[196] Although Leontius, himself almost certainly a Christian, saw nothing objectionable or explicitly "pagan" in the ancient festival, to Hypatius the Olympics were "a festival of Satan" that would encourage pagans in their idolatry and lead Christians into sin.[197]

> Hypatius became very angry, rose with groans and lamentations, and cried, "O God, will you allow idolatry to return?" He then said to the brothers, "Anyone who is not prepared to die for Christ should not come with me." About twenty brothers followed him as he went to bishop Eulalios [of Chalcedon]. When the bishop asked, "What is this madness?" Hypatius answered, "Idolatry will take place at the Olympics, and I have decided to go to the theater and die, rather than allow this to happen." The bishop said, "Why die, when no one is forcing us to sacrifice? You are a monk; go back to your monastery and keep quiet and let me deal with this." Hypatius said, "I do not want the people to be dragged back into idolatry. Therefore I am telling you now that tomorrow, I will go into the games with my monks, and I will strike the prefect and knock him down from his presiding seat, and I will die, rather than let these games take place." Hypatius appealed to the other

196. The source for what follows is the *Life of Hypatius* (paragraph 33) written by his disciple Callinicus shortly after the saint's death in 466. See edition by Bartelink; Wölfle 1986, Dagron 1970. The incident can be dated by Leontius' tenure as urban prefect: see *PLRE*, s.v. Leontius 9. *PLRE* suggests he may be identical with Leontius 10, praetorian prefect of Illyricum in the 440s, who sponsored a shrine to St. Demetrius in Thessalonica and was therefore certainly a Christian.

197. On the Olympic games, and their cessation in late antiquity, see Bengtson 1972, Finley and Pleket 1976. Although most cities' Olympic celebrations died out over the course of the third century, those of Antioch continued into the early sixth century: Liebeschuetz 1972, pp. 136ff. We may assume that Leontius merely wished to provide the imperial capital with a civic entertainment already enjoyed by another of the empire's chief cities. By that time, of course, the festivals would long since have given up sacrifices or any other explicitly pagan trappings, and most Christians would have found them unobjectionable. Still, the more extremist monks and clergy considered such games to be irredeemably tainted by paganism. Callinicus tells us that Hypatius knew very little about the Olympics, until he met a man named Eusebius who was circulating some sort of written tract denouncing the games on religious grounds (*Life of Hypatius* 33).

archimandrites: "Come, do battle along with me against the devil; let us die for God." They all rejoiced and obeyed him like a father. When the prefect Leontius heard of their plan, he feigned illness and stayed in Constantinople, and thus the games did not take place.

Hypatius had declared his intention to assault a high-ranking imperial official, to throw him down from his chair of office, in a public place, before thousands of witnesses—an act that would not normally be received as anything less than high treason, to which the imperial government would not normally respond with anything less than an immediate and gruesome public execution.[198] And yet Hypatius was a holy man, a religious leader of considerable stature, respected and venerated by the emperor himself.[199] The execution of such a man would certainly have provoked considerable outrage. Rather than face such an impossible dilemma, Leontius wisely called in sick.[200]

Had Hypatius gone ahead with his plan, and died in the cause of suppressing "pagan" games, he might have hoped to be venerated as a martyr in the same manner as a Syrian monk named Telemachus, who journeyed to Rome early in the reign of the emperor Honorius with the intention of putting a stop to the bloody spectacle of gladiatorial combat.[201] He stepped into the arena and interposed his own body between the dueling combatants. He was immediately killed—not by the heavily armed gladiators, but by the enraged

198. Such was the fate of Ammonius, an Egyptian monk and over-zealous follower of the Alexandrian patriarch Cyril, who threw a stone at the prefect Orestes, hit him in the head, and drew blood. Orestes had him seized and publicly flogged to death. Cyril's attempt to declare Ammonius a martyr "as one who had fallen in defense of piety" and venerate him under the name "Thaumasios" ("Miraculous") was not well received: "But more sober-minded Christians did not accept this, knowing that he had suffered his fate due to rashness, and had not perished for refusing to deny Christ" (Socrates *HE* 7.14). Eventually Cyril dropped the issue. In this case, a claim to justify violence through religious zeal failed to override respect for secular law and order. See discussion in the next chapter, pp. 220–222.

199. See, e.g., *Life of Hypatius* 37, 40, on Hypatius' contacts with Theodosius II and his sisters, and especially with Pulcheria; cf. Holum 1982, pp. 134–138.

200. We may presume that Hypatius warned the bishop of his plans with the full knowledge that word would get to Leontius, thus offering the prefect a chance to back down and avoid the confrontation.

201. The source is Theodoret *HE* 5.26, who gives the story in his narrative immediately after the death of Theodosius I and accession of Honorius (395) and before the ordination of John Chrysostom in Constantinople (398). In 398, incidentally, the emperor Honorius would have been only fourteen years old, and still under the tutelage of the *magister militum*, Stilicho. It should be noted that the *Martyrologium Hieronymianum* (in *Acta Sanctorum*, November, v.ii.2, p. 19), preserves a slightly different account: the monk is here called Almachius, not Telemachus; he was killed at the orders of the prefect, not stoned by the spectators; it happened under Theodosius I, not Honorius: see Delehaye 1914, Kirsch 1912. These differences

spectators, who, "inspired by the mad fury of the demon which delights in those bloody deeds," stoned him to death. When the emperor heard the news, he "numbered Telemachus in the army of victorious martyrs" and outlawed the games. So, at least, ran the legend—contradicted, however, by ample evidence that gladiatorial games continued well into the fifth century.[202] If the incident did in fact happen as described, we may suspect that whatever ban Honorius decreed was probably temporary and limited to the city of Rome, intended to rebuke the people for their disorderly conduct. Still, the story offered a warning for Christians everywhere against the "demonic" nature of the games. Opposition to gladiatorial combat in late antiquity, in both pagan philosophical and Christian circles, did not concern itself so much for those killed or maimed in the games as it did with the degrading and dehumanizing effect that witnessing such gratuitous bloodshed was thought to have on spectators.[203] It is in the context of such concerns—strikingly similar to modern debates about television violence—that Theodoret's description of the "demonic fury" driving the crowd should be understood. Gladiatorial combats, even more so than Olympic games, were festivals of demons, who possessed spectators by playing upon their basest instincts. In this case, the fury of the demons drove the crowd to cross the line from merely observing violence to actually committing it.

---

of detail do not affect the interpretations presented here. On gladiatorial games generally, and their disappearance in late antiquity, see Ville 1960 and 1979; Wiedemann 1992, esp. pp. 128–164.

202. See Wiedemann 1992, pp. 128–164. The idea that martyrial status could be bestowed by imperial decree can also be found in Theodosius' response to the Alexandrian riots of 391, described above, p. 179. The assertion that Telemachus' death prompted a ban on gladiatorial combat is not directly supported by any extant piece of imperial legislation, although there is some evidence (see *Reallexikon für Antike und Christentum* 11.27–28 and 40–44) for a closure of gladiatorial schools by Honorius in 399. Constantine had already outlawed the games in 325 (*C.Th.* 15.12.1), but with little effect, as demonstrated by several later edicts in *C.Th.*, Title 15.12, regulating various aspects of the games and issued over the course of the fourth century.

203. Wiedemann 1992, pp. 128–164. The most famous statement of this fear was Augustine's description of his friend Alypius, dragged to see the games against his better judgment: "For, directly he saw that blood, he therewith imbibed a sort of savageness; nor did he turn away, but fixed his eye, drinking in madness unconsciously, and was delighted with the guilty contest, and drunken with the bloody pastime. Nor was he now the same he came in, but was one of the throng he came unto, and a true companion of those who had brought him thither . . . " Augustine, *Confessions* 6.8.13 (trans. NPNF). For the violence of the arena see Barton 1993, esp. chap. 1. Ironically, there is no indication that the increasingly gruesome and sometimes near-pornographic depictions of the sufferings of the martyrs in texts of the late fourth century and later were thought to be anything other than edifying to the listener.

From the point of view of the monk who offered up his own life in order to defeat the demons in this place of their greatest power, the games—both gladiatorial and Olympic—had an additional significance. By stepping into an actual arena, Telemachus (and Hypatius, at least in intention) relived the triumphs of the classical martyrs and affirmed the often-stated symbolic link between monk and martyr in an unusually literal way. Both Olympic and gladiatorial events, as worldly "games," here stood in opposition to the martyrs' status as "athletes" of Christ and to their victories over demons in the arena of the spirit. The single significant difference between the act of Telemachus and the plan of Hypatius was the latter's use of aggressive violence, a physical attack on the person of the prefect, which would have served both as a means to martyrdom and as a provocative revelation of Christian truth that would put an end to "pagan" games.

Augustine and Chrysostom were only the most famous among many Christian preachers who tried to steer their congregants away from games, theater, races, gambling, and other immoral pursuits by stigmatizing these common leisure activities as "pagan" customs.[204] Holy men like Hypatius and Telemachus said with their actions what the preachers said in words. Augustine and his colleagues could only lament the inability of most Christians to recognize the "true" nature of practices regarded by the majority as harmless and religiously neutral. Violent provocation, its proponents hoped, would tear away such pretense and reveal the truth for all to see. It would force the government to choose sides, either playing the persecutor by making a martyr of a Christian holy man, or proving the sincerity of its Christian faith by withdrawing support for such manifestations of "cultural paganism."

TRUTH AND FALSEHOOD

Extremist violence targeted what it regarded as the hypocrisy of tolerance and compromise. It sought to expose and condemn pretense, the sin of not being what one seems, of not matching actions to intentions and values. The extremist's obsession with sincerity was itself a reflection of a broader ascetic imperative to perfect the self, a "totalizing" program aimed at transformation of human nature.[205] The language of truth and falsehood defined the

---

204. See, e.g., Augustine *Ep.* 22, along with *Sermon* 198 (Mainz 62); Chrysostom's *Address on Vainglory.*

205. For the implications of asceticism as "totalizing discourse" and the influence of ascetic values and discourses upon late antique politics and society, see Cameron 1995.

Christian holy man. Hagiographers praised their subjects because they matched words to deeds and appearances to realities. When Pachomius spoke, "His mouth matched his mind."[206] Gregory of Nazianzus said of Basil, "His aim was ever to be, not to seem, most excellent."[207] Alexander the Akoimete, upon setting fire to a temple, announced, "We demonstrate the truth of our speech through our actions."[208] Syrian ascetics such as Symeon the Stylite understood every wound and mortification that they endured in their bodies as a true and visible representation of their inner spiritual triumphs, outward appearance faithfully reflecting higher reality.[209] Monastic leaders were known in particular for their powers of discernment, their ability to see into the hearts of others and reveal their hidden sins.[210] The violent acts of extremists, in their own eyes, similarly served to reveal truth—exposing hypocrisy, heightening contradictions, and challenging "tolerance."

But hatred of hypocrisy is a dangerous ideology, a weapon that can easily rebound against its users.[211] The higher a standard of purity or authenticity extremists demand of others, the more vulnerable they themselves become to accusations by their enemies of betraying their own values—a trap into which Donatists, and other perfectionist ideologues, often fell. We shall see next how the same discourses of authenticity against hypocrisy, and truth against falsehood, could be turned back against the zealots themselves. Their claim to act as agents of God's will came under withering attack, with critics arguing that their raging fury was merely a pretense of godly zeal, a mask for selfish impulses and criminal behavior.

206. *Primary Greek Life* 29, with comments by Brown 1983, p. 8 (trans. Veilleux).

207. Gregory of Nazianzus, *Or.* 43.60 (trans. NPNF). See discussion in Vaggione 1993, p. 186.

208. *Life of Alexander the Akoimete* 11.

209. This idea of body as visible display of spirit, rather than the more Hellenistic opposition between body and soul emphasized by Greek sources such as Theodoret's *Historia Religiosa*, is the proper paradigm for understanding Syrian asceticism: see, e.g., Harvey 1988b.

210. Miracles of discernment, e.g., in Besa's *Life of Shenoute* at 13, 34, 36, 42–52, 154–159.

211. A point emphasized by Shklar 1984, esp. pp. 48–49.

6. "The Monks
   Commit Many Crimes"
Holy Violence Contested

"The monks commit many crimes." This remark, by that most Christian emperor Theodosius I, testifies to the difficulties faced by the practitioners of holy violence when they sought to convince the world of the legitimacy of their actions.[1] Central to their justification was the belief that godly zeal overrode secular law, that they themselves possessed this zeal, and that God would lend sanction to their deeds by miraculous demonstrations. Holy men, as presented by hagiography, embodied the values and fulfilled the expectations of the idealized Christian community. Their acts of righteous violence helped to define that community by marking its boundaries, separating the true Christians within from the heretics, hypocrites, pagans, and Jews beyond. The problem, however, lay in the proper definition of "community," and in determining who had the right to define it. While holy zealots and their hagiographers could afford to map their world entirely in terms of religious identity, the imperial administration—as piously Christian as much of its leadership was by this time—had to take other factors into consideration. Much as Theodosius would have liked "that all the peoples who are ruled by the administration of Our Clemency shall practice that religion which the divine Peter the Apostle transmitted to the Romans,"[2] the emperor was also responsible for upholding law and order and regulating rela-

---

1. *Monachi multa scelera faciunt:* quoted in Ambrose *Ep.* 41. "Legitimacy" here means the acceptance of one's claims to authority and one's actions by others, and specifically by others in positions of power and authority—in this case, the imperial government, the church establishment, local secular elites, etc. This concept of legitimacy draws on that defined by Stinchcombe 1968, pp. 149–162, and elaborated on by Tilly 1985, p. 171: "Legitimacy is the probability that other authorities will act to confirm the decisions of a given authority."

2. *C.Th.* 16.1.2 (Pharr trans.).

tions among the countless local interest groups and religious communities that made up the Roman Empire. The theme of this chapter, then, is restraints on extremism: the limits imposed by practical reality on the idealistic vision of the pure; the strategies of criticism and discipline used by opponents and authorities to denounce and delegitimize violent zealotry and uphold law, order, hierarchy, and stability. Where the previous chapter took the point of view of the zealots and their sympathizers, this chapter takes the perspective of their antagonists, and explores the ways in which arguments for violence could be contested and rejected.

The Callinicum incident, as we saw in the last chapter, dramatized the confrontation between pious zeal and public order. At least in the immediate case, Ambrose had gotten his way. When the bishop raised the issue again in church, the emperor admitted that he had "decided too harshly" and promised to forgo the punishment and end the investigation. At the same time, Theodosius made it clear that his forgiveness of the bishop of Callinicum was a one-time display of imperial *clementia*, and was not intended to legitimize the attack on the synagogue or to encourage similar behavior in the future.[3] Ambrose's initiative brought no permanent change in imperial policy, and edicts prohibiting attacks on synagogues continued to appear over the following decades.[4] Although the repetition of these edicts probably testifies to the frequency with which they were being disobeyed, their language does show us some of the outlines of a rhetoric of law and order that might be deployed in opposition to religious violence: "You will restrain the excesses of those who in the name of the Christian religion presume to commit unlawful acts and attempt to destroy and to despoil the synagogues."[5] Religious fanaticism should not take precedence over property rights: "No one shall dare to violate, or occupy and retain [synagogues], since all persons must retain their own property in undisturbed right, notwithstanding arguments of religion or worship."[6]

Even as he granted Ambrose's request for clemency, Theodosius remarked,

---

3. As McLynn 1994, p. 308, emphasizes, though he probably goes too far in calling Ambrose "the loser in this unhappy affair."

4. *C.Th.* 16.8.9 (393), 16.8.12 (397), 16.8.20 (412). That of 393 is addressed to the *magister militum per orientem*, suggesting that similar disturbances continued in the same region.

5. *C.Th.* 16.8.9 (Pharr trans.).

6. *C.Th.* 16.8.20 (Pharr trans.). Religious considerations gained somewhat greater influence in later decades, when it was stated that synagogues that had been seized by Christians would be returned to the Jews only if they had not yet been consecrated as churches, but if they had, then the Jews were to be financially compensated and allowed to rebuild somewhere else: *C.Th.* 16.8.25 (423).

"The monks commit many crimes."[7] The emperor's words invoke what seems to have been a common prejudice, current among many Christians as well as pagans. Probably the most famous statement of this view was made by Libanius in 386, complaining about gangs of monks who wandered the Syrian countryside demolishing pagan shrines and terrorizing peasants.[8]

> This black-robed tribe, who eat more than elephants and, by the quantities of drink they consume, weary those that accompany their drinking with the singing of hymns, who hide these excesses under an artificially contrived pallor—these people, sire, while the law yet remains in force, hasten to attack the temples with sticks and stones and bars of iron, and in some cases, disdaining these, with hands and feet. Then utter desolation follows, with the stripping of roofs, demolition of walls, the tearing down of statues and the overthrow of altars, and the priests must either keep quiet or die. After demolishing one, they scurry to another, and to a third, and trophy is piled on trophy, in contravention of the law. Such outrages occur even in the cities, but they are most common in the countryside. Many are the foes who perpetrate the separate attacks, but after their countless crimes this scattered rabble congregates and they are in disgrace unless they have committed the foulest outrage.[9]

Libanius, a pagan orator, addressed a Christian emperor to complain about the activities of Christian militants and to demand action against them—potentially a very delicate and difficult request. But as we shall see, Libanius was able to make reference to negative stereotypes of monks common to both pagans and Christians, and draw upon elements of several different polemical strategies that opponents of the monks could deploy against them in order to delegitimize their actions.

First of these strategies is what can be called the "discourse of *latrocinium*," the characterization of the monks as mere "bandits" or criminals.[10] Libanius suggested that the monks were using the suppression of paganism merely as an excuse for plunder and pillage. They seized goods and even land from the peasants, on the pretext that it had belonged to a pagan tem-

---

7. Ambrose *Ep.* 41. The general Timasius, also present, was considerably more abusive in his remarks about the monks, but Ambrose did not repeat his words.

8. Libanius, *Oration* 30, "For the Temples." Since these events presumably took place in the countryside around Antioch, we may surmise that the monks who destroyed the Valentinians' chapel (Ambrose *Ep.* 40, above) derived from the same groups of Christian zealots condemned by Libanius. On the date: Petit 1951.

9. Libanius *Or.* 30.8–9 (trans. Norman).

10. *Latrocinium* is the Latin word usually translated as "banditry"; Libanius uses its Greek equivalent, *lesteia*. The latter term passes into Syriac and Coptic as *lestaya* and *mnt-lestes*, respectively. See introduction, pp. 20–21.

ple or had been used in illegal sacrifices: "And if they hear that an estate has something worth looting, it is straightaway [alleged to be] involved in sacrifices and is committing all manner of crimes: an armed visitation is called for. . . ."[11] *Latrocinium/lesteia* did not restrict its meaning to "robbery," but also conveyed general lawlessness, and particularly illegal violence. In late Roman political discourse, *latrocinium* served as a code word for "private violence" not sanctioned by the state and therefore illegitimate.[12] When Shenoute and his monks ransacked the house of a prominent pagan landlord in search of idols to smash, the pagan denounced him as a *lestes*. Shenoute's claim, "There is no crime *[mnt-lestes]* for those who have Christ," did not go uncontested.[13]

Since the monks' assaults and seizures could have destructive consequences —economic losses, for small farmers, might lead to poverty, serfdom, or even starvation—the victims could plausibly characterize the experience as "violent" even if their persons were spared.[14] Libanius went out of his way to emphasize for Theodosius (who could not, after all, be expected to have much regard for the sacrality of pagan shrines) the material and economic consequences of the monks' lawless zealotry against pagan peasants who were, after all, law-abiding citizens and taxpayers.[15] Roman society had always recognized, if not legally condoned, the fact that landowners might resort to violent force to defend or recover their property if official justice were unable or unwilling to help them. Libanius closed his oration with a thinly veiled threat that pagans might be forced to take the law into their own hands if Theodosius did not act to restrain the monks.[16]

For pagans, obviously, the destruction of temples was not just an issue of property damage. Attacks on religious places or objects were normally seen as far worse than simple theft or trespass, a uniquely violating assault

11. Libanius *Or.* 30.11
12. On *latrocinium* as a polemical concept, see B. Shaw 1984. Cf. p. 6: "Almost every kind of violent opposition to established authority short of war was subsumed under the catch-all rubric of *latrocinium*, with little or no conscious differentiation of the subcategories of violence beneath that umbrella term." On the concept of "private violence," see also Bagnall 1989.
13. Shenoute, *Letter to a Pagan Notable*. Shenoute, by way of response, pointed to the pagan's own misdeeds as justification: "If what I did was improper in making a public example of idolaters, then how much greater condemnation it is for you to trespass in the Forty Days and in the great holy Pascha!" (trans. Barns)
14. Compare Hannah Arendt's criticism of activists who destroy property while calling themselves "non-violent" (Arendt 1970, p. 71): "violence" need not necessarily entail bodily harm.
15. *Or.* 30.9–10, 20.
16. On "self-help": see Lintott 1968, esp. pp. 8–34. Libanius: *Or.* 30.55.

on the sacred. The crime of "sacrilege," in a legal sense, traditionally applied only to significant public temples, not private shrines—but the distinction would have been small comfort to those who owned or worshipped
at such shrines.[17] Christians and pagans alike were profoundly sensitive to
any perceived assault on the sanctity of their own places of worship, and
correspondingly insensitive to any such complaints on behalf of the other
side. Those who suffered such attacks tended to blur any distinction between
property damage and physical violence, seeking in their petitions and
protests to emphasize the wrongful and violating nature of the deed. The
temple was the dwelling place of the god, in the same way that the church
was understood to represent the body of Christ.

The attackers and their apologists, on the other hand, went out of their
way to stress that their targets were "only" buildings or statues, in order
both to minimize their own legal culpability and also to deny their victims'
claims to religious legitimacy. Thus Athanasius defended himself against
charges that his agent had overturned a Melitian altar by responding that
the schismatics did not possess a true church or altar, but merely a house
and a table.[18] The Christian government, while it normally opposed lawless and disorderly demolitions, likewise sought to de-sacralize pagan temples, stripping them of cult objects and closing them to worshippers, while
attempting where possible to preserve them as cultural monuments or as
valuable buildings that might be put to other uses.[19]

Downplaying the religious dimension in such incidents also served the
purposes of civil authorities whose main concern was to preserve public order and avoid exacerbating tension between different religious groups. In the
case of Callinicum, the government's initial response was to treat the burned
synagogue as a simple case of property damage that could be made good by
monetary compensation. But such a strategy did not necessarily preserve
peace: during the pagan backlash under Julian, property claims (for buildings or goods allegedly seized from pagan temples over the previous generation) often became occasions for extortion and violence against Christians.
Julian mocked Christians' complaints by sarcastically reminding them of their
religion's commandments not to value worldly possessions.[20]

Religion made persons, places, and objects holy. Religious conflict required

17. On attitudes toward sacralization and desecration of religious space in late
antiquity, see Caseau 1999.
18. Athanasius, *Apology Against the Arians* 14.
19. See generally Caseau 1999 and 2001; Lepelley 1994.
20. See, e.g., Julian, *Ep.* 40.

that each side claim such holiness for itself and deny the same status to the other. Along with physical violence, then, came a battle of definition: were temples and churches sacred space, or merely buildings? Were their destroyers holy zealots or sacrilegious criminals?

Pagans lamenting the fate of their temples were not the only ones who found cause to complain about the violence of Christian monks. John Chrysostom, en route to his exile at Cucusus in 404, stopped at Cappadocian Caesarea and quickly found an unpleasant welcome:

> Suddenly towards dawn a rabble of monks (for so I must call them, indicating their frenzy by the expression) rushed up to the house where we were, threatening to set fire to it, and to treat us with the utmost violence unless we turned out of it. And neither the fear of the Isaurians, nor my own infirmity which was grievously afflicting me, nor anything else made them more reasonable, but they pressed on, animated by such fierce rage that even the proconsular soldiers were terrified. For they kept threatening them with blows and boasted that they had shamefully beaten many of the proconsular soldiers. The soldiers having heard these things, sought refuge with me, and entreated and beseeched me, saying "Even if we are to fall into the hands of the Isaurians, deliver us from these wild beasts."[21]

Even the governor was unable to disperse the monks, and it soon became clear that they were acting on the instructions of Pharetrios, the local bishop. Seleucia, a wealthy lady of the local aristocracy, sheltered Chrysostom at her suburban estate, ordering her steward to assemble and arm her laborers in case the monks should attack. But she too was eventually intimidated by the threats of the bishop, and had to send Chrysostom on his way in a harrowing midnight escape.[22] All this happened against a background of continuous danger posed by the raids of the Isaurians, a more conventional sort of bandits, whose depredations were afflicting much of Cappadocia and northern Syria during these years.[23] John's frequent references to the Isaurians in this narrative serve to highlight the savagery of the monks, explicitly characterized as "worse than the Isaurians."[24] Both the governor and the local landed elites, two agencies normally responsible for maintaining law and

---

21. Chrysostom, *Letters to Olympias* 14.2 (NPNF trans.).
22. *Letters to Olympias* 14.3.
23. On the Isaurians generally, see B. Shaw 1990.
24. "Worse than the barbarians" was a common polemical characterization when complaining of an adversary's violence: see, e.g., Augustine's remark that "not even the barbarians" could have imagined the Circumcellion practice of blinding priests (Augustine *Ep.* 111.1 [409]).

order in the countryside, found themselves powerless against the unruly "private" violence of Pharetrios and his monks—a point deliberately emphasized by Chrysostom.

Greed, banditry and violence came together in the accusation that the charity solicited by these monks was actually a form of extortion. Opponents of the monks charged that they extracted "charitable" contributions through intimidation or threats of violence.[25] Zosimus complained that "under the pretext of giving everything to the poor, they have reduced almost everyone else to beggary."[26] This attitude probably reflects the resentment that older elites, both pagan and Christian, felt against the new patterns of charity and wealth distribution practiced by the church establishment as it gained in power and resources over the course of the fourth century.[27] Certain groups of monks who practiced a lifestyle of "apostolic" poverty, wandering from place to place, renouncing manual labor and living from charity, were accused of "aggressive" begging. Nilus of Ancyra brought this charge against a monk, "Alexander," who may plausibly be identified as Alexander the Akoimete.[28]

All these polemical strategies, which can be considered as part of the discourse of *latrocinium*, serve the key function of dismissing or downplaying any religious significance or pious purpose for the activities condemned, making religious zealots themselves vulnerable to the same charges of hypocrisy they routinely hurled at others. Once pious justifications disappeared, the targets of polemic could be painted as simple criminals. Itinerant, begging monks, in the eyes of critics, were not really driven by literal obedience to the commands of the gospel, but simply wanted a free meal. Libanius claimed that the monks used the laws against pagan sacrifice merely as an excuse to steal goods and seize property. Turning Christian martyrial discourse on its head, he even argued that the abuses suffered by pagan peas-

25. This fear of "coercive begging" can be seen, perhaps, as the counterpart to the "coercive almsgiving" that characterized Macarius' mission to the Donatists: see chapter 4, pp. 135–136.

26. Zosimus 5.23.

27. Compare Chrysostom, *Against the Opponents of the Monastic Life* 2.4, remarking that some (Christians as well as pagans) were offended by the sight of rich men spending money at the command of monks. Their complaints centered not on the fact that charity was being asked and given, but that it was taking place outside of the usual civic or episcopal channels. On the ideology and practice of charity, see now Brown 2002.

28. Nilus of Ancyra, *Ep.* 1.129 (PG 79.137C). The same Alexander is mentioned in Nilus' treatise *On Voluntary Poverty* (PG 79.997). Gribomont 1972 identifies him as Alexander the Akoimete. But see also Alan Cameron 1986. On Alexander the Akoimete and accusations of "aggressive begging," see Caner 2002, chap. 4.

ants would only strengthen their faith.[29] Chrysostom reduced the motives for Pharetrios' enmity to mere envy, asserting that the local bishop was simply made jealous by the attention the prominent citizens of Caesarea had lavished on John.[30] Pharetrios, if offered the chance to tell his side of the story, would undoubtedly have cited far more substantive reasons, such as the long and highly detailed list of misconduct charges brought against Chrysostom by the Synod of the Oak in 403, or the provocative and potentially "tyrannical" manner in which Chrysostom had seen fit to surround himself with armed soldiers.[31]

The discourse of *latrocinium*, when addressed to state authorities, could draw upon a rhetoric of law and order that emphasized the emperor's paramount duty to uphold the law and keep the peace. Such polemic took care to emphasize the uncontrolled and extralegal nature of the monks' violence. Libanius reminded the emperor at great length that the destruction of temples had not been ordered by any imperial edict, and therefore should be considered unlawful.[32] This representation of illegality was undercut somewhat by the fact that some high-ranking imperial officials—most notably Cynegius, praetorian prefect of the east in 384–388—were actively sponsoring and encouraging the monks, and had even destroyed a few temples themselves.[33] Libanius then asserted that these officials, because they went beyond the letter of the law, were "usurping" imperial authority—invoking a second polemical strategy, closely related to the discourse of *latrocinium*, which we may call the discourse of usurpation.

Eunapius, complaining of the *tyrannike exousia* (tyrannical power) of the monks, expressed the many ways in which their exercise of power stole authority away from those to whom it legitimately belonged, or undermined traditional forms and expressions of authority—in a word, usurpa-

29. *Or.* 30.26.

30. *Letter to Olympias* 14.3. For envy as a characteristic of the "tyrant-bishop," who pursues personal grudges under the pretext of fighting for orthodoxy, see chapter 7, pp. 279–281.

31. List of charges preserved in Photius, *Bibliotheca* 59. A translation is provided in Appendix C of Kelly 1995. Reliance on armed guards was characteristic of a "tyrant-bishop," in ecclesiastical polemic: see next chapter, pp. 275–276.

32. For the relevant laws in force by 386, see *Theodosian Code*, Title 16.10.

33. On the activities of Cynegius and other zealous Christians in the Theodosian administration, see Fowden 1978; Matthews 1967 and 1975, pp. 100–145; *PLRE*, vol. 1, s.v. Cynegius 3. Another Cynegius, possibly a younger relative, led the imperial troops sent to assist in the destruction of temples in Gaza in 402: Mark the Deacon, *Life of Porphyry of Gaza* 51, 63. *PLRE*, vol. 2, s.v. Cynegius 2.

tion.[34] This highly conservative discourse was an understandable reaction against the concentration of authority in the persons of Christian bishops and holy men whose blunt *parrhesia* increasingly supplanted the cultured *paideia* of traditional elites over the course of the fourth century.[35] The monks of the Antiochene region gained particular notoriety for their interventions in judicial cases. To some extent this practice was simply one aspect of the larger process by which the Christian church sought to temper the harshness of the Roman judicial system through highly public appeals for clemency in particular cases.[36] Some of these Christian interventions, such as claims for the right to sanctuary in churches, came to be explicitly recognized in law.[37]

But while the same concern for mercy may have motivated a dramatic disruption of a trial by black-robed, psalm-chanting monks just as much as a respectful letter of appeal from a bishop to a magistrate, the two methods of approach were perceived quite differently. When the monk Macedonius, "an old man in rags," grabbed the cloak of one of the imperial commissioners sent to Antioch to supervise trials after the Riot of the Statues in 387 and forced him to dismount, he was exercising a far more confrontational approach in his appeal for clemency than did Libanius in the studied orations that he composed for the emperor on the same occasion.[38] Chrysostom argued that the monks' unique authority derived from their willingness to "martyrdom," as evidenced in their fearlessness in challenging judges and executioners.[39]

Although the imprisoned defendants undoubtedly appreciated the efforts

34. Eunapius, *Lives of the Sophists* 472: "For in those days every man who wore a black robe and consented to behave in an unseemly fashion in public, possessed the power of a tyrant *[tyranniken exousian]*, to such a pitch of virtue had the human race advanced." (Wright trans.)

35. This shift in the nature of authority concurrent with the Christianization of Roman society is the theme of Brown 1992.

36. Augustine appealed to the *comes* Marcellinus not to execute or torture certain Donatist prisoners, even though they had been involved in murderous attacks against his own Catholic clergy: Augustine *Ep.* 133 (412). See discussion in chapter 4, pp. 141–142.

37. For laws on sanctuary in churches, see *C.Th.* 9.45.1–5.

38. Macedonius: Theodoret *HE* 5.9. Libanius' *Orations* 19–23 deal with the riots.

39. *Homilies on the Statues* 17.4: "Tell me not that they were not slaughtered, that they did not pour forth their blood, but that they used as much boldness with their judges as it was likely that no other men would do, but such as had already renounced their own lives . . . For, indeed, if they had not before prepared themselves against every sort of slaughter, they would not have been able to speak freely before the judges." (NPNF trans.)

of Macedonius and other monks, the imperial magistrates clearly perceived it as a usurpation of their own judicial authority. The governor Tisamenus, hearing the chanting of hymns by approaching monks, abruptly jumped up from his seat, adjourned court, and fled from Antioch, claiming that "justice cannot be exercised once they have appeared."[40] When the monks arrived in large numbers to disrupt court sessions, or to rescue prisoners by simply grabbing them away from their guards, the threat of riot and violence was not far beneath the surface. In 398, the emperor Arcadius decreed that clerics and monks should not be permitted to "vindicate or hold by force" any condemned persons, and judges were to be heavily fined if they tolerated any such "usurpation." The next clause is a frank admission of the frequent helplessness of local officials in the face of such demonstrations: "But if the audacity of the clerics and monks is so great that it is thought the outcome will be a war rather than a judicial trial, let the case be referred to us."[41]

Such disruptive violence, when carried out by anyone other than the authorized agents of the state, was in and of itself a usurpation. By stressing the monks' disorderly behavior in their confrontations with imperial officials, critics could present them not just as undisciplined toughs but as a serious challenge to the very authority and legitimacy of the imperial government. As much as Libanius emphasized the uncontrolled, lawless, and chaotic quality of the monks' attacks on the temples, he also made it clear that they were able to get away with what they did precisely because of their close connections with legal and ecclesiastical authorities. The praetorian prefect Cynegius certainly encouraged the monks by his example. Those who had been victimized by the monks sought redress, interestingly, at the episcopal court of Flavian, bishop of Antioch. The bishop praised the monks for their zeal against paganism and sent the petitioners away telling them that they had been lucky to get off so lightly.[42] It is worth asking why the aggrieved pagans came to the bishop: the monks may have claimed that they could not be judged by a secular court, or the petitioners may have felt they

---

40. Libanius, *Or.* 45.26, "For the Prisoners," dated to 386: *hos ouk on dikaion ekeinon phanenton ton dikaion ti poiein.*

41. *Si tanta clericorum ac monachorum audacia est, ut bellum potius quam iudicium futurum esse existimetur, ad clementiam nostram commissa referetur:* C.Th. 9.40.16, dated 27 July 398, and addressed to Eutychianus, praetorian prefect of the east. The edict goes on to threaten, in not very specific terms, that bishops will be held responsible for their failure to punish such misdeeds by monks in their dioceses.

42. Libanius, *Or.* 30.11.

had even less hope of a favorable hearing from officials such as Cynegius.[43] Clearly, however, all understood that if the monks looked to any authority, it was that of the bishop. The claim of the monks, apparently accepted by the bishop, was that they were taking into their own hands the enforcement of various imperial laws against pagan sacrifice. Libanius accepted neither the idea of private individuals undertaking to "enforce" the law, nor the claim of episcopal courts to jurisdiction:

> Moreover, if this really and truly was a crime [pagan sacrifice], it was their [the monks'] job to show that the accused deserved to be punished, but it was the magistrates' job to impose the penalty. And a magistrate was not far to seek, for all the provinces are under such. This is how the kinsfolk of any murdered man get the murderers punished—by their presentation of the case and by the sentence of the magistrates. Nobody draws his sword against the murderer and puts it to his throat, employing force in place of the forms of law [*anti tou dikasteriou tei kheiri*] nor does he do so against the desecrators of tombs, or traitors or any other criminal offender, either past or future, but the place of swords is taken by impeachments and processes, civil and criminal. The magistrate, too, I believe, is satisfied for the penalty to be exacted by agents defined by law. But these people here were the only ones ever to judge the cases of those whom they accuse and, having passed judgment, themselves to play the executioner's part.[44]

Such displays of private violence, even when perpetrators claimed to be acting in support of the law, presented a direct challenge to the magistrates charged with enforcing that law, and could thus be seen as an intolerable usurpation of the state's legitimate authority.

Chrysostom, despite his complaints about the lawless conduct of the Cappadocian monks, was himself no stranger to the exercise of extralegal power. During his tenure as bishop of Constantinople, and also during his years of exile in Cucusus, he sponsored and encouraged groups of monks and clergy who forcibly demolished temples and replaced them with churches in the countryside of Phoenicia Libanensis.[45] At the turn of the fifth century this area was still predominantly and militantly pagan, and the monks both inflicted and suffered violence. Although Chrysostom's letters presented

43. Lamoreaux 1995 argues, however, that pagans as well as Christians often went to the bishops' courts by preference, finding them less procedurally complicated and expensive, and more equitable, than secular justice. On episcopal courts see now Mathisen 2001, especially the contributions by Harries, Lenski, and Dossey.

44. Libanius, *Or.* 30.25–26 (trans. Norman).

45. Theodoret *HE* 5.29; Chrysostom *Epp.* 21, 28, 53–55, 69, 123, 126, 175, 221 (all in PG 52).

these monks as fired by godly zeal, worthy of the martyrdom that they risked every day, seen through the eyes of a hostile source they would look no different from Libanius' "bandits."

In the course of the ecclesiastical conflicts of the fourth century, bishops frequently "usurped" imperial power when they commanded magistrates, soldiers, jailors, and torturers to persecute their rivals—essentially hijacking the state's coercive apparatus for use in their sectarian or personal conflicts.[46] By the latter half of the century, many of the more powerful bishops could bypass the state altogether and assemble veritable private armies to back them up in a confrontation, calling on monks, lower clergy, gravediggers, hospital attendants, able-bodied paupers, and others dependent on the patronage of the local church establishment in much the same way that aristocratic Roman patrons had been able to call upon their clients for physical support in the political struggles of the late Republican period.[47] Bishops who used such methods could be denounced with the name of "tyrant," the same label employed in late Roman political discourse to describe unsuccessful, and therefore illegitimate, rebels who attempted to usurp the imperial throne.[48]

These twin discourses of *latrocinium* and of usurpation, if successful, distracted attention away from the religious credentials of the subjects by emphasizing the legal and political implications of their violent and unruly behavior. Instead of holy men, divinely inspired with zeal for God, they were to be seen as criminals and rebels. This shift of focus away from the religious made it easier to contemplate opposition to such groups, and to argue for their repression by force. While the suppression, capture, trial, and execution of bandits and other criminals constituted a normal duty for Roman magistrates, no one was eager to employ such violence against a holy man. It was commonly believed that those who raised the sword against a true saint would be paralyzed, or stricken blind, or afflicted with some horrible disease—a belief reinforced by frequent repetition in hagiography.[49]

46. See chapter 2.
47. Bishops' ability to mobilize followers: see generally Brown 1992, chap. 3; MacMullen 1990a, with critical remarks by McLynn 1992; on the patriarchs of Alexandria, among the most notorious for such activities, see Haas 1997. On the Republican period, see Lintott 1968.
48. See next chapter.
49. There are numerous examples: see, e.g., *Life of Martin of Tours* 15, a man who attacks him with a knife is violently thrown down; *Life of Shenoute* 81–82, a pagan who strikes Shenoute in the face is suddenly grabbed by a mysterious angelic figure and dragged into the river to drown; *Syriac Life of Symeon the Stylite* 100, three robbers try to attack him but are paralyzed; *Lausiac History* 31, the virgin Pia-

To be sure, displays of a saint's power that hagiographers claimed as "miraculous" might be used by less friendly sources as grounds for an accusation of sorcery.[50]

Another more substantial factor that limited the ability of the secular authorities to use force against those regarded as "holy" was the fear of creating martyrs. The emperor Julian had for the most part refrained from direct violence against Christians for precisely this reason. The martyr's crown could potentially fall upon any Christians who had suffered in a way that others perceived as unjust, even if there had not actually been any religious issues involved.[51] The urban prefect Leontius, as we have seen, wisely chose to back down from a confrontation with the archimandrite Hypatius rather than be put into a position where he might be forced to execute a revered holy man with powerful connections at the imperial court.[52]

Such claims to martyrdom were not, however, always successful. In 415, the rivalry between bishop Cyril of Alexandria and the prefect Orestes erupted into violence when about five hundred Nitrian monks "of a very fiery disposition" entered the city to support Cyril.[53] Confronting the prefect in his chariot, they began insulting him, calling him an "idolator" even though he was a baptized Christian. One of the monks, Ammonius, went so far as to throw a stone that struck the prefect on the head and drew much blood. His guards fled in terror. But the people of Alexandria, who apparently were not particularly well disposed toward the Nitrian monks, rescued the prefect and drove away the monks.[54] Ammonius was captured and

---

moun is able to "transfix" and hold fast a party of hostile villagers through her prayers. Elm 1994, p. 316, associates this power of "transfixion" with the gift of prophecy and with pre-Christian, Hellenistic Egyptian beliefs.

50. The gruesome death of Arius, presented in lavish detail by a variety of Nicene sources as an example of divine justice in action, was thought by the Arians to have resulted from sorcery or poisoning: Sozomen *HE* 2.29.

51. Such as the "Innocentes," minor officials executed by Valentinian on corruption charges, and thereafter venerated as martyrs by the Christians of Milan (Ammianus 27.7), or the "Holy Notaries" of Constantinople, executed on false charges during the reign of Constantius (Sozomen *HE* 4.3, who added that their claim to martyrdom was later validated by miracles that took place at their burial site).

52. Callinicus, *Life of Hypatius* 33; discussion in previous chapter, pp. 203–204.

53. The source for what follows is Socrates *HE* 7.14. These were the same anti-Origenist monks whom Theophilus had previously armed against the four Tall Brothers (Socrates 6.7). See discussion on Cyril and the violence in Alexandria associated with his episcopate in Haas 1997, pp. 295–315.

54. Why did the people of Alexandria side with the prefect in this case? Haas 1997, p. 306, suggests: "We may surmise that the prefect was saved by the Alexandrians' abiding deference for traditional forms of authority, as well as by the long-

handed over to the prefect, who immediately had him tortured to death, and soon afterwards sent a report to the emperor. The prefect presumably would have characterized the incident as an outbreak of lawless violence, and would have reported that the criminal who had dared to assault the emperor's representative had been punished as the law demanded. But Cyril also wrote to the emperors, and in his subsequent actions he attempted to impose a very different interpretation on the incident: "[Cyril], causing the body of Ammonius to be deposited in a certain church, gave him the new appellation of Thaumasios ["wonderful" or "miraculous"], ordering him to be enrolled among the martyrs, and eulogizing his magnanimity in church as that of one who had fallen in a conflict in defense of piety." In this case, however, the attempt to claim martyrdom went too far: "But the more sober-minded, although Christians, did not accept Cyril's prejudicial estimate of [Ammonius]; for they knew well that he had suffered the punishment due to his rashness [*propeteia*], and that he had not lost his life under torture because he would not deny Christ. And Cyril himself being conscious of this, suffered the recollection of the circumstance to be gradually obliterated by silence."[55]

The legitimacy of a claim to martyrdom, which would have validated Ammonius' violent action and incidentally painted the prefect, Cyril's rival, as an enemy of the faith, depended on its recognition and acceptance by a broad audience and particularly by those in positions of authority. The Alexandrian people, Christians included—a very important audience for a patriarch of Alexandria—did not see things Cyril's way. Cyril may have addressed his petition to the imperial court in the hope that Theodosius II would recognize Ammonius as a martyr in the same way that the elder Theodosius had decreed martyrial status for Christians killed in the riots that preceded the destruction of the Serapeum in 391.[56] But the two cases were far different. In 391, Christians had been killed at the hands of pagans and could therefore plausibly be seen as having died for their faith.[57] But no im-

---

standing animosity of the city dweller toward intrusive and disorderly rural elements." As we shall see in other cases, violent activity by monks was particularly likely to meet opposition when monastic, wandering outsiders intruded into a local community and disrupted local arrangements and balances of power.

55. Socrates *HE* 7.14 (trans. NPNF).

56. As Haas 1997, p. 307, suggests.

57. It is clear from Rufinus that Theodosius' decree bestowed the title of martyr specifically on those Christians who had been seized by the pagans, held hostage in the Serapeum, tortured, and then killed in an explicit attempt to make them renounce Christ and sacrifice to idols—an ordeal that would satisfy even the most

perial government, however pious, could afford to legitimate or even tolerate physical assault against the persons of its high-ranking officials.[58] The punishment that Orestes imposed was the expected response to such an offense, and the imperial government did not question his judgment. Socrates himself, not generally enthusiastic about Cyril, took care to distinguish such violent fanatics from true holy men. In describing the brutal murder of Hypatia, which took place shortly afterwards, Socrates characterized the killers as driven by "hot-headedness" [to phronema enthermoi], not to be confused with the "divine zeal" by which holy men performed and legitimated acts of religious violence in the service of God—rejecting precisely the argument that the perpetrators of the deed might well have invoked to justify themselves.[59] Although the monks of Nitria may have remembered Ammonius as a martyr, most Christians did not.[60] Cyril may perhaps have chosen the name "Thaumasios" in the hope that stories of miracles might become attached to the "martyr" and thus lend his claims some legitimacy. If there were such stories, they did not spread far enough to make it into any of our sources. In a case such as this, the discourse of law and order prevailed over Cyril's religious claims.[61]

---

narrow and exacting definition of Christian martyrdom: Rufinus HE 11.22. It is not clear whether their veneration came by extension to cover also those Christians who had merely been killed by pagans in the street fighting that sparked the crisis. Socrates HE 7.13 does not mention any attempt to claim martyrial status for Alexandrian Christians killed by Jews in the bloody episode of communal violence that preceded the Ammonius incident. Nevertheless, Rufinus' version implies an expectation on the part of contemporary Christians that "martyrs" could be proclaimed by imperial decree—striking testimony to the degree to which all parties in religious conflicts valued the legitimacy that could be conferred by imperial recognition.

58. Compare Hypatius' threat against the prefect Leontius, discussed in chapter 5, pp. 203–204.

59. Socrates HE 7.15. It should be pointed out that the mob that lynched Hypatia was not actually composed of the same Nitrian monks, but rather of elements of the Alexandrian Christians, led by Peter, a reader. Socrates generally did not support the use of violence in matters of religion; cf. his remark on Hypatia's death, "and surely nothing is further from the spirit of Christianity than the allowance of massacres, fights, and transactions of that sort." On Socrates as church historian see Chesnut 1977 and Urbainczyk 1997.

60. John of Nikiu in the late seventh century, presumably drawing upon Coptic monastic tradition, does preserve some vestige of Cyril's side of the story: "Cyril was wroth with the governor of the city . . . for his putting to death an illustrious monk of the convent of Pernodj [Nitria] named Ammonius, and other monks also." Chronicle 84.94 (trans. Charles).

61. The ninth-century "martyrs" of Cordoba faced a similarly unenthusiastic reception from the local Christian establishment: see discussion in previous chapter, pp. 200–202.

We may gain additional insight into the contested nature of martyrial assertions made by violent zealots by examining another incident in which a claim of martyrdom might conceivably have been made, but was not. The series of violent upheavals connected with John Chrysostom's expulsion from Constantinople are amply described in a variety of sources.[62] One incident, however, mysteriously absent from all Christian sources, is known to us only through the pagan historian Zosimus.[63] When John left the city for his first exile, there were great disturbances among the people. At this point a rather unusual episode of violence erupted:

> While the city was in an uproar, the Christian church was taken over by the so-called monks. (These men renounce lawful marriage and fill populous colleges of bachelors in cities and villages: they are useless for war or any other service to the state. Moreover, from that time to this, they have taken over most of the land and, under the pretext of giving everything to the poor, have reduced almost everyone else to beggary.) These men, then, took over the churches and hindered the people from coming in for their customary prayers. This enraged the commoners and soldiers, who, anxious to humble the monks' insolence, went out when the signal was given, and violently and indiscriminately killed them all, until the church was filled with bodies. Those who tried to escape were pursued and anyone who happened to be wearing dark clothes was struck down, so that many died with them who were found in this garb because of mourning or some other tragic chance.[64]

The identity and allegiance of the various warring groups mentioned in this passage has been subject to some debate. Although it is well known that the people of Constantinople were in large part enthusiastic followers of Chrysostom, while much of the lower clergy and most of the city's monastic establishment had turned against him because of his overzealous reform efforts, the suggestion that the soldiers sided with the people against the monks might seem confusing given that the imperial government at that time was trying hard to get rid of Chrysostom and would soon turn to brutal persecution of his followers. Timothy Gregory offers a plausible reconstruction of events. Shortly after John departed for his first exile, the em-

62. Palladius, *Dialogue on the Life of Saint John Chrysostom*, passim; Socrates *HE* 6.9–19; Sozomen *HE* 8.14–24; Theodoret *HE* 5.34. Cf. also T. Gregory 1979, esp. chap. 2; Kelly 1995, pp. 191–253.

63. For what follows, Zosimus 5.23. T. Gregory 1973 argues convincingly that Zosimus' report should be taken seriously. This section, like much of Zosimus, seems to have been drawn directly from Eunapius, who would have been an eyewitness to the events described.

64. Zosimus 5.23 (trans. Ridley).

press Eudoxia was alarmed by the loud demonstrations in his favor and changed her mind, sending her eunuch to bring John back. When the monks heard that John was returning, they registered their protest by seizing the Hagia Sophia and disrupting services. At that point the more zealous popular supporters of John combined with Eudoxia's soldiers to expel the monks. Other sources, which do not mention this incident specifically, do however make general references to attacks by the people against the monks who had come with Theophilus from Alexandria. When Theophilus departed for Egypt in order to escape the hostility of Chrysostom's supporters, the monk Isaac, a leader of Constantinopolitan monasticism, felt it necessary to flee with him.[65]

That the soldiers sided with John's supporters in this case, while in several later incidents they would be opposed to them, should not in and of itself be surprising when we remember that the imperial government's first concern was not taking a consistent side but rather maintaining law and order. In this case, the monks, by illegally seizing and occupying the city's main church and disrupting services, were overthrowing both public and ecclesiastical order within sight of the imperial palace. Such a usurpation could not be tolerated, and so soldiers were sent to expel the offenders. Chrysostom's popular supporters, meanwhile, performed a usurpation of their own: seizing the opportunity, they took the law into their own hands and turned what was supposed to be a police action against a specific group of rebel monks into a general massacre of monks, or even of anyone who happened to look like a monk. In later incidents, similar acts of lawlessness attributed to John's supporters—most notably the burning of the same Great Church—drove the imperial government to turn against them and begin a harsh campaign of repression.

Monks, zealous men of Christ, had been slaughtered by the dozens if not more, their blood spilled within the very precincts of the Hagia Sophia, at the hands of an enraged mob and of armed soldiers. Such a lurid picture of sacrilegious violence within church walls might recall other massacres, such as the attack that fell upon John's supporters in their church in the middle of baptismal rites a few months later, or the brutal assault made by the Homoian bishop Lucius against the Nicene congregation of Alexandria thirty years previously.[66] And yet no Christian source reports any expression of sympathy for the victims of this massacre, and there is certainly no evidence

---

65. Sozomen *HE* 8.19.
66. Chrysostom, *Letter to Pope Innocent.* Alexandrian incident described in letter of Bishop Peter, quoted in Theodoret *HE* 4.22; see chapter 2, pp. 81–82.

that the slain monks were venerated as martyrs or even that any such claim was ever made on their behalf.

In fact, no surviving Christian source mentions the incident at all—a surprising omission considering the great attention and detailed presentation given by all the fifth-century church historians, as well as other sources, to other events in the turbulent months surrounding Chrysostom's deposition and exile. One possible explanation for their silence is that this incident would have pointed up an embarrassing problem in historiographical presentation. To put it simply, the fifth-century church historians, like most religious historiographers, preferred to write Christian history around clear-cut distinctions between heroes and villains—Christians versus pagans, Nicenes versus Arians. The case of Chrysostom was considerably complicated by the fact that not only John but also several of his most bitter opponents came to be venerated in later Christian tradition as saints.[67] If both sides in such a battle could claim the mantle of holiness, their disputes could not easily be presented as struggles on behalf of the faith and could at best cause confusion and embarrassment. Socrates' report of the confrontation between John and Epiphanius, monk and bishop of Salamis, presented the curious spectacle of two holy men, equally beloved by God, hurling curses at each other. Epiphanius prophesied that John "will not die a bishop" and John countered with the prediction that Epiphanius would never again see his home country.[68] The holy man's curse, a public prediction or invocation of divine vengeance upon an evildoer, is a common feature in hagiography. But in this case, the cursing was reciprocal. Since both men were saints, both predictions came true: John was soon deposed, and Epiphanius died on his way back to Cyprus.

Some of Chrysostom's most implacable enemies also happened to be the stars of Constantinopolitan monasticism, such as Isaac, revered (at least in Nicene orthodox tradition) as the founding father of monasticism in the imperial capital.[69] Isaac was only the first in a series of Constantinopolitan ar-

---

67. Even his archrival bishop, Theophilus, though not fondly regarded by Socrates or Palladius, enjoyed a considerable reputation as a champion of the Christian faith against paganism, due largely to his role in the destruction of the Serapeum in 391. Later Coptic ecclesiastical tradition, as represented by the seventh-century John of Nikiu, preserves no memory of any bad blood between the saintly bishop John and the equally saintly bishop Theophilus.

68. Socrates *HE* 6.14.

69. Homoiousian or "Eustathian" ascetic foundations in the capital preceded Isaac's arrival by several decades, but their memory was conveniently forgotten in the hagiographical tradition that grew up around Isaac and his followers: see Dagron 1970.

chimandrites to seek the assistance of a patriarch of Alexandria in order to challenge the authority of a patriarch of Constantinople.[70] But in this case the hagiographical traditions of the Constantinopolitan monks did their best to downplay or ignore any conflict between bishop and monastic leaders.[71] Although Isaac was probably not among the monks who seized the Hagia Sophia, those monks would have looked to him as their spiritual leader and would have believed that they were acting in support of him or perhaps even at his direction. But Isaac's spiritual authority could not match the veneration that the people of Constantinople felt for their bishop. Eventually this veneration forced both imperial government and church establishment to rehabilitate John's memory and to return his relics to the city.[72] In such a climate, any significant veneration for the slain monks, outside of their own monasteries, was unlikely.

Indeed, evidence for claims of holy zeal and righteous violence survive not for the monks, but from John's side. Chrysostom, in a sermon thought to have been given on his return from the first exile, praised his supporters for their steadfast loyalty and bravery in his absence. In a likely reference to the battle at Hagia Sophia, he remarked: "The soldiers were armed, not only did the church become a military camp, but the city a church. . . . You have secured the cooperation of the empress . . . she went about everywhere, not indeed in person, but through her own military escort." John then made an explicit declaration as to which side had acted legitimately: "I say these things not to lead you into insurrection, for theirs is the insurrection, while yours is zeal."[73] The violence of the monks was an act of usurpation, and

70. This pattern would be followed by Dalmatius, who sided with Cyril against Nestorius, and later by Eutyches, who sought the assistance of Dioscorus against Flavian. See chapter 8, pp. 289–297. On Alexandrian-Constantinopolitan ecclesiastical rivalry, see Baynes 1926.

71. See, e.g., Callinicus, *Life of Hypatius* 11, which mentions the "great love" between Chrysostom and the monks. Only Palladius, most devoted to Chrysostom, ventured to attack Isaac, "that street idler, the guide of the false monks," by name: *Dialogue* 6.

72. John was officially restored to the diptychs by bishop Atticus shortly after 412, despite the strenuous objections of Theophilus' nephew and successor Cyril, who angrily remarked that he would sooner restore Judas: Cyril, *Ep.* 76. Official annual commemoration at court was introduced by bishop Nestorius in 428 (Marcellinus Comes, *ad annum* 428) and Chrysostom's relics were finally returned from Asia Minor and formally deposited in the Church of the Holy Apostles in 438.

73. *Stasis gar ta ekeinon, ta de humetera zelos:* Chrysostom, *Sermo post redditu ab exsilio* (PG 52, 443–448), (trans. here from T. Gregory 1973, pp. 79–80). Although the authenticity of the sermon has been questioned, T. Gregory 1973 argues that "it probably represents a valid historical tradition." Holum 1982, p. 75 n. 107, considers the doubts unfounded; Kelly 1995, pp. 233–234 accepts the sermon as authentic.

John assured his supporters that they had acted rightly—with godly zeal—in punishing them.[74]

In June of 404, once John had been exiled again (this time not to return) these same zealous followers of his were accused of setting fire to the Great Church, creating a conflagration that also consumed the nearby senate house and even threatened the palace. The imperial authorities used the suspicion of arson as an excuse to begin a harsh repression of John's supporters. The church historians were unsure as to where to assign responsibility for the fire. Socrates simply said that the "Johannites" set the fire, but Sozomen reported that the fire broke out, perhaps accidentally, in the confusion during a battle between the Johannites and their opponents in the church—an equally plausible scenario.[75] Palladius, who can reasonably be called John's hagiographer, offered a very different explanation for the fire. When John left the church, the "angel of the church" had gone with him, leaving only a dark and deserted sanctuary:

> After this unutterable and inexplicable darkness there appeared a flame in the middle of the throne where John used to sit. It was just as the heart situated in the middle of the body controls the other members and communicates the oracles of the Lord. The flame looked for the expounder of the Word, and not finding him, it consumed the church furnishings. Then it took shape like a tree and grew up through the rafters to the very roof. . . . It was as though God were paying the wages of iniquity for the penalty assigned, to chide and warn those who would not be warned except by the sight of these calamities. . . . The fire as though endowed with intelligence leaped over the people in the street like a bridge and destroyed first of all the part closest to the church, but the part on the side of the royal palace. So we cannot say that it really burned because of the proximity of the structures, but it showed that it was only too clear that it had come from heaven. . . . In that whole crowd there was no loss of life, not of man or of beast. But the dirt of those who had carried on in such foul fashion was cleansed by the fire.[76]

The fire came not from John's supporters on earth, but from heaven, to express God's anger at the wrong done to his holy man. To John's follow-

---

74. See discussion in previous chapter of John's zealous exhortations regarding imitation of the martyrs, p. 171.

75. Socrates *HE* 6.18; Sozomen *HE* 8.22. Theodoret did not mention the incident. Zosimus 5.23, like Socrates, stated that John's followers set the fire.

76. Palladius, *Dialogue on the Life of St. John Chrysostom* 10 (trans. Meyer). The *Dialogue* can certainly be considered as hagiography in intention, if not in literary form. Cf. discussion in previous chapter of "fire from heaven" miracles, pp. 185–186.

ers there could be no greater witness to the right of their cause. The monks previously slaughtered in the same church received no such legitimation, and were quietly forgotten by Christian sources who held reverence for both Chrysostom and his opponents, embarrassed by the fact that these zealous men had been enemies of the great saint. Only a pagan observer, who held equal contempt for both parties, cared to report that story.

Without a valid claim to martyrdom, the slain monks lost much of their claim to be considered holy men. Chrysostom's followers, together with the imperial authorities, saw them as criminals and usurpers and punished them accordingly. When monks lose their claim to holiness, they are no longer true monks. The rhetorical distinction between "true" and "false" monks formed an integral part of the polemical arsenal of critics both pagan and Christian, leading to what we may call the "discourse of false pretenses."

Opponents regularly used accusations of pretense and falsehood to undermine the monks' claims to religious authority. Libanius alleged that their famed ascetic practices were a sham: they pretended to fast, but by night they ate "more than elephants." He even charged that they applied white makeup to their faces in order to mimic the "ascetic pallor" commonly thought to be produced by excessive fasting.[77] The classical science of physiognomy had long assured its practitioners that they could "tell just by looking," reading the inner character of others based on their outward appearance and demeanor.[78] Disciples and pilgrims marveled at the visible holiness that radiated from the faces of famous ascetics.[79] Praise for sincerity and authenticity, of course, went hand in hand with fear of hypocrisy, creating an urgent need for ways to distinguish the truly holy from fakers and posers.

Other critics might accept the monks' practices but question their motives. The emperor Julian referred to monks as "people who make small sacrifices in order to gain much"—they thought fasting and chastity an easy price to pay (after all, he himself practiced both) in return for the status, influence, and wealth they gained through the patronage of Christian sec-

77. Libanius, *Or.* 30.8–9, quoted above, p. 210. While "pallor" was typically associated with fasting, Evagrius Ponticus (*Praktikos* 11) warned that it might instead be a physical symptom of unhealthy and festering anger.

78. On physiognomy see Gleason 1995. Gleason emphasizes the function of physiognomic discourses in the context of status-competition between rival members of social elites. She points out the extremely arbitrary ways in which physiognomy could work in practice, with the same characteristics being interpreted in opposite ways depending on the needs of the moment. Early Christian uses of physiognomy are discussed by T. Shaw 1997 and 1998.

79. See Frank 2000, esp. chap. 5.

ular elites who were impressed by their lifestyle.[80] The Christian Jerome warned in nearly identical terms against certain so-called ascetics in Rome who impressed wealthy women with their black cloaks, long hair, bare feet, and chains, who pretended to fast but feasted at night.[81] A common prejudice, shared by the Christian emperor Valens, held that many people became monks simply from "idleness" or in order to escape municipal service responsibilities.[82] Many Christians feared that their religion's commandment to charity might encourage freeloaders.[83] Paulinus of Nola complained of "swarms of wandering beggars" who pretended to be monks.[84] For John Chrysostom, nothing could demonstrate more clearly the value of the true monastic life than the lengths to which pretenders would go to "counterfeit" it.[85]

Although Christians and pagans alike could discredit ascetics by the simple expedient of attributing worldly motives to them, the discourse of false pretenses had much deeper and more sinister connotations in a Christian context, where it was intimately linked to fears of heresy and corruption. True holy men in Christian imagination embodied a perfect sincerity, matching words to deeds and surface appearance to inner nature.[86] Enemies of the faith, by contrast, carried deception in their very being.[87] Christ himself had warned his followers to "[b]eware of false prophets, who come to you in sheep's clothing but inwardly are ravenous wolves."[88] The more successfully these deceivers mimicked the outward appearance of true Christians, the more insidious a danger they posed. The fifth-century Roman *Sacramentary of Pope Leo* included a prayer for deliverance from "false confessors."[89] A pretense of holiness need not be merely a cover for

---

80. Julian, *Or.* 7.224.

81. Jerome, *Ep.* 22.28 *(Letter to Eustochium)*.

82. Valens, *C.Th.* 12.1.63 (370): "Certain devotees of idleness *[ignaviae sectatores]* have deserted compulsory municipal service, have betaken themselves to secret places, and under pretext of religion *[specie religionis]* have joined with the hermit *monazontes*." (Pharr trans.) More discussion of Valens' edict below, pp. 231–232.

83. This concern can be seen as early as the second-century *Didache* (12.1).

84. Paulinus of Nola, *Carmen* 24.325–328. Wanderers were particularly suspect, and the early western monastic rules were very concerned with careful screening of visitors. See Dietz 1997, Caner 2002.

85. Chrysostom, *Homily on Acts* 33.

86. See previous chapter, pp. 206–207.

87. Rousseau 1995, pp. 241–258, discusses fear of deception and heresy in Egyptian monastic communities.

88. Matthew 7:15 (RSV trans.).

89. *Sacramentary of Pope Leo:* PL 55, p. 28. See commentary in Duchesne 1956, pp. 135–144. Brown 1969 links this to fear of Manichaean infiltrators. Cf. Maier 1996.

worldly greed. Instead it might conceal a dangerous fanaticism, an extremism motivated by an incorrect or overliteral understanding of divine commandments.[90]

The warning against "false prophets" and "wolves in sheep's clothing" provided a means by which a Christian audience could challenge or reject an individual's claim to personal holiness. True holy men, in hagiography, protected the faith by confronting, exposing, and overthrowing these false prophets. As Elijah had confounded the priests of Ba'al, and as Simon Peter had disposed of Simon Magus, so late antique holy men called upon divine miracle to unmask these pretenders and punish them violently.[91] The Egyptian monk Copres, entering the city to find a Manichaean preaching to the people, challenged the crowd to light a great fire and see which one of them could endure it unharmed. When Copres entered the fire and emerged whole, the enthusiastic crowd seized the Manichaean and threw him into the flames.[92] Righteous violence inspired by a true holy man served to punish a false one; divine zeal exposed and punished the hypocritical pretense of a heretic.

But just as righteous violence was the prerogative of true holy men, so lawless "latrocinial" violence was held to be characteristic of false monks as they attempted to usurp religious authority. Ecclesiastical and state authorities constructed a set of stereotypes which categorized ascetics who wandered from place to place, "Messalian" enthusiasts, or monks who lived in *martyria*, as undesirable and undisciplined radicals prone to disobedience and violence.[93] These stereotypical "bad monks" stood in opposition to the ideal monks who lived in well-regulated monasteries under the firm authority of bishops and clergy, and who refrained from meddling in worldly affairs. The attempt to define a normative style of monasticism, though perhaps of limited success in regulating actual contemporary practice, exercised

90. Cf. the Donatist Tyconius, characterizing Circumcellions as driven by *superstitio*, or excessive devotion: see chapter 3, p. 122.

91. Elijah: see discussion in previous chapter, pp. 183–185. Peter and Simon Magus: Acts 8:9–24, with later elaborations in the apocryphal acts.

92. *History of the Monks in Egypt* 10.30–32. On this incident cf. Lim 1995, pp. 79–81. Macarius of Tkow likewise threw the pagan priest Homer into the fire: see discussion in previous chapter, pp. 187–188. Death by fire, incidentally, was the penalty that Roman law had prescribed for Manichaeans since the time of Diocletian: *Edict* of 297, in *Fontes Iuris Romani Anteiustiniani*, 2nd ed., vol. 2 (Florence 1940–1943), pp. 544–589.

93. See Dietz 1997 and now Caner 2002. On Messalians see also Stewart 1991; Elm 1994, pp. 190–233; Fitschen 1998. The same characterizations and polemical strategies, of course, were employed by Augustine to delegitimize the Donatist Circumcellions in North Africa: see chapter 3, pp. 111–114.

a tremendous influence upon later Christian tradition's memory of monastic origins and even upon modern historiography.[94]

Ideological efforts to define asceticism in terms of stereotypical "good" and "bad" models went hand in hand with institutional attempts by both church and state to regulate the monastic movement. By the time of Chalcedon, imperial legislation and church regulation of monasticism had come together in a coherent program that attempted to force all asceticism into organized coenobitic forms under careful episcopal supervision.[95] Over the course of the late fourth and early fifth centuries, however, efforts at control pursued a variety of tactics.

The first extensive attempts by the imperial government to regulate the practice of monasticism took place in the reign of Valens. In 370, the emperor instructed the praetorian prefect of the east and the *comes orientis* to hunt down certain "devotees of idleness" who had fled to join monastic hermits "under pretext of religion" in order to escape curial duties.[96] Although no edict survives, there is evidence that around 375 Valens ordered monks to be seized and drafted into the army. According to Jerome, those who refused were to be clubbed to death.[97] Attempts to enforce this edict, coupled with persecution of Egyptian Nicenes who refused communion with the Homoian bishop Lucius, led to a massacre of monks in the monasteries of Nitria.[98] It must be kept in mind that all our information on Valens' religious policies comes to

94. I have been using "ascetic," "monk," and "holy man" interchangeably. Although later tradition eventually came to restrict the term "monk" to those who lived in organized coenobitic communities, precise distinctions between the terms are rather anachronistic for the fourth and fifth centuries (as Elm 1994, p. 14, argues). Scholarship in the last few decades has recently begun to recognize the wide diversity of ascetic practices that characterized the early Christian centuries. See esp. Goehring 1992; Rousseau 1995; Elm 1994; Griffith 1995; Caner 2002. On the origin and evolution of the term *monachos*, see Judge 1977.

95. Monastic legislation at Chalcedon is discussed in chapter 8, pp. 316–317.

96. *C.Th.* 12.1.63, 1 January 370.

97. Jerome, *Chronicle, ad annum* 375: *Valens lege data ut monachi militarent nolentes fustibus iussit interfici.* Cf. Socrates *HE* 4.24. Lenski 2002, pp. 256–257, argues that Valens did in fact pursue such a policy, citing that emperor's well-known hostility toward the largely Nicene and Athanasian monks of Egypt and also Valens' pressing military manpower needs and intense recruitment efforts in the final years of his reign.

98. Sources: Socrates *HE* 4.24, Jerome *op cit.*, Cassian *Conferences* 18. Valens had at first left the Egyptian Nicenes alone, not wishing to challenge Athanasius' popularity. But when Athanasius died in 373, Valens installed the Homoian bishop Lucius in Alexandria by military force, expelling Peter, the Nicene congregation's choice as successor to Athanasius. Peter's detailed and highly charged account of the persecution inflicted by Lucius is preserved in Theodoret *HE* 4.22: see discussion in chapter 2, pp. 76–77.

us through Nicene sources who considered him to be a heretic and a persecutor. Nicene orthodox tradition saw these policies quite simply as an attempt
to destroy monasticism entirely. It stood to reason that since all true monks
were good Nicenes, Valens as enemy of the faith would seek to suppress them.

This polemical representation surely oversimplifies. Valens placed great
emphasis on ensuring the economic well-being of cities and on strength-
ening his military forces, and pursued a rigorous enforcement of curial and
military service obligations. Clearly, for him these concerns carried greater
weight than any respect he might have had for the "higher calling" that
drove monks to abandon the distractions and obligations of worldly life. But
we must keep in mind that those monks who fled human society and withdrew into the desert were not the only, nor even the most numerous, ascetics. Their *anachoresis,* in the third quarter of the fourth century, was still
a relatively new phenomenon, a dramatic contrast to the lifestyles of older
and well-established groups who managed to practice a pious *askesis* without abandoning the lay communities that supported them.[99] In the Roman
East, these groups were largely associated with the Homoian position favored by the majority of bishops and by Valens himself. It is entirely prob-
able that Valens shared the feelings of many other mainstream Christians
at this time who found the lifestyles of the desert hermits to be a disagree-
able and socially disruptive innovation.[100] When the goatskin-clad Syrian
hermit Aphrahat approached Valens' palace in Antioch, the emperor challenged him. To Aphrahat's declaration, "I have come here to pray for you
and your empire," Valens answered, "You ought to go home and pray alone
like a monk."[101] Although the story of this confrontation may well be fictional, Valens' rebuke nevertheless serves to illustrate contemporary prejudices against the disruptive behavior of monks who attempted to step outside their proper roles and usurp spiritual authority.[102]

99. See Griffith 1995.
100. The disgust many secular Christians felt for the hermits who dwelled in
the mountains around Antioch is colorfully described by Chrysostom, *Against the
Opponents of the Monastic Life.* Valens, who resided in Antioch for most of his reign,
may have formed his negative impression of anchoritic monasticism based on en-
counters with these hermits.
101. Theodoret *HE* 4.23; cf. *HR* on Aphrahat. Theodoret adds that one of the
emperor's grooms, who threatened the monk violently, subsequently fell into boil-
ing water and died while preparing the emperor's bath—a manifestation of divine
judgment intended to make clear to the audience which side had the right of the
confrontation.
102. Compare Valens' remark to that of the bishop of Chalcedon in 434/5 who,
when he learned of Hypatius' plan to confront the prefect Leontius, told him, "You

By the time of Theodosius I, the emperor and his court seem to have grown more comfortable with ascetic holy men. The Theodosian court aristocracy established particularly close ties with the prominent Nicene ascetics of Constantinople.[103] Rather than prevent monks from abandoning worldly society, Theodosian policy heartily encouraged them. The main concern now seems to have been the trouble caused by errant monks who left their proper seclusion and returned to the cities to meddle in secular affairs. In 390 Theodosius ordered that "if any persons should be found in the profession of monks, they shall be ordered to seek out and inhabit desert places and desolate solitudes."[104] Government authorities of the Theodosian period seem to have felt, contrary to earlier prejudices, that a monk's proper place was in the desert. Monks' intervention in judicial cases seems to have been one of the primary concerns.[105] Complaints about the violent campaigns of the Syrian monks against pagans and Jews may also have motivated the edict, which came only a few years after Libanius' petition on behalf of the temples (386) and the incident at Callinicum (388). The replacement of the zealous Christian Cynegius by the pagan Tatianus as praetorian prefect of the east in 388 would have created a climate favorable to at least a gesture at restraining the excesses of the monks.[106] Libanius' discourse of law and order may have had some effect.[107] But it seems to have been little more than a gesture: only two years later, a second edict quickly reversed the first and allowed the monks free entry into the cities.[108]

Since attempts to restrain the monks and to bar them from the cities had

---

are a monk, go back to your monastery and keep quiet." (Callinicus, *Hypatius* 33, discussed in previous chapter, p. 203.) Cf. Nestorius' challenge to Shenoute at Ephesus: "What business do you have in this synod? You are not a bishop, but only a monk!" (Besa, *Life of Shenoute* 128–130, discussed in chapter 7, p. 252).

103. See generally Matthews 1975, pp. 100–145. The older Eustathian/ Macedonian ascetic foundations, meanwhile, were gradually suppressed or legislated out of existence: *C.Th.* 16.5.11–13, in 383–84; Socrates *HE* 5.8; Sozomen *HE* 7.7; discussion in Elm 1994, p. 221.

104. *C.Th.* 16.3.2 [*CJ* 1.3], 2 September 390, addressed to Tatianus, praetorian prefect of the east. The decree was revoked two years later (*C.Th.* 16.3.3; 17 April 392), presumably under pressure from supporters of the monks.

105. See discussion above, pp. 215–217. Such intervention is mentioned in *C.Th.* 16.3.3 of 392, and especially 9.40.16 of 398, quoted p. 217 above.

106. Cynegius: references above, p. 217. Tatianus: *PLRE*, vol. 1, s.v. Tatianus 5.

107. Although there is no specific evidence for any response to Libanius' *Or.* 30, Liebeschuetz 1972, pp. 23–39, argues that Libanius' orations generally did reach the ears of the emperors to whom they were addressed, and emphasizes that Libanius continued to enjoy close connections with the imperial court even under Theodosius.

108. *C.Th.* 16.3.3.

not enjoyed great success, at least some authorities felt that it would be more profitable to co-opt them into the church establishment. The edict of 398, after denouncing the "audacity" of the monks with regard to judicial interventions, and threatening to punish bishops who did not restrain their excesses, added that from among these same monks, "the bishops shall ordain clerics when they see a need for them."[109] The holy man's escapes from attempts by congregations and bishops to ordain him are a common feature of hagiography.[110] John Chrysostom, who as a priest of Antioch sang the praises of the Antiochene hermits and glorified them particularly for their fearless confrontations with secular authorities, now as bishop of Constantinople found independent monastic holy men to be a disciplinary headache. He attempted to force monks who dwelled in the *martyria* or who moved freely around the city into organized coenobial monasteries, and tried to restrict their contacts with secular patrons. He also attempted to bring many of these monks directly under his disciplinary authority by ordaining them, in some cases against their will.[111] This seems to have been a fairly common policy by which bishops attempted to exert some control over the monastic movement. The Roman pope Siricius (384–399) warned that some of his fellow bishops were recklessly ordaining wandering strangers, "who may or may not really be monks, as they call themselves," without checking into their backgrounds or establishing their orthodoxy or even confirming that they had been baptized.[112] The monks, for their part, were wise to resist an ordination that would place them under the bishop's control. Before the canons of the Council of Chalcedon subjected monasteries to episcopal authority, a bishop theoretically had no more disciplinary jurisdiction over non-ordained monks than he did over any other Christian laypeople.[113] The holy man derived his spiritual authority directly from God. Once he be-

109. *C.Th.* 9.40.16, quoted above, p. 217.

110. Most famous of these was certainly Ammonius, who cut off his own ear rather than be ordained, and when the people wanted to ordain him anyway, threatened to cut out his tongue: Palladius, *Lausiac History* 11. *Historia Monachorum* 20.14 mentions "three pious brothers," unnamed, who also cut off their ears to escape ordination.

111. Chrysostom: see generally Kelly 1995, pp. 115–127. Forced ordinations: Callinicus, *Life of Hypatius* 11, who notes that one monk resisted ordination by biting Chrysostom's finger when he came to lay hands on him!

112. *Sive simulent, sive sint monachi, quod se appellant:* Siricius, *Ep.* 4.2 (PL 13.1165–1166).

113. At least not with respect to church canons prior to Chalcedon (on which see chapter 8, pp. 316–317). On the other hand, both Theodosius' response to the Callinicum incident (see above, pp. 208–210) and also the language of *C.Th.* 9.40.16 show that bishops could be held responsible for the misdeeds of monks in their dioceses

came a presbyter, that same authority would now be mediated through the person of the bishop. When Athanasius came to visit the monasteries of Tabennesi, Pachomius wisely hid until he had left, knowing that the bishop wished to ordain him.[114]

These various attempts to bring monasticism under control testified to the fear felt by both church and state of independent holy men and the challenges they might bring to established structures of authority. The same violence of the monks that harassed pagans and Jews could also be turned against public order and even against the church hierarchy. Theophilus of Alexandria, threatened by a mob of anti-Origenist monks who had marched from Nitria into the city, saved his authority and possibly his life only by a quick doctrinal about-face that allowed him to co-opt their violent zeal and later deploy it against his own enemies.[115] John Chrysostom was only the first in a long series of bishops to run afoul of the powerful and independent monks of Constantinople.[116]

Secular and ecclesiastical authorities worked hard to impose external regulation on monks. They promoted stable and organized coenobitic institutions, and attempted to channel all forms of ascetic expression into them. Monastic leaders, meanwhile, did their part to impose constraint and discipline within their communities. We are struck by the jarring contrast between the disorderly and violent behavior attributed to many monks in the incidents described earlier in this chapter, and the humble and obedient qualities promoted by normative monastic texts.

Coenobitic monasticism went out of its way to stress the importance of hierarchy, authority, and deference to elders. In this context, the master/disciple relationship placed a higher premium on obedience than on emulation. Two of the fifth century's most famous ascetic innovators, Symeon the Stylite and Alexander the Akoimete, both began their careers by leaving more conventional monastic communities whose abbots feared that their extreme behavior might provoke jealousy or a dangerous competitive spirit

---

and therefore imply that bishops were thought in practice to have some authority or influence over monks.

114. Pachomius: *Bohairic Life* 28. Macedonius, a Syrian monk, was ordained by a visiting bishop. Because the monk did not speak Greek, he did not understand what was happening until after the ordination had been performed. Once it was explained to him, he flew into a rage, struck the bishop, and stormed off: Theodoret *HR* 13.

115. Socrates *HE* 6.7, Sozomen *HE* 8.11. Haas 1997, pp. 260–265.

116. On John's conflict with Constantinopolitan monks see Dagron 1970, and now the thoughtful analysis of Elm 1998.

among the brethren.[117] The radical practices that might later be lauded by a hagiographer were not to be imitated. Rules, *praktikoi, apophthegmata,* and similar texts embodied the values and principles thought most important for the success of communal life. They warned against the dangers of unchecked ascetic zealotry, which could all too easily lead its practitioners into sinful pride. The "desire" that might otherwise lead to martyrdom was to be steered into a more passive *askesis,* drawing near to God through humility and submission.[118]

John Cassian advocated strict ascetic discipline as a means to moderate all the passions. For him, all sin derived from the unchecked desires of the flesh. Gluttony, the most basic of these desires, was to be subdued by rigorous fasting. This, in turn, would tame lust. Fear of bodily impulses reached an extreme in some monastic circles with a worried fixation on the moral implications of nocturnal emissions.[119] Success at controlling the body would, it was hoped, translate into control of greed, anger, and pride. Monastic ideology elevated chastity as a source of purity and strength, a means to victory in the ascetic struggle.[120] But chastity's importance made the consequences of its failure all the more severe. Lustful thoughts could undermine the monk's defenses and leave him vulnerable to the very demons he hoped to battle against.

Anger, also, worried the monks. Evagrius called it the "most fierce" of the passions.[121] Unrestrained anger could poison relationships and threaten the fragile peace that characterized an ideal monastic community. In the *Apophthegmata,* the determination to avoid any interpersonal conflict was taken to such an extreme that some monks warned against rebuking their brethren even if they caught them in sin. The fear was that any judgment or criticism of others—no matter how justified—could only lead to grief.[122]

117. Symeon: Theodoret *HR* 6.5. *Life of Alexander* 7–8.
118. Female ascetics, particularly, were encouraged to channel their impulses in this direction: see Brakke 1995a, pp. 17–79, and generally Elm 1994.
119. Brakke 1995b. On Cassian, see now Leyser 2000, pp. 33–61.
120. Parallels can be found in contexts both more ancient and modern for a connection between extremism and ideologies of sexual purity. Old Testament law demanded that warriors abstain from sex and undergo purification rituals prior to engaging in holy war: see von Rad 1991, pp. 41–50. Compare the elaborate rules for holy war laid out in the Dead Sea Scrolls, e.g., *War between the Sons of Light and the Sons of Darkness.* Juergensmeyer 2000, pp. 195–207, finds that an extreme fear of sexuality and a virulent homophobia coexist with intense male bonding in several modern extremist groups.
121. Evagrius, *Praktikos* 11.
122. See Gould 1993, esp. pp. 107–138. In later medieval centuries, it was considered appropriate for the monastery as an institution to express its collective anger

Physical violence, although not unheard of, was hardly the worst consequence of anger. Syriac monastic legislation addressed the problem of fistfights between brothers, but generally did not consider it a terrible crime. Penances were typically far more severe for verbal offenses such as gossip or mockery, which posed much greater danger to tight monastic communities.[123] Coenobitic rules and ideals expected and enforced a "coercive harmony" to which dissensus was perceived as the greatest threat. The restraint of dangerous zeal and the suppression of corrosive interpersonal conflict demanded a tremendous disciplinary effort, which in some cases required a moderate degree of corrective violence.

Disciplinary beating seems to have been fairly common in monastic settings. Palladius described seeing at Nitria three date palms reserved for the scourging of transgressors.[124] Many ascetics regularly applied severe physical punishments, including scourging, to themselves as part of their self-discipline. In a more organized and regulated coenobitic setting, discipline resided less in oneself and more in the relationship between abbot and ordinary monk, spiritual director and disciple—and so physical punishment found its place, though not always without controversy.[125]

Although monastic discourse steeped itself in metaphors of spiritual combat and battle against demons, nevertheless it conveyed a keen sense of concern that such zeal could get out of control if not properly guided. The impulse to ascetic excellence could all too easily lead to pride, envy, and a destructive spirit of competition among brothers. Novice monks might be unable to tell the difference between godly zeal and personal hatred, just as they might also mistake demonic apparitions for angelic visions. Only the advice of their more experienced elders and superiors could save them from such traps.[126]

---

at external enemies through liturgical cursing—even though the traditional disapproval of anger still applied to individual monks: see Little 1998.

123. Vööbus 1960b, p. 283, *Anonymous Canons for the Monks* #23–24: three months of solitary fasting for the monk who strikes his brother, and one month for the other if he hits back. But the monk who slanders or causes quarrels is to be expelled permanently. On p. 287, Rabbula's *Canons for the Monks* #10: he who raises his hand against his companion shall be demoted to twelfth in rank, but he who mocks and gossips shall be demoted to sixtieth.

124. Palladius, *Lausiac History* 7.3.

125. For disciplinary beating generally, see chapter 4, pp. 140–143. For controversy over physical discipline by clergy, see next chapter, pp. 257–260. On physical discipline in both episcopal-juridical and monastic contexts, see now Dossey 2001.

126. On the dangers of deceptive visions see, e.g., *Life of Antony* 21–43.

As we have seen, both secular and ecclesiastical establishments feared ascetic zealotry out of control, and mistrusted the credentials and motives of monks who found themselves on the wrong side—even while the same critics might praise the holiness of ascetics in other contexts. Clearly, there were "good" and "bad" monks, and all parties were very concerned to differentiate one from the other. The stereotypes we have discussed in this chapter—*latrocinium*, usurpation, false pretenses—certainly slant the reports of our sources. Political or sectarian prejudice undoubtedly led to exaggeration in accounts of particular incidents. Nevertheless, there seems to have been a common perception that monks were prone to violent, disorderly behavior, an assumption shared not just by pagan sources like Libanius and Eunapius, from whom we might expect a uniformly negative perspective, but also by Christians such as Chrysostom who were quick to praise the work of monks when it suited their interests to do so. Complaints from critics of rowdy behavior together with endorsements of "holy violence" in hagiography combine to produce a picture of aggressive and violent ascetics. The apparent contrast between this disorderly conduct, and monastic institutions' seeming emphasis on order and obedience, begs for explanation. Was there something in the nature of ascetic institutions and groups that made their members particularly prone to extremism?

Some useful insight may be found in Mary Douglas' definition of a "sectarian" mentality based on her analysis of modern religious and political groups.[127] "Sectarian bias," according to Douglas, means "polarized arguments, persons shown in black and white contrasts, evil and good, and nothing in between."[128] "The sectarian outlook has three positive commitments: to human goodness, to equality, to purity of heart and mind. The dangers to the sectarian ideal are worldliness and conspiracy. . . . The remedies most easily proposed in such organizations are to refuse to compromise with evil and to root it out, accompanied by a tendency toward intolerance and drastic solutions."[129]

Many of the characteristics described here by Douglas resemble those displayed by the late antique Christians whom this study has characterized as "zealous" or "extremist." Douglas' main contribution is her argument that a group's relationship with the outside world—its "worldview"—is deter-

---

127. The argument is spelled out most explicitly in Douglas and Wildavsky 1982, esp. chap. 6. See also Douglas 1996, esp. the introduction to the new edition, and chap. 7; Douglas 1986; Douglas 1982, pp. 183–254; Douglas 1992, esp. chap. 1. For critical reaction to Douglas see Fardon 1999.

128. Douglas 1996, pp. xix–xx.

129. Douglas and Wildavsky 1982, pp. 10–11.

mined, or at least greatly affected, by its internal structure and organization. A strong sense of separation from the world, and an egalitarian ideology—manifested in mistrust of ambition, property, and competitive individualism—tend to correlate with an extremist outlook, expressed as a contempt for secular society, a refusal to compromise, and a sharp sense of distinction between good and evil. Some aspects of this model may be relevant to the late antique monastic communities that concern us here. Although coenobitic institutions emphasized the master/disciple relationship and demanded submission to the authority of the abbot, they tended to shun the more formal power structures of the outside world. Many monks, fearing subordination to the episcopate and entanglement in worldly affairs, went out of their way to avoid ordination.[130] In reality, of course, it was impossible for monks to separate themselves completely from the world. Monasteries depended on complex connections both with local economies and with civil and ecclesiastical power structures.[131] Nevertheless an ideology and an ideal of separation prevailed: the outside world was evil, a source of constant temptation. While bishops and preachers lived within the secular world and believed in their ability to change it, monks opted to preserve their purity by withdrawing from it. To ascetic zealots, even the Christian church establishment was irredeemably corrupted by its worldly compromises.

The mainstream church, as it gradually reconciled itself to coexistence with secular society and to the fact of a Christian empire, placed greater emphasis on embracing as many believers as possible, even if that required some compromise. The highest standards of ascetic perfection were simply not possible for most ordinary people. Rather than make the perfect the enemy of the good, church leaders such as Augustine accepted the limits of human nature when they reassured their congregants that marriage, while not quite as praiseworthy as virginity, would nevertheless earn its own recognition in the hereafter. Some would see their efforts rewarded thirtyfold, some sixtyfold, some a hundredfold.[132] Augustine spoke of a "mixed church," a worldly institution that in this life included elements of both heavenly and earthly "cities," a mixture of wheat and tares—and it was for God alone to know which was which.[133] Athanasius, likewise, invoked biblical typology

---

130. See pp. 234–235 above, and further examples cited in next chapter, pp. 261–263; also Brakke 1995a, chap. 2.

131. These interconnections are well explored by Wipszycka 1994.

132. Following the parable of the sower, Matthew 13:8.

133. Augustine, *On Christian Doctrine* bk. 3, commenting on Tyconius' second rule of exegesis, the "twofold division of the Lord's Body." See also, e.g., *City of God* 18.49.

in dividing Christians into three groups: beginners, advanced, and perfect.[134] Such a system necessarily implied a need for compromise at the earlier stages, and also aimed to discourage ascetics, consecrated virgins, or other "elites" from thinking themselves better than ordinary believers and thus falling prey to the sin of pride. Monastic institutions, for their part, were conflicted. On the one hand, they demanded a perfect discipline and enforced an equality among the brethren that was intended in theory to wipe away the social distinctions of the outside world. At the same time, however, they recognized the need for differentiating experts and beginners and subjecting the latter to the firm guidance of the former.[135]

The monks' fear of individual achievement, and their ambivalent attitude toward ordination, clashed uneasily with their institutions' professed devotion to hierarchy and obedience. Mary Douglas predicts that groups that deny the legitimacy of disagreement and conflict will have no mechanisms for resolving it, and groups that distrust leadership, ambition, and personal excellence will have difficulty choosing leaders and governing themselves. Unless some coercive pressure works to hold the group together, internal conflicts and disputes over leadership frequently end in schism.[136] Inability to tolerate disagreement was a problem for the late antique church generally, but all the more so for world-renouncing ascetic groups who placed such a high premium on maintaining internal harmony. While the modern examples used in Douglas' studies clearly differentiate between egalitarian and hierarchical forms of organization, late antique monasteries mixed elements of both. Egalitarianism manifested itself in a conscious effort to erase the social distinctions of the outside world, and in a thoroughgoing distrust of personal ambition, together with a desire to restrain the "competitive" atmosphere that might result from the unrestrained ascetic zeal of individual monks. Hierarchy, meanwhile, found support in the institution's emphasis on humility and obedient submission to one's spiritual mentors. It existed partly as a consequence of monastic communities' own respect for their founders, elders, and teachers; partly, too, it was imposed from outside by the necessity of submission to episcopal authority.

The tension between these two principles, between respect for authority and mistrust of it, could not be addressed directly without threatening the harmony of the community. The same passions and conflicts that were care-

---

134. Brakke 1995a, pp. 170–182.
135. Thus John Cassian, discussed in Leyser 2000, pp. 55–59.
136. See, e.g., Douglas and Wildavsky 1982, pp. 119–122, 147, 178; Douglas 1986, pp. 23, 40.

fully suppressed within the monastery could more safely be directed against external foes, whether real or imagined. Douglas finds that groups with a "sectarian" mind-set tend to preserve their unity by focusing on "demonic" external forces, whether literally (through fears of magic and witchcraft) or figuratively (by "demonizing" human adversaries.)[137]

It took no special effort to persuade monks—who regularly warned each other against demon-inspired false visions, and blamed the devil for their lapses and bouts with temptation—that they were engaged in a struggle against cosmic evil.[138] Zealots who smashed idols and destroyed temples believed that they were battling the demons in their very lairs.[139] How easy was it to distinguish between spiritual and worldly enemies? "Demonization" in the literal sense—the identification of worldly opponents with Satan—has been argued to be a defining characteristic of early Christian mentality.[140] For monks, in light of their day-to-day battles with the demonic, the temptation must have been particularly strong. This, perhaps, may go some way toward explaining the apparent prominence of monks in extremist attitudes and behavior.

Extremism in the pursuit of holiness needed to be regulated and directed into proper channels, lest it get out of control. Ecclesiastical authorities were concerned either to restrain the zealots' behavior, or to exploit it and redirect it against the right targets. The monks' obsessions were not necessarily those of their bishops. Athanasius made great efforts to urge the monasteries to take theological controversy more seriously, rebuking them for a well-meaning "hospitality" that allowed them to harbor Arians or Melitians.[141] Against paganism, meanwhile, the monks apparently needed little encouragement. Athanasius and his successors went out of their way to enlist monks in their struggles against both. But even the powerful patriarchs of Alexandria could themselves be vulnerable to monastic zeal, as Theophilus found when he was forced to yield before a threatening mob of anti-Origenist monks.[142]

Because of their relative distance (both geographical and moral) from secular life and urban centers, monasteries were well positioned to take religious and political stances that might contradict the policies of imperial and episcopal authorities. In the late fifth and sixth centuries, Egyptian and

137. See, e.g., Douglas 1996, chap. 7.
138. See generally Coyle 1998, pp. 229–249.
139. See previous chapter, p. 180.
140. Pagels 1995.
141. Brakke 1995a, p. 134. See also Goehring 1997, pp. 61–84.
142. Socrates *HE* 6.7.

Syrian monasteries would become centers of anti-Chalcedonian resistance.[143] In ninth-century Spain, most of the "martyrs" seem to have emerged from country monasteries rather than from among the more assimilated Christians of Cordoba proper.[144] In modern times, leaders of extremist groups typically belong to educated elites, in many cases receiving their intellectual formation in a single-sex school environment steeped in religious texts and developing a strong sense of resentment against the corruptions of popular culture.[145]

The more tightly organized monastic institutions that have left us *Rules* and other normative texts went out of their way to impose discipline and hold back zealous behavior. Ascetic groups and communities with a looser structure, less firmly under hierarchical control, might have been even more conducive to extremism and certainly less able to restrain it. The key, Mary Douglas argues, is separation from the world, if not in practice then at least in ideology. Extremist violence of the sort described in this chapter, so far as we can tell, seems to have been particularly associated with monks who "lived apart"—whether in regimented communities or in looser *lavra*-style groupings—as opposed to *apotaktikoi*, *qyama* and other ascetics who remained integrated into worldly society.[146]

Most dangerous of all, in the eyes of the establishment—perhaps to a lesser extent in reality—were those monks who refused to confine themselves to an institutional context. Monastic groups who wandered from place to place, recognizing the authority of no particular bishop, were thought to pose especially disruptive influences as they intruded into local communities and upset existing power relations and authority structures. To be sure, local authorities often found it convenient (as in Antioch after the Statue Riots of 387) to avoid culpability by blaming civil disorder on travellers, rustics, beggars, and other outside agitators.[147] Prejudices of observers against these "extremists"—and against monasticism in general—no doubt affect the accounts provided in our sources.[148] Those who disapproved of the zealots' lifestyle would not have neglected any opportunity to call atten-

143. See conclusion, p. 327.

144. See previous chapter, p. 202.

145. See Juergensmeyer 2000, pp. 187–215. For the biographical and intellectual background of some key figures in modern Islamic extremism, see Kepel 1984 and now Kepel 2002.

146. On *apotaktikoi* ("renouncers"), *qyama*, and their relation to coenobitic monasticism, see Griffith 1995, Rousseau 1995, Goehring 1992, Judge 1977.

147. Antioch: Chrysostom, *Homilies on the Statues* 3.3; Libanius *Or.* 19.

148. On the prejudices even many mainstream Christians held regarding radical asceticism, see John Chrysostom, *Against the Opponents of the Monastic Life.*

tion to examples of their extreme behavior—even while similar violence carried out by more familiar and less marginalized groups such as *parabalani,* circus factions, or rowdy urban youths might attract less notice.[149]

Nevertheless, zealous wanderers and outsiders often did provoke explosions of violent conflict. Alexander the Akoimete, whom we have already encountered as a destroyer of temples, provides an excellent illustration of this problem. Alexander based his ascetic lifestyle of wandering, apostolic poverty upon a literal application of gospel precepts.[150] Like Antony, he had first been inspired to the monastic life by Christ's command, "Go, sell all you have and give it to the poor."[151] At first Alexander joined a settled monastic community, but quickly took offense at their ownership of property and their worldly concerns.[152] Confronting the abbot, he asked, "Is what is written in the gospel true?" They all thought he had been possessed by a demon. He explained, "Because none of you are living according to it!" and angrily left.[153] After several years alone in the desert had strengthened his faith, he began his career of holiness by burning a temple, risking martyrdom, and converting a village of pagans.[154] Again living as a hermit in the desert, he began to accumulate disciples and to formulate an ascetic program.

As Christ had instructed the apostles to do, Alexander and his followers wandered from place to place, having nothing but one tunic apiece. They "took no thought for tomorrow,"[155] which meant that they made no provision for their own livelihood but remained continually dependent upon the charity they begged from others. They praised God "day and night" in the perpetual hymnody that became the distinctive trademark of the Akoimete monks.[156] Unlike the Egyptian monks, who supported themselves and

149. The *parabalani* were a company of several hundred strongmen employed by the Alexandrian patriarchs as "stretcher bearers" for the hospitals, who were frequently implicated in urban violence: see *C. Th.* 16.2.42 and 43.

150. My discussion of Alexander here relies upon that of Caner 2002, chap. 4, who offers a thorough analysis of the notion of "apostolic poverty" as practiced in the fourth and fifth centuries.

151. Matthew 19:21; *Life of Alexander* 5–6. Cf. *Life of Antony* 2.

152. His criticisms seem thus to have echoed those of Isaac of Antioch on fifth-century coenobitic practice in Syria: see Vööbus 1960a, vol. 2, pp. 146–150.

153. *Life of Alexander* 7–8.

154. Discussion in previous chapter, p. 187. Not content with merely converting them to Christianity, Alexander attempted also to convert them to the ascetic life. He instructed them to sell their goods and follow him into the desert for a day to be fed by miracles. "I have given you the milk," he said, "and now you will be ready for solid food." *Life of Alexander* 18–19.

155. Matthew 6:34.

156. *Life of Alexander* 27–30.

occupied much of their time weaving baskets, Alexander and his followers disdained manual labor because it would interrupt their perpetual prayer and because they thought it incompatible with the command "take no thought for tomorrow." This refusal to work was particularly objectionable to contemporary critics and to the church establishment, who used the issue to measure these disorderly wanderers against the ideal of settled Pachomian-style coenobitism. Rejection of labor was condemned as one of the defining characteristics of the Messalian "heresy."[157]

This combination of wandering and dependence on charity that Alexander called "apostolic" could easily develop into an intolerable social burden, particularly in the towns and military outposts on the margins of the Syrian desert through which the Akoimetes began their movement. Communities that hardly managed to feed their own people could scarcely be expected to support large groups of begging strangers who were able-bodied but refused to work. The citizens of Palmyra closed the gates to them, saying, "How can we feed this mob? If they enter, we will starve."[158]

Strain on food supplies was not the only problem that complicated relations between these wandering monks and the communities they visited. In Antioch, Alexander and his followers occupied an abandoned public bath in the center of the city, even though the bishop, Theodotus, had already made it clear that they were not welcome. The Antiochenes were confronted with the prospect of a group of ill-clad strangers who took over public space in the heart of the city (most of the Antiochene monks tended to live well outside of town) and lived as squatters and beggars. Their pleas for charity, if Nilus of Ancyra is to be believed,[159] could be highly confrontational and even violent. In blatant disregard for existing local power structures, Alexander challenged and usurped the authority of both secular and ecclesiastical elites by public demonstrations of blunt *parrhesia* on behalf of the city's poor. Although ordinary people flocked to him, the clergy hated him because he was depriving them of followers and undercutting their own claims to spiritual authority.[160] Violence soon erupted. When the bishop attempted

---

157. Epiphanius, *Panarion* 80; Theodoret *HE* 4.11. On this characterization of Messalianism see Caner 2002, chap. 3.

158. *Life of Alexander* 35, cursing the Palmyrenes as "Jews, even though they called themselves Christians." Cf. 34: A band of "rich scoundrels" asked, "Have you come to impoverish us?" and Alexander punished their lack of faith by inflicting a three-year drought on the area, following perhaps the example of Elijah. On Alexander's itinerary in Syria, see Gatier 1995.

159. Nilus of Ancyra, *Ep.* 1.129 (PG 79.137C), discussed above, p. 214.

160. *Life of Alexander* 38–41. The subdeacon Malchus called Alexander "a magician."

to expel the Akoimetes by extralegal means, sending a band of *lecticarii* (muscular "stretcher-bearers" attached to the church's hospitals) to assault them, the Antiochene poor who had flocked to Alexander rose in his defense. Only an appeal to the *magister militum per orientis* secured Alexander's expulsion.[161]

When the Akoimetes reached Constantinople, events followed a similar pattern. Again they took over public space at the very heart of the city, this time the martyrium of Menas (originally a temple of Poseidon) on the acropolis of old Byzantium, within sight of the Hagia Sophia and the imperial palace.[162] The established monasteries of Constantinople tended to be situated toward the edges of the city, and, more importantly, had generally been founded on land donated by powerful secular patrons at the imperial court.[163] Alexander enjoyed no such patronage, and indeed seems to have resumed his usual practice of publicly rebuking the wealthy and powerful, "for he was zealous to the extreme."[164] Although Alexander arrived with only twenty-four followers, their number soon swelled to three hundred as other monks left nearby monasteries to join them. This poaching of followers from existing monastic establishments was profoundly irritating to the local archimandrites and clergy. Having turned both secular and ecclesiastical authorities against himself, Alexander was expelled from the city. The *Life of Alexander* is deliberately vague on this point, but the official pretext for his expulsion seems to have been a formal charge of heresy (probably "Messalianism") brought against him before the city prefect.[165] The *Life of Hypatius* describes how the Akoimetes, having been beaten and chased from the city by a mob, took refuge at Rufinianae. The bishop of Chalcedon then sent a gang of *lecticarii, decani*, beggars, laborers, and clerics to threaten violence against both Alexander and Hypatius. This dependence on private hired muscle, rather than government authorities or imperial soldiers, suggests that the bishop was acting outside the law, albeit probably with the tacit approval of some high imperial officials. But a timely dispatch of troops by the empress Pulcheria drove away the mob. Pulcheria's intervention should be understood as a gesture of support for Hypatius rather than for

161. *Life of Alexander* 41.

162. For the events in Constantinople, *Life of Alexander* 43–50; cf. also *Life of Hypatius* 41. On the location: Dagron 1974, pp. 395–396; Janin 1953, pp. 345–347.

163. For example, the monastery of Dalmatius, in Psamathia several miles to the southwest, or that of Hypatius, across the Bosporus at Rufinianae near Chalcedon.

164. *Zelotes gar en eis akron*: *Life of Hypatius* 41.

165. *Life of Alexander* 48–49: "It was reported to the prefects that Alexander was a heretic come to ravage the church."

Alexander—there is no evidence that the ascetically-minded empress made any attempt to prevent Alexander's condemnation or expulsion from Constantinople. The imperial authorities, while tolerating brutal violence against a troublesome outsider with no powerful protectors, stepped in to prevent that violence from falling upon an established monastic foundation whose revered leader had close ties to the imperial court.[166] The Akoimetes eventually reestablished themselves in a new and less provocative location some distance outside the city. After the death of Alexander, they gradually evolved into a more "respectable," settled monastic establishment, retaining only their perpetual hymnody as a distinctive feature.[167]

Alexander's sojourns in Antioch and Constantinople demonstrate the ways in which bands of wandering zealots could strain resources and usurp the authority of local elites, creating tense confrontations that could easily explode into violence. The Syrian monk Barsauma, whose fifty-four year ascetic career alternated between phases of fixed residence in a monastery near Samosata and periods of wandering through the Roman east, created even more confrontational situations as he and his followers moved across Palestine. Like Alexander, Barsauma understood himself to be performing a holy duty, although in this case the scriptural model seems to have been not so much the missionary apostles as the army of Joshua in the land of the Canaanites. The new "Canaanites" were the Jews, Samaritans, and pagans who occupied the Christian holy land, and Barsauma and his followers destroyed their temples and synagogues wherever they found them.[168] It is no wonder, then, that these wandering monks aroused violent opposition nearly everywhere they went. After the bloody incident in which Barsauma's monks stoned and killed Jews who were praying at the Temple site, the local Christian clergy and Christian magistrates joined together with the Jews to complain to the empress Eudocia, then in residence in Bethlehem: "Many brigands have descended from Mesopotamia, dressed in the respectable habit of monks, and they have made war upon the city and devastated it."[169] Local authorities and residents put aside religious differences

---

166. On Hypatius' ties to Pulcheria and to the emperor, see Holum 1982, pp. 134–138.

167. On the Akoimetes after Alexander: *Life of Marcellus* (trans. Baguénard); cf. Baguénard 1988, pp. 219–240; Dagron 1970; Bacht 1951.

168. See discussion on Barsauma in previous chapter, pp. 188–189. On the Joshua comparison, cf. assorted statements in monastic literature comparing the Israelites in Sinai to monks in the desert, e.g., Chrysostom, *Against the Opponents of the Monastic Life* 3.6.

169. *Life of Barsauma*, miracles 61–66. See discussion in previous chapter, pp. 188–189.

for the moment, considering the age-old opposition of *ecclesia* and *synagoga* to be of little importance next to the clear and present danger that this band of violent intruders posed to public order and to law-abiding citizens of all faiths. The language of *latrocinium* and the discourse of false pretenses served the situation well: Eudocia was persuaded to send soldiers against the monks, arresting them as common criminals and murderers.[170]

It did not necessarily take a large group of such zealots to stir up trouble. The monk Fronto accomplished this all by himself when he arrived in the quiet Spanish town of Huesca near Tarragona as a one-man inquisition determined to root out hidden "Priscillianism."[171] Acting on the ill-considered advice of Consentius,[172] who relayed Fronto's report to Augustine, Fronto at first feigned sympathy for "Priscillianist" beliefs and gained the confidence of an old woman in order to uncover information that he used to launch a blistering series of accusations first against Severus, a prominent local priest, and then against several bishops supposedly guilty of shielding him. A true holy man, it was commonly expected, would not fear to confront the powerful if they had done wrong. Hypocrisy and hidden evil had to be exposed, even at the risk of martyrdom. Alexander the Akoimete deserved praise above all because "he did not fear the imperial power, nor the threats of prefects, nor the evil counsels of bishops."[173] Fronto, however, had set his sights particularly high: the presbyter Severus, in addition to being a prominent and well-respected community leader in his own right, just happened to be a relative of the *comes* Asterius, supreme military commander of Spain. Fronto, by contrast, was a mere monk, and an outsider as well, only recently arrived in Tarragona to begin a monastery there.[174]

170. They would have been quickly executed as such, had not God intervened (as Barsauma's hagiographer claimed) with timely miracles: *Life of Barsauma*, op. cit.

171. The source is Fronto's own account of his adventures, which he sent to Consentius, then living in the Baleares. Consentius in turn relayed the story to Augustine, where it is preserved as *Ep.* 11* in the Divjak collection. My remarks here follow the analysis of Van Dam 1986. Van Dam dates the incident to 418 or early 419, Consentius' letter to late 419, and Augustine's highly unsympathetic answer (the treatise entitled *To Consentius, Against Lying*) to c. 420. Van Dam argues forcefully that Fronto's accusations are not to be taken as evidence for the actual existence of any sort of "underground" Priscillianist movement in early fifth-century northern Spain.

172. Consentius, incidentally, also had at least an indirect connection to the anti-Jewish riots on Minorca organized in 418 by bishop Severus, whom Consentius mentions in his next letter to Augustine (*Ep.* 12*). On the Minorca incident see Bradbury 1996, Demougeot 1982, E. D. Hunt 1982.

173. *Life of Alexander* 3.

174. His connections with bishop Patroclus of Arles (412–426), who encouraged his efforts, may perhaps suggest that he had originally come from that region.

Although Consentius praised Fronto as "a man in whom the Holy Spirit kindles the most ardent flames of zeal for the faith," the people of Tarragona were even less receptive to this characterization than was Augustine.[175] All parties quickly closed ranks around Severus. Fronto, threatened violently on several occasions, was lucky to escape with his life. Had he been killed, Consentius would no doubt have held him up as a martyr. As the controversy continued, the unified opposition to Fronto eroded somewhat. The *comes* Asterius, despite his close connections to the accused, nevertheless seemed to recognize Fronto's status as a holy man: he attempted to guarantee the monk a fair hearing, restrained the tempers of others who wished to do him violence, and even entreated his prayers for the success of the army.[176] Still, Fronto's difficulties offer ample illustration of the various ways in which a would-be holy man's claims to act with divine approval might be contested by an unsympathetic audience. Even a "miraculous" event—a lethal stroke that befell a man who had violently threatened the monk, which for Fronto signified divine action against an enemy of the faith—could be challenged. His rivals promptly accused him of having killed the man with magic, demanding that he be punished as a sorcerer as well as a calumniator.[177]

Through these examples we may begin to discern a pattern by which the intolerance of individual zealots frequently ran into opposition in local communities that closed ranks against the outsider in defense of their internal peace.[178] While holy men were expected to give thought only to the faith, those who lived in communities and particularly those responsible for maintaining order at the local level had to balance religion against the more prosaic concerns of getting along with one another on a day-to-day basis. Consentius may have thought that the threat of hidden Priscillianism was enough to make "the barbarians seem trivial by comparison"—a singularly inapt

175. This incident seems to have inspired Augustine to address to Consentius the treatise *On Lying*, in which he argued that deceit and dishonesty of the sort used by Fronto could never be justified even in the service of a good cause.

176. *Ep.* 11*.12: "Forgive, I pray you, servant of Christ, if by chance, we have in anything offended, and when you see me marching off to battle with the army, accompany us with the power of your prayers." (Eno trans.)

177. *Ep.* 11*.13. There were even a few people, "most lacking in faith," who said that it was nothing more than coincidence. See remarks on this incident in Brown 1995b, p. 71.

178. Cf. Rita Lizzi's remark on the three clerics killed by pagans at Anaunia in 397, as described in Maximus of Turin, *Sermons* 105–106 (see discussion of this incident in previous chapter, pp. 173–174): "The Church immediately learnt that it was still dangerous to send to a rustic community extraneous members, evidently ignorant of local political and religious alliances." Lizzi 1990, p. 173.

statement considering the situation in 418–19 as Vandals, Sueves, and Visigoths ravaged the Iberian peninsula—but the local secular and ecclesiastical authorities in Tarragona were more interested in maintaining public harmony than in tracking down heretical books that a respected priest and community leader might or might not have had discreetly hidden in his library. These "limits of intolerance," in the words of Peter Brown, formed the basis for opposition to the disruptive and often violent efforts of zealous monastic wanderers.[179]

Undisciplined itinerant holy men such as Alexander and especially Barsauma were the obvious inspiration for the fearsome image of the violent monk, a popular stereotype common to Christians as well as pagans. With their black robes, their ragged hair, their bare feet and clanking chains, their faces pale from fasting, and above all their chanting of hymns, monks stood out in popular imagination as symbols of the violence that was so intimately associated with Christian zeal.[180] As "soldiers of Christ" they occupied an appropriate place in the vanguard of violent Christianization and seem to have had a particular symbolic association with the downfall of temples and synagogues. Theodore, leader of the Jewish community of Minorca, dreamed in 418 that he saw his synagogue in ruins and occupied by hymn-singing monks. A few weeks later, the synagogue was destroyed. What is particularly striking about Theodore's vision is that monks played no actual role in the demolition, which was carried out by local Christians led by their bishop Severus.[181] Even though there is no evidence for any actual monastic presence on Minorca, still the image of the psalm-chanting monk was the most

179. Brown 1995d, p. 50: "Spasmodic, largely unpredictable violence of this kind was inconsistent with the perpetual, controlled violence of a heavily governed society. If violence was to happen, it was essential that the traditional elites should not lose the monopoly of such violence. They did not want it to slip into the hands of erratic outsiders." Brown's argument here can be supplemented with Judith Shklar's emphasis on the dangers of hypocrisy (Shklar 1984, esp. pp. 48–49): the intolerant, zealous, and anti-hypocritical nature of the violence practiced by these "outsiders" rendered its own perpetrators vulnerable, providing the means to undermine their legitimacy. The more extreme the standard they demanded of others, the more liable they became to accusations of failing to meet it themselves.

180. Various elements of the stereotype: Jerome, *Ep.* 22.28; Libanius, *Or.* 30, quoted above, p. 210. The chanting of the monks terrified the governor of Antioch, causing him to adjourn court and flee the city: Libanius *Or.* 45.26. Cf. Basil *Ep.* 207 (c. 375), defending his monks' practice of psalmody against certain bishops who saw it as a dangerous innovation, and Chrysostom, *Against Opponents of the Monastic Life* 2.2, reporting accusations that the monks "bewitched" youths with their psalmody.

181. *Letter of Severus* 16. See bibliography cited above, n. 172.

common symbolic representation of the process by which Christians seized control of worship space from older faiths.[182] Olympius, leader of the pagan faction that had barricaded itself inside the Alexandrian Serapeum in 391, heard voices inside the temple singing "alleluia"—a practice at that time most commonly associated with monks—and understood it as an omen that the temple would soon fall. Although monks bearing relics of John the Baptist eventually arrived to occupy the ruins, the actual demolition had been carried out by imperial soldiers under the orders of bishop Theophilus.[183] But here again, the monks served best as symbols of Christian triumph.

The monks thus played a double role within the imagination of the Christian audience. The same holy men whose hymnody signalled the downfall of idols and the triumph of the faith could easily turn their zealous violence against Christian targets—at which point they came more to resemble Eunomius' polemical caricature of Eustathius: a false ascetic, "pale with fasting and murderous with rage, cloaked in black, a saint accursed."[184] The Christian holy man can be understood as the embodiment, in a single person, of the religious values and expectations of the Christian community. As a "moral catalyst," in the words of Peter Brown, the saint's role was to express these values in an absolute way, unencumbered by the needs of ordinary people or worldly authorities to balance them against practical considerations.[185] Alexander the Akoimete could follow the gospel to the letter, taking no thought for tomorrow, and Barsauma could rid the holy land of the infidel. It is no paradox that Christian authorities glorified the holy man's divine zeal even while they did their best to restrain the excesses of actual monks. The holy man inspired ordinary Christians precisely because he never compromised in the ways that they themselves often had to.

182. Cf. the miniature depicting bishop Theophilus standing upon the ruins of the Serapeum: Bauer and Strzygowski 1906.

183. Olympius' vision: Sozomen *HE* 7.15. Generally on the riots of 391 and the destruction of the Serapeum: Rufinus *HE* 11.22–30, Socrates *HE* 5.16–17, Sozomen *HE* 7.15, Theodoret *HE* 5.22.

184. Eunomius, *Second Apology,* quoted and challenged by Gregory of Nyssa, *Against Eunomius* 1.5 (trans. NPNF). See discussion of this remark in Vaggione 1993, p. 203. Compare Evagrius, who explained "malnutrition and its attendant pallor" as a symptom of smoldering anger (*Praktikos* 11, trans. Bamberger).

185. This is the theme of Brown 1983. Cf. the sociologist Edward Shils, quoted by Brown on p. 7: "What sociologists and social anthropologists call the central values or belief system of a society can be lived up to only partially, fragmentarily, intermittently and only in an approximate way . . . For the rest of the time, the ultimate values of the society, what is sacred to its members, are suspended amidst the distractions of concrete tasks." Shils 1975, p. 4.

7. "Sanctify Thy Hand by the Blow"

Problematizing Episcopal Power

This chapter examines how Christians sought to regulate power within the church, the right and wrong ways in which violence might be used, and the proper relation between religious authority and secular power. Where chapter 2 saw Christians using the interpretive framework of martyrdom and persecution to try to define a proper role for the Christian emperor within the church, this chapter treats the opposite problem: the assumption of secular power by leaders of the church. Over the course of the fourth century, Christian bishops came more and more to exercise varieties of power—political, economic, judicial, even on occasion military—traditionally regarded as "secular" or "worldly." Fourth-century Christians conceived of this power as being violent in nature. Powerful bishops who used force to intimidate rivals or silence critics were seen to be corrupted by their exercise of such power, in a creeping secularization that threatened to undermine the spiritual authority that defined their position within the Christian community. Classical political discourses about power and rulership, legitimate government and tyranny, and the corrupting potential of unchecked power came in the late fourth and early fifth centuries to be translated into the religious sphere in order to describe the conduct of bishops who acted more and more like secular potentates. This chapter outlines the polemical construction of the "tyrant-bishop" as defined against his counterpart, the idealized bishop of hagiography who manages to combine the charismatic zeal of the holy man with the effective power of the institutionalized episcopate. Violence, and its representation, offers us a window into the ways in which late antique Christians constructed and contested different models of religious authority. Stories of violence helped to define the limits of such authority, by revealing what contemporaries considered to be right and wrong uses of power.

A single blow of the hand is certainly a far less dramatic manifestation of violence than gruesome martyrdoms, deadly riots, or spectacular destructions of temples. It can, however, prove to be every bit as significant for our purpose. Particularly informative are those examples that illuminate the margins of acceptability—actions and practices that were not consistently accepted or condemned but rather subject to endless controversy. Two stories, describing what is essentially the same relatively minor act— one person raising his hand to strike another—demonstrate how the same physical fact of violence may be presented in completely opposite ways, to be celebrated or condemned depending upon where one stands.

In the first example, a hagiographer praises a saint's zealous blow against heresy and blasphemy. Besa's *Life of Shenoute* tells of a confrontation that supposedly transpired at the Council of Ephesus in 431:

> It happened on one occasion that our holy fathers convened a synod to anathematize the impious Nestorius, and my father the prophet Apa Shenoute was also there together with the holy Cyril, the archbishop of Alexandria. When they went into the church to set out the seats and sit down, they set out in the middle of the assembly another seat and placed upon it the four holy Gospels.[1] When the impious Nestorius came in with a great display of pride and shamelessness, he then picked up the four holy Gospels, placed them on the ground, and sat down in the chair. When my father Apa Shenoute saw what Nestorius had done, he leaped quickly to his feet in righteous anger in the midst of our holy fathers, seized the Gospels, picked them up from the ground, and struck the impious Nestorius in the chest, saying, "Do you want the Son of God to sit on the ground while you sit on the chair?" In reply, the impious Nestorius said to my father Apa Shenoute: "What business do you have in this synod? You yourself are certainly not a bishop, nor are you an archimandrite or a superior, but only a monk!" Our father replied and said to him: "I am he whom God wished to come here in order to rebuke you for your iniquities and reveal the errors of your impiety in scorning the sufferings of the only-begotten Son of God, which he endured for us so that he might save us from our sins. And it is he who will now pronounce upon you a swift judgment!" At that very moment Nestorius fell off his chair onto the ground, and in the midst of the synod of our fathers, he was possessed by the devil.[2]

1. A standard practice at church councils, symbolizing Christ's presence and presidency over the synod.

2. Besa, *Life of Shenoute* 128–130 (trans. Bell). The story probably could not have happened exactly as told, if only because Nestorius never actually appeared before the Cyrillian-dominated synod. However, Shenoute was in fact among the many

Much can, and will, be said of this passage, but for now it should be read in juxtaposition with another story. Palladius, in his *Dialogue on the Life of John Chrysostom*, describes this confrontation between John's archenemy, bishop Theophilus of Alexandria, and the so-called Tall Brothers, monks who followed the controversial teachings of Origen:

> Certain monks went down to Alexandria with their priests to ask Theophilus to state the reason why they were condemned to be cast out. He regarded them like a dragon with bloodshot eyes. He glared like a bull. With his temper beyond control he was at first livid, then sallow, and then smiling sarcastically. He snatched the pallium from the aged Ammonius, and twisting it around his neck he inflicted blows upon his jaw, making his nose bleed with his clenched fists, and kept crying out, "Anathematize Origen, you heretic!"[3]

The depiction of Theophilus by Palladius, a devoted supporter of John, offers us an excellent example of polemical construction. Theophilus here stands for the "tyrant-bishop," a figure who is made to speak to the unease felt by a Christian audience at the corrupting influence of secular power within the church, an embodiment of the ways in which that power could be abused. The tyrant-bishop of polemic is defined in opposition to the idealized bishop-saint and holy man of hagiography, and the tension between the two reveals the interaction between hopes and fears of how religious authority and episcopal power ought or ought not to be used.

These stories offer two views of what is essentially the same event: one person moved by anger to strike another. But they are seen from opposite perspectives, and endowed with opposite meanings. Shenoute, a zealous holy man, was driven by a divinely inspired outrage to strike down one who had committed blasphemy and sacrilege. Theophilus, a tyrant-bishop, himself thoroughly corrupted by power and wealth, gave way to base and unworthy impulses of anger, jealousy, and megalomania, and assaulted a venerable monk. These two stories represent alternative and opposing ways of presenting and interpreting a single act of violence, appropriate either for justification or for condemnation. In the tangled religious conflicts of the fourth and fifth centuries, these styles of representation found effective use in the hagiographical and polemical literature of opposing sides, such that the same act by the same person might be seen in opposite ways.

Egyptian archimandrites and monks who accompanied Cyril to Ephesus, as known from references in his own writings; cf. Emmel 1993, pp. 4–6. We will return to this legend in the next chapter.

3. Palladius, *Dialogue* 6 (trans. Meyer).

What was contested was not the fact of the deed, but rather its motivation and moral context.

Shenoute's confrontation with Nestorius fit the pattern of holy violence outlined in chapter 5. Nestorius, seen by our pro-Cyrillian source, embodied both the pernicious error of a heretic and the arrogant pride of a corrupt tyrant.[4] Nestorius' refusal to call Mary "Mother of God" *(Theotokos)* was construed by critics as a denial of Christ's divinity. In this story, his cavalier treatment of the Gospel—itself, as the Word of God, symbolizing the presence and presidency of Christ over the council—served as visible expression of the blasphemous teachings commonly attributed to his name. This act of blasphemy then provoked Shenoute to a "just wrath" *[djont ndukeon]*. He took up the Gospels with one hand and struck Nestorius with the other. When Nestorius fell to the ground in a fit of demonic possession, it was clear to all that God had passed judgment—a miracle declared the rightness of Shenoute's deed, divine violence confirming human.[5]

Theophilus' attack on the aged Ammonius could have been made to look the same way. If we had a hagiographical account of the Alexandrian bishop written by someone who shared Theophilus' bitter opposition to Origenism, it might have commended the bishop's "holy zeal" in striking down a "false monk" who concealed dangerous heresy under the pretense of holiness. Instead, we see the unjust act of a man who has lost control to base emotions. Theophilus raged like a bull, glared like a dragon: animal imagery underlined his "bestial" rage, his inability to keep within the proper limits of decorum and civilized behavior. Persecutors, in martyrological texts, were commonly represented in similar animalistic terms. The more torture the martyrs endured, the more the magistrates would scream, growl, and gnash their teeth as if they themselves were suffering pain.[6] Ideals of elite conduct,

---

4. On pride/arrogance as an attribute of the heretic, see Rousseau 1995, pp. 249–252. In the heresiology and polemical literature of the fifth century, Nestorius became an "arch-heretic," comparable in notoriety to Arius in the fourth century. "Arianism" and "Nestorianism" served as polemical constructions, embodying views far more extreme than had ever actually been held by their namesakes. Nestorius, much of whose own writing has survived, vehemently denied one of the most common charges against him, that he divided the person of Christ into "two Sons." On Arius as "arch-heretic," see Lyman 1993.

5. This particular paradigm of holy violence persisted in hagiography well into the Byzantine period. The tenth-century saint Luke of Steiris angrily struck a man who had insulted and mocked a pious stylite, and the man then fell to the ground in a fit of demonic possession: *Life of Luke of Steiris* 36.

6. Persecutors described in animalistic terms: see, e.g., *Acts of the Abitinian Martyrs.*

shared by pagans and Christians alike, condemned such unseemly displays of anger and losses of control.[7]

But in a late antique Christian setting, to be carried away by anger was not necessarily a bad thing. The context, the cause, and the target all mattered. Righteous outrage, in reaction to a blasphemy or other perceived insult or injury to the faith, was understood to come from God.[8] Shenoute did not so much lose control of his temper as yield it to the divine will. But when the anger comes not from God but from one's own flawed human nature, when rage is expressed against faith and justice and not on their behalf, then it becomes a defining characteristic of tyrants and persecutors.

The distinction between violent zeal on behalf of the faith, and violent rage against it, can be seen in another pair of examples. We have seen the emperor Valens portrayed in Nicene sources as a tyrannical persecutor of the orthodox. During a confrontation with the Nicene congregations of Edessa, those sources tell us, Valens gave way to an unseemly display of rage thoroughly typical of a tyrant-persecutor. When he heard that the Nicenes whom he had expelled from the churches were continuing to meet in a field outside the city, "it is said that he became so angry that he struck his praetorian prefect with his fist for not having driven them from there too."[9] Valens then ordered that all who continued to assemble there would be put to death. But the prefect Modestus, though himself a pagan,[10] had sufficient sense to delay executing the order and warn the Nicenes. When he found the entire congregation resolved to defy the emperor and die as martyrs, he then persuaded the emperor to back down.[11] Modestus, whose wise restraint prevailed even though he himself had suffered an indignity from the emperor, even though he himself was not one of the orthodox, is held up by

7. On norms of elite behavior: Brown 1992, pp. 48–58, and 58–61 on emperors specifically; Matthews 1989, pp. 231–252; Harris 2001.

8. See discussions of divine anger in chapter 1, pp. 31–32, and of holy zeal in chapter 5, pp. 179–191.

9. Rufinus *HE* 11.5. Compare Socrates *HE* 4.18 and Sozomen *HE* 6.18.

10. According to Rufinus; Sozomen however calls him an "Arian," presumably meaning a member of the Homoian church favored by Valens. *PLRE*, s.v. Modestus 2, speculates that he may have converted to Christianity at some point during Valens' reign. But the confusion may simply represent Nicene sources' common polemical strategy of equating Arians with pagans: see D. H. Williams 1997.

11. A parallel may be drawn between Modestus' role in this episode, that of the wise advisor who moderates the emperor's anger, and that of the quaestor Eupraxius before Valens' brother, Valentinian, in the case of the *Innocentes* of Milan: see Ammianus 27.7–8.

the Nicene sources in order to provide a sharp contrast to Valens' disgraceful behavior.[12]

Nicene sources also used Valentinian, a supporter of their cause, as a positive contrast to the heretic and persecutor Valens. Although Valens' angry display at Edessa finds close parallel in Ammianus' accounts of Valentinian's lethal temper, ecclesiastical historians are interested in drawing contrasts, not parallels, between the two brothers, and thus they give opposite meaning to similar behavior.[13] During the reign of Julian, Valentinian had been an officer in the pagan emperor's bodyguard. One day, Theodoret says, the emperor went to sacrifice in the temple of Fortune. A temple attendant sprinkled purifying water on those who entered; when a few drops fell on Valentinian's cloak, he exclaimed, "I am not purified, but defiled!" and struck the priest. Julian exiled him for this offense. In the context of Christian ecclesiastical historiography, there was nothing inappropriate about Valentinian's angry outburst. This story serves to introduce the future emperor and establish his credentials as a devout Christian, who stood up to the persecutor, bore witness to the faith, and was not afraid to endure exile, a mild form of martyrdom.[14] Valentinian's violence, unlike that of Valens, served a good cause.

When the Monophysite holy man Sergius entered the main church in the city of Amida, interrupted services, seized and then struck in the face a Chalcedonian presbyter who was performing the liturgy, the Monophysite

12. This despite the fact that the same Nicene sources also make Modestus responsible for carrying out many other atrocities against the Nicenes, most notably the burning of a boat with eighty priests on board: Socrates *HE* 4.6, Sozomen *HE* 6.14, Theodoret *HE* 4.24; with commentary by Brennecke 1988, pp. 225–226, and Barnes 1993, p. 291 n. 90. The story, by the early fifth century, had grown considerably in the telling: Gregory of Nazianzus, a much more contemporary source, alludes to the incident (*Or.* 25.9–10 and 43.46) but implies only a single victim.

13. On Valentinian's anger see, e.g., Ammianus 27.7, 29.3, 30.6, 30.8.

14. Theodoret *HE* 3.16. Although Theodoret's version is the most elaborate, nearly all Christian histories covering Julian's reign seem to have felt compelled to account for Valentinian's actions under the brief interlude of pagan rule, showing him standing firm in his faith while many other Christians lapsed and sacrificed in the hope of winning imperial favor. Sources without a strong Nicene bias allow a similar heroism for Valens. Sozomen *HE* 6.6 says that Valentinian ostentatiously tore off the part of his cloak that had been touched by the water. Socrates *HE* 3.13 says that Valentinian, Valens, and Jovian chose to resign their commissions voluntarily, to protest Julian's policies—for Jovian this could not be true, because he was still present in a high-ranking post when Julian died. Other sources say that Valentinian was exiled for reasons more traditional in the context of Roman imperial politics—various omens had predicted that he would one day be emperor: Philostorgius *HE* 7.7 (by Constantius); *Chronicon Paschale* p. 364 (by Julian). See Brennecke 1988, pp. 126–127.

hagiographer and historian John of Ephesus praised the deed—which a Chalcedonian source would surely have called a horrible sacrilege—and recounted it as yet another proof of Sergius' sanctity.[15] When John Chrysostom reportedly struck a certain Memnon with his fist in the Church of the Apostles, and then forced him to take communion while still bleeding from the mouth, the incident appeared as one article of indictment among numerous other charges of misconduct brought against John at the Synod of the Oak. No explanation was offered as to what Memnon had done to provoke John's anger; to John's accusers, the mere fact of the incident was enough to demonstrate that he was unfit to hold episcopal office.[16] The Syrian holy man Macedonius was once visited by a bishop who sought to ordain him against his wishes. Macedonius, who spoke no Greek, did not understand what was happening until the ceremony was complete. When he found out how he had been tricked, he flew into a rage, struck the bishop with his staff, and stormed off. Theodoret, Macedonius' hagiographer, avoids giving a clear endorsement or condemnation of the saint's behavior, but rather presents it as proof of the innocence, simplicity, and contempt for the world typical of the ascetic hermit.[17]

Beating for the sake of discipline played a pervasive role in enforcing social and religious norms, as we have seen.[18] Within a specifically ecclesiastical context, attitudes toward disciplinary beating seem to have been far more complicated and troubled. Under what circumstances, if any at all, was it appropriate for religious authorities to use physical force for the purpose of discipline? There does not seem to have been any consistent or coherent canonical view that could be characterized as the authoritative position of late antique Christianity on the issue. Conflicting views on the legitimacy of such violence served as weapons in larger debates over the limits of episcopal power and particularly in envisioning the ways in which that power could be abused.

The *Apostolic Canons,* a collection probably deriving from the mid- or late fourth century Antiochene church, condemned the practice entirely: "If any bishop, presbyter or deacon strikes believers for having sinned, or un-

---

15. John of Ephesus, *Lives of the Eastern Saints* (Brooks ed., pp. 102–103). Cf. Harvey 1990a, pp. 72–73.

16. This is twenty-seventh of the twenty-nine charges brought against Chrysostom by John the Deacon. *Acts of the Synod of the Oak* preserved in summary by Photius; see translation in Kelly 1995, pp. 299–301. Memnon's rank is not specified and he is not otherwise known.

17. Theodoret *HR* 13.4.

18. See discussion in chapter 4, pp. 140–143.

believers for having done wrong, and does this to instill fear in them, we order that he shall be deposed: for in no way did our Lord teach this—indeed he was struck and he did not strike back."[19] The existence of the rule suggests that some bishops and clergy were in fact claiming the right to discipline others by beating, and implies that they did so not just within their own congregations but also against non-Christians. In nearby Edessa, the rules attributed to bishop Rabbula (412–435) for the clergy and *bnay qyama* apparently allowed for the use of force under certain circumstances: "Do not scourge anyone, but if there is a reason because of which you are compelled to scourge, either scourge to frighten, or send the guilty ones to the judges of the world [the secular magistrates]."[20]

John Chrysostom, himself accused of using inappropriate violence, on another occasion offered an explanation that suggests how he might have justified such an act. In a sermon preached to his Antiochene congregation on the eve of the Riot of the Statues in 387, Chrysostom exhorted fellow believers to confront and rebuke those who blasphemed in public:

> I desire to ask one favor of you all . . . which is, that you will correct on my behalf the blasphemers of this city. And should you hear anyone in the public thoroughfare, or in the midst of the forum, blaspheming God; go up to him and rebuke him; and should it be necessary to inflict blows, spare not to do so. Smite him on the face; strike his mouth; sanctify thy hand with the blow.[21]

Here blasphemy, an offense or insult against the faith, provides sufficient cause to justify a violent response, and in such a context the Christian who strikes back apparently need not hold a position of authority over the target that would normally allow for disciplinary beating. By this reasoning, the monk Shenoute could strike the bishop Nestorius, or Sergius the Chal-

19. *Apostolic Canons* 8.47, Canon 27.

20. *Rules of Rabbula for the Priests and Qyama*, #35, ed. and trans. in Vööbus 1960b, p. 45. Cf. Blum 1969, p. 54. The *Life of Rabbula*, on which more below, also hints at the use of physical discipline. On ecclesiastical discipline, see now Dossey 2001.

21. Chrysostom, *Homilies on the Statues* 1.32 (trans. NPNF). Exactly what kind of "blasphemy" would justify such a public rebuke is not made clear, but the fact that the passage somewhat later refers to "Jews and Hellenes" as potential targets would seem to imply that a Christian could claim a fairly broad mandate in using his fists to defend the honor of the faith. Palladius (*Dialogue* 5.101–103) describes John using both the "pipe of reason" [*logikes syringos*] and the "staff of reproach" [*elegktike bakteria*] to discipline his clergy in Constantinople, and the charges brought against him at the Oak would seem to indicate that the latter was meant literally—while reference to his application of the "sword of reproach" [*tou elegktikou xiphous: Dialogue* 5.151] against the rich was to be understood metaphorically.

cedonian presbyter. But even an exercise of violent discipline that did not overturn normal lines of authority could be subject to controversy, as indicated by the inconsistent and contradictory canonical opinions on beating.

Inappropriate personal violence featured prominently in charges of misconduct brought against bishops. Although some authorities clearly allowed disciplinary beating, it was apparently sufficiently controversial that a bishop's political opponents could point to it as proof that he was "abusing" his ecclesiastical power. Chrysostom's accusers at the Synod of the Oak, not greatly concerned with consistency, managed to condemn him *both* for beating someone, *and* for wrongly suspending a deacon who had beaten one of his own servants.[22]

Bishop Rabbula, whose own canons allowed for some degree of disciplinary beating, himself ran into trouble on this issue—and the resulting controversy sheds considerable light on the ways in which such behavior might have been both justified and condemned. Barhadbeshabba Arbaya, in his *History of the School of Nisibis*, recounts an episode when Rabbula had travelled to Constantinople to participate in a synod and found himself accused of hitting clerics. Rabbula allegedly defended himself by invoking the example of Jesus driving the money changers out of the Temple. But Theodore of Mopsuestia, the great Antiochene teacher, contradicted him: Jesus overturned their tables, and ordered them to leave, but he never hit anyone.[23]

Barhadbeshabba, a writer in the pro-Nestorian Antiochene tradition, presented this story in order to hold up Theodore as a great and saintly interpreter of scripture, and to contrast him against Rabbula's tyrannical behavior. Rabbula had attacked Theodore as the chief source of the heresy of Nestorius, ordered the burning of Theodore's books, and persecuted members of the Antiochene-leaning and pro-Nestorian school of Edessa.[24] Ibas, Rabbula's successor as bishop, denounced him as "the tyrant of Edessa." Barhadbeshabba's story served to show that Rabbula's vendetta against Theodore and the Antiochenes arose from nothing more than personal hatred and pettiness: Rabbula was angry that the teacher had reprimanded and corrected

22. Charge #27: Chrysostom struck Memnon (see p. 257 above). Charge #1: Chrysostom improperly removed the deacon John (one of Chrysostom's principal accusers) on the grounds that he had beaten his own servant, Eulalius.

23. Barhadbeshabba Arbaya, *Cause de la fondation des écoles*, pp. 66–67. Barhadbeshabba, a member of the Dyophysite or "Nestorian" church in Persia, was bishop of Helwan (in Mesopotamia) in the sixth century.

24. Eventually in 489 they were forced out of Edessa altogether, relocating across the Persian frontier to Nisibis, where they became a dominant center of learning in the Persian Dyophysite church: Vööbus 1965, pp. 24–32.

him.[25] As biased and problematic as this account may be, the original accusation bears a certain ring of authenticity. Rabbula's own canons did allow for beating, and reference to Christ and the money changers would have been a plausible way of defending the practice.[26] But such an exegesis could also just as easily be challenged: the actual gospel text is sufficiently ambiguous to support either Rabbula's reading or Theodore's.[27]

THE IDEAL BISHOP

The example of Rabbula, seen through contrasting views of hagiography and polemic, offers an opportunity to explore in more detail the interaction between the ideals expressed in the image of the sainted bishop/holy man, and the fears of corruption and abuse implicit in the construction of the tyrant-bishop. The *Life of Rabbula*, written by a disciple during the turbulent years after the bishop's death in 435, attempts to address a problem that had beset Christianity since the days of Constantine: the reconciliation of holiness and power.[28] In an age when bishops came more and more to resemble secular

25. See Blum 1969, pp. 54–55. Since Theodore died in 428, the trip to Constantinople mentioned here cannot be the same one described in the *Life of Rabbula* during which Rabbula supposedly preached against Nestorius (Overbeck 1865, pp. 198–199)—whose controversial statements on the *Theotokos* only began toward the end of that same year. Nau 1931 suggests that the argument between Rabbula and Theodore took place at a synod in Constantinople in 426, and that Rabbula made another visit to Constantinople sometime after 429 but before the Council of Ephesus, at which time he preached against Nestorius—the visit described in the *Life*. Barhadbeshabba does represent what later Nestorian tradition believed about Rabbula and about the causes of his hatred for Theodore. His account is supported in a more contemporary source, Ibas' *Letter to Mari* (see p. 269 below), written during Rabbula's lifetime, which charges that Rabbula turned against Theodore "because he had once reprimanded him in open synod."

26. "Cleansing the Temple" imagery is also used by Gregory of Nazianzus (*Or.* 21.31) to describe Athanasius' efforts against the Arians.

27. Matthew 21:12 says only that he drove them out *[exebalen]*. John 2:14–16 says that he used a whip of cords *[phragellion [= flagellum] ek skhoinion]*, but it is not clear whether he used the whip against the people or only—as Theodore claimed—on the livestock. Nau 1931 suggests that Theodore's interpretation reflects the same school of thought that produced the *Apostolic Canons'* blanket condemnation of physical discipline (see pp. 257–258 above). But Rabbula was not alone in his interpretation of the gospel story. Palladius, *Dialogue* 20.649–654, expressed hope that the enemies of John Chrysostom would be chastised by divine justice, just as "those who corrupted the law of Moses were driven out of the Temple by the Savior with a whip made of cords." (Meyer trans.)

28. *Life of Rabbula:* Overbeck 1865, pp. 159–209. Translations from the *Life* are mine. On Rabbula generally: Nau 1931, Peeters 1928, Blum 1969, Drijvers 1996, Har-

potentates, commanding great wealth, political influence, legal jurisdiction, and even organized violence, how could they avoid compromising their spiritual authority through the corrupting influence of worldly power?

Any religious movement that saw itself as a chosen "elect" group, a righteous minority in an unbelieving and sinful world, faced two choices: it could safeguard its own purity by segregating itself from the influences of secular society, or it could attempt the far more ambitious strategy of converting and reforming the world, bringing all people up to the same standard of holiness, envisioning an idealized universal community of believers. While much Christian thought ultimately looked toward the latter outcome, the nascent monastic movement of the early fourth century had chosen the former path. Antony, and many others who followed his example, chose to separate themselves from worldly society and its temptations by withdrawing into the desert. The ascetic saints' notorious aversion to ecclesiastical ordination, meanwhile, emphasized their desire to keep themselves apart from a clerical establishment increasingly compromised by its involvement in secular affairs. The ecclesiastical hierarchy, for its part, sought to circumscribe the potentially dangerous, independent, charismatic authority of these holy men within the regulated institutional framework of coenobitic monasticism.[29]

The *Life of Rabbula* sought to overcome this dichotomy by offering its subject as a different kind of holy man, a monk-bishop, who combined the charismatic holiness and ascetic virtue of the saint with the organized power and hierarchical legitimacy of the late antique episcopacy in a single ideal of leadership for the Christian community. Rabbula's early career as a monk and desert hermit served to establish his qualifications for the episcopacy, and his divine zeal and ascetic discipline offered an inspiring example to all the people of Edessa, transforming the entire city (in the idealized presentation of the *Life*) into the veritable image of a monastery. Where Antony found holiness in withdrawal from the world, Rabbula—who consciously modeled his early ascetic career after that of the famous Egyptian saint— used his sojourn in the desert to establish an authority that he could take back into the government of city and church. His renunciation of the world made him uniquely qualified to return and lead it: "Once I, listening to

vey 1994. My analysis of the *Life of Rabbula* is greatly indebted to that of Susan Ashbrook Harvey, who has kindly allowed me to use her unpublished paper, "Bishop Rabbula: Ascetic Tradition and Change in Fifth-Century Edessa."

29. This dichotomy was of course in considerable part a rhetorical construction, and actual monastic/clerical relations were much more complicated. Brakke 1995a, pp. 99–110 offers an excellent treatment of this issue.

Christ's word, gave up this evil world and followed him completely, to keep his commandments, and so now also I take up his command in faith and return again to the world in his strength."[30]

Holy men like Rabbula were considered such desirable candidates for ordination precisely because they did not desire it. The idea that power is best entrusted to those who do not seek it has a long history in political discourse and moral imagination, and stems from a fundamental distrust of human ambition. If "authority" is understood as a combination of power and legitimacy, then an appearance of dignified disinterest in power offers a promising way to legitimize one's exercise of that power. Roman emperors in the first centuries of the Principate were expected to assume imperial power only after a carefully choreographed show of reluctance that might include several public refusals—a practice that came to be imitated by many candidates for Christian episcopacy in the fourth century and after.[31] A religious system such as Christianity, which stressed the subordination of one's own will to that of God, was especially fearful of the destructive consequences of human pride –understood as rebellion against God—and ambition. When these desires drove men to compete with one another for ecclesiastical office, blood could be spilled within the walls of the church.[32] Leadership of the religious community was a duty to be reluctantly assumed when called by God, not a prize to be won. Ambition and lust for power, as we shall see, are defining characteristics of the tyrant-bishop. In Rabbula's case, ambition for church office was so alien to his character that he had to be dragged forcibly from his monastery to be ordained bishop of Edessa, and in the end submitted only because a miracle had made it clear that such was God's will:[33] "No desire for this honor ruled in my soul, and longings for it did not disturb my

---

30. Rabbula's words upon submitting to ordination: Overbeck 1865, pp. 171–172.

31. For an analysis of this motif in Roman imperial historiography see Béranger 1948. Cf. Plato, *Republic* 6.489b–c: "It is not the natural course of things that the helmsmen should beg the crew to be guided by them . . . everyone who needs to be governed should go to the door of the man who knows how to govern. The ruler should not implore his subjects to let themselves be ruled." (Desmond Lee trans. [London 1955]) As for those who displayed reluctance at ordination, some were very sincere (e.g., Ammonius, who cut off his ear and threatened to cut out his tongue if they would not leave him: Palladius, *Lausiac History* 11) and others perhaps less so (e.g., Ambrose, discussed by McLynn 1994, pp. 1–52).

32. Many of the violent riots for which fourth-century church history became notorious centered around disputed episcopal elections, such as those between Damasus and Ursinus in Rome or Paul and Macedonius in Constantinople: see generally T. Gregory 1979, MacMullen 1990b, McLynn 1992.

33. When the bishops had assembled in Antioch to discuss a replacement for the deceased bishop, Diogenes of Edessa, the Holy Spirit came upon them "as once it

heart. Thus I believe without a doubt that these things in truth have come from God."[34]

Because he had freely renounced his own wealth and property, he could be entrusted with the wealth and property of the church. Bishop Rabbula presented himself as a champion for the interests of the poor, and steered the ample material resources of the Edessene church into the provision of charity.[35] His own monastic experience of renunciation and deprivation provided the model for the regime of material austerity, physical asceticism, and moral discipline he sought to impose on church and clergy and ultimately upon all Edessa. Rabbula sold off expensive silver table-settings, and refrained from constructing any new lavish or monumental church buildings, in order to conserve money for charity.[36] Even as bishop, Rabbula continued to live like a monk—we are told of his rigorous but not excessive fasting and his simple table service, his plain and austere clothing and "miserable" bed[37]—and his own example inspired or shamed those around him to follow suit. The *Life* describes his ascetic discipline radiating outward as if in concentric circles, enumerating its salutary effects upon, successively, those in his own household, who soon came to present, like him, the char-

---

had upon David" and caused them all to speak Rabbula's name with one voice: "I have found my servant Rabbula suitable to my service; through your hands I will anoint him with my holy oil." Overbeck 1865, p. 171.

34. Overbeck 1865, pp. 171–172. The monk-turned-bishop Apphy feared that while God had helped him as a solitary, he would now have to depend only upon the help of men: *Apophthegmata Patrum*, Greek alphabetical collection, discussed in Brakke 1995a, p. 103. The belief that religious leadership was best sought among those who did not desire it also ran strong in Islamic tradition. Compare this *hadith* attributed to the Prophet Muhammad: "Oh Abd al-Rahman, do not seek command. For if you are given it because you asked, you will bear the full responsibility. But if you are given it without asking, God will assist you in it." (Bulliet 1994, p. 1)

35. On Rabbula's charitable enterprises see Harvey 1994. "The poor" as objects of charity, for Rabbula, included not only the usual widows, orphans, invalids, and other unfortunates, but also the "holy poor," the monks and ascetics who had voluntarily chosen poverty for the sake of Christ. More generally on late antique bishops' rhetoric of alignment with the poor, see Brown 1992, chap. 3, and now Brown 2002.

36. So says the *Life*, at least: Overbeck 1865, pp. 172–173 and 190. But the legend of the "Man of God" of Edessa depicts Rabbula engaged in expensive building projects: Drijvers 1996, pp. 241–242. The *Life* is trying here to draw a contrast with the lavish spending habits associated with Ibas' episcopacy. Accusations of "excessive" building were often brought by critics of powerful bishops, e.g., Theophilus of Alexandria, credited by Palladius (*Dialogue* 6.22) with a "lithomania" worthy of Pharaoh; and Ambrose (see McLynn 1994, p. 55). Jerome (*Ep.* 52) preached against such excessive building.

37. Overbeck 1865, pp. 182–185.

acteristic ascetic pallor; the clergy of Edessa, who were admonished to shun worldly luxuries, avoid contact with women, and abstain from worldly quarrels; the *qyama* both male and female, and also coenobitic monks, subjected to strict supervision, segregation of the sexes, precise rules of dress and grooming, and separation from the world; and finally the laity, who were brought to such shame by his example that they thereafter shunned theater, circus, and arena, not to mention divorce, second marriages, gluttony, and luxury:

> Who . . . would dress himself in fine and elegant garments, to show himself boastfully on the streets of the city, without being ashamed of himself and despising his inclination toward pride, when he saw in what poor clothing that venerable one [Rabbula] stood at the head of the people? Or what immoderate person, taken over by the awful domination of gluttony, would consider the table of that holy one, who never even stilled his hunger, and would then remain inclined to eat greedily or drink immoderately?[38]

Rabbula, in essence, sought to make all Edessa into a monastery.[39] The Christian community, commonly imagined as the idealized "body" of Christ, became for him an ascetic body in need of discipline.[40] But Rabbula's definition of that imagined body/community was an expansive one. He sought to incorporate even those who normally lay outside it—heretics, pagans and Jews—by whatever means were necessary. The narrative of Rabbula's life before ordination begins with his own conversion from paganism, and ends with his dramatic attack on the idol temple of Heliopolis/Baalbek,

38. Overbeck 1865, p. 189. The *Life's* presentation of Rabbula's disciplinary legislation parallels fairly closely the contents of the actual *Canons* attributed to Rabbula, ed. and trans. in Vööbus 1960.

39. The ascetic rule that Rabbula sought to impose bore much greater resemblance to the firmly disciplined coenobitic monasticism of Egypt than the more dramatic and idiosyncratic Syrian traditions represented by Symeon the Stylite or the hermits of Theodoret's *Historia Religiosa*. The ascetic impulse was to be firmly subordinated to the authority of the bishop and to the service of the poor: ostentatious displays such as wearing chains were forbidden, and monks were confined to their monasteries. Rabbula's canonical regulations for the close episcopal supervision of monasteries and charitable institutions bear no small resemblance to those later adopted at Chalcedon, on which see discussion in chapter 8, pp. 316–317.

40. Cf. Harvey "Bishop Rabbula," p. 14: "This text [the *Life*] equates the body of the self with the body of the congregation in no uncertain terms . . . to defeat hunger, pain and suffering in one's own body was incomplete unless these were also defeated in the whole body of Christ: the congregation." Rabbula's idealized disciplinary regime could be understood as an example of the totalizing "ascetic discourse" identified by Cameron 1995 as a defining characteristic of late antique state and society.

both episodes prefiguring the great success bishop Rabbula will later have in converting unbelievers.[41]

Having done battle with the serpents and scorpions of the desert that personified Satan's temptations, Rabbula stood ready to defend his flock against the false teachings of heretics. The divinely inspired voice that proclaimed his worthiness for ordination went on to set the tone for his episcopate: "My hand will help him and my arm will strengthen him. I will annihilate the enemies of truth for him, and crush those who hate him."[42] The *Life* sought to present Rabbula above all as a fighter for orthodoxy. After he had vanquished a long list of heretical sects, there arose what this Monophysite-leaning text regarded as the ultimate enemy: the Antiochene Christology of Theodore of Mopsuestia, regarded by many as the "poisonous root" of Nestorius' "blasphemy" against the Mother of God.[43] Although the *Life* undoubtedly exaggerates Rabbula's role in the fight against Nestorius, and covers up the fact that Rabbula definitively aligned himself with the Cyrillian camp only at a very late stage in the controversy, nevertheless Cyrillian and later Monophysite sources regarded the Edessene bishop as a champion of their cause.[44] Rabbula, as Ibas and later Barhadbeshabba complained, burned the writings of Theodore and did his best to drive his followers out of the city.[45] Cyril himself praised Rabbula for his actions against "Nestorians" in Osrhoene: "Your holiness, my lord, has always indeed shone round

41. Harvey "Bishop Rabbula," p.11, links Rabbula's early attack on Heliopolis/Baalbek to his later actions as bishop, when he demolished several pagan temples in Edessa and used their stones to build a hospital.

42. Overbeck 1865, p. 171. Ironically, the episcopacy of Nestorius—Rabbula's chief adversary in this text—began on a similarly aggressive note: see Socrates *HE* 7.29.

43. Overbeck 1865, p. 196: "Then the spirit of lies let bloom from a poisonous root, namely Theodore—about whom reliable men were sure, that the fire of lust had consumed the flower of his youth, until his pampered body was in old age snatched away through death, rotted and turned into dung in the earth—a cursed shoot, Nestorius, the evil pupil of Theodore, and laid in his mouth the deadly, hidden, poisonous fruit [of heresy]." The insinuations of youthful excess and sexual indiscretion against Theodore here serve to draw as strong a contrast as possible with the ascetic virtues that support and define Rabbula's holiness. Nau 1931, p. 102, speculates that the slur may have some basis in the fact that Theodore, who as a young man had been a fellow-student of John Chrysostom at the feet of the great teacher Diodore of Tarsus (Socrates *HE* 6.3), had briefly "lapsed" from the ascetic life, returning to family business and contemplating marriage, until Chrysostom persuaded him back to virtue, addressing to him the treatise *Ad Theodorum Lapsum*. On Theodore and Chrysostom, see Kelly 1995, pp. 22–23.

44. Rabbula commemorated in later Monophysite calendars: Nau 1931, p. 100.

45. Rabbula's persecution of Antiochenes: Nau 1931, pp. 109–115; Blum 1969, pp. 165–195.

about, but most especially now when you have become the pillar and base of the truth [cf. 1 Timothy 3:15] for all the inhabitants of the East, and are driving out like a deadly disease the abominable and newly sprouted blasphemies of Nestorius which are derived from another root, I mean, Theodore of [Mopsuestia in] Cilicia."[46]

The violent zeal that the young Rabbula had displayed in his attack on the temple at Heliopolis/Baalbek, strengthened and legitimized by his readiness to suffer martyrdom, bore witness to his orthodox faith and undergirded the episcopal authority he later used in his persecution of pagans, Jews, and heretics in and around Edessa. Rabbula destroyed several pagan temples, seized a synagogue for conversion into a church, and confiscated the meetinghouses and exiled the leaders of a variety of heterodox Christian sects.[47] In this manner, the *Life* claims, he brought about the conversion of "thousands of Jews and tens of thousands of heretics."[48] In his attacks on unbelievers, bishop Rabbula had recourse to the same Old Testament models as did the zealous and violent holy men we have previously seen:

> For he was, in his way and in his time, another Moses, whose just zeal was hateful and repugnant to sinners, and whose understanding gentleness seemed contemptible and degrading to the proud. But he resembled Moses not only in this respect, but imitated him in everything. In his difficult battles against many false teachings he resembled Joshua the son of Nun, and also the zealot Josiah. For it was said to him by his Lord, as once to Joshua, "Be courageous and strong and fear not, for I am with you, to help you." Like once Joshua son of Nun, and later Josiah, who found the land of Canaan overgrown with the brambles of paganism, so he found the whole Edessene region densely overgrown with all the thorns of sins.[49]

Toward the rich and powerful, as toward heretics and unbelievers, Rabbula exercised the same confrontational *parrhesia* characteristic of holy men like Symeon the Stylite, backed up with the added sanction of judicial

46. Cyril *Ep.* 74 (trans. McEnerney). The letter is preserved in Syriac together with the *Life* and various writings attributed to Rabbula. Note the striking similarity of language describing Theodore and Nestorius—poisonous roots, sprouting blasphemies—to that from the *Life*, Overbeck 1865, p. 196. For correspondence of Cyril and Rabbula see also Cyril *Epp.* 73 and 101.

47. Overbeck 1865, pp. 193–194. Synagogue: *Edessene Chronicle* 51. It was transformed into a church for St. Stephen, a figure commonly associated in the early fifth century with forcible conversion of Jews in incidents such as that at Minorca in 418, on which see Bradbury 1996.

48. Overbeck 1865, p. 193.

49. Overbeck 1865, pp. 191–192. Cf. chapter 5, esp. pp. 188–189, on Barsauma's invocation of Joshua in Canaan to justify murderous attacks on synagogues.

power through the episcopal court.[50] The hagiographer presents Rabbula's violent and coercive style of leadership as a consequence of his great love for his flock. Rabbula, in a metaphor commonly used to justify disciplinary force,[51] was like a doctor compelled reluctantly to inflict painful treatments in order to save the patient's life, or soul:

> Always he understood, as an expert physician, the appropriate remedies to apply for different kinds of diseases of the soul. Sometimes he cut out the pus-filled wound with a merciful, useful punishment as with a sharp iron, to rescue from death through pain. Sometimes he healed through threatening words, sufficient for the rejection of foolishness, to help a difficult injury to atonement, as with strong [medicinal] roots. At times also he healed the injury of illness through peaceful admonition in soft, useful words for the improvement of those gone astray, to strengthen and console them all as with invigorating medicine. For in every way he was concerned only that sinners be brought through his careful teaching to salvation through the atonement which leads back to life.[52]

Violent coercion, gentle persuasion, and leadership by example all came together as different ways in which Rabbula "healed" the embodied Christian community. His own asceticism, understood as violence against the self, set the model for the violent discipline he applied to others.[53]

The *Life of Rabbula* offered an idealized way in which charismatic holiness and episcopal authority ought to be combined. The violent zeal of a holy man—prefigured by a martyrial assault on paganism that sets the stage for his later battles on behalf of orthodoxy—is wedded to episcopal authority and strict hierarchical control, resulting in a government for the

50. On Symeon's confrontations with the powerful, see chapter 5, pp. 184–185, Elijah's violent apparition (Syriac *Life of Symeon* 42–43). Harvey 1994, p. 57, explicitly compares Rabbula and Symeon as "two paradigms of ministry to the poor."

51. See discussion of disciplinary violence in chapter 4, pp. 146–147.

52. Overbeck 1865, pp. 180–181. Augustine, in particular, made frequent use of such medical imagery: see discussion in chapters 3 and 4, pp. 129 and 146–147. Cf. similar language used by Palladius of John Chrysostom (*Dialogue* 5.151): "He applied the sword of correction against the rich, lancing the abscesses of their souls."

53. The connection between violence and the healing of the soul is particularly stressed by Harvey "Bishop Rabbula," p. 14: "[Rabbula used] external violence (violence against others) for the same reasons that some ascetics chose internal violence (violence against the self): that is, because the disciplining of the body of Christ, whether singular or corporate, was seen to be an inherently violent matter." Harvey (p. 11 n. 72) notes the strong symbolism in the fact that Rabbula used the stones of destroyed pagan temples to build a hospital for the care of the sick (Overbeck 1865, p. 203). A similar imagery of "disciplining the [collective] body" can be found in Shenoute: cf. Krawiec 2002, pp. 66–69.

church that is both responsible and divinely inspired. But the *Life* does more than merely combine these qualities: it presents ascetic virtue and divine zeal as the main legitimate basis for episcopal authority. *Askesis,* charity, and combat against enemies of the faith all come together to define leadership for the Christian community.[54]

THE TYRANT-BISHOP

Defining an ideal also allows one to envision its opposite. The *Life of Rabbula* has long been recognized as a thinly disguised polemic against Rabbula's successor Ibas, written by a devoted follower of Rabbula probably around 449, at a time when Ibas faced a rising tide of opposition that culminated in his condemnation at the Second Council of Ephesus.[55] When one reads the *Life* side by side with the charges brought against Ibas in 449, each of Rabbula's virtues and good deeds seems to find an antithesis in the conduct of Ibas. Where Rabbula eschewed lavish building and forced material austerity upon his household in order to dedicate resources to the support of the poor, Ibas appropriated for his own use money given to the church for the redemption of captives, and diverted other church funds to the pockets of his relatives. Where Rabbula crushed idolatry and destroyed temples, Ibas accepted bribes from pagans and turned a blind eye to their continued sacrifices. Where Rabbula defended the faith against heresy, Ibas befriended Nestorius, and himself uttered blasphemous statements.[56] The imperial *comes* Flavius Thomas Chaereas, sent to Edessa in April 449 by the emperor Theodosius II to investigate reported unrest, submitted a long report recording violent demonstrations in which crowds chanted acclamations that alternated excoriation of their cur-

54. The "ideal bishop" defined by the *Life of Rabbula* can in this sense be likened to the idealized picture of how an emperor ought to govern: clemency, generosity, and reconciliation of conflicts for those within the boundaries of the empire, but continual warfare and military triumph against "barbarians" outside.

55. Nau 1931, p. 99, makes this point; most recently reiterated by Drijvers 1996, pp. 245–246. See the *comes* Chaereas' detailed report on the noisy demonstrations against Ibas at Edessa, and the charges against him, reviewed at the Second Council of Ephesus: Flemming 1917, pp. 14–54. Ibas was condemned and deposed there by the partisans of Dioscorus, but rehabilitated and restored to his see by the Council of Chalcedon in 451 (see esp. sessions 10 and 11). He finally died in 457. On the episcopacy of Ibas, see Segal 1970, pp. 93–95 and 130–133. More on the councils of 449 and 451 in chapter 8.

56. Charges against Ibas, originally brought by clergy of Edessa at the synod of Berytus, recorded in Chalcedon Session 11, *ACO* 2.1.11.73.

rent bishop—"No one accepts the Nestorian Ibas! Give us another bishop! He despoils the temple of God; let him return to the church and to the poor the things that he has taken!"—with passionate invocations of "Holy Rabbula!"[57] The followers of Rabbula conceived a hatred of Ibas that persisted in Monophysite literature long after his death. A full century later, the emperor Justinian based an attempted reconciliation with the Monophysites upon a proposal for formal condemnation of Ibas and two other long-dead objects of Monophysite scorn, Theodore of Mopsuestia and Theodoret of Cyrrhus.[58]

But a simple change of perspective will show what a fine line distinguished the zealous violence with which a holy bishop such as Rabbula might pursue enemies of the faith from the angry violence of a tyrant, whose persecution might fall unjustly upon believers and unbelievers alike. Ibas, for his part, had this to say of Rabbula:

> Many persons, who had not God before their eyes, assumed zeal on behalf of the churches as a pretext, and eagerly took the opportunity to manifest by act the hatred which they secretly entertained in their hearts. One such person was the tyrant of our metropolis [Rabbula], a person not unknown to you, who under pretext of the faith not only wreaked his revenge on the living, but on those likewise who had departed to the Lord, amongst whom is the blessed Theodore, that preacher of the truth, that doctor of the church, who, not in his lifetime only, stopped the mouth of heretics with the true faith, but has done so also after his death, by leaving to the sons of the church a spiritual armory in his writings. Now [Rabbula], who exceeds everybody in audacity, has openly in the church dared to anathematize [Theodore], who, out of zeal for God, not only led back his own city from error to the truth, but who has also instructed by his teaching churches that are far away. And as regards his writings, there was everywhere a great search for them [in order to burn them], not on account of their being alien or adverse to the true faith—for certainly, while he [Theodore] was living, [Rabbula] constantly eulogized him, and used to read his writings—but because of the enmity [Rabbula] had secretly entertained towards him for having reprimanded him openly in synod.[59]

57. Acclamations: e.g., Flemming 1917, pp. 14–16.

58. The writings of the three formed the so-called Three Chapters condemned at Justinian's ecumenical council of 553: see Frend 1972, pp. 280–282; Meyendorff 1989, pp. 235–245.

59. Syriac version in Flemming 1917, pp. 48–52, Greek in *ACO* 2.1.11.138. (Trans. Perry 1881, pp. 117–118.) Ibas' *Letter to Mari the Persian* was written after the reconciliation of Cyril and John of Antioch in April 433, and before Rabbula's death in August 435. The letter was introduced into evidence against Ibas in

Rabbula's crusade against Theodore, Ibas argued, resulted not from zeal for the faith but from personal animosity, apparently referring to the same episode described by Barhadbeshabba. Rabbula's abuse of power, and Ibas' abuse of church resources, come together to define the "tyrant-bishop," polemical counterpart to the idealized saint-bishop type constructed by the *Life of Rabbula*. A tyrant-bishop, who not only lacks but actually contradicts the ascetic virtues upon which true sanctity must be based, cannot be regarded as a "true" bishop—he is an impostor, a usurper. If the qualities of a holy man are postulated as the foundation of episcopal authority, then the absence of those qualities can be used to undermine that authority. The discourse of false pretenses thus constructs a "false bishop" against whom legitimate opposition, and even violent resistance, becomes imaginable and justifiable.[60]

The rhetorical construction of the tyrant-bishop formed one of the ways in which Christians problematized the exercise of power within the church. The tyrant-bishop was essentially a polemical model, and as such it owed much to secular political discourse, which had long employed a standard vocabulary of images and stereotypes to describe and delegitimize "bad" emperors, usurpers, and other secular villains.[61] Within the context of Christian thought, the tyrant-bishop needs to be distinguished somewhat from another type, that of the persecutor, with which we have dealt in chapter 2. Different polemical strategies were appropriate depending upon whether or not Christian communities perceived themselves as living in a time of persecution. Christian historical reflection upon the time of pagan persecution, or upon the reigns of fourth-century Homoian emperors, as remembered by the largely Nicene tradition, employed the category of "persecutor" as the most obvious way of depicting those thought to be enemies of the church. Fourth-century Nicene polemic focused first upon emperors such as Constantius or Valens, and attacked "Arian" bishops mainly insofar as they depended upon or sought to influence the imperial power. Athanasius, in challenging his rivals who contested the Alexandrian episcopacy, found it most useful to present them as mere creatures of the emperor, who enjoyed no support from God

---

449, and formed one of the grounds for his condemnation at that time and again in the sixth century, mainly because of its unflattering remarks about the conduct of Cyril, who by 449 was already regarded as a sanctified "father of the church" against whom no criticism would be tolerated. See D'Alès 1932. On the rapid "canonization" of Cyril, see Gray 1989. On Ibas' condemnation in 449, see the next chapter.

60. Cf. chapter 6, pp. 228–231, for the "discourse of false pretenses" and its application to "false monks."

61. See, e.g., MacMullen 1963, Paschoud and Szidat 1997.

or among the people and who could only be installed and maintained in office by the intervention of imperial soldiers.[62] When one understands the world to be polarized into martyrs and persecutors, Christians and pagans, or orthodox and heretics, then a fairly straightforward polemical strategy is appropriate: the individual target of polemic must be assimilated to an already-defined group known to both author and audience as an enemy, such as "Arians." Polemic thus consists mainly of exposing the target's connections to the defined group. Less attention is paid to the target's personal character, because it is assumed that all members of the group are similarly depraved by nature. We might call this a "wartime" style of polemic.

But the requirements of "peacetime" polemic—when one must challenge a bishop's conduct without benefit of a larger context of persecution or doctrinal controversy—are different. Here "persecutor" gives way to "tyrant." Whereas the persecutor was simply an external enemy, the tyrant-bishop posed a more complicated problem, forcing Christians to recognize the ease with which one of their own might "go bad" if his impulses and passions were not sufficiently restrained. The target of polemic must be judged and condemned as an individual, rather than as a member of a predefined group, though of course there were still established models and stereotypes that could be drawn upon. The focus of polemic shifted from exposure of allegiances to examination of personal character, constructing a narrative in which an individual "goes bad" through the corrupting influence of power—a path more in line with classical political representations of tyrants and bad emperors. Imperial historiography had much to say of the ways in which an absolute monarch might fall prey to the influence of flatterers, or give way to unrestrained and destructive displays of anger. Late Roman political discourse constructed a special polemical category—the "tyrant-usurper"—for those who tried to seize imperial power and failed. Such characters were distinguished by their dangerous ambition for power and their willingness to use illegal violence *[latrocinium]* in its pursuit. This concept in turn traced its ancestry back to political discourse of the Late Republic, rhetorical strategies used to denounce unscrupulous men suspected of plotting to seize dictatorial power by unlawful means.[63] All of these ideas, of course, reflected the broad-based prejudice that those who sought power too eagerly were inherently unfit to hold it.

---

62. See chapter 2, pp. 76–77.
63. On absolute monarchs corrupted by absolute power see, e.g., Plutarch and Curtius on Alexander the Great; Suetonius and Tacitus on various Julio-Claudian emperors. For the Republican period, Cicero's orations against Catiline are paradigmatic:

The image of the tyrant-bishop allows us to explore Christian discourses about power within the church, the ways in which it could corrupt and the ways in which it could be abused. Much of our evidence for the reported conduct of tyrant-bishops necessarily comes from hostile sources, particularly accounts of charges brought against bishops at ecclesiastical synods. Such charges have commonly been dismissed as biased, exaggerated, or downright invented, and many of them probably were. But our purpose here is not to decide whether bishops such as Athanasius, Theophilus, Chrysostom, Ibas, or Dioscorus were guilty or innocent of particular accusations against them. The evidentiary value of these charges is not limited to a simple question of their truth or falsehood in specific cases.[64] They are far more important for what they can tell us about the expectations of the audiences to which they were addressed, and they inform in two ways. First, we may assume that accusations, even if false in a particular case, needed to be plausible. They had to fall within the realm of the audience's expectations and fears regarding the sorts of things a powerful and unscrupulous bishop might do, or memories of what other bishops in similar situations were thought to have done in the past. Second, and more importantly, polemical charges offer us a window into the moral expectations and values that governed Christian thought on the exercise of power, by showing exactly what might be considered "wrong." Which uses of episcopal power constituted "abuse" of that power? If one overriding principle can be extracted from the great variety of specific examples that will be treated below, it is that ecclesiastical power is abused when it is used for one's own ends, to satisfy one's base human desires, instead of serving the interests of God and of the church and congregation.

Where the persecutor-bishop was understood to be dependent upon the emperor's power, the tyrant-bishop is seen as wishing to seize and control aspects of that secular power for himself. Palladius offered a compelling portrait of episcopal corruption: "At present we have men who claim to be bishops [*dokountes episkopoi*]—a lowly breed who have bogged down in acquiring money and military operations and striving for honorable positions. They transgress the law which says, the priests shall not give their sons to the rulers,

---

see Vasaly 1996. Cf. B. Shaw 1984 on the politicized meaning of *latrocinium*, also discussed in the introduction and chapter 6, pp. 20–21 and 210–215. On late Republican political violence both in legal theory and in practice, see Lintott 1968. These Roman discourses, in turn, owed much to classical Greek political philosophy. See especially Plato's remarks on the moral character of the tyrant, in *Republic* 9.8–9.9 (562–576). See discussion in introduction, pp. 16–17.

64. A useful analogy may be found in the study of sorcery accusations in Brown 1972b.

and them that run beside the king. They squander the things of the Spirit in intrigue, in various miserable plots, in imprisonments, and in banishments."[65]

The appearance of secular power, the spectacle of a bishop acting like a worldly potentate, constituted a significant element of polemic. Even before the conversion of Constantine dramatically increased the possibilities for clergy to exercise real power, the ways in which bishops might seize and abuse such power could already be imagined. One of the earliest portraits of the "tyrant" can be found in the synodal letter of the bishops who condemned Paul of Samosata in 268 for his conduct as bishop of Antioch:

> Although formerly destitute and poor, and having received no wealth from his fathers, nor made anything by trade or business, he now possesses abundant wealth through his iniquities and sacrilegious acts *[anomion kai hierosulion]* and through those things which he extorts from the brethren, depriving the injured of their rights and promising to assist them for reward . . . 'supposing that gain is godliness.'[66]
>
> He is haughty, and is puffed up *[hos hypsela phronei kai hyperertai]*, and assumes worldly dignities, preferring to be called *ducenarius*[67] and struts in the market-places, reading letters and reciting them as he walks in public, attended by a body-guard, with a multitude preceding and following him, so that the faith is envied and hated on account of his pride and haughtiness of heart *[dia ton ogkon autou kai ten hyperephanian tes kardias]*. . . . He contrives to glorify himself, and deceive with appearances, and astonish the minds of the simple, preparing for himself a tribunal and lofty throne, not like a disciple of Christ, and possessing a *secretum*[68] like the rulers of the world, and so calling it. . . .
>
> Because of these things all mourn and lament by themselves; but they so fear his tyranny and power, that they dare not accuse him.[69]

Paul of Samosata's heretical teachings were almost beside the point. He demeaned his episcopal office by surrounding it with the trappings of secular magistracy, striding through the agora with a great entourage, sitting on a high throne like a governor—all of which served no purpose beyond the gratification of his pride and arrogance.[70] Monastic communities discouraged their members from accepting clerical office, fearing that it would inevitably lead to destructive ambition and rivalry. Pachomius warned his disciples: "The

---

65. Palladius, *Dialogue* 20.561–571 (trans. Meyer).
66. 1 Timothy 6:5.
67. *Ducenarius:* a procurator, roughly equivalent in rank to a provincial governor.
68. *Secretum:* a magistrate's private audience chamber.
69. Their letter is preserved in Eusebius *HE* 7.30 (trans. NPNF).
70. On Paul of Samosata see Millar 1971, Burke 1975, Norris 1984, Burrus 1989. Millar and others have discredited the earlier belief that Paul actually was a *duce-*

beginning of the thought of love-of-command is ordination."[71] Sulpicius Severus remarked sarcastically that his contemporaries sought bishoprics as assiduously as the ancient martyrs had sought death.[72] In sharp contrast to the studied reluctance of true holy men to accept priestly honors, "tyrants" would seize episcopal office in the ecclesiastical equivalent of a *coup d'état,* taking over a church by night and barricading the doors for an illegal and secret ordination.[73] Mistrust of episcopal ambition underlay fourth-century debates over the issue of "translation," the practice by which bishops ordained to one see sought to exchange it for another. As Ossius of Cordoba reminded the bishops at Sardica: "No one ever seeks to transfer from a greater city to a lesser one. This shows that they are aflame with the fire of greed, and that they are slaves to ambition."[74] Although rules against translation were never consistently enforced—witness the example of Athanasius' adversary Eusebius, a quintessential "court bishop" who moved first from Berytus to Nicomedia and then from Nicomedia to Constantinople—they were nevertheless available as grounds for denouncing an unpopular prelate. Gregory of Nazianzus' short-lived tenure as bishop of Constantinople was derailed in large part by controversy over his previous ordination to the see of Sasima.

The tyrant-bishop's lust for power drove him to overstep the normal boundaries of his episcopal authority and interfere in the business of other dioceses and provinces. When powerful figures such as the Alexandrian patriarchs Theophilus, Cyril, and Dioscorus reached outside their own diocese

---

narius, holding civil office alongside ecclesiastical, during the short-lived imperium of Zenobia. The thrust of the bishops' polemic is that he *acted* like such an official, in a way they felt was incompatible with office in the church.

71. Pachomius, *Primary Greek Life* 27: *arkhe logismou philarkhias, ho kleros.* Similar sentiments can be found in his *Bohairic Life* 25. John Moschus, *Spiritual Meadow* 44, invites the reader to imagine bishops roasting in hell.

72. Sulpicius Severus, *Chronicle* 2.32.

73. Examples include Novatian's attempt to seize the bishopric of Rome (Eusebius *HE* 6.43.5–10); the disorderly election of Silvanus of Cirta by a mob of "gladiators and prostitutes" (*Gesta apud Zenophilum* 16); the hasty and irregular ordination of Athanasius, as alleged by Philostorgius *HE* 2.11 (but denied by Nicene accounts, e.g., Sozomen *HE* 2.17; cf. Barnes 1993, pp. 18–20 and 37); Porphyrius of Antioch, as described by Palladius, *Dialogue* 16.104–109. One might compare Ammianus' belittling and farcical presentation of the usurper Procopius' attempt to elevate himself to imperial rank, an attempt retroactively delegitimized by the fact that it ultimately failed: Ammianus 26.6, with commentary by Matthews 1989, pp. 193–195; Lenski 2002, pp. 73–74.

74. *Canon* 1 of the (western) Council of Sardica 343 (trans. Stevenson). Cf. *Canon* 15 of Nicaea, and later *Canon* 5 of Chalcedon. Socrates *HE* 7.37 argued against a blanket prohibition, citing many examples of translation from the fourth century.

and intervened in the affairs of Constantinople or Antioch, opponents could censure their actions as the result of ambition or greed. Theophilus, for his part, could cast John Chrysostom's attempt to extend Constantinopolitan jurisdiction into Asia in the same light, charging that John was so "power-hungry" that he deposed sixteen bishops in a single day.[75]

The tyrant-bishop's greed betrayed itself in his love of luxury and pursuit of secular ostentation.[76] The epithet "Pharaoh" had a particular way of sticking to the Alexandrian patriarchs, most powerful among bishops.[77] Theophilus, like the Pharaoh of Exodus, oppressed and exploited God's people in order to satisfy his vainglory by building grand monuments to himself. This craze for building, *lithomania,* led Theophilus to misappropriate funds given to the Alexandrian church for the support of the poor. When his elderly steward Isidore confronted him over the matter, Theophilus contrived a trumped-up charge of sodomy against him.[78]

Tyrant-bishops resorted to violence, legal or otherwise, in order to satisfy their greed and ambition. A bishop who relied excessively upon secular power forfeited his claim to religious authority, especially when that secular power manifested itself in violent form. The damning image of the bishop who surrounded himself with soldiers continued to feature in polemic. Chrysostom, writing to Pope Innocent about a bloody attack upon his supporters in their church, condemned his adversaries as "bishops who were acting the part of soldiers [and] were not ashamed to have officers marching ahead of them in place of deacons."[79] Intrusion of secular power into the church was seen to be inherently violent.[80] By the late fourth century, bishops in the larger cities often had access to their own means of violence independent of secular authorities, relying instead on the organized muscle of *parabalani, lecticarii,*

---

75. *Philarkhias pathei kinoumenon.* Theophilus' accusation is reported by Palladius, *Dialogue* 13.129–130, who answers in John's defense that there were only six, not sixteen, and they all deserved it. Kelly 1995, pp. 163–180, discusses the incident.

76. Luxury: charges against Ibas, above; and against his nephew Daniel, bishop of Harran: Flemming 1917, pp. 68–72.

77. On the Alexandrian episcopacy generally see Haas 1997, Martin 1996, articles in Wipszycka 1996a. On the Alexandrian Patriarch as "Pharaoh" see Adshead 1998.

78. Palladius, *Dialogue* 6.57–64. Cf. Sozomen *HE* 8.12, where Isidore is reported to have said: "It is better to restore the bodies of the suffering, which are more rightly to be considered the Temples of God, and for which end the money had been furnished, than to build walls." (NPNF trans.) Shouts of "Pharaoh" against Dioscorus at Chalcedon: e.g., *ACO* 2.1.1.530.

79. Chrysostom, *First Letter to Pope Innocent.* See discussion of this incident's symbolism in chapter 2, pp. 80–83.

80. See chapter 2, pp. 79–83.

fossores and similar groups.[81] Bishops' associations with disreputable and violence-prone groups such as gladiators, circus factions, or theatrical claques formed yet another ground for condemnation.[82]

Constantine had granted the bishops sweeping new secular powers by formally recognizing the *episcopalis audientia* as a judicial forum whose decisions were to be enforceable by law.[83] Some bishops complained that the result was nothing more than endless distraction and annoyance, as they found their time eaten up by congregants' petty quarrels.[84] But while such sentiments may have helped their authors convey a politically correct lack of enthusiasm for their office, it is clear that other bishops used these powers effectively and often.[85] Bishops' judicial and disciplinary power could easily be abused in a violent manner. Basil of Ancyra was condemned at the Council of Constantinople in 360 on charges that he had ordered secular authorities to sentence clerics to imprisonment or exile, and that he used judicial torture to force a slave to testify against her mistress.[86] Chrysostom allegedly had opponents flogged, beaten, and left to die in prison.[87] Prim-

---

81. The *parabalani* were stretcher carriers for the hospitals of the Alexandrian church; similar workers elsewhere were called *lecticarii; fossores* were grave diggers employed by the church in Rome. On their use by bishops in urban violence, see Brown 1992, pp. 102–103.

82. As, e.g., Silvanus of Cirta, in *Gesta apud Zenophilum*. On the bishops' new role as secular potentates within the late antique city, see Peter Brown 1992, esp. chaps. 3 and 4; and now Liebeschuetz 2001, esp. pp. 137–168. For Alexandria, see Haas 1997, esp. chaps. 7–9.

83. Constantine's edict: *Sirmondian Constitutions* 1. See Lamoreaux 1995, and now articles by Harries, Lenski, and Dossey in Mathisen 2001.

84. This point is emphasized by Drake 2000, pp. 344–346. See, e.g., Augustine, *On the Work of Monks* 37; Synesius of Cyrene, *Epp.* 57 and 105.

85. Thus Flavian of Antioch used his jurisdiction to block any prosecution of the monks who destroyed rural pagan shrines: Libanius, *Or.* 30.15–19.

86. Charges detailed in Sozomen *HE* 4.24. See commentary by Barnes 1996. Judicial torture of slaves and *humiliores* was standard practice in secular courts, but it was commonly thought that baptized Christians and especially clerics had no business ordering or supervising such procedures. When Ambrose, then a provincial governor, wished to demonstrate his reluctance to accept ordination as bishop of Milan, he performed two highly public actions meant to show his "unfitness" for clerical office: he invited prostitutes to spend the night at his house, and he presided over several bloody judicial examinations: Paulinus, *Life of Ambrose* 7–8, with commentary by McLynn 1994, pp. 44–46. Augustine's letter to Marcellinus, discussed in chapter 4, pp. 141–142, would seem to imply that (at least in North Africa) judicial torture was not normally used in episcopal courts, where beating with rods was the most severe physical sanction available. See now Dossey 2001.

87. Charges brought at the Synod of the Oak, by the deacon John: #2, #19; charges brought by Isaac: #1, #16.

ian, Donatist bishop of Carthage, was condemned by his Maximianist rivals for an assortment of violent abuses.[88] Although the sensational charge that Athanasius had murdered the Melitian bishop Arsenius and chopped off his hand for sorcerous purposes was later disproven when the alleged victim turned up alive and uninjured, the success of Athanasius' adversaries in pressing the accusation in several consecutive venues suggests that it did not fall far beyond the bounds of what people believed a powerful bishop might be capable of doing.[89] Athanasius did apparently use considerable violence against the Melitian schismatics, on one occasion even sending his men to raid a military camp where Melitian bishops had taken refuge:

> The adherents of Athanasius, hearing of it [the presence of the Melitians], came bringing with them soldiers of the Dux and of the camp; they came in a drunken state, at the ninth hour. . . . When [the Melitian bishops] could not be found, they went out and found four brethren coming into the camp, and they beat them, and made them all bloody, so that they were in danger of death. . . .
>
> I have written to you in order that you might know in what affliction we are; for he carried off a bishop of the lower country and shut him in the meat-market, and a priest of the same region he shut in the lock-up, and a deacon in the principal prison, and till the twenty-eighth of Pachon, Heraiscus too has been confined in the camp—I thank God that the scourgings which he endured have ceased—and on the twenty-seventh, he caused seven bishops to leave the country.[90]

The eastern bishops assembled at Sardica in 343 had this to say of Athanasius' conduct:

> Athanasius was charged with unlawful acts, with the use of force, with murder and the killing of bishops. Raging like a tyrant even during the most holy days of Easter, he was accompanied by the military and officials of the imperial government who, on his authority, confined

---

88. *Letter of the Council of Cebarsussa*, 24 June 393 (text in Maier 1987–1989, *Dossier*, vol. 2, pp. 73–82; trans. from Stevenson 1989, pp. 217–218): "#4, that he caused the presbyter Fortunatus to be thrown down a drain; #7, that [he] sent a large gang [Circumcellions?] to wreck the homes of Christians; #8, that bishops [and] other clerics were shut up by him and afterwards stoned by his partners in violence; #9, that in a basilica senior persons were beaten; #11, [that he refused to answer our charges,] by blocking the doors of basilicas with [guards;] #13, [that he seized] various pieces of property, first by force and then with official support."

89. The hand of Arsenius: e.g., Sozomen *HE* 2.25.

90. *Letter of the Melitian Callistus to the priests Paeiou and Patabeit* (335) = *P. London 1914*, ed. and trans. Bell 1924, pp. 58–63, with commentary.

some to custody, beat and whipped some and forced the rest into sacrilegious communion with him by various acts of torture.[91]

The charges of Melitians and others against Athanasius bear a somewhat different tone from those made by Athanasius and his camp against "Arians." Because Athanasius sought to delegitimize them by emphasizing their connections to the condemned beliefs of Arius, he could deploy the familiar rhetoric of martyrdom and persecution in order to accuse them of attempting to force a heretical doctrine upon the church.[92] Athanasius' opponents, however, who generally denied any connection to Arius, attacked Athanasius not for his doctrine but for his behavior. In their minds Athanasius was a tyrant, who acted not in order to defend the faith but rather to indulge his own personal animosity, ambition, greed, and lust for power.

A tyrant was defined in large part by his inability to restrain his temper. Uncontrolled anger could lead to violence that was not only cruel and inappropriate but even sacrilegious. When Theophilus, in his rage, set fire to the dwellings of the Origenist monks, he inadvertently burned the holy scriptures they kept in their cells.[93] Theodoret of Cyrrhus, according to accusations brought against him in 449, displayed his "audacity" by seizing a volume containing the decrees of Nicaea and Ephesus I and throwing it into a fire, an act that "no pagan, Jew or heretic" had ever dared, after some Monophysite-leaning clerics had produced the text in order to challenge him on a point of baptismal practice. In this case, we are told, God did not tolerate the sacrilege: the fire was miraculously quenched.[94] Athanasius' agent Macarius allegedly smashed a liturgical chalice and overturned an altar in a Melitian church—an act of sacrilege committed because Athanasius' pride and anger led him to disregard the sanctity of the church, the same sort of

---

91. *Letter of the Eastern Bishops at Sardica*, in Hilary of Poitiers, *Against Valens and Ursacius* 1.2.6 (trans. Wickham), in which Athanasius and his allies are accused, among other things, of stripping holy virgins. Compare Nicene sources' accusations of similar behavior by bishop Macedonius of Constantinople: Socrates *HE* 2.27 and 2.38, Sozomen *HE* 4.2–3 and 4.20–21.

92. See discussion in chapter 2, p. 72.

93. Palladius, *Dialogue* 7.40–44.

94. As soon as the book was thrown in, the fire surged up and melted a bronze cauldron hanging above, which caused water to spill down and quench the fire, leaving the book unharmed: *libellus* submitted by the presbyter Cyriacus, Flemming 1917, p. 116. Oddly, this evidence was presented during the action against Domnus of Antioch, to condemn him for his association with Theodoret, and not during that against Theodoret himself. Accusations involving the burning of holy texts naturally invoked powerful memories of *traditio*, when bishops in time of persecution had betrayed Christ by handing over scriptures to be burned.

violation of ecclesiastical space that formed a dominant theme in his own anti-Arian polemic.[95] This was violence against the very body of Christ. Athanasius answered the charge by invoking orthodoxy to justify his violence. The churches of heretics and schismatics were not true churches, merely houses. The altars were only tables, the chalices just cups. Christ was not truly present in any of these, and therefore action against them could not be considered sacrilege.[96]

The tyrant-bishop persecutes others in order to feed his anger, ambition, and greed, and uses doctrinal issues merely as a pretext for indulging personal vendettas. Such a polemical presentation allowed critics to dismiss and ridicule the tyrant's claims to be acting on behalf of orthodoxy. Theophilus was "by nature impetuous, rash, bold, seeking quarrel above reason" and he "proceeded with mad fury."[97] In such a narrative, Rabbula's crusade against Theodore and Antiochene theology could be reduced to the level of a mere grudge. Canonical legislation allowed that personal motives might unfairly influence a bishop's disciplinary actions, and outlined procedures for appeal in such cases.[98] At the height of the Nestorian controversy, Isidore of Pelusium warned Cyril that even many people who agreed with his theology felt that he was going too far in pursuing his adversaries. He risked becoming the image of his uncle and predecessor, Theophilus:

> Many of those who were assembled at Ephesus speak satirically of you as a man bent on pursuing his private animosities [*oikeian amunomenon ekhthran*], not as one who seeks in correct belief the things of Jesus Christ. "He is sister's son to Theophilus," they say, "and in disposition takes after him. Just as the uncle openly expended his fury against the

95. For images of violation of ecclesiastical space, see chapter 2, pp. 79–83. Mareotis incident: e.g., Athanasius, *Apology Against the Arians* 14; discussion by Barnes 1993, pp. 27–30.

96. Cf. the monk Barsauma's defiant assertion (*Life of Barsauma*, 70th miracle), "I never killed any *true* bishop."

97. Palladius *Dialogue* 9.22–32. Palladius and other hostile sources took great care to point out Theophilus' reversal of position on Origenism, in order to stress that Theophilus' claims to act against "heresy" were not to be taken seriously. Elm 1998, pp. 72–73, recognizes this as a conscious polemical strategy on the part of Theophilus' critics. On the late fourth-century Origenist controversy, E. Clark 1992.

98. Cf. Sardica *Canon* 14, allowing that if a bishop condemned subordinates because he was "quick to anger," they could seek refuge with the metropolitan. In 448, in order to resolve a dispute between Ibas of Edessa and several of his clerics who had brought charges of heresy and misconduct against him, Domnus of Antioch forced Ibas to suspend his normal disciplinary power over them. So that no one might think he was punishing them for their previous opposition, any future action taken by Ibas against them would have to be confirmed by Domnus: *ACO* 2.1.10.7.

inspired and beloved John [Chrysostom], so also the nephew seeks to set himself up in his turn."[99]

These images of angry, tyrannical behavior could even be used by critics who had no theological differences with their targets, to rebuke them for over-zealous pursuit of orthodoxy that risked destroying the peace of the church. Socrates, who explicitly defended Nestorius against charges of theological error, nevertheless attacked him as a "firebrand" whose determination to root out heresy would only lead to violent disorder.[100] Socrates represented a school of Christian thought largely unsympathetic to claims of "holy" violence, believing that at least in some cases, peace ought to be valued above doctrinal purity.[101] "Tyrants" such as Theophilus or Rabbula, by contrast, pursued controversy even beyond the grave. Defenders of Origen in the late fourth century, and of Theodore of Mopsuestia in the fifth, argued against posthumous attacks upon the writings of those who had "died in the peace of the church," whose orthodoxy had never been challenged during their lifetimes.[102]

Because such "tyrants" normally justified their own actions in terms of enforcing orthodoxy, critics could undermine their legitimacy—and avoid potentially divisive theological debate—by shifting the focus to issues of personal character and temperament.[103] As we shall see in the next chapter, theological division could amplify personal rivalry into something far worse, a destructive "civil war" within the church. Dioscorus, held up at Chalcedon as the ultimate tyrant-bishop, would in the end be convicted of misconduct,

99. Isidore of Pelusium, *Ep.* 1.310 (trans. Stevenson). Cf. Theodoret's vitriolic posthumous assessment (*Ep.* 180), suggesting that a large stone be placed on top of Cyril's grave lest the demons find him so intolerable that they expel him from hell!

100. Socrates *HE* 7.29–32. Nestorius' very first sermon upon being ordained bishop of Constantinople in 428 included the promise, "Give me, o emperor, the earth purged of heretics, and I will give you heaven as a recompense. Assist me in destroying heretics, and I will assist you in vanquishing the Persians." For Socrates, this was proof of Nestorius' "levity of mind" [*to kouphon tes dianoias*] and "violent and vainglorious temperament" [*to thumikon en tauto kai kenodoxon*].

101. On Socrates' perhaps unusual views, see Urbainczyk 1997. Cf. the plea of Pope Liberius (after succumbing to considerable pressure from Constantius) for "the peace and concord which has prior place to martyrdom": Hilary of Poitiers, *Against Valens and Ursacius* 2.9.1 (Wickham trans.).

102. Origen: E. Clark 1992. Theodore: Ibas, *Letter to Mari*, p. 269 above. Nestorius, *Bazaar of Heracleides*, p. 332 [454–455] condemns Cyril for "rising up against dead Fathers," i.e., Diodore and Theodore. Such struggles over the orthodoxy of long-dead theologians could be seen as a symptom of what Gray 1989 calls "patrification," the selective pruning of the patristic legacy to produce a narrow authoritative canon of "Fathers."

103. Elm 1998, discussing the conflict between Chrysostom and Theophilus, argues that in some circumstances, misconduct charges offered a safer arena for epis-

not heresy—even though Chalcedon condemned the one-nature Christology that he continued to proclaim. But the discourse of episcopal misconduct should not be taken as a mere contrivance intended to substitute for more "serious" doctrinal charges: it spoke to real concerns about the use and abuse of power within the church.

CONSEQUENCES

We have already seen in previous chapters how Christian emperors, facing resistance that expressed itself in the language of martyrdom, sometimes moderated their policies in measurable ways so as to avoid the unwelcome label of "persecutor." Similarly, models of ideal episcopal conduct—and critiques of ecclesiastical "tyranny"—had some impact upon the behavior and self-presentation of bishops. The hagiographic discourses discussed earlier in this chapter did their best, naturally, to present episcopal exercise of power in the best possible light. The ideal bishop acted from selfless motives, and even his harshest disciplinary measures were understood to derive from a charitable concern for the well-being of his congregation. Still, late antique churchmen were painfully aware of the ease with which such an ideal could be corrupted. Even as polemicists invoked the discourse of tyranny against ecclesiastical opponents, others attempted to forestall such criticism by subjecting themselves to a stricter scrutiny.

Cyprian, addressing his episcopal colleagues at the Council of Carthage in 256, reassured them: "For neither does any of us set himself up as a bishop of bishops, nor by tyrannical terror does any compel his colleague to the necessity of obedience." In its immediate context—a division within the church over how to treat those who had lapsed during persecution—the statement was an implicit rebuke to Rome's bishop, who claimed for himself the title *episcopus episcoporum*.[104] Cyprian's remark reflected a deep uneasiness within the church regarding the proper limits of episcopal power, and a particular discomfort with hierarchical principles that allowed some bishops to

---

copal rivalry than accusations of heresy, particularly when the doctrines involved had not yet been definitively endorsed or condemned.

104. *The Seventh Council of Carthage under Cyprian* (trans. in ANF, vol. 5, p. 565). The criticism echoes an earlier complaint in Tertullian, *On Modesty* 1, regarding the Roman bishops' claims to ecclesiastical primacy. On Cyprian's ideas of episcopal authority see Rives 1995, pp. 285–310. Lane Fox 1986, pp. 493–517, offers an excellent discussion of the role of the bishop in the third century. On the term "bishop of bishops" as applied to emperors, see Rapp 1998a, Girardet 1977.

claim authority over others. By the fifth century, when much greater degrees of wealth and power were at stake, church leaders feared the emergence of ecclesiastical "tyrants"—such as Dioscorus of Alexandria—who would set themselves up as "bishop of bishops" and subject the rest of the church to their rule. The Council of Chalcedon, as we will see in the next chapter, attempted simultaneously to strengthen the episcopacy as an institution while quietly adopting measures to curb the power and ambition of individual bishops.[105]

The anonymous author of the Pelagian treatise *On Bad Teachers* turned the polemical discourses of ecclesiastical tyranny toward a cautionary self-criticism:

> What are we to make of the fact we strive to conceal our cruelty and savagery under the name of religion and commit the crime of ungodliness under the name of godliness? For when we wish to hurt one of our brethren or to weigh down his life with a heavy burden of infamy, we boast that we are doing this because of our zeal for righteousness and religion and faith, in order that we may appear in the eyes of men to have done our unrighteous deeds in a righteous manner and be accounted holy in the sight of outsiders, when we are most wicked first in the sight of God and then in the judgment of our own conscience.[106]

Different discourses about power and violence could endow a single act with different or even opposite meanings: the healthy discipline of a zealous saint-bishop, or the arrogant and reckless brutality of a tyrant. In like manner, the previous two chapters outlined a hagiographic model of holy men's holy violence, and explored ways in which that representation could be challenged and contested. The tension between ideals and realities of episcopal leadership and ascetic zeal formed one of the main driving forces behind the catastrophic conflicts and schisms that divided the eastern church in the early fifth century.

---

105. *Canon* 26 of Chalcedon, for example, mandated that *oikonomoi* were henceforth to oversee church finances, so that the bishop would no longer be directly responsible for money—and presumably, then, less vulnerable either to temptation or to accusation in financial matters. Compare *Canon* 3, a more general prohibition on bishops and clergy engaging in secular business.

106. *On Bad Teachers* 11.4 (trans. Rees 1991, pp. 231–232). Rees dates the text between 411 and 415. Toward the end of the sixth century, Pope Gregory the Great expressed similar worries about the dangers of ecclesiastical power and urged his fellow bishops to subject their own motives to the strictest scrutiny, lest "vices pass themselves off as virtues." *Pastoral Rule* 2.9. On Gregory and ecclesiastical leadership, see now Leyser 2000, chaps. 6 and 7.

8. *Non Iudicium sed Latrocinium*

Of Holy Synods and Robber Councils

In late 428 or 429, just as Nestorius' pronouncements on the *Theotokos* were beginning to stir controversy, an ominous event befell the church of Constantinople. Several slaves, fleeing from an abusive master, sought protection in the sanctuary of the Great Church. But their claim to refuge was tarnished by the fact that they had seized the altar with drawn swords. For several days they remained there, threatening all who approached, so that the sacraments could not be performed. Finally the standoff ended in a bloodbath, when the fugitives first murdered a priest and then slew themselves. Although the slaves' quarrel had nothing to do with Nestorius, Cyril, or the *Theotokos,* nevertheless the significance was clear. Blood had been spilled within the sanctuary and indeed upon the very altar, an ultimate act of desecration in Christianity's holiest space.[1] It could only be a grim portent for the future of the Christian church as it headed into a long period of schism and division, an ecclesiastical "civil war" waged through successive ecumenical councils.[2]

Socrates had no great respect either for the "firebrand" Nestorius or for the violent and power-hungry Cyril. There was no true doctrinal issue at

---

1. Socrates *HE* 7.33, who deliberately interrupts his narrative of the *Theotokos* controversy in order to cover this apparently unrelated incident and thus underlines its ominous significance. Socrates' historical narrative emphasized "correspondence" between secular and ecclesiastical events, such that disorder in the church meant trouble in civil society, and vice versa: Urbainczyk 1997, pp. 69–79. The law of 431 on sanctuary in church (*C.Th.* 9.45.4 = *CJ* 1.12.3, abbreviated versions, with full text in Schwartz, *ACO* 1.4, pp. 61–65; trans. in Coleman-Norton 1966, pp. 654–662), which explicitly denies refuge to those who bear arms, may perhaps have been inspired by this incident.

2. On language of "civil war" in the church, cf. Tyconius' characterization of the Donatist schism as *bellum intestinum:* Gennadius, *De Viris Illustribus* 18. See also Halton 1995.

stake between them, only mischaracterization and distortion, "like a battle in the dark."[3] The rivalries of powerful bishops could only lead to grief. Palladius believed that the "civil wars" in the church that resulted from such ambition were all the more regrettable because there was no serious doctrinal issue at stake: "For the serpent, the inventor of lawlessness and the cultivator of the worst form of evil, did not find a newer type of heresy. So he infuriated those in authority in the church to mutual slaughter to satisfy their desire for the episcopal office and even the primacy in the episcopate. It was for this they tore the church asunder."[4]

At the First Council of Ephesus in 431, charges of "tyranny" echoed back and forth, alongside doctrinal accusations, between Cyril and Nestorius.[5] The *Life of Rabbula* painted Nestorius as an illegitimate pretender who had tricked his way to the throne and then attempted to impose his heresy by force:

> [Nestorius] had already early taken on the accursed seed through the
> instruction of Theodore [of Mopsuestia] and through his company,
> but had held it suppressed and hidden in the field of his heart, so long
> as he was held back by the fear of men. But he found an opportunity
> to take over the throne and residence of the exalted bishop of the capital,
> where he hoped for a door leading to error through his pride; he was
> able without further ado to seduce everyone to his blasphemy through
> the weighty power of his authority and with the support of the secular
> magistrates.[6]

When Rabbula confronted him, therefore, it was with the courage of a holy man exercising *parrhesia* before a fearsome secular tyrant: "Although that one still, inflated with pride and arrogance, sat on the elevated throne of rulership, nevertheless Rabbula preached fearlessly to his face before the eyes of all the assembled congregation, the correct word of truth, with a loud voice."[7]

Besa's *Life of Shenoute*, in the scene that opened the last chapter, presented a similar picture. Nestorius, striding in "with a great display of pride and

---

3. Socrates *HE* 7.32.

4. Palladius, *Dialogue* 20.579–584 (trans. Meyer). This is an interesting extension of the commonly expressed belief in Christian historiography that after Satan tried and failed to destroy Christianity through the direct assault of pagan persecution, he turned to the more insidious strategy of dividing the church against itself through heresies and schisms: cf. the opening remarks (1.1) of Theodoret's *Ecclesiastical History*.

5. Cf. *ACO* 1.1.5.143, petition of Basil, Thalassius, and other monks, describing how Nestorius had ordered magistrates and *decani* to beat, imprison, and exile priests, monks, and laymen who denounced his heresy.

6. Overbeck 1865, p. 196.

7. Overbeck 1865, p. 198.

shamelessness," usurped the seat and insulted the very person of Christ, by throwing the Gospels on the floor. In response to such sacrilege, Shenoute's violent riposte was entirely justified. That dramatic scene was almost certainly fictional: in reality, Cyril and Nestorius never confronted each other in person. Cyril and his supporters had arrived first, and proclaimed themselves in session without waiting for John of Antioch and the eastern bishops, who were expected to support Nestorius. The bishop of Constantinople, sensing that he had no hope of a fair hearing before Cyril's council, refused the synod's repeated summons and was quickly condemned in absentia.[8] When the Antiochenes finally arrived, the result was two separate conclaves, each excommunicated by the other.[9] John of Antioch complained in a letter to the emperor that he had arrived in Ephesus only to find the church "disrupted by civil war."[10] Once again, a council that had been called in order to unite the church managed only to exacerbate division.

Envoys, sent by the Cyrillian synod to summon him the canonical three times, reported that Nestorius had barricaded himself in his house, surrounded by armed soldiers who harassed and threatened Cyril's representatives. To the Cyrillians, this typically "tyrannical" display of secular force was proof of Nestorius' arrogance and contempt for the lawful ecclesiastical authority of their synod, and only confirmed the rightness of their action against him: "Since a body of soldiers surrounds his house, and they will not permit anyone to approach, it is clear that it is not with good conscience that he refuses to appear before the holy council."[11] The bishops' complaint was in its way a preemptive accusation: by calling attention to Nestorius' armed guards, and insinuating that he might try to use them to seize control of the synod, they hoped to make it more difficult for him actually to attempt any such thing.

Nestorius, well aware of the prejudicial spectacle created by his resort to military protection, did his best to deflect the charge. Cyril, not he, was the

8. "Without trial or investigation," as Ibas complained in his *Letter to Mari*.

9. The *Acts* of the First Council of Ephesus are in Schwartz, *ACO* 1. For the events of the council see generally Holum 1982, pp. 147–174; Scipioni 1974; McGuckin 1994, esp. pp. 1–125; Sillett 1999.

10. *Letter to Theodosius: ACO* 1.5.124.

11. Juvenal of Jerusalem, after the third summons, at the first session on 22 June 431: *ACO* 1.2.43. See also *ACO* 1.3.3–5, report of the Cyrillian bishops to the emperor: "He surrounded his house with soldiers, even though there was no threat of disturbance in the city." *Letter of Cyril to Comarius, Potamon, Dalmatius et al.* in Constantinople (Cyril *Ep.* 23): "A second and third time we summoned him, but he had the soldiers of Candidianus surrounding his house, armed with clubs, an extraordinary thing." (McEnerney trans.)

true tyrant, and the soldiers were needed to protect him against Cyril's violent followers:

> You see of how much tyranny I made use and how far I was liable to accusation, because, for the purpose of rescuing myself from the conspirators who rose up against me, I had need to post soldiers around my house to guard me, that they might not come against me with violence and destroy me! You accuse me of posting soldiers around my house: [it was] not that they might do any wrong to you, but that they might hinder you from doing wrong to me. From the fact that you reproach us with posting soldiers, it is clear that if they had not first been posted around me and been a wall for me, I would have been destroyed by violent men.[12]

Cyril had brought with him to Ephesus a large body of zealous and fanatical Egyptian monks, who joined forces with the followers of Cyril's ally, bishop Memnon of Ephesus, to roam the streets of the city, occupy the churches so as to monopolize worship space for the Cyrillian party, and terrorize Antiochene bishops.

> They did all things such as take place in wars. And the [followers] of the Egyptian, and those of Memnon by whom they were aided, were going around the city, girded and armed with rods, stiff-necked men, who rushed upon [the Antiochenes] with the clamor of barbarians and forcibly emitted from their nostrils a spirit of anger with fearful cries . . . breathing [anger] without self-control, with all pride, against those whom they knew to be not in agreement with the things which were done by them. . . . All of those things which were taking place were [matters] of astonishment and fear, so that they blocked all the ways and made everyone flee and not be seen, and were behaving arbitrarily, giving way to drunkenness and to intoxication and to a disgraceful outcry. And there was none hindering, nor even bringing assistance, and thus [men] were amazed.[13]

Although Nestorius, who initially enjoyed the favor of the emperor Theodosius II, had arrived in Ephesus in the company of the *comes domesticorum*, Candidian, and an impressive military escort, this display of secular force

---

12. Nestorius, *Bazaar of Heracleides*, p. 135 [199–200]. Nestorius composed this long apologia during his years of exile in the Great Oasis of the Egyptian desert. References to events preceding Chalcedon indicate its completion by 451; Nestorius is thought to have died shortly thereafter. The text survives in a sixth-century Syriac translation. Quotations here are taken from the English translation of Driver and Hodgson 1925. Page citations from Nestorius refer first to Driver and Hodgson, followed by those from Bedjan's Syriac text in brackets.

13. Nestorius pp. 266–267 [367–369]. Cf. similar complaints by Theodoret (*Ep.* 169), John of Antioch (*ACO* 1.1.3.97).

had little effect upon the outcome of the council. Theodosius had instructed Candidian to keep order, and above all "to remove from the city the laypeople and monks who have assembled there in order to incite disturbances and disrupt the work of the council."[14] But Candidian could only send a series of increasingly plaintive complaints back to Constantinople as Cyril's bishops defied his repeated orders that they not convene while John and the Antiochenes were still absent.[15]

Nestorius had arrived bearing all the trappings of a secular tyrant, and could still be faulted for that, but the intrusion of state power into church affairs, as polemically charged as it still was, counted for surprisingly little at the Council of Ephesus. Real power lay in the hands of the monks, whether brought by Cyril from Egypt or recruited from circles opposing Nestorius in Constantinople—violent zealots of the same sort described in chapters 5 and 6. To Nestorius, these were false monks, concealing disorderly brigandage under the pretense of holiness, "supposed on account of their having the *schema* of monks to be acting with religious zeal" so that they might "seem righteous, rather than merely troublesome."[16] The monks' point of view is perhaps better reflected in the story told by the *Life of Shenoute*. Though it could not have happened exactly as described, Shenoute's violent challenge to Nestorius probably captured the spirit of many street confrontations between Cyrillian monks and Antiochene bishops, and certainly expressed the zealous Egyptian ascetics' understanding of their mission in Ephesus: to strike down with God's holy anger those who dared to offend the faith.[17]

RIGHTEOUS REBELLION: MONKS AGAINST BISHOPS

The story of Shenoute and Nestorius, at first glance, might seem to embody a classic Weberian formulation of charisma versus hierarchy. Nestorius' an-

14. *ACO* 1.1.31.

15. Candidian's letters: *ACO* 1.1.1 pp. 120ff. and 1.4.30–33. For Candidian's advocacy of Nestorius see *PLRE* vol. 2, s.v. Candidianus 6; Holum 1982, pp. 163–171.

16. Nestorius pp. 288–289 [397–399]. See discussion of polemic against "false monks" in chapter 6, pp. 228–231. The monks at Ephesus of whom Nestorius complained may have been the same sort of disorderly, *martyria*-dwelling ascetics he had previously clashed with in Constantinople: see Caner 2002, pp. 212–223. *Schema* here refers not only to the distinctive physical garment of the monks but also implies "seeming" or "surface appearance" and thus connotes deception and pretense. It would best be translated by "costume," with a similar double meaning.

17. Though a face-to-face encounter with Nestorius seems unlikely, given that bishop's careful avoidance of any venue dominated by the Cyrillians, Shenoute did in fact accompany Cyril to Ephesus: Emmel 1993, pp. 4–6.

swer, "You are not a bishop, but a mere monk," challenged Shenoute's right to speak on hierarchical grounds. Shenoute, for his part, claimed authority directly from God, to express the righteous outrage he felt: "I am he whom God has sent, to rebuke you for your impiety." Shenoute invoked violent *parrhesia* as the answer to institutional rank, an alternative justification for his right to speak—and as a forceful act that suppressed Nestorius' blasphemous speech. Here Bruce Lincoln's analysis of authority in terms of struggles over "authorizing stages" and "authorized speakers" becomes very relevant: much of the violence we will see in connection with the fifth-century councils will revolve around determining, and contesting, who is and is not authorized to speak in the supremely authoritative forum of an ecumenical synod.[18] Normally, only bishops spoke at councils. Shenoute offered a challenge to that rule both in his own "unauthorized" speech and in his suppression of the normally "authorized" speech of the bishop, Nestorius.

We might be tempted to apply the simple paradigm of charisma versus hierarchy more broadly. At first glance, the events of 448–49 can easily be seen as a rising monastic movement in revolt against episcopal authority, from Eutyches' confrontation with Flavian to the fearsome deeds of Barsauma, "slayer of bishops," and the hordes of club-wielding monks who terrorized bishops at Ephesus II.[19] But we must keep in mind that much of this terrifying image comes from complaints brought later at Chalcedon by bishops who had been on the receiving end of this violence. The bishops at Chalcedon, who sought to institutionalize, regulate, and generally "tame" the monastic movement through comprehensive canonical legislation, had as much interest in constructing an alarming, polemical image of violent fanaticism as had Libanius when he had written his infamous portrait of the "black-robed tribes" of monks in the 380s.[20] The eastern bishops, who came under attack by followers of Barsauma, Eutyches, and Dioscorus, appealed to the imperial authorities and to the pope in Rome for support in the starkest possible terms, presenting their assailants as part of a dangerous move-

18. Lincoln 1994, esp. pp. 7–13 and 74–76. Cf. p. 75: "They [incidents of violence] were catalyzed either by the entry of an unauthorized person into the privileged sphere . . . or alternatively, when it appeared that an authorized person . . . would make use of his access to say things judged intolerable. In all cases, the period of crisis ended in violence: violence deployed by people who were determined to prevent an act of speech that threatened not only their interests, but also their relative monopoly on access to the privileged sphere."

19. See discussion below, pp. 290–299.

20. See chapter 6 for discussion of polemical constructions of "false monks." Chalcedonian legislation on monasticism is discussed below, pp. 316–317.

ment that threatened to overthrow all ecclesiastical hierarchy and secular law and order.[21]

The reality, of course, was far more complicated than could be explained in terms of conflict between the monastic movement and the episcopal hierarchy. Diverse factions of Syrian Christians, including monks but also ordained clergy as well as laypeople, revolted against their own bishops, but did so in alliance with another bishop, Dioscorus. They challenged their bishops for a variety of reasons, partly doctrinal—the bishops, adherents of the Antiochene school of Christology, were thought to be closet "Nestorians"— but also for allegations of misconduct and misrule specific to each case. The charges brought against Ibas, Daniel, Sophronius, Theodoret, Domnus, and others were undoubtedly presented in a slanted and exaggerated manner. Nevertheless, we may assume that any powerful bishop must have had a certain number of critics, frustrated rivals, or personal enemies within his clergy or congregation, who might be predisposed to see any number of "abuses" in his government of the local church. But the bishop had considerable disciplinary power over those under his authority, and such people normally had little voice, or access to any authorizing forum in which they could make their grievances known.[22] Only when broader controversies or rivalries erupted on an ecumenical stage might there appear a sympathetic audience willing to entertain minor clerics' accusations against their own bishops. Dioscorus, following in a long Alexandrian tradition in his efforts to extend his power at the expense of the rival sees of Constantinople and Antioch,[23] encouraged independent and rebellious behavior from monks and clergy in those sees that he would never have tolerated in Egypt—where he reportedly treated opposition with the same heavy hand as had Athanasius, Theophilus, and Cyril before him.[24]

One cannot, therefore, reduce the events of Ephesus II and Chalcedon to a simple paradigm of charismatic Monophysite monks versus hierarchically-minded Chalcedonian/Antiochene bishops. Strong and equally militant monastic factions featured prominently in the Chalcedonian camp, most notably the Akoimetes of Constantinople, who would repeatedly challenge the

21. As, e.g., in Theodoret *Ep.* 113, to Leo, or Flavian's appeal to Leo (*ACO* 2.2, p. 78), both of which followed very much in the rhetorical tradition of John Chrysostom's letter to Pope Innocent or Athanasius' appeals to Julius: see chapter 2, pp. 79–82.

22. Cf. Nestorius p. 362 [496–497]: for monks to accuse their bishops was like slaves bringing charges against their own masters.

23. On which see Baynes 1926.

24. Charges brought against Dioscorus are discussed below, pp. 318–321.

authority of both patriarch and emperor in the decades after Chalcedon to prevent any compromise with Monophysite "heretics." And of course both Chalcedonian and Monophysite camps would fight hard to win the support of charismatic "stars" such as Symeon the Stylite.[25] Chalcedon's crackdown on monasticism was made possible in part by a split in the Constantinopolitan monastic movement between followers of Eutyches and those of archimandrites such as Faustus and Martin who had remained loyal to Flavian.[26] The bishop had allowed these friendly archimandrites to sign their names to the decree condemning Eutyches—such signatures normally being the prerogative of bishops.[27] At Chalcedon, the monastic foundations led by Faustus and Martin supported the episcopal hierarchy and the imperial government in their legislative attempt to define one form of monasticism, regulated coenobitism, as the only true and legitimate variety, and called for the suppression of alternative movements that remained outside their control, naming them mere "troublemakers" and "false monks."[28]

We may conclude, then, that neither adherence to a principle of rank and hierarchy nor resort to charismatic authority appears consistently on one side or another. Nevertheless they are not without importance. Each represented a certain style of self-presentation, a rhetorical stance available to be invoked when the situation demanded it. The confrontation between Eutyches and Flavian at the *synodos endemousa* of 448 will illustrate some of the ways in which these different paradigms could be brought to bear in a contest over religious authority. Eutyches was a powerful and revered Constantinopolitan archimandrite with important connections at court. When bishop Eusebius of Dorylaeum—himself a "firebrand" who twenty years earlier had been one of the first to charge Nestorius with heresy[29]—accused him of holding heretical beliefs on the incarnation, it created a difficult situation for bishop Flavian. Though as a presbyter Eutyches fell under Flavian's disciplinary authority, Flavian approached the case with some discomfort and

25. On these events see Bacht 1951.

26. Caner 2002, chap. 6, discusses these events.

27. Flavian did however preserve one important distinction: whereas the bishops signed "I have defined and subscribed" [*horisas hupegrapsa*], the archimandrites wrote merely *hupegrapsa*, "I have subscribed." Signatures at *ACO* 2.1.1.552, fifty-three subscriptions in all. Cf. Eutyches' complaint to Pope Leo about the novelty of such signatures: Leo *Ep.* 21.

28. This conflict could be seen most clearly in Session 4, where the loyalist archimandrites challenged the credentials of those who pleaded on behalf of Eutyches: see below, pp. 316–317.

29. On Eusebius' previous role in the Nestorian controversy see *PLRE*, s.v. Eusebius 15; Holum 1982, p. 155.

tried unsuccessfully to persuade Eusebius to drop the matter.[30] The ensuing scene displayed the ambiguity of the relation between ecclesiastical and secular law on judging matters of faith. Were accusations of heresy to be handled as a simple matter of clerical discipline, or according to the inquisitorial model of a judicial trial? Flavian tried to present it as a disciplinary exercise, in which he took the role of a loving ecclesiastical "father" correcting a misguided disciple. This would have the effect both of softening the tone of the proceedings—for he feared Eutyches' powerful backers—and at the same time firmly subordinating Eutyches, casting the elderly monk as a "child" before his fathers. It would have allowed Eutyches an easy way to back down, should he wish to: he could be forgiven for having fallen into error, as long as he was willing to yield to the judgment of those better qualified to decide matters of faith:

> Let him come here. He will come before fathers and brothers, before those who are not ignorant of him, who persevere in amity for him. . . . We are men; many great men have stumbled and have fallen through imprudence and inexperience even though they believed themselves to possess the truth. There is no shame in repentance, but there is shame in persisting in sin. . . . Let him come here, let him confess and anathematize his error, and we will pardon him all his past errors.[31]

But Eusebius insisted on making a legal case of it: "Guilty people are always evasive and seek pretexts for delay. . . . I demand that the authority of the holy canons exercise its vigilance against the accused, and proceed against him."[32]

This had the effect of putting Eusebius, a bishop, and Eutyches, a "mere monk," on an equal footing as prosecutor and defendant and also necessitated strict adherence to judicial procedure—which in turn allowed Eutyches subsequently to appeal his condemnation on the grounds that proper procedure had not been followed.[33] A judicial paradigm would also require a clear winner or loser: either Eutyches would be convicted and stripped of rank, or Eusebius would suffer the legal penalties appropriate to a false accuser.[34]

In his answer to the charges against him, Eutyches sought to present himself as a simple monk, an anchorite who had separated himself from the world. "From earliest childhood," he later said in his petition to the Second

---

30. *ACO* 2.1.1.419, Flavian: "You know the zeal of the accuser. Fire seems cold to him, next to his zeal for piety. God knows that I admonished him and begged him, 'Please, give it up.' But when he pressed on, what was I to do?" Cf. also 2.1.1.231–235.
31. Flavian: *ACO* 2.1.1.417.
32. *ACO* 2.1.1.400.
33. Eutyches' complaints: e.g., *ACO* 2.1.1.185, 220, 572, 834.
34. As Eusebius protested several times, e.g. *ACO* 2.1.1.423, 425, 477–486.

Council of Ephesus, "I have wanted nothing more than to lead a quiet life, free from worldly affairs and from disturbance."[35] At first he refused the summons, saying that he had sworn an oath never to set foot outside his monastery but to live there as if in a tomb.[36] This protest of simplicity had the effect of elevating his personal ascetic devotion to a higher level of authority than the official, canonical command of a synod of bishops. When he finally arrived at the synod, he protested a simple faith based on allegiance to scripture, Nicaea, First Ephesus, and Cyril, and claimed to have little understanding or patience for the complex theological questioning with which he felt the bishops were trying to entrap him.[37]

Although he had previously refused to say, as the bishops demanded of him, that Christ was consubstantial to us in his humanity,[38] now Eutyches made an exaggerated show of obedience and deference to the bishops: "I said that I did not profess this before, but now since your Sanctity teaches it, I will say it too—even though I do not find these teachings in Scripture or in the Fathers."[39] Pretending to bow to the bishops' authority, he in fact went on record accusing them of the cardinal sin of "innovation." Eutyches knew that he would be condemned by Flavian's synod, but also that his powerful allies in the imperial court and in Alexandria would ensure him a far more sympathetic hearing at which he would be able to turn the tables on his accusers. He manipulated the course of his trial in order to ensure that evidence was entered into the record, which could later be used to his advantage, and to set the trap, which was later sprung at Ephesus II, when both Eusebius and Flavian would be condemned on the same charge of innovation.

Eutyches' self-presentation as a "mere monk" was belied by the obvious signs of his powerful connections at court. He arrived in the company of the silentiary Magnus and a military escort, bearing letters indicating the emperor's personal interest in the case. As godfather to the powerful court eunuch Chrysaphius, and spiritual advisor to the emperor, Eutyches had *parrhesia* and he wanted the bishops to know it. Eusebius of Dorylaeum, the

35. *ACO* 2.1.1.157.

36. *ACO* 2.1.1.359.

37. Cf. Lim 1995, pp. 182–216 for analysis of stories from the Council of Nicaea that presented the simple, creed-based faith of the unlearned Christian triumphing over theological "sophistry."

38. The "heresy" associated with the name of Eutyches was an extreme version of Monophysitism, downplaying or even denying the human element in Christ— but Eutyches' often confused and contradictory statements in the trial record make it difficult to determine exactly what the archimandrite believed. On the theological background to Chalcedon see Grillmeier 1975, Frend 1972.

39. *ACO* 2.1.1.535.

accuser, claimed that Eutyches had threatened him: "I fear his tricks. I am poor and without resources. He has threatened me with exile; he is resourceful. He has depicted me in the Oasis."[40] Eusebius and his allies attempted to invoke the sinister language of "tyranny" against the defiant archimandrite who entered his trial surrounded by soldiers. Eutyches was accused of fomenting rebellion among the monks of Constantinople,[41] circulating credal statements to the other archimandrites and warning them, "If Flavian crushes me, he will come after you next."[42] The archimandrite Martin's response embodied the proper behavior of a respectful and obedient monk: he declined to sign Eutyches' statement—"It is only for bishops to sign creeds"—and promptly reported the matter to Flavian.[43] After the synod, Eutyches refused to accept the legitimacy of his condemnation, and challenged Flavian both in the secular courts and on the streets. Flavian complained to Pope Leo:

> You should be told that this same Eutyches, after suffering just and canonical deposition, instead of appeasing God by tearful repentance, has made every effort to throw the most holy church of [Constantinople] into confusion: setting up in public placards full of insults and maledictions, and beyond this addressing his entreaties to our most religious and God-loving emperor, and these too overflowing with arrogance and insolence, whereby he has tried to overthrow the divine canons in everything.[44]

For Flavian, the simple act of appealing to the emperor was an unacceptable transgression against the canonical authority of the bishop. Eutyches, like the Arian bishops of the fourth century, had in effect summoned the secular powers into the church. Nestorius, observing the events of 448–51 from the distant and embittered vantage point of his exile in the Egyptian desert, invoked the discourses of usurpation and tyranny most succinctly: "Because he was not a bishop, Eutyches set himself up by the authority of the emperor to act as bishop of bishops."[45]

Further examples of these competing paradigms of authority could be

40. The Great Oasis of Egypt, a notorious destination for exiles (Nestorius was already there). *ACO* 2.1.1.481. Cf. Nestorius p. 341 [467–469] on the intimidation and "persecution" that Theodosius undertook against Flavian on Eutyches' behalf.

41. As charged by Eusebius: *ACO* 2.1.1.436.

42. *ACO* 2.1.1.436. But Eutyches' followers later denied that he had ever made any such inflammatory statement: 2.1.1.685.

43. *ACO* 2.1.1.436. On the rivalry between Eutyches and the other archimandrites, see Caner 2002, pp. 223–241.

44. Flavian, letter to Leo: Leo *Ep.* 26 (NPNF trans.).

45. Nestorius p. 336 [459]. On the implications of the title "bishop of bishops" see discussion in chapter 7, pp. 281–282.

seen at the fourth session of Chalcedon, when the presiding authorities tried and failed to force acceptance of the controversial *Tome of Leo*—regarded by Monophysites as unacceptably "Nestorian"—upon two groups of recusants: Constantinopolitan monks who still supported Eutyches, and Egyptian bishops loyal to Dioscorus. The monks articulated their refusal in charismatic and confrontational terms—they set their own understanding of the faith above that claimed by the council, and rejected its condemnation of Dioscorus as unjust: "The condemnation which was made against Dioscorus is utterly unreasonable. . . . If your holiness should oppose the things which we thus legitimately seek . . . then shaking off our garments we remove ourselves far from communion with you. For when the creed of the faith of the 318 [Fathers of Nicaea] is abolished, we do not suffer to remain in communion with those who have abolished it."[46]

The Egyptian bishops, meanwhile, used an excessive show of devotion to the principle of episcopal hierarchy to justify what was in fact the same act of resistance. They refused to accept the *Tome of Leo* because, they claimed, ancient custom and canonical legislation allowed them to take no such step without the permission of their leader, the bishop of Alexandria.[47] Since Dioscorus had at this point been legally deposed and was already on his way into exile, and no replacement had yet been elected, the Egyptian bishops were in essence invoking obedience to an absent authority in order to justify their disobedience to the present authority of the council. Furthermore, they feared that if they signed the controversial *Tome* they would be killed upon their return to Egypt.[48] The Chalcedonian bishops, not normally eager to encourage the privileging of individual judgment over the authority of

46. *Libellus* presented by Carosus, Dorotheus, and a number of other monks: *ACO* 2.1.4.88.

47. Bishop Hierakis said: "Regarding the letter of the most holy and God-beloved archbishop Leo, all of you most holy fathers know that in everything we wait upon the decision of our most holy archbishop [of Alexandria], and we beg your philanthropy to await the decision of our president, for we follow him in everything. This also the 318 holy fathers who gathered in Nicaea legislated, that all the diocese of Egypt should follow the archbishop of the great city of Alexandria, and nothing should be done without him by any of the bishops under him." *ACO* 2.1.4.31. Canon 6 of Nicaea stated: "Let the ancient customs in Egypt, Libya and Pentapolis prevail, that the Bishop of Alexandria have jurisdiction in all these." (NPNF trans.)

48. The Egyptian bishops cried: "We will be killed, have mercy on us. . . . We do not wish to disobey the synod, but we will be killed in our homeland: have mercy on us. You have the authority: we submit, we do not resist. Better that we should be killed by the lord of this world and by your excellences and by the holy synod than there. For God's sake have mercy on our gray hairs." *ACO* 2.1.4.56. Though the Chalcedonians ridiculed this claim—"See, how will they make martyrs of their own bish-

tradition and hierarchy, found themselves in the odd position of ridiculing the Egyptians for their lack of personal initiative and martyrial zeal.[49]

These two examples demonstrate the ways in which individuals and groups could profess their submission to established authority while in fact exercising considerable choice as to which "authorities" they wished to recognize and obey. Loyalty to one could be invoked in order to justify rejection of another. Eutyches and the monks at Chalcedon offered an absolute reverence for Nicaea—a long-past council of 318 long-dead and collectively canonized "holy fathers"—as grounds for disobeying the bishops at the present council, whom they accused of "innovating" upon a pure faith that Nicaea had decided for all time.[50] The Egyptian bishops, meanwhile, invoked obedience to a vacant episcopal throne to the same end. All parties couched their claims in terms of reverence for authority, but these confrontations bore revolutionary implications.[51] Persons without clerical rank, without the legitimacy conferred by apostolic succession, took it upon themselves to decide which authorities to obey. All sides claimed to be following the faith of Nicaea, but the monks claimed to understand that faith better than their bishops. The earliest stage of what would later be termed the "Monophysite" opposition to Chalcedon presented itself not so much in terms of one-nature Christology but rather what could be called "Nicene fundamentalism"—an absolute privileging of tradition, and invocation of that tradition to justify opposition to anyone judged as "innovating" upon it. But the Chalcedonian bishops could, and did, answer that taking such judgment upon oneself was in itself an act of rebellion, a usurpation of authority that lawfully be-

---

ops?" (2.1.4.55)—the lynching of bishop Proterius in 457 suggests that their fears were not entirely exaggerated. On this incident see Evagrius Scholasticus *HE* 2.8, Zacharias of Mytilene *Chronicle* 4.2; with commentary in T. Gregory 1979, pp. 163–201.

49. "Paschasinus [papal representative] said: For how many years have they grown old as bishops in the churches until this moment, and still not knowing the orthodox and catholic faith, and hanging upon another's judgment?" *ACO* 2.1.4.38.

50. The Council of Nicaea, which in fact probably brought together somewhat fewer than three hundred bishops, by the late fourth century had come to be associated with the biblically significant number three hundred and eighteen (the number of the followers of Abraham in Genesis 14:14): see Aubineau 1966, with commentary by Henry Chadwick in the same volume, pp. 808–811.

51. Rousseau 2000 argues for fifth-century monasticism that "One did not base one's life on loyalty to a specific written rule or even to a permanent community. The fundamental social component of the ascetic life was still the relationship between master and disciple." This tendency helps to explain why some Egyptian bishops and Constantinopolitan monks could privilege their personal devotion to Dioscorus or Eutyches at the expense of any sense of loyalty toward the church hierarchy or the council as an institution.

longed to bishops. The language of tyranny found use even here. The *Apostolic Canons* had ordered that any presbyter who "despised his bishop" and set up a separate congregation was to be deposed "as one who loved power" [*hos philarkhos*], "for he is a tyrant."[52]

The principles of hierarchical authority and charismatic *parrhesia* could be deployed and invoked flexibly, according to the needs of the moment. The *Life of Shenoute* went to bizarre extremes to emphasize the importance of obedience to episcopal authority. "One day," Besa tells us, "our father Shenoute and our Lord Jesus were sitting down talking together." The bishop of Shmin, passing by the monastery, wished to meet the abbot. When Shenoute sent word that he was busy and could not come to the door, the bishop grew angry and threatened to excommunicate him for disobedience:

> The servant went to our father [Shenoute] and said to him what the bishop had told him. But my father smiled graciously with laughter and said: "See what this man of flesh and blood has said! Behold, here sitting with me is he who created heaven and earth! I will not go while I am with him." But the Savior said to my father: "O Shenoute, arise and go out to the bishop, lest he excommunicate you. Otherwise, I cannot let you enter [heaven] because of the covenant I made with Peter, saying 'What you will bind on earth will be bound in heaven, and what you will loose on earth will be loosed in heaven' [Matthew 16:19]." When my father heard these words of the Savior, he arose, went out to the bishop and greeted him.[53]

Not even Christ himself, it seems, would disregard the authority of an ordained bishop. And yet the same text later praises Shenoute for doing exactly that in his confrontation with Nestorius. Shenoute's violence constituted not so much a revolt against episcopal authority, but rather a challenge to Nestorius' right to that authority. The ideal bishop combined his institutional power with the virtue and zeal of a holy man—but Nestorius, and the "Nestorian" bishops of Syria, forfeited their claim to episcopal office through their heretical beliefs and tyrannical conduct. The story from Ephesus, ironically, ended with Shenoute's incorporation into the same hierarchy he had just assaulted. Perhaps in answer to Nestorius' challenge, "You are not a bishop, or even an archimandrite, but a mere monk," Cyril kissed

52. *Apostolic Canons* 31, in *Apostolic Constitutions* 8.47.31. Cf. a similar injunction in *Canon* 5 of the Council of Antioch (341), invoked at Chalcedon to threaten these monks: *ACO* 2.1.4.90.
53. Besa, *Life of Shenoute* 70–72 (trans. Bell). On the context of this story see Behlmer 1998, esp. pp. 353–354.

Shenoute, gave his own stole and staff to the monk, and made him an archimandrite on the spot.[54] In this narrative, Shenoute's act of defiance against a "false" bishop only demonstrated his obedience to his true and lawful bishop and to God—both of whom, the story makes clear, approved.

If we look more closely at the "monastic rebellion" of 448–49, we see similar attempts to assimilate these holy men into the very hierarchy they were challenging—a pursuit, perhaps, of the "holy man/bishop" ideal expressed in the *Life of Rabbula*. The Theodosian dynasty and court had always been known for its patronage of, and devotion to, charismatic ascetic figures such as Isaac, Dalmatius, and Hypatius, who presented a locus of spiritual authority more or less independent from the organized church and bishops in Constantinople.[55] Theodosius II took this devotion to a new extreme, from the aftermath of Ephesus I through Ephesus II in 449, siding decisively with ascetic figures such as Dalmatius or Eutyches, even against the bishops of his own capital. As Nestorius complained bitterly, "The *schema* of the monks was very dear to him."[56] It was the dramatic appeal of the venerable Dalmatius, emerging from his cell for the first time in forty years, that finally convinced Theodosius to abandon his support of Nestorius.[57] Ironically, Theodosius' reverence for the *schema* had brought Nestorius to power in the first place. Wishing to bypass the squabbling factions among the Constantinopolitan clergy who were competing to place one of their number on the vacant episcopal throne in 428, Theodosius— apparently having in mind an episcopal ideal similar to that of the *Life of Rabbula*—decided that a pious monk would make the best bishop. He had offered the job first to Dalmatius, who had refused. So he sent to a monastery outside Antioch for another monk "famous for his preaching and for his manner of life"—Nestorius.[58] If Theodosius had hoped for a saintly ascetic whose example would bring peace to the church, he was to be gravely disappointed. That mounting disillusionment presumably lay behind his eventual break with Nestorius and his passionate hatred of the very name

54. *Life of Shenoute* 130.
55. For the reign of Theodosius I, see Dagron 1970; Matthews 1975, pp. 100–145; discussion in chapter 6, p. 233.
56. Nestorius p. 272 [375].
57. *ACO* 1.1.2.65–69 and 1.1.3.14–15; Nestorius pp. 272–278 [375–383]; commentary in Dagron 1970, pp. 267–268. A similar spectacle was accomplished some decades later when Daniel the Stylite climbed down from his pillar to confront the short-lived emperor Basiliscus over his support for Monophysitism: *Life of Daniel* 73–75.
58. Nestorius pp. 274–277 [377–382], putting those words in the emperor's mouth in his retelling of the conversation between Theodosius and Dalmatius in 431.

of the man he had once chosen. But even as Theodosius turned decisively against the Antiochene bishops in 449, his reverence for monastic holy men only deepened. Theodosius praised the Syrian archimandrite Barsauma lavishly, and invited him to take an unusual role at the Second Council of Ephesus:

> It has not escaped our piety in what kind of conflict the godliest and holiest archimandrites in districts of the east have been placed, fighting for the orthodox faith in opposition to certain bishops in eastern cities who are sick with the impiety of Nestorius, and when the orthodox laypeople share in the struggle along with the most godly archimandrites. Therefore, since your holiness, also, both has sustained such great toil on account of the orthodox faith and has come to our piety's notice, we consider it to be just for your sanctity, respected for purity of life and for orthodox faith, to go to the city of the Ephesians, and, occupying the place of all the most godly archimandrites in the east, to sit down with the holy synod ordered to convene in that place, and with the other holy fathers and bishops to decree matters pleasing to God.[59]

Although it was not unusual for prominent ascetics or laypeople to attend ecumenical councils, Barsauma's role seems to have been largely unprecedented in that he was to be seated among the bishops, take an active part in the proceedings, and attach his signature to the *Acts* alongside those of the bishops.[60] Barsauma was to represent "all the monks and pious people of the east"—in place of their bishops, who would normally be expected to represent them. The imperial letter explicitly condemned these eastern bishops, and effectively endorsed open rebellion against them. The emperor himself seems to have supported an attempt to set up an alternative hierarchy in which pious and proven archimandrites substituted for corrupt and heretical bishops. Theodosius supposedly even offered to make Barsauma patriarch of Antioch, apparently not caring that the see was already occupied.[61] Barsauma, seated among the bishops at Ephesus, in the official tran-

---

59. *Letter of Theodosius to Barsauma*, 14 May 449: *ACO* 2.1.1.48 (trans. adapted from Coleman-Norton).

60. There were, of course, common situations in which a presbyter or deacon sat as a proxy on behalf of a bishop who was absent or ill, or spoke as an interpreter for a bishop who could not communicate in Greek. But Barsauma attended in his own right.

61. By Domnus, one of the bishops who would soon be deposed at the Second Council of Ephesus in August 449. *Life of Barsauma*, 70th miracle. The *Life* places Barsauma's meeting with the emperor immediately before Ephesus II. The offer is attested only in this late source, but is quite consistent with other examples of Theodosius' reverence for monastic holy men.

scripts signed his name last and made an exaggerated show of deference to the judgment of his superiors.[62] The official transcript, of course, did little justice to the true scope of his role at Ephesus II.

In August of 449, approximately 140 bishops assembled at the church dedicated to Mary *Theotokos* for the Second Council of Ephesus.[63] The council presented itself as a celebration of unity and consensus achieved by the exclusion of a predefined "Nestorian" enemy. Theodosius' edicts convening the synod made clear that its purpose was not to reconcile but to "root out," not to define faith but to condemn heresy. Such an unquestioning endorsement of one side was a departure from the more typical "centrist" strategy of coercive compromise that had been pursued by emperors in the fourth century and that would reappear at Chalcedon two years later. "The impious Nestorius' blasphemous case against God occasioned the synod already previously held in Ephesus. . . . But since even now another controversy against the divine faith has awakened, we have ordained this second synod to be held in Ephesus, for we are eager in every way that evil's root should be excised."[64]

In its official records, the council sought above all to present an appearance of unity under the firm guidance of a single presiding bishop, Dioscorus of Alexandria. Leading Antiochene theologians such as Theodoret and Ibas were barred from the council: by imperial order, they were to have "no freedom of speech."[65] It was to be a show trial with a predetermined outcome, in which "heretics" would be exposed and condemned without opportunity to defend themselves. We may call this the "Alexandrian" model for an ecumenical council: it is what Cyril had aimed for at the First Council of Ephesus, and the *acta* of his own synod gave a similar impression of unity. But where Cyril had had to share the stage and compete for imperial recognition with an alternative conclave organized by John and the Antiochenes, now

---

62. As, e.g., from the first session, approving the reinstatement of Eutyches: "I also, Barsauma, as a child following my fathers, give my agreement and approval . . ." (read back at Chalcedon: *ACO* 2.1.1.884, #112).

63. On the Second Council of Ephesus: Acts of the first session, containing the case of Eutyches and Flavian, were read back at Chalcedon's first session two years later, and are preserved in the transcripts of that council, *ACO* 2.1.1. The second session, dealing with the Antiochene bishops, has survived only in a sixth-century Syriac translation, ed. Flemming 1917; English trans. Perry 1881. Discussion in Frend 1972, pp. 35–46; Murphy 1952, pp. 12–24; T. Gregory 1979, pp. 129–161; Bacht 1951, pp. 221–231.

64. *ACO* 2.1.1.49, memorandum to Elpidius, *comes* of the sacred consistory (trans. adapted from Coleman-Norton).

65. *Letter of Theodosius to Dioscorus*, 6 August 449: *ACO* 2.1.1.52.

Dioscorus, enjoying the full support of the imperial authorities, was able to run the council exactly as he pleased. The official transcript presents the assembled bishops alternating unanimous acclamation of Dioscorus with unanimous denunciation of the "Nestorian" defendants. These acclamations were extremely vehement and violent—"Let those who say Christ has two natures be cut in two!"—and Dioscorus showcased his complete control of the proceedings as he alternately fanned and moderated the flames of their zeal.[66]

At the first session, on 8 August, Flavian and Eusebius found the tables turned upon them as they were placed on trial and condemned for their earlier action against Eutyches. Dioscorus' notaries read back the transcripts from Flavian's *synodos endemousa*, which were subjected to a withering barrage of challenges. Although Eutyches' allies condemned statements of "two natures" made at Flavian's synod, their criticism also employed an elaborate rhetoric of judicial unfairness in order to undermine the legitimacy of Eutyches' condemnation: accusers were allowed to sit as judges, the accused were not given notice nor permitted to defend themselves, condemnations were written up in advance of the trial, transcripts were falsified.[67] Such charges, which allowed the losers in one judicial arena to challenge the legitimacy of the judgment against them, featured prominently in accusations brought by different parties throughout the controversy. Even as Eutyches complained that Flavian had treated him in such a manner, so the bishops at Chalcedon two years later would charge Dioscorus with doing the same to Flavian.[68] The unfortunate bishop of Constantinople found both his disciplinary authority and his theological competence repeatedly second-guessed, as he was denounced and condemned first for his harsh actions against Eutyches and his followers—actions that, under normal rules of hierarchical discipline, were entirely within his power but that in this context were characterized as the abuses of a tyrant-bishop—and then for his "innovation" upon the faith of Nicaea.[69]

---

66. Examples from the first session at Ephesus II, as read back at Chalcedon: *ACO* 2.1.1.136–137 and 141–148; 303–304; 491–494.

67. Eutyches' complaints: *ACO* 2.1.1.185, 220 (challenging the papal representatives as "biased" because they lodged with Flavian), 572, 834.

68. See ,e.g., Theodoret *Ep.* 138. Cf. the charge against Chrysostom at the Synod of the Oak (1.26): "He acts as accuser, as witness and as judge."

69. The bishops at Ephesus gave a warm reception to the plaintive appeal of Eutyches' followers "unjustly excommunicated and forced to mourn while the rest of Christendom celebrated Easter": *ACO* 2.1.1.887–894. After Eutyches had been formally rehabilitated, Dioscorus brought up for acclamation the canon from Ephesus I, which condemned any innovation upon Nicaea—and then surprised most of the assembled bishops by invoking it against Flavian: *ACO* 2.1.1.905–964.

At the second session, on 22 August, it was the turn of the Syrian bishops. Ibas, Daniel, Sophronius, Theodoret, Domnus, and several others were all condemned in rapid succession, their real crime being that they all belonged to the Antiochene party, which had opposed Cyril and which continued to arouse suspicions of "Nestorianism." But the rationales for condemnation included not only heresy but also a great variety of misconduct charges encompassing nearly every form of behavior associated with the polemical type of the tyrant-bishop: luxury and waste, heavy-handed persecution of opponents, consorting with Jews and pagans, sorcery, sexual misconduct, and sacrilegious violence.[70] Unlawful corruption of the written record and violent coercion of witnesses featured in these accusations, as they had in Eutyches' appeal: the presbyter Pelagius submitted a long and rambling *libellus* charging that Theodoret and Domnus had beaten him into signing a false and heretical confession of faith.[71] Such typically tyrannical abuses would, of course, feature prominently in later complaints about Dioscorus' council. Theodoret himself was tried and condemned on the basis of examination of "heretical" passages in his writings, as Nestorius had been at the First Council of Ephesus. In the interval between the two councils, Cyril had become a standard of orthodoxy, such that Theodoret and Ibas could be condemned as heretics simply because their writings could be shown to disagree with those of Cyril—or because they had criticized Cyril's conduct and character, as Ibas had done in his *Letter to Mari*.[72] "Heresy," in this style of judgment, could be found not just in one's own explicit doctrinal statements, but might also inhere in one's personal relationships: friend-

70. Ibas, for blasphemy, misuse of church funds, taking bribes from pagans, abuse of power: Flemming 1917, pp. 6–68. Daniel of Harran, Ibas' nephew, for sexual misconduct, luxury, theft: Flemming 1917, pp. 68–72. Irenaeus of Tyre, for bigamy, uncanonical ordination, and prior friendship with Nestorius: Flemming 1917, pp. 72–76. Sophronius of Tella, for sorcery, astrology and divination, and also for calling in soldiers to suppress an anti-Jewish riot: Flemming 1917, pp. 80–84. Theodoret, largely for heresy on the basis of his own writings: Flemming 1917, pp. 84–112. Domnus of Antioch, partly for heresy and abuse of power but also in large part for his support of Ibas, Theodoret, and others already condemned: Flemming 1917, pp. 114–150.

71. Pelagius' complaint is given in the action against Theodoret, Flemming 1917, pp. 84–90. The same incident is referred to again in the action against Domnus, where Pelagius' allegedly "forced" confession is given: Flemming 1917, pp. 128–130.

72. Charge #11 against Ibas: "That he is a Nestorian, and that he calls holy Cyril a heretic." *ACO* 2.1.11.73, #11. An old letter of Theodoret's (Theodoret *Ep.* 151), containing similar criticism of Cyril, was likewise produced as evidence against him: Flemming 1917, pp. 90–104. The letter, written in 431 to a group of eastern monks, contained a refutation of Cyril's Twelve Anathemas. This letter in turn became one of the "Three Chapters" condemned in the sixth century.

ship with a known heretic such as Nestorius, or demonstrated hostility to an "orthodox father" such as Cyril, was enough.

This rationale of guilt by association also fueled Ephesus' handling of misconduct charges. The bishop or metropolitan was held responsible not only for his own sins but also for the misdeeds of those ordained by or otherwise dependent upon him. Ibas was condemned for having elevated his dissolute nephew, Daniel, to the episcopacy of Harran, and Daniel's own colorful abuses were charged both against himself and also against his uncle. Several of the other charges against Ibas likewise faulted him for having ordained adulterers and thieves as priests and deacons.[73] The practice of holding bishops to account for the misdeeds of their subordinate clergy was not new to Ephesus. Athanasius was held just as liable for his presbyter Macarius' alleged attack on a Melitian church as if he had done it with his own hands. At the Synod of the Oak, likewise, a significant proportion of the charges against John Chrysostom actually referred to actions done by his subordinates, or the disreputable character of those ordained by him.[74] But Ephesus II took guilt by association to a new extreme. Domnus, bishop of Antioch, was deposed almost entirely on grounds of his friendship, patronage, and protection for other bishops already condemned by the council.

> Domnus, the bishop of Antioch . . . has from the beginning manifested the fruit of his partiality for Theodoret, the bishop of the city of Cyrrhus, in that he has continually lived with him, and he encouraged him so far as to assist his impiety, openly, instead of revering God; and what is worse than all, whilst seated on the episcopal throne, he is continually clapping his hands in church at the blasphemies [of Theodoret] against the Lord of all, Christ; and by fulsome praises, he has rendered him presumptuous and arrogant in his impiety. . . . Also, when it was resolved to depose Irenaeus of Tyre from the ministry, the aforenamed Domnus did not eject Irenaeus from his communion. . . . And as for Theodoret, it was at the instance of this man that he [Domnus] aided and abetted the impious Flavian.[75]

The sensational book-burning charge against Theodoret surfaced not during Theodoret's own trial—where his doctrinal writings provided more than

---

73. *ACO* 2.1.11.73, #5: he ordained as deacon one Valentius, "an adulterer and a boy-lover."

74. *Acts of the Synod of the Oak:* 1.10 (he ordained a grave-robber); 2.16 (he ordained runaway slaves); cf. 1.18, 1.29, 2.9.

75. *Libellus* presented by the presbyter Cyriacus at the action against Domnus: Flemming 1917, pp. 114–116 (trans. here from Perry 1881).

sufficient grounds to convict him—but rather during the action against Domnus.[76] The exact sequence of condemnations at the second session thus carried significant weight: only after Ibas and Theodoret had been condemned and deposed could cause be found to act against Domnus on the basis of his association with them. This may perhaps represent more than just a cynical strategy by Dioscorus to bring down as many of his opponents as possible by whatever means he could manage. Dioscorus' charges against the Antiochene bishops, as contrived and invented as many of them probably were, nevertheless had to appeal to a concept of guilt and a model of episcopal misconduct that at least some of his fellow bishops would find plausible. In them we see a logic of culpability that looked not just at the deeds, character, or beliefs of the individual but also at his connections, allegiances, or enmities with others. In contradistinction to the Donatists, whose concept of *traditio* had postulated a taint passed downwards from the original *traditor*-bishops to all those subsequently ordained by them, the judicial rationale of Ephesus II envisioned sin propagating in the opposite direction, up the hierarchy, as the crimes of subordinates rebounded on those who ordained them.[77]

Ephesus II can be understood as a council driven above all else by holy zeal: it subordinated normal considerations of ecclesiastical hierarchy and judicial fairness to the single-minded pursuit of orthodoxy. Here we see an oppositional or "sectarian" mentality, the zealot's strategies of division and exposure, now threatening to take over the entire church. Dioscorus, occupying a position of tremendous institutional power, but guided by fundamentally extremist attitudes, posed an exceptional danger to ecclesiastical order. In his own words:

> I have been brought to admire the Divine Scripture which exclaims "Make peace with all men" [Romans 12:18] . . . [but] with any of those people [heretics], because it is a necessity, and impossible for me to escape it, I do find myself in direct conflict, being reminded of the wise man who indicates this in saying "Everything is good in its season, there is a time for war and a time for peace, a time to serve and be zeal-

---

76. Book-burning: Flemming 1917, p. 116, discussed in previous chapter, p. 278.

77. A similar concept of culpability can be found in John Chrysostom, *Homilies on the Statues* 1.1, expounding upon Paul's warning, "Do not be hasty in the laying on of hands, nor participate in another man's sins" (I Timothy 5:22, RSV trans.). John commented: "[Paul] explained the grievous danger of such a transaction, by showing that so men will undergo the punishment of the sins perpetrated by others, in common with them, because they confer the power on their wickedness by the laying on of hands." (NPNF trans.)

ous for the Lord." [Eccles. 3:11 and 8]. "Be clothed in the armor of God," Paul never ceases to cry out to us [Ephesians 6:13]. Too short would be the time for me, if I wished to quote and point out sentences of Divine Scripture which stimulate us to the propriety and duty of resisting manfully, and of turning our faces from, and hating, those who hate our Lord.[78]

It was a holy zeal that brought with it a considerable amount of violence. The official documentary *acta*, carefully prepared and edited by the Alexandrian notaries of Dioscorus, sought to present a unified chorus of orthodox fathers passionately denouncing proven heretics.[79] But that transcript itself came under attack two years later at Chalcedon, and the investigations on that occasion revealed a "hidden transcript" that cast Ephesus II in a far different light.[80] Pope Leo, writing from Rome to the empress Pulcheria in July 451, gave Dioscorus' council a name that would stick: *latrocinium*, a "Robber Council."[81] The word, which we have previously seen applied to particular acts of illegal violence or to the misbehavior of "false" monks or tyrant-bishops, now labelled an entire ecumenical council as a single act of "violence" against the church. The physical violence that characterized the workings of the council matched the metaphorical violence done by its many violations of ecclesiastical and secular law. Its results were accomplished by force, and were therefore invalid: faith coerced is not true faith.[82]

More than anything else, the violence of the "Robber Council" manifested itself in the production of the official transcript. Dioscorus and his supporters used physical force to compel speech, by coercing bishops to assent to the decrees of the council; to suppress it, by silencing dissident voices

78. Dioscorus' first letter to Domnus, read back at the action against Domnus: Flemming 1917, p. 132 (trans. Perry).

79. Normally each metropolitan would have his own notaries making independent copies, whose accuracy could later be carefully checked. Cf. Lim 1995, p. 78, on the importance attached to accurate written records of disputations and other adversarial proceedings. For fourth-century procedure see Amidon 1979; and an excellent analysis by B. Shaw 1992 of the politics of transcript-production at the Conference of Carthage in 411. Even in the official record from Ephesus, one can find some hints that the bishops were not really speaking with such confident unanimity: at the action against Domnus, among other acclamations, we hear bishops shouting, "Those who remain silent are heretics!" (Flemming 1917, p. 122).

80. The notion of the "hidden transcript" is of course taken from Scott 1990.

81. Leo *Ep.* 95. Cf. also Theodoret's *Epp.* 113 and 147, complaining of the violence at Ephesus.

82. Cf. Arendt 1970, p. 4: "The very substance of violent action is ruled by the means-end category, whose chief characteristic, if applied to human affairs, has always been that the end is in danger of being overwhelmed by the means which it justifies and which are needed to reach it."

and by preventing the accused from speaking in their own defense; and finally to control the recording and authentication of speech, by monopolizing the notarial production of an authoritative transcript. Theodoret and Ibas, regarded as "Nestorian" troublemakers, were simply kept away— Theodoret was ordered by imperial edict to remain in his own diocese, while Ibas was held in "twenty prisons in forty places," as he later complained.[83] Flavian, present at the first session, protested repeatedly that he felt himself unable to speak freely; the official transcript shows Dioscorus and the other senior bishops mocking his complaints:

EUTYCHES: Your piety has seen that the re-reading of the documents has proven that the transcripts were falsified. . . .

FLAVIAN: It is a lie.

DIOSCORUS: If the God-beloved archbishop knows any thing that supports his opinion, let him say it in writing.

FLAVIAN: You have barred me from making any plea of defense.

DIOSCORUS: The synod knows if I have forbidden anything to you. If you know anything useful to you, say it.

FLAVIAN: The second session [at Constantinople] had nothing forged, Thalassius knows it, Eusebius knows it.

THALASSIUS OF CAESAREA IN CAPPADOCIA: No one prevents your sanctity from speaking. If then you have anything that is useful to you, say it.

DIOSCORUS: Master Eusebius, tell: have I prevented him from speaking?

EUSEBIUS OF ANCYRA IN GALATIA: God knows, we pray you to speak.

JUVENAL OF JERUSALEM: Now again, if you want anything, say it.[84]

Pope Leo's letter to Flavian, which confirmed the judgment against Eutyches and firmly endorsed a two-nature Christology, was received and qui-

---

83. *ACO* 2.1.11.1. Cf. the emperor Theodosius' order that Ibas, Theodoret, and their allies were to have "no freedom of speech" at the council: imperial letters to Dioscorus, 30 March 449 (*ACO* 2.1.1.24) and 6 August 449 (*ACO* 2.1.1.52).
84. *ACO* 2.1.1.865–876.

etly filed away, despite repeated requests by the pope's envoys that it be read out loud to the council. The Alexandrian notaries, enforcing a strict monopoly over the production of the transcript, attacked and savagely beat the secretaries of another bishop who were secretly taking notes.[85] Bishops later claimed that they had been forced to place their signatures upon blank pages, which were then to be filled in with whatever Dioscorus ordered—the blank documents symbolized the emptiness and illegitimacy of the council's decrees: "The eastern bishops shouted: We agreed to nothing, force was used, force with beatings. We subscribed on blank sheets. We were threatened with deposition and exile. Soldiers were standing around and threatening us with clubs and swords. We subscribed from terror. With clubs and swords, what kind of synod is it?"[86]

In many cases, it seems, the actual remarks of bishops were altered or forged to make them appear more supportive of the leadership: several of those bishops, at Chalcedon, challenged or recanted their own words in the transcript, testifying that their true condition at Ephesus had been one of confusion and hesitation rather than the confident and militant unanimity of the official record.[87]

The bishops, as they later claimed, found themselves terrorized by zealous monks, followers of Eutyches, Barsauma, and Dioscorus:

> All those with Eutyches—they were monks—were in great liberty
> and authority, such that whatever men wished to be done by authority
> was done by them, so that they also delivered unto their leaders and
> unto the inhabitants of Ephesus all those who were indicated to them.
> For every man was made subject to them, and they were ministering
> to them whether they were willing or whether they were unwilling. For
> what was being done was displeasing to many of them, but they were
> constrained and were weeping. And by every means [the monks] were
> doing the things which were commanded; and they were carrying off

---

85. *ACO* 2.1.1.128–130. Stephen of Ephesus: "My notaries had taken notes, Julian bishop of Lebedus and Crispinus the deacon; and the notaries of Dioscorus came up and erased their tablets and almost broke their fingers trying to seize them and the pens. And I did not get the record of the proceedings, nor do I know what became of it."

86. *ACO* 2.1.1.54; cf. 62 and 131–134; cf. Dioscorus' denial at 65: "They say that they had not heard the sentences passed and the decisions taken, but they simply signed a blank sheet which was given to them. They should not have signed without being assured that these were the pronouncements of the council, since matters of faith were at stake. On the other hand, if they say that they signed blank sheets, who then took them back and wrote the proceedings on them?"

87. See, e.g., *ACO* 2.1.1.62 (Theodore of Claudiopolis in Isauria); 308–329 (Aitherichus of Smyrna); 545–548 and 850–854 (Basil of Seleucia).

men, some of them from the ships and others of them from the streets
and others of them from the houses and others of them while praying
in the churches, and were pursuing others of them that they fled; and
with all zeal they were searching out and digging even after those who
were hiding in caves and in holes in the earth. And it was a matter of
great fear and danger for a man to speak with the adherents of Flavian,
on account of them.[88]

After the condemnation of Flavian, the first session dissolved into chaos
as Dioscorus' followers used brutal force to coerce the assent of the reluctant bishops. The bishops at Chalcedon denounced Barsauma as a "murderer" who had "destroyed Syria" and "sent a thousand monks against us."
The *Life of Barsauma* made him answer that charge in a manner worthy
of Elijah: "I have never killed any *true* bishop."[89] But Dioscorus also played
the tyrant in a more traditional manner, summoning soldiers into the church
to enforce his will:

ONESIPHORUS
OF ICONIUM: Dioscorus said, "Give me the notaries," and they
came forward and read out the condemnation
of blessed Flavian. Taking the other bishops with
me I rose and embraced his knees, saying, "No,
by the feet of your piety. He has done nothing
to merit condemnation. If he deserves reprimand,
let him be reprimanded." Then he rose from his
seat and stood on a footstool, saying: "Are you
rebelling against me? Call the *comites!*" And then,
in fear, we subscribed.

DIOSCORUS: He lies, let him suffer the penalty. I did not say
"Call the *comites!*" Give me the ones who say this.

WHEN MARINIANUS
OF SYNNADA ROSE,
DIOSCORUS SAID: Did I ever threaten you, saying "Call the
comites"?

MARINIANUS: When the sentence was given, I arose along with
Onesiphorus and Nunechius of Laodicea and
others, and we embraced your knees. . . . But
[Dioscorus] said, "Even if they cut out my tongue
I will not pronounce any different sentence." Then

88. Nestorius pp. 351–352 [482–483].
89. Bishops' shouts against Barsauma: *ACO* 2.1.4.77–81. His answer: *Life of Barsauma*, 74th miracle. On Elijah's massacre of "false prophets" as a model for zealous holy men, see chapter 5, pp. 183–185.

> a mob burst in but we continued to cling to his
> knees and supplicate him. He said these words:
> "Where are the *comites?*" I speak loving truth.
> The *comites* entered and they brought in the
> proconsul with a great mob, and with chains,
> and after that each of us subscribed.[90]

Dioscorus clearly felt the need to deny such a particularly damning accusation: "I never said, 'Call the *comites!*'"[91] The deacon Hilary, Pope Leo's envoy and himself a future pope, considered himself lucky to have escaped with his life and later set up an inscription thanking John the Evangelist for his salvation.[92] Flavian was not so fortunate: dragged from the sanctuary by force and placed under arrest, he was apparently so badly mistreated that he died shortly thereafter on his way into exile. The bishops at Chalcedon hailed him as a martyr.[93]

Dioscorus acted in every possible manner as a tyrant, destabilizing legitimate authority in two ways: he encouraged rebellion by subordinates against other bishops, while he attempted to set himself up as sole hierarch, overstepping the legitimate bounds of his episcopal authority as he deposed every significant colleague and rival. At Ephesus he had brought down both Constantinople and Antioch, and two years later, in a small caucus of Egyptian bishops on the eve of Chalcedon, he took the final step, formally condemning and excommunicating Pope Leo as a "Nestorian" heretic. This ultimate

90. *ACO* 2.1.1.858–861.

91. Dioscorus: "There were not only ten or twenty or thirty or a hundred; from this number I can produce witnesses who will prove that nothing he has said is true!" *ACO* 2.1.1.862.

92. Hilary's letter to Pulcheria, *ACO* 2.4, pp. 27–28 = Leo *Ep.* 46: "The bishop of Alexandria, most skilled in the condemnation of innocent men . . . tried to force me to the council with threats and tricks, so that he could either make me consent to the condemnation of the saintly Flavian, or stay there to oppose it, since I was not allowed to leave . . . With Christ's help I preserved myself from having to take part in the condemnations of the innocent; no beating or torment could force me; but abandoning everything I departed through unknown and trackless places to return to Rome." The inscription *(liberatori suo beato Iohanni)* is published in Ernst Diehl, *Inscriptiones Latinae Christianae Veteres* 980, and can be seen today in the baptistery of St. John Lateran in Rome.

93. *ACO* 2.1.1.280. Chadwick 1955 shows that the bishops' use of words like "murder" and "killing" *[phoneuo]* were not always meant literally—in some instances they seem simply to describe the wrongful condemnation of bishops, e.g., Theodoret, complaining of "the butcheries *[tas sphagas]* directed against me": *ACO* 2.1.1.34. This offers an intriguing example of how such "violations" of law and custom came to be imagined as "violent" even in the absence of actual bloodshed.

act of arrogance seems to have been the last straw for many of Dioscorus' enemies, rising to the top of a long list of charges when he himself was brought to trial at Chalcedon. The papal envoys, not surprisingly, considered this to be the most serious of his misdeeds.[94] In the end Pope Leo, first to use the word *latrocinium* to describe Dioscorus' council, had the last word:

> But how contrary to my warnings and entreaties were their actions then, it is a long story to explain, nor is there need to put down in the pages of a letter all that was allowed to be perpetrated in that meeting, not of judges but of robbers *[non iudicium sed latrocinium]* at Ephesus; where the chief men of the synod spared neither those brethren who opposed them nor those who assented to them, seeing that for the breaking down of the catholic faith and the strengthening of execrable heresy, they stripped some of their rightful rank and tainted others with complicity in guilt.[95]

NON IUDICIUM SED LATROCINIUM: FROM HOLY SYNOD TO "ROBBER COUNCIL"

The death of Theodosius in July 450 brought an end to the alliance of pious emperor, zealous monks, and tyrant-bishop that had made possible the Second Council of Ephesus. Although the emperor—not present at the council—had been the least visible partner, his willingness to cede complete authority to Dioscorus had been instrumental. Now Theodosius' sister, Pulcheria, took over, elevated her new husband Marcian to the throne, and joined forces with Pope Leo to overturn everything that had been done at Ephesus. Anatolius, who had been Dioscorus' *apocrisiarius* until installed in Flavian's place as the new bishop of Constantinople, now decided to place the interests of his own see above those of his Alexandrian patron. Pulcheria quickly arranged for the "martyred" Flavian's remains to be brought back to Constantinople and buried with due honors, and allowed bishops exiled after Ephesus to return to their sees and await the convocation of a new council.[96]

94. See, e.g., *ACO* 2.1.3.47, a *libellus* presented by the Alexandrian deacon Theodore, and the formal condemnation of Dioscorus at 2.1.3.94.

95. Leo to Pulcheria, 20 July 451 = Leo *Ep.* 95 (trans. NPNF). Similar characterizations: e.g., Cyril of Scythopolis, *Euthymius* 27 and *Sabas* 56. Palladius *Dialogue* 18 described the Synod of the Oak as an "assembly of transgressors" *[synodon athetounton]*, a gathering of false prophets, quoting Jeremiah 9:2.

96. Flavian's remains: Pulcheria's letter to Leo, 22 November 450 [Leo *Ep.* 77]. On Pulcheria's role see generally Holum 1982, pp. 195–216.

In October of 451, several hundred bishops convened in the basilica of the martyr Euphemia in the city of Chalcedon.[97] The Council of Chalcedon explicitly set out to reverse everything that had been done at Ephesus— "things that were done by violence and fear"[98]—restore lawful hierarchy and canonical order, and end disputes about the faith. If Ephesus stood for holy zeal, Chalcedon represented the triumph of the hierarchical establishment. Chalcedon presented itself as a council of law and order, restoring peace to a church that had been gravely disturbed by the excesses of Ephesus. The secular and episcopal authorities who dominated the council understood themselves to be reacting against two equally serious threats: the anarchy represented by the uncontrolled violence of zealous monks, and the tyranny resulting from excessive episcopal power in the hands of one dangerous man, the "Pharaoh" Dioscorus. Their answer, consistent with longstanding imperial tradition, was to seek a middle way between these two extremes, a centrist strategy that emphasized order and stability.[99]

Step by step, each session of Chalcedon addressed itself to undoing decisions taken at Ephesus. At the first session, transcripts from Ephesus' first session (which in turn included the documentary *acta* from Flavian's synod of 448) were read back and challenged, and the bishops formally rehabilitated Flavian and thus confirmed the original condemnation of Eutyches. The second session featured a reading of Leo's *Tome*, which had been suppressed at Ephesus, and its quick establishment as a touchstone of orthodoxy. At the third session, Dioscorus was put on trial for various acts of tyranny and misconduct, and finally deposed when he refused to appear and face the charges against him. The fourth session attempted, unsuccessfully, to convince a number of disobedient Constantinopolitan monks and reluctant

97. *Acts of the Council of Chalcedon* in Schwartz, *ACO*, vol. 2. A complete English translation of the Greek *Acts* will soon be available: Price and Gaddis, forthcoming 2005. Festugière's French translation is complete only through the sixth session. Murphy 1952 offers a detailed session-by-session summary of the council's proceedings. On Chalcedon generally see the massive collection of articles in Grillmeier and Bacht 1951; Frend 1972, pp. 1–49; Holum 1982, pp. 208–216; Meyendorff 1989. On the number of bishops in attendance: Chalcedonian tradition later claimed exactly 636, in order to double the 318 of Nicaea. But the synod's final letter to Leo (Leo *Ep.* 98) spoke of 520, while attendance- and signature-lists from each session never seem to have more than about 300–350 bishops actually present: see Schwartz 1937, Honigmann 1942.

98. Leo *Ep.* 45 = *ACO* 2.1, pp. 47–48.

99. One might say that the "Chalcedonian establishment"—the alliance of ecclesiastical and imperial authorities that guided the course of the council—followed in a tradition of classical political discourse that presented aristocratic oligarchy as the only sensible middle way between the opposite extremes of anarchy and tyranny.

Egyptian bishops to accept Leo's *Tome*. The fifth session saw the adoption of a definition of faith based largely upon Leo's two-nature Christology, while at the sixth, bishops convened to acclaim a speech by the emperor Marcian. In subsequent sessions, the council adopted canonical legislation to deal with church discipline and particularly with monastic issues; resolved jurisdictional quarrels or disputed episcopal seats; and rehabilitated—over considerable opposition from many bishops—Theodoret and Ibas. In the process, the zealous monks of Ephesus were redefined as false monks, Dioscorus as a false bishop, and the entire Ephesian synod as an illegitimate and therefore "false" council.

The authorities at Chalcedon were concerned above all to project an appearance of legitimacy, fairness, and respect for proper judicial procedure. A committee of high-ranking civil and military officials and senators directed the sessions as if presiding over a secular judicial inquiry. In contrast to Ephesus, the notaries at Chalcedon took scrupulous care to guarantee the accuracy of the transcript, carefully recording even dissident voices. Where the acclamations of bishops at Ephesus had been written up so as to imply unanimity, at Chalcedon we are privileged to hear unexpurgated shouting matches between rival factions:

AFTER THEODORET HAD BEEN SEATED, THE EASTERN PARTY [OF BISHOPS] SHOUTED:	He is worthy!
THE EGYPTIAN PARTY [OF BISHOPS]:	Do not call him a bishop, he is no bishop. Throw out the one who fights against God. Throw out the Jew.
THE EASTERN PARTY:	The orthodox one to the synod. Throw out the troublemakers. Throw out the murderers.
THE EGYPTIAN PARTY:	Throw out the God-fighter! Throw out the one who insults Christ! Many years to the Augusta! Many years to the orthodox emperor. He [Theodoret] has anathematized Cyril!
EASTERNERS:	Throw out Dioscorus the murderer!
EGYPTIANS:	Long live the Senate! He [Theodoret] has no voice. He was deposed before the whole council. . . . Theodoret accused Cyril. We throw out Cyril if we receive Theodoret, we throw out the canons. God turns away from him.

> JUDGES AND SENATORS: These vulgar outbursts are not becoming to bishops, nor useful for either party. Allow the full acts [from Ephesus] to be read.
>
> EGYPTIANS: Throw out that one, and we will listen to everything. We scream for the sake of piety. We say these things for the orthodox faith.
>
> JUDGES AND SENATORS: By God, allow the hearing to take place, and let everything be read in good order![100]

The treatment of acclamations seems in this instance to bear some resemblance to the longstanding administrative requirement that local officials accurately record and forward popular acclamations to the imperial court, even—or especially—when they were unfavorable.[101]

Chalcedon presented itself as a council of moderation and consensus, seeking to achieve doctrinal unity not through ruthless exclusion—as at Ephesus—but through persuasion and compromise. Just as the bishops' disciplinary measures sought to find a path for governing the church that steered between the twin extremes of anarchy and tyranny, so Chalcedonian doctrine presented itself as the sensible middle ground between the heretical extremes of Nestorius—accused of making Christ a "mere man"—and Eutyches—accused of denying Christ's humanity altogether.[102] In Christian heresiological tradition, there were essentially two ways of envisioning the relationship between orthodoxy and heresy. One, the most common, might be called a "two term" model, which contrasted good and evil, right doctrine and wrong doctrine. Most useful when confronting a single heretical target, this zealot's outlook was the polemical strategy of Athanasius and the Nicenes against "Arians" and of Dioscorus and the Alexandrians against "Nestorians."[103]

Chalcedon, by contrast, invoked what might be termed a "three term" model, a "centrist" theology that defined orthodoxy as the correct middle way between two opposite extremes of doctrinal error. In like manner, the

---

100. *ACO* 2.1.1.36–46.

101. Decreed, e.g., by Constantine in 331: *C.Th.* 1.16.6 = *CJ* 1.40.3. On acclamations generally see Rou+ché 1984.

102. The doctrines condemned as "Nestorianism" and "Eutychianism" of course represented significant exaggerations and distortions of what their respective namesakes actually believed. Nestorius, for his part, wrote that he found two-nature Christology entirely in line with his own beliefs (e.g. Nestorius p. 370 [508]: "Let Nestorius be anathematized, so long as they believe what I believe")—a claim that Monophysite propaganda, for entirely different reasons, was all too willing to repeat.

103. On polemical strategies in fourth-century doctrinal conflict, see Lyman 1993.

moderate Homoians of the mid-fourth century, with the support of emperors Constantius and Valens, had presented themselves as a sensible compromise between radical Anomoian Arians and equally extreme Nicene Homoousians.[104] Where the two-term model privileges purity and zeal, aiming for exposure and condemnation of heretics, the "middle way" paradigm allowed a valid role for moderation and compromise in the hope that the two extremes might be brought together—a strategy more in line with what emperors had traditionally sought (but usually failed) to accomplish through the mechanism of ecumenical councils.[105] The doctrinal and synodal history of the next two centuries after Chalcedon consisted largely of imperially-sponsored attempts to effect a reconciliation between the firm Monophysitism of Egypt and much of Syria, and the equally hardline Dyophysite convictions of Rome and Constantinople.[106] The Chalcedonian authorities, and later theologians, went to great effort to defend the legitimacy of the Christological definition produced by the council—which did, after all, contain many things that could not be found in the sanctified creed of Nicaea. It was necessary, they argued, to "define more exactly" certain things that previous councils had left unclear.[107] The defensive tone of such arguments testified to the polemical strength of the charge of "innovation" that Eutyches and then Dioscorus had brought against Flavian, and with which Monophysite sources would never tire of attacking Chalcedon.[108]

When one looks closely at the actual workings of the council, then the irony of Chalcedon becomes apparent: its theological result was achieved to a significant degree by non-theological means. This should not be taken to downplay the importance of the doctrinal issues, or the sincerity of the beliefs of those involved. Rather, it was precisely *because* different factions

---

104. On fourth-century Homoians see Brennecke 1988, pp. 1–4.

105. Cf. discussion of fourth-century councils in chapter 2, pp. 74–75, and of "disciplinary" or "centrist" violence in chapter 4.

106. On the history of the Christological controversies after Chalcedon, see conclusion, pp. 323–330; also Frend 1972; Meyendorff 1989; Grillmeier 1987, 1995, 1996.

107. See, e.g., *ACO* 2.1.1.160, Diogenes of Cyzicus: "It is misleading that [Eutyches] claims to rely on the [creed of the] council of Nicaea, since additions were made to it by the Fathers in order to combat the heresies of Apollinarius and Valentinus and Macedonius and others . . . Apollinarius also accepted the council of Nicaea. But he took its language according to his own lawlessness, and fled from the Holy Spirit and the Virgin, so that in no way did he confess the union of the flesh. The holy Fathers therefore had to explain the 'and was made flesh' of Nicaea, and they clarified it by saying 'from the Holy Spirit and from the Virgin Mary.'" Cf. also 2.1.1.451–456, 525 ("we are not making an innovation!"); 2.1.4.98; 2.1.5.34.

108. Polemic against, and apology for, Chalcedon: see Gray 1979.

held such passionate convictions on the question of Christ's nature that the imperial and ecclesiastical authorities sought at all costs to avoid a bitterly divisive, open debate on the respective theological merits of Antiochene and Alexandrian Christologies. Chalcedon's final product had to allay the concerns of many eastern bishops—who, fearing above all the specter of "Nestorianism," were deeply suspicious of the formula "in two natures"— but also needed to satisfy Pope Leo and his representatives, who cared little about "Nestorianism" and felt "two natures" was the only sure way to refute what they regarded as the far greater threat of Eutychian Monophysitism. The safest and least disruptive way to secure a compromise between these two positions was not to debate them in open synod. Accordingly, at the fifth session the imperial commissioners directed Anatolius and the papal representatives to gather a select committee of leading bishops— only twenty-three out of the hundreds present at Chalcedon—in order to draft a credal statement.[109] This was, significantly, to be done off the record, in a telling exception to Chalcedon's otherwise scrupulous documentation. The Chalcedonian bishops, already bruised by charges of "innovation," felt that faith was not something that ought to be seen as a work in progress. At the fifth session, the final result was presented to the assembled synod for acceptance as a *fait accompli*.

Leo's blanket denunciations of Ephesus II as *latrocinium* were calculated to invalidate everything that had been said and done there. The one-nature Christology endorsed at Ephesus could therefore be discredited simply by its association with Dioscorus, *latrocinium*, tyranny, and violence, without any consideration of its theological merits. The imperial commissioners and the pope's representatives pressed wavering eastern bishops to sign the *Tome of Leo* less with reference to its theological content and more in personal terms. It was, they argued, nothing more than a choice between Leo and Dioscorus: "Dioscorus said, 'I accept "from two natures" but I do not accept "two."' The most holy archbishop Leo says that there are two natures. . . . Now who do you follow, the most holy Leo, or Dioscorus?"[110]

Those who would rather submit to the tyranny of Dioscorus were welcome to withhold their signatures. The bishops signed. The personal authority of Cyril helped to convince those in doubt, once they were shown that passages from Leo's writings agreed with those of Cyril.[111] This method of proof

109. *ACO* 2.1.5.29.
110. *ACO* 2.1.5.26.
111. *ACO* 2.1.2.24–26.

by reference to person could cut both ways, of course: Monophysite polemicists would later argue that the doctrines of Chalcedon *must* be wrong simply because they could be shown to be similar to the teachings of Nestorius.
The adoption of a creed, a document intended to serve future generations as
a foundation of orthodoxy, was accomplished in large part by non-doctrinal
arguments, but once established, of course, then it became entirely a matter
of doctrine. Thereafter, those who questioned it could be called heretics, even
though many of the bishops who ratified it had done so with grave doubts.

But doctrinal closure was not the only task facing the council. Chalcedon
also needed to restore the law and order of the church that had been violated by Dioscorus and his allies. Herein lay Chalcedon's second great irony.
In the fourth century, as we saw in chapter 2, Christians conceptualized the
intrusion of secular power into church affairs—symbolized by the image
of armed soldiers within the sacred space of the church—as the ultimate
sacrilege, emblematic of everything that could go wrong in the relationship
between the emperor and the church. At Chalcedon, by contrast, the bishops were begging for such intervention. Pope Leo, who at first had suggested
to Pulcheria that the new council be held in Italy, reluctantly agreed to send
his envoys to a synod in the east only in return for a firm guarantee that
the emperor and empress would themselves be present and keep order at
the council. The imperial couple kept their promise. Pulcheria issued strict
instructions to local officials that the lawlessness of Ephesus was not to be
repeated:

> Certain persons—as we have learned—of those wont to disturb and
> confound God's dear discipline, have needlessly introduced themselves
> into the city, clergy and monks and laymen, and are trying to create an
> uproar by disputing earnestly against the matters approved by us, [so]
> we have sent this pious letter to your splendidness, so that you should
> expel . . . those clergymen dwelling there without our citation or deci-
> sion of their bishops, whether they happen to be in that rank or even
> certain ones of them [having already been] removed by their bishops;
> or monks or laymen, whom no reason calls to the council, so that with
> all discipline, when the holy synod has sat in consultation, the matters
> relating to Christ the Lord may be confirmed by all.[112]

Originally called to meet in Nicaea, to "complete" the work of Constantine's council, the synod was transferred to Chalcedon, across the straits from

112. Pulcheria's letter to the governor of Bithynia, *ACO* 2.1, p .29 (trans. Coleman-
Norton).

the capital, so that the imperial authorities could supervise the proceedings more closely. Not even the depredations of the Huns—raiding along the Danube even as the council opened—prevented Marcian from appearing in person at the sixth session.[113]

At previous councils, formal presidency had devolved upon a bishop chosen according to the apostolic rank of his see. One or two imperial officials might be present, charged with maintaining order and reporting back to Constantinople, but their role was usually minor or—in the case of Candidian at the First Council of Ephesus—utterly ineffective. The bishops arriving at the first session of Chalcedon, however, found an unprecedented spectacle. Center stage belonged to a committee of no fewer than nineteen of the highest military and civil officials in the empire: the *magister militum*, the praetorian prefect, the urban prefect, the master of offices, the *comes domesticorum* and the *comes* of the *res privata*, along with a number of *illustrissimi* senators and patricians also distinguished as former holders of those same offices. The "most glorious judges and most magnificent senators," as they are designated in the *acta*, displayed their names ahead of even the most senior bishops on the official lists, set the agenda, questioned witnesses, silenced disorderly arguments among the participants, and generally ran the proceedings with an iron hand to ensure that everything would be done according to proper judicial procedure.[114] "Soldiers" had not simply entered the council's church—they had sat down and taken the presidency. Why did the bishops invite such an intrusion?[115] Because at Ephesus II they had seen the alternative. The violence unleashed within the church by Dioscorus, Barsauma, and Eutyches had proven to be far more destructive than the orderly and respectful violence of the state. Bishops begged the emperor to restore order in the church because they were incapable of doing it themselves.[116]

To address the problem of monastic discipline, the bishops adopted a program of canonical legislation for which they welcomed both imperial

113. Cf. Marcian's letter to the synod, *ACO* 2.1, p. 30.

114. On these officials, see the detailed prosopographical analysis by Delmaire 1984.

115. Compare how Athanasius had reacted to a similar spectacle in the fourth century: "How dare they call it a council, when a *comes* presided?" *Synodal Letter* of 338, 8.3.

116. Urbainczyk 1997, pp. 121–126 and 139–167, discusses the church historian Socrates' generally positive attitude toward imperial intervention in church affairs (at least when such intervention was carried out by Nicene orthodox emperors such as Theodosius I and his successors). For Socrates, the emperor's influence could be a welcome restraint on the divisive factionalism of bishops.

suggestions—Marcian himself proposed at the sixth session an early draft of what was quickly adopted as the fourth canon—and, more importantly, imperial enforcement. The canons, which subsequent imperial edicts decreed to have the force of secular law, firmly subordinated the monastic movement to episcopal authority. No one was to found a monastery without the permission of the bishop. Monks were to fast and pray quietly within the walls of their monasteries, busying themselves with neither secular nor ecclesiastical affairs. Monasteries' economic activities were sharply limited, the better to ensure their financial dependence upon the bishop.[117] The normative model of organized coenobitism now acquired the force of law, a rhetorical construction of "true" and "false" monks serving as a discursive means of enforcing hierarchical and institutional control. The *martyria* of Constantinople, home to many of those undisciplined "false" monks, were to come under strict episcopal oversight.[118] The canons also reinforced episcopal authority against challenges from subordinate clergy, in one instance drawing an explicit analogy from secular models of tyranny and usurpation: "The crime of conspiracy or banding together [*sunomosias e phratrias*] is utterly prohibited even by the secular law, and much more ought it to be forbidden in the Church of God. Therefore, if any, whether clergymen or monks, should be detected in conspiring or banding together, or hatching plots against their bishops or fellow-clergy, they shall by all means be deposed from their own rank."[119]

Problems of monastic discipline could easily be addressed, if never truly solved, through canonical legislation. Bishops, as rulers of the church, could lay down the law for their subordinates just as the emperor did for all his worldly subjects. But the problem of the tyrant-bishop, equally dangerous to the peace of the church, proved more difficult. The tyranny of Dioscorus resulted from an extreme application of the same episcopal power and au-

117. *Canon 4.* Caner 2002, pp. 210–212, reads the clause "the bishops shall provide *pronoia*" to refer to material support, not simply "attention," and argues an intent to curtail the economic independence of monasteries—if true, a program strikingly similar to that of the canonical legislation of Rabbula.

118. See chapter 6 for discussion of monastic stereotypes. At Chalcedon, they were most clearly in view at the fourth session, as archimandrites friendly to Flavian challenged the credentials of those claiming to speak for Eutyches. Faustus said: "Elpidius is the guard at the memorial of Procopius. Photeinus, we do not know who he is. Eutychius is in the *martyrium* of Celerine and does not have a monastery . . . Moses we do not know . . . Leontius is from the bearkeepers . . . Paul the Bithynian lives alone in a tomb." *ACO* 2.1.4.64.

119. *ACO* 2.1.7, *Canon 18* (trans. NPNF). Cf. *Canon 21:* clerics or laymen who brought charges against bishops were not to be received without careful examination into their own character.

thority that underlay the legitimacy of the council. Having just asserted a near-absolute episcopal authority over subordinate monks and clergy, the bishops did not want to turn around and legislate too many controls over that same authority. A few canons attempted to restrain some of the more common episcopal abuses. Ordinations for money were condemned.[120] Henceforward, the finances of every church were to be managed by an *oikonomos* rather than by the bishop himself—"so that the administration of the church may not be without a witness, and the goods of the church may not be squandered, nor reproach be brought upon the priesthood."[121] Still, the canons made no direct reference to the tyrannical abuses of Dioscorus. But the council's overall effort to convey a tone of legality, procedural order, and judicial fairness can be seen as a more subtle attempt to limit the effect that one man's ambition and zeal could have within the church.

What, then, were they to do with Dioscorus? Wishing to avoid divisive theological debate, the bishops did not attempt to condemn him for heresy, even though he continued to pronounce a doctrine that would be deemed heretical according to Chalcedon's definition of orthodoxy. The polemical construction of the tyrant-bishop, on the other hand, allowed a means to convict Dioscorus as an individual without opening a troublesome examination of the larger movement of which he had been a part. Ephesus II was retroactively condemned as *latrocinium,* and Dioscorus, held up at Chalcedon as the quintessential tyrant, was now made its sole architect. In this way, the more than one hundred bishops who had signed the decisions of Ephesus, and particularly men such as Juvenal of Jerusalem and Thalassius of Caesarea, who had shared with Dioscorus in the leadership of the council,[122] were able to save their reputations and their jobs through a timely repentance.[123] They had been deceived, they claimed, or coerced:

120. *Canon 2.*

121. *Canon 26* (trans. NPNF).

122. As Dioscorus protested: "You heard that the emperor entrusted the judgment not to me alone, but also to the good bishops Juvenal and Thalassius. We judged what was to be judged, and the whole synod agreed. Why are these accusations brought against me alone? The authority was given equally to us three, the whole council assented, in their own voices and with their subscriptions, and it was reported to the late emperor, who confirmed all the decisions of the holy synod with a general law." *ACO* 2.1.1.53.

123. Cf. the dramatic spectacle in the first session when Juvenal and a succession of others stood up and moved away from the Egyptians, crossing over to the side of the Eastern bishops: *ACO* 2.1.1.282–298. Juvenal's "betrayal" of Dioscorus would come back to haunt him, once he returned home to Palestine to face a full-scale armed rebellion by local monks: sources in Bacht 1951, pp. 244–255. On Juvenal's career, see the detailed study of Honigmann 1950.

"We have sinned!"[124] Never mind that a substantial majority of the bishops at Ephesus seem to have supported Dioscorus willingly.[125] The complicity of the emperor Theodosius II, without whose support the *latrocinium* could not have taken place, was discreetly and politely forgotten: the imperial family would not tolerate any insinuation of heresy against one of their own.[126]

At the third session of the council, preparations were made to try Dioscorus for his tyrannical actions. As Dioscorus had encouraged the monks and clergy of Syria to bring forward accusations against their bishops, so now a parade of Egyptian witnesses lined up to testify regarding the theft and violence that characterized his own episcopal administration: "No one has not had experience of his cruelty and inhumanity. Some have seen their lands devastated when their trees were cut down, others have had their houses destroyed, others have been exiled, and others hit with fines, still others have been chased out of the great city of Alexandria as if that city were the personal property of Dioscorus."[127]

Many of the plaintiffs were friends and relatives of Cyril, who during his tenure had obtained wealth and rank that Dioscorus, upon his succession in 444, had attempted to take back. Speaking to an audience of bishops who continued to uphold the late Cyril as a canonized "father," the accusers made a point of stressing their Cyrillian connections in order to undermine Dioscorus' own claims to the mantle of his predecessor.[128]

The final accusation took the rhetoric of tyranny to such an extreme as to insinuate that Dioscorus had designs upon imperial as well as ecclesiastical power. Ever since the days of Augustus, emperors had taken care that

---

124. Variations on "We have sinned!": 2.1.2.39–41 (Illyrian bishops); 2.1.1.265–269 (Eustathius of Berytus); 2.1.1.181–184 (assorted others).

125. This estimation is based on the remark of Theodore of Isaurian Claudiopolis, describing the synod's reaction when Dioscorus read the condemnation of Flavian: "We were one hundred and thirty-five in all: forty-two obeyed the order to keep silent, the rest were Dioscorus and Juvenal and the unruly mob; we [those who protested] were left with no more than fifteen." *ACO* 2.1.1.62. If these numbers are approximately accurate, it would imply that somewhat less than two thirds of the bishops needed no coercion to follow Dioscorus.

126. Cf. their careful, patient, and indulgent treatment of the empress Eudocia, who supported the rebellion of Monophysite monks in Palestine and continued to reject Chalcedon until 455: Holum 1982, pp. 217–225. See conclusion, p. 326.

127. A representative example, from the *libellus* presented by the deacon Ischyrion: *ACO* 2.1.3.51. On the ecclesiastical politics of Alexandria see Haas 1997; and specifically on the episcopacy of Dioscorus see T. Gregory 1979, pp. 175–192.

128. *ACO* 2.1.3.47, Theodore, ordained by Cyril; 51, Ischyrion, who served Cyril; 57, Athanasius, Cyril's nephew.

Egypt's tremendous wealth never be entrusted to any man of high rank and ambition.[129] That wealth now supported the power of the Alexandrian bishops or "Pharaohs." Although Constantine had previously shown little patience when Arians and Melitians brought numerous accusations of violence, sorcery, plunder, and sacrilege against Athanasius, the mere suggestion that Athanasius might be plotting to block Alexandrian grain shipments to Constantinople was enough to make the emperor turn against the bishop and order his exile.[130] Cyril, as Socrates put it, sought to command not only ecclesiastical but also secular power.[131] Now, at Chalcedon, Dioscorus' accusers alleged that he had tried to block Marcian's proclamation as emperor in 450:

> I am prepared to prove that the most revered bishop Dioscorus . . .
> is guilty of crimes of treason. When, for the good of humanity, the
> wreathed portraits of the emperor [Marcian] were introduced into the
> great city of Alexandria, he did not fear to have Agorastus, Timothy
> and others distribute bribes to many people to have the imperial
> images removed from the city. He was angered that the emperor
> should have been declared to be master of the whole world; for he
> wanted rather that he himself should be the one who ruled in the
> diocese of Egypt.[132]

This accusation seems somewhat implausible: it is hard to imagine what Dioscorus could have hoped to accomplish by such a treasonous action, since there is no evidence that he was attempting to back any alternative candidate for the throne. Such a charge would be ridiculous if brought against a less powerful bishop, but the fact that people apparently were willing to believe it of an Alexandrian "Pharaoh" such as Dioscorus, testifies to the long shadow cast by the rhetorical image of the tyrant-bishop across the imagination of fifth-century Christians. Such insinuations were made with the intent of presenting Dioscorus as a threat to the state as well as to the church and thus persuading the emperor to take action against him.[133]

In the end, most of these charges were not pursued: the council deposed

---

129. Augustus had prohibited men of senatorial rank from setting foot in Egypt: Cassius Dio 51.17.

130. Socrates *HE* 1.35, Theodoret *HE* 1.29; cf. Barnes 1993, p. 24.

131. *Kai gar ex ekeinou he episkope Alexandreias pera tes hieratikes taxeos katadunasteuein ton pragmaton elabe ten arkhen*: Socrates *HE* 7.7.

132. *Libellus* presented by Sophronius, a layman of Alexandria: *ACO* 2.1.2.64.

133. Ephesus II had employed similar insinuations of treason in its condemnation of Theodoret and Domnus: numerous witnesses were brought forward to report

and condemned Dioscorus simply for his failure to present himself after being summoned the canonical three times. This outcome was arguably best for all parties. The authorities did not wish to provide him another opportunity to defend "one nature" in open synod, and Dioscorus certainly would not have looked forward to a rigorous investigation of his administration in Egypt. By incurring deposition for failure to appear, Dioscorus avoided conviction on more serious charges. By choosing not to attend, he signalled that he did not accept the authority of a court he regarded as an unfair tribunal dominated by his enemies. Once sent into exile, he could be venerated by followers as a martyr. The authorities, meanwhile, were free to interpret his silence on the charges against him as proof of his guilt, obtained without the effort and trouble of an actual trial. Leo's deputies, in turn, could claim that they had deposed Dioscorus for his defiance of the pope, and thus congratulate themselves for upholding the principle of papal supremacy that was suffering serious challenges in other sessions of the council.[134]

The council's convenient but fundamentally indecisive judgment upon Dioscorus did nothing to resolve the underlying problem of secular power in the hands of religious leaders. Dioscorus abused his position in a very destabilizing way. Envy, greed, and hatred drove him to use violence, both in the physical sense and also in his "violation" of law and order, both secular and ecclesiastical, to expand his own power at the expense of other legitimate authorities in the church. The ecclesiastical and imperial authorities demanded his condemnation, but did not wish to be too precise about the reasons. Worried also about protecting episcopal authority in the face of rebellious monks and disobedient clergy, they did not want to make it easy to undermine that authority by bringing charges against bishops in future.

Since the time of Constantine, the steady encroachment upon secular power by religious leaders had been building up to its inevitable outcome: a true "civil war" within the church. From the time of Theodosius I onwards, particularly, state authorities showed an increasing reluctance to use their

---

that when the imperial decree banning the books of Theodore was read aloud in the church of Antioch, Theodoret and Domnus reacted approvingly to certain voices in the crowd who shouted the potentially treasonous protest, "Throw out the edict! No one believes by imperial decree!" Flemming 1917, pp. 56–58 and again at 118.

134. *Canon 28*, ratified over the strenuous objections of the papal legates, claimed for the bishop of Constantinople, "New Rome," privileges equal to those of the pope.

potentially formidable coercive power to restrain the holy violence of zealots or the tyranny of bishops, for fear that such action might be seen as "persecution." But the church proved unable to control the escalating violence that resulted from its own assumption of power. The bishops at Chalcedon invited the emperor back in: better that worldly power be exercised by the ruler of the world than that the leaders of the church be further corrupted by it. The rule of the emperor in the church was far less dangerous than the rule of a bishop who tried to act like an emperor.[135]

135. Because the emperor, as a layman, had no claim to sacerdotal authority, he could not be suspected—as a bishop might be—of excessive ambition in that department. By a similar logic emperors found it convenient to trust both eunuchs and barbarians in positions of high authority, because neither could ever hope to occupy the imperial throne themselves.

Conclusion

"We are not deceived by the name of 'Council.'"[1] This verdict—pronounced by the exiled Nestorius upon hearing of the "Robber Council" held at Ephesus—could just as easily have captured the Monophysite indictment of Chalcedon.[2] Nestorius claimed that the *Tome of Leo*, which subsequently formed the basis for the council's own definition, vindicated his own beliefs.[3] It was an endorsement the council's architects would not have appreciated.[4] Chalcedon, intending to unite the church, had instead produced divisions that would eventually harden into permanent schism. To its opponents, Chalcedon represented an unacceptable innovation upon a faith that had been defined for all time at Nicaea. Its condemnation of Eutyches—who was, admittedly, a heretic in the eyes of most of those who would come to be called "Monophysites"—was merely a pretext for reintroducing the far more sinister doctrine of Nestorius. Chalcedon "introduced and increased the heresy of Nestorius, and shook all the world."[5]

The authorities at Chalcedon had already shown themselves to be very

1. Nestorius, *Bazaar of Heracleides*, p. 371 [509] (trans. Driver and Hodgson).
2. On the history of the post-Chalcedonian schism, see generally Frend 1972; Meyendorff 1989; for theological developments, Grillmeier 1975–1996 is fundamental.
3. Nestorius, p. 370 [508]: "Let Nestorius be anathematized, so long as they believe what I believe."
4. Other unwelcome endorsements included Satan, telling monks that they should worship him now that the bishops at Chalcedon had done so: John Rufus, *Plerophoriae* 9. Cf. a forged letter where "Jews" supposedly congratulate Marcian for declaring Christ a mere man and thus clearing them of the charge of deicide: Michael the Syrian, *Chronicle* 8.12, cited in Frend 1972, p. 148.
5. Zacharias of Mytilene *Chronicle* 3.1 (trans. Hamilton and Brooks). The lost Greek original of this work, written c. 492–495, survives in a reworked Syriac version by an anonymous editor of the late sixth century: Grillmeier 1987, p. 56.

sensitive to the charge of "innovation" and had taken great care to argue that they were merely "defining more precisely" matters not explicitly addressed in the Nicene Creed.[6] That defensive attitude persisted in the emperor's pronouncements following the synod. Marcian's correspondence with Egyptian clerics and Palestinian monks fused an emperor's usual tone of command with an unusual concern to engage the opposition and patiently explain the rationale behind Chalcedon.[7] In the immediate term, Marcian and Pulcheria got their way. Nearly all bishops present signed the definition. A few complaints of coercion notwithstanding, Chalcedon seems to have avoided the explicit brutality that had marred Ephesus II.[8] But the initially scattered opposition fed upon a growing sense of betrayal on the part of clergy, monks, and laypeople who refused to accept that the bishops who compromised and "innovated" were authorized to speak for them. Chalcedon, its opponents argued, had betrayed Nicaea. They in turn justified their defiance of conciliar and episcopal authority by clinging to the more sacrosanct authority of an earlier council.[9] Both sides competed to cloak themselves in Nicene legitimacy. Later Chalcedonian tradition claimed that with 636 bishops in attendance it had doubled Nicaea's 318.[10] Monophysite tradition countered that divine providence had ensured the council would meet at Chalcedon and not Nicaea, "so that it might not be the meeting-place of rebels."[11]

Official explanation and definition had to compete with rumor, revelation, and vision. Pope Leo complained of mistranslations—or perhaps deliberate forgeries—of his *Tome* that falsely attributed to him a "Nestorian" division of Christ into two persons.[12] Even the imperial couple did not escape: anti-Chalcedonian sources preserve accusations that Pulcheria had broken

6. See previous chapter, pp. 312–314.

7. See, e.g., postconciliar correspondence of Marcian and Pulcheria at *ACO* 2.1.3.26–31.

8. Eustathius of Berytus claimed to have signed under duress, and Amphilochius of Side was allegedly beaten by the archdeacon Aetius: Zacharias 3.1.

9. An interesting modern parallel can be found on the fringes of conservative Catholicism, where opposition to the "innovations" of Vatican II has expressed itself in an intense devotion to the sixteenth-century Council of Trent as the "authentic" basis of the faith. This sentiment manifests itself along a spectrum ranging from simple preference for the Latin "Tridentine" Mass, all the way to "Catholic Separatists" who have broken with Rome in the belief that the modern church has been hopelessly corrupted by popes they reject as heretical impostors. See Cuneo 1997, esp. pp. 81–119.

10. This number was certainly inaccurate: see Honigmann 1942.

11. Zacharias 3.1.

12. Leo, *Epp.* 130 and 131 in March of 454. This division of Christ into two *prosopa* or persons was the common caricature of "Nestorianism," even though Nestorius himself explicitly denied any such idea: Nestorius, p. 374 [513].

her vow of virginity and that Marcian had usurped the throne.[13] John Rufus' *Plerophoriae* enlisted God among the opponents of the council, compiling accounts of visions and prophecies denouncing its participants.[14] God's vengeance fell upon both Nestorius and Pulcheria, as it had upon earlier heretics.[15] No less an avenger than John the Baptist, answering the prayer of a monk, ordained the death of Marcian.[16] For Proterius, meanwhile, installed by the imperial authorities to replace Dioscorus in Alexandria, human vengeance came in the form of a lynch mob.[17]

Dueling miracles of the Word, dutifully reported by the developing Chalcedonian and Monophysite traditions, summed up the conflict between what were rapidly becoming separate Christian communities. The martyr Euphemia, patron saint of the council that met in her basilica, indicated her preference between two definitions of faith by clasping the Chalcedonian one to her breast and leaving the other beneath her feet. But Monophysites could counter with stories of the bones of dead monks crying out against the *Tome of Leo*, and their own documents overcoming that hated text in a trial by fire.[18]

An observer familiar with the previous century's religious controversies might have been forgiven for thinking that history was repeating itself. Both Dioscorus and his successor Timothy Aelurus cast themselves as the new Athanasius, finding "martyrdom" in defiant exile, while their rival Proterius met the same unfortunate fate as the "Arian" bishop George had done a century earlier.[19] Increasingly embittered by the government's attempts to impose a Chalcedonian solution, Monophysites assembled numerous tales of martyrdom and resistance. Macarius of Tkow, according to sixth-century tradition, was beaten to death by imperial officials for his refusal to sub-

13. Burgess 1993–1994.

14. On the *Plerophoriae* see now Steppa 2002. The text can likely be dated to 512–18: Steppa pp. 77–78.

15. For Nestorius, e.g., *Plerophoriae* 33, 36; Pulcheria, *Life of Barsauma*, 76th miracle.

16. *Life of Barsauma*, 97th miracle.

17. Cf. Bishop Seleucus of Amasia's letter to Emperor Leo, *ACO* 2.5.41, pp. 84–86; Evagrius Scholasticus *HE* 2.8; Zacharias 4.2; with commentary in T. Gregory 1979, pp. 163–201 and Haas 1997, pp. 316ff.

18. Euphemia: told in the *Synaxarion of Constantinople*, ed. H. Delehaye (Brussels 1902), pp. 811–813. According to Monophysite tradition, troops sent by Juvenal came to a monastery and demanded agreement with the *Tome of Leo*, but the bones of the monastery's dead fathers cried out in opposition: *Macarius of Tkow*, pp. 54–59. Cf. Rufus *Plerophoriae* 46 for a similar anecdote in which dueling creeds compete in a trial by fire.

19. A considerable hagiographical tradition developed around the figure of Dioscorus, first apparent in the late fifth century in Theopistus' *Life of Dioscorus* and continued in the sixth century in the *Life of Macarius of Tkow*.

scribe to the *Tome of Leo*.[20] Peter the Iberian, in Oxyrhynchus, was inspired by a vision to tear up Proterius' edict before a statue of the emperor—mocking the "triumphs of Goths and Sarmatians" once again.[21] John of Ephesus, in the late sixth century, catalogued many exemplary tales of Monophysite holy men resisting Chalcedonian persecution. As in previous decades, the willingness to martyrdom went hand in hand with holy violence against enemies of the faith. The monk Sergius, who had made an earlier career of burning synagogues, charged single-handedly into church and assaulted a Chalcedonian preacher, an act that earned him torture and imprisonment. Sergius' act served to rebuke not only the Chalcedonians but also his fellow orthodox who saw no wrong in attending Chalcedonian services as long as they did not actually take communion.[22]

As earlier persecution had done, Chalcedon produced *traditores* as well as martyrs. Juvenal, whose timely abandonment of Dioscorus had signalled the turning of the tide at the first session of Chalcedon, faced a full-scale rebellion by Palestinian monks upon his return to Jerusalem.[23] Chalcedonian authorities applied the usual discourses of delegitimization, characterizing the monks' leader Theodosius, who had proclaimed himself bishop and effectively seized both ecclesiastical and secular power in Jerusalem, as both "false monk" and "usurper." The imperial government nevertheless showed far more restraint than it might have done against a secular rebellion, recognizing that it was dealing with religious zealots regarded by many—including the empress Eudocia—as holy men. Marcian and Pulcheria spent many months in negotiation and patient argument with supporters of the rebels before finally resorting to force.[24] Their restraint was not appreciated by Monophysite sources, which celebrated the slain monks as martyrs and charged that the imperial government had conspired with Jews and Samaritans to massacre them.[25]

By the sixth century the Chalcedonian church had come in Syriac-speaking circles to be called *Melkite*—"the emperor's church"—associated,

20. *Life of Macarius of Tkow* 15, pp. 94–96.

21. John Rufus, *Life of Peter the Iberian* 62; discussed by Steppa 2002, p. 70. See chapter 1, pp. 29–30, for the fourth-century antecedent.

22. John of Ephesus, *Lives of the Eastern Saints*, pp. 84–111; cf. discussion in Harvey 1990a, pp. 52–53, 72–74.

23. On Juvenal see Honigmann 1950.

24. *ACO* 2.1.3.26–31; Zacharias 3.3–6; for summary of events see Honigmann 1950, pp. 247–257; Steppa 2002, pp. 1–11; for the role of Eudocia see Holum 1982, pp. 217–225.

25. Zacharias 3.6, adding that a blind Samaritan was cured, and converted, after smearing his eyes with the spilled blood of the "martyrs."

despite its best efforts at self-justification, with the taint of secular power and with persecution. In the tradition of both Donatists and Athanasius, Monophysites celebrated their defiance of worldly authorities and condemned opponents for their association with secular violence, even as they themselves welcomed the occasional support of emperors more sympathetic to their cause.[26] Each outbreak of persecution, such as that described by the chronicler Pseudo-Dionysius of Tel-Mahre in the reign of Justin I, added to a growing tradition of martyrology, which shaped a distinctive anti-Chalcedonian identity and ultimately a separate church.[27] The schism developed over several generations. In response to the refusal of many Monophysites to accept sacraments from Chalcedonian bishops, leaders such as Jacob Baradaeus moved secretly from one congregation to the next, ordaining a separate and parallel hierarchy. Driven from the cities, the defiant bishops found refuge in monasteries. Monophysite leaders, in the eyes of their disciples and hagiographers, were holy men whose actions combined martyrial resistance and ascetic withdrawal. The hated Council of Chalcedon, in turn, came to signify compromise with worldly power.[28]

"Monophysite" opponents defined their identity less by a common theological program than by what they were against—Chalcedon, and the corruption and betrayal associated with it. But having turned their backs on imperial and conciliar authority, they themselves became vulnerable to further disagreement and schism within their own ranks. Moderate leaders who attempted to reach accommodation found themselves challenged by extremists who demanded nothing less than the condemnation of the hated council. Having rejected Chalcedon, and having made a virtue out of their defiance of episcopal and imperial authority, how could Monophysites in turn deal with disagreement and dissent and maintain order within their own ranks? Without the consistent support of the coercive state, Monophysite unity could not be sustained. Resistance to Chalcedon spread across a spectrum that included moderates as well as extremists, divided mainly by their willingness or unwillingness to consider reconciliation. For the Chalcedonian authorities, Monophysite disunity was an unending source

26. These emperors included the short-lived Basiliscus, and Anastasius; Zeno's position, as expressed in the *Henotikon*, was at least neutral. See Frend 1972, chaps. 4 and 5.

27. Pseudo-Dionysius (trans. Witakowski, pp. 21–41). On the emergence of a separate Monophysite church see Harvey 1988a.

28. This is the thesis of Steppa 2002, esp. pp. 135–141 and 163–174, perhaps exaggerated somewhat by the high representation of monastic and ascetic sources among surviving anti-Chalcedonian texts.

of frustration, because there was no one empowered to speak on behalf of all in negotiating and making the necessary compromises for the restoration of ecclesiastical unity. The beliefs of most Monophysite leaders seemed orthodox, in Chalcedonian eyes, and yet they inexplicably "hesitated" (diakrinomenoi) to join communion. Hard-line anti-Chalcedonians, of course, would disown anyone who did attempt such compromise. Moderate bishops such as Severus of Antioch, who were willing to work with emperors when possible, agreed with their Chalcedonian counterparts in condemning the extremists as "separatists" (aposchistai) for their rejection of hierarchical authority and their narrowly sectarian mentality. For Severus, the dreams and visions they claimed in support of their defiance were simply a predictable tactic of those excluded from ecclesiastical power.[29] Their defiance of legitimate leadership, or "headlessness," could only reflect the anarchy and disorder long thought characteristic of heretics and schismatics.[30]

Hierarchy mattered—and to none more so than the shadowy author known to us as Pseudo-Dionysius the Areopagite, who saw it as a central organizing principle for both heaven and earth. The ecclesiastical ranks and rituals of the worldly church reflected the physical order of the universe. In his *Eighth Letter*, Pseudo-Dionysius castigated a monk named Demophilus who had taken it upon himself to confront and challenge a priest for excessive leniency toward sinners, and who had apparently justified his disobedience by making reference to biblical exemplars of holy violence:

> It is not permitted that a priest should be corrected by the deacons,
> who are your superiors, nor by the monks, who are at the same level
> as yourself, and this is so even if it could be shown that he had violated
> some other regulation. Even if disorder and confusion should under-
> mine the most divine ordinances and regulations, that still gives no right,

29. "One might hear them relating certain dreams and prophecies, on account of which, as they said, they hesitated to communicate with the holy churches in Egypt . . . Who is there who will not (and very rightly) pronounce against us as senseless, if we set ourselves against such prophecies and dreams, and while occupying ecclesiastical thrones forget these things, but, when we are outside and are expelled and driven out, again attend to dreams and repeat dreamy prophecy?" Severus of Antioch, *Ep.* 5.11 (trans. Brooks, p. 327), referring to monks who broke with their bishops over the *Henotikon* of 482. Rejecting it not for unorthodoxy but simply because it did not explicitly condemn Chalcedon and Leo's *Tome*, they were called *Akephaloi:* Frend 1972, p. 180. Cf. discussion by Steppa 2002, p. 48.

30. Compare Tertullian's mockery of earlier sects, in which "today one man is their bishop, tomorrow another": *Prescription Against Heretics* 41. Cf. Douglas on the disadvantages of sectarian mentality for effective government, discussed in chapter 6, pp. 238–241.

even on God's behalf, to overturn the order which God himself has established. God is not divided against himself. . . .

In your bold letter you say over and over again that you were looking for God's vengeance, not your own. But tell me, is it by wrongdoing that one avenges the good? . . . So, then, we will not put up with these onslaughts of yours, however zealous they may be and however often you cite the examples of Phinehas and Elijah.[31]

Pseudo-Dionysius' writings are famously difficult to fix in time and space, and there is no way to tell if the letter referred to an actual incident, or was even written to a real person.[32] It nevertheless served to make a broader point, a defense of order and episcopal authority against anarchic extremism. Denying the legitimacy of "holy zeal," and labelling rebellion a result of pride, arrogance, and uncharity, lent support to the centrist strategy and disciplinary ideology of the secular and ecclesiastical establishment.[33] Principles of order, hierarchy, and unity created counter-discourses against extremism, delegitimizing the holy zeal claimed by those who valued purity above comity.[34]

The Roman state's response, in the two centuries after Chalcedon, followed a familiar pattern. Emperors made a series of attempts to end the schism that combined compromise formulae with a muscular enforcement of consensus, ironically the same strategy that had led to Chalcedon in the first place. Predictably, such measures angered hard-liners on both sides and often created new divisions. The Chalcedonian side, for its part, had strong vested interests demanding unwavering loyalty to the council. For the Roman popes, questioning Chalcedon meant questioning the *Tome of Leo* and was therefore unacceptable. The patriarchs of "New Rome," meanwhile, could not allow any challenge to the legitimacy of the council whose twenty-eighth canon had ratified their own status as the equals of Rome. Constantinopolitans, led by the powerful Akoimete monks, violently opposed any compromise, rioting in response to an attempt to introduce the Monophysite addition "who was crucified for us" to the Trisagion.[35] Daniel the Stylite climbed down from his pillar to confront the usurper Basiliscus and force him into a reversal of ecclesiastical policy.[36]

---

31. Pseudo-Dionysius, *Letter to the Monk Demophilus* 5 (trans. Luibheid).

32. For the context and possible dating of the letters, see Rorem 1993, pp. 3–46.

33. See discussion of "disciplinary" violence in chapter 4.

34. See, e.g., the discourses used against ascetic zealots in chapter 6, and against "tyrannical" bishops in chapter 7.

35. On the role of the Akoimetes in Constantinople see Baguénard 1988, chap. 4; Bacht 1951. Trisagion riots: Evagrius *HE* 3.44.

36. *Life of Daniel the Stylite* 73–75.

In the face of such resistance, some emperors tried to seize the middle ground, searching for a formula on which they thought all could agree, imposing that solution by force, and banning further discussion. Zeno's *Henotikon* of 482 took the safe tack of proclaiming Christ "one and not two," made no mention of "nature" and deliberately refused to take a position on Chalcedon's orthodoxy, simply anathematizing "those who teach differently, whether at Chalcedon or at any other synod." The intention was to turn the clock back, and restore the peace that had existed before the divisive questions of "nature" had been raised. But that, of course, was impossible. The *Henotikon*'s refusal to condemn Chalcedon failed to convince hard-line Monophysites, while its failure to endorse the same council alienated the Roman popes, who broke communion with Constantinople in a schism that did not end until 518.[37] In the mid-sixth century Justinian attempted, with similarly divisive results, to appease Monophysite opinion through condemnation of writings by Theodore of Mopsuestia, Theodoret of Cyrrhus, and Ibas of Edessa, the so-called Three Chapters. The seventh century, in turn, produced new attempts at Christological reconciliation under the ill-fated doctrines of Monoenergism and Monotheletism.[38] In each instance, much of the ecclesiastical establishment went along with the compromise once the emperor's wishes became clear. But such attempts at moderation earned only contempt from those, on both sides, who took theological purity more seriously. Each attempt at unity produced heavy-handed coercion and corresponding resistance. Leaders such as Maximus Confessor—mutilated and exiled for his opposition to Monotheletism—took up a now time-honored tradition of martyrdom.

The seventh century, then, brings us to the twin catastrophes of Persian wars and Arab conquests. In the wake of the collapse of the Roman state across large parts of the Middle East, the way was opened for the elaboration of alternative models of religious government. This study has illuminated the centrist paradigm of disciplinary violence through which Christian Roman emperors struggled to maintain the unity and conformity of faith and practice they believed God demanded. But did imperial unity necessarily dictate a single and uniform religious orthodoxy?[39] The Sasanian Persian Empire,

37. Text of *Henotikon*, e.g., in Evagrius *HE* 3.14. See generally Frend 1972, chap. 4. In the mid-fourth century, the Homoian party likewise tried to reconcile hardline Nicenes and Anomoians by striking a moderate position and deliberately avoiding any discussion of *ousia*.

38. See generally Meyendorff 1989, chaps. 7–10.

39. The link between monotheistic religion and universalizing ideologies of empire is the theme of Fowden 1993. Momigliano 1986, meanwhile, discusses the

Rome's rival in many spheres, offered another way. The King of Kings co-operated with the Magian priestly class to protect Zoroastrianism's superiority over competing religions and its exclusive monopoly on the faith of the Iranian ruling elite, severely punishing apostasy from or proselytism toward the ruling class while generally tolerating religious diversity among the common population. Different sects were organized into separate confessional communities, governed under their distinct laws and customs by a compliant state-sponsored religious leadership. Khusro II, after forcibly occupying much of the Roman Near East, skillfully played Monophysites, Nestorians, Chalcedonians, and Jews against one another in order to weaken their allegiance to Constantinople.[40] The traditionally Roman maxim "divide and rule," at least in the religious sphere, was more effectively practiced by Rome's eastern rival.

This Sasanian strategy, which arose as a practical solution to governing a religiously diverse population, was later adopted and elaborated by Muslim conquerors, who articulated a theological justification for tolerating rival faiths as "Religions of the Book." Islam, initially limited to the numerically small Arab ruling class, received a privileged status guaranteed by legal prohibitions on apostasy to or proselytism from other religions. Christians, like Jews and other *dhimmi*, suffered continual reminders of their subordinate status. They were not to ride horses, bear arms, build new houses of worship, or display crosses. So that the inequalities of gender would support and not undermine the inequalities of religion, Muslim men could marry *dhimmi* women but Muslim women could not marry *dhimmi* men, and the children of mixed marriages were claimed for Islam. Nevertheless, the *dhimmi* system explicitly recognized the rights of subordinated religious communities to exist. This was a formal tolerance, however oppressive, to be distinguished from the temporary and situational "forbearance" of Christian Roman emperors who assumed and expected with increasing impatience that all would eventually see the light.[41] Early Muslim regimes, financially dependent on the taxes collected from the Peoples of the Book, showed little interest in mass Islamization. In such a system, state violence against the *dhimmi* intended neither to annihilate them nor to co-

---

alternative possibility of universalist imperial ideologies founded on Rome's traditional polytheism; cf. comments by Fowden 1993, pp. 59ff. Christian critiques of polytheism and empire seem to have been more common than pagan endorsements of it.

40. On the religious policies of the Sasanians see Asmussen 1983; Morony 1984, pp. 277–430.

41. Forbearance: see Digeser 2000 and my discussion in chapter 1, pp. 64–66.

erce or discipline them towards conversion, but simply to keep them in their place. Incidents of forcible conversion, officially discouraged, were rare though not unheard of—but Muslim jurists were of divided opinion as to whether those who had been compelled to recite the *shahada* at swordpoint could return to their former faiths without incurring charges of apostasy.[42] The Muslim system offered, in contrast to Christian Rome's coercive harmony, a paradigm of repressive pluralism.[43] It depended upon administrative practices and legal traditions derived from the Sasanians, and reflected the demographic fact of inheriting rule over Christian populations that had already, as a result of the endless Christological controversies, evolved into separate confessional churches.[44] Finally, Islam's own understanding of itself as both following and surpassing the other "Religions of the Book" allowed the Muslims to see themselves as inheriting the best of Judaism and Christianity while transcending the limitations of those faiths. Islam, according to a tenth-century commentator, was the "middle way" between the "deficiency" of the Jews and the "excess" of the Christians— a centrist discourse reflecting the self-confidence of those in power.[45] Islam itself, lacking the tightly-organized and hierarchical priestly class that dominated and unified the Christian church, developed looser definitions of orthodoxy that left more room for legitimate disagreement between different schools of thought, and therefore less scope for conflict over fine points of doctrine. But Islam's fusion of secular and religious authority in the person of the Caliph meant that political rebellions often took on religious overtones, and vice versa—with the result that divisions of faith contributed

42. In later centuries, church authorities in Christian Europe would profess equal uncertainty over the status of Jews who had been forcibly baptized.

43. On the religious policies of early Islam see Morony 1984, pp. 431–506; Choksy 1997; Ye'or 1996.

44. Sawirus al-Muqaffa in the mid-eighth century described the curious spectacle of rival Chalcedonian and Monophysite bishops arguing their respective cases and comparing historical grievances before an audience of Muslim judges: *History of the Patriarchs of Alexandria* 1.18, p. 376 (trans. Evetts).

45. Tabari, quoted and trans. in Peters 1990, vol. 2, p. 353: "I regard the word 'middle' in this context [commenting on Qur'an 2:143] as signifying the mean between two extremes. God described the Muslims as a people of the middle path because of their middle position in religion. They are neither people of excess like the Christians, who went to extremes in their monastic practices as well as in what they said concerning Jesus, nor are they people of deficiency like the Jews, who altered the Book of God, killed their prophets, gave the lie to the Lord, and rejected faith in Him. Rather they are people of the middle path and of balance in their religion. God characterized them as people of the middle path because the things which God loves most are those of the middle position."

far more directly to fragmentation of empire than had been the case for Christian Rome.[46]

The surviving rump of the Byzantine Empire, meanwhile, struggled to preserve the Constantinian paradigms of imperial Christianity. Emperors still quarrelled with patriarchs and presided over councils. The controversies that divided the empire now raged more over practice—as with the eighth century's arguments over the veneration of icons—and less over doctrine.[47] The catastrophes of the seventh century, by largely killing off the ancient system of classical education, had put an end to the culture of philosophical discourse and sophistic argument from which, Christians believed, new heresies arose.[48] With Christendom irretrievably divided into separate Chalcedonian, Monophysite, and Dyophysite churches, Constantinople lost its claim to religious universalism even as the "universal empire" of Rome shrank within smaller and smaller horizons. But the truncated empire continued to exercise a profound religious and cultural influence beyond its borders, as newly emergent societies on the peripheries of Europe and the Middle East adopted Christianity from Constantinople. In these new "commonwealths," as some scholars have described them, Christianity itself adapted to local conditions, translating scripture into indigenous languages and in some cases inventing new alphabets.[49] Outside the frontiers of empire, effectively independent or "autocephalous" national churches fostered a diversity of language and religious practice while maintaining communion with the old imperial centers.

Alternative schemes for relations between secular power and ecclesiastical authority developed in the fragmented west, with slightly different results in each of the post-Roman successor states. In North Africa, the Catholic

46. For Fowden 1993, chap. 6, the early Islamic Caliphate constituted the ultimate expression of monotheistic empire, and its later devolution into a politically fragmented "commonwealth" illustrated empire's weaknesses.

47. A beleaguered community, constantly threatened by the superior armies of Islam, could no longer support the simple Constantinian equation of Christianity with military victory. God gave power to the infidel, they believed, in order to punish Christians for their sins. Early in the eighth century, some Christians—perhaps influenced by Muslim polemic on the subject—identified idolatry as the sin and icon veneration as the culprit. On Iconoclasm see generally Herrin 1987, chaps. 5 and 8.

48. For this explanation of the "root causes" of heresy, see, e.g., Tertullian, *Prescription against Heretics* 7.

49. The term "commonwealth" was first used by Obolensky 1971 to describe Byzantium's sphere of cultural and religious influence over Slavic Eastern Europe, the Balkans, and Russia. Fowden uses "First Byzantine Commonwealth" to describe an arc of mainly Monophysite Christian polities stretching from the Caucasus in the north, through the Fertile Crescent, to Southern Arabia and Ethiopia. The Latin West, of course, could also be described as a "commonwealth": Fowden 1993, p. 169.

church faced brutal persecution by the conquering Arian Vandals, bringing an effective and ironic end to the Donatist schism. The Donatist church hierarchy had already been badly damaged by imperial crackdowns in Augustine's time. The fact of foreign invasion and Arian persecution against both Donatists and Catholics removed the rationale for schism—the Catholics themselves, and not by choice, had now become a "Church of the Martyrs."[50] But Africa was the exception, and more benign examples of Arian rule over Catholic majorities could be found in Ostrogothic Italy, and in Visigothic Spain prior to 589. The Gothic warrior elites accepted the practical limits of their situation as a ruling minority—more interested in maintaining their distinct identity than in attempting to enforce conformity on all—and went to their own Arian churches while leaving the Catholic majority alone.[51] But when the Spanish Visigothic kings converted to Catholicism in 589, they joined with the bishops and summoned councils in a new attempt to revive the imperial model of religious unity through a crackdown on heretics and Jews. As before, consensus could not be had without resort to coercion.[52]

In Gaul, meanwhile, the slow erosion of imperial authority in the fifth century had forced the bishops into a more overtly secular role as they became, by default, the patrons of their cities. These bishops, though a number of them did claim suitably ascetic credentials, represented the same elite families that owned the land and filled civic offices. As Roman rule in the West broke down, the bishops themselves had effectively *become* the secular government at the local level, part of a process that has been described as the "draining away of the secular."[53] For this reason, perhaps, they did not enjoy the same luxury of agonizing about their proper role in worldly affairs that we have seen in the comparatively sheltered environment of the fifth-century East.[54]

At the local level, throughout the West, bishops had to combine secular power with their spiritual authority as a matter of practical necessity. Gregory the Great, whose career embodied the tension between the desire for ascetic withdrawal and the demands of ecclesiastical service, worried deeply

---

50. On Catholic martyrdom under the Vandals see Victor of Vita, *History of the Vandal Persecution*. On the apparent end of the Donatist-Catholic schism see Markus 1991.

51. The best study on the much-debated issue of ethnic identity in the post-Roman West is Amory 1997. On the peculiar ecclesiastical organization of the Germanic Arian churches see Mathisen 1997.

52. See Stocking 2000.

53. Markus 1990, esp. pp. 1–17. Compare Cameron 1995.

54. On the secular roles and responsibilities of bishops in Gaul, see Mathisen 1989 and Mathisen 1993, esp. chap. 9. On the ascetic formation of Gallic bishops see now Leyser 2000, esp. chaps. 2–4.

about the consequences. Unlike some later medieval popes, Gregory was keenly sensitive to the dangers of power and pride implicit in his office. His *Pastoral Rule* adapted classical discourses on kingship to comment on the role of the bishop. The "ruler" of the Christian community had the responsibility both to correct the faults of others and, more critically, to monitor his own conduct in a relentless and almost ascetic self-examination. Apparent virtues, he warned, could all too easily be twisted into vices: "Often inordinate laxity is believed to be loving-kindness, and unbridled wrath is accounted the virtue of spiritual zeal."[55]

Gregory occupied an office whose claims to primacy aimed at a status that Cyprian might have described as "bishop of bishops."[56] The papacy in later centuries paid little attention to Gregory's warnings. After the seventh century, the Roman popes were effectively beyond Constantinople's reach and thus left to develop independently of imperial influence. Although at this stage it had little effective power outside Italy, the papacy remained the cultural and religious center of the Latin West. Alliance with the Carolingians would later lead to revival of a new "western empire" in which popes crowned a succession of Germanic kings as "Emperors of the Romans." Rome's universalist claims over the church and its insistence on papal supremacy would ultimately lead to schism with Constantinople, the end of a centuries-long estrangement that had begun with Chalcedon's twenty-eighth canon. In the West, the idea of Rome came to be contested between "Roman" emperors and the popes who bestowed their title upon them—and claimed that what they had given, they could take away. Thus the groundwork was laid for the imperial papacy of the high medieval centuries, when popes not only saw themselves as "bishop of bishops" commanding the church and deciding doctrine, but indeed claimed the same supremacy in the secular realm that an emperor would have exercised in centuries past. Constantine himself, as filtered through distorted legend four centuries after his death, had given *imperium* over the West to Pope Sylvester, in gratitude for being cured of leprosy, before transferring the seat of empire to the East.[57] The fifth-century councils had worried about bishops usurping the emperor's role, corrupted by desire for secular power. The popes of the high middle ages, brandishing one of his-

---

55. *Pastoral Rule* 2.9 (trans. NPNF).

56. Cyprian, speaking at the Seventh Council of Carthage in 256. See discussion in chapter 7, pp. 281–282.

57. The *Donation of Constantine*, an eighth-century forgery, can be read alongside Lorenzo Valla's withering commentary in Coleman 1922. On the ideological use of the text see Alexander 1963.

tory's most famous forgeries, would exercise that power in the firm belief that the first Christian emperor had himself offered to share it with them.

Late antiquity's most significant innovation was the establishment of religious allegiance, in an exclusive sense, as the new defining characteristic of both individual and collective identity—the consequence of monotheistic religion acquiring broad political power. Christian imperial unity came crashing down along with the fall of the empire, leaving in its wake a Mediterranean world fragmented into separate communities distinguished by language and culture but above all by religion—the Latin West, the Byzantine Orthodox East, and the Islamic South, divisions that persist to this day. The combination of exclusivity with the need for precise definition of orthodoxy tended to drive these confessional groupings toward further schism.[58] Late Roman Christianity fragmented into mutually antagonistic Chalcedonian and Monophysite churches—just as, a thousand years later, Latin Christendom would divide between Catholics and Protestants. These "imagined communities," which with the passage of time came to identify themselves in ethnic and linguistic terms as well as religious, hardened their sense of identity and difference from one generation to the next by repeating stories of martyrdom and persecution. Modern nationalism, like religion, builds community through shared history, using narratives of past triumphs and heroic sacrifices—"martyrdoms"—to shape a patriotic identity for its citizens.[59]

Monotheistic religion, for its most zealous adherents, brought with it a sense of cosmic struggle between good and evil, a conviction of the necessity to do God's will, and a certainty in its claims to understand that will—in a word, extremism. Modern religious terrorists follow closely in patterns defined by late antique zealots. The same sense of apocalyptic struggle against demonic adversaries, a persecution complex that in turn inspires the rhetoric and practice of martyrdom, creates an extremist exegesis that interprets religious tradition in the direction of endorsing lethal violence.[60] Secular extremists, meanwhile, even those driven by explicitly anti-religious ideologies, have not escaped habits of thought that are broadly religious in their origins—the rejection of a corrupt world, the repudiation of compromise, the strategy of "forcing the contradictions" by provoking the state to

---

58. Cf. Mary Douglas on the sectarian mentality's natural tendency to schism, discussed in chapter 6, pp. 238–241.

59. On modern nationalism: Anderson 1991.

60. On modern religious terrorism: Juergensmeyer 2000. On contemporary radical Islamism see Kepel 2002.

retaliation, pursuing radical change through violence with the certainty that things must get worse before they can get better.[61] The zealous holy men of late antiquity, as we have seen, displayed a similar attitude in their attacks on what they perceived as the false and hypocritical "tolerance" of an overly moderate regime.

The violence of the establishment, backed by the coercive resources of the state, has historically taken a far greater toll than that employed by extremists. The consensus ideology of the imperial state was not unique to the Christian empire—it had driven the persecutory initiatives of Constantine's predecessors—but Christianity changed the nature of the unity to be enforced. The new religion's exclusivist quality, its emphasis on scriptural authority and careful concern to distinguish truth and falsehood, meant an ever-narrowing definition of orthodoxy. As the scope for legitimate difference and disagreement contracted over time, the state found itself compelled to become involved in regulating the process of argument and definition. Where pagan persecutors had rested content to compel specific acts of observance and had not seen the need to forbid alternative devotions, authorities enforcing Christian unity had to demand a more exclusive practice and profession of faith. Christian preachers such as Augustine understood "Christianization" as a never-ending process, necessitating a total transformation of daily life in order to escape the distractions of the secular. In like manner, ascetic theology and discipline demanded constant self-examination and exertion in order to battle temptation and strive toward perfection. When such totalizing discourses were linked to the universalist mandate of the Christian imperial state, there was, in theory, no limit to the disciplinary application of "compassionate" coercion.

Christianity, of course, outlived the collapse of Christian empire. Later Christian potentates, both secular and ecclesiastical, followed similar universalizing ideologies that led them inexorably toward similar practices of discipline and coercion. These models of violence showed up again and again, in the various contexts of the papal inquisitions, the militant ideologies of crusade and imperialism, and the persecutions of Reformation-era magistrates.[62] Spain in 1492 celebrated its newfound political unification by an attempt— following in the footsteps of the Visigoths—to compel a corresponding religious unity. The same year led the Spanish toward the conquest of a new empire in the New World, in which European missionaries—upon en-

61. See Ellis 1998.
62. On holy war, the crusading impulse, and its relation to imperialist ideologies, see Partner 1997. On the Reformation: B. Gregory 1999.

countering, for the first time in centuries, idol-worshipping pagans—turned to the ancient pages of Augustine and other late antique writers for advice on the encouragement of Christianization.[63] All of the political and religious power structures of Christendom—some openly claiming to be direct heirs of Rome—drew explicitly or implicitly upon the political and religious legacy of the late antique Christian empire. The secular regimes of more modern times, even though no longer frankly admitting to Christian ideological underpinnings, also follow, broadly speaking, the same patterns of "centrist" violence, justifying sometimes lethal force in corrective or disciplinary terms, for the sake of their paramount goal of maintaining stability and order.

Far worse than the traditional violence of the center, in modern times, might result when extremist ideology seizes control of the state's apparatus of coercion and begins the project of exposing, denouncing, and annihilating its "enemies." Thus, for instance, the terror phase of the French Revolution, which foreshadowed the far more bloody convulsions of the twentieth century.[64] At the level of state power, the difference between centrist and extremist corresponds to Arendt's distinction between authoritarian and totalitarian.[65] The one uses violence in measured degrees to maintain existing order and coerce obedience; the other uses it without restraint, to identify and then destroy its chosen scapegoats, whether defined by race (Nazism) or by class (Communism). Totalitarian terror governments put aside the state's traditional emphasis on order, harmony, and conservatism, and enlisted its lethal power in the service of revolutionary ideological projects. The twentieth century gave rise to the murderous combination of the center's monopoly on force with the extremist's totalizing vision of transforming the world by any means necessary.[66]

Our own age has seen violence on a scale unmatched in ancient times—not because of any difference in human nature, but because premodern violence was constrained by technological limits. Zealous individuals, or fringe groups with few followers, could use their own deaths as a dramatic spectacle but had no way to take large numbers of innocents with them. Antiquity offered no precise equivalent to the suicide bomber. Mass murder

---

63. On the Spaniards in the New World see Clendinnen 1987, MacCormack 1991, Mills 1997. In the early sixteenth century, Francisco de Vitoria offered an extraordinarily nuanced exploration of the pros and cons, both moral and practical, of religious coercion: in Mills and Taylor 1998, pp. 52–64.

64. See now A. Mayer 2000.

65. See Arendt 1967, esp. pp. 460–479.

66. Rummel 1994 describes in stark and graphic terms the human toll of such totalizing visions.

needed masses of armed men, an army or at least a mob. Ancient governments, of course, could murder by the thousands, but even they could not begin to approach the millions killed by twentieth-century regimes with all the tools of modern bureaucratic organization and weaponry at their disposal. But violence, then as now, had to be committed by human actors with human motivations. Their patterns of behavior, their worldviews, and their styles of justification and contestation have remained broadly similar across centuries. Late antiquity, as we have seen, set precedents in these areas that extend into modern times.

Religious violence, in the Christian Roman Empire, reflected a clash between the authorities' determination to preserve unity and extremists' vision of absolute truth. Christian religious tradition contained grounds both for violent aggression and for the condemnation and repudiation of the same violence. In its late antique context, it gave those in power an imperative to use their might to uphold an ever more narrowly-defined orthodoxy, and forced them to ever more vigilant interventions to maintain that unity in the face of continual challenges from the religion's own tendency for divisive controversies. Extremists, meanwhile, gained from religion the ideological tools—ascetic discipline, the discourse of martyrdom, a sense of opposition to a corrupt world—to inspire resistance against secular powers.

Much can be learned by studying the intentions, worldviews, and ideologies of those who commit violence. But we must not forget that violence is a dangerous tool that, once unleashed, cannot easily be undone. As Hannah Arendt cautions, the means of violence have a tendency easily to overwhelm the ends for which it was employed, with consequences far beyond the intentions or imaginations of those using it.[67] Ancient political and moral discourse emphasized the danger of hubris, which, in a Christian context, shaded into the deadly sin of pride. The arrogant zeal of extremists, who sought to impose their own vision of God's will, found its match in the equally arrogant paternalism of establishment authorities, the "benevolent, medicinal, kindly-meant cruelty" with which they carried out their Christian duty.[68]

The imperial state displayed its characteristic form of hubris first in the Diocletianic persecutions, then in post-Constantinian attempts at unity, and finally through the debacle of Chalcedon and its aftermath. Pagan authorities sought to create a patriotic unity through compulsory religious observance, a project that necessitated coercive violence against recalcitrant Christians. This in turn provoked a Christian resistance articulated in martyrial

67. Arendt 1970, p. 4.
68. Shklar 1984, p. 240; cf. p. 29.

terms, a movement that later lent its moral force to Christian violence against paganism. The Christian government, in its turn, employed violence to promote religious unity and forestall the heresies and schisms it saw as threats to peace. This official violence provoked a counter-reaction, again couched in terms of martyrdom, that in some instances forced the authorities to back down. But when the state yielded too much—as it often did particularly from Theodosius onward—then the result was a power vacuum in religious government, into which the bishops brought their own tyrannical abuses. The result, either way, was a church hierarchy feared to be dangerously corrupted by its entanglements and compromises with worldly power.

The use of force to settle religious disputes necessarily created casualties, adding strength to ideologies of martyrdom that in turn further fueled distrust and resistance. The discourse of Christian martyrdom had particularly divisive consequences under Christian government. The power of the state, now on the Christian side, made a very tempting tool—but it brought violence within the walls of the church in a much more damaging way than the pagans had ever managed. Many Christians circulated and celebrated hagiographic stories of zealous holy men attacking enemies of the faith, smashing idols, burning temples and synagogues, and thereby making converts to the faith. But when the same zealotry turned against the church establishment, the result was ecclesiastical "civil war" and frantic appeals for state intervention. Bishops were endowed with a tremendous degree of secular power that they might use to do good and to advance the faith, but the same power could easily corrupt them. Violence was often used with the best of intentions, by extremists certain that they were doing God's will, and by authorities convinced that they acted out of both necessity and compassion.

In the middle of this struggle, of course, was caught everyone else—the vast majority of ordinary people for whom religious imperatives took a back seat to the day-to-day business of getting along. Both establishment authorities and zealous extremists were guilty of what Judith Shklar calls the hypocrisy "that the ideological needs of the few correspond to the moral and material interest of the many."[69] Most of those involved, if asked, would have believed that their descent into violence was not the result of a conscious moment of decision but rather the logical and seemingly inevitable consequence of their religious duty as they understood it. Many would have denied culpability, insisting in all sincerity that they did nothing more than answer the evil deeds of others—righting perceived wrongs, whether for the sake of retaliation, deterrence, correction, or plain destruction. Their

69. Shklar 1984, p. 66.

adversaries, in their own turn, would make the same excuses for the same behavior. Amid all the desires and impulses late antique Christians feared and sought to discipline, the temptation to bring violence into the church was the greatest and most treacherous of all. As Hannah Arendt warns:

> The danger of violence . . . will always be that the means overwhelm the end. If goals are not achieved rapidly, the result will be not merely defeat but the introduction of the practice of violence into the whole body politic. Action is irreversible, and a return to the status quo in case of defeat is always unlikely. The practice of violence, like all action, changes the world, but the most probable change is to a more violent world.[70]

This study has taken as its purpose to explore not only the practice of violence but also its meaning: the intentions of those who used it, the complaints of those who suffered it, and the reactions of those who witnessed it. Every event was, potentially, subject to struggle over its meaning. The moral, religious, and political traditions available to late antique Christians offered a wealth of possibilities for reaching judgment, so that the same acts praised by some might be condemned by others. Shenoute's claim—that there is no crime for those who have Christ—did not go uncontested.

70. Arendt 1970, p. 80.

Bibliography

PRIMARY SOURCES

Acta Conciliorum Oecumenicorum [ACO]. Eduard Schwartz, ed. Berlin, 1927–. French trans. of Ephesus I and of first two sessions of Chalcedon in A. J. Festugière, *Ephèse et Chalcédoine: Actes des Conciles*. Paris, 1982. French trans. of Chalcedon, sessions three through six, in Festugière, *Actes du Concile de Chalcédoine: Sessions III–VI (La Définition de la Foi)*. Cahiers d'Orientalisme 4. Geneva, 1983. See now *Acts of the Council of Chalcedon*, trans. Richard Price and Michael Gaddis. Liverpool, forthcoming 2005.

Actes de la conférence de Carthage en 411. Ed. with French trans. Serge Lancel. SC, vols. 194, 195, 224, 373. Paris, 1972–1991.

Acts of the Second Council of Ephesus. Syriac text ed. J. Flemming, *Akten der Ephesinischen Synode vom Jahre 449*, with German trans. Georg Hoffman. Abhandlungen der königlichen Gesellschaft der Wissenschaften zu Göttingen, philologisch-historische Klasse, n.s., vol. 15. Berlin, 1917. English trans. S. G. F. Perry. *The Second Synod of Ephesus*. Dartford, England, 1881.

Alexander the Akoimete, *Life* of. Ed. E. de Stoop, "Vie d'Alexandre l'Acémète," PO 6.5, 645–705. Paris, 1911. French trans. in Jean-Marie Baguénard, *Les Moines Acémètes: Vies de Saints Alexandre, Marcel et Jean Calybite*. Spiritualité Orientale, vol. 47. Bellefontaine, 1988. English trans. in Caner 2002.

Ambrose of Milan. *Letters*. PL 16. *On Virgins*. Ed. E. Cazzanica. Turin, 1948. Both trans. in NPNF, 2nd ser., vol. 10.

Ammianus Marcellinus. *Res Gestae*. Ed. and trans. John C. Rolfe. LCL, 3 vols. London, 1935–1939.

Aphrahat. *Demonstration 4*, "On Prayer." Trans. in Sebastian Brock, *The Syriac Fathers on Prayer and the Spiritual Life*. Cistercian Studies, vol. 101. Kalamazoo, 1987.

Apostolic Canons. In *Apostolic Constitutions*, ed. with French trans. Marcel Metzger. SC, vols. 320, 329, 336. Paris, 1987.

Athanasius of Alexandria. H. G. Opitz, W. Schneemelcher, and M. Tetz, eds., *Athanasius Werke*. 3 vols. Berlin, 1934–1938. English trans. of historical-polemical works (e.g., *Historia Arianorum; De Decretis; Encyclical Letter; Apology for His Flight, Apology against the Arians*) in NPNF, 2nd ser., vol. 4. *Life of Antony*, trans. Robert C. Gregg, *Athanasius: The Life of Antony and the Letter to Marcellinus*. Classics of Western Spirituality. New York, 1980.

Athenogenes, *Passion* of. Ed. with French trans. Pierre Maraval, *La passion inédite de S. Athénogène de Pédachthoé en Cappadoce (BHG 197b)*. Subsidia Hagiographica 75. Brussels, 1990.

Augustine of Hippo. Most major works ed. with French trans. in the series *Bibliothèque Augustinienne: Œuvres de Saint Augustin*. Paris, 1949– . Main anti-Donatist works ed. G. Finaert in vols. 28–32. Paris, 1963–1968. English trans. of many of these in NPNF, 1st ser., vols. 1–8. *De Haeresibus*, trans. Liguori G. Muller. Washington, DC, 1956. English trans. of letters Wilfrid Parsons. FOTC, vols. 12, 18, 20, 30, 32. Washington, DC, 1951–1956. New letters (distinguished in numbering sequence by *) ed. with French trans. Johannes Divjak in *Œuvres de Saint Augustin*, vol. 46B. Paris, 1987. English trans. Robert B. Eno. FOTC, vol. 81. Washington, DC, 1989. New sermons ed. with French trans. François Dolbeau, *Augustin d'Hippone: Vingt-six sermons au peuple d'Afrique*. Collection des Études Augustiniennes, Série Antiquité 147. Paris, 1996. English trans. Edmund Hill, *Works of Saint Augustine: A Translation for the 21st Century* Part III, vol. 11. Hyde Park, NY, 1997.

Barhadbeshabba Arbaya. *Cause de la fondation des écoles*. Ed. with French trans. Addaï Scher. PO 4.4. Paris, 1907.

Barsauma, *Life* of. Excerpts ed. with French trans. François Nau, "Résumé de monographies syriaques" in *Revue de l'Orient Chrétien*, 2nd ser., 8 (18) (1913): 270–276, 379–389; 9 (19) (1914): 113–134, 278–289.

Basil of Caesarea. *Letters*. Ed. and trans. Roy J. Deferrari. LCL, 4 vols. Cambridge, MA, 1926.

Bedjan, Paul, ed. *Acta Martyrum et Sanctorum Syriace* IV. Paris and Leipzig, 1894. German trans. in G. Hoffman, *Auszüge aus syrischen Akten persischer Märtyrer*. Abhandlungen für die Kunde des Morgenlandes VII. 3. Leipzig, 1880; and in O. Braun, *Ausgewählte Akten persischer Märtyrer*. Bibliothek der Kirchenväter 22. Kempten-München, 1915.

Besa. *Life of Shenoute*. Bohairic Coptic text ed. J. Leipoldt and W. E. Crum. *Sinuthii Archimandritae Vita et Opera Omnia*. CSCO 41, Scriptores Coptici 1. Paris, 1906. Latin trans. H. Wiesmann and L. T. Lefort in CSCO 129, Scriptores Coptici 16. Paris, 1951. English trans. David N. Bell. Cistercian Studies, vol. 73. Kalamazoo, 1983.

Caesarius of Arles. *Sermons*. Ed. Marie-José Delage. SC, vols. 175, 243, 330. Paris, 1971. English trans. Mary Magdalene Mueller, *Saint Caesarius of Arles: Sermons*. FOTC, vols. 31, 47, 66. Washington, DC, 1956–1973.

Callinicus. *Life of Hypatius*. Ed. with French trans. G. J. M. Bartelink. SC, vol. 177. Paris, 1971.

Chronicon Paschale. Ed. L. Dindorf. 2 vols. Bonn, 1832. English trans. Michael Whitby and Mary Whitby, *Chronicon Paschale 284–628 AD*. Liverpool, 1989.

Clement of Alexandria. *Stromateis.* Ed. C. Mondesert et al. SC, vols. 30, 38, 278–279, 428, 446, 463. Paris, 1951. English trans. ANF, vol. 2.

Coleman-Norton, P. R., ed. and trans. *Roman State and Christian Church: A Collection of Legal Documents to A.D. 535.* 3 vols. London, 1966.

Collectio Avellana. Ed. Otto Guenther. CSEL vol. 35.1. Vienna, 1895.

Constantine, Emperor. *Oration to the Assembly of the Saints.* Appended to Eusebius' *Life of Constantine,* English trans. in NPNF, 2nd ser., vol. 1.

Cyprian. *On the Lapsed; On the Unity of the Church; Letters.* Ed. in CCSL vols. 3, 3A. English trans. ANF, vol. 5.

Cyril of Alexandria. *Letters.* Trans. John I. McEnerney, *St. Cyril of Alexandria: Letters.* FOTC, vols. 76, 77. Washington, DC, 1987.

Daniel the Stylite. *Life.* Ed. H. Delehaye, *Les saints stylites.* Brussels and Paris, 1923. English trans. in Elizabeth Dawes and Norman H. Baynes, *Three Byzantine Saints.* Crestwood, NY, 1977.

Donation of Constantine. In Christopher B. Coleman, ed. and trans. *The Treatise of Lorenzo Valla on the Donation of Constantine.* New Haven, 1922.

Elvira, *Canons* of. Ed. J. Suberbiola Martinez, *Nuevos concilios Hispano-Romanos de los siglos III y IV: La coleccion de Elvira.* Malaga, 1987.

Eunapius. *Lives of the Sophists.* Ed. and trans. Wilmer Cave Wright. LCL. Cambridge, MA, 1922.

Eusebius of Caesarea. *Ecclesiastical History [HE].* Ed. Mommsen, *Eusebius Werke.* GCS 2. Leipzig, 1903. Trans. in NPNF, 2nd ser., vol. 1, along with *Martyrs of Palestine, Panegyric to Constantine [LC]* and *Treatise on the Holy Sepulcher [SC]. Life of Constantine [VC].* Ed. F. Winkelmann, *Über das Leben des Kaisers Konstantin.* GCS 1.1. Berlin, 1975. English trans. Averil Cameron and Stuart G. Hall. Oxford, 1999.

Evagrius Ponticus. *Praktikos.* Trans. John Eudes Bamberger. Kalamazoo, 1981.

Evagrius Scholasticus. *Ecclesiastical History [HE].* Ed. Joseph Bidez and Leon Parmentier, *The Ecclesiastical History of Evagrius with the Scholia.* London, 1898. English trans. Michael Whitby. Liverpool, 2001.

Firmicus Maternus. *On the Error of the Pagan Religions.* Trans. Clarence A. Forbes, ACW, vol. 37. New York, 1970.

Gregory of Nazianzus. *Orations Against Julian [Orations 4 and 5].* Ed. Jean Bernardi, SC, vol. 309. Paris, 1983. Trans. in C. W. King, *Julian the Emperor.* Bohn's Ecclesiastical Library. London, 1888.

Gregory the Great. *Pastoral Rule.* Ed. B. Judic and F. Rommel. SC, vols. 381–382. Paris, 1992. Trans. NPNF, 2nd ser., vol. 12.

Hilary of Poitiers. *Against Valens and Ursacius* and *Letter to Constantius.* Ed. Alfred Feder. CSEL vol. 65, 41–205. Vienna, 1916. English trans. in Lionel R. Wickham, *Hilary of Poitiers: Conflicts of Conscience and Law in the Fourth-century Church.* Liverpool, 1997. *Against Constantius.* Ed. and French trans. in André Rocher, ed., *Hilaire de Poitiers: Contre Constance.* SC, vol. 334. Paris, 1987.

Jerome. *Letters.* Ed. I. Hilberg. CSEL vols. 54, 55, 56. Vienna, 1910, 1912, 1918. English trans. NPNF, 2nd ser., vol. 6.

John Cassian. *Conferences*. Ed. E. Pichery. SC, vols. 42, 54, 64. Paris, 1955–1959. English trans. NPNF, 2nd ser., vol. 11.

John Chrysostom. Text of most works can be found in PG vols. 47–64, with French translations in the series *Oeuvres Complètes de S. Jean Chrysostome*. Paris, 1865. English translations of many texts fill NPNF, 1st ser., vols. 9–14. *Homilies on the Statues:* text in PG 49, trans. in NPNF, 1st ser., vol. 9. *Letters* from exile and *Letters to Olympias:* ed. with French trans. Anne-Marie Malingrey. SC, vols. 103 and 13bis. Paris, 1964 and 1968. English trans. in NPNF, 1st ser., vol. 9. *Discourse on Babylas*, and *Homily on Babylas, Against Julian:* ed. with French trans. Margaret A. Schatkin. SC, vol. 362. Paris, 1990. English trans. of the *Discourse* in Margaret A. Schatkin and Paul W. Harkins, *Saint John Chrysostom Apologist*. FOTC, vol. 73. Washington, DC, 1983. English trans. of the *Homily* in NPNF, 1st ser., vol. 9. *Panegyric on Juventinus and Maximinus:* PG 50, 571–578. *Against the Opponents of the Monastic Life:* ed. F. Dübner, *Sancti Joannis Chrysostomi opera selecta*. Vol. 1. Paris, 1861. Trans. David G. Hunter. Lampeter, 1988. *Sermo post redditu de exsilio:* PG 52, 443–448. See now a new selection of translated sermons in Wendy Mayer and Pauline Allen, eds., *John Chrysostom*. London and New York, 2000.

John of Ephesus. *Lives of the Eastern Saints*. Ed. and trans. E. W. Brooks. PO 17–19. Paris, 1923–1925.

John of Nikiu. *Chronicle*. Ed. H. Zotenberg. Paris, 1883. English trans. Robert Henry Charles, *The Chronicle of John, Coptic Bishop of Nikiu*. London, 1916.

John Rufus. *Plerophoriae*. Ed. with French trans. F. Nau. PO 8. Paris, 1912. *Life of Peter the Iberian*. Ed. and trans. J. Raabe, *Petrus der Iberer*. Leipzig, 1895.

Lactantius. *Divine Institutes*. Ed. P. Monat. SC, vols. 204–205, 326, 337, 377. Paris, 1973–1992. *The Anger of God*. Ed. C. Ingremeau. SC, vol. 289. Paris, 1982. *On the Deaths of the Persecutors*. Ed. J. Moreau. SC, vol. 39. Paris, 1954. All trans. in ANF, vol. 7.

Leo, Pope. *Letters*. Ed. in Schwartz, *ACO*, vol. 2.4. Berlin, 1932. English trans. NPNF, 2nd ser., vol. 12.

Libanius. Select *Orations*. Ed. and trans. A. F. Norman. LCL, 2 vols. Cambridge, MA, 1969 and 1977.

Luke of Steiris, *Life* of. Ed. and trans. Carolyn L. Connor and W. Robert Connor. Brookline, 1994.

Macarius of Tkow, *Panegyric* on. Ed. and trans. D. W. Johnson, *A Panegyric on Macarius, Bishop of Tkow*. CSCO Scriptores Coptici 41–42. Louvain, 1980.

Maier, Jean-Louis, ed. *Le Dossier du Donatisme*. 2 vols. Texte und Untersuchungen zur Geschichte der altchristlichen Literatur. Berlin, 1987–1989.

Malalas. *Chronicle*. Ed. L. Dindorf. Bonn, 1831. English trans. Elizabeth Jeffries, Michael Jeffries and Roger Scott, *The Chronicle of John Malalas: A Translation*. Byzantina Australiensia 4. Melbourne, 1986.

Marcellus the Akoimete, *Life* of. Ed. G. Dagron, "La vie ancienne de saint Marcel l'Acémète." *AB* 86 (1968): 271–321. French trans. in Jean-Marie Baguénard, *Les Moines Acémètes: Vies de Saints Alexandre, Marcel et Jean Calybite*. Spiritualité Orientale, vol. 47. Bellefontaine, 1988.

Mark the Deacon. *Life of Porphyry of Gaza*. Ed. Henri Grégoire and M.-A. Kugener, *Marc le Diacre: Vie de Porphyre évêque de Gaza*. Paris, 1930. English trans. G. F. Hill, *The Life of Porphyry Bishop of Gaza*. Oxford, 1913.

Maximus of Turin. *Sermons*. Ed. Almut Mutzenbecher. CCSL 23. 1962. English trans. Boniface Ramsey, *The Sermons of St. Maximus of Turin*. ACW, vol. 50. New York, 1989.

Munier, C., ed. *Concilia Africae a.345–a.525*. CCSL 149. 1974.

Musurillo, Herbert, ed. and trans. *The Acts of the Christian Martyrs*. Oxford, 1972.

Nestorius. *Bazaar of Heracleides*. Syriac text ed. Bedjan, *Nestorius, Le Livre d'Héraclide de Damas*. Paris, 1910. English trans. G. R. Driver and Leonard Hodgson. Oxford, 1925.

Nilus of Ancyra. *Letters* and *On Voluntary Poverty*. Text in PG 79.

On Divine Law, and *On Bad Teachers*, anonymous Pelagian treatises. Trans. in B. R. Rees, *The Letters of Pelagius and his Followers*. Woodbridge, 1991.

Optatus. *Against the Donatists*. Ed. with French trans. Mireille Labrousse, *Optat de Milève: Traité contre les Donatistes*. SC, vols. 412–413. Paris, 1995. English trans. Mark Edwards, *Optatus: Against the Donatists*. Liverpool, 1997.

Origen. *Commentary on John*. Ed. Cécile Blanc, *Origène Commentaire sur Saint Jean*. SC, vols. 120, 157, 222, 290, 385. Paris, 1966–1992. English trans. in ANF, vol. 9. *Against Celsus*. Ed. M. Borret. SC, vols. 132, 136, 147, 150, 227. Paris, 1967–1976. Trans. in ANF, vol. 9. *Exhortation to Martyrdom*. Ed. P. Koetschau. GCS 2. Leipzig, 1899. English trans. Rowan Greer. Classics of Western Spirituality. New York, 1979.

Pachomius, *Life* of. Bohairic version ed. L.-T. Lefort, *S. Pachomii vita bohairice scripta*. CSCO 89. Louvain, 1925. Primary Greek version ed. F. Halkin, *Sancti Pachomii Vitae Graecae*. Subsidia Hagiographica 19. Brussels, 1932. English trans. of both in Armand Veilleux, *Pachomian Koinonia*. Cistercian Studies vols. 45, 46, 47. Kalamazoo, 1980–1982.

Palladius. *Dialogue on the Life of John Chrysostom*. Text ed. Anne-Marie Malingrey. SC, vols. 341–342. Paris, 1988. English trans. Robert T. Meyer. ACW, vol. 45. New York, 1985. *Lausiac History*. Ed. G. J. M. Bartelink, *Palladio: La Storia Lausiaca*. Fondazione Lorenzo Valla. Milan, 1974. English trans. Robert T. Meyer. ACW, vol. 34. New York, 1964.

Panegyrici Latini. Ed. and trans. C. E. V. Nixon and Barbara S. Rodgers, *In Praise of Later Roman Emperors: The Panegyrici Latini*. Berkeley, 1995.

Philostorgius. *Ecclesiastical History [HE]*. Ed. Joseph Bidez, *Philostorgius Kirchengeschichte*. 2nd ed. rev. Friedhelm Winkelmann. GCS 21. Berlin, 1972. English trans. Edward Walford, *The Ecclesiastical History of Sozomen and the Ecclesiastical History of Philostorgius*. Bohn's Ecclesiastical Library. London, 1855.

Possidius. *Life of Augustine*. Ed. Herbert T. Weiskotten, *Sancti Augustini vita scripta a Possidio episcopo*. Princeton, 1919. English trans. in F. R. Hoare, *The Western Fathers*. New York, 1954.

Prudentius. *Peristephanon*. Ed. and trans. H. J. Thomson. LCL. Cambridge, MA, 1953.

Pseudo-Dionysius of Tel-Mahre. *Chronicle* Part III. English trans. Witold Witakowski. Liverpool, 1996.

Pseudo-Dionysius the Areopagite. English trans. Colm Luibheid, *Pseudo-Dionysius: The Complete Works.* Classics of Western Spirituality. New York, 1987.

Rabbula of Edessa. *Life of Rabbula.* Ed. J. J. Overbeck, *S. Ephraemi Syri, Rabulae episcopi Edesseni, Balaei aliorumque opera selecta.* Oxford, 1865, 159–209. German trans. G. Bickell, *Ausgewählte Schriften der syrischen Kirchenväter Aphraates, Rabulas und Isaak v. Ninive.* Kempten, 1874. *Canons* attributed to Rabbula. Ed. and trans. in Arthur Vööbus, *Syriac and Arabic Documents Regarding Legislation Relative to Syrian Asceticism.* Stockholm, 1960.

Rufinus. *Ecclesiastical History.* Ed. Theodor Mommsen. Leipzig, 1908. English trans. Philip R. Amidon, *The Church History of Rufinus of Aquileia.* Oxford, 1997. *History of the Monks in Egypt (Historia Monachorum).* Text ed. Eva Schulz-Flügel, *Tyrannius Rufinus Historia Monachorum sive De Vita Sanctorum Patrum.* Patristische Texte und Studien 34. Berlin, 1990. English trans. Norman Russell, *The Lives of the Desert Fathers: The Historia Monachorum in Aegypto.* Cistercian Studies, vol. 34. Kalamazoo, 1981.

Sawirus al-Muqaffa. *History of the Patriarchs of Alexandria.* English trans. B. Evetts. PO 5. Paris, 1910.

Severus of Antioch. Ed. and trans. E. W. Brooks, *The Sixth Book of the Select Letters of Severus Patriarch of Antioch.* 4 vols. London, 1904.

Severus of Minorca. *Letter on the Conversion of the Jews.* Ed. and trans. in Bradbury 1996.

Shenoute of Atripe. Coptic text ed. with Latin trans. J. Leipoldt and W. Crum, *Sinuthii Archimandritae Vita et Opera Omnia.* CSCO vols. 42, 73, 96, 108, 129. English trans. of "Letter to a Pagan Notable" in John Barns, "Shenute as a Historical Source." In Jozef Wolski, ed., *Actes du Xe congres international de papyrologues.* Warsaw and Cracow, 1961, 151–159.

Socrates Scholasticus. *Ecclesiastical History [HE].* Ed. Günther Christian Hansen, *Sokrates Kirchengeschichte.* GCS, neue Folge 1. Berlin, 1995. English trans. NPNF, 2nd ser., vol. 2.

Sozomen. *Ecclesiastical History [HE].* Ed. Joseph Bidez, *Sozomenus Kirchengeschichte.* 2nd ed. rev. Günther Christian Hansen. GCS, neue Folge 4. Berlin, 1995. English trans. NPNF, 2nd ser., vol. 2.

Stevenson, J., ed. *A New Eusebius: Documents Illustrating the History of the Church to AD 337.* Rev. ed. W. H. C. Frend. London, 1987.

———, ed. *Creeds, Councils and Controversies: Documents Illustrating the History of the Church AD 337–461.* Rev. ed. W. H. C. Frend. London, 1989.

Sulpicius Severus. *Life of Martin of Tours.* Ed. Jacques Fontaine, *Sulpice Sévère: Vie de Saint Martin.* SC, vols. 133–135. Paris, 1967–1969. *Letters, Chronicle.* Ed. C. Halm. CSEL vol. 1. Vienna, 1866. All trans. in NPNF, 2nd ser., vol. 11.

Symeon the Stylite. *Syriac Life.* Trans. in Robert Doran, *The Lives of Symeon Stylites.* Cistercian Studies 112. Kalamazoo, 1992.

Teresa of Àvila. *Autobiography.* Trans. J. M. Cohen, *The Life of Saint Teresa of Àvila.* London, 1957.

Tertullian. *On Martyrdom; On Flight from Persecution; On Spectacles; Prescription Against Heretics; Apology; Scorpiace.* Texts ed. in CSEL vols. 69–70. Vienna, 1939–1942. Trans. in ANF, vols. 3–4.

Theodoret of Cyrrhus. *Ecclesiastical History [HE].* Text ed. Leon Parmentier, *Theodoret Kirchengeschichte.* 3rd ed., rev. Günther Christian Hansen. GCS, neue Folge 5. Berlin, 1998. English trans. in NPNF, 2nd ser., vol. 3. *Historia Religiosa* or *Philotheos [HR].* Text ed. Pierre Canivet and Alice Leroy-Molinghen, *Théodoret de Cyr: Histoire des Moines de Syrie.* SC, vols. 234, 237. Paris, 1977–1979. English trans. R. M. Price, *A History of the Monks of Syria.* Cistercian Studies 88. Kalamazoo, 1985. *Letters.* Ed. with French trans. Yvan Azéma, *Théodoret de Cyr: Correspondance.* SC, vols. 40, 98, 111, 429. Paris, 1955–1998. English trans. in NPNF, 2nd ser., vol. 3.

Theodosian Code [C.Th.]. Ed. Th. Mommsen and E. Meyer. Berlin, 1905. Trans. C. Pharr, *The Theodosian Code.* New York, 1952.

Theopistus. *Life of Dioscorus.* Ed. and trans. F. Nau, "Histoire de Dioscore, patriarche d'Alexandrie." *Journal Asiatique* 10 (1903): 5–108, 241–310.

Tilley, Maureen A., trans. *Donatist Martyr Stories: The Church in Conflict in Roman North Africa.* Liverpool, 1996.

Tyconius. Extant fragments ed. in T. Hahn, *Tyconius-Studien.* Leipzig, 1900.

Victor of Vita. *History of the Vandal Persecution.* English trans. John Moorhead. Liverpool, 1992.

Zacharias of Mytilene. *Chronicle.* Trans. F. J. Hamilton and E. W. Brooks. London, 1899.

Zosimus. *History.* Ed. F. Paschoud. Paris, 1971. English trans. Ronald T. Ridley. Sydney, 1982.

MODERN WORKS

Adshead, K. 1998. "Patriarch and Pharaoh: A Lexical Approach." In T. W. Hillard et al., eds., *Ancient History in a Modern University,* vol. 2, 350–356. Grand Rapids, Michigan.

Alexander, P. 1963. "The Donation of Constantine at Byzantium and Its Earliest Use against the Western Empire." *Zbornik radova Vizantoloskog Instituta* 8: 11–26.

Amidon, Philip R. 1979. *Studies in the Procedure of Church Synods of the Third and Fourth Centuries.* D.Phil. Thesis, Oxford University.

Amory, Patrick. 1997. *People and Identity in Ostrogothic Italy 489–554.* Cambridge.

Anderson, Benedict. 1991. *Imagined Communities: Reflections on the Origin and Spread of Nationalism.* Rev. ed. London.

Ando, Clifford. 1996. "Pagan Apologetics and Christian Intolerance in the Ages of Themistius and Augustine." *JECS* 4: 171–207.

Arendt, Hannah. 1967. *The Origins of Totalitarianism.* New ed. New York.

———. 1970. *On Violence.* New York.

Asmussen, J. P. 1983. "Christians in Iran." In Ehsan Yarshater, ed., *The Cambridge History of Iran*, vol. 3, 924–948. Cambridge.

Atkinson, J. E. 1992. "Out of Order: The Circumcellions and *Codex Theodosianus* 16.5.52." *Historia* 61: 488–499.

Aubineau, M. 1966. "Les 318 serviteurs d'Abraham (Gen., XIV, 14) et le nombre des Péres au concile de Nicée (325)." *Revue d'histoire ecclesiastique* 61: 5–43.

Avi-Yonah, Michael. 1976. *The Jews under Roman and Byzantine Rule*. New York.

Bacht, Heinrich. 1951. "Die Rolle des orientalischen Mönchtums in den kirchenpolitischen Auseinandersetzungen um Chalkedon (431–519)." In Grillmeier and Bacht 1951, vol. 2, 193–314.

Bagnall, Roger. 1989. "Official and Private Violence in Roman Egypt." *Bulletin of the American Society of Papyrologists* 26: 201–216.

Baguénard, Jean-Marie. 1988. *Les moines Acémètes: Vies des saints Alexandre, Marcel, et Jean Calybite*. Bellefontaine.

Barnard, Laurette. 1995. "The Criminalisation of Heresy in the Later Roman Empire: A Sociopolitical Device?" *Legal History* 16: 121–146.

Barnes, M., and D. H. Williams, eds. 1993. *Arianism After Arius: Essays on the Development of the Fourth-Century Trinitarian Conflicts*. Edinburgh.

Barnes, Timothy D. 1968. "Legislation against the Christians." *JRS* 58: 32–50.

———. 1981. *Constantine and Eusebius*. Cambridge, MA.

———. 1984. "Constantine's Prohibition of Pagan Sacrifice." *American Journal of Philology* 105: 69–72.

———. 1992. "The Constantinian Settlement." In H. W. Attridge and Gohei Hata, eds., *Eusebius, Christianity, and Judaism*, 635–657. Detroit.

———. 1993. *Athanasius and Constantius: Theology and Politics in the Constantinian Empire*. Cambridge, MA.

———. 1994. *From Eusebius to Augustine: Selected Papers 1982–1993*. London.

———. 1996. "The Crimes of Basil of Ancyra." *JTS*, n.s., 47: 550–554.

———. 1998. *Ammianus Marcellinus and the Representation of Historical Reality*. Ithaca.

Barns, John. 1961. "Shenute as a Historical Source." In Jozef Wolski, ed., *Actes du Xe congrès international de papyrologues*, 151–159. Warsaw and Cracow.

Barton, Carlin A. 1993. *The Sorrows of the Ancient Romans: The Gladiator and the Monster*. Princeton.

———. 1994. "Savage Miracles: The Redemption of Lost Honor in Roman Society and the Sacrament of the Gladiator and the Martyr." *Representations* 45: 41–71.

Bauer, Adolf, and Josef Strzygowski. 1906. *Eine alexandrinische Weltchronik: Text und Miniaturen eines griechischen Papyrus der Sammlung W. Goleniscev*. Vienna.

Bauer, Walter. 1934. *Orthodoxy and Heresy in Earliest Christianity*. Tübingen. English trans. Philadelphia Seminar on Christian Origins. Philadelphia, 1971.

Bauman, Richard A. 2000. *Human Rights in Ancient Rome*. London and New York.

Baynes, Norman H. 1926. "Alexandria and Constantinople: A Study in Ecclesiastical Diplomacy." *Journal of Egyptian Archaeology* 12: 145–156.

———. 1937. "The Death of Julian the Apostate in a Christian Legend." *JRS* 27: 22–29.

Behlmer, Heike. 1998. "Visitors to Shenoute's Monastery." In David Frankfurter, ed., *Pilgrimage and Holy Space in Late Antique Egypt*, 341–371. Leiden.

Bell, Harold Idris. 1924. *Jews and Christians in Egypt: The Jewish Troubles in Alexandria and the Athanasian Controversy.* London.

Bengtson, H. 1972. *Die olympischen Spiele in der Antike.* 2nd ed. Zürich.

Béranger, Jean. 1948. "Le refus du pouvoir: recherches sur l'aspect idéologique du principat." *Museum Helveticum* 5: 178–196.

Birley, A. R. 1987. "Some Notes on the Donatist Schism." *Libyan Studies* 18: 29–41.

Blum, Georg Günter. 1969. *Rabbula von Edessa: Der Christ, der Bischof, sein Theologie.* CSCO Subsidia vol. 34. Louvain.

Bowersock, Glen W. 1978. *Julian the Apostate.* Cambridge, MA.

———. 1995. *Martyrdom and Rome.* Cambridge.

———. 2001. "The Syriac Life of Rabbula and Syrian Hellenism." In Tomas Hägg and Philip Rousseau, eds., *Greek Biography and Panegyric in Late Antiquity*, 255–271. Berkeley.

Boyarin, Daniel. 1999. *Dying for God: Martyrdom and the Making of Christianity and Judaism.* Stanford.

Bradbury, Scott. 1995. "Julian's Pagan Revival and the Decline of Blood Sacrifice." *Phoenix* 49: 331–356.

———. 1996. *Severus of Minorca: Letter on the Conversion of the Jews.* Oxford.

Brakke, David. 1995a. *Athanasius and the Politics of Asceticism.* Oxford.

———. 1995b. "The Problematization of Nocturnal Emissions in Early Christian Syria, Egypt and Gaul." *JECS* 3: 419–460.

Braun, René, and Jean Richer, eds. 1978. *L'empereur Julian: De l'histoire à la légende.* 2 vols. Paris.

Brenk, Beat. 1991. "Die Umwandlung der Synagoge von Apamea in eine Kirche." In *Tesserae: Festschrift für Josef Engemann*, Jahrbuch für Antike und Christentum, Ergänzungsband 18, 1–25. Münster.

Brennecke, Hanns Christof. 1988. *Studien zur Geschichte der Homöer: Der Osten bis zum Ende der homöischen Reichskirche.* Tübingen.

Brock, Sebastian. 1982. "Christians in the Sasanian Empire: A Case of Divided Loyalties." In Stuart Mews, ed., *Religion and National Identity*, Studies in Church History 18, 1–19. Oxford. Reprinted in Brock, *Syriac Perspectives on Late Antiquity*. London, 1984.

———. 1993. "Fire from Heaven: From Abel's Sacrifice to the Eucharist. A Theme in Syriac Christianity." *SP* 25: 229–243.

Brock, Sebastian, and Susan Ashbrook Harvey. 1998. *Holy Women of the Syrian Orient.* 2nd ed. Berkeley.

Brown, Peter. 1961. "Religious Dissent in the Later Roman Empire: The Case of North Africa." *History* 46: 83–101. Reprinted in Brown 1972a, 237–259.

———. 1963. "Religious Coercion in the Later Roman Empire: The Case of North Africa." *History* 48: 283–305. Reprinted in Brown 1972a, 301–331.

———. 1964. "St. Augustine's Attitude toward Religious Coercion." *JRS* 54: 107–116. Reprinted in Brown 1972a, 260–278.

———. 1969. "The Diffusion of Manichaeism in the Roman Empire." *JRS* 59: 92–103. Reprinted in Brown 1972a, 94–118.

———. 1971. "The Rise and Function of the Holy Man in Late Antiquity." *JRS* 61: 80–101. Reprinted in Brown 1982, 103–152.

———. 1972a. *Religion and Society in the Age of Saint Augustine.* London.

———. 1972b. "Sorcery, Demons and the Rise of Christianity: From Late Antiquity to the Early Middle Ages." In Brown 1972a, 119–146.

———. 1976. "Town, Village and Holy Man: The Case of Syria." In D. M. Pippidi, ed., *Assimilation et résistance à la culture gréco-romaine dans le monde ancien,* 213–230. Bucharest. Reprinted in Brown 1982, 153–165.

———. 1981. *The Cult of the Saints: Its Rise and Function in Latin Christianity.* Chicago.

———. 1982. *Society and the Holy in Late Antiquity.* Berkeley.

———. 1983. "The Saint as Exemplar in Late Antiquity." *Representations* 1: 1–25.

———. 1988. *The Body and Society: Men, Women and Sexual Renunciation in Early Christianity.* New York.

———. 1992. *Power and Persuasion in Late Antiquity: Towards a Christian Empire.* Madison.

———. 1995a. *Authority and the Sacred: Aspects of the Christianization of the Roman World.* Cambridge.

———. 1995b. "Arbiters of the Holy: The Christian Holy Man in Late Antiquity." In Brown 1995a, 57–78.

———. 1995c. "Christianization: Narratives and Process." In Brown 1995a, 3–26.

———. 1995d. "The Limits of Intolerance." In Brown 1995a, 29–54.

———. 2000a. *Augustine of Hippo: A Biography.* 2nd ed. Berkeley.

———. 2000b. "Enjoying the Saints in Late Antiquity." *Early Medieval Europe* 9: 1–24.

———. 2002. *Poverty and Leadership in the Later Roman Empire.* Hanover, NH.

Bührer-Thierry, Geneviève. 1998. " 'Just Anger' or 'Vengeful Anger'? The Punishment of Blinding in the Early Medieval West." In Rosenwein 1998, 75–91.

Bulliet, Richard W. 1994. *Islam: The View from the Edge.* New York.

Burgess, Richard W. 1993–1994. "The Accession of Marcian in the Light of Chalcedonian Apologetic and Monophysite Polemic." *BZ* 86–87: 47–68.

Burke, John. 1975. "Eusebius on Paul of Samosata: A New Image." *Kleronomia* 7: 8–20.

Burns, J. Patout. 2002. *Cyprian the Bishop.* London.

Burrus, Virginia. 1989. "Rhetorical Stereotypes in the Portrait of Paul of Samosata." *VC* 43: 215–225.

———. 1991. "The Heretical Woman as Symbol in Alexander, Athanasius, Epiphanius and Jerome." *HTR* 84: 229–248.

———. 1994. "Word and Flesh: The Bodies and Sexuality of Ascetic Women in Christian Antiquity." *Journal of Feminist Studies in Religion* 10: 27–51.

———. 1995. "Reading Agnes: The Rhetoric of Gender in Ambrose and Prudentius." *JECS* 3: 25–46.

Burton-Christie, Douglas. 1993. *The Word in the Desert: Scripture and the Quest for Holiness in Early Christian Monasticism.* Oxford.

Butterweck, Christel. 1995. *"Martyriumssucht" in der alten Kirche? Studien zur Darstellung und Deutung frühchristlicher Martyrien.* Tübingen.

Cameron, Alan. 1986. "The Authenticity of the Letters of St. Nilus of Ancyra." *GRBS* 17: 181–196.

Cameron, Averil. 1991. *Christianity and the Rhetoric of Empire: The Development of Christian Discourse.* Berkeley.

———. 1995. "Ascetic Closure and the End of Antiquity." In Wimbush and Valantasis 1995, 147–161.

Cameron, Averil, and Lawrence I. Conrad, eds. 1992. *The Byzantine and Early Islamic Near East: Problems in the Literary Source Material.* Studies in Late Antiquity and Early Islam 1. Princeton.

Caner, Daniel. 2002. *Wandering, Begging Monks: Spiritual Authority and the Promotion of Monasticism in Late Antiquity.* Berkeley.

Canivet, Pierre. 1977. *Le monachisme syrien selon Théodoret de Cyr.* Paris.

Caseau, Beatrice. 1999. "Sacred Landscapes." In Glen W. Bowersock, Peter Brown, and Oleg Grabar, eds., *Late Antiquity: A Guide to the Post-Classical World,* 21–59. Cambridge, MA.

———. 2001. *"Polemein Lithois:* La désacralisation des espaces et des objets religieux païens durant l'antiquité tardive." In Michel Kaplan, ed., *Le sacré et son inscription dans l'espace à Byzance et en Occident,* Byzantina Sorbonensia 18, 61–123. Paris.

Castelli, Elizabeth A. 1996. "Imperial Reimaginings of Christian Origins: Epic in Prudentius' Poem for the Martyr Eulalia." In Elizabeth A. Castelli and Hal Taussig, eds., *Reimagining Christian Origins: A Colloquium Honoring Burton L. Mack,* 173–184. Valley Forge.

Cayrel, P. 1934. "Une Basilique donatiste de Numidie." *Mélanges d'archéologie et d'histoire de l'école française de Rome* 51: 133–136.

Cecconi, Giovanni A. 1990. "Elemosina e propaganda: Un'analisi della 'Macariana persecutio' nel III libro di Ottato di Milevi." *Revue des études augustiniennes* 36: 42–66.

Chadwick, Henry. 1955. "The Exile and Death of Flavian of Constantinople: A Prologue to the Council of Chalcedon." *JTS,* n.s., 6: 17–34.

Chaffin, C. E. 1970. "The Martyrs of the Val di Non: An Examination of Contemporary Reactions." *SP* 10: 263–269.

Chesnut, Glenn F. 1977. *The First Church Historians: Eusebius, Socrates, Sozomen, Theodoret and Evagrius.* Paris.

Chitty, Derwas. 1966. *The Desert a City: An Introduction to the Study of Egyptian and Palestinian Monasticism under the Christian Empire.* Crestwood, NY.

Choksy, Jamsheed K. 1997. *Conflict and Cooperation: Zoroastrian Subalterns and Muslim Elites in Medieval Iran*. New York.

Christensen, Arthur. 1944. *L'Iran sous les sassanides*. 2nd ed. Copenhagen.

Christys, Ann. 2002. *Christians in al-Andalus (711–1000)*. Richmond, Surrey.

Cimma, Maria Rosa. 1989. *L'episcopalis audientia nelle costituzioni imperiali da Costantino a Giustiniano*. Turin.

Clark, Elizabeth A. 1992. *The Origenist Controversy: The Cultural Construction of an Early Christian Debate*. Princeton.

Clark, Gillian. 1998. "Bodies and Blood: Late Antique Debate on Martyrdom, Virginity, and Resurrection." In Dominic Montserrat, ed., *Changing Bodies, Changing Meanings: Studies on the Human Body in Antiquity*, 99–115. London and New York.

Clendinnen, Inga. 1987. *Ambivalent Conquests: Maya and Spaniard in Yucatan, 1517–1570*. Cambridge.

Cohen, Jeremy. 1976. "Roman Imperial Policy toward the Jews from Constantine until the End of the Palestinian Patriarchate." *Byzantine Studies* 3: 1–29.

Coleman, K. M. 1990. "Fatal Charades: Roman Executions Staged as Mythological Events." *JRS* 80: 44–73.

Coope, Jessica A. 1995. *The Martyrs of Córdoba: Community and Family Conflict in an Age of Mass Conversion*. Lincoln, NE.

Courcelle, P. 1936. "Une seconde campagne de fouilles à Ksar el Kelb." *Mélanges d'archéologie et d'histoire de l'école française de Rome* 53: 161–183.

Coyle, J. Kevin. 1998. "Early Monks, Prayer, and the Devil." In Pauline Allen, Raymond Canning, and Lawrence Cross, eds., *Prayer and Spirituality in the Early Church*, vol. 1, 229–249. Everton Park, Queensland.

Cuneo, Michael W. 1997. *The Smoke of Satan: Conservative and Traditionalist Dissent in Contemporary American Catholicism*. Oxford.

Dagron, Gilbert. 1970. "Les moines et la ville: le monachisme à Constantinople jusqu'au concile de Chalcédoine." *TM* 4: 229–276.

———. 1974. *Naissance d'une capitale: Constantinople et ses institutions de 330 à 451*. Paris.

———. 1996. *Empereur et prêtre: étude sur le "césaropapisme" byzantin*. Paris.

D'Alès, A. 1932. "La lettre d'Ibas à Marès le Persian." *Recherches de science religieuse* 22: 5–25.

Davis, Natalie Z. 1973. "The Rites of Violence: Religious Riots in Sixteenth-Century France." *Past and Present* 59: 53–91. Reprinted in Davis, *Society and Culture in Early Modern France*, 152–187. Stanford, 1975.

de Bruyn, Theodore S. 1999. "Flogging a Son: The Emergence of the *pater flagellans* in Latin Christian Discourse." *JECS* 7: 249–290.

De Gaiffier, Baudouin. 1956. " 'Sub Iuliano Apostata' dans le martyrologe romain." *AB* 74: 5–49.

Delehaye, Hippolyte. 1907. *The Legends of the Saints: An Introduction to Hagiography*. Trans. V. M. Crawford. London.

———. 1909. *Les légendes grecques des saints militaires*. Paris.

———. 1912. *Les origines du culte des martyrs*. Brussels.

———. 1914. "Saint Almachius ou Télémaque." *AB* 33: 421–428.

Delmaire, Roland. 1984. "Les dignitaires laïcs au concile de Chalcédoine: notes sur la hiérarchie et les préséances au milieu du Ve siècle." *Byzantion* 54: 141–175.

Demougeot, Emilienne. 1982. "L'évêque Sévère et les Juifs de Minorque au Ve siècle." In *Majorque, Languedoc et Roussillon de l'antiquité à nos jours: actes du LIIIe congrès de la federation historique du Languedoc et du Roussillon*, 13–34. Montpellier.

Dietz, Maribel. 1997. *Travel, Wandering and Pilgrimage in Late Antiquity and the Early Middle Ages*. PhD Dissertation, Princeton University.

Digeser, Elizabeth DePalma. 2000. *The Making of a Christian Empire: Lactantius and Rome*. Ithaca.

Dossey, Leslie. 2001. "Judicial Violence and the Ecclesiastical Courts in Late Antique North Africa." In Mathisen 2001, 98–114.

Douglas, Mary. 1966. *Purity and Danger*. London.

———. 1982. *In the Active Voice*. London.

———. 1986. *How Institutions Think*. Syracuse.

———. 1992. *Risk and Blame: Essays in Cultural Theory*. London.

———. 1996. *Natural Symbols: Explorations in Cosmology*. Rev. ed. London.

Douglas, Mary, and Aaron Wildavsky. 1982. *Risk and Culture: An Essay on the Selection of Technological and Environmental Dangers*. Berkeley.

Drake, Harold A. 1995. "Constantine and Consensus." *Church History* 64: 1–15.

———. 1996. "Lambs into Lions: Explaining Early Christian Intolerance." *Past and Present* 153: 3–36.

———. 2000. *Constantine and the Bishops: The Politics of Intolerance*. Baltimore.

Drijvers, Han J. W. 1996. "The Man of God of Edessa, Bishop Rabbula, and the Urban Poor: Church and Society in the Fifth Century." *JECS* 4: 235–248.

Droge, Arthur J., and James D. Tabor. 1992. *A Noble Death: Suicide and Martyrdom among Christians and Jews in Antiquity*. San Francisco.

Du châtiment dans la cité: Supplices corporels et peine de mort dans le monde antique. 1984. Collection de l'École française de Rome, vol. 79. Rome.

Duchesne, L. 1956. *Christian Worship: Its Origin and Evolution*. Trans. M. L. McClure. 5th ed. London.

Duri, A. A. 1983. *The Rise of Historical Writing Among the Arabs*. Trans. Lawrence I. Conrad. Princeton.

Duval, Yvette. 1982. *Loca Sanctorum Africae: le culte des martyrs en Afrique du IVe au VIIe siècle*. Rome.

Ellis, Richard J. 1998. *The Dark Side of the Left: Illiberal Egalitarianism in America*. Lawrence, KS.

Elm, Susanna. 1994. *Virgins of God: The Making of Asceticism in Late Antiquity*. Oxford.

———. 1998. "The Dog That Did Not Bark: Doctrine and Patriarchal Authority in the Conflict between Theophilus of Alexandria and John Chrysostom of Constantinople." In Louis Ayres and Gareth Jones, eds., *Christian Origins: Theology, Rhetoric and Community*, 68–93. London.

Emmel, Stephen Lewis. 1993. *Shenoute's Literary Corpus*. PhD Dissertation, Yale University.

———. 2002. "From the Other Side of the Nile: Shenute and Panopolis." In A. Egberts, B. P. Muhs, and J. van der Vliet, eds., *Perspectives on Panopolis: An Egyptian Town from Alexander the Great to the Arab Conquest*, 95–113. Leiden.

Fardon, Richard. 1999. *Mary Douglas: An Intellectual Biography*. London.

Finley, Moses I. 1999. *The Ancient Economy*. Updated ed. Berkeley.

Finley, Moses I., and H. W. Pleket. 1976. *The Olympic Games: The First Thousand Years*. London.

Fitschen, Klaus. 1998. *Messalianismus und Antimessalianismus: ein Beispiel ostkirchlicher Ketzergeschichte*. Göttingen.

Foucault, Michel. 1977. *Discipline and Punish: The Birth of the Prison*. Trans. Alan Sheridan. New York.

Fowden, Garth. 1978. "Bishops and Temples in the Eastern Roman Empire." *JTS*, n.s., 29: 53–78.

———. 1993. *Empire to Commonwealth: Consequences of Monotheism in Late Antiquity*. Princeton.

Frank, Georgia. 2000. *The Memory of the Eyes: Pilgrims to Living Saints in Christian Late Antiquity*. Berkeley.

Frankfurter, David. 1990. "Stylites and Phallobates: Pillar Religions in Late Antique Syria." *VC* 44: 168–198.

———. 1993. *Elijah in Upper Egypt: The Apocalypse of Elijah and Early Egyptian Christianity*. Minneapolis.

———. 1998. *Religion in Roman Egypt: Assimilation and Resistance*. Princeton.

Frend, W. H. C. 1965. *Martyrdom and Persecution in the Early Church*. Oxford.

———. 1969. "Circumcellions and Monks." *JTS*, n.s., 20: 542–549.

———. 1972. *The Rise of the Monophysite Movement: Chapters in the History of the Church in the Fifth and Sixth Centuries*. London.

———. 1984. *The Rise of Christianity*. Philadelphia.

———. 1985. *The Donatist Church: A Movement of Protest in Roman North Africa*. Rev. ed. Oxford.

———. 1988. "The Donatist Church: Forty Years On." In Frend, *Archaeology and History in the Study of Early Christianity*, 70–84. London.

———. 1997. "Donatus 'paene totam Africam decepit.' How?" *JEH* 48: 611–627.

Friedland, Roger, and Richard Hecht. 1991. "The Politics of Sacred Place: Jerusalem's Temple Mount / al-haram al-sharif." In Jamie Scott and Paul Simpson-Housley, eds., *Sacred Places and Profane Spaces: Essays on the Geographies of Judaism, Christianity, and Islam*, 21–61. New York.

———. 1998. "The Bodies of Nations: A Comparative Study of Religious Violence in Jerusalem and Ayodhya." *History of Religions* 38: 101–149.

Garnsey, Peter. 1970. *Social Status and Legal Privilege in the Roman Empire*. Oxford.

———. 1984. "Religious Toleration in Classical Antiquity." In W. J. Sheils, ed., *Persecution and Toleration*, Studies in Church History 21, 1–27. Oxford.

Garnsey, Peter, and Richard Saller. 1987. *The Roman Empire: Economy, Society and Culture.* Berkeley.

Gatier, Pierre-Louis. 1995. "Un moine sur la frontière: Alexandre l'Acémète en Syrie." In Aline Rousselle, ed., *Frontières terrestres, frontières celestes dans l'antiquité,* 435–457. Paris.

Gay, Peter. 1993. *The Cultivation of Hatred: The Bourgeois Experience Victoria to Freud Volume III.* New York.

Geanakoplos, D. J. 1965. "Church and State in the Byzantine Empire: A Reconsideration of the Problem of Caesaropapism." *Church History* 34: 381–403.

Giardina, Andrea. 1983. "Banditi e santi: un aspetto del folklore gallico tra tardo antichità e medioevo." *Athenaeum,* n.s., 61: 374–389.

Girardet, Klaus M. 1977. "Kaiser Konstantius II als 'Episcopus Episcoporum' und das Herrscherbild des kirchlichen Widerstandes." *Historia* 26.1: 95–128.

Gleason, Maud W. 1995. *Making Men: Sophists and Self-Presentation in Ancient Rome.* Princeton.

Goehring, James E. 1992. "The Origins of Monasticism." In Harold W. Attridge and Gohei Hata, eds., *Eusebius, Christianity, and Judaism,* 235–255. London.

———. 1997. "Monastic Diversity and Ideological Boundaries in Fourth-Century Christian Egypt." *JECS* 5: 61–84.

Gould, Graham. 1993. *The Desert Fathers on Monastic Community.* Oxford.

Gray, Patrick T. R. 1979. *The Defense of Chalcedon in the East (451–533).* Leiden.

———. 1989. " 'The Select Fathers': Canonizing the Patristic Past." *SP* 23: 21–36.

Greenslade, S. L. 1953. *Schism in the Early Church.* London.

Gregory, Brad S. 1999. *Salvation at Stake: Christian Martyrdom in Early Modern Europe.* Cambridge, MA.

Gregory, Timothy E. 1973. "Zosimus 5.23 and the People of Constantinople." *Byzantion* 43: 63–81.

———. 1975. "Novatianism: A Rigorist Sect in the Christian Roman Empire." *Byzantine Studies/Études Byzantines* 2: 1–18.

———. 1979. *Vox Populi: Popular Opinion and Violence in the Christological Controversies of the Fifth Century A.D.* Columbus.

Gribomont, J. 1972. "Le dossier des origines du Messalianisme." In J. Fontaine and C. Kannengiesser, eds., *Epektasis: Mélanges patristiques offerts au Cardinal Jean Daniélou,* 611–625. Paris.

Griffith, Sidney H. 1995. "Asceticism in the Church of Syria: The Hermeneutics of Early Syrian Monasticism." In Wimbush and Valantasis 1995, 220–245.

Grillmeier, Alois. 1975, 1987, 1995, and 1996. *Christ in Christian Tradition.* 4 vols. London.

Grillmeier, Alois, and Heinrich Bacht, eds. 1951. *Das Konzil von Chalkedon: Geschichte und Gegenwart.* 3 vols. Würzburg.

Grubbs, Judith Evans. 1995. *Law and Family in Late Antiquity: The Emperor Constantine's Marriage Legislation.* Oxford.

Haas, Christopher. 1997. *Alexandria in Late Antiquity: Topography and Social Conflict.* Baltimore.

Hackel, Sergei, ed. 1981. *The Byzantine Saint.* London.

Halton, Thomas. 1995. "Ecclesiastical War and Peace in the Letters of Isidore of Pelusium." In Timothy S. Miller and John Nesbitt, eds., *Peace and War in Byzantium: Essays in Honor of George T. Dennis*, 41–49. Washington, DC.

Hanson, R. P. C. 1985. "The Transformation of Pagan Temples into Churches in the Early Christian Centuries." In Hanson, *Studies in Christian Antiquity*, 347–358. Edinburgh.

———. 1988. *The Search for the Christian Doctrine of God: The Arian Controversy 318–381*. Edinburgh.

Harries, Jill. 1999a. "Constructing the Judge: Judicial Accountability and the Culture of Criticism in Late Antiquity." In Richard Miles, ed., *Constructing Identities in Late Antiquity*, 214–233. London and New York.

———. 1999b. *Law and Empire in Late Antiquity*. Cambridge.

Harris, Lee. 2002. "Al Qaeda's Fantasy Ideology." *Policy Review* 114 (August 2002): 19–36. Available online at http://www.policyreview.org/aug02/harris.html.

Harris, William V. 2001. *Restraining Rage: The Ideology of Anger Control in Classical Antiquity*. Cambridge, MA.

Harvey, Susan Ashbrook. 1988a. "Remembering Pain: Syriac Historiography and the Separation of the Churches." *Byzantion* 58: 295–308.

———. 1988b. "The Sense of a Stylite: Perspectives on Simeon the Elder." *VC* 42: 376–394.

———. 1990a. *Asceticism and Society in Crisis: John of Ephesus and the Lives of the Eastern Saints*. Berkeley.

———. 1990b. "The Edessan Martyrs and Ascetic Tradition." *V Symposium Syriacum 1988*, 195–206. Orientalia Christiana Analecta 236. Rome.

———. 1994. "The Holy and the Poor: Models from Early Syriac Christianity." In Emily Albu Hanawalt and Carter Lindberg, eds., *Through the Eye of a Needle: Judeo-Christian Roots of Social Welfare*, 43–66. Kirksville, MO.

———. 1998. "The Stylite's Liturgy: Ritual and Religious Identity in Late Antiquity." *JECS* 6: 523–539.

———. Unpublished. "Bishop Rabbula: Ascetic Tradition and Change in Fifth-Century Edessa."

Helgeland, John, Robert J. Daly, and J. Patout Burns, eds. 1985. *Christians and the Military: The Early Experience*. Philadelphia.

Herrin, Judith. 1987. *The Formation of Christendom*. Princeton.

Hjort, Øystein. 1993. "Augustus Christianus—Livia Christiana: *Sphragis* and Roman Portrait Sculpture." In Lennart Ryden and J. O. Rosenqvist, eds., *Aspects of Late Antiquity and Early Byzantium*, 99–112. Stockholm.

Holmes, Stephen. 1995. *Passions and Constraint: On the Theory of Liberal Democracy*. Chicago.

Holum, Kenneth G. 1977. "Pulcheria's Crusade (AD 421–422) and the Ideology of Imperial Victory." *GRBS* 18: 153–172.

———. 1982. *Theodosian Empresses: Women and Imperial Dominion in Late Antiquity*. Berkeley.

Honigmann, Ernest. 1942. "The Original Lists of the Members of the Council of Nicaea, the Robber Synod and the Council of Chalcedon." *Byzantion* 16: 20–80.

———. 1950. "Juvenal of Jerusalem." *DOP* 5: 209–279.

———. 1954. *Le couvent de Barsauma et le patriarcat jacobite d'Antioche et d'Syrie*. CSCO Subsidia vol. 7. Louvain.

Hopkins, Keith. 1998. "Christian Number and its Implications." *JECS* 6: 185–226.

Howard-Johnston, James, and Paul Antony Hayward, eds. 1999. *The Cult of the Saints in Late Antiquity and the Middle Ages: Essays on the Contribution of Peter Brown*. Oxford.

Humphries, Mark. 1998. "Savage Humour: Christian Anti-panegyric in Hilary of Poitiers' *Against Constantius*." In Mary Whitby, ed., *The Propaganda of Power: The Role of Panegyric in Late Antiquity*, 201–223. Leiden.

Hunt, David. 1993. "Christianising the Roman Empire: The Evidence of the Code." In Jill Harries and Ian Wood, eds., *The Theodosian Code: Studies in the Imperial Law of Late Antiquity*, 143–158. Ithaca.

Hunt, E. D. 1982. "St. Stephen in Minorca." *JTS*, n.s., 33: 106–123.

Janin, R. 1953. *La géographie ecclésiastique de l'Empire byzantin, v.3: Les églises et les monastères*. Paris.

Jones, A. H. M. 1949. *Constantine and the Conversion of Europe*. London.

———. 1959. "Were Ancient Heresies National or Social Movements in Disguise?" *JTS*, n.s., 10: 280–296.

Jones, A. H. M., J. R. Martindale, and J. Morris, eds. 1971. *The Prosopography of the Later Roman Empire*. [PLRE] Cambridge.

Judge, E. A. 1977. "The Earliest Use of *monachos* for 'Monk' (P. Coll. Youtie 77) and the Origins of Monasticism." *Jahrbuch für Antike und Christentum* 20: 72–89.

Juergensmeyer, Mark. 2000. *Terror in the Mind of God: The Global Rise of Religious Violence*. Berkeley.

Kakar, Sudhir. 1996. *The Colors of Violence: Cultural Identities, Religion, and Conflict*. Chicago.

Kedar, Benjamin Z. 1984. *Crusade and Mission: European Approaches Toward the Muslims*. Princeton.

Kelly, John N. D. 1995. *Golden Mouth: The Story of John Chrysostom—Ascetic, Preacher, Bishop*. London.

Kepel, Gilles. 1984. *Muslim Extremism in Egypt: The Prophet and Pharaoh*. Berkeley.

———. 2002. *Jihad: The Trail of Political Islam*. Cambridge, MA.

Kirsch, J. P. 1912. "Das Ende der Gladiatorenspiele in Rom." *Römische Quartalschrift* 26: 205–211.

Klingshirn, William. 1994. *Caesarius of Arles: The Making of a Christian Community in Late Antique Gaul*. Cambridge.

Kofsky, Aryeh, and Guy G. Stroumsa, eds. 1998. *Sharing the Sacred: Religious Contacts and Conflicts in the Holy Land*. Jerusalem.

Kötting, Bernhard. 1979. "Martyrium und Provokation." In Adolf Martin Ritter, ed., *Kerygma und Logos: Beiträge zu den geistesgeschichtlichen Bezie-*

hungen zwischen Antike und Christentum. Festschrift für Carl Andresen, 329–336. Göttingen.

Krawiec, Rebecca. 2002. Shenoute and the Women of the White Monastery: Egyptian Monasticism in Late Antiquity. Oxford.

Kriegbaum, Bernhard. 1987. Kirche der Traditoren oder Kirche der Märtyrer? Die Vorgeschichte des Donatismus. Innsbruck.

Krueger, Alan B., and Jitka Maleckova. 2002. "Does Poverty Cause Terrorism? The Economics and the Education of Suicide Bombers." The New Republic, June 24: 27–33.

Krueger, Derek. 1997. "Typological Figuration in Theodoret of Cyrrhus' Religious History and the Art of Postbiblical Narrative." JECS 5: 393–419.

———. 1999. "Hagiography as an Ascetic Practice in the Early Christian East." Journal of Religion 79: 216–232.

Labourt, J. 1904. Le christianisme dans l'empire perse sous la dynastie sassanide (224–632). Paris.

Lamberigts, M., and P. Van Deun, eds. 1995. Martyrium in Multidisciplinary Perspective: Memorial Louis Reekmans. Louvain.

Lamoreaux, John C. 1995. "Episcopal Courts in Late Antiquity." JECS 3: 143–167.

Lancel, Serge. 1989. "Le sort des évêques et des communautés donatistes après la Conférence de Carthage en 411." In C. Mayer and K. H. Chelius, eds., Internationales Symposium über den Stand der Augustinus-Forschung, 149–165. Würzburg.

Lane Fox, Robin. 1986. Pagans and Christians. New York.

Lawless, George. 1987. Augustine of Hippo and his Monastic Rule. Oxford.

Le Boulluec, Alain. 1985. La notion d'hérésie dans la littérature grecque, IIe–IIIe siècles. 2 vols. Paris.

Leipoldt, Johannes. 1903. Schenute von Atripe und die Entstehung des national ägyptischen Christentums. Leipzig.

Lenski, Noel. 2002. Failure of Empire: Valens and the Roman State in the Fourth Century A.D. Berkeley.

Lepelley, Claude. 1980. "Iuvenes et circoncellions: Les derniers sacrifices humains de l'Afrique antique." Antiquités africaines 15: 261–271.

———. 1994. "Le musée des statues divines: La volonté de sauvegarder le patrimoine artistique païen à l'époque théodosienne." Cahiers archéologiques 42: 5–15.

Leyser, Conrad. 2000. Authority and Asceticism from Augustine to Gregory the Great. Oxford.

Lieberman, Saul. 1946–47. "Palestine in the Third and Fourth Centuries." Jewish Quarterly Review 36: 329–370 and 37: 31–54.

Liebeschuetz, J. H. W. G. 1972. Antioch: City and Imperial Administration in the Later Roman Empire. Oxford.

———. 2001. The Decline and Fall of the Roman City. Oxford.

Lieu, Samuel N. C. 1989. The Emperor Julian: Panegyric and Polemic. Liverpool.

Lim, Richard. 1995. Public Disputation, Power, and Social Order in Late Antiquity. Berkeley.

Lincoln, Bruce. 1989. *Discourse and the Construction of Society: Comparative Studies of Myth, Ritual and Classification.* Oxford.

———. 1994. *Authority: Construction and Corrosion.* Chicago.

Linder, Amnon. 1987. *The Jews in Roman Imperial Legislation.* Jerusalem.

Lintott, Andrew. 1968. *Violence in Republican Rome.* Oxford.

Little, Lester K. 1998. "Anger in Monastic Curses." In Rosenwein 1998, 9–35.

Lizzi, Rita. 1990. "Ambrose's Contemporaries and the Christianization of Northern Italy." *JRS* 80: 156–173.

Löhr, Winrich A. 1993. "A Sense of Tradition: The Homoiousian Church Party." In Barnes and Williams 1993, 81–100.

Lyman, Rebecca. 1993. "A Topography of Heresy: Mapping the Rhetorical Creation of Arianism." In Barnes and Williams 1993, 45–62.

MacCormack, Sabine. 1991. *Religion in the Andes: Vision and Imagination in Early Colonial Peru.* Princeton.

MacMullen, Ramsay. 1963. "The Roman Concept Robber-Pretender." *Revue internationale des droits de l'antiquité*, 3rd ser., 10: 221–225.

———. 1974. *Roman Social Relations 50 BC to AD 284.* New Haven.

———. 1990a. "The Historical Role of the Masses in Late Antiquity." In MacMullen, *Changes in the Roman Empire: Essays in the Ordinary*, 250–276. Princeton.

———. 1990b. "Judicial Savagery in the Roman Empire." In MacMullen, *Changes*, 204–217.

———. 1997. *Christianity and Paganism in the Fourth to Eighth Centuries.* New Haven.

———. 2000. *Romanization in the Time of Augustus.* New Haven.

Maier, Harry. 1996. " 'Manichee!' Leo the Great and the Orthodox Panopticon." *JECS* 4: 441–460.

Malone, E. E. 1950. *The Monk and the Martyr: The Monk as Successor to the Martyr.* Washington, DC.

Mandouze, André. 1976. "Le donatisme représente-t-il la résistance à Rome de l'Afrique tardive?" In D. M. Pippidi, ed., *Assimilation et résistance à la culture gréco-romaine dans le monde ancien: Travaux du VIe congrès international d'études classiques Madrid 1974*, 357–366. Paris.

———. 1982. *Prosopographie chrétienne du Bas-Empire v. 1: Afrique (303–533)* [*PCBE*]. Paris.

Mango, Cyril. 1963. "Antique Statuary and the Byzantine Beholder." *DOP* 17: 55–75.

Marcuse, Herbert. 1969. "Repressive Tolerance." In R. P. Wolff, B. Moore, and H. Marcuse, *A Critique of Pure Tolerance*, 81–123. Boston.

Markus, Robert A. 1988. *Saeculum: History and Society in the Theology of St. Augustine.* Rev. ed. Cambridge.

———. 1990. *The End of Ancient Christianity.* Cambridge.

———. 1991. "The Problem of 'Donatism' in the Sixth Century." In *Gregorio il Magno e il suo tempo*, Studia Ephemeridis "Augustinianum" 33, 159–166. Rome. Reprinted in Markus, *Sacred and Secular*. London, 1994.

Martin, Annick. 1974. "Athanase et les Melitiens (325–355)." In Charles Kannengiesser, ed., *Politique et Theologie chez Athanase d'Alexandrie*, 31–61. Paris.

———. 1996. *Athanase d'Alexandrie et l'église d'Égypte au IVe siècle (328–373)*. Collection de l'École française de Rome 216. Rome.

Mathews, Edward G. 1990. "On Solitaries: Ephrem or Isaac?" *Le Muséon* 103: 93–110.

Mathisen, Ralph W. 1989. *Ecclesiastical Factionalism and Religious Controversy in Fifth-Century Gaul*. Washington, DC.

———. 1993. *Roman Aristocrats in Barbarian Gaul: Strategies for Survival in an Age of Transition*. Austin, Texas.

———. 1997. "Barbarian Bishops and the Churches 'in barbaricis gentibus' during Late Antiquity." *Speculum* 72: 664–695.

———, ed. 2001. *Law, Society, and Authority in Late Antiquity*. Oxford.

Matthews, John. 1967. "A Pious Supporter of Theodosius I: Maternus Cynegius and His Family." *JTS*, n.s., 18: 438–446.

———. 1975. *Western Aristocracies and Imperial Court AD 364–425*. Oxford.

———. 1989. *The Roman Empire of Ammianus*. London.

Mayer, Arno J. 2000. *The Furies: Violence and Terror in the French and Russian Revolutions*. Princeton.

Mayer, Wendy. 1998. "John Chrysostom: Extraordinary Preacher, Ordinary Audience." In Mary B. Cunningham and Pauline Allen, eds., *Preacher and Audience: Studies in Early Christian and Byzantine Homiletic*, 105–137. Leiden.

Mazzucco, Clementina. 1993. *Ottato di Milevi in un secolo di studi: problemi e prospettive*. Bologna.

McGlew, James F. 1993. *Tyranny and Political Culture in Ancient Greece*. Ithaca.

McGuckin, John A. 1994. *St. Cyril of Alexandria: The Christological Controversy. Its History, Theology and Texts*. Leiden.

McLynn, Neil B. 1992. "Christian Controversy and Violence in the Fourth Century." *Kodai* 3: 15–44.

———. 1994. *Ambrose of Milan: Church and Court in a Christian Capital*. Berkeley.

Meeks, Wayne. 1983. *The First Urban Christians: The Social World of the Apostle Paul*. New Haven.

Merkt, Andreas. 1997. *Maximus I von Turin: Die Verkündigung eines Bischofs der frühes Reichskirche im zeitgeschichtlichen, gesellschaftlichen und liturgischen Kontext*. Leiden.

Meyendorff, John. 1989. *Imperial Unity and Christian Divisions: The Church 450–680 AD*. Crestwood, NY.

Micka, Ermin F. 1943. *The Problem of Divine Anger in Arnobius and Lactantius*. Washington, DC.

Millar, Fergus. 1971. "Paul of Samosata, Zenobia and Aurelian: The Church, Local Culture and Political Allegiance in Third-Century Syria." *JRS* 61: 1–17.

———. 1977. *The Emperor in the Roman World 31 BC–AD 337*. Ithaca.

———. 1992. "The Jews of the Greco-Roman Diaspora between Paganism and

Christianity." In Judith Lieu, John North, and Tessa Rajak, eds., *The Jews among Pagans and Christians*, 97–123. London.

Miller, William Ian. 1993. *Humiliation, and Other Essays on Honor, Social Discomfort, and Violence*. Cornell.

Mills, Kenneth. 1997. *Idolatry and Its Enemies: Colonial Andean Religion and Extirpation, 1640–1750*. Princeton.

Mills, Kenneth, and William B. Taylor, eds. 1998. *Colonial Spanish America: A Documentary History*. Wilmington.

Momigliano, Arnaldo. 1986. "The Disadvantages of Monotheism for a Universal State." *Classical Philology* 81: 285–297.

Monceaux, Paul. 1912. *Histoire littéraire de l'Afrique chrétienne depuis les origines jusqu'à l'invasion arabe*. 5 vols. Paris.

Moore, R. I. 1987. *The Formation of a Persecuting Society: Power and Deviance in Western Europe, 950–1250*. Oxford.

Morony, Michael. 1984. *Iraq After the Muslim Conquest*. Princeton.

Murphy, Francis X. 1952. *Peter Speaks Through Leo: The Council of Chalcedon A.D. 451*. Washington, DC.

Nader, Laura. 1990. *Harmony Ideology: Justice and Control in a Zapotec Mountain Village*. Stanford.

———. 1996. "Coercive Harmony: The Political Economy of Legal Models." *Kroeber Anthropological Society Papers* 80: 1–13.

Nau, François. 1927a. "Deux episodes de l'histoire juive sous Théodose II (432 et 438) d'après la vie de Barsauma le syrien." *Revue des études juives* 83: 184–206.

———. 1927b. "Sur la synagogue de Rabbat-Moab (429) et un mouvement sioniste favorisé par l'impératrice Eudocie (438) d'après la vie de Barsaume le syrien." *Journal Asiatique* 210: 189–192.

———. 1931. "Les 'belles actions' de Mar Rabboula, évêque d'Edesse." *Revue d'histoire religieuse* 103: 97–135.

Nicholson, Oliver. 1994. "The 'Pagan Churches' of Maximinus Daia and Julian the Apostate." *JEH* 45: 1–15.

Nirenberg, David. 1996. *Communities of Violence: Persecution of Minorities in the Middle Ages*. Princeton.

Norris, Frederick W. 1984. "Paul of Samosata: *Procurator Ducenarius*." *JTS*, n.s., 35: 50–70.

Obolensky, Dimitri. 1971. *The Byzantine Commonwealth: Eastern Europe 500–1453*. London.

Overbeck, M. 1973. "Augustin und die Circumcellionen seiner Zeit." *Chiron* 3: 457–463.

Pagels, Elaine. 1995. *The Origin of Satan*. New York.

Partner, Peter. 1997. *God of Battles: Holy Wars of Christianity and Islam*. Princeton.

Paschoud, François, and Joachim Szidat, eds. 1997. *Usurpationen in der Spätantike*. Stuttgart.

Patlagean, Evelyne. 1977. *Pauvreté économique et pauvreté sociale à Byzance 4e-7e siècle.* Paris.

Peeters, Paul. 1909. "Une passione arménienne de SS. Abdas, Hormisdas, Sahin (Suenes) et Benjamin." *AB* 27: 399–415.

———. 1928. "La vie de Rabboula, évêque d'Édesse." In Peeters, *Recherches d'histoire et de philologie orientales,* 139–170. Brussels.

Pellegrino, M. 1981. "Martiri e Martirio in S. Massimo." *Rivista di storia e letteratura religiosa* 17: 169–192.

Perkins, Judith. 1995. *The Suffering Self: Pain and Narrative Representation in the Early Christian Era.* London.

Peters, F. E. 1990. *Judaism, Christianity, and Islam.* 3 vols. Princeton.

Petit, P. 1951. "Sur la date du *Pro Templis* de Libanius." *Byzantion* 21: 285–310.

Price, Richard. 1983. *First-Time: The Historical Vision of an Afro-American People.* Baltimore.

Ragette, Friedrich. 1980. *Baalbek.* Park Ridge, NJ.

Raikas, Kauko K. 1990. "St. Augustine on Juridical Duties: Some Aspects of the Episcopal Office in Late Antiquity." In Joseph C. Schnaubelt and Frederick Van Fleteren, eds., *Collectanea Augustiniana: Augustine, "Second Founder of the Faith,"* 467–483. New York.

Rajak, Tessa. 1997. "Dying for the Law: The Martyr's Portrait in Jewish-Greek Literature." In Mark J. Edwards and Simon Swain, eds., *Portraits: Biographical Representation in the Greek and Latin Literature of the Roman Empire,* 39–67. Oxford.

Rapp, Claudia. 1998a. "Imperial Ideology in the Making: Eusebius of Caesarea on Constantine as 'Bishop'." *JTS*, n.s., 49: 685–695.

———. 1998b. "Storytelling as Spiritual Communication in Early Greek Hagiography: The Use of *diegesis.*" *JECS* 6: 431–448.

Rives, J. B. 1995. *Religion and Authority in Roman Carthage.* Oxford.

Roberts, Michael. 1993. *Poetry and the Cult of the Martyrs: The Liber Peristephanon of Prudentius.* Ann Arbor.

Rorem, Paul. 1993. *Pseudo-Dionysius: A Commentary on the Texts and an Introduction to Their Influence.* Oxford.

Rosenwein, Barbara H., ed. 1998. *Anger's Past: The Social Uses of an Emotion in the Middle Ages.* Ithaca.

———. 2002. "Worrying about Emotions in History." *AHR* 107.3: 821–845.

Roueché, Charlotte. 1984. "Acclamations in the Later Roman Empire: New Evidence from Aphrodisias." *JRS* 74: 181–199.

Rousseau, Philip. 1995. "Orthodoxy and the Coenobite." *SP* 30: 241–258.

———. 1999. "Ascetics as Mediators and as Teachers." In Howard-Johnston and Hayward 1999, 45–59.

———. 2000. "Monasticism." In Averil Cameron, Bryan Ward-Perkins, and Michael Whitby, eds., *The Cambridge Ancient History Vol. 14: Late Antiquity: Empire and Successors, A.D. 425–600,* 745–780. Cambridge.

Rubenson, Samuel. 1995. *The Letters of St. Antony: Monasticism and the Making of a Saint.* Minneapolis.

Rubin, Zeev. 1995. "Mass Movements in Late Antiquity—Appearances and Realities." In I. Rubinsohn and Z. W. Malkin, eds., *Leaders and Masses in the Roman World: Studies in Honor of Zvi Yavetz*, 129–187. Leiden.

Rudé, George. 1964. *The Crowd in History: A Study of Popular Disturbances in France and England, 1730–1848*. New York.

Rummel, R. J. 1994. *Death by Government*. New Brunswick, NJ.

Russell, Frederick H. 1999. "Persuading the Donatists: Augustine's Coercion by Words." In William E. Klingshirn and Mark Vessey, eds., *The Limits of Ancient Christianity: Essays on Late Antique Thought and Culture in Honor of Robert A. Markus*, 115–130. Ann Arbor.

Salomonson, J. W. 1979. *Voluptatem Spectandi Non Perdat Sed Mutet: Observations sur l'Iconographie du martyre en Afrique Romaine*. Amsterdam.

Sansterre, J.-M. 1972. "Eusèbe de Césarée et la naissance de la théorie 'césaropapiste'." *Byzantion* 42: 131–195, 532–594.

Saradi-Mendelovici, Helen. 1990. "Christian Attitudes toward Pagan Monuments in Late Antiquity and Their Legacy in Later Byzantine Centuries." *DOP* 44: 47–61.

Satran, David. 1995. *Biblical Prophets in Byzantine Palestine: Reassessing the Lives of the Prophets*. Leiden.

Sauer, Eberhard. 1996. *The End of Paganism in the North-Western Provinces of the Roman Empire*. British Archaeological Reports International Series 634. Oxford.

———. 2003. *The Archaeology of Religious Hatred in the Roman and Early Medieval World*. Charleston, SC.

Saxer, Victor. 1980. *Morts Martyrs Reliques en Afrique chrétienne: Les témoignages de Tertullien, Cyprien et Augustin à la lumière de l'archéologie africaine*. Paris.

Schatkin, Margaret. 1974. "The Maccabean Martyrs." *VC* 28: 97–113.

Schwartz, Eduard. 1937. *Über die Bischofslisten der Synoden von Chalkedon, Nicaea und Konstantinopel*. München.

Scipioni, Luigi I. 1974. *Nestorio e il concilio di Efeso*. Milan.

Scott, James C. 1985. *Weapons of the Weak: Everyday Forms of Peasant Resistance*. New Haven.

———. 1990. *Domination and the Arts of Resistance: Hidden Transcripts*. New Haven.

Segal, J. B. 1970. *Edessa: The Blessed City*. Oxford.

Shaw, Brent D. 1984. "Bandits in the Roman Empire." *Past and Present* 105: 3–52.

———. 1990. "The Isaurians." *Journal of the Economic and Social History of the Orient* 33: 237–269.

———. 1992. "African Christianity: Disputes, Definitions and 'Donatists'." In M. R. Greenshields and T. A. Robinson, eds., *Orthodoxy and Heresy in Religious Movements: Discipline and Dissent*, 5–34. Lampeter. Reprinted in Shaw 1995.

———. 1995. *Rulers, Nomads and Christians in Roman North Africa*. London.

———. 1996. "Body/Power/Identity: Passions of the Martyrs." *JECS* 4: 269–312.

Shaw, Teresa M. 1997. "Wolves in Sheep's Clothing: The Appearance of True and False Piety." *SP* 29: 127–132.

———. 1998. "Askesis and the Appearance of Holiness." *JECS* 6: 485–499.

Shils, Edward. 1975. *Center and Periphery: Essays in Macrosociology.* Chicago.

Shklar, Judith N. 1984. *Ordinary Vices.* Harvard.

Sillett, Helen M. 1999. *Culture of Controversy: The Christological Disputes of the Early Fifth Century.* PhD Dissertation, University of California, Berkeley.

Simonetti, Manlio. 1975. *La crisi Ariana nel IV secolo.* Rome.

Spieser, J.-M. 1976. "La christianisation des sanctuaires païens en Grece." In Ulf Jantzen, ed., *Neue Forschungen in griechischen Heiligtümern,* 309–320. Tübingen.

Stancliffe, Clare. 1983. *St. Martin and his Hagiographer: History and Miracle in Sulpicius Severus.* Oxford.

Stark, Rodney. 1996. *The Rise of Christianity: A Sociologist Reconsiders History.* Princeton.

Stead, Christopher. 1976. "Rhetorical Method in Athanasius." *VC* 30: 121–137.

Ste. Croix, G. E. M. de. 1963. "Why Were the Early Christians Persecuted?" *Past and Present* 26: 6–38.

———. 1981. *The Class Struggle in the Ancient Greek World.* London.

Steppa, Jan-Eric. 2002. *John Rufus and the World Vision of Anti-Chalcedonian Culture.* Piscataway, NJ.

Stewart, Columba. 1991. *Working the Earth of the Heart: The Messalian Controversy in History, Texts and Language to AD 431.* Oxford.

Stinchcombe, Arthur L. 1968. *Constructing Social Theories.* New York.

Stocking, Rachel L. 2000. *Bishops, Councils, and Consensus in the Visigothic Kingdom, 589–633.* Ann Arbor.

Stroumsa, Guy G. 1993. "Le radicalisme religieux du premier christianisme: contexte et implications." In E. Patlagean and A. Le Boulluec, eds., *Les retours aux Écritures: fondamentalismes présents et passées,* 357–382. Louvain.

———. 1999. *Barbarian Philosophy: The Religious Revolution of Early Christianity.* Tübingen.

Swift, Louis J. 1983. *The Early Fathers on War and Military Service.* Wilmington.

Teitler, H. C. 1985. *Notarii and Exceptores: An Inquiry into the Role and Significance of Shorthand Writers in the Imperial and Ecclesiastical Bureaucracy of the Roman Empire.* Amsterdam.

Telfer, W. 1950. "Paul of Constantinople." *HTR* 43: 31–92.

Tengström, Emin. 1964. *Donatisten und Katholiken: Soziale, wirtschaftliche und politische Aspekte einer nordafrikanischen Kirchenspaltung.* Göteborg.

Thelamon, Françoise. 1981. *Païens et chrétiens au IVe siècle: l'apport de l'Histoire Ecclésiastique de Rufin d'Aquilée.* Paris.

Thompson, E. P. 1971. "The Moral Economy of the English Crowd in the Eighteenth Century." *Past and Present* 50: 76–136.

Thornton, T. C. G. 1986. "The Destruction of Idols—Sinful or Meritorious?" *JTS,* n.s., 37: 121–129.

Tilley, Maureen A. 1991a. "The Ascetic Body and the (Un)Making of the World of the Martyr." *Journal of the American Academy of Religion* 59: 467–479.

———. 1991b. "Dilatory Donatists or Procrastinating Catholics: The Trial at the Conference of Carthage." *Church History* 60: 7–19.

———. 1997a. *The Bible in Christian North Africa: The Donatist World.* Minneapolis.

———. 1997b. "Sustaining Donatist Self-Identity: From the Church of the Martyrs to the *Collecta* of the Desert." *JECS* 5: 21–35.

Tilly, Charles. 1985. "War Making and State Making as Organized Crime." In P. Evans, D. Rueschemeyer, and Th. Skocpol, eds., *Bringing the State Back In,* 169–191. Cambridge.

Trombley, Frank R. 1993–94. *Hellenic Religion and Christianization c.370–529.* 2 vols. Leiden.

Trout, Dennis. 1994. "Recontextualizing Lucretia: Cultural Subversion in the *City of God.*" *JECS* 2: 53–70.

Urbainczyk, Theresa. 1997. *Socrates of Constantinople: Historian of Church and State.* Ann Arbor.

Vaggione, Richard P. 1993. "Of Monks and Lounge Lizards: 'Arians', Polemics and Asceticism in the Roman East." In Barnes and Williams 1993, 181–214.

———. 2000. *Eunomius of Cyzicus and the Nicene Revolution.* Oxford.

Van Dam, Raymond. 1985. "From Paganism to Christianity at Late Antique Gaza." *Viator* 16: 1–20.

———. 1986. "Sheep in Wolves' Clothing: The Letters of Consentius to Augustine." *JEH* 37: 515–535.

Van Rompay, Lucas. 1995. "Impetuous Martyrs? The Situation of the Persian Christians in the Last Years of Yazdgard I (339–420)." In Lamberigts and Van Deun 1995, 363–376.

Vasaly, Ann. 1996. *Representations: Images of the World in Ciceronian Oratory.* Berkeley.

Ville, G. 1960. "Les jeux de gladiateurs dans l'Empire chrétien." *Mélanges d'archéologie et d'histoire publiés par l'école française de Rome* 72: 273–335.

———. 1979. "Religion et politique: comment ont pris fin les combats de gladiateurs." *Annales ESC* 34: 651–671.

Vivian, Tim. 1988. *St. Peter of Alexandria: Bishop and Martyr.* Philadelphia.

von Rad, Gerhard. 1991. *Holy War in Ancient Israel.* Grand Rapids, MI.

Vööbus, Arthur. 1948. "La Vie d'Alexandre en grec: un témoin d'une biographie inconnue de Rabbula écrite en syriaque." *Contributions of the Baltic University* 62: 1–16.

———. 1958, 1960a, 1988. *History of Asceticism in the Syrian Orient: A Contribution to the History of Culture in the Near East.* 3 vols. CSCO Subsidia 14, 17, 81. Louvain.

———. 1960b. *Syriac and Arabic Documents Regarding Legislation Relative to Syrian Asceticism.* Stockholm.

———. 1965. *History of the School of Nisibis.* CSCO Subsidia 26. Louvain.

Walker, Joel Thomas. 1998. *"Your Heroic Deeds Give Us Pleasure": Culture and

Society in the Christian Martyr Legends of Late Antique Iraq. PhD dissertation, Princeton University.

Weber, Max. 1947. *The Theory of Social and Economic Organization*. Trans. A. M. Henderson and Talcott Parsons. New York.

———. 1963. *The Sociology of Religion*. Trans. E. Fischoff. Boston.

Wiedemann, Thomas. 1992. *Emperors and Gladiators*. London.

Wiegand, Theodor, ed. 1921–1925. *Baalbek: Ergebnisse der Ausgrabungen und Untersuchungen in dem Jahren 1898–1905*. 3 vols. Berlin and Leipzig.

Wiles, Maurice. 1996. *Archetypal Heresy: Arianism through the Centuries*. Oxford.

Wilken, Robert L. 1984. *The Christians as the Romans Saw Them*. New Haven.

Williams, D. H. 1997. "Necessary Alliance or Polemical Portrayal? Tracing the Historical Alignment of Arians and Pagans in the Later Fourth Century." *SP* 29: 178–194.

Williams, Stephen. 1985. *Diocletian and the Roman Recovery*. New York.

Wimbush, Vincent L., and Richard Valantasis, eds. 1995. *Asceticism*. Oxford.

Winlock, H. E. and W. E. Crum. 1926. *The Monastery of Epiphanius at Thebes, Part 1: The Archaeological and Literary Material*. New York.

Wipszycka, Ewa. 1994. "Le monachisme égyptien et les villes." *TM* 12: 1–44.

———. 1996a. *Études sur le christianisme dans l'Égypte de l'antiquité tardive*. Rome.

———. 1996b. "Les clercs dans les communautés monastiques d'Égypte." *Journal of Juristic Papyrology* 26: 135–166.

Wolf, Kenneth B. 1988. *Christian Martyrs in Muslim Spain*. Cambridge.

Wölfle, E. 1986. "Hypatius und Alexander." *BZ* 79: 302–309.

Woodward, E. L. 1916. *Christianity and Nationalism in the Later Roman Empire*. London.

Ye'or, Bat. 1996. *The Decline of Eastern Christianity under Islam: From Jihad to Dhimmitude*. London.

———. 2002. *Islam and Dhimmitude: Where Civilizations Collide*. Cranbury, NJ.

Index

Abda of Hormizd-Ardashir, Bishop, 197; death of, 198, 199
Abitina, martyrs of, 40, 41n49, 56
Acclamations, transcriptions of, 18
Acts of Peter, 37
Agnes (martyr), 166
Agonistici (circumcellions), 123
Akoimetes. *See* Monks, Akoimete
Alaric, sack of Rome, 156
Alexander of Alexandria, Bishop: and Constantine, 58, 59
Alexander the Akoimete, 214, 248, 250; ascetic career of, 187n143; burning of temples, 185, 187; confrontation with pagans, 154; death of, 246; desert solitude of, 243; disciples of, 243–46; discourse of truth, 207; and Empress Pulcheria, 245; expulsion from Constantinople, 245, 246; in monastic community, 235; *parrhesia* of, 244; in Syria, 244n158; wandering by, 243–44. *See also* Monks, Akoimete
Alexander the Great, 22n69
Alexandria: attack on church at, 79–80, 83; bishops of, 275n77, 320; destruction of Serapeum, 95, 117n55, 156, 157, 186n139, 221, 225n67, 250; ecclesiastical politics of, 319n127; episcopacy of, 275n77; martyrs of, 221, 222n57; monastic

establishment of, 223; pagans of, 12n37, 190n152
Altar of Victory controversy, 195
Alypius, 205n203
Amachius (governor of Phrygia), 92, 93n69
Ambrose of Milan, Bishop: on apostasy, 196, 199; and Callinicum incident, 157, 198, 209; and Theodosius I, 63, 102, 148, 195–96, 198; reluctance for ordination, 276n86; and torture, 63n145
Ammianus Marcellinus: account of Valentinian, 256; on Procopius, 274n73; on temple of Apollo, 90n63
Ammonius (Egyptian monk), self-mutilation of, 234n110, 262n31
Ammonius (Origenist monk), Theophilus' assault on, 253, 254
Ammonius ("Thaumasios"), 204n198, 220–21; martyrdom of, 221, 222
Amphilochius of Side, 324n8
Anachoresis (withdrawal), 38; of fourth century, 232
Anarchy: extremist, 329; *versus* tyranny, 16
Anatolius (*apocrisiarius*), 309
Anaunia (Italy), martyrs of, 173–74, 178n98
Anderson, Benedict, 2, 44; on simultaneity, 69n4

Text: 10/13 Aldus
Display: Aldus
Compositor: Integrated Composition Systems
Indexer: Roberta Engleman